MY LIFE

Louis Nizer

IN

COURT

Martino Publishing
Mansfield Centre, CT
2012

Martino Publishing
P.O. Box 373,
Mansfield Centre, CT 06250 USA

ISBN 978-1-61427-376-9

© *2012 Martino Publishing*

Cover design by T. Matarazzo

Printed in the United States of America On 100% Acid-Free Paper

MY LIFE

Louis Nizer

IN

COURT

1961

Doubleday & Company, Inc.

GARDEN CITY, NEW YORK

Design: Alma Reese Cardi

CONTENTS

PROLOGUE

OPENING THE GREEN DOORS

The layman's impression of a trial frequently comes from stage, motion picture, and television sources, which, while invariably exciting, are a pale simulation of a real trial. My quarrel with these presentations is not that they are technically incorrect, but that they are substantively inadequate. They lack emotional authenticity. They tend to become stereotyped. Their falsity largely defeats their authors' purpose because the excitement, surprise, and meaningfulness of a real court contest are incomparable and elude imagination. In fictional court scenes one sharp contradiction often breaks the witness, who then hysterically screams a confession. In real life the witness's fortitude in the face of exposure is as remarkable as a human body's resistance to incredible torment. The need to survive creates desperation, and desperation makes possible survival. This circle of determination is not easily broken, and in the succeeding pages one will find dozens of entrapments and startling contradictions, leaving the witness no retreat and compelling him to admit his error. Yet he continues to fight back and clutch for the remote chance that the tide will turn and he will not go under. Sometimes it does, and the bizarre developments that bring it about are also beyond inventiveness. This gruesome struggle exceeds the artificial concept of authors of what constitutes court drama in the same way that true human experience in any sphere exceeds the patterned concept of some fiction.

A trial, however, is more than the thumping excitement of contest, where the weapons are words and the defenses are wits. It is the search for truth. Diogenes and his lantern might well constitute a symbolic replacement for the blindfolded figure of Justice. The lawyer's task is to reconstruct past events and adduce the persuasive facts for his client. He is like the archeologist who must find and exhume old evidence. How does he know where to search, and for what? This is the supreme test of preparation and, as any trial lawyer will admit, proper preparation is the be all and end all of trial success. "The stupid man it will make bright, the bright, brilliant, and the brilliant, steady."

Ordinarily the lawyer turns to observation and memory to obtain the truth. Too often they are feeble indexes to its reconstruction. Tests have been conducted at Harvard University and elsewhere to determine the accuracy of observation. Actors have appeared suddenly before classrooms and enacted violent scenes in which, after explosive dialogue, one of the actors was stabbed or shot. The students were then asked to write what they had just seen and heard. Their reports demonstrated that it was rare for two students to record the same version. Even more astonishing were the variations indicating distorted and imaginative impressions. The eye may focus on one sector of the scene and be hypnotized by it to the exclusion of all else. It is not the visual sense alone which is directional. Sympathy or bias may transform what we do see into what we would like to see. The tests proved that observation is a weak reed upon which to lean when the observer is under emotional excitation.

It is just as hazardous to rely on memory. Ordinarily we cannot even recall what we did a month ago, not to speak of years ago. John Locke urged that recall depended largely on association of ideas. However, when we have no reason to make the association, we do not readily do so. Sigmund Freud's thesis was that we never really forget anything. The unconscious refuses to unlock the memory to the conscious mind for fear of the conflict it will create.

My own observation has been that all of us have extraordinarily good memories and also very bad memories. It depends on the degree of concentration we bring to our memories. If, for example, we have witnessed an entrancing play that riveted our attention, we can recite the plot developments, including large segments of dialogue, in correct sequence. On the other hand, have we not all been embarrassed at some time by being introduced to the same person twice in a few minutes at some cocktail party and not remembering the name? I know that when I am concentrating in the courtroom, I can thereafter recite hundreds of pages of the record by memory. Yet, in other directions I have an atrocious memory and have even developed some small reputation for absent-mindedness.

Since one rarely anticipates litigation, he has no reason to concentrate upon the events he is living through and which he may be required to recall years later. It is the lawyer who must nevertheless assemble the facts from those who should know, but who are beset with vagueness or, still worse, complete blankness. Yet, how can he persuade the jury when he cannot make the reality of the past come to life before them? Of course, contemporaneous documents and interviews with participants aid in the reconstruction of the factual edifice. But often they are missing, and above all, the great dilemma is the uncertainty of what evidence exists somewhere, either oral or in writing, of which the searcher is unaware.

Every lawyer dreams of the ultimate electronic invention that could recapture from the airwaves the words spoken in the past. Then we would hear the original Sermon on the Mount, Shakespeare's sonnets read by him, Lincoln's Gettysburg Address, and other great words proven to be deathless in more than the symbolic sense. We could also be certain of what every witness said years before the trial. In the meantime there is a technique that serves almost as well. I shall call it the rule of probability. It tells me what facts to seek. It leads me to witnesses and documents which I did not know existed. It points out the vulnerable area of the hostile witness's testimony and suggests cross-examination. It is an all-potent weapon in the contest for truth. Let me illustrate:

Konrad Bercovici sued Charles Chaplin for plagiarism of the motion picture *The Great Dictator*. I represented the plaintiff. The claim was that Chaplin had approached Bercovici to produce one of his gypsy stories as a motion picture and in the course of those friendly negotiations Bercovici gave him an outline of *The Great Dictator* story about a barber who looks like Hitler and is confused with him. Chaplin denied ever having negotiated for the gypsy story and also denied the rest of the claim. To develop the origin of the incident that was the basis for the plagiarism claim, I wanted to know how far the gypsy-story transaction had progressed. Had Chaplin discussed the price for the story? Had he engaged writers for the script? Had he started to cast the picture? To all of which Bercovici replied in the negative. It seemed highly improbable to me that something more had not been done with the gypsy story to form the background for the submission of a script on *The Great Dictator*. Nevertheless, my client persisted in saying it had reached nothing but the idea stage.

One day, upon my continuous inquiry, Bercovici suddenly had a flash of memory. He recalled that he had met Chaplin in a theater in Hollywood and that Chaplin had pointed out a Russian baritone in the audience whom he thought might play the leading role in the gypsy story. Bercovici believed that they spoke to the singer that evening and that he might possibly be a witness. What was the name of the baritone? He didn't know. Where did he live? He didn't know. It was 12:30 A.M. at my home. At 2 that morning that baritone was in my home. The events were these. I called the Russian Tea Room and inquired about a Russian baritone of the given description. The owner said I probably was referring to a singer named Kushnevitz. "Where is he?" I asked. "Oh, he is performing some place in Canada, but he is coming in tonight for the Russian New Year and I will see him within an hour." "Will you please tell him to call me when he arrives?" He came. I asked him if he had ever met Chaplin. He recalled the incident vividly, for this, as he put it, was one of the great moments in his life—the possibility that he would star in a Chaplin picture. Chaplin had called him down the aisle of the theater and had given him his private telephone number. He pulled out a little black book from his back pocket and he still had the number written in it. He was a perfect witness in view of Chaplin's denial of any interest in Bercovici's gypsy story. The rule of probability had led me directly to him.

This is how the rule of probability performs its miracles. Through cumulative experience we can anticipate with reasonable certainty how people will react to certain stimuli. By applying this "knowledge" to any set of facts, we can judge whether the conduct described is probable. If implausible, it must be rejected as untrue no matter what assurance the client or witness gives of his recollection. Either he is innocently inaccurate, or he is deliberately lying, or there are surrounding circumstances which make the implausible plausible. (A proven eccentric in other matters may perform a bizarre act without challenging credence; a tendency to alcoholism may explain a lapse in communication, etc.) The rule of probability rarely misleads. I cite another illustration.

John Garfield, the motion picture star, was subpoenaed before Senator Joseph McCarthy's Committee to testify about his political activities. It was claimed that he had contributed money to a Communist front called The American Committee for Jugoslav Relief. Even Red Channels had quoted Garfield's earlier statement in the press that the Marshall Plan was "killing Communism in Europe and that's good," and my own investigation of his affairs, before I undertook to represent him, fully confirmed his service to democracy. It was therefore highly improbable that he had helped "finance" a Communist organization.

He could recall nothing about the incident, even though I found his personal check to the Jugoslav Committee. The date indicated that he was starring in a motion picture production at the Warner Brothers studio at the time. The probability was that he had been visited there and solicited for a contribution. If so, it must have been an important committee which could interrupt a production schedule. It turned out that a Jugoslav committee visiting this country, accompanied by a representative of the State Department, had been escorted to several motion picture studios. I had a search made for the photographs in the Warner files and we found the customary pose of the committee with various stars on the lot. Then only did Garfield recognize the Jugoslav colonel and recall the entire incident.

During the war Garfield had headed a USO troupe to the Italian war zone. He was flown in the dark of night to a mountain region where Jugoslav partisans were in preparation for an assault. He entertained them. After the war, our State Department arranged with Tito to receive his representatives, at the head of which was the colonel whose troops Garfield had once entertained.

In Hollywood the colonel asked specifically for John Garfield. He greeted the bewildered star with embraces appropriate to comrades in arms. While Garfield did not remember him in the new lighted setting, he responded courteously and inquired what the colonel's mission was. He learned that he was raising funds for Jugoslav orphans. Garfield authorized his agent to send a check for $200. This was the extent of his contribution to a "Communist front." The rule of probability had removed the curtain of forgetfulness and brought back the innocent details.

Time and again I have insisted that a client must have written a letter because surrounding circumstances indicated his need to express his position. Time and again the client has persisted that he had looked through all of his files and records and there was none and he could not recall writing. Yet later such letters have been found. On one occasion the client called me excitedly to say that he was visiting his sister in Philadelphia and had found the letter in a file taken from his father's office after he died. Before he read it to me, he said, "It is word for word what you said I probably wrote on that occasion. How did you know?" A couplet could well commemorate the answer:

> *How do you know?*
> *The rule of probability told me so.*

On several occasions, witnesses whom I have cross-examined have later inquired how I had learned about the facts that I had dug out of them. Earl Carroll once sued Paramount Pictures Corp. involving the motion picture version of his *Vanities*. I represented Paramount and observed that at a particular point in his direct testimony Carroll's hand covered his mouth—a frequently occurring psychological gesture meaning "I would prefer not to say what I am about to say." In addition, his statement violated the rule of probability. I marked this passage of his testimony for concentrated cross-examination. It was extremely fruitful and probably accounted for his loss of the case. When he stepped from the witness stand, he stopped at my seat in apparent cordial conversation for a few minutes. The jury and our adversaries must have been perplexed. What he said was not amiable at all. Addressing me with a choice epithet, he wanted to know how we had found out about certain facts that he thought were known to no one but himself. I would only have mystified him more if I had told him that the intelligence agent who gave me the knowledge with which to place the unerring question was called the rule of probability.

The magical qualities of this rule are endless. The jury decides the case because of the rule of probability. It accepts one version as against another because it accords with its own standard of experience. The judge, when he is faced with conflicting testimony, decides on the basis of probability. We talk of the credibility of witnesses, but what we really mean is that the witness has told a story which meets the tests of plausibility and is therefore credible.

The corollary of this proposition is that to be plausible a witness must recreate the emotion at the time of the original incident. The psychologists call this "abreaction." Once more, the rule of probability is the surest guide. If a witness, testifying to events five years old which no longer inflame his mind, gives his answer flatly and without emotion, I know it is unlikely that he would have reacted that way under the original circumstances. He must be stirred to re-create the feelings that swept him at that time. If I follow this clue, I am invariably rewarded, sometimes with considerable amusement. I recall a vital witness telling us how the defendant had attempted to bribe him to change his story. "What did you say?" we asked him in the privacy of our room. "I told him I wouldn't do it," he said in a matter-of-fact manner. "Was that your answer when he made this dishonest proposal to you?" I asked. After repeating that it was, he finally smiled and said, "Well, you don't want me to tell you what I really said, do you?" We told him that was precisely what we wanted. He then cut loose with a series of expletives which would have made the most hardened briber blush with shame. He was told that when he testified in court not to resort to the filthy language he had employed to express his anger, but to say simply that he had told the culprit in no uncertain language what he thought of him. The cross-examiner objected to characterization and insisted upon having the precise conversation. He got it. The effect in the courtroom was explosive, not because the walls were seared by unaccustomed diction, but because the truth of the whole incident became evident from the outraged naturalness of the man's retort to an insidious proposal.

The rule of probability functions best when it is applied by one who has good insight into the motivations and reactions of people. Education, culture, and breeding have little to do with it. Anyone who has lived an uncloistered life and has come in contact with people in diverse experiences necessarily acquires considerable knowledge of common behavior. Indeed, it is to a great extent an automatic acquisition, and the judgment based upon it is usually exercised spontaneously in small and large matters alike every day. It is what gives the jury that sixth sense to decide correctly on the evidence presented, as almost all trial lawyers and judges will agree. It is what makes the common sense of the average man so uncommonly sound. It is the reason democracy, again on the facts presented to the electorate, functions as wisely as it does in comparison with rule by a few, elite or not.

Most people apply the rule of probability without analysis or even awareness of its use. Watch an audience in the theater. So long as the characters behave plausibly under the circumstances in which they are placed, interest is held. At some point the action or dialogue may be false. The spell is immediately broken. The audience is jolted into the realization that it is only watching a play. Coughing and restlessness take over. The discerning critic may be able to analyze the defect in the play's character development, action, or dialogue, but the audience has reacted automatically. The rule of probability has done its deadly work. If the credibility of fiction must meet the inexorable test of the rule of probability, how much more is the sworn testimony in the courtroom subject to its radar accuracy in measuring plausibility? I shall in this book sometimes refer to the rule of probability. I hope that this introduction to it will make it a familiar friend when it is encountered in the course of preparation for trial or at the witness stand or in the jury box.

The Inns of Court in London are built in such a way that one who enters must bend his head low. This architectural compulsion for respect for our historic profession is an interesting symbolism. My own symbolism of awe and reverence for the law stems from a boyhood memory and involves my standing on tiptoe rather than bowing. While working as a delivery boy during summers for the Regal Shoe Stores, I used to wander over to the Supreme Court building nearby. I had dreamed of being a trial lawyer when I grew up, and the lure of famous lawyers appearing in special summer Parts was as irresistible as the announcement that Enrico Caruso would sing. (I managed to stand in the balcony to hear him, being sure that the tones sounded better as they reached me near the high ceiling of the Metropolitan Opera House.)

The Supreme Court building to me was glamorous beyond compare. The moment I entered it, the cool marble floor, the frescoes on the ceiling which commemorate the great lawgivers (if you could crane your neck upward enough), the brief cases of all sizes and colors which seemed to be marching up and down the corridors attached to the hands of lawyers, the musty smell of old law books which emanated from the library on the ground floor, and the wooden signs with gold lettering sticking out at right angles from the walls reading "Special Term, Part III" or "Trial Term, Part I"—all were magically beautiful and exciting. I have read so often about a child's thrill when visiting the circus for the first time. I believe it does not compare with my enthrallment when walking through the courthouse.

But the most wonderful of all were the doors that led into the courtroom. They were the mystic gates. They were huge and covered with dark green leather. They had brass plates where one was to push them open, but the spot underneath was always dark from use. Each door had oval glass panes on top through which one could peer. They were just too high for me, and I would stretch on my toes so that I could look into the room as other children must have looked through a knothole in a fence at baseball games. What I saw was breathtaking, even though at times there was hardly any motion at all. The court clerk might be marking a large sheaf of papers as exhibits, and everyone sat or stood around while he did so. But every stamp he put upon a sheet seemed to me highly dramatic.

I would look at the lawyer whose reputation had drawn me there. Almost always he seemed to be doing nothing, just sitting back in his seat, relaxed and watching. I was sure his motionlessness was full of wisdom. Sometimes a witness was being questioned. I could hear no sound, and the pantomime inflamed my imagination. I watched the jury as it reacted to the witness, saw a lawyer jump up apparently to make an objection, saw the Judge's mouth move, and the lawyer sit down. Sometimes I came upon a summation. I saw the lawyer walk up and down before the jury, his jaws moving furiously, waving a paper in front of it, and breathing hard as emotion swept him. I could tell through the window how he was faring. If the jurors bent forward and listened intently, he was making persuasive inroads into their minds. If they sat back in varying postures of disinterest, I knew he was in trouble.

Even when I dared, on a few occasions, to go into the room, I still had to be guided by visual impressions because the words that came in the midst of the case seemed to hang incomprehensibly in mid-air. Almost always I was outside standing on my toes, with my neck stretched to reach the window. This was the symbol of my prayerfulness, as if I were on bended knee. Some day, I was certain, I would push those doors open and enter as a lawyer participating in the highest function of all, the administration of justice. Since then I have fulfilled this dream. I have opened hundreds of courtroom doors in many states, but the excitement has never diminished. Indeed it has grown. The challenge is ever new. The contest is ever intense. Surprise is ever present. The satisfactions of a noble calling are unique and bright.

I offer the reader the opportunity of opening those doors. The reader will not sit on the rear bench of the courtroom during a number of significant trials, but at the counsel table itself, sharing the thoughts of the lawyer as he improvises strategy when confronted with inevitable surprises. He will experience the ardor of the persuasive effort and the excitement of mental combat. He will participate in the scene behind the scene. He will be taken to the lawyer's office during trial preparation to hear the problems of the case discussed and the attempted solution designed. He will even accompany the lawyer on long trips throughout many parts of the world as the evidence is prepared for the trial. He will learn in advance about the cross-examination attacks, because the ancient trial by ordeal in which the witness was required to walk barefoot and blindfolded over red-hot plowshares laid lengthwise at unequal distances has been replaced by a stream of burning questions which a cross-examiner may hurl at the witness to drag from him the concealed truth. He will observe the witness combat this effort desperately, and see with what success. He will experience that breathless moment when the foreman of the jury announces who has prevailed. He will be alongside the lawyer when he argues the subsequent appeal in a higher court. He will learn much about human nature, for nowhere else are the nobility and cupidity of man more revealed than when he struggles for his rights in a judicial arena.

The green doors are open.

MY LIFE IN COURT

REPUTATION

Chapter One

THE LIBEL CASE OF

QUENTIN REYNOLDS

VS. WESTBROOK PEGLER

On a Tuesday morning there burst across the nation in 186 newspapers with a circulation of twelve million, a full-length Westbrook Pegler column attacking Quentin Reynolds with unprecedented virulence. It seared Reynolds in every aspect of his professional and private life. It constituted not one, but at least fifteen separate and different libels. With resourceful invective it described Reynolds as having a "mangy hide" which was "peeled" and "nailed to the barn door with the yellow streak glaring for the world to see." It asserted that Reynolds had a "protuberant belly filled with something else than guts." It charged Reynolds with being "an absentee war correspondent," of having posed as an intrepid reporter because he once "covered the ghastly Dieppe raid from a battleship," a distant vantage point of safety.

It ridiculed Reynolds as a man who had "fallen in love with himself as a celebrity," and "by forceful opportune promotion, became one of the great individual profiteers of the war."

It suggested that he was a slacker who, "though six feet five, weighing 250, in the prime of life and health," had attacked "a woman on the home front [Clare Boothe Luce] who had actually seen more fighting than he, and closer up, while high school boys were pushing back the Nazi in the war he had been asking for for the last ten years."

It combined slurs of pro-Communism and war profiteering (a fine brew) by stating that when "the pressure on his Russian friends" was relieved during the war, he was "safe in the United States cleaning up . . . in the movies, in vaudeville, on the radio, and on the lecture circuit."

It asserted that Reynolds was discharged as an editor of *Collier's* magazine when his "medicine grew too strong even for" *Collier's* and after it had "seen the light and faced about," thus charging both *Collier's* and Reynolds with communistic propaganda and an eventual falling out between them.

It accused Reynolds of having "cleaned up $2000 of the ill-gotten loot of the Garsson brothers who, with Congressman May, later were convicted of fraud in war contracts."

Having thus raked Reynolds fore and aft in his professional work, called him yellow, denounced his patriotism, made him out to be a war profiteer, and sharer of loot from men convicted of fraud in war contracts, Pegler then launched a venomous attack on Reynolds's morals, painting him as a filthy, lecherous ogre of indescribable evil.

He charged that Reynolds was a member of the "parasitic, licentious lot" which surrounded Heywood Broun; that Reynolds was a member of the nudist group consisting of Broun and "his friends of both sexes," in which "there was no color line and a conspicuous Negro Communist of the present day . . ." had "seduced a susceptible young white girl at Heywood Broun's"; that "Reynolds and his girl friend of the moment were nuding along the public road" and Broun feared that if the "Yankee neighbors . . . saw Reynolds and his wench strolling along together, absolutely raw, they would call the State police and give him and his place a bad name."

The column asserted that "Connie Broun, Heywood's widow, for whom Reynolds now expresses noble sentiments, reflecting credit on himself, related that, as Reynolds was riding to Heywood's grave with her, he proposed marriage. But she said that some time later, after he had made an artificial reputation as a brave war correspondent in the London blitz, he snubbed her publicly and barely knew her. That would be credible."

After describing Broun as a "voluptuary," a "sneak," a "dirty fighter," a "fellow-traveler," a hypocrite, and unclean, Pegler's column said that "Reynolds was a coat-holder for Broun and imitated his morals, and his equally frowsy physical sartorial corpus . . . that he was sloppy and ran to fat."

He called Reynolds a "fourflusher" and "a sorry mediocrity." The column plumbed every depth, not overlooking a religious slur against Broun, who, he said, had "worshiped at all shrines," then "embraced Catholicism and was funeralized with éclat by Monsignor Fulton J. Sheen at St. Patrick's Cathedral."

The corollary of the proposition that a big lie is more believed than a small one is that a newspaper would not print such daring accusations without *some* proof. Not only had Pegler prided himself on being a good reporter who checked facts (he had won the Pulitzer prize for his exposé of labor racketeering), but the Hearst chain of newspapers was an established organization cognizant of the laws of libel. Would it be so reckless as to publish such a column if it weren't true? Thus brazenness begets its own credibility. Even Reynolds's friends may have had lingering doubts about some of the wide variety of accusations. Surely the public could be misled. *Collier's* magazine, after seventeen years of association, during which Reynolds had written more than 330 feature stories, terminated its relationship with him and did not order another article. His radio and television work dried up instantly. The column was so devilishly clever in its inventive abuse that it was torn out by readers and passed on as an illustration of audacious writing.

People laugh when a man slips on a banana peel and winds up in an undignified posture with foolish shock on his face. The same perverse trait will cause people to chuckle at the discomfiture of a public figure who is belabored for "his protuberant belly filled with something else than guts" and his "mangy hide hung on a barn door with the yellow streak glaring for all to see," etc. I have seen similar Pegler columns of calumny against Mrs. Eleanor Roosevelt, President Dwight D. Eisenhower and others passed along by reader to reader with a chuckle and some conscience-saving comment about the originality of its vituperation. Libel seldom causes as much public indignation as it does private anguish.

Quentin Reynolds and his wife Ginny sat before me. Her eyes, belying her composure, revealed hours of recent crying. His face was pained and pale except for red blotches of anxiety. They had sought me out to sue Pegler and the Hearst companies. My office had made a preliminary examination of the facts. I have undertaken the representation. Now one warning remained to be given. I would prosecute their suit, but I hoped they understood that this would be a legal war without quarter given or asked. It would not be easy to bring Pegler down from the arrogant columnist's perch on which he sat, and where for so many years he had been impregnable. Nor would the Hearst chain of newspapers yield without a counteroffensive. Every moment of Reynolds's life (he had been a bachelor for forty years) would be explored by an army of investigators. Economic and other pressure could be expected to be exerted upon him and perhaps me.

It would take years to prepare this case in the manner I thought it should be, including extensive examinations before trial of Pegler himself. We would be opposed by the ablest libel counsel in the country, and delay tactics might very well be exploited, while thousands of dollars of expense for stenographers' minutes and trips abroad to gather in witnesses was incurred. Then, in the event of victory, there might be only a nominal award. This possibility could not be ignored in view of the fact that Pegler's column had been written in answer to what he would claim was a provocative attack made upon him by Reynolds in a review of a book about Broun by Dale Kramer which appeared in the *Herald Tribune*. Finally, even if we won a substantial award, there would be appeals to the higher courts and the consequent delays of such procedures.

What was called for was not their present fiery determination, stimulated by immediate pain and humiliation, but long-range endurance. If I read the signs rightly, Pegler and the Hearst press might respond to a suit with a new series of vindictive articles. The strategy of the defendants might well be to brazen it out and crush the spirit of the plaintiff. A libel, like sickness, comes on horseback but leaves by foot. The processes of justice are slow. Would Reynolds and his wife feel as determined a year or two or three after this conference? Would their nerves crack? They were undertaking a litigation that challenged an ensconced literary tyrant and a newspaper empire. They had meager resources with which to do battle, but these might be enough if their spirits could hold out. I urged them to think this over carefully. I wanted no heroic answer. I had given full warning of the ordeal ahead and they ought to weigh the advisability of abstaining from battle, as many distinguished victims of Peglerization had done. If they decided to become the champions of challenge to this kind of journalism, they had to be ready to suffer the consequences of a protracted contest. This was the price of possible vindication.

Both gave solemn assurances that they could make the sacrifices required and that they would not weaken in their resolve. Reynolds had the fortitude to keep his promise. Ginny, however, out of her desperate love for her husband, broke under the strain, as we shall see.

After we instituted suit against Westbrook Pegler and the two Hearst Corporations which published the New York *Journal-American* and syndicated the column through various newspapers in the United States, we received the first confirmatory shock that the defendants intended to bludgeon Reynolds into submission. It is customary for defendants in a libel suit to be contrite if they have erred, to give assurance of lack of malice, to publish some retraction, thus diminishing damages. That is why 6 cent verdicts have so often occurred in libel actions. Of course we expected the defenses of "fair comment," and "qualified privilege," as well as a claim that Reynolds had "provoked" the contest by his book review.

But I had not anticipated that instead of the traditional answer composed of formal allegations, there would be served upon us another Pegler diatribe actually enlarging the libel. I am sure no such pleading has ever before been filed in any court. It asserted that "at his home in Connecticut the said Broun permitted and encouraged the practice of nudism, not only by members of his family, but by dozens of visiting literateurs and practitioners of belles-lettres without distinction as to race, color, age or sex. The atmosphere of the aforesaid nudist practices was equally shabby with regard to morality and squalid with regard to sanitation. Interracial seduction was regarded as a mere incident by these prophets of the coming classless and collectivistic society, and the general atmosphere and aroma was in no substantial manner different from that of a pen of animals."

It enlarged the original accusation by then asserting that Reynolds "was a willing and enthusiastic participant in the aforesaid orgies with certain secret reservations as to some of the interracial aspects thereof."

The answer elaborated in the most lurid language the other libels of the original column. To the charge that Reynolds was a war profiteer was added the claim that he "appeared as a vaudeville actor in connection with a motion picture show and appeared on the stage in a spotlight, emerging from a trap door wearing a steel helmet, with intended terrific histrionic impact."

The earlier accusation that Reynolds took $2000 of the "ill-gotten loot" of the Garsson Brothers was enlarged by asserting that "the said plaintiff appeared at a celebration conducted by the aforesaid Garsson Brothers [who swindled and defrauded the United States in connection with the production of munitions] at an all-day carouse. Plaintiff herein was the principal attraction of the aforesaid Garsson burlesque for which the taxpayers of the United States paid $16,000."

It embroidered the original claim of a ghoulish proposal in a funeral car with: "The said plaintiff had sought the hand of the widow of the aforesaid Heywood Broun at his funeral, but his enlarged self-importance and increased earning power led him to other circles and to a discontinuance of his attentions to that lady."

The document ranged from unbelievable references about "the tenets of nudism as laid down by one Parmelee, the father of Gymnosophy, wherein said Parmelee advocated as one of the principal advantages of nudism its facilitation of communistic experiments" to the venomous assertion that "it had become the familar custom in the Book Review Section of the 'Herald Tribune' to select for review for the most part such books as tended to further the socialistic, if not downright communistic ideology."

Finally Pegler counterclaimed against Reynolds for libel! He asserted that Reynolds's review of the book on Broun claimed "that some doctor told Broun he could recover from pneumonia by relaxing and would recover if he could sleep, but said Broun was unable to do so and died as a consequence of defendant Pegler's misconduct and that in effect defendant Pegler was morally guilty of homicide in some unstated degree."

So Pegler pleaded he "was libeled in his reputation and sustained legal injury."

Pegler was so pleased with this answer that he printed portions of it as a column.

Several associates in my office were quick to point out that we could obtain an order from the court striking out most of the answer as improper in law. We had done so in other cases under far less offensive circumstances. The legal authorities were clear that an answer in a lawsuit must allege only ultimate facts in such a way as to clarify the issues. The plea of truth, fair comment, denial of malice, all of which were contained in Pegler's answer, were properly asserted as the defendants' contentions, but he had no right to use his pleading as a cloak for harangue, insult, alleged evidence and malicious opinion.

I surprised my partners and associates by saying: "I don't want a word of that document touched. Leave it just as it is. What better evidence of malice will we have, particularly against the Hearst corporations, than that they filed such a pleading?"

This strategy turned out to be sound. Not only did this unorthodox, discursive document open the door more widely in examining Pegler, but it established the malevolence of all the defendants out of their own mouths. Years later I was able to argue before the Federal Court of Appeals: "Four months after the complaint had been served, the corporate defendants, as well as Pegler, had an opportunity to retract. Nevertheless, the answer . . . not only repeats the lie, but deliberately indulges in new libels of even greater ferocity. . . ."

As for the counterclaim filed by Pegler, this put *his* reputation on the line for the first time!

I am sure that Pegler must have chuckled when he published part of his "legal answer" as a column. It gave him the momentary satisfaction of thumbing his nose at our suit and saying, "How do you like that?" There was to be a day of reckoning, however. In the meantime my heart went out to Reynolds and his wife. The contest had barely begun and they were in worse trouble than before.

I really got down to work.

I went to London to determine whether some of Reynolds's friends in high places would give testimony to contradict the charge that he was a coward, an absentee war correspondent, and a war profiteer.

During the war Reynolds had become one of the most admired figures in England. In a popularity poll among the British people he had ranked third after the King and Winston Churchill. There were reasons for this and I wanted to have them in sworn testimony.

I was granted a conference with Lord Louis Mountbatten. But when I arrived at the gray stone Admiralty building which had the stained and musty look of a castle in Lord Nelson's day, and I had passed through the many preliminary chambers presided over by differently uniformed officers, I was told by Lord Mountbatten's aide that my allotted time was three minutes.

I used the three minutes as I would under similar restriction in court, not to persuade but to excite his interest. He sat at his desk in white uniform, uprightly relaxed, and looked at me with the friendly but remote air of a man who was about to perform a necessary formality and proceed to more important things. In answer to his opening, "How is Quentin

Reynolds?" I startled him by answering literally: "He is fighting for his reputation and honor and needs your help." I quickly listed the charges which had been hurled at Reynolds in an American newspaper, and reminded Mountbatten of those desperate days when, as the leader of the British commandos, he had planned a daring raid on the German-held port of Dieppe and Reynolds had used every possible influence to get himself assigned to the exploit so that he could report it firsthand. His very light blue eyes appeared to become darker as memory filled them. The look of casualness peeled off his face and he began to concentrate and communicate on the business at hand. In a little while excitement pushed him up from his chair and he began to walk around the room. He belonged to that small coterie of men (like Schweitzer, Einstein, Hughes) whom nature had endowed with appearance suitable to their calling. He had the tall, lean figure that an artist would have drawn for a leader of commandos and was handsome withal. As I questioned him, he became warmer and friendlier. I was taking notes. He said, "Why don't I summon my secretary and dictate to him? It will be easier."

He became more animated and eager as the recollection of Reynolds's heroism came to him. He agreed to provide his own testimony as he had dictated it and suggested that I ought to talk to Rear Admiral J. Hughes-Hallet who had commanded the flagship, the *Calpe*, at the Dieppe raid. He arranged for my appointment with Rear Admiral Hughes-Hallet. Two hours and twelve minutes after I entered the office I left.

The testimony of Lord Louis Mountbatten was later formally recorded by interrogatories submitted by me, and cross-interrogatories put by the defendants' lawyers.

After qualifying himself as Earl Mountbatten of Burma, and Fourth Sea Lord of the Admiralty, and as having had "the over-all responsibility for the Dieppe raid under the British Chiefs of Staff," he testified that Col. Jock Lawrence of General Eisenhower's headquarters staff had, at the behest of Quentin Reynolds, interceded for his permission to have Reynolds assigned to the flagship on what was then an unrevealed mission. "I told him," testified Mountbatten, "that from the nature of this operation it was bound to be extremely hazardous, and particularly so if he went in the Headquarters ship." Reynolds came to him personally and, despite the warning that this would be "a sticky wicket," pleaded for the assignment. Mountbatten granted it.

When asked what reputation Reynolds enjoyed as a journalist and author in Great Britain during World War II, he replied, "It was the very highest."

When Pegler's lawyers put questions designed to show that the flagship was the safest place to be, they were sharply rebuffed. Lord Louis testified that the enemy could always identify a flagship because all instructions for battle emanated from her. "It is inevitable in naval actions for the flagship or headquarters ship to be in the greatest danger. All history shows that flagships and flotilla leaders have suffered most in naval actions. Any ship other than the *Calpe* would have been a safer place."

The defendants pressed and elicited even more damaging testimony. "The *Calpe* [on which Reynolds was] suffered about 25 per cent casualties from the Nazi planes in spite of the R.A.F. air umbrella."

When, on cross-examination, he was asked whether at least the journey home wasn't peaceful, he replied: "There were several bombing attacks on the way home."

Since Pegler's column charged that Reynolds had observed the Dieppe raid from a distance in the safety of a battleship, his attorneys asked whether being on the destroyer *Calpe* was more dangerous. Mountbatten said it was because "she was going in close owing to her shallower draft and was entirely unarmoured."

Then I visited Rear Admiral Hughes-Hallet (who had also been in charge of naval operations on D day) in his home at Bath, Somerset.

He gave a firsthand account of Reynolds's heroism under fire. The *Calpe* had been attacked by Dorniers, Messerschmidts and Focke-Wulfs. Men were hit all around Reynolds. Of the four people standing closest to him, two were killed and the other two were injured.

There were 278 wounded Canadians picked up from the sea and Reynolds "tended the wounded and displayed calmness and efficiency. He acted bravely and honorably in the heat of battle."

When asked about Reynolds's reputation, he testified that he "enjoyed high reputation for integrity and accuracy as a journalist and author. His B.B.C. broadcasts made him a national figure."

I then proceeded to Lord Beaverbrook's home at Cherkley, Leatherhead, in Surrey.

He was stretched out on a bed suffering from gout, but the pain did not appear to reach his head. He was full of good humor and waived aside my apology for imposing on him when ill. Like Churchill, his face was another version of John Bull. He was eagerly chatty and interested in the fact that I was born in London. I had, in all honesty, to break the tie of affinity by telling him that I came to the United States when I was only two years old and considered myself undilutedly American.

He testified that he and Averell Harriman had headed the Anglo-American Lend-Lease mission to Moscow. "Mr. Reynolds was attached to Mr. Harriman [in order to get into Russia and the fighting front]. I recall that he did excellent service there."

The most remarkable deposition came from General Sir Frank Messervy. It was a vivid description of Reynolds under fire given under oath by the major-general in command of 200,000 men on service in the Western Desert of Egypt and Cyrenaica for two years and later in Burma for two years. He had commanded five divisions, including the 7th Armoured Division, known as the Desert Rats. His list of extraordinary decorations included the Distinguished Service Order, Order of Companion of the Bath, Knight Commander of the British Empire and the Knight Commander of the Star of India, all presented by King George, and Citation of the Legion of Merit presented by President Truman for his services in Burma against the Japanese, where he also directed two American Air Force units called Air Commandos. He testified: "I met Quentin Reynolds at Western Omar. Our troops had just captured the Omars, but Rommel's Nazi armoured divisions had counterattacked. We were in the midst of a fierce and prolonged battle. When we ultimately held the Omars we were able to advance and relieve Tobruk. During this struggle Colonel Desmond Young, Mr. Quentin Reynolds, and Captain Clive Burt arrived on a journey through the German lines. In order to reach our Headquarters they had passed through the mine fields and German positions in a decidedly dangerous journey."

The General was walking with me on the grounds of his farm and gardens as he related these events. He was wearing a typical country tweed suit with leather elbows, and smoking a pipe. The serenity of the lazily swaying grass fields, livened occasionally by patches of brilliantly hued flower beds, was a proper background for his scholarly mustached face. But the unemotional formality of his recital actually heightened the effect of his blood and cannon-thunder story. His deposition brought the scene to life: "Mr. Quentin Reynolds stayed in this hot spot of fighting for two or three days, interviewing our officers and men. Like the troops in actual combat, he was under fire of all sorts. On one occasion during a very heavy air raid he was wounded by a splinter in the knee and sustained other cuts. He was treated and bandaged, but continued to keep up the morale of all with whom he came in contact by his cheerful manner. Mr. Quentin Reynolds and Colonel Young advised me that they intended to travel back in the darkness of night through the German lines to Army Headquarters when they could proceed to Cairo. I warned them that this was a hazardous undertaking since Rommel's Panzer divisions were all around us in a swirling battle. They had to pass through extensive mine fields and dodge parties of Nazi tanks which were on the move in all directions. Mr. Quentin Reynolds insisted nevertheless on passing through the German lines in order that he might send immediate dispatches on the developments. In view of the fact that they insisted on carrying out their plan, I asked them whether they would take back military dispatches to Headquarters. They left at night and I learnt later that they had successfully traversed the mine fields, evaded all enemy tanks and returned to British Army Headquarters."

In answer to a final question came this reply: "From my personal observations I am able to state that Mr. Quentin Reynolds at all times, under extremely hazardous conditions of war, demonstrated great courage, calm, and exemplary morale in conditions of a fierce battle with all its attendant dangers. I felt then, and do now, that Mr. Quentin Reynolds's conduct was brave, intrepid, and up to a high standard of soldierly conduct under fire."

Little wonder that Pegler and the Hearst defendants waived their right to cross-examine General Sir Frank Messervy. How could they challenge his veracity and, short of that, what could they ask?

Now I drove on even more eagerly to obtain the testimony of an eyewitness to Reynolds's journey through the Nazi lines.

He was Captain Clive Burt, a barrister at the English bar for twenty-five years, who was Captain in the Scots Guards during the war. In November 1941 his troops were engaged in the battle in the Western Desert. On his way to join his regiment: "I became attached to Colonel Desmond Young as his navigator to guide him and his motorized detachment through the desert to the scene of the battle. The word 'navigator' refers to the fact that in the desert one had to find one's way largely by compass and by the sun and stars. . . . Mr. Quentin Reynolds was advised by us of the risk, but nevertheless insisted upon accompanying us."

Only twenty minutes separated this trio from capture or death, for they "learnt that about twenty minutes after we had left the 4th Indian Division Headquarters on our way forward, General Rommel's German tanks had broken through and overrun the Headquarters."

They were bombarded as they picked their way through the mine fields. Then the Nazi planes sighted them and attacked. "Colonel Young, Mr. Reynolds, and myself took cover in a slit trench which had been made by an enemy. It was about four or five feet deep. [It was night so] flares were dropped at first by the enemy planes, followed at a short interval by a stick of bombs—five or six in number. This was repeated about half a dozen times, and the bombing was accurate and fairly destructive. We were showered with sand and stones from the explosion of bombs, which were extremely close. One bomb blew the back out of Colonel Young's truck, which was standing alongside our trench, and an ammunition truck about fifty yards away went up in flames and the ammunition in it continued to explode for the next quarter of an hour. One stick of bombs fell only a few yards from us. The flares which preceded the bombing hung slowly in mid-air as they descended and lit up the area so that the bombing would be as accurate as possible."

With characteristic and deliberate understatement, Captain Burt testified: "It was not a very pleasant experience to feel that one was being subjected to searchlight effects and then knowing that bombs were going to be dropped on us. There were a number of serious casualties in our immediate vicinity as a result of this bombing. Mr. Quentin Reynolds received an injury in his knee from flying bits of rock or bomb fragments and received other cuts from which he was bleeding. Colonel Young personally treated Mr. Quentin Reynolds's knee and bandaged it."

After this night, in which they were pointed out by searchlight fingers and shot at individually, came daylight but not surcease. They were shelled by long-range guns, and casualties were suffered. In the afternoon Nazi tanks came up from the rear and attacked. "This attack was beaten off with difficulty, the guns firing over open sights, which means firing at point-blank range."

After the battle of Sidi Omar was won, Colonel Young and Reynolds wanted to get back to Army Headquarters near Fort Maddelena to send off their dispatches to Cairo. Captain Burt described this trip briefly in his testimony: "Flares were being sent up continuously by the Germans which lit up the area in order to prevent vehicles from passing through. We steered our way between these lights and between the shadowy forms of the German tanks, many of which had been knocked out and were being repaired. There was light shelling during the night. We ultimately succeeded in passing through the Germans, and at daybreak arrived at Army Headquarters."

What was Captain Burt's evaluation of Reynolds's conduct? "He was calm and unruffled, and was a great encouragement to the troops on the ground around us. During lulls in the shelling he cheered up the troops, visiting them and telling them of his experiences in London, which was 'back home' to the troops, and also encouraging them by telling them that reports of their gallant doings would be broadcast to the world by him and others. Mr. Quentin Reynolds's conduct during these trips was the exemplary conduct of a courageous man who, in the course of performing his duty as a war correspondent, sought out places of danger that he was under no obligation otherwise to encounter. It was upon his own insistence that he shared the experiences I have described."

"Absentee war correspondent," "yellow," "gutless"—indeed!

While in London I endeavored to obtain evidence to contradict Pegler's slur that Reynolds was a "war profiteer."

Even before the United States entered the war, many American fliers had volunteered to fight in the English sky, which they considered a mere extension of the American sky. They became known as the Eagle Squadron. Quentin Reynolds, who had seen two hundred fires sown in London by Nazi incendiary bombs in a single night, had an affection for the R.A.F. heroes which burst into adulation for the young American boys who had invited themselves into the desperate sky battle. At his own expense he set up suites of rooms for these American youngsters. Food, drinks, theater tickets—for them and their girls—were all on him. It was a sort of one-man USO reception center, but on a lavish scale, suitable to the emotions which ruled him. To Quent, fervently American, sympathetically British, and sentimentally Irish, there was nothing too good for those boys, and he no more calculated the enormous expense of his undertaking than the fliers calculated the thirty per cent risk of no return over a period of six months. Certainly, as his literary agent, Mark Hanna, later testified, he was oblivious to his income taxes which were piling up despite these lavish expenditures. Since he continued this unlimited treat over a long period of time, even while he was away in Russia, he wound up not only broke, but in serious debt to Uncle Sam. This was the man Pegler denounced as a "war profiteer."

I visited Arthur Christiansen, editor of the *Daily Express*, whose circulation of four million made it the largest daily newspaper in the world. He later testified in his deposition: "I know that Mr. Reynolds was constantly providing entertainment on a lavish scale for members of the Armed Forces, and particularly for airmen in the Eagle Squadron who were spending a few days leave in London. I remember that on more than one occasion I saw Mr. Reynolds's bills at the Savoy Hotel and these sometimes exceeded £200 a week. I remember hearing Mr. Reynolds on many occasions direct one of his secretaries to go down to the restaurant with visiting airmen and make arrangements for their bills to be charged to his, Reynolds's account."

I also obtained the deposition of Jack Beddington, a leading industrialist, who during the war was the Director of the Films Division of the Ministry of Information. He was an Honorary Fellow of the Society of Industrial Artists, and the King had appointed him, a wounded veteran, Commander of the British Empire. He testified: "I knew and was present on more than one occasion at Mr. Quentin Reynolds's apartments in London. He kept open house. The brave American fliers who volunteered their services and were fighting to protect British skies, were given free rein by Mr. Quentin Reynolds to use his rooms, to order food, drinks, tickets for theaters, all at his expense. I knew that he was an intensely brave man. Reynolds had achieved the reputation of one who sought the most dangerous missions in order to give firsthand account of the actual news."

Reynolds's generosity took other forms too, because it was a form of recklessness inspired by larger values emanating from the life-and-death struggle around him. For a long while whatever money he earned he contributed to the R.A.F. and Eagle Squadron benevolent funds.

He had given a commentary on a film called *London Can Take It.* It became famous throughout the free world. While the motion picture recorded the roaring flames, collapsing buildings, siren wails rising to hysterical crescendo, and women and children running through the flickering smoky night with incongruous bundles in their arms, Quent's vibrant low voice described the scene with immeasurable calm. It was a contrapuntal tour de force. The film earned huge sums. Reynolds gave everything to the fliers' families.

Beddington testified that *London Can Take It* was widely shown throughout the United States "and raised a large sum of money for the R.A.F. Benevolent Fund. Again Reynolds declined to receive compensation for his efforts and contributed all the substantial sums for the families of deceased or disabled R.A.F. fighter personnel." Indeed, he pointed out that "the two great voices in England to which the people listened over the radio were first Mr. Winston Churchill and, second only to him, Mr. Quentin Reynolds."

Reynolds also made special broadcasts on the B.B.C. addressed to Hitler under his real name, Mr. Schicklgruber, and one to Dr. Goebbels. They struck deep into the Nazi hide with the fiercest of weapons, ridicule. The English received a corresponding chuckle and lift in morale.

I obtained the deposition of Sir Walter Monckton, Minister of Labor in the British Cabinet and a distinguished lawyer. He confirmed Reynolds's contributions of all his earnings to Spitfire and Eagle Squadron funds. So did Lord Alfred Duff Cooper, who also identified the original signature of Winston Churchill on a letter to Reynolds:

My dear Sir,

I should like you to know how admirable I thought your broadcast last Sunday. I know that I was far from being alone in my enjoyment of it and that your words have given real pleasure and encouragement to a great many people in this Island.

Yours faithfully,
Winston Churchill.

I also conferred with Brendan Bracken, Prime Minister Churchill's secretary, whose thinning red hair gave me the impression of violence reduced to witty resignation. He arranged a meeting for me with Winston Churchill, but unfortunately this was the time when the Prime Minister suffered his first—then undisclosed—illness, and my appointment was canceled. Thus I missed not only the crowning confirmation of Reynolds's reputation and courage, but also the fulfillment of my own ambition to share, no matter how briefly, the presence and mind of the greatest figure of our century.

When I returned to the United States we arranged to take the deposition of Captain Harry Butcher, General Eisenhower's personal aide during the war, who had written a book about him. He testified that Reynolds had a uniquely high standing with General Eisenhower and "with the higher echelons of the Army and Navy, including Supreme Headquarters."

So we had obtained testimony from unimpeachable sources of Reynolds's courage and generosity. Ultimately we buttressed these depositions with twenty-one witnesses who appeared on the witness stand. Many of these surprised the defendants. But then they had some surprises for us too, including the appearance on the witness stand of a famous general, an admiral, and the priest of the only Roman Catholic church in Moscow.

Now the time had come to examine Westbrook Pegler before trial. I had brought the suit in the Federal Court rather than in the State Court because broader examinations before trial are permitted there. Even though I knew that in the Federal Court a verdict required the agreement of all twelve jurors, whereas in the State Court ten out of twelve was sufficient, I accepted this heavier burden of persuasion for the privilege of a more liberal examination of Pegler. The law permits a searching exposure of both parties by each other before the trial, so as to reduce the element of surprise and make possible the fullest preparation on the merits. Pegler's testimony, so taken, could be used in one of two ways. I could either read it into the record at the trial, or I could confront him with it at the trial if his testimony varied from it. In short, such an examination has the virtue of pinning down the witness. As we shall see, there was such pinning down that at the trial Pegler over and over again retracted his prior testimony, protested that he had been misled, wriggled and wiggled, but admitted *dozens* of times that he had been incorrect under oath.

But it was not easy to get Pegler to submit to testimony under oath. He sought delays because he had professional duties to perform in Washington and other places, because he had to be in Arizona due to his father's illness, because he had to travel to Europe, etc., etc. Finally, when I had exhausted the courtesies of delay, I insisted upon his appearance. When he failed to obey the court order, I moved to punish him for contempt. Judge William Bondy declared him in default and ordered a default judgment unless he appeared for examination. Then he came. At last we had taken him out of his private office, where he fashioned his verbal thunderbolts with impunity, and put him out into the open, under oath, for full inquiry.

Examinations before trial are judicial proceedings, but no judge presides. When a ruling is required, the attorneys visit the judge in chambers. Since such requests for rulings are usually accumulated until the end of the examination, the practice has grown up of having the examination conducted in the office of the examining attorney where a court stenographer attends. This suits the convenience of both the lawyers and the litigants, and such arrangements are usually stipulated.

Newspaper reporters have the right to attend because the examination is still a court proceeding. I preferred that they didn't, because a witness who is testifying in the presence of the press strikes poses, and is doubly reluctant to make an admission. I had no right to exclude the reporters, but I found that by promising each that no other reporter would be present, they were content to stay away until the trial itself. For the same reason that I did not wish to inflame Pegler into unnecessary resistance, I asked Reynolds and his wife not to attend these sessions. So only Pegler's attorney, Mr. Charles Henry, his assistant, Mr. James E. Bowden, and one or two of my partners, Mr. Walter Beck or Mr. Paul Martinson, were present as week after week over a period of more than a year I dug into the defendant with thousands of questions. Before we were finished we had over 5000 pages of his sworn testimony and had marked several hundred exhibits. Before we were through, his attorneys had made applications to Federal judges to terminate the examination because

I was charged with being too far afield and repetitious. The motions were denied and Pegler was ordered back for further examination.

The examination was held in my office and when he appeared the first time, I made a quick reading of the man. He was imposingly tall, but his erectness was marred by girth. He had very bushy blond eyebrows, and they were cultivated to point upwards. But somehow this effort at Mephistophelean ferocity failed in the same way that waxed mustaches seldom succeed in producing the appearance of refined sophistication. His voice, as is usually the case, gave the truest impression. It was weak and quavered with nervousness. When he spoke, his cheeks seemed to catch the tremor of his voice and quivered too. He would gulp as he neared the end of a sentence and his eyes stared momentarily as he caught his breath.

He drank water during these sessions. In the morning his hand was fairly steady. But as the day progressed with hundreds of searching questions, he shook so violently as he filled or lifted the glass that the water spilled on my desk. At the end of the day my secretary observed the wet trail of testimony with horror, for she was more concerned with the desk's polish than with Pegler's discomfiture. One day she placed a towel underneath the glass. Pegler deemed this a personal insult and protested. I ordered it removed. This incident reminded me of an anecdote Mike Todd once told me about the opening night of *South Pacific*. After the final curtain he went backstage where, together with hundreds of others, he was being pushed in all directions by an enthusiastic mob of well-wishers. He came across Molly, the seamstress who took care of costumes, sitting in a corner crying quietly. She was one of the veterans of show business and he greeted her with appropriate exuberance until he discovered hers were not tears of joy.

"What's the matter, Molly?" he asked.

"The show's a flop. And after so much work."

"A flop! Are you crazy? Haven't you heard the ovation? Why this is the biggest thing that's ever hit Broadway."

She was unconsoled. "It's a flop," she insisted. "I stood out front for a while and watched the show. I tell you, Mr. Todd, you can see every seam on those dresses!"

Apocryphal or not, this was quite a sermon on the significance of perspective. I am sure that to my secretary the Reynolds–Pegler case was a disaster because it ruined the polish on my desk. Fortunately there were to be many days when she would be distressed.

Just when the case was nearing trial, Pegler burst forth in his column again. He had read that Reynolds was to deliver a lecture to the New York Credit and Financial Management Association. This was a paid engagement, and Pegler wanted to draw the economic rope tighter around Quent's neck. So he wrote in his column: "As a public service I provide herein information concerning Quentin Reynolds which may be a guide to any organizations which may desire to hire him. . . . It may also help the radio and television publics to evaluate his statements."

There followed a nasty and false diatribe about Reynolds joining the Harriman–Beaverbrook mission to Russia ". . . to thrust on the Soviet dictators the riches of the United States," and concluding that Reynolds's attitude toward Congressional investigations of Soviet propaganda was "exactly what the Communist traitors in the United States have been arguing for years."

In splitting a boulder one never knows which blow will crack it open. Hundreds may rain upon it without any visible sign of effect. Then one more swing and it splinters wide. Apparently Quent and Ginny had been under pressure from the first attack. Doors of all kinds had been slammed in their faces. Quent had to shift his efforts in new directions to earn money. Even loyal friends were a constant reminder of his banishment, because their attitude was one of sympathy rather than eagerness. I had no idea that one more column would crack the façade of resistance.

But a few days later Reynolds telephoned me. "Lou, I have some bad news to tell you." His voice had the low vibrant timbre and ominous calm of his commentary in *London Can Take It*. But this time I imagined it was several years of preparation and his case which had been burnt to the ground.

"What has happened?"

"I just learned that Ginny went to see Pegler yesterday and pleaded with him to let up on me. I know she shouldn't have done it, but his last column made her hysterical. She is afraid she has destroyed the case and that you won't ever talk to her again. I want to put her on the phone so she can tell you what happened. Please don't be angry with her, Lou."

"Did she sign anything?" I asked. I could hear the question repeated, and I hung on the intervening moment's silence. Then he said she had not. Again he asked whether I would talk to her. She was sobbing as she got on the telephone.

"I know, Lou, I have done something terrible. I know I shouldn't have done it, but I just couldn't stand it any longer. What does he want of us? Why won't he let us alone?"

I calmed her and asked for a description of what had occurred. Between inconsistent cries of bitter self-condemnation and efforts at exculpation, I was able to piece together the incident. After she read Pegler's column, she telephoned him and asked to see him. Surprised, he consented. She came to his office and wept that she could not stand Quent being destroyed by his attacks. Why did he not let up? Why did he want to destroy them? Pegler explained that it was Reynolds who was suing him, that Reynolds had originally attacked him in the *Herald Tribune Book Review* of the book about Broun, and that the whole matter could be settled if Reynolds would drop his suit; then Pegler would never write about him again. She was too distressed to know what to do and said she would come back and let him know. She had signed no document and made no promise. Of course she understood she had no authority to do so anyway. But she realized full well that she had revealed to Pegler her distress, and had given him the impression that Reynolds had sent her to surrender. Now it dawned on her that she should not have acted without Quent's knowledge and permission, or mine. She was in panic because she feared she might have destroyed the case in a moment of hysteria.

I assured her she had not. Though I sympathized inwardly with her plight, and even admired her loyalty to Quent which had set her off course, I felt I had to give her a stern rebuke for meddling in a matter beyond her province. I therefore told her that she had done immense psychological harm. Now the defendants would consider that Quent's resistance had collapsed and, if we pursued the suit, they might be encouraged to wage more written attacks in order to exploit her vulnerability and, through her, his. I was willing to overlook the incident provided I had her assurance that she would not do anything in the future, no matter what the provocation, without my knowledge and consent. She was relieved that she had not caused more harm, and only too eager to escape with a reprimand. She lived up to her promise. She later sat through the trial silently, adding her beautiful presence to the scene of her husband's ordeal.

As for the defendants, their psychological advantage was offset by their miscalculation. Pegler reported to his attorney that the case was settled. It would be discontinued, and he would refrain from any further attacks. When Mr. Henry, his counsel, so advised me, I disabused him of his impression. I told him I knew of Mrs. Reynolds's tearful approach to Pegler, but that this did not represent Reynolds's views. I told him, disbelieving though he was, that Reynolds had not sent his wife on her mission, and that he disavowed her action. Furthermore, Mrs. Reynolds herself was horrified by her impulsive conduct and had pleaded for forgiveness for her unauthorized interference in the case.

All this only convinced the defendants that it was I who was standing in the way of a speedy and painless disposition of the case. This is often the lot of the lawyer. No matter what the plot, he is readily cast by the adversary in the role of the villain. Pegler was so convinced that the Reynoldses had no stomach for the case that his secretary called Ginny to ask when she would return to close the matter as she had promised. She rejected all overtures and refused to take any more calls. The Hearst Company likewise probed for a surrender. Mr. Richard Berlin, its president, arranged a conference with me through an intermediary in which he, too, advocated that Pegler and Reynolds had had a writer's quarrel and could well shake hands as men in the profession do, and call off the whole thing.

I believe that the defendants clung so tenaciously to the "settlement"

Ginny had instigated, that they didn't really believe the case would ever be tried. How could Reynolds, who already was suffering from his wife's hysteria, face with her the struggle which would be his when he took the stand?

But they misread Quent's litigation courage as they had misread his war correspondent's courage. He faced all accusations, ranging from cowardice to nudism and Communism, with dignity and self-assurance. Could Pegler do the same?

The breathless anxiety of actors on the opening night of a play has been written about and depicted frequently. But it is nothing compared to the nervous excitement on the opening day of a court trial. The air is laden with anticipatory fears and hopes. Both sides have prepared for years, and now in the actual clash the strength of the contending forces will be revealed for the first time.

Reynolds, like Pegler, had been examined before trial to the extent of some 5000 pages of testimony. Hundreds of exhibits had been gathered. Witnesses from all parts of the United States and some from Europe had been flown in.

Tension had been mounting steadily as the trial date approached. Reynolds, our first witness, had spent weeks at my home into the early hours of the morning reviewing every sentence he had written in his many books which might be the subject of cross-examination. He was prepared to ward off the blows, fair and foul, which would rain upon him from all sides.

The actor knows his lines. He need not improvise. He is not required to face surprise verbal attacks. Most actors and actresses are terrified if they have to make a three-minute speech of their own creation at some public function. They are articulate and confident only when they have the shelter of memorization of an author's words.

This, then, will indicate the plight of a witness who knows that a trained, hostile lawyer will examine him for days on end and he must be capable of coping with the attack, known and unknown. To add to his terror is the knowledge (represented by a pain in the pit of his stomach) that if he makes one slip, he may destroy his case. He is as concerned about unwittingly betraying his own lawyer by his stupidity as injuring his cause.

On the morning of the trial all the physical indicia of unbearable trepidation are evident. Hands are clammy, brows are wet, cheeks are either flushed or sickly pale, eyes are red-rimmed, voices are froggy, there are artificial yawns, dry lips and, indelicate though it be to relate, frequent visits to the toilet.

This is the time when the lawyer, although he may be suffering from the same symptoms, and his own pulse is rapid, must bring confidence to his distressed army. I greet clients and witnesses with hearty cheerfulness.

I engage them in light jests. They must be comforted by my easy serenity. They clutch at it and derive strength from it. At all times the lawyer must be the central bower of strength upon which all lean. And if he can create around him an atmosphere of sureness, it is like oxygen which relieves the strain of breathing. Ultimately the jury, too, is enveloped by the confident air of counsel, and the psychological play upon its convictions is incalculable.

The setting of the courtroom drama is also awesome. The courtrooms in most federal courts are high-paneled in walnut grains. There are two large specially constructed tables one in front of the other, each seating as many as eight lawyers and assistants. The first table is occupied by the plaintiff's counsel, the other by the defendant's. In front of counsel table is an elevated platform and desk at which sits the court clerk, who marks documents in evidence. On the side, on another platform facing the counsel tables, are fourteen swivel seats for a jury of twelve and two alternates—in case a juror should become ill.

At the end of the jury box, elevated on a still higher platform, is the lone seat for the witness, with a small table in front of him for documents or the glass of water, which he needs if his tongue is not to cling to the dry roof of his mouth. And towering above all on a magnificently carved platform is the Judge's chair. It is built like a throne with a huge brown leather back topped by graceful wooden carving. Behind that chair is a high wall designed in paneled wood with the seal of the Federal Government engraved into the walnut. And at one side stands a huge silk American flag with gold fringe, the only brilliant touch of color in the austere surroundings.

Then, three knocks on the door alongside the Judge's bench. Everyone in the crowded courtroom springs to his feet respectfully. The Judge, robed in black, mounts the three steps toward his seat and remains standing. The clerk intones the announcement with solemnity reminiscent of prayer, while all stand rigidly still: "Hear ye, hear ye, hear ye. All having business before this Court, come forth, give your attention and you shall be heard. God save these United States and this Honorable Court."

The Judge nods an undirectional greeting, and sits down. There is a shuffling, scraping noise as jurors, lawyers, and visitors in the fifteen fine wooden benches in the rear of the court also sit down.

The clerk calls out: "Quentin Reynolds against the Hearst Corporation and Hearst Consolidated Publications, Inc."

"Plaintiff ready," I say.

"Defendants ready," says a voice from the table behind me.

Judge Edward Weinfeld announces that he will question the jurors to determine their impartiality. The lawyers may submit questions through him, if they wish. I consider this a serious setback. I like to question jurors myself. It is an invaluable opportunity to make personal contact with the juror and gauge his personality and mind. By speaking individually to each juror, one can get behind the face's mask. Sometimes a hard face lights up in a warm smile, or a kindly face becomes forbidding as the lips curve during an answer. The voice and diction are always revealing. During personal questioning one may sense a sympathetic bond or, conversely, resistance. All the psychological arts can be employed to evaluate the juror's leanings. But when a number of jurors merely shake their collective heads in answer to the Judge's formal questions, observation gives very limited clues.

Each lawyer has three challenges to excuse a juror, even though the juror has not shown prejudice calling for disqualification. These arbitrary challenges are precious because they permit the lawyer to use his discretion in weeding out anyone from the jury whose occupation, personality, or age do not suit him. Pegler's lawyers asked for additional challenges because there were three defendants and only one plaintiff.

COURT: On the representation of Mr. Henry that at least one defendant is in a different position from the other defendants, while not altogether compelling or even persuasive, I am going to allow the defendants two additional challenges and the plantiff one additional challenge.

NIZER: I think that does me a great injustice, your Honor. In view of the fact that I must have a unanimous verdict to get a verdict at all, the problem facing the plaintiff is far, far greater than that which faces the defense.

COURT: That is true in every case. You need a unanimous verdict.

NIZER: That is correct. Therefore I say when your Honor exercises his discretion in this matter, anything which throws the weight of the additional challenge to the defendant is magnified many fold in its injury to the plaintiff. If anything, since the defendant could well afford, for example, to have two or three biased jurors, theoretically speaking, and still be all right, I can't afford to have one biased juror and be all right.

I do not think it is fair to give 2 to 1 on any such additional claim. The corporations are one and the same interest. They are simply divided for a pure matter of corporate structure.

COURT: Well, I am accepting Mr. Henry's statement with respect to the alleged different positions.

This was a serious blow. Though I hoarded my challenges as carefully as possible, I ran out of them and was obliged to accept two jurors who were steady readers of Hearst's *Journal-American* and Pegler's column. They insisted that this would not cause them to favor the defendants and that they would decide solely on the evidence presented. They could therefore not be challenged for cause, and I missed the two extra arbitrary challenges which the defendant had exercised. I felt that we had a tough jury to convince, and we had to win the mind of every one of them.

The swearing in of the jury is a solemn rite. At that moment the housewife and shopkeeper become judges—judges of the facts. The presiding judge is supreme in determining the applicable law, but even he cannot interfere with jurors in their exclusive right to decide the facts.

The Judge then nods to the plaintiff's lawyer. "You may address the jury." The purpose of the opening addresses is to acquaint the jurors with the nature of the case and what each side intends to prove. In this way the jury obtains a preliminary view of the entire case and the respective contentions of plaintiff and defendant. It is then better able to follow the testimony as it comes piecemeal from the witness stand.

It is an old theory that opening statements should be conservative and not promise too much. There is an illustrative anecdote about the trial lawyer who permitted his young assistant to make the opening address to the jury. Thus thrown into the limelight, the young man delivered an emotional oration that set the courtroom aflame. When he was finished, the client jumped up to congratulate him. "What a magnificent opening statement," he exulted.

"It certainly was," said the experienced lawyer sadly. "He has opened the case so wide, I don't know how in hell I'll ever be able to close it."

But if the attorney stays within his capacity to perform, the opening statement can be an invaluable forensic weapon. By a skillful presentation of what he intends to prove, set opposite the issues in the case, he can convert a mere informative exercise into a persuasive plea. Of course he should not tell all. Indeed, he may even spread some leaves over the traps, so that his adversary will tread more readily over them. But the opportunity to condition the jury favorably is as limitless as the attorney's art.

I believe in an extensive opening statement. I speak without a note, but I have thought through my address very carefully. It is an early opportunity to look each juror in the eye and by sincerity and earnestness make contact with him. It is interesting to observe the bland look on a juror's face when you begin, perhaps even a cynical smile, and how he is caught up in the drama of your recital, his face responding properly with varying emotions of sympathy or resentment as the arguments make inroads upon him. Finally, when you walk up and back, and his eyes follow and are riveted upon you, the persuasive effort has begun successfully.

When my opening statement was almost completed, I turned the jury's attention to Pegler himself. I knew how effective Reynolds would be, and what an extraordinary series of witnesses was ready to testify on his behalf. But I wanted the jury to know that it was Pegler we were waiting for, and I wanted Pegler to know it, too.

So, after explaining Pegler's counterclaim against Reynolds, I said: "Now we are very glad in a way, ladies and gentlemen—it is a curious thing to say, but we are very glad that we have a counterclaim in this action, because Mr. Pegler thereby puts his reputation and character on the line. He says that his reputation and character have been injured, and when the time comes we are going to examine Mr. Pegler's reputation and character, and what he does and what he writes, and what he stands for from the beginning of his life to now, at least to the date of the libel article. We don't mind putting Mr. Reynolds under a microscope. We are going to do it—anything at all that they wish to ask him. But we are going to take the same privilege and put Mr. Pegler under a microscope in this court and find out what his reputation and character are. I invite you, ladies and gentlemen, I entreat you, to wait for the time when Mr. Pegler takes the stand and watch him carefully. Listen to every word carefully."

As I turned from the jury for a moment, I caught a glimpse of Pegler. His eye was twitching.

There is that unsurpassed moment in the theater when anticipation, made mysterious by darkness, bursts into light as the curtain rises.

All preliminaries in the courtroom, concluding with the opening statements, are like an overture. Then comes that breathless moment when the curtain rises on the trial itself. "Your Honor, I call Mr. Quentin Reynolds to the stand."

He walks from behind the balustrade that separates the attorneys from the spectators and mounts the steps to the lonely witness chair. The clerk announces that all must be seated and silent while the oath is administered. His left hand on a Bible, his right hand raised in vow, he is given the oath of truth. He sits down and every eye in the room is on him.

Reynolds would be a distinguished-looking man even if his voice did not persuade you he was. He is as tall, broad, and powerful as a former Brown University football star and boxing champion should be. His pert face has earned the lines it needed to give it character. It is a trusting face, not pinched with cynicism. What must have been called sandy-colored hair when he was a youngster is now hued with indistinct gray, which gives it an unfamiliar tan-gray blend. It is thick, curly, and parted on the right side. His kindliness dominates him. He is eager to be friendly and bestow praise on others. Hearst executives with whom he has worked are given his unqualified appreciation as "wonderful" newspapermen. His early friendship with Pegler himself is recited with sincere sentiment. Whenever he is required to relate his own experiences as a war correspondent, he cannot be stopped from volunteering that other correspondents did as much and more. He is extrovertedly hearty and generous. There could not be a sharper personality contrast than between the two antagonists in this contest.

I begin casually with uncomplicated questions. Even one as experienced in public appearances as Reynolds must be put at ease and given confidence, for a long ordeal awaits him. After describing his schooling, he testifies: "So my first job was that of a lifeguard over in a pool in Newark in Dreamland Park. I didn't last very long because I couldn't take the sun, and they didn't like the fact that a lifeguard spent most of the time in the shade." This is an early reference to his peculiar allergy to sunlight, which we were to develop fully as a refutation to his "nuding along with a wench."

Damon Runyon recognized in him the makings of a newspaperman and took him to the head of King Features and International News Service. Soon he was sent to Germany where Hitler had just come to power. "Being lucky, I found myself in Nuremberg when a young girl, Anna Fuess, who was engaged to a German Jew refused to give him up and she was paraded through the streets by the storm troopers. The whole populace was out to taunt this girl, whose head was shaven. [She went insane.] I got the story as an eyewitness to such an atrocity perpetrated, and I sent the story back to the United States." It was reprinted all over the world. The Nazis denied it, but Reynolds had two reliable witnesses with him, the son and daughter of the American ambassador.

Reynolds covered the trial of Van der Lubbe and others accused of setting fire to Reichstag. Soon he was engaged by *Collier's* magazine. "For the first year I was with *Collier's* I wrote thirty-seven articles, and with the decent generosity that is always characteristic of them, they broke their original arrangement and paid me a retainer of $10,000 and $500 an article."

Through the years he wrote three hundred and eleven feature articles for *Collier's*.

Reynolds was assigned to the French Army, then battling with the desperation that precedes collapse. To hide their plight, the Army officials sent correspondents on "conducted tours." He was not to be so side-tracked. Through Ambassador Bullet he and Kenneth Downs, a Hearst reporter, received a four-day pass to the front lines. They walked "five miles under sporadic shell fire" to a camouflaged slit in a hill where artillery spotters observed the effect of shells on the Nazi lines. His article for *Collier's* was entitled "Front Seat in Flanders."

The Nazis broke through at Montmedy. Reynolds got back to Paris and could not get another pass to the front lines. But he met his old friend actor Robert Montgomery, who was driving an ambulance, and he and Kenneth Downs stowed away in it. They arrived at Beauvais, which was in flames. Montgomery and his two "assistants" helped load stretchers with wounded onto the last train as dive bombers strafed them. He described these scenes of chaotic rescue in an article, "The Wounded Don't Cry": "After dawn two hundred Nazi planes gave another unmerciful beating to this very tired old city which wasn't a military objective at all; it was a cathedral city, but they killed the city that morning with this bombing."

He returned to Paris. I asked:

Q. Who was the last American correspondent to leave Paris before the Nazis actually occupied it?

A. As far as I know, I was. . . .

He fled to Tours, describing in his next *Collier's* article, "The Army of Despair," the shooting down of the fleeing, bewildered refugees.

He and Downs backed into Bordeaux and before the Nazis took the port they escaped to England on a Dutch freighter, the last boat to leave France. It was bombed.

There was a rumor that the Germans would invade Ireland. Reynolds was sent there to observe the parachute landings. But the alarm was unwarranted and he wrote "The Irish Don't Believe It."

In this manner I continued to take him through his exploits and resulting articles, which were offered in evidence. Since all his dispatches were carefully censored, first by France and later by England, there could be no doubt about their accuracy. As we proved later, Pegler had read most of them and therefore knew how false were his slurs of "absentee war correspondent," Reynolds's "mangy hide with a yellow streak," and all the rest of his fulminations.

Then Reynolds was accredited as a war correspondent to the British Army, to the R.A.F., and to the Navy. Lord Haw-Haw, a Nazi radio broadcaster, boasted that the North Sea and the English Channel belonged to the Luftwaffe. Reynolds testified: "I had seen some of these convoys, and although a great many of the ships had been hit by German air attacks and by shelling from Boulogne and Calais, some were getting through."

He decided to go on one of these convoys and "nail one of Dr. Goebbels's lies."

The Admiralty would not permit it. Ambassador Joseph Kennedy did not want an American involved in a sinking. But Reynolds prevailed on him and on the editor of the *Daily Express*—who was promised that the article would be his—to arrange permission for him. He signed the usual "blood sheet" absolving the English Government in the event of his death. He sailed on the convoy down the North Sea and then the length of the English Channel to Portsmouth. They traveled at six knots, "tuned to the speed of the slowest ship." It was called the Bacon convoy, because "bacon was used for bait in the channel by fishermen and they were hoping this would look like bait to the Germans, because the Air Force was making a special effort to cover this convoy, and if we were attacked by air, as we hoped, the Spitfires could do a great deal of damage to the German Air Force. The captain also said he hoped we were attacked by submarines and by the guns from Boulogne and Calais because there would be aircraft higher up above to watch for the flashes of the guns and they could actually pinpoint where they were so they could be bombed out of existence. In short, we were a decoy sort of convoy."

The Nazis bit. Their planes attacked. The Spitfires fought them wildly at random in the skies. A bomb hit Reynolds's boat, but the convoy got through. *Collier's* featured his next article, "It's Still Churchill's Channel."

War can change the meaning of seasons. Spring was the time for the Blitz and death. Winter became the season of life. In January 1941 there was a lull in manmade thunder, and Reynolds returned to the United States for several months. But in April he returned to England, visiting London, Plymouth, Hull, Coventry, and Liverpool to record the highest soldierly qualities of non-uniformed men, women, and children when their homes, shops, and streets become the front line of a war. During four months of the first Blitz, 25,000 were killed and injured. Reynolds lived in Lansdowne House, only a quarter of a mile from the Houses of Parliament. They were a prime target. At one period explosive and incendiary bombs were aimed at this district for forty-one consecutive nights. Parliament was struck. Reynolds's hotel suffered one direct hit. It was set on fire and three apartments were gutted. One dawn, when he returned to his room after dragging victims from burning buildings all through the night and treating the wounded strewn in the streets, he found a bomb fragment in his bed. It had burned a hole through a pillow on which he slept.

Reynolds also fought with his voice. In addition to recording *London Can Take It, Christmas Under Fire*, and broadcasts to "Dear Doctor Goebbels," he raised funds for St. Bartholomew's Hospital. A wing of the hospital was named in his honor. I drew from him his contributions to the Eagle Squadron boys. He spent about $40,000 providing entertainment for them. Ironically, he had to pay income taxes in England. Since he hadn't earned enough money to meet these expenses, he cabled Mark Hanna, his agent, to sell the furniture in his New York apartment. But he still owed income taxes to the United States because the money he gave to the Eagle Squadron boys and the Spitfire Pension fund was not deductible. I read to the jury the charge in Pegler's column that Reynolds was a war profiteer, and took a long look at them before going on to another subject.

Articles continued to click out of his typewriter even under these harrowing conditions. *Collier's* featured "Direct Hit" and "Nobody is Better off Dead." He would work at his typewriter even during raids. One night a bomb fell so near that his windows crashed in. He jumped, fell over a chair, and broke two ribs. His chest was strapped, but within a few days he kept an appointment with a demolition squad that played Russian roulette with a bomb; either they would all be blown to unrecoverable fragments, or the bomb would be tamed into a harmless chunk of iron.

Pegler, as we shall see, did not fail to ridicule the rib injury, suggesting that our war hero had an extra drink and was attacked by a chair. His malicious chuckle stuck in his throat because it gave me an opportunity to examine Pegler's war activities during the First World War, when he was only twenty-three years old, single, and eligible for service. But that shall come later.

During the few months respite in the United States, Reynolds came face to face with a few economic realities. Except for several dollars in the bank, he was stone-broke. His brother Jim, his agent, Hanna, and two editors of *Collier's*, Colebaugh and Chenery, got together to add solvency to his sentiment.

At that time *Christmas Under Fire*, a motion picture written and narrated by Reynolds, was being shown at the Strand Theatre in New York City. If Reynolds would appear in conjunction with this exhibition he could earn several thousand dollars a week. When it was pointed out that the box office receipts for the motion picture would be enhanced, and therefore that the proceeds for the R. A. F. Benevolent Fund would be increased, he consented. *Collier's* waived its rule forbidding a staff writer to take outside engagements.

Then I read to him from Paragraph 7 of the answer filed by the defendants in the lawsuit in which they had enlarged the original libel that he was a phony: "The said plaintiff appeared as a vaudeville actor in connection with a motion picture show and appeared on the stage in a spotlight emerging from a trap door, wearing a steel helmet, with intended terrific histrionic impact."

None of this ridicule was warranted. He had appeared in ordinary civilian clothes. He wore no helmet. He did not emerge from any trap door. As the curtain went up he was found seated at a desk. He gave an eight-minute talk, which was an introduction to the motion picture about to be shown. The Strand Theatre had taken camera shots of Reynolds while performing. I obtained the originals from their photographer and they were offered in evidence.

Even though this was an engagement—held over for a second week—to help resuscitate Reynolds financially, he gave 20 per cent of his earnings of this and other lectures during this period to the Spitfire Fund. When his agent, Mark Hanna, later testified, we learned that Reynolds had received $750 for a talk in Seattle, Washington, but finding that the American Red Cross Drive was taking place in the city, he donated his fee to it. Hanna sighed helplessly as he explained that he had to pay the expenses for the trip and Reynolds owed an income tax on the fee.

The second Blitz of England during the spring and summer of 1941 killed 43,000 civilians and maimed 50,000 men, women, and children. The Germans sent 700 bombers nightly to evacuate their load of death over London. But the Spitfires saw to it that bombers as well as bombs fell over England. Each night fewer of the dwindling German planes and crews returned to report. In one final gritted effort to kill the largest city in the world, the Nazis sent 1200 bombers over London on Sunday, May 10, 1941.

Reynolds and another correspondent, Ed Blattner, stood on the roof of the Savoy Hotel and saw all London turn blood-red. Two thousand fires ringed them. The Nazi radio announced that London had ceased to exist. But the next morning a dauntless populace emerged from the flaming wreckage and cindered lava, while the Nazi bomber squads, further decimated, fell back exhausted. Reynolds wrote his stories "Full Moon over London" and "Plymouth Fights Back" to record the nobility as well as the sadistic stupidity of man. Pegler read these eyewitness accounts. How could he have called Reynolds "an absentee war correspondent"?

One can imagine how a people drenched in blood and death would react to Reynolds's broadcasts to Dear Dr. Goebbels and to Mr. Schicklgruber. The boastless taunts, subtle defiance, and witty ridicule addressed to their tormentors were a miraculous medicine for their spirit.

Winston Churchill invited Reynolds to have dinner with him, his wife Clemy, his daughter Mary, and Harry Hopkins at Chequers. The talk until ten o'clock that evening was warm and uninhibited, but this was one occasion when Reynolds censored himself. In his article "Dinner with Churchill" he omitted many revelations made in candid intimacy. As he explained, it was a point of honor to consider certain matters off the record, though not so stipulated, and he had practiced such self-restraint whenever he dined with General Eisenhower. Since Reynolds's reputation was a key factor in the litigation, how impressive it was that a war correspondent had achieved the confidence of the Prime Minister and had shared the hearth with his family.

The air raids on England petered out, but Russia was being crushed by the huge Nazi glacier that moved over the land with unprecedented mechanized speed. *Collier's* thought Reynolds ought to leave England, gasping in respite, and get to the Russian front. But how? Russia would not permit any more correspondents to enter. Even Harry Hopkins and Averell Harriman could not manipulate a visa from the Soviet Embassy in Washington. Finally when Harriman and Beaverbrook were assigned to a lend-lease mission to Moscow, Reynolds got himself designated as their official press attaché.

Now he was in a strategic position to obtain news and, in cherished newspaper tradition, he shared it with the press corps stationed at the Metropole Hotel. Even the farewell dinner tendered by Stalin to the Commission, which Reynolds attended, was reported by him to his professional associates. Little wonder then that the defendants' attempt to present proof of Reynolds's unpopularity among the newsmen in Moscow came a cropper.

When Harriman and Beaverbrook left Moscow, Reynolds quit their mission and stayed behind. He had successfully arranged a strange hitchhike into Moscow. He wrote "City of Courage," and a story about war hospitals called "Life by the Pint." But with maddening illogic, his stories were so severely censored that he despaired of writing at all.

By October 1955 General Von Bock's army had advanced to within fifty-four miles of Moscow. The city was being bombed nightly. It seemed to be Reynolds's self-imposed fate to flee to places about to be devastated. The Russians wanted him to do a film with Sergei Eisenstein about Moscow, like *London Can Take It*. He refused all proffers of money, but said he would accept if he could have an interview with Stalin. Before it could be arranged, the government, diplomatic and press corps had to be evacuated and moved to Kuibishev, six hundred miles away, one hundred and five hours by train. The Nazis sped the group by a bombing although a heavy snow storm was sweeping the countryside.

Kuibishev's two hundred thousand people suddenly swelled to one million. There was not enough water or food. Sanitary conditions were odorous and unspeakable. Shrapnel can be clean and merciful in its wounds. There are worse kinds of war injuries. Reynolds picked up almost every ailment possible—dysentery, scabies (bugs under the skin), and carbuncles. The latter had to be opened, but there was no anesthetic; ethyl chloride was used, and he fainted from the pain. Then his gums became infected. For eight years he was under constant treatment, but ultimately he lost every tooth in his head.

In his book *Only The Stars Are Neutral* (what a gift Reynolds had for titles), he gave his impressions about Russia. Under the impact of our ally's heroism (General Douglas MacArthur had said the fate of civilization rested on banners of the Red Army), he wrote passages which ten years later sounded differently than when written. Hindsight is prognostication with all the errors removed. But there are always those who ignore the intervening time and set standards for original conduct based upon knowledge since acquired. The error of anachronism was once enshrined by an amateur playwright. He had a French obstetrician leave home in the early hours of numbingly cold dawn to attend a delivery. When he returned home exhausted, his sympathetic wife gave him hot tea and inquired:

"Did all go well?"

"It was a very difficult delivery," he said, "but it was worth it. You know who was born today? Victor Hugo!"

Should we wait for the cross-examiner to reveal the passages in Reynolds's book which in retrospect did not seem as wise as when written? A bold strategy was called for. We decided to take the wind out of our opponent's sails on direct examination.

So it was I who asked him about religion in Russia. Although the government had converted churches to warehouses, the people remained religious and on Easter Sunday one million people crowded into the churches. General Bedell Smith and Lord Beaverbrook had made similar observations. That is why Reynolds wrote that Russia was not atheistic.

Why had Reynolds spoken favorably of the Russian purge of its generals? Because, unlike France, there was no fifth column in Russia. The Nazis could not find a Quisling.

However he had also seen the sordid facts about Russia. He had depicted its slave labor, with thousands of women wielding shovels on roads. Molotov, as well as other leaders, was universally distrusted. "After twenty-five years of life the Soviet Union has not yet discovered free speech," Reynolds wrote.

Also Reynolds set off a storm of protest against censorship. When his story on Kuibishev, which had no security data in it, was cut from twenty-five hundred words to four hundred, he asked Sir Walter Monckton, who had just arrived, to protest to the Government. It did no good. Reynolds cabled *Collier's* that he wanted to go to a fighting sector where he could write. He got out of Russia on Monckton's plane which flew with Ambassadors Laurence Steinhardt and Maxim Litvinoff (just appointed Ambassador to the United States) to Cairo.

There followed his escapades with Clive Burt and Desmond Young across the desert to General Messervy's headquarters in Sidi Omar. We had depositions from all these witnesses. But Reynolds paused here to tell about his sensitivity to the sun.

Whenever he was on the desert, and despite the burning heat, he wore a scarf which was swathed around his face and over his helmet. He also wore gloves. Since he could not take these precautions during battle conditions, he was exposed to the sun for a few minutes in Libya. Immediately he contracted sun poisoning, with its concomitant rashes, swelling, and fever. The poisoning turned septic and his face looked as if it had been chewed up by insects.

We offered in evidence a photograph taken of Reynolds prior to his illness, standing next to a tank. Despite the heat he was covered as if in freezing climate. He peered through the scarves which were wrapped around his face. This was the man who, Pegler testified, splashed around nude in Broun's lake during weekends and once climbed into Connie Broun's rowboat stark naked.

Suddenly Reynolds was no longer a foreign correspondent. A deluge of bombs over Pearl Harbor had made the United States a bleeding participant. Reynolds, Downes, Bob Lowe, and other correspondents rushed to get home. Reynolds got to London on top priority as a King's messenger. The only way to reach home was on a convoy of fifty ships from Wales. He was abroad the *Loch Katrine* which took twenty-three days to reach New York. Several boats in the convoy were left at the bottom of the sea. On the return voyage the *Loch Katrine* was sunk with all aboard.

Though forty years of age, Reynolds instantly tried to enlist. He was told he was too old to be an active soldier, and a desk job would certainly not afford the opportunity for front-line service which a correspondent had. He asked Harry Hopkins to get him into the fight, but was told that such men as he and Ed Murrow could do more for our cause by broadcasts and articles from the battle front. Hopkins had just read Reynolds's two stories in *Collier's* describing desert tank battles, and he asked, "How much nearer can you get to the fight than this?"

By this testimony Reynolds refuted Pegler's charge that he had permitted "high school boys to push back the Nazi in the war he had been asking for for the last ten years."

Collier's consulted the Government and Reynolds was assigned to the home front for several articles. They were "We Will Make It," on steel production, "Here's Where You Come In," and "Manpower at Home."

War, like age or disease, brings consciousness of imminent death. So we grasp for living values. That is why so many marriages are contracted during war, at the most unpropitious time when separation is certain. Whether such an impulse or the coincidence of being overwhelmed by love at this particular time was the reason, Quentin Reynolds surrendered his bachelorhood and married Ginny on March 30, 1942. While the couple was honeymooning in Sun Valley, *Collier's* advised Reynolds that a large military operation of some kind was rumored in England and that he was to hurry there. Shades of Hollywood's oldest cliché, our newspaperman left his bride behind, after only ten days of their idyl, to answer his editor's call for a great international story. It turned out later that the tip was correct. It was the Dieppe raid. But it was postponed at that time because of weather.

Reynolds visited General Eisenhower who arrived with his staff in England. He interviewed him and arranged to be accredited to the American Army. While waiting for the mysterious operation, Reynolds flew with the R.A.F. over France and wrote "Night Flight." At General Eisenhower's request, he and Ernie Pyle reported on the morale of our troops in Ireland. Eisenhower corrected their gripes.

At this time there was a growing uproar in England and elsewhere for a Second Front to aid Russia. Not only the Communists, but Lord Beaverbrook and other conservatives were demanding that we attack to shorten the war. A poll showed that 80 per cent of the British people favored the opening of a Second Front. The clamor in the United States was similarly persistent. Reynolds was assigned to write several articles which would advocate "the popular front."

But when he interviewed General Eisenhower, General Carl Spaatz, Ambassador A. J. Drexel Biddle, Jr., First Lord of the Admiralty Albert V. Alexander, General Sir Hastings Ismay, and Admiral Louis Mountbatten, he found that the emotional and political view was overruled by practical military considerations. He warned of a channel turned red with blood if the attack were ill-timed. *Collier's* published his two articles called "Second Thoughts on a Second Front" in July 1942. They were widely reprinted and reduced the fever for an immediate offensive. The Communists, of course, hurled abuse at Reynolds, for he had supported the caution of the unprepared military against the emotion of the uninformed. Pegler had read these articles and filed them in a folder he kept under the title of "Reynolds." I had obtained his copies of these articles during the examination before trial. I offered them in evidence. They contradicted his theories of Reynolds's sympathies toward Communism and opened the door to telling cross-examination.

Sensing that a Commando raid of large proportions was not far off, Reynolds applied to Lord Mountbatten to be taken along. We had the depositions of Lord Louis and others which traced his participation in what became known as the Dieppe raid.

Reynolds now told the story on the witness stand from his own vantage point. The plan was to land six thousand troops and tanks against a fortified harbor, destroy its installations and coastal defenses, remain eight hours and withdraw with knowledge of the equipment and landing tactics necessary for the real D day. The Nazis had placed magnetic and acoustic mines in the channel which would be drawn to the hulls of the ships to explode, or would be touched off by sound. Careful mine sweepers preceded, while all on the invading boats maintained strict silence. After an hour, the loud clanging of a bell was joyous news that the sea lanes were cleared. But fate was cruel to the daring venture. By sheer accident a small trawler discovered the armada of ships and signaled the Nazis of their approach. Surprise, the chief asset of such an attack, was lost. The Nazi coast defenses opened up. Dorniers, Messerschmidt 109s, and Focke-Wulfs, used as dive bombers, streaked down from the sky. The flagship *Calpe*, on which Reynolds was stationed, blinked its signals furiously to the circling and evading boats, and thus revealed itself as the command ship. It was singled out by the Germans for special attention. Planes dived at it, their machine guns and cannon open with death. Reynolds and crew members crouched behind protective plates which were tattooed with hails of consecutive bullets. Bombs scored direct and near hits. Debris shot high into the air fell back on the crew, as if even the friendly parts of the ship had turned hostile.

Air Commodore A. T. Cole, Lieutenant Boyle, and Reynolds were standing together when a Focke-Wulf jammed through the umbrella of Spitfires, ignored the flak, dived from 5000 feet to 300 feet in a few seconds and raked the *Calpe* from stem to stern with its machine guns, before dropping its bomb on deck. Two crew members alongside of Reynolds toppled over dead. Air Commodore Cole was severely wounded. Lieutenant Boyle had a deep shrapnel cut in his neck and a head wound. The blast flung Reynolds through a passageway. He suffered only a concussion and spat out a gold inlay. But the rattling shock to his teeth, loosened by his Kuibishev gum infection, made their salvage impossible.

The destroyer *Berkeley*, four hundred yards away, suffered a direct hit. Six men at a gun station were set afire. The boat heaved as if taking a last breath and dove under the water. The *Calpe* picked up 278 wounded. They were placed on wooden mess tables in the wardroom, but were thrown to the floor as the boat lurched. Reynolds and the doctor tended the wounded under these maddening conditions of bomb screeches magnified in the hold of the ship and the constant impression that the sharp turns were the capsizing or final plunge of a sinking vessel.

Eight and one-half hours later there was a message to withdraw for all but the *Calpe*. It went toward shore to pick up the last survivors. It searched so near the land that German machine guns and small arms fired at it.

Then, with one quarter of its crew dead, the *Calpe*, harrassed by bombers, sailed off homeward. I read a passage from the defendant's legal answer filed in court: "The casualties of said raid were enormous, the chances of success infinitesimal, and the results nil, as said plaintiff then and there well knew, having witnessed the same from some distance while aboard a warship, although other correspondents went ashore."

I asked Reynolds:

Q. Is this statement that you were on a warship and witnessed the raid from some distance correct?

A. It is completely false. Since 5000 of the 6000 troops were Canadians, two Canadian reporters had accompanied them ashore.

Q. Did any American correspondent go ashore at Dieppe?

A. No.

Q. Did any officer or crew member from *Calpe* land?

A. No.

During direct examination it is wise for the lawyer to be out of sight and focus attention on the witness, particularly one like Reynolds. I make it a practice to stand at the far end of the jury box while questioning. The jury's heads naturally turn in the opposite direction toward the witness. After a while the lawyer is blotted out of view, only his voice being heard.

In cross-examination, the technique is different. I walk forward toward the witness, often stand in front of the jury, and permit them to observe the emotions of both the lawyer and the witness. Every reaction of the duelists plays upon the other and gives the jury a better insight into the truth.

As I led Reynolds on in his recitals, I could see the effect he was having upon the jurors. Their faces turned intently toward him and mirrored his ordeals. They were caught up not only in his deeds, but by his personality. Interest was becoming admiration. Here was an author who was also a man of action. His huge imposing figure was devoid of severity. His light eyes showed that he was accustomed to humor. His modesty and kindliness were natural. He was winning the sympathy of the jurors, even jurors numbers nine and ten, the regular Hearst readers.

I encouraged this favorable process by weaving Reynolds's account of his further activities into a continuous pattern. He told of his next visit to Russia, his difficulty getting in, and his difficulty getting out (on Eddie Rickenbacker's special plane); his trip on a P.T. boat from Bizerte to Sicily; his accreditation to General George Patton's Seventh Army in Sicily; his flight on the new British Beaufighter, a night fighter equipped with radar; and his successful effort to be assigned to the Command ship *Ancon* as "the pool man" to report to all naval correspondents for the combined British and American press.

Collier's cabled him to come home for a rest, but it did not know why Reynolds refused. Security provisions prevented him from telling his editors that a big story was in the wind.

The *Ancon* was commanded by Admiral H. Kent Hewitt. General Mark Clark was aboard. It was a converted luxury liner, but was equipped with extra masts for radar and wireless, and was therefore identifiable as the flagship that would give orders.

Three hundred ships were under its command. After they had sailed, Reynolds was given the unique honor and assignment of addressing the crew over a loud-speaker to break the suspense and mystery of the undertaking. After briefing by the English commander, as well as by General Clark and Admiral Hewitt, he was introduced by the Captain. He revealed that the mission was the invasion of Salerno. He bolstered the morale of the crew by revealing the extent of the air support and the landing plans. A Canadian correspondent, Lionel Shapiro, was also aboard. He later appeared as a witness for Reynolds because Pegler claimed Reynolds had fled from the scene when the fighting got heavy.

H hour was 3 A.M. As the armada approached, the Germans began their barrage from land batteries and by all-out plane attack. This battle lasted two days and two nights. The cruiser *Savannah* was steaming past the *Ancon*, two hundred yards away, when a radio-controlled bomb, used for the first time by the Germans, scored a direct hit. It burst aflame.

In the communications room of the *Ancon*, General Clark's experts were monitoring conversations among Nazi fliers. They had identified the *Ancon* and were instructed to "get that ship with the funny mast." The Nazi planes seemed to do an acrobatic dance of death over the *Ancon*, swirling and pirouetting in graceful patterns. The near misses almost rent the boat apart. On D+2 day Reynolds, together with thousands of soldiers, headed for shore in landing craft. General Clark and the other commanders stayed on the *Ancon* to direct the battle. The beachhead was secured.

There were no radio facilities to send back a story of the successful

invasion. General Clark sent dispatches by motor launch to General
Bernard Montgomery in Pizzo, southern Italy. Reynolds got permission to
go along and was aided by General Montgomery in reaching Algiers, the
nearest censor and radio center. There he cabled two articles entitled
"Bloody Salerno."

It so happened that after Reynolds left the captured beachhead, the
Germans counterattacked, and for a while it appeared we might be driven
into the sea. Reynolds's absence during this period was seized upon by
Pegler and the Hearst defendants as proof of flight from combat. They
even presented a surprise witness, Admiral Richard Conolly, but how he
fared on cross-examination I shall leave for later recital.

The libel article had stated: "Reynolds's medicine grew too strong
even for *Collier's* which I am told incidentally 'has seen the light' and
faced about. He is no longer an editor of *Collier's*."

I asked Reynolds to explain how his name came to be dropped from
the masthead of *Collier's* as Associate Editor.

When Reynolds returned to the United States in the fall of 1943, he
was ill and virtually penniless. The editors of *Collier's* agreed with Hanna
that he ought to be permitted to earn some money for Ginny and himself
by accepting lucrative radio offers. But it had been a standing rule at
Collier's that no editor or staff writer could accept commercial sponsorship, because this might interfere with *Collier's* advertisers. To permit
Reynolds to accept an offer of the Goodyear Company to do a half-hour
weekly program called "Salute to Youth," *Collier's* editors, William L.
Chenery and Charles H. Colebaugh, arranged to take his name off the
masthead, cancel his $10,000 retainer, but increase his price per article
from $1500 to $2000, to make up the difference. In short, it was a device
to avoid conflict in advertising. But Reynolds continued to write articles
for *Collier's*, some fifty-one over the next six years. Obviously his
"medicine" was not "too strong" for *Collier's*.

In ten years Reynolds had written 260 articles for *Collier's* comprising
about one and a half million words, and not one line had been deleted.
Nor was there any reason to do so, for where they touched political
theory they were in the tradition of American democracy. The accusation
that *Collier's* had turned its back on Reynolds because his "medicine
grew too strong" was a concoction. We presented Chenery and other
Collier's editors as witnesses to these facts.

Another charge had to be answered. How was it that "Reynolds, the
intrepid war correspondent, was in the United States during the great
invasion of France?" Why, if he was not an "absentee correspondent,"
had he skipped the big show on D day?

The answer was that President Roosevelt had invited Reynolds to
the White House in May 1944 and asked him to speak at the Democratic
Convention to be held in July in Chicago. At that time the exact date

of D day was a closely guarded secret. Reynolds and many experts thought August was the likely month, because the Dieppe raid had also been timed for August, when the Channel is at its best. Reynolds therefore expected to be in Europe for the great invasion. In any event, the request by the President and Commander-in-Chief, while not obligatory in a military sense, was in effect an order. One could not say "No" to the President, particularly when he was conferring an honor by his invitation. Reynolds delivered an oration entitled "G. I. Joe" at the July convention. It was carried on a national radio network. But after having participated in many of the thrilling and dangerous operations in preparation for the invasion for freedom, he was chafing in his hotel room writing his speech when, on June 6, the greatest flotilla of sea, air, and land in the history of the world forced its way on to the Normandy beaches, just so many inevitable steps to Hitler's bunker.

Secretary of the Navy James Forrestal, who had known Reynolds for many years, requested him and Ernie Pyle to cover the Navy in the Pacific. Pyle went to Okinawa and was killed there.

Reynolds went to Pearl Harbor where he boarded the aircraft carrier S.S. *Saratoga* from which emanated his article "Sarah Has a Birthday." While visiting Guam, Kwajalein, and Johnston Island, he found that several hundred Japanese had not yet surrendered and the Marines were flushing them out. He went along on one of these hunts and, while straggling, he was suddenly surprised by a bedraggled Japanese soldier eager to surrender. He wrote a tongue-in-cheek article, "You Too Can Capture a Jap," but the defendants humorlessly attacked this story as representing false bravery.

When he returned to the United States, Forrestal assigned him to board the aircraft carrier *Franklin*, which secretly had limped into port. Half of the crew had been killed. It was listing and brutally damaged by continuous bombing, but its courageous crew refused to abandon it and brought it home. Reynolds discovered that the hero of this saga was Father Timothy O'Callahan. He wrote a story entitled "Chaplains Courageous." It was republished in *Reader's Digest*, the *Catholic Weekly*, and in publications of many other countries. It was among the one hundred best stories compiled for *Reader's Digest Reader* from thirteen thousand published in the thirty years of the magazine's existence.

This incident involving Reynolds's private visit on the S.S. *Franklin* unexpectedly became a pivotal point in the case. The defendants produced newspaper clippings indicating that Reynolds could not have boarded the ship several days before other reporters because it arrived on the day they were all invited on board. They charged him on cross-examination with having invented the story that he had been given priority by Secretary Forrestal. The accusation that he had lied cast a shadow over his other testimony. We shall see later the bizarre outcome of this attack and why it became a symbol of the entire trial.

Now we turned to the sentence in the libel article which read: "He cleaned up $2000 of the ill-gotten loot of the Garsson brothers who, with Congressman Andy May later were convicted of fraud in war contracts."

The Hearst defendants, as well as Pegler, had asserted in their answer filed in court: "Among the other receipts of Reynolds was $2000 from certain Garsson brothers who swindled and defrauded the United States in connection with the production of munitions."

This was the charge. What was the truth?

During the war the Army and Navy conferred "E" awards (E for excellent) to outstanding war plants. These ceremonies encouraged production and stimulated morale on the vital industrial front. It was the practice for the proud owners of such plants to arrange a celebration attended by the workers at which important Army and Navy officers presented the E pennant, which was raised on a flagpole while martial music played. Professional bands, singers, and actresses were hired to entertain and add to the patriotic fervor of the occasion. Stars such as Helen Hayes appeared at these functions. Reynolds had appeared at the Eastman Kodak "E" award celebration held at Rochester. His agent offered him a similar paid engagement at Batavia, Illinois, where the Garsson munitions plant was situated. Brilliantly uniformed officers of the Army and Navy appeared to present the award. Congressman Andrew J. May, then head of the Armed Services Committee, spoke. So did Reynolds.

How was he to know that several years later the Garsson brothers and Congressman May would be convicted for defrauding the Government in obtaining war contracts? By omitting the surrounding circumstances of the "E" award, Pegler gave the impression that Reynolds had shared "the ill-gotten loot of the Garsson brothers," and had participated in their fraud.

We shifted to the absurd accusation that Reynolds had proposed marriage to Connie Broun in the funeral car. He made short shrift of this invention. He revealed that Bishop Fulton Sheen (then Monsignor) and Heywood Broun's son were seated with them on the way to the cemetery.

After Reynolds had analyzed his loss of income from previous sources, although more than replaced by new successes in his books and a new lecture program, I announced that he was ready for cross-examination.

For eight days Pegler's and Hearst's lawyer battered at Reynolds. There are numerous strategies in breaking down a witness. The classic one is to "go for the jugular," to skip the unessential and concentrate on the essence of the direct testimony. Another technique is to demonstrate that the witness has told a series of untruths which, though trivial individually, cumulatively discredit his veracity. There are combinations and variations of such strategies. If the cross-examiner relegates himself to unimportant detail, he must at least be successful if he is to gather momentum. If his battle is pitched on inconsequential terrain and he is rebuffed, he looks ridiculous in retreat. Another favorite strategy in cross-examination is to begin with a strong contradiction, shaking the witness at the outset and bleeding him of his confidence.

I was therefore concernedly alert when almost the first line of questioning was about the S.S. *Franklin*. This subject was quite out of the ordinary sequence of Reynolds's testimony. There must be a reason why it was first on the cross-examiner's agenda. It soon developed.

Q. When the *Franklin* limped into New York, is it your testimony that it stayed tied up at the dock four or five days before the story was released?

A. As I recall, the full story, yes.

Q. So you interviewed the crew on the *Franklin* before the Navy issued a press release?

A. I am not positive. That is my best recollection.

After long preliminaries, the trap was beginning to be discernable.

Q. Mr. Reynolds, don't you know that the United States Navy had a press conference at 90 Church Street *on the day the ship docked*, and thirty newspapermen were there?

A. Yes.

Reynolds continued to insist that he had been continuously on the ship three or four days before the press conference. The attack resumed:

Q. Isn't it a fact, Mr. Reynolds, that Secretary Forrestal did not request you to do anything, that you interviewed these men after an official United States Navy press conference at which any newspaperman could have appeared if he wanted to?

A. You asked me two or three questions there. The first is, isn't it a fact that what?

Q. Nobody requested you to write this story?

A. I have already explained that Forrestal said this would be a great story for the Navy. I said, "I would love to do it, but I want authority to talk to the fellows. I just don't want a press handout." He told Markey, his captain in charge of public relations, to fix it up for me. So when I went on the ship, they were on notice that I had the confidence of the Navy Department and the men could talk freely to me.

Now the cross-examiner was ready for the revealed challenge.

Q. Mr. Reynolds, don't you know this story was published in complete detail all over the United States *on the day that ship docked*?

A. The story that I wrote for *Collier's* that was picked up by *Reader's Digest* and *Catholic Digest*? Why weren't these stories picked up by these various magazines? Why was mine singled out?

COURT: You are arguing with counsel now.

WITNESS: Forgive me . . .

Q. I show you a story from the *Journal-American* dated May 18th and I ask if that doesn't contain the facts as to Father O'Callahan's heroism?

A. It is a brief outline, yes. What date did you say this was?

COURT: May 18th.

WITNESS: May 18th.

Reynolds was shown a similar clipping in the *Herald Tribune*. It, too, was dated May 18. They were both offered in evidence and received as defendants' Exhibits A-1 and A-2.

Then the defendants' counsel piled it on. He offered in evidence clippings from the *New York Times* and *Daily News* to demonstrate "that the story was released on the very day the *Franklin* reached Brooklyn Navy Yard." They, too, were dated May 18.

How then could Reynolds have been on the ship, as he insisted, three or four days before that to interview the crew? And if that was a lie, could not his story about Secretary Forrestal, who now was dead, also be an invention? I saw suspicion spread over the faces of several jurors. They were giving Reynolds a look of new appraisal.

That night after court we traced down Captain Leslie Gehres of the S.S. *Franklin* in San Diego. He did not remember dates, but he confirmed that Reynolds had been on the ship *before* there was any press conference at Navy headquarters. Would he fly to New York? That was impossible. Still the mystery remained. How could all of the newspaper clippings be wrong in stating that the S.S. *Franklin* came into dock on May 18, the very day of the press release?

I usually sleep well during a trial. I have trained myself to blot out the excitement and anxieties of court contest. My method is so childish I am ashamed to confess it, but I find that if I concentrate on something unworthy of concentration, but pleasant, I will not be stimulated to remain awake. So, for example, I play an imaginary round of golf, each shot superb. The birdies, and an occasional eagle, roll off my clubs. I rarely, however, reach the eighth or ninth green. My perfection becomes boring, and I slumber off. I have found other Walter Mitty sports achievements a fine discipline against returning to the problems of the day. But though I have trained my conscious mind, I have not mastered my subconscious. In the middle of that night I awoke, a picture in my mind of an incident at counsel table when Reynolds was being cross-examined. As the newspaper clippings were being called for by Mr. Henry, his assistant Mr. Bowden, a large bald man, had handed them to him. Mr. Henry, after selecting several, had returned the others to Mr. Bowden. I observed from a corner of my eye that he pushed these clippings into a folder. I could see no significance in this at the time, but apparently my mind's eye had taken a snapshot of the scene. I awoke with that picture vividly before me.

Was it possible that the other newspaper accounts of that day had some reference to the ship having arrived secretly a few days earlier?

As soon as I could reach an assistant, without waking him in the middle of the night on a mere hunch, I ordered that all newspapers morning and night of May 18 and immediately thereafter, be obtained.

That afternoon at the end of the day the following took place:

NIZER: Your Honor, I have asked for several of those clippings so that I can make a comparison with the article.

COURT: What is the problem?

NIZER: One that shouldn't exist. I asked Mr. Bowden for copies of those exhibits, the clippings, so that I can make a comparison of the articles, but he won't give them to me.

COURT: They are in evidence, you know. Anything that is in evidence, of course, must be available to counsel on all sides.

On redirect examination I asked Reynolds:

Q. Did you do anything to check the facts as to whether the S.S. *Franklin* arrived at the yard in Brooklyn on May 18th or whether it arrived much earlier in April, as your recollection had been?

A. I did, that very same night when I left this courtroom.

Q. What did you do?

A. I got in touch with Captain Leslie Gehres.

Q. Where was he?

A. San Diego, California. I phoned him.

Q. Don't tell us the conversation. That would be hearsay, but you spoke to him, did you?

A. Yes, I did.

Q. And after you spoke to him, did you have any further check made of the date on which the S.S. *Franklin* got into the Brooklyn Navy Yard?

A. Yes, I did.

NIZER: Now I call upon counsel to produce Exhibits 2-A, B, and C.

HENRY: We will produce any exhibits you wish, but they are not all handy at this minute.

NIZER: I will wait for them. May the record show that I have also called for the production not only of that exhibit, *but for the other newspaper clippings which counsel had in his hand?*

We waited while Mr. Bowden fetched the documents from the anteroom. Silence added to the suspense.

HENRY: I have here Defendants' Exhibit A-1, Defendants' Exhibits B and C.

NIZER: Thank you. Now I ask for the production of the other clippings which counsel had in his hand, and which he did not offer in evidence. May I have those too, please?

HENRY: If they are produced, I wish to offer them in evidence.

NIZER: Will you please offer in evidence the *Daily News* of May 18.

COURT: Well, has it been received?

NIZER: Not yet. I wish to make a statement about it. It has the left column cut off. I don't object to it, but I am going to offer in evidence the complete page of the *Daily News* of the same date with the complete column in it and offer both.

I showed both to the jury. The clipping originally offered in evidence had been scissored so as to leave only the byline story. In cutting the story out of the page, the headline which ran across the whole page had been cut so that it read "Blasted—772 Lost," instead of "U. S. Carrier Blasted —772 Lost." I then presented the entire page which I had obtained from the newspaper morgue. In that section which had been cut out was a statement that the S.S. *Franklin* had "arrived here *April 26th* after a 12,400-mile voyage from the scene of her disaster and triumph; censorship forbade mention of the facts until now."

Not only was Reynolds completely confirmed, but on summation I was able to argue that an incomplete exhibit had been offered by the defendant, and to analyze the significance of this incident.

Once more the value of complete concentration had been demonstrated. Had my associates been talking to me at the time the ordinary procedure of offering the clippings in evidence had taken place, my eye would not have caught the picture of Bowden putting the clippings back into a folder. The sensitized mind, eye, and ear may pick up messages which only the antenna of complete concentration can receive.

In preparation of Reynolds for cross-examination, I had struggled with his propensity for loving everybody, even his enemies. He thought all the Hearst executives were just "great guys." But when he saw the truth devoid of his emotional standards of friendship, he reacted firmly. Witness the following when Mr. Henry tried to capitalize on Reynolds's sentimentality:

Q. During your employment did you ever have any trouble with your superiors?

A. The very reverse. They were personal friends of mine as well as my bosses, and I hope Barry Faris is still, the present INS chief.

Q. You have a great number of friends who work for those companies, both on the *Journal* and at King Features, do you not?

A. Yes, indeed.

Q. You are well acquainted with Bill Corum, Louis Sobol, Seymour Berkson?

A. True.

Q. Dick Berlin and others?

A. Yes.

Q. What others: Bob Considine?

A. Yes; practically the whole staff of the *Journal* I have known at one time or another.

Q. Is not the malice in this case, if any, entertained by Mr. Pegler and you? I say, if any.

A. Well, all I know is that Pegler made the bullets and the Hearst papers shot them. That is all I know. I don't know the meaning of malice in its legal sense.

I could almost see the cross-examiner reel from this blow. But he asked for more.

Q. Well, in the ordinary sense isn't it true?

A. In the ordinary sense?

Q. Yes.

A. Until what to me was a pretty horrible answer which you made to our complaint, and I couldn't conceive of the Hearst executives even implying their approval of this column written by Pegler, but in the answer which was signed by you as the representative of the corporations, I was horrified to find that in effect this was signed by these top executives of the Hearst organization whom I knew, and who knew me and who knew better.

Reynolds had actually put Henry on the defensive.

Q. It was signed by me who knew you?

A. It was signed by you on their behalf.

Q. It was signed by me, yes.

A. And of course they must be credited with knowledge of it. That is what horrified me—that men like Berlin, who knew better than to think I was this grotesque moral degenerate pictured by Mr. Pegler.

Q. Well . . .

NIZER: May I request that the witness be permitted to finish the answer?

HENRY: I thought he had finished.

WITNESS: No, I did not.

A. (continuing) They knew better than to believe the statements made in the column. . . .

HENRY: I move to strike it out as not responsive.

COURT: I think it is responsive to the question. It was a pretty broad question.

HENRY: Yes, it was.

Reynolds was gaining confidence with every moment. At one point he turned a cross-examination attack into a burst of laughter from the courtroom, aided, I must admit, by the defense's humorlessness.

In one of his books, Reynolds had described his effort to obtain authority from a minor French official to get to the front. When he was balked, he wrote a cable:

Dear Uncle Franklin:

Am having difficulty getting accredited to French Army. Time is important. Would you phone or cable Premier Renaud and ask to hurry things up. It was grand of you to phone me last night. Please give my love to Eleanor.

Quent.

The solemnity of the cross-examiner's attack made it even more heavy-handed.

Q. Did you intend for this French official to believe that President Roosevelt was your uncle and Mrs. Roosevelt was your aunt?

A. Mr. Henry, I have to confess that I did intend that, yes, and it hurried my accreditization considerable. . . . If you want me to admit that perhaps I used a journalistic device to hurry my way toward the front, I will be glad to admit it. . . .

Q. Did you intend to deceive him? . . .

A. I exercised whatever journalistic enterprise I was capable of and that I had learned from my friend Barry Faris at INS in order to facilitate my accreditization. . . .

Q. Did you intend for him to believe that you were the nephew of President Roosevelt?

A. Well, I didn't think he would be that fool enough—I hoped he would though, yes.

(Laughter)

COURT: Please. There has got to be order in the courtroom. Go ahead.

Q. You hoped that he would believe you were a nephew of President Roosevelt?

A. That's right. This was a minor dignitary. I was not under oath or making any statement, mind you, to a responsible person. This was a real bureaucrat in the French office who arbitrarily was holding up these accreditizations for not only me, but for other men.

What made the incident even funnier, was that the Frenchman actually sent the cable to the White House.

A similar instance occurred when the cross-examiner quoted from Reynolds's book that in the face of approaching Nazi troops, Knicker-bocker, Downs, and he decided "the better part of valor was to run like hell. We ran." Also, to get to the border they "stole gas from the deserted American Embassy" on the ground that "if Mr. Bullitt had been there he would have been glad to give it to us."

To charge that running was cowardice or taking gasoline was stealing in the circumstances of a nation dying and its conquerors swooping down upon American correspondents trying to escape was, I felt, ineffectual literalness.

Reynolds continued to strike back at such spurious attacks. Because his book stated that he had reported to President Eamon de Valera about parachutists, he was asked;

    Q. You had never seen a parachutist, had you?

    A. I have never seen a whale, Mr. Henry, but I know something about it. I knew something about parachute troops from having been in France and hearing the stories of what they had accomplished.

It turned out that Mr. Henry was somewhat of an authority on modern Canadian history, and he therefore engaged in lengthy cross-examination to establish the catastrophic results of the Dieppe raid, particularly to the Canadian troops. Pegler, too, had written that Dieppe was a ghastly failure. Reynolds was ready with a quotation from Winston Churchill's volume, *The Hinge of Fate*: "Dieppe taught us to build new types of craft. . . . All these lessons were taken to heart. . . . Honor to the brave who fell. This sacrifice was not in vain."

When the cross-examiner persisted in analyzing the tactics at Dieppe, I objected and the Court ruled: "The issue . . . is the statement of which he complains, that he covered the ghastly Dieppe raid from a battleship . . . and that the plaintiff had a yellow streak. That is the real issue with respect to this Dieppe raid. Shouldn't your question be confined to that inquiry? Otherwise you are constituting the jury-sort of Monday morning quarterbacks and armchair strategists."

I had hoped that sooner or later the cross-examiner would goad Reynolds into real anger. His bear-like goodness was appealing, but we were attempting to show that the libel had eviscerated him. If only he could be stirred to the hurt and compressed fury he had evinced on the day he retained me. The moment came unexpectedly.

In his book *Only the Stars are Neutral*, Reynolds had told the remarkable story of an English scientist who was taken ashore by the Commandos at Dieppe to examine a new radar device which the Germans had developed. The instructions were that if he were captured he was to kill himself or the Commandos were to kill him, because he knew too much to fall into German hands. Reynolds explained in a preface that for security reasons he had used a fictional name, Wendell, for the scientist.

Mr. Henry claimed that the whole story was a melodramatic invention:

    Q. Do you know the name of the scientist that you say went ashore at Dieppe?

    A. I don't know his name, and he did go ashore at Dieppe.

    Q. Well, the whole incident of this scientist is fiction, isn't it?

    A. The what?

    Q. The whole incident is nothing but fiction.

    A. Don't call me a liar, Mr. Henry.

    Q. I am not calling you a liar. You know that very well.

    A. You certainly are—I am fighting for my life here—

This was Reynolds's most effective moment. Sincere righteous indignation is a favorite vehicle of persuasion. I suspect the psychological reason is that a justifiable outburst of anger touches the emotions as well as the mind. Its impact upon reason is thus doubled.

Later witnesses, such as Colonel Justus Lawrence, aide to General Eisenhower, confirmed the accuracy of the story about the scientist. Indeed, considerable detail was added. The new German radar equipment for the first time detected even low-flying planes. Four Commandos had been assigned to guard the scientist, but at his own request were to kill him if he could not be brought back. Furthermore, Reynolds's book had passed through stringent wartime censorship and also Lord Mountbatten's office. While some matters had been deleted, those that were left had to be accurate. Finally, the World Almanac, which Mr. Henry was fond of quoting, stated that the secret radar equipment stationed at Dieppe was one of the reasons it had been selected for the raid. So it wasn't the testimony that was important. It was Reynolds's furious outburst that mattered. The desperation of his plight had broken through his self-discipline and good nature. He really was fighting for his life. All he had ever achieved as a writer, correspondent, and public figure was in the balance. Unless he won this case, his reputation would be irretrievably lost. Men have found such a blank wall, particularly after high achievement, unfaceable. It was literally a struggle for survival and against most powerful forces.

One morning after the case had been in progress for three weeks, the revelation burst into the open that someone was tampering with a juror. Judge Weinfeld held private hearings in chambers after court sessions to trace down this nefarious effort to poison a juror's mind against Reynolds. The testimony was recorded in the minutes, but kept secret in order not to destroy the continuation of the trial. It has never before been revealed.

Mr. Henry is a fairly tall, very thin man, with a gaunt face furrowed with deep vertical lines. His low-pitched voice and gray hair add to his solemnity. One morning he asked for a conference of counsel in Judge Weinfeld's robing room. He seemed more pale than usual. He advised the Judge that an FBI man had called him to say that a juror had been approached. The Judge made immediate inquiries of the FBI investigator, Mr. ——, Pegler, and Henry's assistant, Bowden. Their statements mentioned Mr. Frank Conniff, an editor of the defendant Hearst Company, which publishes the *Journal-American*.

Judge Weinfeld announced that he was initiating his own proceedings out of the presence of the jury to ferret out the facts. He called for the appearance of Mr. Conniff, who came without subpoena. He was sworn in, and stated, "The man contacted me, told me that he had heard that a juror was making telephone calls concerning the case."

COURT: Who is the man that contacted you?

A. Well, I will have to plead the Fifth Amendment of the newspaper business, I would say, and respectfully refuse to answer on the grounds that it is an ancient practice of our business not to divulge a source. . . .

COURT: I am determined and I tell you now, to get at the bottom of this thing.

The information I have is that a person communicated with you and allegedly stated that you had heard from this person to the effect that he had talked with a juror; that such person is a prominent man in the City of New York. As far as I am concerned I don't care who he is, and there will be no protection of any person.

This is a very serious matter and I am impressing upon you that the inquiry goes to the heart of the administration of justice.

Conniff still refused to divulge the name of the very prominent person who had called him. In answer to other questions, he said that he had called Pegler, but denied telling him about this matter.

COURT: You say you didn't discuss this at all with Mr. Pegler?

A. Not a word, sir. Then or until this moment.

Q. Did you tell Mr. Pegler that a member of the jury had been discussing the trial?

A. No, sir. . . .

Q. You are sure of that?

A. Positive.

Q. And if Mr. Pegler made that statement to me, would you say he was incorrect?

A. I would have to say he was incorrect, sir.

COURT: Mr. Pegler, I'm going to ask you to be sworn.

Pegler took the oath and then contradicted Conniff. "Mr. Conniff told me that he had heard a report that a juror was talking about the case. . . ."

COURT: Well, Mr. Conniff, you understand that it is important for me to get the name of the person who conveyed this information to you. . . .

A. Yes, sir.

COURT: I direct you to answer the question, and if you desire time before answering . . . to confer with your attorney, I will give you time.

Judge Weinfeld then sent for the United States Marshal, to arrest Conniff for contempt if he failed to answer.

The Judge had a fine balance of severity and fairness, so that his action could not be mistaken for mere threat. His thin ascetic face, under a high bald forehead, was a judicial mask of impassivity. Only his deep black eyes betrayed his emotion.

Mr. Henry pleaded for more time because "I think Mr. Hearst ought to be consulted as to what he wishes to do about it." This request was granted.

Finally Conniff appeared with special counsel. He had been advised that there was no journalistic Fifth Amendment available to him and he was ready to reveal the name of the man who called him. We waited breathlessly for the disclosure of "the very prominent man, whose name everybody would immediately recognize."

CONNIFF: The man, the name of the man who called me was John Griffin, G-r-i-f-f-i-n. I believe he lives in Fifth Avenue. It is in the phone book. . . .

COURT: What is Mr. Griffin's business, if you know.

CONNIFF: I believe it is in public relations.

COURT: Is he the man that you referred to as a very prominent man?

CONNIFF: I don't believe he is prominent. . . .

COURT: My recollection is both Mr. Pegler and Mr. Bowden, I think Mr. Bowden particularly stated that in this conversation you informed him that the man was a very prominent man in New York City, and the minute you mentioned his name, which you didn't, he would know him.

CONNIFF: Well, he should know him. . . . Mr. Griffin's father was, I believe in the Hearst organization at one time, and I believe that explains it. . . .

There followed a most involved and contradictory series of statements by the various witnesses.

Conniff claimed that the juror, who was identified as William M. LeFevre, sitting in seat two, had called Griffin because he wanted to know "what was this about Mr. Reynolds and assertions of his involvement with Communism? Something as plain as that."

But when the juror LeFevre was called to testify he was emphatic that he had not inquired about this, but on the contrary the suggestion that Reynolds was pro-Communist was foisted upon him over his protest.

LEFEVRE: Griffin then said his father didn't think too kindly of Reynolds and I told him, "Please, after all. I am on the jury. . . ." Whatever opinion he had of Reynolds I didn't want to know it.

So LeFevre contradicted Conniff's version. He also refuted Griffin's testimony.

GRIFFIN: LeFevre said, "Didn't your dad at one time have some sort of run-in with Reynolds?" I said . . . I believed dad thought Reynolds was slightly pro-Communist in some articles he had written. . . .

I said on several occasions when my father was alive that I had mentioned to him where I had been—at the Reynolds's home, and he would say, "Fine, but don't get involved with the man because I don't believe that his thinking is all American."

COURT: This was your father?

GRIFFIN: My father talking to me.

COURT: Which you told to Mr. LeFevre?

GRIFFIN: Yes. . . .

COURT: In any event you told him your dad informed you he believed Quentin Reynolds was pro-Communist?

A. Yes, sir.

Q. And also that your dad told you not to have anything to do
with him?

A. That's right.

But when LeFevre was on the stand, the Court asked:

Q. Who originated the discussion about the viewpoint of his father
with respect to Quentin Reynolds.

A. Griffin did.

Q. Did you ask him whether or not his father at one time had had
a run-in with Quentin Reynolds?

A. I didn't ask him that, no, sir. . . . I gathered that the opinion
of his father was detrimental to Mr. Reynolds. That is why I didn't
want to hear any more of it.

Conniff testified that Griffin concealed from him the fact that it was Griffin rather than some other person who was talking to the juror. But the
Judge asked Griffin:

Q. Did you conceal from Mr. Conniff that you were the person
who had talked with the juror?

A. No. . . .

Q. In other words, it was crystal clear . . . that you had a conversation with the juror that you were relating to Mr. Conniff?

GRIFFIN: Correct, sir.

Not only did Griffin report to Conniff about his conversation with the
juror, but thereafter he took the juror out to lunch to engage him in
further conversation. Was he encouraged to continue his effort? Griffin
himself testified that: "Frank [Conniff] said, 'Well, if you hear from him
again, keep me posted. I think I ought to tell the Hearst lawyers that a
juror has talked to you.' . . . Maybe once later he [Conniff] said, 'Have
you ever heard from your friend again?' "

Had Griffin followed up LeFevre to have a second conversation or, as
he claimed, had LeFevre called him on a Saturday to take him to lunch?
LeFevre contradicted Griffin vehemently on this point by stating that the
luncheon invitation came from Griffin.

When Mr. Henry's assistant, Bowden, was sworn in by the Judge, he
contradicted Mr. Henry:

COURT: . . . May 25th was the day that Mr. Henry received the
information from the FBI.

BOWDEN: Mr. Henry is mistaken. I was the one who received it. I
was the one who told him to call the FBI at their request.

Bowden said Conniff had told him that a juror was being talked to. He
knew it for a week before the FBI man called. Why, then, asked the
Judge, didn't he tell his superior, Mr. Henry, about it? Bowden replied
that Mr. Henry had been under tremendous strain with the case and he

did not inform the Judge because he did not think he would have much standing with the Court.

In recognition of Mr. Henry's high standing at the bar, the Judge was quick to clear him of any complicity in the matter:

COURT: . . . I am sure nobody in this case has any idea in the world that Mr. Henry acted in any way other than as an honorable member of the bar. I am sure that is concurred in by plaintiff's counsel and also by Mr. Reynolds.

NIZER: I certainly do, sir.

COURT: You have no concern about that.

HENRY: I don't understand why the FBI didn't communicate with the Court.

COURT: Well, there are other elements I don't understand, too, which I am going to make inquiry about. . . .

The most extraordinary fact of all in this maze of contradictions was that it was Pegler himself who had tipped off the FBI. He testified that he did learn from Conniff that a juror was contacted. This, combined with the mysterious suggestion that he pretend he was never called, was all he needed. He notified the FBI, not realizing what strange consequences would follow.

When Bowden testified, he could not contain himself about Pegler's conduct, which had exposed the effort to reach a juror. He said:

I didn't have any conversation with Mr. Pegler about this incident until after the FBI called here the other day on the telephone . . . and gave me some inkling as to what it was all about, and I went to Mr. Pegler and— May I use the word?

COURT: Go ahead.

BOWDEN: —and I said, "Pegler, what the hell have you done?" Then he told me.

When the Judge had concluded his inquiry, he commented that the testimony was "quite in conflict." He referred the matter to the U. S. Attorney for criminal investigation. He discharged LeFevre from the jury and fined him $250 for contempt of court for violating repeated instructions to all jurors not to discuss the case with anyone. He disqualified him from ever serving as a juror again.

But now another critical question faced us. Could the trial continue with one of the two alternate jurors available in any emergency, or would there have to be a mistrial?

Mr. Henry insisted that the jury would learn of the incident now that LeFevre was dismissed and fined. I replied: "There has been injury, perhaps even irreparable injury so far as expense, time, and effort are concerned. My client is now a poor man and we have exhausted ourselves in this case in every way, efforts, financial, and time. I have felt so strongly about the justice of this case that I have had as many as six and eight lawyers working on this case for weeks, exclusively. . . . We have also brought witnesses here. I am most eager to proceed subject to your Honor's quite sound observation that if there has been prejudice so far as the jury is concerned, all other considerations must fall, but I think every effort should be made to salvage this jury. . . . If it turns out that they are prejudiced, then, of course, I realize that there is no other thing to do, but I hope very much that this one bad apple hasn't spoiled the rest of the barrel."

The Judge decided to question each juror separately to discover whether LeFevre had passed on the contagion he had contracted from huddling with Griffin. He advised the jurors that LeFevre had been removed from the jury because he had violated the Judge's instructions against discussing the case with anyone, but by agreement with counsel he carefully avoided informing them that it was the defendants' representatives who were involved. Each juror responded satisfactorily to the Judge's meticulous questioning and promised that he could continue to sit without this incident affecting his judgment. Mr. Henry nevertheless continued to press for a mistrial: ". . . I fear . . . that LeFevre has identified himself to other jurors as a defense sympathizer. Furthermore, human nature being what it is, there is absolutely no doubt in my mind that the other jurors will address themselves to the cause of his disqualification and in some manner discuss it. The defense will then be regarded by them as having engaged in some irregularity, will be held in disfavor, and the other jurors will perhaps be fearful and will lean over backwards not to favor the defendant in any way."

I concluded my reply by saying: ". . . it is clear that whether this amounts to a tampering or stupidity and foolishness, a juror was told that my client is pro-Communist, and to be distrusted. If he indicated this to any other juror . . . then the risk is mine rather than Mr. Henry's. . . . The administration of justice also requires that these three weeks be not wasted, that the time of the Court and counsel and witnesses be not wasted, including that of the jurors."

The Judge ruled: "After a further study of the minutes and much reflection, I am satisfied . . . that this jury can continue this trial and live up to their oaths of office and decide the issues fairly and impartially. The case has now continued for three weeks and there really is no substance or basis on which to grant the motion. Accordingly, it is denied."

The Judge also submitted the entire record of his inquiry to the U. S. Attorney, but no action was ever taken.

We caught our breath again and went back to trial, but not without misgivings. Would the jury speculate as to who had tampered with LeFevre and perhaps come to the wrong conclusion that it was the plaintiff's doing? This was not impossible, particularly if LeFevre, before he was improperly talked to, had expressed some favorable views about Reynolds. Indeed, my observation and that of my associates was that LeFevre was deeply impressed by Reynolds. If so, the jury might conclude that it was

Reynolds's representative who had talked to him and caused his downfall. On the other hand, we had to agree that the Judge should not reveal the true facts to the jurors, for then they would be hopelessly prejudiced against the defendants and a mistrial would have been inevitable.

Offsetting these calculated risks was the realization that only by the margin of a telephone call (by Pegler) had we escaped disaster. We would never have known that a hung jury or a verdict for the defendants was the result of an invasion of the jury box. This is the only time in thirty-five years that I experienced an attempt to influence a juror improperly. I was outraged that years of preparation and effort should have been so endangered. A trial is a contest in accordance with rules designed by legal philosophers over the centuries. The scales of justice are maintained in balance by a sensitive mechanism, adjusted with such nicety that they record the minutest evidentiary weight. But if a heavy hand of influence can be secretly laid upon one of the scales, to what purpose all the painstaking craftsmanship derived from ancient tradition? The resulting cynicism is an invitation to self-help—the resort to violence.

The civilized procedure of trial by jury is slow, painful, and expensive, but it takes man one more step away from the jungle. It is as essential to democracy as voting, because the judgment of the jury is but another way of obtaining the consent of the governed.

We were more eager than ever to come to grips with the defendant in cross-examination. It was obvious that an emotional explosion was building up.

> Now the cross-examination of Reynolds took on a red hue.
>
> HENRY: Were you friendly with the Communists you met?
>
> A. The only Communist I ever met whom I actually sat down and talked with at any length was in the House of Commons, the Communist member, Willie Gallagher, whom I was anticipating doing a story on. . . .
>
> He also was the head of the Prohibition Party in England. He was a Scotsman. . . . He studied for the ministry. He was a great friend of Churchill's.
>
> Q. Was he a great friend of yours?
>
> A. No, not a great friend of mine. I met him, and when I listened to the nonsense he talked, I didn't think he would be a worthy story.

Reynolds pointed out that Lord Beaverbrook, the Conservative, had joined with the Communists Gallagher, Pollitt, and Montague, demanding a Second Front.

> HENRY: Did you write as follows, page 109: "I'd heard my Communist friends, Willie Gallagher, the MP Harry Pollitt, leader of the Party; Ivor Montague; Ambassador Maisky and others voice telling arguments."?

A. I said they were writing articles for the Sunday papers.

Q. No, did you write this as I read it?

NIZER: Will you read the next sentence?

HENRY: Yes, I will read the next sentence. "The British Communists are not the long-haired, wild-eyed creatures so often caricatured by American political cartoonists. No greater patriots exist in the British Empire than Willie Gallagher or Harry Pollitt. . . . These fellows seemed to be Englishmen first and Communists second. Churchill often spoke very affectionately of old man Gallagher and other men in the House did too.

Until he studied the subject and wrote his article against the Second Front, Reynolds admitted he had written: "I was as ardent a Second Fronter as anyone."

Q. Did you write "to such an extent that men like Willie and Harry thought of me as a sort of unofficial member of the party?"

A. Yes. That is a facetious commentary on how I felt.

Q. You were just joking?

NIZER: Read the next sentence.

WITNESS: The next sentence shows how I was kidding Willie Gallagher. I told him "Russia is the only country in the world where there is no Communism." I said that is why I liked Russia.

The cross-examiner continued to press the Second Front issue, even though Reynolds had incurred the enmity of Gallagher, Pollitt, Lord Beaverbrook, and the Russian Government for having written a keen analysis explaining why such a front should not then be opened.

In his book *Dress Rehearsal* he had recorded: "I wrote a different story from the one I had planned and called it *Second Thoughts on a Second Front*. When it appeared in *Collier's* I was panned unmercifully by left-wing friends both in Britain and America."

Finally, I objected to this line of questioning.

COURT: Sustained. What is the relevancy of this, Mr. Henry? Suppose he did advocate a Second Front? If you will explain it.

HENRY: Well, we got some vague claim of pro-Communist association and this would seem to be—

COURT: Because a man advocated a Second Front or was an armchair strategist, that would suggest affiliation with a Communist group? Is that your idea?

HENRY: Yes, indeed.

COURT: Is that what you want to argue to the jury?

In one of his books, Reynolds explained the difficulty of getting a visa into Russia, which he was eager to visit. Every word he had written, as we had anticipated, was put under a microscope and examined. The cross-examiner played upon this mercilessly:

Q. You said you would have joined the Communist Party, which I grant is only an exaggeration and figure of speech; isn't that so?

A. Yes, like I said last night, "I would give my right arm to see the Giants win the pennant, but if they do, I don't think Durocher would like to have my right arm in a flower box."

Q. And you so used the expression, that you would join the Communist Party to get a visa?

A. I said I would join the Communist Party, I would sell my two brothers into slavery; I would learn to speak Russian and do everything else to get a visa. . . .

Now Reynolds had to explain his observations about religion in Russia.

Q. Did you write: "The Government by merely ignoring religion, although not forbidding worship, has most certainly hoped to see it eventually die out. . . . ?"

A. Yes, I wrote that.

NIZER: The next sentence, please, if you are going to read it.

I knew practically by heart almost every sentence in every book that Reynolds had written and I attempted to force the cross-examiner to read an off-setting or explanatory passage, which would mollify or nullify the part he had read. Where I could not succeed in making him read it immediately, I made a note to refer to the desired passage in redirect examination after Mr. Henry had finished his cross-questioning. In this instance, Mr. Henry acceded to the pressure that he read on.

HENRY: Very well, I will read it: "God has been a strict absentee in the educational program of the youth here in Moscow, but despite that, parents have never stopped implanting the faith of the Russian Orthodox Church into the hearts and minds of the young. . . . By now the Government probably realizes that attempting to kill faith is like trying to punch a hole in a pillow."

A. Yes, I wrote that.

In one of his books Reynolds had quoted the English Communists' demand that the subways be opened as deep shelters since the poor people in the East End of London had no other shelters. The cross-examiner equated Reynolds's approval of this position with Communist tactics of disruption. But I inserted another "Will you please read from page so and so," and it appeared that the Queen had joined the demand and the subways were thereafter used during air raids. Furthermore, Reynolds had also written that London's Communist newspaper, the *Daily Worker*, would sooner or later have to be suppressed. He wrote: "They hate Hitler apparently and they hate fascism, these Communists, but they will do everything except fight."

After every word in any of his books that referred to Russia had been dissected, Mr. Henry put a final encompassing question:

Q. Now toward the end of this book . . . about your stay in

Russia, did you say that after spending three months there . . . you didn't know a damned thing about the country?

A. Yes, the British ambassador was over and asked me questions about Russia and I couldn't answer them. I said: "After I'd been in Russia three weeks I knew everything about the place. I could have written a book about it. But I made the mistake of staying there three months. After three months I realized I didn't know a damned thing about the country."

That is why all of those paragraphs about Russia are . . . little bits of a jigsaw puzzle, like candid camera shots I was taking in an attempt to get a well-defined picture. . . . I wasn't making judgment in this book. I said this is what I saw.

One of the most frequent errors in cross-examination is to try to squeeze an admission out of a witness at the cost of opening the door for him to make a harmful answer. Good judgment must be exercised in determining whether the exchange is worthwhile. Time and again I have seen a witness score a devastating blow that could have been anticipated, but the cross-examiner's narrow vision was concentrated only upon some minor admission and disregarded the consequences. A good illustration was Reynolds's answers when he was questioned scornfully about not having joined the fighting forces:

HENRY: How long were you dive-bombed at Sidi-Omar?

A. Oh, it seemed about fifteen or twenty years. I suppose it was only about thirty-five minutes, fifty minutes, something like that. . . .

Q. Did you express some regret at that time that you were not with the New York 69th Regiment?

A. If you quote—it rings a bell.

Q. Well, maybe I don't quote it correctly, but at the bottom of page 271, did you write: "When you are under sentence of death, as I thought all of us were there in the chill, tortured desert, you think of things like that. And I felt a little sick because these magnificent men of Britain . . . who emptied their machine guns and rifles and revolvers so futilely every time the Hun dove at us, were not men of New York's 69th. They would, I felt, have been just as good and as truculent and as disdainful of both death and the Hun as these farmers and sons of farmers of the First Royal Sussex. Life would be so much happier if we could only pick those with whom we wanted to die. As it is we are only granted the lesser boon of being allowed to pick those with whom we want to live."

Was it worth reading this passage to Reynolds for the gain of asking him why he hadn't joined the 69th if he yearned so for them? Now Reynolds also had an opportunity to answer.

A. . . . I never made any secret of my love for the British and my admiration for the way the British had fought and suffered, but if you are born in the Bronx and brought up in Brooklyn and worked in New York most of your life, I have but one loyalty, one allegiance, and that is to the much maligned sidewalks of New York and to our whole country. Then I was saying, when you think you are going to die, as we literally thought during this dive-bombing attack, one regret I had was that as long as I had to go I wasn't going with an American outfit.

Q. What effort did you make to join the 69th Regiment, New York National Guard?

NIZER: Objection, sir.

COURT: Objection sustained.

So the cross-examiner did not even get the crumb that had cost him a loaf of bread. I thought to myself, "Have you had enough?" The answer obviously was "No," because the question that followed was:

Q. Did you express a further regret that your brother was not present at this affray?

A. I believe I did. I got to thinking of my two brothers, Don and Jim. One was in the Army; the other was later in our Navy; and I remember this in a nostalgic sort of way, looking backward, that I wished they had been with me.

With the suddenness of a plane diving thousands of feet, we found ourselves discussing Sally Rand, the fan dancer. How were we catapulted from the sublime to the preposterous?

Mr. Henry had an early article written by Reynolds for *Collier's* about this lady. He desired to show how inaccurate Reynolds was. The Court doubted the relevancy but permitted the article to be placed in evidence. Perhaps everybody, including the jury, was relieved to get away from politics and war and bloodshed to enjoy a lighter moment.

Q. Did not the editors of *Collier's* make any inquiry of you as to why you had referred to Sally Rand as having almost a million dollars, whereas two months later she admitted she had nothing and was grossly insolvent?

NIZER: Objection—is counsel testifying? If he would like to take the stand on this, I would like to examine him.

A. I was out at San Francisco and wanted to do a story about the World's Fair, and they said: "Well, the smartest one out here is this girl, Sally Rand. She is the only person making money out of the Fair. She has an exhibit in the Fair; she has a night club in San Francisco. Why don't you see her?"

In redirect examination I used the Sally Rand testimony to pry open the door to J. Edgar Hoover.

Q. Out of 200 articles which you wrote for *Collier's* before World War II, Mr. Henry picked the one on Sally Rand. Two months before that had you written an article for *Collier's* called "J. Edgar Hoover on Death in the Headlines?"

A. Yes.

Q. Mr. Reynolds, how many times did you meet Miss Sally Rand?

A. Just once, the day I interviewed her out in San Francisco.

Q. Had you ever seen her before or since?

A. No.

Q. How long had you known Mr. J. Edgar Hoover?

A. Oh, I have known him twenty-five years. He is one of my oldest friends.

Q. . . . Is there anything in that article on Sally Rand that says she is a millionaire or on her way as a millionaire?

A. I don't think so.

Q. The only thing that refers to her wealth is in the headline, is that right?

A. That is right.

Q. Did you write that headline?

A. No, I did not.

Q. Did you have anything to do with its composition?

A. Nothing, no.

The cross-examination shifted to a far more important lady.

Q. Isn't it a fact, Mr. Reynolds, that you made grave charges against Clare Booth Luce in that campaign?

A. . . . I answered something that she said; she made a grave attack on the President, and at that time I was answering such attacks to the best of my ability.

Q. What did you say in answer?

A. She . . . had attacked the President for leading us into war. She said he had promised never to get us into a foreign war and he had done so. I felt that was a vicious attack on the President not warranted by the facts.

Q. What did you say in answer?

A. So I said that this is not the first time someone bearing the name Booth has attacked the President of the United States. . . .

Q. Isn't it a fact that John Wilkes Booth assassinated President Lincoln by creeping up behind him and shooting him in the head?

NIZER: Objection.

COURT: Objection sustained.

Q. May I have the reply which Mrs. Luce made to you? . . .

A. I was not aware she had made a reply until I saw it in Mr. Henry's office [during examination before trial]. She and I were good friends. We often laughed over this incident.

Pegler's indiscriminate hate articles had included Mrs. Luce. She, among so many others, had reason to be aggrieved, and we arranged to take her deposition in favor of Reynolds. However, since she was Ambassador to Italy, the rigmarole of taking an official's testimony in Rome, and having it properly authenticated, caused such delay that we could not obtain it in time for the trial, despite the heroic efforts of my associate counsel in Italy, Count Graziadei.

Combat between a witness and cross-examiner may injure one as much as the other. Though it is rare, the lawyer may reel back from the witness's counterblows and decide to quit. The witness must be prepared to avail himself of the opportunity to take the offensive. A classic illustration of such a strategem was a series of answers made by Reynolds which virtually forced the cross-examiner to conclude his questioning.

I had anticipated that the defense would claim that it was Reynolds who had initiated the quarrel with Pegler by writing a hostile book review. It was not too remote to expect that a good cross-examiner would endeavor to prove that Reynolds had deliberately selected the unfriendly passages in Kramer's book and thrown them at Pegler.

To prepare Reynolds for such cross-examination, I marked the many paragraphs in the Kramer book which were inimical to Pegler, but which Reynolds had not mentioned in his book review. This would enable Reynolds to answer with assurance that had he had a malicious eye for Pegler, rather than just writing a fair book review, he could have quoted these devastating passages. Furthermore, if by any good fortune Reynolds should be challenged to demonstrate these other passages he would be ready to do so. I went over the matter carefully with Reynolds. He made notes with the numbers of the pages he would wish to refer to, if the great opportunity should come.

HENRY: Isn't it a fact, Mr. Reynolds, that every mention of Westbrook Pegler in this book is unfavorable and hostile?

A. I don't think so. There are many unfavorable references to Mr. Pegler which I carefully kept out of my review because I wanted to present a balanced review.

Q. What unfavorable reference to Mr. Pegler in this book did you carefully keep out of your review?

The bait had been taken, Reynolds straightened up in his chair, as a witness does when he is fully prepared for an answer and is eager to make it. The Broun biography was not admissible in evidence. But now it was proper for Reynolds to read to his heart's content from the book and its deadly references to Pegler. Reynolds placed in front of him the sheet with page references and proceeded to answer the question.

A. On page 249 where Kramer referred to the "often brutal tone" of Pegler's writing. I kept that out. On page 250 where he discussed—

Q. Pardon me I haven't found the reference.

A. He said, "Despite the often brutal tone of Pegler's writing, a sulky mouth, and sometimes angry defensive eyes, he was known as 'fun guy'; Broun liked him." I kept that out about the brutal tone of his writing. That is one of the many instances in this book.

Q. You kept this out of your review in order to do what, you said?

A. To give a well-balanced review of the book.

The cross-examiner did not know how to stop.

Q. Now did you not notice another reference—

A. Well, I haven't answered your question in full, sir. You asked me where in the book are there adverse criticisms of Mr. Pegler that I kept out of the review. There are any number of them. . . .

NIZER: May I ask the witness to finish his answer.

WITNESS: May I, Mr. Henry?

Q. What are you reading from, Mr. Reynolds?

A. From the book.

Q. Have you got any other material in the way of notes?

A. Yes, I have.

Q. Did you take the index of the book and find every reference to Pegler and prepare yourself to reveal that you had not put them into your review?

A. No. I just went through the book.

Q. All right. Go ahead, what is the next reference?

A. On page 250 where the writer refers to a rather famous column of Pegler's in which he virtually condones lynching.

The Court granted Mr. Henry's motion to strike out this answer unless Reynolds read from the book.

NIZER: Would you be good enough to read, sir.

A. "A few days before Pegler's arrival a mob in San Jose, California, had lynched and mutilated two men accused of kidnaping and murdering a Santa Clara University student, an action which Gov. James Rolph Jr. described as 'a fine lesson for the whole nation.'

In his third column for the *World-Telegram*, Pegler in the rowdy brutal style of his sports-writing days raked over the affair, finding himself in agreement with Rolph. The storm of protest from the liberal readers of the Scripps-Howard papers almost blew him out of his new home."

I swiveled to take a glance at Pegler. His face was fierce and flushed, but I thought it was with anger not embarrassment. Henry's face was a study of frustration and confusion. He tried to get out of the trap by pushing forward.

Q. Have you read the column in question?

A. When it came out I was as shocked as anyone who knew Pegler. . . . Shall I go on, Mr. Henry?

Q. Yes. What is the next page?

A. Page 270 . . . "Broun stated a belief that an income tax had bitten Pegler severely at an early age and suggested that the man who had named Pegler's column had also titled near beer. Once Pegler after a particularly cutting attack on Broun came up to him in a night club and suggested they forget what they wrote during the day and be pals at night.

'What I write by day,' Broun said, 'I live by night.'"

That kind of thing is completely left out of my review.

Q. What is the next?

COURT: Mr. Henry, the only reason I am letting this in is because you put the direct inquiry.

HENRY: I am quite content with it, sir.

A. On page 287.

HENRY: Oh, no, you are right. This is not what I thought it was. Go ahead.

A. I want to oblige you.

Reynolds was almost purring with politeness. He continued to quote chapter and verse. Shortly thereafter Mr. Henry announced, "I have no further questions."

I was now given the opportunity of redirect examination. Its purpose is to explain matters that may have been elicited on cross-examination. It is generally regarded as a rehabilitation task. In Reynolds's case, despite his eight days of cross-examination, there were only two major matters that required further development.

One was to cite passages from his books which negated the impression Henry had attempted to create by truncated quotations. For example:

Q. You recall that Mr. Henry asked you whether you had made the statement, to quote him, that you were other than proud to be an American.

A. Yes. I do.

Q. In the first place, what is the sentence that he is referring to?

A. Well, it is on page 85. It reads exactly this way: "I am not very proud of being an American *tonight*, Ken," I said [Mr. Henry had left out tonight].

Q. Will you please read the passage of the book which explains the context. . . .

A. "People finally realized that it was all over. . . . As dusk fell, Downs and I sat at a table outside a café. We felt as bad as the thousands of weary refugees who passed ghost-like in the gloom. Now and then we heard mutterings as people noticed 'American War Correspondent' on the shoulders of our uniforms. America had promised so much—and had done so little. Speeches by prominent Americans promising help for France had been printed every day in the papers. The French people were foolish enough to have believed them. . . .

We felt as if we were attending a wake . . . and tried to rationalize what had happened. 'Why did France collapse?' 'I am not very proud of being an American tonight, Ken,' I said. 'I am not either.'"

In this way I took him over dozens of quotations, most of which when originally put to him on cross-examination had been unfinished, or had a different meaning in full context. The process not only cast a shadow upon the technique that had been employed to discredit Reynolds, but actually revived the impact of his testimony by repetition.

There remained only one other major task on redirect examination. It was to lay the ghost, once and for all, of the Communist issue. Fortunately we had the perfect weapon to do so.

Reynolds had written a book on the evils of Communism. It was called *Leave It to the People*. Significantly it had been published in 1947, one year before Pegler's libel article, so that it could not have been planned as an aid to the suit. Reynolds had traveled throughout Europe, interviewed heads of state and common people and made a definitive study of the expansionist dictatorship that was hidden under the fake idealism of Communism. He analyzed its true moral and intellectual nihilism. It was a brilliant work, devoid of demagoguery, and stated with heart-felt conviction that Communism was a threat to world order and peace. I read several passages to the jury, and they were obviously moved, not only by its truth, but by the simple eloquence with which the American credo was set forth.

I stated I was through, but a night had passed and the defendants had gathered their forces for a final attack. Mr. Henry announced he wished to have re-cross-examination.

Q. Isn't it a fact, Mr. Reynolds, that you took a vow never to fire a shot in defense of the United States? . . .

A. Oh, nonsense, Mr. Henry.

Q. Have you ever stated in your writings that you are a conscientious objector as far as firearms are concerned?

A. Of course not. I recounted an incident of how I almost shot my brother's eye out and how ever since then I have been scared stiff of guns. . . . But I hadn't anticipated that my country would ever be endangered. This is a vow I made when I was eight or nine years old.

Q. Now the incident you referred to was shooting your brother with a Daisy air rifle, wasn't it?

A. That's right; something that horrified me.

Q. And at the time you grew up, isn't it a fact that 20 or 30 per cent of the kids of the United States shot each other or got shot with Daisy air rifles; sometimes both?

NIZER: Objection, sir.

COURT: Objection sustained. Mr. Henry, this is to be strictly re-cross-examination limited to the testimony that was elicited upon the redirect.

Nevertheless, the cross-examiner continued to press this matter, until Reynolds surprised us all by dropping his deferential manner and yelling:

A. Don't shout, Mr. Henry. I can't hear you when you talk so loudly.

A moment later, the re-cross-examination of Reynolds was finished. Neither counsel had any further questions. He walked from the witness stand to a seat at the far end of the counsel table to become an observer.

We called Edward R. Murrow to the stand. After qualifying him as a member of Phi Beta Kappa, the holder of honorary degrees of Doctor of Laws from Washington State College and the University of North Carolina, as an Honorary Officer of the Most Excellent Order of the British Empire appointed by King George VI, as European Director of CBS for nine years with headquarters in London, he testified that Quentin Reynolds was regarded as a most important American correspondent, of the highest integrity.

To demonstrate Reynolds's reputation for courage, he told of the night Reynolds, Vincent Sheean, and Murrow himself were driving through Trafalgar Square in the midst of a heavy enemy raid. The flames illuminated the area so brightly that Reynolds bet fifty dollars he could read a newspaper in their light. Sheean stopped his car. Reynolds stepped out, read the newspaper and won the bet, while bombs were still bursting around them.

Perhaps it was a childish and reckless prank to disguise heroic defiance of the Hun, but surely it was not a picture to conjure up a "belly filled with something else than guts."

When Murrow was asked on cross-examination about Reynolds having "cleaned up $2000 of the ill-gotten loot of the Garsson brothers," he replied with clipped resonance in his most imperturbable television manner that he did not see how Reynolds could have had the prescience to foretell what would happen to the Garsson brothers two years later, when the United States Government hadn't been able to do so. And that was that.

John Gunther was our next witness. He was prosaic enough when he recited his achievements as newspaperman, war correspondent and author of the famous "Inside" books, but his voice quavered with emotion as he testified: "From the very first time I knew him [Reynolds] in Berlin, one of his outstanding qualities was courage. . . . He was the leader of the foreign correspondent corps in London."

Kenneth Downs, at one time chief of the Paris Bureau of Hearst's International News Service, testified: "I have traveled with men in the Army and with correspondents under hazardous conditions for quite a long while during the war, and I never saw any one who behaved better in conditions of danger than Mr. Reynolds, nor a finer companion, nor steadier comrade."

In reciting the escapades he had shared with Reynolds in France, he revealed that he had participated in the "stealing" of the gasoline from the deserted American Embassy. So a Hearst man was in on the "theft."

Sidney Bernstein, a member of the British Ministry of Information, whom we had flown in from Britain to testify, told the jury that at

Reynolds's request he had aided him in getting on a bombing mission over Berlin. He confirmed the fact that Reynolds had applied to Wing Commander Billy Bishop to enlist as an R.A.F. pilot, but, because of his age, was rejected and offered only a desk job. He refused and chose to remain an active war correspondent. This disposed of Pegler's charge that Reynolds had shirked war duty while "high school boys were pushing back the Nazi in the war he had been asking for for the last ten years."

The next witness, Halvorsen, had been a fighter pilot in the Eagle Squadron and had been in Reynolds's room when the biggest blitz of all crushed London into rubble and ashes. Reynolds had disdained going to a shelter and was "calmly sitting at a typewriter." Halvorsen asserted with actual tears in his eyes that Reynolds was revered by the pilots and that his name was "a household word in the service among the Americans." The jury was deeply moved by the young man's obvious hero worship.

Reynolds had not been asked a single question on cross-examination about the charge that he "and his girl friend of the moment were nuding along the public road . . . absolutely raw," and that he participated in nudist practices where "there was no color line"; nor had the cross-examiner asked a single question about the charge that Reynolds proposed marriage to Connie Broun while in the funeral car, though later, having "made an artificial reputation as a brave war correspondent . . . he snubbed her publicly and barely knew her."

Reynolds's denial of these accusations, therefore, stood unchallenged. The burden of establishing truth is on the defendants. Nevertheless we were not content to take advantage of the defendants' default on cross-examination. We put Mrs. Connie Broun on the stand. She was prettily tiny, the kind of wife a huge man—like Heywood Broun—so often takes. Her devoutness gave her an earnest manner that seemed in strange contrast to her flashing dark eyes and fresh countenance, eager to smile.

She told of her shock and intense grief which made her ill for weeks after her husband died. In the funeral car with her were Monsignor Fulton Sheen, her stepson, Heywood Hale Broun, and Quentin Reynolds. Tears rather than conversation were the bond of sorrow. Pegler's claim that Reynolds proposed marriage to her in that car was denied by her with simple vehemence, while her face registered incredulity as well as horror at the lie. Nor had Reynolds ever snubbed her. She said that the first time these preposterous statements had come to her attention was when they appeared in the libel column.

There was no nudism ever practiced at her Stamford home. She explained that Broun was in many respects puritanical. If the word "damn" slipped out of his mouth, he would excuse himself even though no one else was present but Connie. He never told a dirty story in his life.

On such occasions as Heywood and his son would take a dip in the lake they wore swimming trunks, even though the spot was completely sheltered and was like a swimming hole.

She explained that Reynolds was rarely near the water because he was "terribly allergic to the sun." He was usually in the house with a book or using her husband's typewriter.

In a sworn affidavit which Connie gave me in preparation for trial she said: "Since the whole story is an invention, it becomes unnecessary to deny each detail, but I consider the reference to Quentin Reynolds walking with a nude "wench" and being observed by neighbors, vicious and untrue. Not only was there no such incident . . . but in every other way the story is fictional. . . ."

She explained that Reynolds frequently brought his parents to their home, because Heywood was very fond of them and would invite them even when Quent was not available. Also Quent's brothers and sister were often weekend guests. This was hardly a setting for miscegenational orgies. As to Pegler's reference in the libel article to Connie's having "cleaned out the parasitic, licentious lot" surrounding Broun and turning him "respectable," she swore: "The entire statement is malicious and vicious and untrue. Heywood had wonderful friends, men and women who had some of the foremost reputations in the nation. Just to cite a few people who come to mind and houses we visited and who were friends of Heywood's before and after I married him, there were: Herbert Bayard Swope and his wife Margaret, Paul de Kruif and his wife Rhea, W. Averell Harriman and his wife Marie, John Steinbeck, Mrs. Eleanor Roosevelt, who visited us at Stamford and whom we visited at Hyde Park, Aldous Huxley, Harry Guggenheim and his wife Alicia and her father, Captain Joseph Patterson of the *Daily News*, Robert Benchley, Gene Tunney, Harry Hopkins, and many others, not excluding President Franklin D. Roosevelt, whom we also visited at Hyde Park and at the White House. . . . To speak of these people, because there could be no others referred to, as a licentious and parasitic group, is as low a use of language as I have ever encountered. To speak of my turning out a group of "bums" is an insult to Heywood's memory and to me. There was no one of low character to turn out. I never had such a problem and never performed such a task."

She branded as a fantastic lie Pegler's statement that a Negro seduced "a susceptible young white girl at Heywood Broun's."

"While I do not wish to imply by this statement that there would be anything wrong in having any colored people as our visitors, the fact is that during all the time that I knew Heywood we were never visited by any colored person, man or woman."

What made Pegler's accusations as puzzling as they were false was the fact that, during this very period, he and his wife visited the Brouns regularly as intimate friends: "We saw each other and visited each other two and three times a week during the summer and I would say an average of once a week during the year. Very often Quentin Reynolds was present on these occasions. . . . We would play poker regularly and we had rivalry in soft-baseball games. . . . Since Peg and his wife and Heywood and I and Quentin Reynolds were one little group of friends, joined frequently by other intimates whom all of us knew in the same way, whom could Peg have been referring to as the licentious and parasitic lot? Has Peg gotten so acidy that he is accusing himself?"

When Connie Broun had finished her testimony, the defendants announced "No cross-examination." This is the most difficult and yet the wisest decision a lawyer must sometimes make. The timid lawyer believes he owes it to his anxious client "to go after the witness." But, where there is no likelihood of contradiction, aimless cross-examination only produces repetition of the harmful story, and heightens its effect. Nothing is more ungainly than a fisherman pulled into the water by his catch.

Instead, the defendants planned to have Pegler, his wife, and others testify to "other" incidents of nudity not asserted in his libel article. The strategy was to let Connie Broun off the stand as quickly as possible and dim the memory of her appearance. Then, by new charges, nullify her denial. Our countermove was to bring Connie back to the stand in rebuttal, and also to produce her daughter Patricia.

In a libel action, the injured person may recover general damages for loss of income and injury to his feelings. This is called compensatory damages. If the defendants were malicious, the jury in its discretion may award punitive damages or, as it is sometimes called, exemplary damages or "smart money." This is not to compensate for actual deprivation of income, but rather to punish the defendants.

We put a series of witnesses on the stand to prove loss of income. Albert E. Winger, Chairman of *Collier's*, William Chenery, its publisher, John Chaplin, an editor, Fred Rohlfs, an attorney, and Mark Hanna, an agent, all sought to establish the damage Reynolds had suffered because of lost income.

The financial records showed that Reynolds had more earnings after the libel than before. How was this possible? There were two reasons. First, his income immediately before the libel was depressed by an arid period while he was writing his nineteenth book, prophetically entitled *Courtroom*. It became a best seller and so his income after the libel article was substantially enhanced. Second, although Reynolds lost his customary revenue from *Collier's*—which the defendants insisted was due to change in management, not to the libel article—he was resilient enough to substitute other earnings for it, from enlarged lecture tours and from commercial writing such as children's books. Of course we gave these explanations and argued that Reynolds had suffered monetary damage. But we were faced with the stark mathematical fact that Reynolds's total gross earnings after the libel article were actually larger than before. This was the defendants' most comforting haven. Even if they lost the case there might be only a nominal award of six cents or one dollar, unless the jury could be made sufficiently angry to award punitive damages. Therefore the duel with Pegler which was now impending had double significance. Not only could we best batter down the defenses through him, but if malice and recklessness could be demonstrated so as to arouse the jury, punitive damages might be obtained.

We rested. After the customary motions to dismiss the complaint had been denied, the defendants were required to proceed with the defense.

"Mr. Westbrook Pegler will take the stand," announced Mr. Henry. We had looked forward to this moment for several years. Pegler took the oath for truth. He was intense, pale, and taut. Within minutes he was off on a rampage.

HENRY: The next paragraph reads as follows: "Like Broun, Reynolds was sloppy and ran to fat but the fact was not to be established until we got the war which he had been howling for, that his belly was filled with something else than guts. Reynolds was a sycophant, a coat-holder for Broun and imitated his morals, and his equally, physical and sartorial corpus."

What to your knowledge was the manner of attire by Mr. Broun when you knew him?

A.   He was filthy, unpressed, uncombed, would go around with his fly open, he would look like a Skid Row bum.

Q.   Is it your testimony that Reynolds did likewise or not?

A.   Reynolds did wear laces in his shoes, and, unlike Broun, he did not go around sometimes with his fly open, as Broun did. He didn't shave, he didn't comb, he was unpressed and frowsy. . . .

Then he launched into an incident that he claimed had occurred in 1932. On a Sunday afternoon Reynolds drove up to his house at Pound Ridge with a girl and "the woman declared that . . . they wanted a shower bath."

HENRY: How were the plaintiff and this young woman dressed when they came to your house?

A.   There was nothing unseemly about his attire, but the young woman had on a sort of vest which I am told is called a bolero, which flaps open and revealed her breasts.

Pegler claimed that Reynolds and the girl went upstairs to take a shower, and although there were two bathrooms in separate wings, they took a shower together.

A.   I observed these two persons naked, displaying themselves on the balcony behind a window which stood open, however, on the second floor of the house. The living room was fourteen feet high and the window gave onto this second floor balcony.

Q.   Did the window open into the living room?

A.   It did.

Q.   Who was present in your home on the occasion to which you have referred?

A. There were present my wife, Julie Pegler, my brother Jack Pegler, and his wife Mabel, his young son, Bud, who was then a small boy, Mrs. Robert J. Bender, a neighbor . . . and her daughter Beverly.

Q. What part of the house were you and these visitors occupying?

A. We were in the living room.

Pegler then recited another instance of nudism, adding a lascivious touch to his story.

A. Mrs. Broun said she was in a rowboat on the Broun lake at North Stamford and that Reynolds was standing in the water and he asked her to take him for a ride in the boat. She said she rowed over to where he was, and believing that he had on swimming trunks, invited him to get into the boat. She said he then got into the boat and she was shocked to discover that he was absolutely naked, and in her phrase, he didn't have on even a hair net.

NIZER: I move to strike all this out.

WITNESS: My answer is not finished. Do I finish it, Mr. Counselor?

COURT: Finish your answer.

A. (continuing) She said she looked around at the trees and the sky, trying to avoid this spectacle but that he sat there with his lavaliere dangling.

The very phrasing seemed to indicate Pegler's inventiveness with words, and I was all the more convinced of this when counsel asked the unusual question:

Q. Did she use that exact phraseology?

A. That is Mrs. Connie Broun's phrase.

NIZER: I move to strike all this out, your honor. . . .

COURT: The jury understands, as I have repeated so often, that this is not received as truth of the occurrence, but simply on the issue of mitigation of damages.

What did the Court mean by that statement? There is a Statute, undoubtedly inspired by newspaper and other publishers, which affords special protection to defendants in libel actions. It permits the defense to offer hearsay evidence, which otherwise would be clearly inadmissible, for the limited purpose of showing what the defendant relied upon when he wrote the libel. In other words, even if the article is false, if the writer thought it wasn't, his motivation was not malicious, and punitive damages ought not to be awarded. So a writer may, under this unique Statute (Sec. 338 of the Civil Practice Act), testify to anything anyone told him, or he may put in evidence any item of columnist gossip or newspaper comment which he says he heard or read and thought was true. It does not matter how false the information is, it goes into evidence if the writer relied on it. Such hearsay and gossip are not admitted to prove the truth of their contents. To do that, the witness who made the original statement would have to be called and an opportunity to cross-examine afforded. It is admitted only to disprove malice, and the sole test is, did the writer rely on this data? If he did, the jury may hear or see it in order to determine whether he was honestly misled and had no malice in his heart.

This is an instance in which the law assumes that the jury possesses extraordinary powers of discrimination. Even though Judge Weinfeld gave clear instructions, was it likely that a jury could read a prejudicial item in a newspaper column and remember that it was not to be considered evidence against Reynolds but only relevant to the subject of punitive damages?

As newspaper clippings and remote hearsay poured into the record I pleaded with the Court to repeat its instructions.

COURT: Mr. Nizer, I don't think it is necessary for me to repeat in each instance something that I hope I had made crystal-clear to this jury.

NIZER: Well, it is so difficult a concept, your Honor, that a document is being received not as to the truth of anything in it but as the reliance on the subject of punitive damages—it is such a difficult concept even for lawyers, I am not sure, with one exhibit following after another, that it is clear that that distinction is made for this particular exhibit as well as the others.

Of course this special legislation explains why it is so difficult for a plaintiff to win a libel action. Many prominent people have been maligned by enemies, sensation seekers, gossip columnists, or notorious magazines. All this irresponsible hearsay becomes admissible to contradict malice. In the meantime the jury's mind is assailed by dozens of these additional nasty libels, while the plaintiff is unable to cope with them because his lawyer cannot cross-examine a clipping or the alleged oral statement of someone who told someone something terrible about the plaintiff and it came to the ears of the defendant, who says he believed it.

I adopted a surprise technique in cross-examination to overcome this burden.

In the meantime the defendants took full advantage of this special privilege. They developed their nudity and marriage-proposal evidence by testifying to what Connie was supposed to have told them, instead of putting her on the stand as a witness. They quoted hearsay evidence by Mrs. Luce and offered newspaper reports of her comments, instead of producing her or taking her sworn testimony in deposition form. The deadly nature of such hearsay made me fight its admissibility on every technical ground that would remove it from the permissive purpose of Section 338.

I objected so strenuously that the Judge called for a legal conference in chambers.

COURT: It is evident that these papers contain many hearsay statements, which, in turn, include hearsay statements from other persons, reports of various groups and comments by various individuals, all of which, there is no question, have been made or issued in the absence of Reynolds, without any hearing, confrontation or right of cross-examination insofar as Reynolds is concerned.

I must recognize that they are of a defamatory nature, and unless the documents are clearly admissible would tend to do incalculable harm and constitute prejudicial matter.

On the other hand, I have up to the present, by reason of Section 338, received in evidence on the issue of absence of malice, under the defense of mitigation of punitive damages, many documents, which, of course, do contain hearsay statements, reports, gossip, and rumor. I am about to put questions to Mr. Pegler preliminarily to determine whether or not he did in fact rely upon these documents in writing the publication in question.

The Judge then referred to the sentence in the libel article that "Reynolds's medicine grew too strong even for *Collier's*. . . . However, a fellow of his politics can do fairly well in Hollywood. . . ."

COURT: I understood Mr. Henry to say the other day that the defendant did not charge the plaintiff with pro-Communism. . . . I find it difficult to understand that the defendant relied on these various documents. I am going to ask Mr. Pegler this question: Will you tell me what you intended to charge particularly by the sentence: However, a fellow of his politics can do fairly well in Hollywood? . . .

A. . . . I meant to convey . . . that he became an aggressive and offensive, in the view of *Collier's*, partisan of a political party to the extent that he alienated persons of other political faiths and was no longer acceptable to them.

COURT: Which political party, if any, were you referring to by that last remark.

PEGLER: The Democratic Party.

COURT: All right. Thank you, Mr. Pegler. [Mr. Pegler leaves the room.]

COURT: On the basis of the answers given by the defendant to the Court's questions I am going to exclude this. . . . I think it would be doing violence to Section 338 to permit the proffered exhibits to go in. They contain statements of the rankest kind of hearsay, in my opinion . . . and also in the light of Mr. Henry's repeated statement that there was no charge against the plaintiff of pro-Communism. So we had succeeded in keeping some of the poison out. But dozens of other clippings went in. Then Pegler was turned over to me for cross-examination.

Within three minutes he was caught in such a serious contradiction that he threatened me. My first questions were:

Q. Mr. Pegler, yesterday and the day before various clippings were shown to you and you were asked whether you had read them and relied on them prior to the time you wrote Exhibit 1 [the libel article], which is November 29, 1949. Do you recall that?

A. Yes.

Q. And before you were asked those questions you were on the stand when his Honor gave a learned instruction to the jury as to the purpose for which this kind of evidence might be accepted, namely, it went to punitive damages and not as to the truth. You heard that?

A. Yes.

Q. And you also heard that if you testified under oath that you had relied on these clippings . . . prior to writing the November 29, 1949, article, then his Honor instructed the jury they would be accepted for that limited purpose. You heard that?

A. Yes.

I then showed him one of the exhibits that he had so qualified and asked him if he had read it before November 29, 1949. He said he had.

Q. You . . . told this court that you remembered reading that article about seven years before you wrote Exhibit 1 in 1949?

A. Yes.

Q. Isn't it a fact, Mr. Pegler, that you never saw that Hinsley article until after the publication of the November 29, 1949, column?

A. No.

I proceeded to contradict him.

Q. You signed an examination before trial in this action?

A. I recall testifying for 2400 pages, more than the entire record of this trial for the first four weeks.

NIZER: I move to strike it out.

COURT: Strike out the balance of the answer. Mr. Pegler, just answer the question. If there is anything on direct your counsel will ask you about it.

Q. Did you read your examination . . . before you signed it?

A. No.

Q. Didn't you make specific changes of particular answers spread over the entire examination before you signed it?

A. The answer to the first part of your question is yes.

Q. Isn't it a fact that you made more than twenty-eight changes directly changing your answer from yes to no, and no to yes, after you read this examination and before you signed it.

A. I do not know how many.

Q. I show you this volume which ends with page 313 and ask you whether that is your signature?

A. Yes.

I had, of course, approached the witness stand to show him his signature. The volume was on the table in front of him. I asked him whether he had read that volume before he signed it. Suddenly he shouted:

A. Don't stand close to me; go down where you belong.

COURT: Please, Mr. Pegler. Please don't tell counsel where to go. I was surprised to have drawn blood so early. We all remained frozen for a moment. Then I said: "It will be a pleasure for me to comply with your request."

I walked back to the counsel table, but pressed the lie upon him.

Q. Do you contradict or disavow your counsel's statement that the Cardinal Hinsley article was given to you after November 29, 1949, and not in 1942, seven years before?

WITNESS: Is that the statement of my counsel?

NIZER: Yes.

COURT: Show it to him.

A. I disavow nothing that my counsel stated.

Q. And you accept this as a statement of your counsel, that the Hinsley article was given to you after November 29, 1949, right?

A. Yes.

So he had lied when he testified originally that he read and relied on that article before he wrote the libel column. I followed this with another illustration of his false "reliance" testimony.

Q. Then . . . your counsel showed you a publication called the *Tablet*, which is now Exhibit UU . . . and you were asked whether you had read this publication and relied upon it—it is dated January 9, 1943. Do you recall those questions, sir, about this exhibit?

A. Yes, I do.

Q. Do you recall that you said you read it at about the time it was published?

A. Yes.

Q. Of course, that wasn't true, was it?

A. Yes.

Q. You are now telling this court . . . that six years before you wrote Exhibit 1 of 1949 that you recalled reading this paragraph in the 1943 issue of the *Tablet*, and relying upon it six years later? Is that what you are telling this court?

A. Yes.

Q. Isn't it a fact that you never saw Exhibit UU, this *Tablet*, until after you wrote the article of November 29, 1949?

A. No.

Q. Didn't you testify under oath that you didn't see it until after November 1949?

A. I don't know.

NIZER: . . . I don't want any doubt about it. I am going to read from your examination before trial.

I then read the passage from the transcript in which he stated that it first came to his attention in April 1950, long after this suit was instituted.

Q. Did you make that answer?

A. I believe I did. If it is this text, I will say yes.

Q. Isn't it a fact, Mr. Pegler, that what you were doing [yesterday] was to accommodate yourself to the law as it had been instructed to the jury, to claim that you relied on Exhibit UU so that you could get that hearsay clipping into evidence? Isn't that the plain fact?

When he answered "No" to the rhetorical question I pummeled him some more on this subject, drawing new admissions, such as the fact that he had sent this exhibit to his lawyer *after* the suit was instituted.

Q. And that was the first time you saw it?

A. Yes, sir.

His covering letter was dated April 1950. We adjourned for lunch. Upon return, I asked:

Q. Before recess you told us that . . . you mailed that to Mr. Henry in April 1950. Do you recall that?

A. No, I don't recall it, but it is all right; I will accept it. I don't recall the date. I remember discussing it.

Q. You don't recall from an hour and a half ago that the date was April 1950 of this letter?

A. No, I certainly do not. I went out and had lunch and I didn't keep the date in my mind, but I am willing to admit if you say it is there on the record, that I said it before lunch, I will let it stand. I do not specifically remember that date even at this time after lunch. Why should I?

Q. Well, why should you remember that you read Exhibit UU six years before you wrote this November 29, 1949, article? Why should you remember that?

HENRY: I object to the form of the question.

COURT: Objection sustained.

At another point, I asked:

Q. You couldn't remember that since Friday?

A. No. Something five minutes ago I couldn't remember.

Q. But you do remember reading Loomis's article in the Brooklyn *Eagle* in 1941?

We struggled through the tunnel of confusion concerning the *Tablet* exhibit, but we finally came out into daylight:

Q. And on June 1950 you had no recollection that you had read either that reprint or any other copy of that article, did you?

A. On that day I did not.

Q. But four years later in 1954 you discovered that you had read it?

A. No. I didn't discover it. I remember that I had read it.

Q. What was there that refreshed your memory, four years later, that you had read something that you didn't remember you read in 1950?

A. Nothing.

I then shifted to the fact that in the very clippings he claimed to have relied upon, there were some favorable comments about Reynolds. Did he also rely on those?

Q. When you read this article did you make a selective choice of the things you were going to rely upon and the things you were not going to rely upon?

A. Yes.

I showed him a clipping from the *New Yorker* which his counsel had introduced and read to him from it.

Q. "After an awkward silence during which we all admired the view of the East River, and some signed photographs of President Roosevelt and General Eisenhower . . ." —do you recall reading that in Exhibit GG?

A. I think I do, yes, I do.

Q. And did you also take into consideration the fact that there were personally autographed photographs from General Eisenhower and President Roosevelt to Mr. Reynolds?

A. Yes, I took it into consideration for what it was worth. It seems to me I also recall something about a mutt in there, a dog.

NIZER: I move to strike out that last statement.

COURT: Strike it out.

I showed him a highly laudatory article about Reynolds written by Damon Runyon.

Q. Do you think Damon Runyon was a reliable reporter?

A. No.

Q. Do you think that he was an honorable man with integrity?

A. No.

I found that one of the easiest ways to reveal Pegler's extremism and irresponsibility was to question him about men who were generally admired and draw his denunciation of them.

Q. Did you rely on General MacArthur with respect to his judgment on this when you read it?

A. No, I don't think he knew head to finger side what he was talking about. . . .

President Eisenhower didn't fare any better in Pegler's lexicon.

Q. Have you ever referred to Eisenhower's Socialistic Republican Party?

A. I think so . . . . I don't believe he knows what he is talking about.

In the examination before trial I read to him from his column: "All the crooks and Communists wanted to give us Ike."

I tested him on one of his own confreres on the *Journal-American*:

Q. Do you recall that this Exhibit 138—this is Louis Sobol's column. Do you consider him reliable?

A. No.

Q. Do you consider the fact that he writes for [Hearst's] *New York Journal* gives him any reliability in his statements?

A. No.

He turned on another Hearst publication with similar unconcern.

Q. Do you think that the appearance of Damon Runyon's article in the Hearst publication, the *Mirror*, gave it any sense of reliability?

A. No.

Even the founder of his co-defendant publications had not escaped his wrath when he wrote for the *World-Telegram*. He referred to William Randolph Hearst as "that never to be adequately damned demagogue and historic scoundrel."

As always his accusations had built-in boomerangs and returned to strike him, for he had also written that one who works for the Hearst organization sells his principles for some dimes. Thereafter, of course, he joined that organization.

He attempted to justify his support of the notorious Gerald L. K. Smith by stating in his examination before trial: "My version was that if you are going to have one lying scoundrel [Walter Winchell] poisoning the air on one side, it is no worse than a proper redress of balance to have a similar rascal propagating the opposite view in similar appropriate time." He testified that the New York *Herald Tribune* was a "heavily pro-Communist" paper. Its support of Eisenhower was "evasive action" and its prior support of Thomas Dewey was "again a camouflage." The New York *Times*, according to him, was in part pro-Communist.

In a final effort to destroy the clippings and "reliance" testimony, I resorted to a daring device. I made photostats of the very clippings which he said he had read and relied on. The photostats had no court-exhibit markings on them so Pegler did not know that these were the same as those which had already been shown to him. I was gambling that he would not remember them:

Q. I show you these clippings and ask you whether you ever read these and then relied upon them.

A. No, I don't think I did.

The day before he had said of originals of these clippings: "Yes. I read them all."

I felt that the corroding prejudice of the hearsay testimony that had entered through the inviting door of Section 338 had been overcome. By various cross-examination techniques we had demonstrated that the claimed "reliance" was mostly fictional. I hoped that the clippings and the "he told me" or "I heard" testimony would be completely discounted by the jury. This neutralizing cross-examination had been chiefly improvised. It was designed as an opening effort to clear away the obstacles, as a football player takes out the interference, so that the runner himself may be tackled. I now addressed myself to the libels.

When Pegler originally testified on examination before trial, he did not mention Reynolds and a woman exposing themselves nude together while taking a shower in his house. Four years later, he added this claim. I asked him:

    Q. And you further testified . . . that the only information you claimed to have on nudism was hearsay from Broun or Mrs. Broun?

    A. I had forgotten this incident apparently.

I read his testimony that he had not personally seen any nudity. He replied:

    A. It was a mistake.

    Q. Another mistake under oath; is that right?

    A. . . . Yes, another mistake under oath.

Had he remembered this shower incident when he originally omitted it?

    A. I had it in my mind, but I didn't recall it.

This was a neat psychiatric poser for the jury. He had fixed the date of this incident as 1933. Knowing that the lady whom Reynolds had escorted to Pegler's home (Reynolds emphatically denied the whole incident otherwise) had left the United States to go to England a year earlier (1932), it was obvious that Pegler had chosen an impossible date. The best way to induce him to stick to it, was to insist that the date he gave might be wrong and that the visit might have been earlier. Perversely enough, he then insisted it could not have happened before 1933.

Witnesses who gauge their answers not by recollection but by the tonal anxiety of the cross-examiner can be lead into such traps. A telling illustration of testimony adjusted to resist the cross-examiner's apparent objective, but which destroyed the witness, occurred in this very case. That error by Pegler became the most widely published incident of the trial. It involved Pegler's self-condemnation as a Communist. But its recital will have to take its place in the later developments on cross-examination. So, wanting Pegler to adhere to the date of 1933, I had asked again in the examination before trial:

    Q. Do you exclude a possibility that . . . it was 1931 or 1932, in other words earlier than 1933?

    A. Yes.

The more I had pressed, the surer he was.

    Q. Then I ask you if it could have been earlier than 1933 and you say no. 1933 was the outside date . . . is that right?

    A. Yes.

Pegler maintained that there were a number of witnesses in his living room who conveniently could see from their orchestra seats the balcony where the male and female nudes were disporting themselves in full view of the audience. He identified these witnesses as his brother, Jack Pegler, and his wife Mabel, his nephew, Bud Pegler, and his present wife, Nancy Hutchinson. But he forgot that this incident was supposed to have occurred twenty-two years before when Bud was only eight years old and his future wife Nancy was not even present:

Q. Well, do you say that the girl who later became his wife was present on that occasion?

A. I did so, but I was mistaken.

Q. . . . That was wrong, you say, under oath?

A. Yes, it was a mistake under oath, an error under oath.

Q. Well . . . let's sum it up briefly. You had the year wrong.

A. Yes.

Q. You had the people wrong?

A. Yes, that was one out of four that was wrong.

And, of course, he had "forgotten" to mention the matter when he first testified. I pushed him further in the direction that this story of the splashing nudes was really a recent invention.

Q. Did you ever talk to Quentin Reynolds personally at any time about this alleged nudism?

A. I don't remember whether I ever did.

Would not a host, subjected to such embarrassment in the presence of his wife and family have protested to his guest about the extraordinary liberties he had taken?

Q. After the shower incident did you invite Reynolds over to the house again?

A. I think so.

Q. Did he come?

A. Yes, he came.

Q. I ask you now . . . did your wife join in the social invitation to Mr. Reynolds to come to your house?

A. I think so.

Would a fine woman like Mrs. Pegler, if she had been subjected to sexual exhibitionism in her own living room and in the presence of her eight-year-old nephew, have invited the offender to visit her home again?

During this cross-examination Pegler once more lost his composure. At one point while I was reading from his former testimony to contradict him, I punctuated my comment with an emphatic gesture of my hand, in which I held my glasses. He stood up and shook his glasses at me in a mocking manner, while imitating my voice. Such an incident could not be recorded in the stenographer's minutes and therefore could not be referred to on appeal to a higher court. I took the precaution of making a statement for the record.

COURT: He is standing on his feet now—

NIZER: Your Honor . . . I am referring to a mannerism of the witness in attempting to shake his finger at me in answering . . . and I ask your Honor to tell the witness not to indulge in that kind of gesture.

COURT: I can't control the gesture of anybody. The jury will make its own observation. . . . As a matter of fact the manner of giving the testimony is an item which jurors may take into account in passing upon the credibility of witnesses.

Yet the very next day, when Pegler was in another squeeze of "I was in error under oath" admission, he exploded again. I was questioning him about the libel column. He invited me to show it to him:

WITNESS: . . . Inasmuch as it is here, why can't I see it?

NIZER: It is right there [indicating].

PEGLER: Get away from me.

NIZER: Please, your Honor.

COURT: Please, Mr. Pegler, I ask you to refrain from these comments.

NIZER: . . . I would like to make a brief statement on the record . . . with your Honor's permission. On several occasions the witness has asked me to hand him something or show him something. When I go up to show it to him, with great insolence he demands that I get away from him, as he said just a moment ago. I also call to your Honor's attention, respectfully, the fact that when I have put questions he has mimicked my manner, or if I have made a gesture with my glasses he has mimicked it, and I respectfully ask the Court to instruct the witness that he is insolent, that his behavior is improper; that it isn't enough merely for the jury to determine what his character or the credibility of his testimony is from his manner, but that I am entitled to the protection of the Court, as an officer of the Court, against that kind of insult and insolence.

COURT: Please do not tell counsel where to go to. I thought I made it clear that this Court is the only one that issues instructions in this courtroom. With respect to the question of his conduct the jury may take into account his manner of testifying. . . .

Politeness is the mark of a gentleman even in legal combat. I have rarely seen a successful trial lawyer who did not practice courteous amenities toward friend and foe alike. Similarly I have warned witnesses always to be respectful toward opposing counsel. They must never permit provocation to unsettle them. The jury evaluates the witness's character as well as his testimony. His credibility can be affected by offensiveness in demeanor. My feelings were ambivalent. On the one hand I felt insulted and was genuinely angered by Pegler's conduct; on the other, I was delighted that he could not stand a searching cross-examination. In his frustration and anger, he could not strike at Reynolds, who was sitting quietly on the side and enjoying the spectacle. So, as is often the case, the witness let out his venom toward his tormentor, the lawyer. I knew that if the questioning could maintain the pressure upon him, his malice might be fully exposed. I did not let up.

Pegler's charge that "Reynolds and his wench were nuding along in the raw" on Broun's property required an enveloping kind of cross-examination. I approached him from different sides in order to pierce his credibility.

Q. Have you ever taken a swim in the nude?

A. Yes.

A. Do you know whether there were any people nearby at the time you did it?

A. Yes.

Q. Did you consider yourself immoral for having taken a dip in the nude?

A. No.

Then, another approach.

Q. According to you, your sole source for the statement in Exhibit 1 [the libel article] that Reynolds and his wench were nuding along in the raw on a public road was pure hearsay, wasn't it?

A. I don't know the legal definition of hearsay.

Q. Haven't you testified that you have used the word hearsay in many columns when you were attacking certain propositions and claiming that it was simply based on hearsay?

A. Well we had a long discussion of that in pretrial examination. It left me with the impression that hearsay was something heard from a third party.

I moved back to the attack.

Q. Now, under your definition you never saw Mr. Reynolds in the nude any place on the Broun estate nuding along with a wench, did you?

A. No.

Q. The only source for that statement in Exhibit 1 according to you was hearsay of Heywood Broun?

A. It was the statement of Heywood Broun to me.

Q. And of course you knew when you wrote this column of November 29, 1949, that Broun was dead, didn't you?

A. Yes. I knew Charlie Duffy was dead, too.

NIZER: I move to strike it out.

COURT: Strike it out.

Now I approached on another flank.

Q. You say you relied on Broun for this alleged information, is that right?

A. Yes.

Q. According to you Broun was a notorious liar, wasn't he?

A. Yes.

Q. And you also called him a sneak?

A. That is right.

Q. Have you ever stated that Broun was in the habit of imagining and creating stories?

A. I may have said that.

Q. And according to you Broun upon whom you relied was also devoid of ordinary veracity, wasn't he?

A. Yes.

Q. . . . And also according to you, Broun, upon whom you relied in this instance, was not only accustomed to being called a liar, but proved a liar continuously?

A. Yes.

Q. And you thought Broun was such a liar that if he had recanted any position of his views you wouldn't believe him any more than you would believe Stalin or Hitler or Browder; that is what you said, too, isn't it?

A. Yes.

Q. You said upon direct examination that he was an abusive liar?

A. Yes.

Q. Didn't you consider that statement abusive of Reynolds?

A. No.

Now, another approach.

Q. Incidentally, you had read, had you not, before you wrote this column . . . that Mr. Reynolds was allergic to the sun?

A. I think I had.

Q. Do you recall the sun poisoning which is described [in *Only the Stars Are Neutral*] before you wrote this column?

A. Yes.

I came at him from a different side.

Q. You were in court when Mrs. Connie Broun testified, weren't you?

A. Yes.

Q. You heard her state under oath that Reynolds was never involved in any nude incidents?

A. I don't remember her words, but that is the effect of what she said.

Q. Did you testify as follows on your examination before trial: "Q. Do you believe Mrs. Connie Broun to be an honest person? A. Yes, sir. Q. And trustworthy and reliable? A. Yes, sir. Q. And certainly you would believe her under oath? A. Yes, sir."

A. I so testified, erroneously.

Q. During all these years that you knew her you found her trustworthy and reliable, up to the time that your counsel told you . . . she was going to testify against you, is that right?

A. That is when I changed my belief, yes.

Then I made a surprise sortie which resulted in one of the most startling answers of the trial. First I asked Pegler whether Mrs. Broun's honesty was such that he would believe her even if she were not under oath. He replied:

A. I think everybody is subject to doubt not under oath.

This opened a new door.

Q. When she is supposed to have told you these things about the rowboat incident [Reynolds climbing in stark naked] she was not under oath, was she?

A. No.

Q. But you believed her?

A. Yes.

Q. And when she was here on the witness stand and she swore that there was no nudism . . . she was under oath, wasn't she?

A. Yes.

Q. But you disbelieved her?

A. Yes, I disbelieved her.

I returned to his cynical answer, "I think everybody is subject to doubt not under oath," and shot two words at him.

Q. Including yourself?

A. Certain people make inexact statements that draw on their imaginations, to be amusing.

Q. And when you say that certain people draw on their imagination and make inexact statements, that has been true about you, has it not?

A. Yes.

Q. You have actually written, haven't you, sir, that it is perfectly all right to create fiction about a real person, because if you do it several years after it happens nobody will know the difference anyhow.

A. Yes, I wrote that.

Incredible as it seemed, Pegler thus admitted that he "drew on his imagination to make inexact statements" and that it was perfectly all right to create fiction about a real person. Could there be a crasser credo? And what could be a more damning admission in a libel action?

I attacked from a different direction.

Q. You never mentioned this alleged rowboat incident that you claim Mrs. Connie Broun told you about at any time during the entire examination before trial, did you?

A. No. I wasn't asked about it.

Q. At page 1129 was not the following question put to you and didn't you make the following answer:

Q. Except for this [shower incident] . . . is there any other incident of alleged nudism that you can recall or wish to charge against Mr. Reynolds?

A. I never saw any.

Q. You did not . . . in the examination, mention a single word about the rowboat incident until you got into this Court and told us about it, did you?

A. No.

While I am endeavoring to give a full account of Pegler's tortuous testimony, its effect upon the courtroom cannot be fully reproduced in writing. The jury was watching him intently and I never ceased watching the jury. Were there signs of sympathy for him? Did any of the jurors think he was being badgered? I could detect no such reaction. I sensed that an atmosphere hostile to the defense was building up. It has been said that an old man has an almanac in his bones. I believe a trial lawyer can tell from the very air in the courtroom when his case is prospering. The "atmosphere" of a case may not appear for weeks. Then it is there and even the court attendants sense it. One side begins to predominate. It is not some particular evidence which creates the winning barometric pressure, but rather the total effect from all that has occurred in the courtroom.

It was important not to dissipate this atmosphere and to keep the defendants in a state of confusion and contradiction. I turned to the alleged marriage proposal in the funeral car.

Q. You knew . . . that Monsignor Fulton Sheen was in the same automobile going to the funeral of Heywood Broun, didn't you?

A. No.

After a few moments of interrogation:

A. However I do believe that Bishop Sheen was there. Let us not quibble about that. I think he was there.

Q. Yes, let's not. . . . You knew before you wrote the [libel] article that Bishop Sheen was in the funeral car? . . .

A. I think not. I think it was after.

After a considerable pummeling:

A. I think I knew that almost at the time of the funeral [ten years before he wrote the article].

He reversed his answers concerning Woody Broun, too.

Q. . . . In the case of Woody you testified a few moments ago that you did know before November 29, 1949 [that he was in the funeral car], right?

A. I believe that is true, yes.

Q. And yet on the examination before trial under oath you said you didn't know it, right?

A. I could have been mistaken under oath.

Q. Not only could you have been, you were again, weren't you?

A. I may have been; I don't know.

Q. And you didn't change that answer, did you?

A. I don't know. Did I?

Q. No.

A. No.

In his examination before trial, Pegler had admitted that had he known Monsignor Sheen and Woody were in the funeral car "that would cast doubt" upon his statement in the libel article that Reynolds had "proposed marriage to Connie Broun while riding to the grave." This being so, the next question was, had he checked with Monsignor Sheen or Woody to "see whether you were accurate about this matter."

A. No, sir.

Q. Did you ask Connie Broun, to be sure you had that statement right?

A. No, sir.

Q. Did you do that before you filed your answer?

A. No, sir.

By that time he knew a suit had been instituted charging the complete falsity of his statement. Yet, without any attempt to verify the facts, he and the Hearst defendants filed answers that repeated and enlarged these incredible accusations. Recklessness is proof of malice. We were making important strides.

Pegler had made the mistake of filing a counterclaim for libel against Reynolds. He claimed that Reynolds's book review had besmirched his reputation and character. So it became relevant—which otherwise it would not have been—to ask what was Pegler's reputation which he said was injured?

We had researched Pegler's life and activities. I had read thousands of his columns and indexed them. I had read everything I could find which had been written about him. Since he accused Reynolds of being a slacker and a coward, it was quite proper to look at Pegler's own war record. This is what cross-examination of him revealed:

Q. At one time in your life you were also a war correspondent, were you not?

A. Yes.

Q. That was during World War I?

A. Yes.

Q. And you were at that time how old, sir?

A. I think twenty-three.

Q. And unmarried?

A. Unmarried.

Q. And healthy?

A. Yes.

Q. . . . When you became a war correspondent, did you first try to enlist as a soldier in the Army?

A. No.

Q. . . . Or any other military branch of service?

A. No.

Pegler's gift for insult and offensiveness got him into trouble as a war correspondent and his accreditation was canceled. He wrote that "Newton Baker [Secretary of War] had come to France and had been quoted in

American papers as having said in a position up at the front 'This is the furthest outpost of democracy,' representing that that was an American outpost, which was a lie because no American outpost was there."

So he had called our Secretary of War a liar, by interpreting "outpost of democracy" to be a representation of an American front.

Pegler also criticized the use by American soldiers of "idiotic British spiral puttees, which consumed millions of man-hours in putting them on and taking them off and rolling them."

After insisting that his accreditation was not canceled, I read to him his contrary statement on the examination before trial. He replied: "Well, I was mistaken. Accreditation was canceled by GHQ."

We skirmished over changes in his testimony and he shouted: "Your Honor, may I be protected from this harassment? Could he stand down there?"

COURT: There has been no harassment.

I returned to the main line of cross-examination. After he was discharged as a war correspondent, what did he do?

Q. Well, during that period that you were in London without accreditation as a war correspondent, and without enlisting, did you consider . . . that you were a coward?

A. No.

Knowing that great infantry battles were impending:

Q. Did you try to enlist in the Marines?

A. No, sir.

Q. In aviation?

A. No, sir.

Q. In the infantry?

A. No, sir.

Q. The only attempt you made to enlist was in the Navy; is that right?

A. That is right.

Although six feet tall and in perfect health, he obtained a clerical job. He was stationed in an office building.

Q. You never had a gun?

A. No, sir.

Q. And the only reason you enlisted in the Navy, the provoking cause for that was the withdrawal of the accreditation, right?

A. No.

Q. Didn't you so testify?

A. No.

Q. Were you asked the following question and did you make the following answer.

HENRY: What page?

NIZER: Sixty-two.

I then read to him from the transcript of his pretrial deposition:

"Q. And was the withdrawal from France the direct provoking cause for your enlisting? A. Yes, I think I can say that."

Q. Did you make that answer?

A. Well, that is a mistake.

Q. That is a mistake too?

A. Yes.

Q. How many have you had so far in your testimony, would you know?

A. Do you know? I don't.

He served as a clerk in the Navy to the end of the war.

Q. When you got the assignment to render clerical service at a hotel office building in Liverpool for the United States Navy, did you protest to anyone?

A. Of course not.

Q. Did you request to be assigned to any fighting ship?

A. No.

Q. Did you request to be transferred?

A. No.

Q. To any fighting service, either in the Navy or in the Army?

A. No, nor to any lecture service back in the United States.

NIZER: I move to strike that out.

COURT: Strike it out.

I summed up his activities in the war; he caviled and dodged. I quoted the following from his examination before trial:

Q. So that it is fair to say, Mr. Pegler, that your war record consisted of being a war correspondent in civilian capacity between 1917 and 1918 when the United States was at war, and at which time you did not enlist, and thereafter when you enlisted, your war service consisted of being a clerk in a hotel building in Liverpool for the United States Navy?

A. That is right.

At this moment the only comment permissible was a meaningful pause. It was not until the testimony was completed and I was permitted to sum up to the jury that I could contrast the forty-year-old Reynolds's participation in the mutilating struggles of the Second World War with the twenty-three-year-old Pegler's service at a Naval typewriter in the First World War. Yet it was Pegler who set himself up as a standard-bearer of patriotism and reviled Reynolds for dodging duty and danger.

During the Second World War Pegler began a campaign for good citizens to remove the bumpers from their cars and give them to the Government to provide strategic materials. He was photographed making his own bumper sacrifice and a special article appeared in *Life* magazine to publicize this exercise of patriotism.

At the very same time, Pegler had applied to the local War Priorities Board for permission to use strategic materials in a $50,000 rebuilding of his Connecticut home. He justified his request on the ground that he was going to engage in farming.

I drew from him the details of the strategic materials that he used in rebuilding his home: copper drain pipes, leaders and gutters, hundreds of feet of water pipe, three bathtubs and a shower, metal lathing (though wooden lathing was available), electrical conduits, an electrical pump, etc. Thirty workmen were employed, fourteen automobiles were on the grounds using up gasoline, etc.

Since his "give away your bumper" campaign did not exactly jibe with his private conduct, Pegler did not hesitate to denounce his own patriotic brainchild.

    Q. And you say that you were mistaken in this campaign; is that right?

    A. Certainly was.

    Q. It was a mistake?

    A. It was a mistake.

    Q. And unnecessary?

    A. Quite unnecessary.

    Q. And of no help?

    A. No help.

    Q. . . . Approximately how long after you ran the columns for that purpose did you discover that you were wrong?

    A. I would think inside of a week or ten days.

    Q. Did you write a column correcting the impression?

    A. I think I did not.

At all times in his testimony Pegler had described his profession as being solely journalism. What about his written representations for income tax deductions and otherwise that he was in the profession of "farming"? Of course, he had never been a farmer before. It was obvious that the cross-examination soil on this subject would be more fertile than he had found the land.

    Q. So that you have no idea whether it was one bushel of potatoes or a thousand bushels that you raised on your farm; is that right?

    A. Yes, sir, I have.

    Q. Will you tell me?

    A. It was more than one bushel and less than ten thousand.

    Q. In between those two figures can you make that more definite?

    A. No, sir.

    Q. Even though you were in full charge of the operation? Were you?

    A. Yes, sir.

HENRY: The only relevant question so far has been whether he cheated the Government on these farming operations. In the first place, anybody who knows a thing about farming will tell you that is not a farm. That is a garden. I was raised on a farm. I know what farms are.

NIZER: Mr. Pegler, do you wish to accept your counsel's statement that what you were operating was a garden rather than a farm?

A. I regarded it as a farm . . . not a garden.

Q. . . . Did you during the time that you were operating this farm, sustain a loss or profit from its operation?

A. A loss.

Q. Did you claim such loss in your regular income tax reports?

A. I believe we claimed a loss.

Q. . . . during the war years?

A. I think so.

While the Court struck out most of the testimony on farming, enough evidence and quotations from the examination before trial remained to cast a strange light on his attacks on Reynolds as a slacker and war profiteer. I probed into other inconsistencies of Pegler.

A. . . . I don't say Reynolds was not loyal and patriotic. I say he is a big dope. He doesn't know the difference.

Q. Now isn't it a fact, Mr. Pegler, that you have joined . . . organizations which you later felt were Communistic?

A. No—oh, the Newspaper Guild, yes.

Q. Well, isn't there another one [Friends of Democracy] that you found is subversive?

A. No, just rotten.

Q. . . . And how long had you been listed as a member on the letterhead before you discovered you were a dope?

A. I didn't say I discovered I was a dope and I never was.

Q. Did you consider . . . that your name on the letterhead committed you morally and politically to that organization?

A. No.

I read to him his answer on the examination before trial in which he said: "A. I joined it, I gave . . . authority to use my name on a letterhead . . . which I consider to have committed me morally and politically to their organization."

Q. Did you make that answer?

A. Yes. I am mistaken now in my present answer.

I quoted some of his prior answers on the Newspaper Guild and elicited the familiar confession:

A. I was mistaken under oath. . . .

And as for being "taken in" by "questionable" organizations, I asked him:

Q. That can happen to any man, can't it?

A. I don't know. Maybe some of them would be smarter than I was.

Q. In any event, your name on the letterhead meant to you that you were being represented as one of the sponsors and supporters of this organization.

A. . . . I am afraid that could have been so.

Why had he waited three years before retiring from a "Communistic organization" he had been roped into? When he couldn't find the explanation, I supplied it from a column he had written: "I know who the Communists are, and I waited for a long time before I became convinced that they were actually enemies of the freedoms which are inherent in Americanism."

Of course, he was more embarrassed by his excuse for waiting than by his original error in joining.

There is such a thing as momentum of contradiction. As the witness is forced repeatedly to retract his answers, the effect upon the jury is increased disproportionately. Each succeeding defeat registers more deeply because of the accumulated impact.

How can the cross-examiner assure himself of the maximum number of triumphs over the witness? There is a technique I have developed to accomplish this.

I prepare my cross-examination notes by writing out the questions on the left-hand side of the page. On the right I fill in the exact answer that the witness has made previously at the examination before trial. If he has given several versions, I write out each with a page reference to the examination minutes. If he has changed his testimony before signing it, I add his changed answer in different colored ink. When he testifies at the trial on direct examination, I obtain the stenographer's minutes overnight and write in his latest answers to the same subject matter in still a different colored ink. And if my cross-examination is lengthy, as for example of Pegler, I obtain the minutes of his cross-examination and add his answers to my notes. The result is a set of notes in red, blue, and green ink representing the witness's various answers in all their refinements. When I ask him a question I may have before me in different colors his previous conflicting answers, so that no matter what reply he makes, he is subject to contradiction. In this way I am able to exploit to the fullest whatever variations there are in his testimony.

Of course, the key to this magic box of contradictions is memory. Questions and answers do not run in predestined orbits. Invariably the witness seeks to evade the question by a tangential answer, and he must be pursued down every alley of his escape. Often I will cross-examine for hours between two written questions in my notes. But such improvisation must be aided by recollection of the hundreds or even thousands of answers given by the witness with respect to other matters. For he is most vulnerable when he is off guard. For example, at one point Pegler unexpectedly blurted out: "My memory is about as good as the next man's. Excellent in some ways."

There swam into my head a contradictory answer in connection with another subject, and the page of my notes upon which it appears came vividly to the forefront. I found it quickly and faced him with an answer he had made: "'I was deceived about my relations with Broun by my own faulty memory. . . .'"

He was obliged to hedge: "Yes, to that extent I will admit that my memory is faulty."

On another occasion he surprised me by claiming he had signed his examination before trial without reading it. A red-ink entry somewhere in my notes beckoned me to a familiar page:

Q. Isn't it a fact that you have testified . . . that you had read the entire deposition? . . .

A. No. In fact, I told you in your office that I had not read it.

Q. Were you asked the following question and did you make the following answer at page 1588: "Q. And you have reread the entire examination recently before you made such changes as you have made? A. Yes."

Often there are valuable by-products. Pegler went on to explain his error. "I knew I was mistaken. . . . I was simply head-weary, brainwashed. . . ."

Once, in a spiteful moment, Pegler volunteered that Broun was physically dirty and Reynolds supposedly emulated him. I remembered an extraordinary column he had written, and overnight I found it. It held forth the theory that cleanliness is a great affectation in America and that being untidy and dirty, short of leprosy, was acceptable. The Court excluded the column as too remote on reputation, but could not wipe out the distressful look in Pegler's eyes, as he found that no statement of his was impervious to contradiction.

When Pegler found himself in a sea of contradiction, he would reach out to any piece of wreckage, but found that it too disappeared under his hand. So he claimed that he was never permitted to correct his testimony until the end of the examination. My memory index led me to a remote passage which I read to him.

Q. So it wasn't correct to say . . . that you never made any changes in the midst of the examination, was it?

A. It was incorrect. It was an error.

In one exchange between us, he insisted that the changes he made were only of major matters. He must have thought that at least this platform was firm and would not collapse. But there were those colored notes waving their hues in my memory. I read to him: "Page 32, where the witness says he believes he recalls that Reynolds lost a tooth at Dieppe, he wishes to change the answer to the effect that he lost a filling."

I also read his change which corrected the number of bathtubs in his new home from three to four, and

Q. Did you on page 92 make a correction to say that you didn't play on a softball team headed by Lowell Thomas, but you played against Lowell Thomas on a softball team?

A. I will accept it.

Q. Did you consider that a vital matter?

A. No.

Where testimony flows to the pole of truth, variations are of little consequence. The facts fall back into the magnetic stream. But when the witness abandons his compass of veracity and is off in any direction which he believes will serve him best, his wanderings lead him into confusing circles. Each new turn toward safety only adds to the misdirection. There were times when Pegler had given one answer on the examination before trial, changed it, reverted to the original answer on direct examination, and changed again on cross-examination.

My colored notes were all in use, sometimes with kaleidoscopic frequency. For example, although Pegler's column charged Reynolds with being a war profiteer, he contradicted himself on his examination before trial by admitting that Reynolds's "profits" from his professional activities were legitimate. He admitted being mistaken when he testified on the earlier occasion, but he made no effort to correct the mistake. Similarly his varying answers at different times recorded in my colored notes compelled him to admit another "mistake," when he placed himself in the untenable position of contending that a nurse who worked overtime because of war conditions was a "war profiteer." He withdrew this too.

Furthermore he denied and then admitted that he himself had earned more money during the war, and therefore he faced the dilemma, according to his own definition, of being termed a war profiteer.

Even I could sympathize with his plaintive comment, "You make me nervous, Mr. Nizer."

I took him through his libelous statement that Reynolds had received part of the "ill-gotten loot" from the Garsson brothers who were convicted of defrauding the Government. He admitted that his omission of the "E" Award setting distorted the meaning of his comment, and that neither the United States nor he nor Reynolds had known at that time of any impropriety by the Garssons. But on the turbulent road to these admissions, he was tossed back and forth between his conflicting statements until at one point, when I asked him whether he had deliberately given a false answer, he replied: "I deliberately gave an erroneous and honestly mistaken answer, not a false answer."

I engaged him for a while in this exercise of metaphysics.

Then he was buffeted between his own conflicting definitions of "ill-gotten" and "loot." When he said they meant dishonest proceeds, he was confessing to libel. When he reversed himself and said: "No, not dishonestly on Reynolds's part, unethically but not illegally," he had to retract "unethically."

When I showed him photographs of the "E" Award ceremony, which had been taken from his own files, and asked him whether they indicated a "carouse" (as charged by him), he conceded they did not, but attempted to salvage his position.

Q. What is there about this picture that makes you call it a carouse?
A. It looks like a merry party.
Q. Anybody dancing?
A. No, sir.
Q. Anybody drinking?
A. I don't see anyone drinking.
Q. By "merry" you mean that one of the gentlemen who was speaking into the microphone has a smile on his face?
A. Yes, sir.

While teetering along the confused roads of his prior testimony, he left a trail of abuse behind him. He called the high officers of the Army and Navy who attended the ceremony, "Briefcase Commanders, who should have been ashamed of themselves."

The momentum of contradictions was reaching crescendo proportions. In rapid succession he testified that answers he gave were "misrepresentative of my thoughts," "my answer was incorrect," "that was a mistake," "it was an error under oath"; and "No—yes, it means that, subject to— I don't know what it means. It means I think that is the case."

After returning from lunch on the thirteenth day of Pegler's cross-examination, he did not take his seat on the witness stand. Instead, his attorney advised the court that a most important witness had arrived from Canada who could not stay in this country long. He therefore wished to put him on the stand before Pegler was finished. The Court excused Pegler temporarily, and counsel called a Mr. R. D. Collins to the stand.

He was a surprise witness from Calgary, Canada. The setting of his story soon developed. A Canadian by the name of George Du Pre had served in British Intelligence during the war. He parachuted into captured France where he posed as a half-wit who had once lived in the village of Turini. His chief mission was to help R.A.F. fliers who had been shot down to escape. He was ultimately captured by the Nazis.

Despite Gestapo inventiveness in devising techniques for pain which would be too excruciating to bear, but not so injurious as to give the release of death, Du Pre would not talk. His detailed descriptions of Gestapo torture methods and his resistance was a thrilling saga of the triumph of the human spirit.

After the war he gave talks on the radio and before dozens of clubs and organizations about his experiences. He was a devout man and gave all income from his lectures to his Church and to charity. Over a period of seven years his fame spread, and the *Reader's Digest* assigned Quentin Reynolds to write a story about Du Pre's exploits. While in Calgary to gather confirmatory data about the amazing story, the editor of the *Calgary Herald* suggested to Reynolds that he might want to write a book about Canada's great hero. Du Pre came to New York and lived with Reynolds while the facts were gathered and checked. Reynolds was caught up in the gruesome but heroic details of one of the greatest sagas of intelligence operations in the history of warfare.

Reynolds wrote the book *The Man Who Wouldn't Talk*. The *Reader's Digest* published its condensation. Both were enormous successes.

A short time later the story broke on the front pages of the world's newspapers that Du Pre had perpetrated one of the greatest hoaxes in literature. The man who had discovered the fraud and exposed Du Pre was the witness now on the stand, R. D. Collins.

He was a short, stocky, handsome man in the late thirties with a high front of otherwise slicked down hair. He had a supercilious grin and cocky manner. He turned to the Court and said:

WITNESS: May I stand up? I prefer to.

COURT: I think I may tell the members of the jury that under English practice witnesses stand. I think the witness prefers to stand for that reason.

WITNESS: Well, I just feel uncomfortable sitting down.

COURT: You may stand.

He recited his impressive war record. He had been captured at Dunkirk, escaped after a year, and ultimately rejoined his troops to cross the Rhine not as a prisoner, but invader.

He looked out at the crowded courtroom with immense satisfaction, as a vain man looks into a mirror. He had apparently read fictional books about trials, or seen stage or motion picture trials, in which the witness convulses the courtroom with witty answers, which rout the confounded cross-examiner. He strove at every turn for this effect, and when, as in real life, the sallies didn't come off, one could never tell it from his face. He registered triumph, even when there was no explosion of laughter to justify it. So he held forth under the friendly hand of direct examination. When I got to work on him in cross-examination, his theatrical charm turned smart-alecky. Once he held up his hand like a traffic cop and said: "OK, take it easy." He testified that, having talked to newspapermen and others in Calgary, he could say that Reynolds's reputation for accuracy "was bad."

His main thesis was that Reynolds, his publisher Random House, and *Reader's Digest* were careless, while he, Collins, by brilliant investigation, had compelled Du Pre to confess. The *Reader's Digest* had published a special article entitled "The Story of an Extraordinary Literary Hoax." It explained how the most distinguished citizens (including the Minister of Mines, Forests and Lands of Alberta, for whom Du Pre had worked) had been taken in by Du Pre's persuasively detailed story and highly purposed and selfless private life. Organizations such as the Calgary R.C.A.F. Squadron had accepted his veracity. Collins considered this *Reader's Digest* article "sloppy."

Having written for the *Reader's Digest*, I knew first-hand its meticulous standards for accuracy. On one occasion, when it published my

"Most Unforgettable Character" about the author Rex Beach, it had corrected my script which referred to a "marble statue" of Beach at Rollins College to read "terra-cotta statue." I asked Collins:

 Q. You call this article sloppy. How long have you been in the newspaper business?

 A. Two years.

 Q. What is the circulation of this newspaper that you had two years' experience with?

 A. About 60,000.

I challenged him to point out the "inaccuracies" in the *Reader's Digest* story. We waited while he read the article to himself. Then he struggled to find discrepancies. The article said that Du Pre had "managed to deceive not only Quentin Reynolds, Random House, and the *Reader's Digest*, but also his employers, his friends and neighbors, newspaper reporters, intelligence officers, and the countless men and women who heard him speak at meetings of church, business, and civic groups over a seven-year period."

 COLLINS: I am not aware that he deceived an Intelligence officer.

 Q. Well, by not being aware, you mean you have no knowledge one way or the other?

 A. Well, if you will allow me to expand—

 Q. No, no, I will allow you to please answer my question first. Do you mean by not being aware that you have no knowledge one way or the other of that fact?

 A. That is right.

His next grievance with the article was that it said Du Pre was anything but a braggart:

 A. He was only a braggart.

Upon questioning he explained:

 A. He was one of those shy and modest men who always brag about what they are doing.

 COURT: Pardon me . . . isn't that something inconsistent?

 WITNESS: My grandfather was Irish, sir, so forgive my inconsistency. The point is . . . there are some people who . . . create the impression that they are wonderful people. . . .

 COURT: That means they are subtle, doesn't it?

 WITNESS: Subtle braggarts, I suppose.

 COURT: You think there is no inconsistency in your prior answer?

 WITNESS: I personally do not, sir.

 NIZER: Well, we will leave it with this: He was shy and modest, but a braggart nevertheless?

 A. Yes.

His other fault-finding with the *Reader's Digest* was even more trifling. His ambition to be a witness-wit led him into delicate areas.

 Q. These distinguished people, such as Bishop Tanner—

A. I suppose you are referring to Mr. Tanner.

Q. He is a bishop, isn't he?

A. He may be a cardinal for all I know, but he was a minister in the Alberta Government and he is at present in the oil industry. I didn't know the oil industry had any bishops.

Q. Well, Mr. Collins, I am sure you don't mean to cast any reflections upon the religious title which this man does earn; he is a bishop, isn't he, in the Mormon Church?

A. . . . He might be a cardinal.

Once more he admired himself in the audience mirror.

Q. Who called you to come to Court, Mr. Collins?

A. I understand Mr. Pegler did.

Q. You understand? Didn't he personally call you?

A. Yes.

It developed that he had come into the city at Pegler's request and expense and was provided accommodations in the Park Plaza Hotel. He protested to Pegler that he was entitled to better quarters and was transferred to the Waldorf-Astoria.

Q. How long have you been comfortably ensconced at the Waldorf-Astoria?

A. Alone?

He grinned at the jury and I am sure mistook their wincing for admiration.

Q. No, no. How long?

A. Thursday, Friday, Saturday, Sunday, Monday, and today is Tuesday. During those days.

So he hadn't just arrived. I dragged from him the amount of the expenses being paid to him by Pegler. Although he repeatedly denied that a job for him was involved in his coming to testify, persistence brought this qualification: "I told Mr. Pegler . . . that I couldn't come because I wasn't prepared to defy my employers. . . . I could only come on the understanding that other employment was found me, not necessarily by Pegler, but anyone else, and eventually Pegler rang up again . . . I believe he phoned the publisher . . . and apparently he agreed to free me for the purpose of coming to New York. . . ."

Then I tried one of the oldest chestnuts on him. After he had reluctantly conceded meeting with Pegler four or five times, "a couple of hours each time," and with Pegler's lawyers, too, I asked:

Q. Did you ever discuss with Mr. Pegler what you were going to testify to in this case?

A. No.

Q. Did you ever discuss with his counsel what you were going to testify to in this case?

A. No.

After Collins had identified himself on the witness stand, Reynolds had telephoned his friends in Calgary to find out what they knew about his surprise appearance. They were indignant that Reynolds should be injured by one of their own. They told him that there were rumors that Collins was taking credit for exposing Du Pre, when the fact was that a man called Kenneth Spencer had provided certain documents to Collins which really exploded the hoax. Although this information was thin and unsubstantiated, I decided that the situation warranted a long cross-examination gamble. I held a folder with a sheaf of papers in my hand and approached him slowly. Then, with careful emphasis, I asked:

Q. Isn't it a fact, Mr. Collins, that you met a former R.C.A.F. friend of Du Pre, a chum of his, quite by accident, and that he gave you a menu which had the signature of Du Pre upon it, and the date, which showed that he couldn't have been in France at the time of that menu? Is that or is that not a fact?

A. Would you mind repeating that question? There is one fact in it I don't quite understand.

NIZER: Read it to him.

The stenographer did, while I moved a step closer.

WITNESS: I got it. It is incorrect—I can't answer that with yes or no because—you have a part in there "quite by accident." . . .

His eyes were upon the folder I was holding in my hand.

Q. Well, Mr. Collins, who is Kenneth Spencer?

A. Kenneth Spencer is, I believe, a man who lives at Edmonton.

Q. And up to this moment, Kenneth Spencer's name has never been mentioned publicly in this matter?

A. That's right.

Q. And you have been keeping the secret buried in your chest that it was Mr. Spencer who gave you the menu and the photograph, which revealed the hoax?

There was an uproar.

HENRY: I object.

WITNESS: No, no!

HENRY: I object to the form of the question.

WITNESS: It is—

COURT: He wants to answer it though.

Collins didn't have sense enough to permit his lawyer to come to his rescue.

A. It is quite incorrect. I can answer that.

COURT: Mr. Henry, do you withdraw your objection?

HENRY: Yes, sir.

Q. Did Mr. Spencer give you—

NIZER: Withdrawn.

WITNESS: Withdraw that.

He was giving mock instructions to the stenographer to poke fun at my having withdrawn a question.

Q. Did Mr. Spencer give to Mr. Allen Bell a menu and a photograph, which were conclusive evidence that Du Pre wasn't where he said he was?

A. No.

Q. Did he give it to you?

A. Yes.

Q. And didn't you take those two documents, which were in themselves proof that Du Pre had not told the truth and confront Du Pre with them?

A. That's right.

Again Mr. Henry tried valiantly to head off the impending disaster.

HENRY: May we have the two documents. He may be confused.

NIZER: He has answered "Yes."

HENRY: Read the question again, please.

COURT: Which two documents were you referring to?

NIZER: The menu and the photograph. That's right, isn't it Mr. Collins? Those were the two?

A. That's right.

Once more he eyed the folder I was holding. I asked him to supply the details that he thought I knew.

Q. How did the menu show that Du Pre had lied?

A. He had signed the menu.

Q. What was its date?

A. 1943.

Q. Did he indicate where?

A. On the S.S. *Bassano*.

Q. And that in itself demonstrated, did it not, that Du Pre couldn't have been where he said he was in all of his talks in 1943?

A. Demonstrated that he couldn't have been where he said he was on that particular date.

Q. That's right. . . . The next document . . . is a photograph. Will you tell us what that was?

A. It depicted six R.C.A.F. officers with Du Pre, taken in Toronto in May 1942.

Q. And that, too, demonstrated physically, by objective evidence, that Du Pre had lied as to being in France?

A. That's right.

Q. Did you confront Du Pre with these two documents?

A. Yes, I did.

We skirmished some more, as he denied that it was really these documents which broke Du Pre. He had been standing erect. As the questions struck him, he grew smaller and leaned heavily on the little table in front of him. I now knew the rumor we had heard was true. I could dare to put the final bold questions:

Q. So it was Kenneth Spencer who produced the two documents which were the objective evidence of Du Pre's chicanery. Right?

A. Right.

Q. And up to this moment you have never given credit to Kenneth Spencer for that?

A. No.

So Collins, who had achieved fame for having exposed one of the greatest literary hoaxes of our time, now stood exposed himself, as a man who had never given credit to Spencer, who had contributed so much to the revelation of Du Pre's fraud.

I have always thought that scenes in a courtroom exceed the boldest imagination of a stage director. Collins did something that none of us could have expected. In very slow motion, as if he were on a screen, he sat down. He just sat down. If he had screamed and toppled over in a faint, it could not have registered his reaction more vividly. The man who had buoyantly insisted on standing, slid in frozen motion into his seat.

There was a pained silence in the courtroom, which eloquently proclaimed the debacle. I extended it for another moment and then interrupted softly. "That is all."

I put the folder, which held nothing but blank sheets, back on the counsel table.

When Collins had been taken through re-direct and re-cross-examination, and dismissed, Pegler returned to the witness stand. He was instantly immersed in difficulty.

Q. Before writing this libel article . . . you did not check to find any facts?

A. . . . What do you mean by check?

Q. Newspapermen use the word "check" to indicate an inquiry for the purpose of verifying a fact; isn't that so, Mr. Pegler?

A. Yes, sir.

Q. And you didn't do that in this case, did you?

A. No, sir.

On another occasion, he changed his answers even at the price of having to reply to the humiliating question: "When you said "No, sir" you meant "Yes, sir?" Once more there came from his lips the now familiar refrain: "I was erroneous under oath."

After a while, I was less interested in what position he took than in the stultifying changeability of his answers:

Q. Didn't you originally testify when you wrote Reynolds had a protuberant belly filled with something else than guts, and a yellow streak . . . that you did not mean by those words to call him a coward?

A. Yes. . . . I changed my opinion.

Q. And didn't you also testify that when you wrote that he had a yellow streak and no guts that you did not mean to impugn his courage?

A. I am afraid I did.

Q. . . . Later you changed those answers to the direct opposite effect, that you did mean to call him a coward, that you did mean to call him yellow . . . is that right?

A. Yes.

The libel column said that Reynolds "though a giant and a bachelor, let several million kids about 18 years old do the fighting," and that he belonged to the "'let's you and him fight' school of heroes."

Q. Did you intend to give the impression that Reynolds shirked his duty to fight in the war?

A. Yes.

He changed this answer to "No." I followed him on his reversed course.

Q. It was not your purpose to brand him as a slacker?

A. No, sir.

This answer was so untenable that he finally abandoned it for a new theory. He said he meant that Reynolds was a moral not a legal slacker.

Q. Did you intend to hurt him with that charge?

A. No.

Nor did he intend that "mangy hide with a yellow streak" should mean that Reynolds was a coward.

Q. You intended to be hateful with those words, didn't you?

A. No, I don't hate anybody, not even you!

A wave of laughter from the packed courtroom inundated us.

COURT: There will be absolute order in the courtroom. If there isn't, I will order the courtroom cleared, and I mean that. There will be no comment of any kind.

In the index of my mind was a column he had written on the subject of hatred. Even the identifying number I had marked on it stood out. I asked one of my associates to get out column 1018 from our cabinet of files. In one moment we had it. "Haven't you written, Mr. Pegler, that your credo, your belief, is in hatred?"

The protective objections of his lawyer were persistent. After Pegler had been permitted to read the column and conceded it was his, the Court ruled: "I will take it on the issue of credibility, in the light of the answer given by the witness about four or five questions back."

I then read from his column: "It is odd that honesty and friendship both are held in such tender sentimental regard considering that both are so little patronized and that their opposites have by far the greater appeal. For myself, I will say that my hates always occupied my mind much more actively and have given me greater spiritual satisfaction than my friendships."

I invited him to take back his previous answer that he never hated anyone, though it was of no moment whether he did or not. Instead, he plunged blindly to the position he had previously abandoned.

Q. When you used the word "yellow" did you intend it to be a hateful word?

A. No.

Q. Did you intend it to be complimentary?

A. No.

Q. . . . Did you intend by the word "yellow" to connote cowardice when you wrote it?

A. Yes.

Thus he was tossed back and forth in a storm of questions which raged unabated for hours. On some points he surrendered and conceded that he could not explain away his inconsistency. For example, the libel column quoted Clare Booth Luce as saying during the 1944 campaign: ". . . What was a dashing war correspondent doing here at home, picking up $2000 from the crooked Garsson munitioneers for lauding their glorious patriotism. . . ."

Since the Garsson incident didn't occur until one year later in 1945, how could Mrs. Luce have referred to it in 1944? Pegler had no defense against the most damning questions: "Isn't it a fact that you made this whole story up . . . and put it into the mouth of Mrs. Luce in 1944, when it couldn't have happened?"

He looked toward his lawyers but they were unable to supply any help. "Will you please tell me how she could have told you in 1944 . . . that Reynolds took $2000 from the Garsson munitioneers when he didn't make the speech [at "E" Award ceremony for which he received the $2000] until 1945?"

He answered resignedly: "I don't know."

There is a psychological time for venturesomeness with a witness. A question put to him when he is vigorously resistant may be ineffectual. The same question thrown at him when he is stunned and low in morale may induce a confession. Similarly in examination before trial a question asked almost casually after a moment of jest and good will, may be conceded with a gesture of candor. The same question, put when the witness is belligerent, will beget defiance. The converse can be true too. If the mood is hostile, the witness may deny his own name, so to speak, and ultimately pay for his foolish anger. The examiner must be sensitive to the moods of the witness and vary his approach in the light of expectations.

The most extraordinary entrapment of the entire trial occurred when I played upon Pegler's venom toward Reynolds and permitted, rather than induced, him to put a noose around his own neck and spring the trap door, too.

I had not planned it. It was improvised out of the peculiar cirstances existing at the examination before trial. At one stage of that examination, I was quoting from Reynolds's book *Leave It to the People* to demonstrate how anti-Communist he was, and the atmosphere was particularly strained.

Q. Would you say that a person who wrote that was writing a pro-Communistic statement?

HENRY: . . . The witness will not answer.

NIZER: You instruct him not to answer?

HENRY: Yes.

When I threatened to take the matter to a Judge for ruling, the attorney relented. We had received a number of prior rulings that boded no good for the defendant. Judge Edward J. Dimock who was then in Motion Part to rule upon questions arising from pretrial examination had said: "I get the impression that Pegler is impeding the examination and does require some sort of admonition, so that I deny the motion for closing the examination, and I direct the witness to continue answering questions. . . ."

Pegler and his lawyer were therefore not too eager to court another rebuke from the Judge. Would Pegler admit that the passage written by Reynolds was anti-Communist?

A. It would depend on the author.

Q. If you wrote that, would that be a pro-Communist statement?

A. I can't imagine myself writing such material.

Q. Will you answer my question? I didn't ask you whether you could imagine it. I said, if you wrote it.

A. . . . I cannot envision such a state of affairs. Pegler could not have written that.

Here, incidentally, was another insight into Pegler. He was the kind of man who referred to himself in the third person. But his challenge that he could not have written such a passage planted a seed in my mind. It took a little time to sprout. In the meantime, the air grew thick with acrimony.

NIZER: I will reserve my rights before the court.

WITNESS: May I hear that?

HENRY: He is going to cite us for contempt and put us in Alcatraz.

NIZER: I didn't say that, and I think you are attempting to inflame the witness, as well as yourself. All I said is I will reserve my rights before the court. I didn't say I was going to move to punish for contempt.

Pegler was in such a frame of mind that I thought he would claim anything Reynolds wrote was Communistic. The amusing idea came into my mind that Pegler might condemn his own writing, if he thought Reynolds was the author. Why not try it?

While continuing the examination, I got my hands on some political columns Pegler had written. Then, without advising him who the author was and reading as if from my notes, I quoted this passage to him:

Q. Would you say that a statement "Communism is the reaction to poverty, oppression, and the exploitation of the masses by the few, and represents the demands of the masses for a strong central authority to curb their enemy" is a pro-Communist statement?

HENRY: Made by Mr. Reynolds in 1949?

Pegler's lawyer was alert. He had interrupted to give warning signals to his client, but Pegler was as oblivious to the subtle hint as when he was advised about the juror and he rushed to the FBI.

NIZER: I am asking my question, please, and I would prefer not to be cross-examined about each question. If you have an objection, you may make it, sir, but I think I ought to be permitted to conduct this examination.

HENRY: I object to the form of the question unless the time is stated and the authorship of the alleged work.

NIZER: May he answer, nevertheless, please?

HENRY: He can.

Pegler still didn't catch the signal. He replied: "It is just utter nonsense." We were already ahead. He had condemned his own writing as "utter nonsense." But I pressed on:

Q. Is it a pro-Communist statement?

A. . . . It is certainly part of the Communist line.

I tried to throw even his attorney off the scent.

Q. Would you say that that was an honest expression of liberalism, or would you say that was pro-Communist propaganda?

Now that I was endeavoring to defend the passage, Pegler was sure that Reynolds was the author. He became more vehement.

A. I would say it is pro-Communist propaganda; it is very familiar in the Communist line. And it is false.

Pegler was calling Pegler a Communist, and at the top of his voice. Mr. Henry was still suspicious.

HENRY: May I ask either on or off the record if this was published in *Collier's* weekly or just in this book *Leave It to the People?*

NIZER: Please let me continue.

I read another passage from one of Pegler's columns, not telling him, of course, who the author was:

Q. I read the following to you: "Communism will never get to first base in the United States because it is strictly a foreign article and identified with atheism. On the other hand there is a good deal of native fascism in the American make-up." Do you consider that a pro-Communist statement, or a statement of liberal American faith?

A. I don't know. . . . It would depend on who made it.

Q. If Reynolds made it, it would be what?

A. Nonsense.

Q. If you made it, what would it be?

A. I couldn't imagine myself making that statement.

Again I defended the passage, thus evoking his condemnation of it. He insisted it was untrue to say, "Communism will never get to first base in the United States":

    A. It certainly did get to first base.

    Q. ". . . and is identified with atheism." You agree with that, don't you?

    A. No. It is not identified with atheism.

I struggled not to reveal my excitement over this spectacle of Pegler turning his vaunted ruthlessness upon himself. There was no time to reflect on the man's unconscious suicidal tendency. Or was this a drama of poetic justice enveloping a wrongdoer in its symmetry? I read another sentence from one of his own columns:

    Q. "But Communism, if it should ever make a break, would be slapped down in a few days." Do you consider that . . . a pro-Communist statement?

    A. I don't know what he is talking about.

    Q. Would you say that statement was false or accurate in 1937?

    A. I would say it was false.

    Q. . . . Do you say that that is a pro-Communist view in 1937?

    A. Yes.

When a man points a finger at someone else, he should remember that four of his fingers are pointing to himself. In this case all five were accusing their owner.

When this session of the examination closed and Pegler left my office, I learned that Reynolds was in a preparation conference with my partners Walter Beck and Paul Martinson. I buoyed them up with this latest development. I could not blame them for being incredulous.

"Wait until you see the minutes," I said. "His self-denunciation is worse than I have told you. The only question is whether he will discover his error before he signs the transcript. Mr. Henry has shown signs of awareness. Even correction will not wipe out entirely the effect of his answers. But should he fail to change his answers, can you imagine the explosion at the trial?"

Before he signed the transcript of his examination, Pegler made 134 changes and corrections (Reynolds made none of his own examination). But he didn't change a comma in his answers in which he called his own writings "the Communist line." Apparently on reviewing the mass of evidence and exhibits, Pegler had not detected his colossal blunder. We had a delayed bomb in our possession, and it was timed to go off at the appropriate time on cross-examination.

That time had arrived. At first, Pegler denied characterizing certain passages as pro-Communistic. This opened the door to the reading at length from his examination before trial. Then:

    Q. Did you make those answers to those questions?

    A. Yes.

I put his own columns before him, containing the very paragraphs he had denounced:

    Q. Do you happen to know, Mr. Pegler, that the statements which you said were the Communist line were written by you? There was a collective gasp in the crowded courtroom, as if all the air were being sucked out of it. The turmoil reflected itself in Pegler's face. He barely looked at the columns in front of him. He behaved like a man who knows his inexorable fate and accepts it quickly.

    Q. . . . The statements which you said were the Communist line were written by you?

    A. Yes.

His answer was understandably so weak it was inaudible. I repeated the question.

    Q. You do know that?

    A. Yes.

    Q. . . . When you said . . . "It is pro-Communist propaganda, it is very familiar in the Communist line; and it is false," were you referring to what you yourself had written in 1937?

    A. I was.

    Q. The statement "Communism would be slapped down in a few days." . . . Do you say that is a pro-Communist view in 1937?

    A. Yes. . . . I was mistaken.

I would have liked to conclude my cross-examination at this point. In dramatic terms anything thereafter might be anti-climactic. But in a legal sense the greatest prize was still to be won—the conclusive demonstration of malice. I knew that punitive damages were our chief hope for recovery, and they could only be granted if the jury believed that the defendants were motivated by malice. This was my last subject for inquiry. What had preceded set the stage favorably for the final onslaught.

    I changed my cross-examination technique to achieve this final objective. No longer did I engage him at every twist and turn as before. I ignored his sallies as if I hadn't heard them and stuck to the main question of malice. The more demonstrative he became, the quieter was my tone. I gave him unfettered leeway to express himself. I shall put at least some brush strokes on the canvas to reveal the nature of the legal painting which emerged.

    Pegler's theory was that his column was merely written in retaliation against Reynolds's attack on him in a book review. Had not Pegler, long before this book review, insulted Reynolds in his columns? If so, this was proof of malice.

    Q. . . . A long time before Reynolds wrote any book review, you had called him in your column an artful check-dodger, didn't you?

    A. I believe I did.

    Q. And also the Ferdinand the Bull of war correspondents?

    A. I don't recall, but that would have been appropriate.

After the suit began, Pegler had warned organizations not to hire Reynolds as a lecturer. His effort to injure Reynolds was also evidence of malice. But he played games with my questions. Had he not inquired about one of Reynolds's paid engagements in order to warn off prospective clients?

Q. The man you talked to . . . was the financial editor of the New York *Journal*, wasn't he?

A. There is no New York *Journal* that I know of, and I don't know the title of the man to whom I talked.

Q. It was the *Journal-American*, one of the defendants in this case?

A. I don't know the title of the man to whom I talked.

Q. Wasn't it a man named Gould?

A. Yes.

Q. You talked to Gould to check up on the circumstances under which this credit association . . . had arranged for Reynolds to give a talk, didn't you?

A. I don't know what you are talking about. Put your question in clear language. I don't understand it.

He finally understood it, but he denied asking Gould anything. It turned out he was quibbling about who asked whom.

Q. He volunteered of his own?

A. Yes, that's my recollection.

When I asked him whether in his column he had not advised other organizations what kind of man he thought Reynolds was so that they would not engage him, he answered "No." The column was in evidence and it said just that.

COURT: Did you write anything on that subject is the question.

A. Not the subject that Mr. Nizer put. I will not assent to that.

NIZER: Well, I am going to give you an opportunity in your own way to tell me what it is you wrote with respect to Reynolds and future lecture engagements.

A. I will wait for my attorney . . . I will wait for my counsel. He is on his feet.

HENRY: I object. . . .

COURT: Overruled.

WITNESS: What is the question? (Question read.)

A. I don't remember what I wrote.

So he continued to slip and slide for dozens of questions. Finally the Judge took a hand.

COURT: Did you ever communicate orally with any person, firm, corporation, or organization with respect to Reynolds's prospective employment?

A. Yes.

Q. That is subsequent to the date of the [libel] article?

A. Yes.

Q. With whom did you communicate?

A. Lowell Thomas.

Q. Will you state the substance of the conversation with him.

A. I told Lowell Thomas that I had been informed that Reynolds was going to do some work in connection with a movie . . . concerning General Doolittle. Shall I proceed?

Q. Yes, give us the entire conversation.

A. I called the attention of Mr. Thomas, who is known as a very patriotic gentleman, to the— I don't recall what I said to Mr. Thomas. I will have to reflect on it. I don't recall at the moment.

Q. Suppose you reflect upon it then and tell us what you did say to him. . . .

A. I can't recall it at the moment, not in a way that would do justice to the subject.

The jury must have observed his flight in the midst of his confession. I took up his motives for communicating with Thomas. Did he know that Reynolds had written a book on Jimmy Doolittle?

A. Well, I only got in this box a minute ago—ten minutes ago— yes, I knew it before I testified here.

Q. How long ago, sir?

A. I can't tell you.

Q. Well, long before the trial began anyhow?

A. Before the trial began.

Q. Well, the reason for your calling Mr. Thomas was to discuss Reynolds's possible employment in doing a picture concerning Doolittle, wasn't it?

A. Yes.

Q. The reason you had this conversation was to see whether Thomas could help in seeing that Reynolds was made an inappropriate choice, wasn't it?

A. No, I just wanted to inform a friend of some facts.

Q. When, about, was it that you spoke to Mr. Thomas concerning Reynolds?

A. You have had your answer to that.

Q. Will you please tell me?

A. No.

COURT: I will direct you to answer the question, please.

WITNESS: I do not know, your Honor, I have told him that.

He also didn't remember writing a column warning organizations not to hire Reynolds. I read it to the jury.

Only a few weeks before the trial began, Reynolds was scheduled to address a public dinner of the Amateur Athletic Union (A.A.U.). We had reason to believe that Pegler attempted to have him removed from the program. As this would be impressive evidence of malice, I questioned him closely, and this resulted in some flaming exchanges.

Q. Mr. Pegler, was there anyone else you ever spoke to concerning Mr. Reynolds's not making a speech?

A. I don't recall any such discussion with anyone.

Q. Did you ever talk to Mr. James Farley after this suit was instituted to urge him to see to it that Reynolds was taken off a speaking program?

A. No.

Q. Did you call Mr. Farley and leave any message or request concerning Mr. Reynolds?

A. No—now wait a minute. You busted that question up. I called Mr. Farley. I didn't leave any message. Leave it with whom? What are you talking about? I called Mr. Farley.

Q. About Mr. Reynolds?

A. How do you know?

Q. I am asking.

A. Well, if I didn't get him, how could I call him about Reynolds?

But when I persisted, the complete story emerged.

Q. Did you talk to anyone else about this Amateur Athletic Union?

A. Yes, I talked to Farley.

Q. I thought you said you didn't talk to Farley?

A. You just don't know how to examine. I called him but didn't get him, but I did talk to him later.

In summation I was able to read his earlier testimony, when I had asked him, "Did you *ever* talk to Mr. James Farley . . ." and he had answered, "No."

But now I would not stop even to point out his contradictions. He admitted he was not a member of the A.A.U. and had not been invited to the dinner.

Q. But you made it your business to call Mr. Farley . . . and spoke to him later about the fact that Reynolds ought not to be a speaker on that occasion, didn't you?

A. Is that so?

He was mocking me.

Q. The facts you gave him, the alleged facts, were they favorable to Mr. Reynolds or unfavorable?

A. . . . I don't know. That is up to Farley.

Q. You have no opinion as to whether what you told Mr. Farley would be helpful to Mr. Reynolds or unhelpful to him; is that right?

A. I don't know how anything I could have said would have been either helpful or otherwise.

A moment later he hurled this barb at Reynolds: "It was an amateur occasion. For once he wasn't getting $3500 from this charity."

It soon turned out that Pegler had also called Robert Moses, the guest of honor on this occasion. After further evasive answers the Judge put a direct question to him.

COURT: Was your purpose in making the call to effect a cancellation of the invitation of Mr. Reynolds as a speaker at that function?

A. No, sir. Let them use their own judgment.

His admissions burgeoned as he strove to avoid them. I asked:

Q. Wasn't it really your intention in making these calls and in writing the column . . . to pursue Mr. Reynolds and cut off his economic income right up to the date of the trial?

A. I haven't read the column you refer to, so I don't know what it says.

The column [his own] had just been read to the jury in his presence.

Q. Did you also speak to Jimmy Powers [sports columnist of the New York *Daily News*] about Reynolds's talk at the A.A.U.?

A. Yes, I did.

He fenced about what he told him.

Q. You just talked to Jimmy Powers so he could use his fair judgment about it?

A. That's right.

Q. Not intending ever that that judgment would be exercised against Mr. Reynolds, of course?

The Court directed him to answer, and there slipped from his mouth the following:

A. I don't know whether fair presentation of the facts would be for or against Mr. Reynolds.

What a curious statement! He would not even assert that the truth would be harmful to Reynolds. The unrestrained violence which had made his column and his testimony exciting, if nothing else, was now diluted by caution. His malice was evident, but it was cloaked in unbecoming timidity.

On the seventeenth day of cross-examination I excused him from the witness stand.

The defendants called as their next witness, Mrs. Ariane Ross, the wife of the editor of the *New Yorker* magazine. She testified hearing Connie Broun tell "many times that Mr. Reynolds has proposed marriage to her." Cross-examination:

Q. Did she tell you that the proposal of marriage was made in the funeral car on the way to the funeral?

A. Mrs. Broun tells a story very well.

Q. No, no, I didn't ask you how well she tells it. . . . Did she tell you that Reynolds proposed marriage to her while in the funeral car while on the way to the grave?

A. Well, I think one time she did.

Q. You think?

A. But she told—

Q. But she kept retelling it to you?

A. Yes.

Q. For ten times or more?

A. Yes.

Q. Did she ever tell you Reynolds proposed marriage to her in the funeral car on the way to the grave?

A. Not as I recall it. Not in the funeral car.

Q. . . . Patricia was present when her mother told this on at least several occasions, if not the full ten times?

A. That would be my guess.

NIZER: That is all.

Arthur James Pegler II took the seat his brother had occupied so long: "I saw Mr. Reynolds and a young woman nude. . . . I saw through the window Mr. Reynolds and a young woman naked."

On cross-examination I established that he was eleven years old at the time, that the windows through which he saw and identified the naked couple were French windows with little panes of glass partitioned by wood, and that Reynolds "may have had a towel in his hand." But my main thrust was to have him confirm that thereafter Pegler, Reynolds, and Broun frequently played softball and poker, visited each other, invested in the newspaper *The Connecticut Nutmeg,* and that his present wife, the former Nancy Hutchinson, was not present on the occasion when Reynolds and his girl supposedly crowded the shower together.

The next relative to stand by Pegler was his wife, Julie. She confirmed the nude incident in the rowboat. Mr. Henry asked:

Q. What did Mrs. Broun say about the rowboat incident at the home of Jack Pegler?

A. Do I have to use her rather unsavory, quaint language?

Q. No, just give the substance of it.

A. She said . . . she was rowing a boat and Quentin had been in swimming and was standing in the water about up to his waist—she said he said to her if she would row over he would get in the boat with her, and to her surprise he got in the boat absolutely naked. I wish I don't have to repeat the rest of the conversation. Do you want me to? Well, anyway she said he had that lavaliere dangling and nothing on, not even a hair net. Those were her words.

Cross-examination was hardly "cross-" of this loyal woman, who everybody thought was a fine lady. She admitted Connie Broun was religious and "a very decent and fine woman." In this way I set the stage for Connie's reappearance on the stand, when for the first time she would deal with this rowboat incident. Then I developed the friendly intimacy among the Brouns, Peglers, and Reynoldses, the poker games, picnics, ball games and bridge, which continued throughout the years after this alleged nude incident.

I showed her a book written by Lowell Thomas on softball. It contained pictures of Pegler, Reynolds, and Broun in gay and friendly association, all after this so-called shocking nudist exhibitionism.

Q. Now, you knew that Connie Broun never went in swimming, don't you?

A. I never saw her in swimming.

Q. She was afraid of the water, wasn't she?

A. I don't know that. I never saw her in their lake there.

Q. . . . Did you ever see her in any kind of rowboat?

A. No, I don't think I did. I am just quoting her story.

We had further prepared the setting for the testimony of Connie and her daughter Patricia.

The defendants called Frank Doyle as their next witness. He was the reporter for the *Daily Mirror* who had written the story of Reynolds's speech at the Democratic dinner honoring Ambassador James W. Gerard, in which he was supposed to have condemned the attacks on Russia made by prior speakers. Doyle yielded readily on cross-examination:

Q. At that time Russia was . . . in the war with the United States and England, fighting not only the Nazis, but the Japanese. . . .

A. Yes.

His story had quoted Reynolds as making a snide comment concerning Gerard as "the once-distinguished Ambassador." Doyle knew that Judge Jeremiah Mahoney who was at that function, was Quent's uncle, and that Gerard was not only a friend of the Mahoneys but of Reynolds. I led him gently to admit that rewrite men sometimes garble a quote sent in by the reporter. Then:

Q. In view of your knowledge of the relationship between Mr. Reynolds and the former Ambassador to Germany, . . . does it suggest to you that what you sent over the wire . . . in referring to Mr. Gerard was "the distinguished former Ambassador to Germany" [not "the once-distinguished Ambassador"]?

A. . . . I frankly can't say whether . . . I gave that in that way and the rewrite man twisted it around . . . from "the former Ambassador." I really can't recall.

COURT: . . . Is it a misplaced modifier?

A. That's right; very possible that it is.

NIZER: . . . You recall . . . that Mr. Reynolds . . . stated that the Communists, so far as they believed in their political theories, were misled and were wrong, but that, he said, this is the time when we need them for fighting?

A. Generally, yes.

I established that his Hearst newspaper "was all out for Russia as an ally." He also acknowledged that "Mr. Winchell, who appeared regularly

in the *Mirror*, was pounding the drums the same way, that Russia was
doing a heroic military job with us, . . . isn't that so?"

A. . . . Yes.

At about eleven thirty and three thirty every day the Judge declared
a fifteen-minute recess. This was the time for an exodus to the corridor,
which buzzed with comment and expertise. One could distinguish between mere visitors who smoked casually and witnesses and lawyers who
lit their cigarettes hungrily and puffed deeply. Legal assistants would keep
an alert eye on the opposition to spot prospective witnesses. On several
occasions we saw Pegler talking earnestly to a tall, funereally clothed
man whose white-powdered face made his Homburg look blacker than it
was. Inquiry revealed that he was Howard Rushmore, a former Communist, then an informing anti-Communist, and editor of the magazine
Confidential. Later he ended his career by suicide. His conferences with
Pegler seemed to be the earnest reports of an investigator, and we sensed
that either he or some other converted anti-Communist might be a
witness for the defense. It was not, therefore, a surprise that Bella Dodd,
the former member of the National Committee of the Communist Party,
who had recognized the profound error of her ways, took the stand. But
when I demonstrated by preliminary objection and question that she had
never met Reynolds personally, or talked to him, the Court excluded her
testimony entirely.

One of Pegler's corridor companions was a priest. Often he accompanied Pegler back into the courtroom, ostentatiously walking with
him to his seat or standing with him in the aisle through which the jurors
passed to their seats. Who was he? Even if he were not a prospective
witness, I was disturbed by such display of clerical garb in front of the
jury box. There were a number of Roman Catholics on the jury, and
though Reynolds, too, was Catholic, no one would have compared his
worldliness with the holy dedication of priesthood. After much difficulty
we learned that Pegler's friend was Father Leopold Braun, the priest of
the only Roman Catholic Church in Moscow during the time Reynolds
was there. Whatever the excuse for his testifying it seemed certain he
would be a witness.

For some time I had debated calling Monsignor Fulton Sheen as a
witness. It was he who had converted Heywood Broun to Catholicism
and had ridden in the funeral car with Connie and Quent. He was an
eyewitness and could give conclusive evidence that Reynolds had not
proposed marriage to Connie during that ride. I knew Monsignor (now
Bishop) Sheen quite well. On numerous occasions I had introduced him
as the speaker at resplendent functions in the Waldorf-Astoria ballroom
in New York City. Several times he had introduced me to audiences.
Whether as speaker or introducer he never failed to thrill his hearers, for
he is a great orator, having "flashing eyes under the philosopher's brow."

He had asked me not to involve him in this litigation and, out of respect for him, and also because Pegler's own admissions that his story about the funeral car proposal appeared improbable, Reynolds and I had decided to spare the good man any embarrassment. But if Pegler was going to parade Father Braun in front of or on the witness stand, I felt it my duty to advise Monsignor Sheen that I would require him to be a rebuttal witness. "I will of course do my duty, Louis," he said, "but I still plead with you not to involve me in this unpleasant lawsuit, if you can possibly help it."

"I will see what happens with Father Braun. If we find that it is not too prejudicial to lose your testimony, of course Quentin Reynolds and I are eager to accommodate you." So we left it. If it became necessary, he would appear and testify.

Father Braun did take the stand. He had been the pastor of a church in Moscow for nine years. Only two Roman Catholic churches out of fifteen hundred had remained open. Out of fifty-four thousand Russian Orthodox churches only about five hundred remained. After Reynolds arrived in Moscow, Father Braun met him only once, accidentally, in the lobby of Hotel National for "between seven and eight minutes." When he proceeded to tell about this conversation, I objected on the ground that it did not relate to any issue in the case.

COURT: Is there any issue of veracity between this plaintiff and the witness?

HENRY: Not at all.

COURT: Is there anything in the column on the subject?

HENRY: Not at all. . . .

The court sustained my objection. But the attorney resourcefully sought to open another door. Perhaps Father Braun had talked to other correspondents so that he could express an opinion about Reynolds's reputation based on their views.

Q. Can you tell us, Father Braun, what the reputation of the plantiff was for accurate . . . reporting among those whom you heard discussing it?

A. The correspondents emphasized the fact that the plaintiff was not a reporter in the full sense of the word, he was a feature writer. . . . They said that among themselves.

But when the Court put the direct question to him, he dropped his hesitation and delivered the answer Pegler had been seeking.

COURT: Father Braun, the question is a very plain and specific one. . . . What was his reputation for accurate reporting?

A. The answer to the question, your Honor, is that it was extremely poor.

I decided not to attack a priest, fearing that I might do more injury to our cause in victory than bowing to the blow. Instead, we flew in from Washington Walter Kerr, for many years editor of the European Edition of the New York *Herald Tribune*, published in Paris, and from 1941 to 1943 its correspondent in Moscow. In rebuttal, he told of the American, British, and French correspondents' delight when they learned that Reynolds was coming to Moscow. Contrary to Father Braun's description of the jaundiced view his colleagues took of Quent, Kerr described the touching scene in which the correspondents "went to the airport to meet him and there was a small impromptu dinner in one of the hotel rooms that night."

Kerr talked proudly of Reynolds as a distinguished member of the profession: "We knew him well; he was a friend of ours; we respected him."

I asked, "What was Quentin Reynolds's reputation for integrity and accuracy and patriotism among the war correspondents whom you knew intimately?"

"I would say it was excellent, sir. I know of no one who would have had a higher one."

Mr. Henry did not cross-examine on this subject and the witness was quickly excused. Thus, in oblique fashion we had countered Father Braun's opinion testimony, without directly attacking him and perhaps offending the sensitivity of some jurors. Surely Walter Kerr, a distinguished correspondent in his own right, knew how the correspondents felt about Reynolds, better than Father Braun who said his opinion was based on overhearing their talk. We believed Father Braun's testimony had been rendered ineffectual.

Not without some misgivings, nevertheless, about the effect of a priest's appearance on behalf of Pegler, we advised Monsignor Sheen that we would grant his wish not to be called as a witness.

The defendants had two more surprises for us.

One can tell when the opponent is about to fire a powerful missile. There is excitement in his ranks. I could feel behind my back, Mr. Henry's assistants scurrying around. There was dashing in and out of the courtroom, and finally the announcement by Mr. Henry: "I call as our next witness Admiral Richard L. Conolly." The jurors' heads turned toward the door in unison.

He was escorted into the courtroom by a lawyer who acted like a destroyer accompanying a dreadnought into battle. Admiral Conolly was now president of Long Island University. Previously he had served in the United States Navy for forty-three years, and had commanded the amphibious task group at Salerno.

His appearance as a defense witness was apparently for the purpose of describing the desperate struggle at Salerno. Since Reynolds had been on the flagship *Ancon*, and had landed on the beach with the troops, the greater the danger, the more heroic his role. But it was the defendants' theory that when Reynolds left Salerno to file his story, he was really fleeing because of the Germans' counterattack. If so, why had he gone on the mission in the first place? *Collier's* had invited him to come home, but he having heard of this operation, refused, and had had himself assigned to it. Furthermore, by this time, Reynolds's intrepidity had been established so firmly, that accusations of cowardice sounded ludicrous rather than merely implausible.

The real reason for putting the Admiral on the stand was psychological. The defendants were throwing uniforms at us in the hope of impressing the jury—first the cloth of the priest, and now the white linen of the Admiral. We did not know it then, but the impressive army khaki of a General was to be added to the assault of uniforms.

The Admiral launched into a vivid description of the hazards of landing troops by sea upon a defended beach. The enemy used radio-controlled bombs for the first time in this sector. But General Montgomery's Eighth Army moved up the peninsula, and the capture of the nearby airfields emptied the air of Nazi bombers which had found the ships inviting targets.

After describing the Admiral's later service in the Pacific, Mr. Henry announced, "You may examine."

I soon established that the witness was in charge of the landing in the northern part of the gulf of Salerno, whereas the *Ancon* was heading the invasion in the southern part of the anchorage.

He confirmed the fact that the *Ancon* "had no armor at all," her purpose as a flagship being to receive and send radio messages to the fleet. Yes, the enemy usually singled out the flagship for attack. Indeed he did not know about the ordeal the *Ancon* was going through.

Q. In other words, you are not familiar with the facts as to what happened to the *Ancon*, itself, since you were in another sector? . . .

A. Until D+3, you could say so.

He readily admitted that the use of radio-controlled bombs made conditions even more hazardous on the *Ancon* and therefore, of course, for Reynolds. He knew that the *Savannah* was hit when less that "1000 yards" away from the *Ancon*.

Now if I could establish that the counterattack by the Nazis occurred after Reynolds left (he believing, as did our commanders, that the beachhead had been made secure), the Admiral's testimony would not harm Reynolds at all. Reynolds left Salerno on D+2 day. I asked:

Q. . . . Unexpectedly . . . the Nazis were able to draw up very large counter-attacking forces, which later created . . . a real crisis; isn't that so?

A. Yes . . . by about D+5, the situation ashore had become critical.

Q. Had become critical?

A. Was considered . . . very serious. The Nazis brought up re-enforcements.

Q. The Nazis did on D+5?

A. About that time.

So Admiral Conolly, who had never met Reynolds, had given a vivid picture of the extreme danger he shared with the troops on the *Ancon* and in storming a defended beach. Despite the contention that Reynolds fled from Salerno because a critical battle was impending, the Admiral established for us that the Nazis' counterattack was a surprise and came after Reynolds had left.

Admiral Conolly's testimony had turned out to be favorable to the plaintiff. Like a glass of champagne which has grown dull, but comes to life with a new spurt from the bottle, the bubbles of excitement rose again behind me. There were stage whispers, "Has he arrived?", "Go out and see." I sensed that the defense was about to wind up its case with its foremost witness. I cannot deny that there was trepidation in our ranks. One can never tell what startling testimony may come from an unimpeachable source to win just one juror, which is all the defendants needed to prevent a verdict. This time Mr. Henry did not announce his name. The suspense was maintained until the last moment.

It was General Albert C. Wedemeyer, planner for General George C. Marshall at the Pentagon, who went to North Africa to execute the invasion of Sicily and supervise General George Patton's earliest adventures in racing through, over, and past enemy troops.

Generals should either be very short, like Napoleon, or very tall, like de Gaulle. Uniqueness becomes them. Average height or average anything else fails psychologically to set them apart. Wedemeyer towered over everyone in the courtroom. He had a basketball player's height and slimness. A weathered, lined face made him look more like a field commander than a planner. But why was he here? I leaned over and motioned to Quent. "Have you any idea what he is going to testify to?"

He shrugged his shoulders in a gesture of perplexity. I leaned forward intently to discover the thrust and ward it off if possible. The General described the invasion of Sicily. "Early in the morning of July 10, beginning at 2:30 A.M., our small landing craft began the assault on the landing beaches of southern Sicily, 1943."

As he developed the tactics, I interrupted:

NIZER: I object to this as irrelevant and immaterial to any issue in this case.

COURT: With respect to what issue is this, Mr. Henry? Would you please enlighten me?

HENRY: The plaintiff's alleged participation in some infantry action in Sicily.

COURT: If you direct it specifically to that issue I will take it.

HENRY: Very well.

But the General went on with his detailed description of operations as if a military history lesson were being given at West Point.

NIZER: I object. . . . I have no quarrel with the distinguished General's recital, but I don't think it has anything to do with this case.

COURT: Yes, Mr. Henry, I allowed certain background information, but you have to get down to the issues that are involved in this case.

HENRY: All right, we are just about there.

He continued to recite the campaign in Sicily, disregarding the admonition. When he reached the battle at San Rosso, I objected again, and once more counsel promised he was approaching relevancy.

Finally the reason for this whole performance was set forth in a few sentences. Quentin Reynolds had been assigned to the 1st Division under General Terry Allen and, said General Wedemeyer: "The 1st Division had experienced very heavy casualties and had been fighting ever since D day, and it was decided that that division would be given a rest." His notes showed that this occurred on July 30. So the inference was that Reynolds, instead of seeing active fighting, had been with the 1st Division about July 30 and thereafter, when it was inactive.

I was more convinced than ever that the calling of these military witnesses was to confer on Pegler the distinction of having war heroes testify "for him," in the sense that they appeared for the defense.

I could have waived cross-examination and relied upon summation to point this out. But a cross-examiner's instinct told me that there were prizes to be had without undue risk.

I decided to tackle General Wedemeyer, despite the misgivings of my associates and even Quent. But of course, the approach was different in tone than to any other witness.

He must have been warned about cross-examination, because his early answers showed some resistance. He soon discovered that I was an admirer. Ultimately he shed his suspicious armor and we traveled in comradeship on a common road. The disarmament process took the following course:

Q. General, was Palermo a dangerous place to be in during this entire time?

A. Well, when you ask me a question like that, it is relative. . . . I would say that it was not severely contested . . . I wouldn't say that our losses were very high.

Q. Well, General, I accept your word for anything you say. I am merely asking this: without going into the matter of degree . . . was it a dangerous place to be from the standpoint of safety to any soldier . . . or any correspondent?

A. . . . No, sir. You made one statement that I might correct: no military commander that I . . . respect ever thinks—no matter what numerical losses you experience—he doesn't take it lightly.

Q. Now, I didn't say that.

A. I misunderstood you then.

Q. So we will clear that up. All I was saying was when you say we didn't suffer severe casualties, but light casualties . . . you were not indicating that that meant no danger.

A. Yes.

Q. I am accepting that. Now my question is, even after Palermo had been captured by our forces, it was under bombing attack from the air, was it not?

A. We had almost undisputed control of the air. There would be desultory intermittent bombing attacks by the Germans, but we were not subjected again to heavy bomb attacks. . . .

Q. General, for this purpose I am again not proceeding into the subject of relative degree of casualties, or severity of bombing; I merely say, if there was intermittent bombing it was a dangerous place from the viewpoint of a soldier or general or correspondent. . . .

A. I go along with that a hundred per cent. . . . I would say any area in Sicily during my period of observation was extremely dangerous.

A few more friendly questions accelerated the disarming process.

Q. Do you happen to recall, General, that in the Palermo harbor there was a bombing raid by the Nazis on one occasion in which a United States destroyer was hit?

A. Yes, sir.

Q. And that was about July 30th?

A. Well, I would accept it.

Q. And also do you recall, General, and if you wish you may refer to any notes that you have, that a munitions ship was also hit and bombed successfully, unfortunately, by the Nazis in Palermo harbor at the very end of July, July 30th?

A. Yes, sir.

I was now emboldened to invite him to join other distinguished witnesses in attesting to the courageous role of war correspondents such as Reynolds. My questions were enveloped in respectful compliments, not because he might succumb to flattery, he was too big a man for that, but rather to herald to him again and again that I was not attacking or contesting with him, but rather eliciting his impartial opinion.

Q. Now in your distinguished career I take it you have had the opportunity to meet with war correspondents who were attached to the various military forces, have you not, sir?

A. Oh, a great deal, yes.

Q. . . . They are sharing the dangers of injury and death, are they not?

A. Yes, sir, in varying degrees.

Q. Do you happen to know during world War II over fifty-odd war correspondents were actually killed while serving?

A. Yes. I lost some in my theater, the China Theater.

Q. . . . You have told us that the 1st Division . . . had pretty tough going and . . . suffered tough casualties . . . in Sicily?

A. Well, it was in combat and suffered normal casualties and rugged going.

Q. Would you say that a war correspondent attached to the 1st Division was sharing in some degree, more or less, those hazards and risk of life. . . .

A. Not necessarily. A division occupies a large area . . . and any area in a combat zone is dangerous, but a war correspondent might be up with the assault echelon, or he might be back near the headquarters.

Q. Less dangerous?

A. Much less dangerous. . . . He may be away back near headquarters.

Q. . . . Without the slightest reflection upon the heroism of our commanders, and particularly yourself, because I know of your distinguished career . . . isn't it a fact that duty requires that you be back farther?

A. I suggested it does.

Q. In order to make plans, and for some peace from bombardment, so you can properly direct the soldiers at the front; that is a necessary military function, is it not?

A. Yes.

Q. You wouldn't say if a person was assigned farther back, even to headquarters, that that was a reflection upon his courage, would you?

A. No, not at all, not if he were assigned.

Q. You have told us of correspondents who go forward more, and those who are stationed back farther. You have never met Mr. Reynolds in your life, have you?

A. . . . No, I didn't see him in Sicily.

Q. There were many correspondents there?

A. That's right.

Q. That you never saw?

A. Yes.

Q. You didn't mean to imply that he . . . wasn't doing his duty faithfully with the 1st Division as a war correspondent?

A. No implication at all.

NIZER: Thank you very much. [Witness excused.]

As he stepped off the witness stand he paused in front of me and shook hands amiably. Then he did the same with Mr. Henry. Not only his testimony, but his impartial leave-taking indicated, I hoped, that he was not a witness against Quentin Reynolds even though he had been brought into court by the defendants. The assault of uniforms had been weathered.

Indeed I was not too sure but that some of the epaulets had remained with us.

The defendants rested. We had the privilege of rebuttal. The jurors had been sitting on this case for eight weeks. They had sacrificed business and other plans to render a service far beyond the ordinary call of jury duty. I knew that its mood was to conclude the case as soon as possible. I made our rebuttal sharp and concise.

We put upon the stand Robert Christie from Calgary, Alberta, Canada. When the editor of the Calgary *Herald*, Allen Bill, heard that Collins, his reporter, had testified against Reynolds, he and the leading citizens of Calgary authorized Christie to come to New York to undo the damage.

Q. Did Mr. Reynolds call you or did you call Mr. Reynolds with respect to this matter?

A. I called Mr. Reynolds.

Q. And who is paying for the expenses of your coming here from Calgary, and staying here and going back?

A. I pay my own expenses, sir.

COURT: In other words, you are saying you volunteered to come here as a witness after you heard the testimony of the witness Collins?

A. Yes, I do.

The jury must have remembered that Collins had exacted a subsidy from Pegler for coming to New York, and then had demanded more luxurious hotel accommodations as befitted a man rendering his service. This was not the only contrast between the two Calgary contestants. Christie, though an author of some distinction, and a former member of the Royal Canadian Mounted Police, and of the Canadian Army for five years, was frightened to death of the courtroom. Unlike Collins, who gloried in its atmosphere, and stood stage center (at least until some questions sat him down), Christie was almost paralyzed into speechlessness by the setting. Repeatedly we all called for his speaking up.

HENRY: The witness drops his voice and I can't hear him.

NIZER: It is very difficult to hear you, sir.

COURT: Talk up, Mr. Christie.

NIZER: Would you like some water, sir?

WITNESS: It would be helpful.

A few moments later:

Q. I can't hear you. I am awfully sorry to badger you. You have taken a long trip in the middle of the night to get here; I suppose that is it.

A. Yes.

He kept addressing the Judge as "Your Lordship" even though the Court modestly disavowed the wigged title. All this, I felt, endeared him to the jury. His testimony spoke loudly even if he didn't. "The men with whom

I discussed Mr. Reynolds included Calgary's leading newspapermen, civic leaders such as Rev. Doctor Gerald Green Switzer, and, of course, with officers of the Royal Canadian Air Force and the Army."

Q. And also with any writers or ministers?

A. Yes, sir.

Q. Radio broadcasters?

A. Yes sir, with Clarrie Hayward, Station CFAC.

Q. You know Mr. Allen Bill?

A. Very well indeed.

Q. Is he one of the men, sir, with whom you discussed Mr. Reynolds's reputation?

A. Well, as recently as the day before yesterday, sir, when I boarded the plane to get here.

Q. Can you tell us what Mr. Reynolds's reputation for accuracy and integrity was and is in Calgary?

HENRY: I object to it as not proper rebuttal.

COURT: Overruled.

A. Well to the best of my knowledge, sir, and as far as everyone I know in Calgary is concerned, Mr. Reynolds's reputation was and remains the highest.

There was a rather severe cross-examination, but Christie's nervousness was not lack of firmness.

Q. When did you first meet Mr. Reynolds, sir?

A. June 1949, sir.

Q. And his reputation was good then, wasn't it?

A. Yes.

Q. And it is good now, according to you?

A. Yes, sir.

Q. . . . You are not aware of any deterioration or damage to his reputation since June 1949 from anything whatever?

A. That's right, sir.

On re-direct examination I endeavored to show why.

A. Mr. Du Pre made a number of speeches all over Canada from the fall of 1946 until the fall of 1953.

Q. Was his story accepted as true during all this period?

A. Astonishingly enough, it was, yes.

Q. Do you know whether that story was also presented to Intelligence officers and others at the time of the checking of this matter?

A. Yes.

The real value of Christie's appearance was not that he counteracted Collins's testimony, for I believe cross-examination had taken care of that matter. The significant and moving fact was that Calgary had risen voluntarily to show its regard for Reynolds. Such was the respect and affection which he evoked.

Connie Broun returned to the stand, barely filling the chair that the towering General Wedemeyer had occupied.

COURT: This will be strict rebuttal.

NIZER: Indeed, Judge.

I asked her whether she had ever told anyone the story of Reynolds climbing into her rowboat nude.

A. I did not, since I never got into a rowboat, since I can't swim, and I loathe the water.

Had she ever told Mrs. Ross or Mrs. Pegler or anyone else that Reynolds proposed marriage to her in the funeral car.

A. I did not, since it never happened.

Q. Did you ever tell anyone that Mr. Reynolds proposed marriage to you any other place than in the funeral car?

A. No, never.

I wanted her to deny Pegler's statement that she had described Reynolds's alleged nudity as "sitting there without even a hair net" and his "lavaliere dangling." I believed it would be more in keeping with the jury's sense of propriety if I made an indirect allusion to this language.

Q. I don't wish to repeat the language which has been attributed to you in this rowboat incident, but I have shown you the minutes at page 2975 and 2976 with respect to what you are supposed to have said to Mr. Pegler or Mrs. Pegler about the nudity of Mr. Reynolds. Have you ever used such words in your life with respect to any such matter?

A. Never.

NIZER: Your witness.

HENRY: No questions. [Witness excused.]

She had been a model of conciseness and forceful direct answers. The defendants did not wish to tangle with her. They wanted to abandon the subject as quickly as possible, but we would not permit them to do so.

Patricia Broun followed her mother on the stand. She was comely, charming, and crisp. At the time of the claimed rowboat story, she was only fourteen years old. Had she ever been present, as the defense testimony claimed, when her mother told the story of Reynolds climbing into the rowboat nude.

A. No, I am positive my mother never said such a thing.

Q. Does your mother know how to swim?

A. No, she—[An objection was sustained.]

Q. Did you have a rowboat at the Broun lake?

A. Yes, we have a very old rowboat that leaked, and it was seldom used except by myself.

Had she ever heard her mother say that Reynolds had proposed marriage to her on the way to Heywood Broun's grave?

A. I never did. I think it is a fantastic story.

Q. Did she ever say in your presence at any time that Reynolds had snubbed her?

A. Never.

NIZER: That is all.

HENRY: No questions.

COURT: You may step down.

The testimony was concluded.

"Plaintiff rests," I announced.

"Defendants rest," came the voice from behind me. The Court excused the jury for the day and called the lawyers into conference. Motions to dismiss, to strike testimony, and other technical matters were disposed of. Then like duelists, arrangements were agreed upon for the battle of summations. Under the rules the defendants sum up first, the plaintiff last. This equalizes the procedure in which during the trial the plaintiff is first and carries the burden, while the defendants are last. Allotment of time was made by the Judge. Each side was to have five hours.

This was another night in which I worked through to morning and returned to court. During that awesome stillness which one can find only in the hours preceding daybreak, I like to "plough deep while sluggards sleep." With my assistants I culled the citations from the record and organized a summation that would predigest the enormous amount of testimony, without sacrificing emotion or lucidity. The excitement of such a task is one of the rewards of a lawyer's life. I have painted, and written music, and I find that the art of constructing a mosaic of persuasion is no less stimulating and affords an unlimited opportunity for creative expression.

Unfortunately, not all adrenal glands react the same to such stimulus, and a few of my associates found themselves in grotesque postures of slumber on the edge of a sofa or on the carpet before the sun rose. But they dared not be drowsy during my oration, so I will not attribute their alertness to anything but loyalty.

The art of summation is as varied as the personalities of men. Mr. Henry, a veteran defender of Hearst publications in libel actions, had achieved a unique record of success. His style was a paradoxical combination of sophistication and country-lawyer hominess, garnished with strong doses of irony, satire, and ridicule. Anticipating our attack upon the bizarre legal answer filed by the defendants he said: "The plaintiff in some way expected after calling us criminal libelers, conspirators and designers of destruction, that we would turn around and palliate the matter and seek some kind of peace. Well, we didn't, and any idea that just because somebody brings a libel action and says his reputation was injured we are going to swoon and enact the part of these Jehovah Witnesses, I hope this answer has destroyed, if it has done nothing else."

He almost looked like a Jehovah's Witness, with his gray hair, ascetically lined face, and booming bass tones. As for the doctrine that "you should be mulcted . . . because you dared to defend yourself," he compared it with the way they used to try witches: "They would take the suspect and throw her in the pond and if she drowned, that was proof of innocence; if not that was conclusive proof of witchcraft and the penalty was exacted accordingly."

He knew how to revive the jury's interest when it flagged. Even if he had to resort to irrelevancy, he took the curse off it by confession (as a skillful playwright has a character protest the improbability of an incident to deprive you of your accusation that it is improbable): "Reynolds went to a front-line airdrome, whatever that may be, at a Parisian race track called Chantilly. Now it is funny what things stick in your memory —absolutely useless; just clutter up your mind. Some of you older gentlemen of the jury may remember that that is the place where John L. Sullivan fought a fellow named Charlie Mitchell, and the reason I remember it, they were fighting on turf with spikes on, and Mitchell tried to stamp on Sullivan's foot, and Sullivan says, 'Try to be a gentleman, Charlie, you so-and-so.' Now if that is of any use to anybody, I don't know, but they do stick in your mind. Anyway, they went there to this front-line airdrome. Nothing happened; I suppose a few bombs dropped. Back to Paris."

So the minimization process continued. "In all my descriptions of the plaintiff's comings and goings, let's have it assumed that the place was absolutely teeming with mine fields; no place he ever went was otherwise, but apparently these mines were of an antiseptic character—they never exploded; they never hurt anybody, and in the case of the Dieppe raid, they probably weren't even there. They were merely suspected. Some aviator possibly having seen the Germans out trying to catch a few herring and suspected they were laying mines, so they swept the area and nobody was hurt, and few apparently were very much frightened."

He poured gallons of sarcasm upon the incident of the English scientist who inspected the radar equipment at Dieppe: "I will leave out about the mad scientist or whatever it was they were going to shoot if he was captured, lest they give him some truth serum. It is a familiar story. I think I heard it before either in *Batman* or *Space Cadet* or some piece of literature of that kind."

As for Lord Mountbatten, "he resembles the fellow I used to play baseball with many years ago, who is said to have had a $10,000 arm and a ten-cent head—he could be useful and he was useful in a subsequent part of the war."

Reynolds's knee injury while on the desert was given the following Henry treatment: "Plaintiff says he got wounded in the knee while lying in a trench, something I leave to you to figure out. The Japs weren't in the war yet; they weren't shooting up through the earth, but he got wounded there from shrapnel or rocks or whatever it may have been."

Mr. Henry told the jury he was convinced Reynolds wasn't: "as sensitive as he would have you believe. That is up to you, of course, the amount of mental anguish he suffered, when, having started this controversy, Pegler, to be brutally correct about it, let him have both barrels after he made this charge of murder. Here is a man who takes this kind of money from the Garssons. They are later convicted. Wouldn't you think that he would have a little embarrassment about it? Wouldn't you think he would stay away from this Toots Shor's place for a few days? That was sort of for writers that can't write and fighters that can't fight. But of course not. Right back with the whole *Collier's* staff and all this other literary assortment. It doesn't betoken to me a very sensitive violet-like character."

Surprisingly, the chief attack was reserved for the Salerno incident. Henry charged that Reynolds's story as to why he left Salerno after the third day was "a complete fake, just as the one about Du Pre, and I will see it we can't develop that right from his own book."

He quoted disconnected passages from here and there, stringing them together with ridicule. "Well, now, on page 311, Mr. Little Alibi Ike gets into form and gives us another one. Somebody mentions Frank Sinatra and asked him who he was. The man said, 'Boy you've been away from home too long. You've missed too many boats.'"

He then referred to Reynolds's description of leaving the *Ancon*. "Then I thought of home and blew a happy kiss to the ship." Well, I have never been in the Navy, but I can't imagine what comfort it was to those fellows out there taking it from the 88s and the aircraft to have a kiss blown at them by the fellow who three days before had given them an inspirational talk over the ship's radio."

It was psychologically instructive that where Henry had a real point, he did not resort to verbal pyrotechnics. "I have never in my life seen such a pretentious front of enormous damages to start with, which came down to evidence of absolutely nothing. You remember, I am sure, the fact that the plaintiff made more money in 1950, 1951, 1952, and 1953 than he made in 1949. There was no loss of income. Any claim that he might have had of a lot more income, of course, is purely speculative."

Henry built to a crescendo as he neared his conclusion. "When Reynolds took on Mr. Pegler, the plain and simple fact is that he overmatched himself, and now he is down here seeking relief from the very contest which he invited and initiated."

He read a quotation from a Chief Justice of England: "I own I cannot feel much sympathy for a man, who, having been the first to make an appeal to public opinion, when he is answered in the same manner by a counter appeal, changes the tribunal which he has himself selected and invokes the aid of the law."

Mr. Henry dealt with the subject of malice like a swordsman who wards off a fatal thrust by deftly pushing it in another direction: Whatever malice there be in the case appears to me to exist for some reason between the defendant Pegler and counsel for the plaintiff, and it appears to be about mutually balanced on each side, the one complaining of the other's insolence, and the other requesting counsel to stay away."

A little later he concluded: "It comes down to this: If you can't take it, don't dish it. That is the situation that we find here in this case. My friends, the more you study and consider these facts, I believe you will come to the conclusion that . . . there was no malice, there was no damage, there was no falsity, there was no libel."

"May it please your Honor, ladies and gentlemen":

I stood before the jury ready to answer Mr. Henry and make my own summation. I felt fresh and eager although I had not touched a bed or closed an eyelid the preceding night. There was no time for tiredness.

It is familiar defense strategy to minimize and ridicule the plaintiff's claim, puncture it with sarcastic humor, and try to laugh it out of court. Mr. Henry had executed this gambit brilliantly.

Such an approach, however, is subject to heavy counterfire. If it is possible to demonstrate that the facts have been ignored by the defendants and that they have toyed with the truth, their frivolous approach becomes calloused and offensive. That is why witty summations, which skirt the evidence, have short lives. As soon as they are subjected to analytical sunshine, they dry up. A jury will resent levity when the truth points to tragedy. I endeavored at the outset to pierce the balloon of risibility which the defendants had floated. My technique was to create an image, which would be understood readily and which would haunt the defendants throughout the summation. I asked:

"What does a defense lawyer do in a case of this kind? He does what Mr. Henry so skillfully did—he attempts from the very first moment to becloud the issue, not to discuss the merits, not to discuss the facts, not to discuss the truth, but to raise every conceivable prejudicial issue he can. I would like to tell you something about an octopus.

"When an octopus is attacked by an enemy, it emits a black inky fluid, and the water around it gets very black, and in the confusion the octopus escapes.

"In this case from the very first moment . . . until this skillful summation, the defendants emitted black fluid to becloud the issues in this case.

"Salerno. The entire summation's point turned out ultimately to be Salerno. Does it make any sense that this man, who several years before we were at war voluntarily goes to England and France, . . . to Dieppe and all the operational flights . . . runs away at Salerno? This becomes the emphasis at the last moment, just black ink of the octopus. That is all that is."

As I analyzed the record and the false issues repeatedly raised by the defendants, which were later abandoned, I kept referring to such tactics as those of the octopus which squirts black fluid to escape in the resulting darkness. The ugly picture of the octopus grew more vivid with each illustration, and after a while I had only to wave my hand as if through dark water and say "black fluid"—and the allusion completed itself.

So on the inflammatory issue of Communism, Pegler in his column said "Reynolds's medicine grew too strong for *Collier's*." We challenged him on this accusation, but Pegler ran away and would not fight: "On examination before trial Pegler says 'I never said he was a Communist. That doesn't mean that. . . . All I meant was that he was a liberal Democrat, that is all I said, and when the Court asked Mr. Henry 'Do you charge Mr. Reynolds with being a pro-Communist?' he said 'Oh, no, your Honor, we have admitted he is a loyal and patriotic American.' Then why was this going on here for three or four weeks—all the cross-examination about Russia—all the insinuations? It was the black ink of the octopus."

Reynolds was accused of stealing gas from the American Embassy in Paris, until it developed that Ken Downs had participated in the act and put the gas in his Hearst car "and that is the last we have heard about stealing gas. . . . That was just some black fluid of the octopus."

I analyzed the extensive accusations about nudity, but pointed out that there was no cross-examination of Connie Broun or Patricia, and that Mr. Henry, while flippant on so many irrelevancies, had not uttered one word in summation on the subject of nudism—just another instance of black fluid.

The defendants charged that Reynolds was an "absentee war correspondent," but: "Colonel Lawrence [Eisenhower's aide] said that if a man served six or seven months in a war zone, he was a war correspondent. If he goes home for the rest of his life, he has earned that title; and if he serves twelve months, he says, he is beyond the average war correspondent. Do you know how many months Quentin Reynolds served? Thirty months. There isn't another war correspondent alive or dead—and I do not exclude the wonderful Ernie Pyle—who served that long on so many fronts and in so many dangerous positions. So you haven't heard anything more about . . . calling this man an absentee war correspondent, simply because he was at home between 1943 and 1944 and then went out to the Pacific."

What had happened to this issue? The defendants attempted to create confusion in which the defendants might escape. It was some more black fluid.

Pegler claimed he was provoked to write the libel column by Reynolds's book review in the *Herald Tribune*. But I read Pegler's columns, published long before that book review, which sneered and clawed at Reynolds. "He wasn't provoked by any book review. That is nonsense. That is more black ink of the octopus."

The defendants charged Reynolds with being a war profiteer. I reviewed his generosity as a one-man U.S.O. center financed by himself:

"This is the fourflusher, this is the tightwad, the man who wouldn't lift a check."

The defendants had challenged Reynolds's story of the British scientist who accompanied the Commandos at Dieppe. But we produced "Colonel Lawrence who said he knew the scientist. That was an actual incident. It occurred as the book said. Colonel Lawrence, who knew the man's name, said "I don't want to mention it." So his Honor protected him and said 'You don't have to.'"

Now Mr. Henry, without referring to the evidence, made facetious comments about "the mad scientist."

Mr. Henry's ridiculing skepticism of the wound Reynolds suffered in the desert near Sidi-Omar afforded me the opportunity to read at length from the depositions of General Messervy and Captain Clive Burt, which expounded his heroism. Here were unimpeachable eyewitnesses whom Mr. Henry had chosen not to cross-examine, but now he substituted sneering disbelief for demonstrated truth. Was this really a funny exercise, or was it a clever, all too clever, resort to the black fluid of the octopus?

So I proceeded through the long record, quoting the overwhelming evidence, often out of the mouth of Pegler himself, and exposing the defendant's technique of ignoring the evidence and substituting chuckle and demagoguery for it. The time came when the defense's mirth had been turned against it. The immensity of Pegler's offense once more hung heavily over the jury box. I put the case back in perspective. "I hope you are conscious of the fact that you are sitting as the judges of one of the historic cases of this generation."

For nothing less was at the stake than the curbing of irresponsible journalism. The freedom of the press was being prostituted by recklessness and sensationalism. The law of libel stood as guardian over our precious rights, and only the sensitivity and keenness of the jury system could prevail over the anarchy of unbridled destruction of citizens' reputations.

When speaking of the defendants, I would occasionally turn half way toward them. I observed that Pegler was not in his seat. At first I thought he had left the room temporarily. But as the summation continued, his absence registered on my consciousness. His seat began to grow larger and more empty. When I was convinced that he was not going to appear, I turned a verbal spotlight on his chair: "Mr. Reynolds was here during the entire summation of Mr. Henry. Anything he had to say, Reynolds looked him in the eye. Where is Mr. Pegler? Where is this man who said we ran away? Why isn't he here to listen to the truth. . . . I am going to quote him many, many times before I am through. He hasn't the courage to sit here."

My summation ran over to the next day. But again Pegler did not show up. Once more I turned to the unoccupied chair: "I notice again Mr. Pegler isn't here today, after he talks about 'dishing it out, but not taking it.'"

I made that empty chair a symbol of Pegler's guilt which made it impossible for him to hear his own testimony quoted, of his insolence in quitting his own trial.

I once witnessed a demonstration of posthypnotic suggestion in which the subject was told that after he came out of his trance he would look for his brother who had left the room. When he awoke, his brother was seated next to him, but he looked at him and saw only an empty chair, while he proceeded out of the room calling for him. The suggestion implanted in him while he was under hypnosis had actually blocked out his vision. As I continued my summation and addressed the imaginary Pegler in the empty chair, I thought of the reverse hypnotic process. I hoped that the jurors would look at the chair and see Pegler there. I contrasted Reynolds and Pegler: "Now you have observed them on the stand—Reynolds courteous, decent, warmhearted, truthful; not once did Reynolds say 'Oh, I take that back. I made a mistake under oath'—not once.

"Pegler—did you ever see a more shifty, uncertain, neurotic, and vicious man? . . . It finally got to the point where his Honor had to instruct the clerk to hand papers to him, because otherwise he might have struck me. I never had any such experience in my life. . . .

"I don't recall ever a witness who took back his words under oath as many times as Pegler, and took it back so ungraciously. At one time we counted up in the record 130 times that he said he made a mistake under oath."

I turned toward the empty chair and just looked at it. I read to the jury Pegler's startling admission:

Q. And when you say that certain people draw on their imagination and make inexact statements, that has been true about you, has it not?

A. Yes.

The chair seemed to be embarrassed. Then I gave the reason for such a devastating confession: "Do you know why this witness made this answer? Because he had learned during this trial if he said no, I could face him with columns in which he admitted that he drew on his imagination to write stories. . . ."

I quoted Pegler's admission that he had not checked the facts of his libel article, and pointing at him as if he were there, I said: "This is supposed to be a responsible reporter."

I pinned the truncated clipping about the S.S. *Franklin* on him. I held up the two newspaper stories dated May 18, one offered by the defendants which was cut out, and the other, the complete original, and I read the following words in the section deleted by the defendants, who contended that Reynolds could not have been on the boat before May 18, because that was when it arrived: "Big Ben arrived here *April 26th* after a 12,400-mile voyage from the scene of her disaster and triumph; censorship forbade mention of the facts until now."

I had never before seen a chair blush. I jogged the jury's memory by reminding them of Pegler's assertion that he had relied upon certain clippings, six and seven years old. He had attempted to destroy Reynolds by getting into evidence dozens of adverse clippings, but it turned out that he had never read those documents, and furthermore many of them contained favorable comments about Reynolds. So the effort boomeranged. "You know—the Chinese say, if you are going to dig a grave, dig two. They got caught in this. . . ."

By this time I could indulge in a bit of ridicule, too. I quoted from the legal document filed by the defendants as an answer to our complaint: " 'According to the principles of Parmelee, on the theory of Gymnosophy, Mr. Reynolds did practice nudism, which is associated with Communistic theory.' "

"Did you ever hear such drivel? Reynolds said he thought Parmelee was a Greek, and it turned out he was some kind of crackpot. Mr. Pegler never heard of him. I have to give Mr. Henry credit for that one. And they file an answer, not only not apologizing for the untruth, but dressing it up with Parmelee's philosophy of Gymnosophy, whatever the devil that is, connecting that with Communism? If that isn't malice—"

I reviewed his brand of patriotism, which permitted him during wartime to use strategic materials for extensive building operations, while urging citizens to turn in the bumpers from their cars; which permitted him to claim he was a farmer, though he confessed his pitiful record with the soil; which permitted him to condemn "E" Award ceremonies, while defending Robert Best, convicted of treason, because "He was just a damn tattletale, hanging around saloons, eliciting harmless gossip from a lot of flannel-mouthed American leaders of the journalistic trade."

During all this his chair stood spotlighted in all its emptiness, while the jury's imagination was given free rein to see Pegler writhe in it. When I analyzed the charge that Reynolds violated sensibilities by proposing marriage to the bereaved widow, I used a different device to bring the enormity of the offense home to the jury. I told them of a script conference in Hollywood in which a brilliant writer suggests how to depict in subtle manner that a married couple is no longer enamored of each other. They get into an elevator. He wears his hat. At one of the stops a beautiful girl enters. He removes his hat.

Then I said: "Now it seems to me that this funeral-car story must have been created by someone as ingenious as that. If you had a story conference among a lot of brilliant malicious people, and you said, 'I want to tear the guts out of Reynolds. I called him everything under the sun, but can you think of a touch that will really make him look like a heel?' and somebody made this suggestion and said, 'Why don't you have him ride with her in the funeral car right to the grave? She is in mourning, she is hysterical, she is sobbing, and he makes a pass at her. . . . Wouldn't that really be pretty low? . . .'

"And what does Mr. Pegler write about this after he tells it. He said, 'That would be credible.' He puts the stamp of credibility on this."

Whenever I sum up, I have the court attendant place a large table in front of the jury box. On it I line up in sequence the many blue-covered volumes of typewritten testimony of the trial and of the examinations before trial. On the other side of the table I put the depositions and dozens of exhibits which I have culled from hundreds for the purpose of citing.

Each volume is marked with a large number in red pencil, which corresponds to my summation notes. I advise the jury that I intend to bear out my assertions from the record, and will read chiefly the words of the defendants and their witnesses, so that I will prove my case out of the mouths of the defendants themselves. As I develop the argument I reach for the particular testimony which has been carefully underlined, so that I will not wander over the page.

The very act of lifting volume after volume of trial minutes and exhibits becomes a manual symbol of the authoritativeness of the argument. In his summation, Mr. Henry had only once read a brief passage from the record. I punctuated every contention with specific citations. The eyes of the jury followed the frequent stretch for different documents, and their ears heard repeated playbacks of testimony given weeks before. Psychologically such a process is especially valuable. If the juror recognizes the quotation, he is pleased with his memory and will sometimes nod assent. He is your partner in the persuasive effort. If he is startled by the quotation because he does not recall it as an isolated bit of testimony but now sees its true significance in the surrounding context, he is gratified to have made a new discovery.

Above all, the repeated use of the typewritten testimony acts as a magic carpet on which the jurors may be taken on an occasional emotional and rhetorical flight. Without the support of the record, such flights will never leave the ground.

The advocate's task of weaving thousands of threads of disconnected testimony into a cloth of persuasive patterns, while at the same time dexterously eliminating those strings which would spoil the design, is difficult enough. But he must also keep an eye out for the threads that are missing. They have a meaning, too.

The semantic device of the empty chair, suggested by Pegler's absence, encouraged me to couple it with another empty chair: "Why did not a single Hearst executive take that stand? They couldn't subject themselves to cross-examination, because if they were asked,"—I turned to the empty witness chair and plied the imaginary witness with questions—" 'Didn't you know that Mr. Pegler was a dangerous writer who had given you trouble? What do you know about the lawsuits that you have had on account of Mr. Pegler's recklessness? Will you answer that. How many columns have you cut out? Did he write a column against the Pope which you cut out, or didn't he? . . . Didn't you know that he was reckless? . . .

" 'What did you do after this suit? . . . Why, Mr. Hearst executive, didn't you make a check of facts? You have Mr. Bowden—who also isn't around right now (I turned to the other empty chair next to Pegler's); you have an investigative staff that no one can equal, the Hearst publications from coast to coast; you have morgues of clippings. Why didn't you say, "Now that we have been sued, we had better check into this. How about it, Peg? Where did you get this story from? How about these facts? Let's do a little checking here." ' "

"They didn't check a thing. Do you know why they didn't? Because they were malicious too. . . . They were out after him.

"Much more important than any witness that appeared in this case is the absence of a Hearst executive from that stand."

The defendants had not produced a single character witness for Pegler. Once more I attempted to make the witness chair look significantly forlorn. I analyzed the reason for such a failure, pointing out in contrast our production of twenty-six witnesses, and concluded: "There are two big holes in this case. Remember those holes—no Hearst executive and no reputation witness for Pegler. . . . I therefore say that if I sat down now I could claim that the defendant has defaulted in this case. All the rest is black ink of the octopus."

Hour after hour I pulled the words out of the cold record and attempted to breathe life into them, to make them glow with sympathy or indignation. I re-created the scenes of Pegler's distress when he discovered that writings he had denounced as the Communist line, turned out to be his own columns, when he admitted that the clippings he claimed to have relied upon were not seen by him until long after he wrote the libel column, and when he quoted Mrs. Luce as referring to an incident that hadn't yet occurred. I brought back by word-pictures the gallery of distinguished men who had appeared for Reynolds, among them, Ed Murrow, John Gunther, Captain Harry Butcher (the night after he had spoken to President Eisenhower), Kenneth Downs, Walter Kerr, Lionel Shapiro, William Chenery, and by deposition, Lord Louis Mountbatten, Sir Walter Monckton, Lord W. M. A. Beaverbrook, Harold Duff-Cooper, General Sir Frank Messervy, Captain Clive Burt, Arthur Christiansen.

I also revived the scenes of Pegler's witnesses, among them Bella Dodd, Louis Waldman, Louis Ruppel, R. D. Collins, Father Broun, Admiral Conolly, and General Wedemeyer and re-enacted the cross-examination of them.

I concentrated on Pegler's malice in attempting to cut off Reynolds's income, right up to the date of trial. "If there ever was a fingerprint of economic murder left in a courtroom, this is it. Pegler is going out to carve up whatever is left of Mr. Reynolds, economically. Here is proof of malice . . . brazenly and in open sunlight."

I unfurled the larger issue again and again. "I have to limit myself to Reynolds, but you have a right to feel that this is a symptom of a kind of disease . . . of a wild-eyed era that we have been having with Pegler. The phrase "Peglerized" has become a word in the dictionary. It is a very vicious, evil word, and well-known from coast to coast."

I concluded: "An assassin and a slanderer, ladies and gentlemen, are the same thing. They use different weapons. The assassin uses a gun and a slanderer uses his pen. When he uses a pen or a printing press and destroys the most precious thing a man has, his reputation, it is time that one of our juries, in their wisdom, made a lesson of that man by awarding punitive damages."

When I sat down, Ginny and others were crying softly. We had done all we could to vindicate Reynolds. Our task was done.

After the lawyers have whipped up a storm in the jury box with their passionate advocacy, the Judge calms the atmosphere with an objective instruction of the law. The Judge's charge, as it is called, enables the jury to apply legal yardsticks to the facts which they, and they alone, will determine. It is part of the genius of Anglo-Saxon jurisprudence that each contestant reveals his profile to the jury, while the applicable law permits the jury to see the truth fullface.

The law of libel is very complicated, much more so than, for example, criminal law. Judge Weinfeld spent almost three hours expounding the legal principles which governed the case.

The defendants had pleaded the defense called the Privilege of Reply. They claimed that Pegler had merely replied to Reynolds's book review, and therefore could not be liable. However reply is only privileged if it is limited in scope to the original attack. If A calls B a thief, B may reply by denying the accusation and belaboring A as a liar. But he may not engage in personal invective dealing with unrelated matters. Therefore Pegler's accusations of immorality, cowardice, and dishonesty were beyond the proper limits of reply and were not privileged. The Judge struck out the defense of reply. He did, however, permit the book review to be considered as a possible provocation, limiting its effect to amelioration of damages.

The defendants had also pleaded the defense of Fair Comment. An individual or a newspaper may in the exercise of free speech comment adversely on a public figure's activities. However, this privilege, too, is restricted by two factors. The comment may express opinion, but if it asserts facts they must be accurate. Also, the comment must be relevant to the subject matter to which it addresses itself. Once more the privilege is lost if the defendant uses it as a license for impertinent slander.

All these privileges are forfeited if the jury finds that the defendants were malicious. The law in its wisdom will throw a protective cloak around the transgressor so long as he acts in good faith and within the limits of the privilege. But he cannot expect the law to hold out a sympathetic hand if venom rather than excessive zeal has motivated his deed.

The Judge also instructed the jury on libel by innuendo. The law recognizes that one may libel another by clever insinuation, rather than by express statement. For example, we had pleaded that Pegler's statement "Reynolds's medicine grew too strong even for *Collier's* which, I am told, incidentally has 'seen the light' and faced about" conveyed by innuendo (particularly in the light of other language in the column, such as "his Russian friends") that Reynolds was pro-Communistic and that *Collier's*, which had also been, had reversed its position and therefore could no longer tolerate him. It was for the jury to determine whether such innuendo could reasonably be read into the language used. If so, it was libelous, otherwise not.

So with lucidity equal to its learning, the Court set forth the legal rules that governed the subjects of compensatory and punitive damages, burden of proof and the like.

At thirty minutes after noon the jury was told to retire and reach a verdict. Within fifteen minutes there was a rap on the door. A court attendant excitedly informed us that the jury was returning. The Judge hastily ascended the bench. I was jubilant. Surely we had done well enough to prevent instantaneous agreement against us. A speedy verdict is a good omen for the plaintiff. It means that there has been no quarrel among the jurors and therefore that the verdict is likely to be high.

The jury filed in, and I looked eagerly at their faces. A favorable jury usually smiles at the victorious attorney. They did! The clerk intoned the customary question, "Ladies and Gentlemen of the jury, have you agreed upon a verdict?"

The foreman arose and said, "No, sir. We would like to have all the exhibits sent to the jury room before lunch."

What a letdown. The Judge instructed the jury that henceforth, if they had any request, they could forward it by a written note. They retired for lunch. We did likewise, our first rush of exhilaration having subsided into a more realistic mood. But we enjoyed our lunch. No one could have reasonably expected that a jury could decide an eight-week trial in a few minutes. Nor were we concerned by the passage of several hours after lunch.

Then with increasing frequency the jury sent notes to the Judge. It wanted to have certain portions of his instructions on the law read to them, or it wanted to hear the cross-examination of certain witnesses re-read. By six o'clock five such written notes had been submitted to the Judge. He answered each, after advising counsel on both sides.

Our anxiety began to mount. The jury had now been out about five hours, and obviously there were decided differences among them. We tried to divine the meaning of each request sent to the Judge, sometimes being filled with hope, at other times disheartened, and often perplexed.

We sat around the courtroom in disrespectful poses, on tables, or in the jury box. Someone brought a container of hot coffee and paper cups;

they seemed to connote a long vigil and made us more restless. Some of us paced the corridor, the nervousness of suspense quickening the pace, until we seemed to be rushing back and forth to no destination at all.

At seven o'clock the blue-coated court attendant advised us that the jury had gone out to dinner and would not return until eight fifteen. Alarm was beginning to set in among my associates, and Quent's friends. At dinner we tried to banter and maintain good spirits, but feeble appetites exposed the real state of affairs.

We returned to the Federal Court House. The building was dark, except for the ninth floor where the jury was closeted in a bare room. The lights in the courtroom seemed yellower when not pitted against the daylight of court sessions. Also, there was an eerie stillness because the banks of elevators were not running, distant typewriter keys were not heard, and the honks and screeches of traffic were not being wafted up through the windows. The absence of customary noises created a disturbing silence. New sounds, otherwise unnoticed, became enlarged as if through a microphone. The footsteps on the marble floor as the pacing continued, the gurgle of the drinking fountain, the lighting of a match, a nervous cough, a forced laugh, all resounded through the corridor in such a way as to remind us of the late hour.

Nine o'clock, ten o'clock, ten thirty, ten forty-five. More messages from the jury for instructions. By now there had been eight.

More and more frequently everyone looked at his wrist watch. It became an automatic gesture; sometimes we looked without seeing the hour. As time peeled off, it left a raw skin of tension. Max Steuer, a famous trial lawyer, once told me that he felt he lost one week of his life every hour the jury stayed out.

Eleven o'clock, eleven ten, eleven twenty-five. Anxiety was now universal among us. A hung jury seemed to be inevitable. Two more messages from the jury to the Judge. Now there had been ten. These notes took on ominous meaning. They seemed to be calls for help from a jury sinking in a morass of disagreement.

As we sat or walked restlessly among the strewn paper cups, evil forebodings set our conversations on the road of panic. Had the priest turned the case against us? Why, oh why had I not called Monsignor Sheen to the stand?

If there was a disagreement, asked Reynolds, would the case be retried, and if so, when? What were the chances on retrial? I waived the questions aside as premature and defeatist, but my manner could not have been too convincing.

Eleven fifty, midnight! No word from the jury. Someone reported hearing quarrelsome noises from their room. More feverish conjecture. Perhaps if we had tried the case in the State Supreme Court where ten out of twelve jurors may render a verdict, those two Hearst readers on the jury might not have blocked a decision. What a severe requirement unanimity was in the Federal Court. One juror could put our heartbreaking effort to naught.

Twelve ten. Twelve twenty. No word. Now I found it difficult to meet the inquiring glances of Quent, Ginny, and a small group of loyal friends who paced the floor nervously with them. My own partners and associates looked to me for a hopeful prediction. But what did I have to present to them?

Twelve thirty. Twelve thirty-five. Suddenly the court attendant dashed into the corridor, his voice like an alarm bell. "The jury is returning. Counsel, please return to the courtroom."

Our hearts beat quickly as we took our usual seats. Mr. Henry and his associates arrived from another floor. Their faces also betrayed the strain they were under, but we imagined they were more hopeful. At this late hour, a disagreement might very well be the announcement we would hear.

In my own mind I could find little solace. Even if there was a verdict, it must have been cut down by the long struggle to a nominal sum. This is the common experience of protracted jury struggles. They breed compromise after compromise, and always downward.

We waited for the Judge, who had kept a midnight vigil in his chambers on the twenty-first floor. The next ten minutes until he arrived were unbearable with suspense. Finally there were three knocks on the door. He ascended the bench while we stood throbbing and impatient.

The jury was summoned. I looked eagerly once more into their faces as they filed into the jury box. Not one greeted me. They all looked angry and flushed, as if harsh words of recrimination still lingered over them.

The clerk, whose face was still asleep, but whose eyes and voice were filled with excitement, put the fatal question. "Ladies and Gentlemen of the jury, have you agreed upon a verdict?"

Mr. Cocks, the foreman, rose and said: "We have. We find for the plaintiff, Quentin Reynolds, in the sum of one dollar."

There was momentary tumult from the small audience. Quent seized my hand and shook it saying: "Well, we won anyhow, chum. Congratulations."

The foreman was still speaking: ". . . We also find for the plaintiff, Quentin Reynolds, in the sum of one hundred and seventy-five . . . dollars punitive damages."

Again the commotion blotted out Mr. Cocks's weak voice. Someone leaned over my shoulder excitedly and said, "Did he say one hundred and seventy-five dollars, or one hundred and seventy-five thousand dollars?"

None of us knew what was happening. Mr. Henry and his associates, too, were straining forward to get the true import of the verdict. We were distressed with uncertainty and new possible hope. The foreman was still speaking: ". . . Twenty-five thousand dollars against the defendant Hearst Consolidated Publications, Inc."

Reynolds seized my shoulder and pressed it.

"Fifty thousand dollars against the defendant the Hearst Corporation."

Reynolds's grip became painfully tight.

"One hundred thousand dollars against the defendant Westbrook Pegler."

Everyone rushed toward Reynolds and smothered him with hugs, slaps, and confused mauling. Ginny, who was crying with the same intensity as if she had lost, was being comforted by her friends.

The clerk was wielding an angry gavel so that he could complete his function. Now we would hear the verdict uninterruptedly and clearly. Said the clerk: "You, the jury in the case of Quentin Reynolds against Westbrook Pegler et al., have reached a verdict in favor of the plaintiff against all the defendants in the sum of one dollar compensatory damages, and in the sum of one hundred and seventy-five thousand dollars punitive damages against the respective defendants in the following amounts:

"Twenty-five thousand dollars, punitive damages against the defendant Hearst Consolidated Publications, Inc.

"Fifty thousand dollars, punitive damages against the defendant Hearst Corporation.

"One hundred thousand dollars, punitive damages against the defendant Westbrook Pegler.

"So say you all."

Mr. Henry asked that the jury be polled. The Judge instructed the clerk to do so. He addressed each juror separately and asked whether the verdict as read, correctly expressed his or her determination. With varying degrees of emphasis, each nodded yes, or called out "I agree," or "It does."

The Judge expressed his gratitude to the jury for their long and dedicated service. He excused them from service for a year and then graciously dismissed them.

Mr. Henry moved to set aside the verdict as excessive and contrary to the evidence. The Judge set down a day for special argument of this motion.

My associates had already left the courtroom to encounter the jurors in the corridor and learn about the events that had mystified and distressed us for twelve hours. Now Reynolds and I joined them.

We were besieged with affection and apology! Eight jurors had held out for a full verdict of five hundred thousand dollars punitive damages. Two stood for three hundred and fifty thousand dollars. But two jurors insisted that they would hold out against any verdict if the punitive damages exceeded one hundred thousand dollars. Respectful disagreement turned gradually into bitter exchanges among them. Each group accused the other of unreasonable stubbornness. Whenever an argument about the law or facts reached feverish heights, they would attempt to resolve it by sending a note to the Judge. That is why ten such requests were sent out of the seething forum as the hours stretched on. Finally by different devices of entreaty and threat, judiciously flavored with appeals to the high purpose of their function and the importance of the case, compromises were effected until unanimity was achieved. But the great majority felt they had yielded to the pragmatic necessity of reaching an inadequate verdict rather than having no verdict at all. That is why they were disappointed in their decision and assured Reynolds and myself that we deserved better at their hands.

What they did not realize was that never in the history of libel actions had a case that warranted only one dollar in actual damage been offset by so large a verdict in punitive damages.

We had a formidable task ahead of us to sustain it.

"No verdict of this amount for compensatory, punitive, or any other kind of damage, or any combination of such damages, has ever been sustained in any appellate court anywhere."

So argued Mr. Henry in support of his motion to have the verdict set aside by the trial judge. "Furthermore, I have never found any verdict for more than $5000 in this country as punitive damages, based on a nominal verdict for compensatory damage."

I replied that there should be no relationship between actual damage and punitive damage. If one's reputation is so impeccable that it is untouched by the libel, the reason for punitive damage is strengthened. Otherwise, men who are impervious to injury to character would be open game for any malicious libeler.

The Judge upheld the jury's verdict in an opinion in which he wrote: "Punitive damages are intended as a deterrent upon the libeler so that he will not repeat the offense, and to serve as a warning to others. They are intended as punishment for gross misbehavior for the good of the public and have been referred to as 'a sort of hybrid between the display of ethical indignation and the imposition of a criminal fine.'"

The Judge analyzed the evidence of malice and found the verdict not excessive, despite the disproportion between compensatory and punitive damages.

We had passed the first test. Now there followed an appeal to the United States Court of Appeals, composed of three Judges. The defendants retained special appellate counsel, Mr. Milton Pollack, to write the brief and argue the cause.

They contended that the column was really not libelous. The handsprings they had to perform in support of such an ingenuous position was pointed out by me in the opening of my argument. "To say that when Pegler wrote 'Reynolds's protuberant belly was filled with something other than guts' was not libelous because it is an equivocal statement referring either to Reynolds or his belly;

"or to say that 'Reynolds's mangy hide was pinned up on a barn door with the yellow streak glaring for all to see' was only a political jest;

"or to say that 'Reynolds was nuding along in the raw with his wench' is not libelous because it does not charge a crime;

"or that 'Reynolds was one of the great individual profiteers of the war' is not libelous because the language is not 'war profiteer' but 'profiteer of the war';

"or that when Pegler wrote 'Reynolds, while in the funeral car on the way to Broun's funeral, proposed marriage to his widow' is not libel because 'under the Mosaic Code it is a courtesy to propose marriage to a widow';

"or that when Pegler called Reynolds a 'sycophant and fourflusher' this was not libel because Webster's dictionary defines a fourflusher as one who plays poker and draws to a flush;

"and all the rest of this nonsense indicates the extremism of the appellant's position on this appeal—the desperate clutching for any contention which would make a straw look like a solid raft."

I pointed out the appellants' failure to describe the evidence, which filled 11,000 pages, while they talked of presenting a blueprint for reversal. I observed: "The result has been a sort of disembodied argument floating around in mid-air in academic abstractions with no roots of reality whatsoever. The appellants have constantly talked of a blueprint for reversal. All I see is a blueprint to nowhere, on a chartless and factless sea."

The appellants had insisted that the Hearst corporations could not have been guilty of malice and therefore that no punitive damages could be rendered against them. But I read from the answer filed by them which "indulges in new libels, of even greater ferocity. I do not believe your Honors have ever read a legal pleading of such unprofessional wording spiked with malice. It is a veritable torrent of abuse."

I referred to new charges in the answer of "interracial seduction" and the "orgies with certain secret reservations as to some of the interracial aspects thereof." I stressed the failure of the Hearst corporations to check and correct facts, concerning the "ghoulish charges," and the recklessness equivalent to malice which this connoted.

Once more we awaited the Court's determination. On June 7, 1955, an opinion written by Judge Harold Medina, and concurred in by Presiding Judge Jerome Frank and Judge Stephen W. Brennan unanimously affirmed the judgment.

The defendants still would not accept their fate. They went to the United States Supreme Court. We filed briefs in opposition to their petition for certiorari, and won.

By this time the costs and interests had increased the judgment to more than two hundred thousand dollars. There were no other steps the defendants could take. It has been said that there is no appeal from the United States Supreme Court except to God, and at least we were of the belief that that Court of last jurisdiction would not be very sympathetic.

The defendants paid a certified check for the full amount of the judgment, costs, and interest.

What Reynolds had not known was that compensatory damages are substitution for lost income and are taxable. Punitive damages are not. Therefore the jury had done better than it thought. The verdict of only one dollar compensatory damages was taxable, but what had grown to $200,000 punitive damages was not and was therefore equivalent in practical terms to well over $400,000.

Reynolds tendered a dinner to me, my associates, and to close friends who had shared his ordeal intimately. We met at a suite in the Carlyle Hotel to celebrate and cerebrate.

What was remarkable were the telegrams and cables which arrived from many parts of the world. Distinguished statesmen, actors, writers, and newspaper executives tendered their congratulations in emotional terms which revealed their pent-up feelings. Famous Americans from the Capitol in Washington, to the remotest regions within our boundaries (not excluding Hearst writers) telephoned to say how significant they thought Quent's victory was, and what a landmark his achievement would be for decent journalism.

The occasion descended understandably to gloating jests. It floated on a sea of camaraderie often experienced by those who share combat, and it rose to heights of mutual sentiment and gratitude. It was a perfect evening for Reynolds, who was at his best when he could disown his gallantry and generously distribute to others the praise due him.

One of my associates read a few sentences from the court minutes of my argument before the United States Court of Appeals: "The purpose of punitive damages is to punish and to act as a deterrent. Unless the damages 'smart,' unless they cause some pain to the defendants, there is no deterrent and no punishment.

"Reckless attacks equivalent to character assassination have become too frequent an occurrence in personal column editorializing. Newspapers are like cannon. They must not be shot carelessly and with abandon.

"This case afforded an opportunity to protect the individual from malicious libel; to inculcate a revived sense of responsibility in newspapers; to encourage the old tradition of checking facts, and to control reckless writers who build circulation by extremism and sensationalism."

In the succeeding months, I was besieged with requests to represent famous men and women in suits against Westbrook Pegler. The columnist, Drew Pearson, had a litigation pending and wanted me to become trial counsel. I refused, and have since refused all such overtures. I did not want it to appear that my representation was the beginning of a vendetta against Pegler, or that I would make a career attacking him or the newspapers which published him. Indeed, I advised Reynolds not to sue the many newspapers which had carried Pegler's libelous column, although each of them was liable in damages to him. A pursuit for more money damages would taint the ideals that had motivated him and me.

He could always be proud of the fact that he had fought for his personal vindication against great odds and in gaining it had scored a significant triumph for responsible journalism.

DIVORCE

Chapter Two

THE "WAR OF THE ROSES"

AND OTHERS

Litigations between husbands and wives exceed in bitterness and hatred those of any other relationships. I have represented defrauded business-men who fight their deceivers for fortune and power. I have seen them pour out their venom against their opponents until they suffered heart attacks or were ulcerated. I have witnessed struggles for the protection of copyrighted property, where the pride of authorship, being dearer than life itself, consumed the creative artist. I have seen public figures libeled or accused of wrongs which could wreck their life's work, strike back at their detractors. I have observed men with spotless reputations who were indicted, suffer nervous breakdowns. I have witnessed children sue their fathers to deprive them of their businesses, or brothers engaged in fratri-cidal contests without quarter. I have seen defendants in antitrust suits beleaguered by plaintiffs seeking treble damages or defending themselves against Government actions aimed to break up their enterprise, pains-takingly built over a lifetime. I have participated in will contests in which relatives were at each others' throats for the inheritance.

All these litigations evoke intense feelings of animosity, revenge, and retribution. Some of them may be fought ruthlessly. But none of them, even in their most aggravated form, can equal the sheer, unadulterated venom of a matrimonial contest. The participants are often ready to gouge out the eyes or the soul of the once loved, without any pity whatsoever.

A man whose sense of honor may be punctilious and whose restraint under extreme provocation may be admirable, will unhesitatingly insist on making charges against his wife which, even if true, would not be entertained by any decent man, particularly against the mother of his children. A woman who all her life has been kindly and gentle may turn so vengeful against her husband that she will write obscene and poisonous letters to his friends, create violent scenes at his office, confront and physically attack him in public places, have him arrested, and write anonymous accusations to the Treasury Department. Either may disregard their children's welfare by making them pawns in the battle, filling their ears with loathing for the other. There is no limit to the blazing hatred, the unquenchable vengefulness, the reckless abandonment of all standards of decent restraint, which a fierce matrimonial contest engenders.

I leave to the psychiatrists the explanation of the volatile transformation from love to hate. The chemical ingredients of rejection, jealousy, and possessiveness certainly play a part in the explosive content. But there is something more, a mysterious element, which unbalances the mind, changes the personality, and distorts the character. It derives undoubtedly from the sexual ties which, if profound and ecstatic, can never be completely severed. The mutual enslavement of love will not tolerate unilateral freedom. Two people joined together in intimacy are often like Siamese twins, the separation of one causing the death of the other. By great exercise of will, the rejected sometimes overcome the unbearable ache and readjust their lives. Even these go through an unsettling period that borders on the irrational. When one reads of a man of good repute and solid business judgment who has shot his wife and two children, or a woman of impeccable rearing and social status who has thrown acid into the eyes of her husband and then shot herself, the insanity of the rejected reaches its extreme manifestation. Short of such criminal violence, but stemming from the same acerbation of emotion, is the matrimonial lawsuit.

The lawyer is often caught in the fires that rage about him. The other half of the erstwhile union cannot of course believe that the gentle person of prior intimate experience has turned out to be so characterless. The conclusion is easy: "It's the lawyer who is putting him up to it. Bill could never do anything so rotten," or "It's the lawyer's scheme. Mary just isn't that kind of a woman." Since the lawyer should serve as a lightning rod, to draw the bolts away from his client, he must consider the injustice done to him a necessary professional sacrifice.

Litigations of this sort are begun by serving written complaints which set forth generally the cruelties or immoral conduct charged. These are inflammatory enough, but usually they are followed by a motion for temporary alimony. In support of such a motion, affidavits are filed reciting the history of the marriage and describing specific instances of cruelty, vile language, drunkenness, sexual aberrations, penuriousness, mistreatment of the children, interference by parents or relatives or whatever the charges happen to be. The incendiary effect of such affidavits upon the accused can hardly be imagined. The outcries of hurt at the distortions and lies fill the room. The war is on. The flames spread in all directions.

Then come the rebuttal affidavits! By this time the last restraints have been dissolved. The process is complete, like the symphony that begins with a faint wail of the flute, develops into a full violin section, is taken over by the wind instruments, and reaches a violent furious crescendo with thunderous tympani and accompanying trumpets which assail the eardrums.

The curious aspect of this progressive stirring-up procedure is that serious accusations may cause little pain, either because they are untrue, or do not affect basic vanity, whereas, some trifling charge may have an infuriating effect which grows and grows, blotting out all relevant matters. The lawyer's effort to restore perspective often meets with rebuff. "How could he say the house was always dirty, and that I was generally slovenly?" "How dare he say it was I who made him late because I took hours to primp and dress." "She's a dirty liar when she says I used foul language in front of the children. Why once when she lost her temper she said right out loud, 'Go and. . . .'" "What a nasty thing to say, that I left an inadequate tip and embarrassed her. That waiter had been insolent so. . . ." "He said the children were never well-dressed. I'll never forgive him for that lie."

There seems to be little relationship between the heinousness of the accusation and its effect. This is true in the artistic world as well. An actress or author may take umbrage at some comparatively minor criticism, while being impervious to the larger expressions of disapproval. Apparently the humiliation quotient is measured by inner sensitiveness rather than by external standards. A partial truth is extremely painful, while a whole lie can be disdainfully dismissed. Even in ordinary social contacts, this inconsistent reaction to criticism is often encountered. Who has not met the woman who is conscious of her ignorance and introduces every other sentence with "I may be stupid, but it seems to me . . ." or in reverse form, who is constantly protesting "You know I'm not that stupid! . . ." To correct such a person and expose her error is to strike a dagger deep into her, while one less sensitive on this score would merely consider the comment a minor phase of the discussion. How then can one adequately measure the pain from affidavits that assert sexual incompetence or cruelty, or unveil hypocritical poses of charitableness, or relate financial meanness toward parents or relatives, or in dozens of ways expose the false personality presented to the world which the accuser claims he or she covered up. There is a humiliation in such revelation which is bitter beyond belief.

We think of the skeleton in the closet as some really scandalous secret. But most homes are filled with little skeletons; the ordinary foibles and weaknesses of men and women; the conspiracy of lies to make an impression on others; the hypocritical poses for the outside world, which cannot be hidden between husband and wife, making one of them at least a silent partner in the deception; the dishonesties in word and deed of people who pride themselves on integrity; the crudeness and unsentimentality of the physical relationship, while in public there is the social grace of gallantry and love; the dignity in public contrasted with the contempt in the private relationship. These are some of the miniature skeletons that fill peoples' closets and are taken out for full airing in a matrimonial litigation. Even when they are viewed in their true perspective, they are hideous enough, for exposed pretense is an ugly sight. But when in addition, fevered imagination throws a silhouetting light upon them, so that they appear to be the enlarged size of their shadows, the retaliation charges and recriminations break all bounds of restraint.

If only the litigants understood that they had exposed themselves long before the legal papers were exchanged, they might feel less humiliated. One need only sit five minutes at the average dinner table to pierce the disguises, which some married couples believe they are wearing successfully. Across the glowing silver candle lights, shining with formal good will, one hears the hostess laughingly sneer at her husband's representations of himself either as a golfer, or good mixer of Martinis, or handy man with tools, or any other trifle. Perhaps he begins to tell a story, and she comments charmingly, "Oh, John, are you going to tell that one again? I've heard it a dozen times." His conduct may be no less revealing, like a good-humored retort that "my wife never thinks I do anything well, do you, dear?"

He may initiate the attack by shifting from an economic discussion to a homey illustration. "Women spend money as if it grew on trees. If they had to earn a dollar, they would appreciate its worth more." This is accompanied by a gracious grin in the direction of the wife, which is supposed to take the sting out of the comment. But she is beyond the influence of his charm, and the answering batteries are unloosed. "Some men cannot get over resentment at providing for the home. We work as hard as they do and are as important in building the home, but we are not as jealous of our contribution as they are."

Sometimes the discussions are in general terms, or even addressed to a third person, but no one is fooled. The generalities are about as unspecific as a poisoned arrow shot by a keen marksman.

The overwhelming impression is that of mutual contempt. It may take many forms, perhaps a pained silence as if the comment was not worth a reply, or a long angry look that says, "I'm too much a lady (or a gentleman) to answer and create a scene," or an exaggerated attentiveness to and admiration of the stranger in the next seat. The air is charged with corrosive bitterness and lack of respect, but such married couples believe at the end of the evening that they have carried off the masquerade successfully and that no one has learned of the inner strains.

The insidious encroachments of contemptuous language in private develop a mutual callousness, so that later husband and wife are insensitive to their denuding themselves verbally in public. The wife will casually shut up her husband, without realizing that she has unfurled a flag of her dominance and contempt, or he will angrily reprimand her for interrupting him. So they revert to their private habits without awareness that the company pose has been dropped for a fatal moment.

Although matrimonial representation is an insignificant fraction of my legal work, and although I have represented dozens of prominent people whose names we succeeded in keeping out of the papers, there were a few cases that blazened into fierce litigation and whose fires lit up the newspapers. I represented many husbands. Nevertheless, the large alimony awards or property settlements on behalf of some of my female clients created the impression that I was a partisan for wives, and their legal benefactor. I have been embarrassed many times upon meeting people socially, by having the wife announce joyfully, "I've often wanted to meet you. I told Henry, here, that you're going to be my lawyer when I sue him for divorce." The husband with equal insensitivity would counter, "I told her, Mr. Nizer, that I am going to get you first. You will be my lawyer, won't you?" These shafts of humorous flattery were supposed to be sophisticated banter, but what did it reveal about their marriage? How could a couple supposedly in love, speak blandly and with scheming jest about the demise of their relationship? I sought to ward off my embarrassment by suggesting that I would not represent either, because they were never going to let go of each other. But what a curious assurance from a stranger.

Similarly insensitive is the talk one hears around many a dinner table, in which husband and wife are so magnificently tolerant of the other's professed hunger for an exciting adultery that one is smothered in supersophistication. She wishes him good hunting. He hopes she will have a good time on her vacation trip, which she will take without him. Once more the self-revelations are vividly etched, but the participants in the discussion seem as unaware of what they are really saying, as if Freud were a German word meaning joy. Sometimes the drawing-room conversation crackles with outspoken jests by the wife about her husband's relative impotence. Bad taste aside, these are the gnawing revelations of the unsteadiness of so many marriages.

I would ordinarily attach no importance to derisive conversation between husband and wife. But when one considers the statistics that one out of every four marriages in this country ends in divorce or annulment and that almost 60 per cent of these are on grounds of cruelty, these gauche verbal displays may not be an insignificant clue.

Litigation contest in matrimonial disputes should be avoided like a plague. There are many areas for sensible resolution which can be successfully explored. Almost all such controversies in which I am counsel yield to the non-contest approach. It is the extremely rare case that runs off the track and heads for the courts, wrecking dignity, self-respect, and privacy in its wild run. This becomes the sensationalized case where the unspeakable venom of the litigants is set forth for millions of people to see as they look into the windows of their newspapers.

The Billy Rose case is a typical example. That situation, like many similar ones, demanded a quiet solution. Previously it had flared with lurid lights in the newspapers of the world. Joyce Matthews, the former twice-married and divorced wife of Milton Berle, had taken a trip to Canada with Billy Rose under the names of Joyce and William Rosenberg. A newspaper reporter had discovered the ruse. They returned hastily. Thereafter, she barricaded herself in his bathroom in his office-apartment on top of the Ziegfeld Theatre and slashed her wrists. Police arrived, shot open the door, and saved her. Rose is supposed to have said, "This is the time to have a wife. I am calling Eleanor." He later denied this, but she did rush to the scene and stand by him.

Shortly thereafter, on a Sunday afternoon, Eleanor discovered her husband and Joyce together again in the same apartment. Feeling twice betrayed, she determined to seek legal relief. Not only were all these events the rawest meat for voracious readers of the tabloids, but the dramatis personae would have delighted the owner of any marquee. Each corner of the triangle was studded with a star. There were Eleanor, a former Olympic swimming star, Joyce, the former wife of an outstanding television star, and Billy Rose, the former husband of Fannie Brice and on impresario and clever columnist in his own right. It was not surprising that, short of a third world war, the headline space of the newspapers would be reserved for the impending "War of the Roses," as they called it.

I convened a conference to stop the hostilities before they got completely out of hand. Rose and his lawyer, Arthur Garfield Hays, met with Eleanor and myself at my desk. What ensued is a typical explanation of why such disputes become contests open for the public gaze.

I proposed, as a basis for discussion, that Eleanor receive alimony in accordance with their past living standards, and that we then consider a property settlement which would be reasonable and well within Rose's acknowledged wealth. Before we could get down to a discussion of amounts, Hays, who was a distinguished lawyer, noted particularly for his admirable civil rights activities, began to express his views. Rose cut him short with a wave of the hand, saying, "Arthur, this is my life and I am going to do the talking."

I was even more surprised at Rose's statement. He announced that he knew the law. He had obtained an opinion from an outstanding lawyer (Hays was sitting next to him and took this, too), and that in New York State no property settlement would be granted by the courts. They had no power to do so, he told me defiantly.

I readily agreed. Indeed, I had already referred to that fact, but then pointed out why, so often, property settlements are voluntarily given and the public policy which approved them, as indicated by tax and other benefits.

He instantly declared that under no circumstances would he pay one cent as property settlement. As for alimony, he was similarly defiant. He proposed an alimony sum that turned out to be less than a third of what the State Supreme Court later granted her.

To set a friendly tone for the conference, I had announced in advance that we were not going to make any references to his conduct. We would preach no morals. Nevertheless, I was stunned by the aggressiveness and insensitivity with which Rose laid down the law. At least the occasion called for words slightly softened by guilt. Yet it was Rose's indignation, and not his wife's, which filled the room, and all with respect to mere money that was to afford her some financial security.

When the conference was over, I told my associates sadly that we had better batten down the hatches. We were in for a long, stormy voyage. It was not the disagreement on the money aspects which discouraged me. Far more definite pronunciamentos have been issued in the course of a negotiation, and then have given way to persuasion and reason. As a matter of fact, it was not entirely unlikely that Rose, who was noted as a shrewd businessman, might have taken this first stance for bargaining purposes. The reason I thought that a bitter contest was inevitable was his lawyer's attitude.

A client, particularly in a matrimonial controversy, is so emotionally involved that he cannot be trusted to have cool judgment. His lawyer must be firm and in full control of the case, or he disserves his client. The lawyer must not be dependent on his client's favor either because of fees or even friendship. What a man in legal trouble needs is not merely a friend, but a counselor. If a client is strongly guided by skillful and loyal hands, he has received also the most significant expression of friendship. Sentiment alone will not do. When the lawyer, in order to please the client, permits him to have his way, he may incur his favor temporarily, but they are both likely to be in trouble at the end.

Under similar circumstances I have taken my client into a private room and talked sense to him; I have advised him to pay a property settlement (over a ten-year period) and clean up the mess he had created; I have pointed out the benefits that would accrue to him from such a decent position (among which were the saving of counsel fees to me and the attorney for the wife); far more important was the peace of mind he would derive from being out of the courts, preventing publicity, and gaining, at least in some measure, the good will of the wife against whom he had committed wrongs. I have then used my skills to obtain the most modest but appropriate terms, and guided him firmly to a solution which never became part of a blazing court drama.

The Rose case, like many others involving more prominent participants, need never have become a public, knockdown and drag-out fight. Since only money stood in the way, it is not inappropriate to point out that ultimately Rose paid far more (including a substantial property settlement) than he could have settled for, and in addition, he had to pay accumulated counsel fees to distinguished counsel, a former gubernatorial candidate, Charles Tuttle, whom he brought into the case, and to me as Eleanor's counsel.

What might also have been foreseen was that Rose, in the course of running the show (an apt allusion because that is the way he must have regarded the matter, judging by some statements he issued), would commit legal and strategic errors galore.

The first test of strength was a motion for temporary alimony which we made on behalf of Eleanor. Rose demanded that this relief be denied completely because she was living in their sumptuous five-story home at 33 Beekman Place and had excluded him from it. There was much ado about the precious paintings that invested the walls, including a Rembrandt, and the risks involved in cancellation of insurance and otherwise if he were barred and limited to his Ziegfeld apartment or his 60-acre estate in Mt. Kisco, New York, called Roseholm. Also, he contended that she had accumulated great wealth from her former performances as a swimming champion at the Aquacades in Texas and New York and chiefly from his gifts. Being able to support herself, there was no need, his attorneys argued in extensive briefs, for temporary relief.

The philosophy behind the doctrine of temporary alimony is that during the pendency of a suit, the wife should not be starved into submission. She is entitled to necessities in accordance with her prior standard of living. It does not matter whether she brings the suit or must defend herself against the suit brought by the husband. In either event, the court may, in its discretion, grant her relief until the trial takes place. Then, depending on who wins the litigation, final alimony is granted or denied.

Temporary alimony does not therefore depend on the merits of the controversy. It is simply a device to prevent economic destruction of the wife while she is waiting for her day in court, which, with our crowded calendars and extensive intermediate procedures—a glimpse of which will be had in the Rose case—may be months or even a year or more away. In so far as temporary alimony is concerned, the wife need not prove that she will win the suit when it is tried. She need only demonstrate that she has a reasonable chance for success.

Temporary alimony in most states is determined on affidavits filed by both sides. There is no trial, no appearance of witnesses, no cross-examination. Since its purpose is to fill in the gap until there is a full-scale trial, the decision on temporary alimony is not conclusive as to final alimony. Sometimes, after trial, the permanent alimony may be far larger than the temporary award, or far smaller, or even eliminated.

Nevertheless, the court's reaction to a full-scale review of the contest in affidavit form has a great impact. Particularly so when Justice Kenneth O'Brien of the New York State Supreme Court granted Eleanor a temporary alimony award of $700 a week with the further proviso that she be permitted to remain in control of the Beekman Place residence and if she did not that she could apply for additional alimony to take care of an appropriate residence for her. The award was equivalent to well over $1000 a week and was hailed by the press as perhaps the largest ever made in New York State.

What could more likely make a defeated husband lose his head, especially if his lawyer was not firm enough to hold it for him?

Rose rushed in with a series of charges. Although he had conceded in his original answer that the formal allegation of his marriage to Eleanor was true, he bethought himself and asserted a new defense. He denied that he was legally married to her over the past thirteen years. Why? Because her divorce from her former husband, Arthur Jarrett, had been illegally obtained. He claimed that Jarrett asserted falsely that he was a resident of California for one year preceding his divorce, as was required by law. Therefore, the argument went, the divorce was defective, Eleanor was still married to Jarrett and her marriage to Rose didn't take. This attack was pressed with extraordinary vigor and resourcefulness. An order was obtained from the New York Supreme Court to take the testimony of Arthur Jarrett, who suddenly found himself neck-deep in a review of his California divorce proceedings thirteen years earlier. He was closely questioned about where he had lived, voted, paid taxes, and performed as an actor. Orders were also obtained for the examination of a former representative of the California Tax Department, of a witness in Texas who claimed Jarrett had told him he intended to become a Texas resident, and of another witness in California who worked for Music Corporation of America who booked Jarrett.

We insisted that these depositions be taken orally so that we could be present to cross-examine. The court granted our motion and directed Rose to pay our travel and counsel fees. Not only did we contend that, legally, Jarrett's divorce could not be collaterally attacked in New York by Rose, but we prepared a surprise for his counsel. Eleanor had not appeared in the original divorce suit, and a third party might therefore claim that the divorce was a nullity. We advised Jarrett to make an application in California to open his divorce proceeding for the purpose of having Eleanor file her appearance, thus conferring unquestionable jurisdiction upon the court so that no third party could challenge it. The California court granted this motion and amended the divorce decree *nunc pro tunc*, which means "as if done at that time." In the meanwhile, there were appeals to the higher courts and the skirmishes spread into furious engagements.

The blunder of Rose's move was that it alienated public opinion, to which he continually addressed his statements. For example, columnist Robert Ruark condemned Rose's attack on the validity of his own marriage as going against the grain of the American notion of fair play.

Despite the extensive publicity constantly given these moves, I instructed Eleanor to keep a strict silence. Occasionally, when the developments got under her skin—and what wife wouldn't be infuriated by the charge that she was never really married at all—I had to keep her morale up by a brief statement on her behalf. On this occasion I sought to strike at the vulnerability of the defense position by saying that Rose's accusation "was not only nonsense but would not rank high among the decent and gracious acts of the year."

Rose and his attorneys continued to scatter their shots in all directions. He launched a divorce action against Eleanor, charging her with misbehavior. He made other serious attacks on her. In support of his accusations, he filed an affidavit of a colored maid of one of their mutual California friends.

I had to go to the Coast at the time to conduct examinations before trial of Abbott and Costello who were then suing my client, Universal Pictures Corporation, on a contract claim. While there, I instituted an investigation of this remarkably belated "revelation" of incidents which were supposed to have occurred a very long time ago. The maid, who had only worked for Eleanor's friend for four weeks, soon confessed that her statement was complete fiction. The matter was referred to District Attorney Ernest Roll who obtained evidence that the statements in the maid's affidavit were concocted and false. On the complaint of her employer, a criminal libel complaint was filed and the California court issued a bench warrant for Rose's arrest. Since the charge was a misdemeanor (although punishable, if found guilty, by six months imprisonment or $500 penalty or both), no extradition from New York could be obtained. But the terrible revelation of the falsity of the charge caused Rose to call a press conference and accelerate the tempo of his battle for public opinion. He promised the press that as soon as the trial in New York was over, he intended to go to California and face the charges. He continued to belabor Eleanor as a faithless wife against whom he would press his divorce charges.

This was another occasion when we could not afford to be silent in the face of his public attack. Eleanor was tormented by the injustice of finding herself the accused in a situation which had become notorious because of the Rose–Joyce Matthews relationship. I assuaged her feelings with a statement that was designed to expose Rose's inconsistency and overcome any impact his press conference might have had. It read as follows:

When Billy Rose flew to Canada with Joyce Matthews, he registered as William and Joyce Rosenberg. At that time he posed as the husband of one to whom he was not married.

Later, Rose attacked Mrs. Rose's prior divorce from Arthur Jarrett; claiming therefore that he was not the husband of the woman to whom he had been married for 13 years.

Now he files papers asking for a divorce from a woman, who, he claims, is not his wife.

So, Mr. Rose, at the same time pretended to be married to Joyce Matthews who was not his wife; argued that he was not married to Eleanor Holm Rose who is his wife, and finally claims that not being married to her, he nevertheless wants a divorce from her.

Apparently he is somewhat confused. We hope the Court will straighten him out.

I suppose the reason ridicule has always been found to be so effective a weapon is that it is aimed at a man's self-importance, rather than at his logic. One suffers more from being exposed as a fool than as a knave. Even wickedness is not inconsistent with a powerful intellect. It may therefore feed the ego. Is this not why the cheapest criminal often glories in the public accounts of his misdeeds? But to be made to look like a fool is the most painful deflation of all. The impact of the statement which revealed Rose running in all directions at once must have been great. He understood instinctively the value of ridicule because in the next episode he turned it on her with consummate cleverness.

In his press interview he had asserted his willingness at all times to settle the controversy, but that Eleanor's unreasonableness had protracted the quarrel. She had charged that his "clenched fist" on a dollar was the only thing that had prevented a financial adjustment. He countered with the following statement to the press:

Eleanor is absolutely right. Compared to me, Scrooge is a philanthropist.

For instance, throughout our marriage we lived in a five-story house on Beekman Place with only one lousy elevator. The furniture was second-hand, designed by Chippendale and other 18th-century carpenters.

The old Crown Derby plates she ate off had occasional cracks, and the antique Paul Storr silver was once slobbered on by King George III.

The pictures on the wall were horrors—the works of hacks like Rembrandt, Hals, Velasquez, and Renoir. During the summer I made her rough it in a 30-room shack in Mount Kisco. This estate had only one swimming pool, only one tennis court, and a private movie theater with only one operator. On our private golf range Eleanor had to play with repainted balls.

When it came to servants, I really put my foot down. I refused to hire more than one butler, one cook, three maids, and two gardeners. What's even worse, Eleanor had only one personal maid and one personal laundress.

She only got $17,000 pocket money a year and I was downright mean when it came to motorcars. When she wasn't using the Cadillac, she had *to put up with a Buick station wagon. On some occasions she even had to ride in a taxi.*

Her clothes were mostly rags, stitched together by cut-rate seamstresses like Hattie Carnegie and Valentina. And sometimes poor Eleanor had to wear the same evening gown more than once. She only had 113 pairs of shoes, 41 sweaters, and 11 fur coats. I confess that at no time did I ever buy her an $80,000 sable.

I was particularly penurious when it came to winter vacations away from me. I never let her spend more than three months in Florida or Nassau, and when I took her on a trip around the world, I made her pay for her own postcards.

When it came to jewelry, it was all last season's stuff—92 different pieces which contained, I am ashamed to confess, less than 200 carats of blue white diamonds. When she asked me to buy her the Hope diamond, I trickily touted her off it by telling her it was bad luck. . . .

The logical answer to this philippic was that it was an amusing satire of his treatment of Eleanor while they were living together, but was no answer to the proposition that if after the Joyce Matthews affair, he had evidenced an iota of similar grandeur, no suit would have existed.

But this was no time for merely logical replies. The balloon of ridicule which he had so skillfully blown had to be pricked with one sharp thrust. It was this:

Mrs. Rose is indebted to Mr. Rose for having provided the evidence of their high standard of living, upon which permanent alimony will be awarded at the trial.

The incident was a good illustration of the errors a client can make when he masterminds his own contest. Also, this illustrates the wisdom of the rule that during a litigation, it is wise to keep one's silence. Self-serving declarations cannot be used at the trial, but if they contain admissions—with which Rose's statement abounded—they can be exploited by the adversary.

The controversy raged on. Rose's lawyers sought an injunction to permit him to take possession of his Beekman home and its treasures. The court denied the injunction.

By this time a feverish air of expectation had been built up around the approaching trial. Rose promised in all his statements that "if it is drama, the other side wants, I will give it to them." He threatened a full exposure, and proof of his many charges and defenses. We did not utter a word about our proof, but it could be anticipated that for the first time there would be a full revelation of the Joyce Matthews episodes. The daily newspaper headlines and feature stories had made this private conflict between husband and wife a serial for public consumption.

Eleanor dedicated herself to final preparation for her testimony with rare singleness of purpose. I had never experienced such concentration in a client. She literally went into training. She would not drink a cocktail.

She ate sparingly. She went to bed at an early hour until the last stages before the trial date when we worked late. I explained to her how to "walk in if the cross-examiner put a question which left the door ajar." She mastered the technique of responding on cross-examination and was insatiable in requesting further drills. The same determination that made her a swimming champion was applied to the unfamiliar task she now faced. Wearing her glasses low on her nose, in studious fashion, she wrote copious notes and trained herself to remember significant dates and the sequence of events which, without documentation, must have become a melted blur to her.

Vital witnesses responded magnificently to Eleanor's plea to tell the facts in court. None wanted to be involved in the controversy. Some feared antagonizing Rose. Nevertheless their compassion and affection for Eleanor surmounted their reluctance. When all witnesses had been fully prepared, I completed my own preparation for a surgical cross-examination of Rose and his witnesses.

Justice James B. McNally was the Judge who was to preside over the trial. Although he is taller and younger than former President Eisenhower, he bears a strong resemblance to him in the open, smooth kindness of his face, its sudden change to severity, the shining dome that seems to smile or frown according to the mood beneath it, and the clipped nature of his speech.

On the day preceding the trial, Rose and his counsel announced their readiness for a full-scale trial. This news was carried prominently on the front pages, as the excitement of the impending contest mounted. It was announced that 100 telephone wires had been installed in the courtroom for reporters who represented American and foreign newspapers. Only twenty seats were reserved for visitors, sixty having been pre-empted for leading publications. On the morning of the trial, front-page spreads announced "War of the Roses Opens." There were pictures, the width of the newspaper, depicting the courtroom, with insets of the participants and the Judge. One newspaper even went to the length of giving the history of the original Wars of the Roses, which lasted thirty years. On the morning of the trial, Rose departing for court, stated that he would tell his story on the witness stand. One newspaper reported he had twenty witnesses.

It was almost impossible to get into the courthouse. Hundreds of people crowded the entrance. We tried a ruse, getting in through the rear, but that entrance too was besieged by reporters, photographers, and a crowd of well-wishers. When we finally pushed our way into the courtroom, Rose and his counsel were there and had placed huge portfolios of documents on the table. It was all a bluff. Hays asked for a conference with Judge McNally. After half an hour, he left the chambers.

The Judge then sent for me. He advised me that Rose was ready to withdraw all his defenses, and counterclaims and concede Eleanor's suit for a separation decree, provided we would limit our grounds to abandonment and cruelty and not specify his conduct with Joyce Matthews. I told the Judge that if this case had not received the notoriety in the press which it had, this would be a satisfactory suggestion. But since the charges made against Eleanor were dastardly and false, and we were ready to prove them so, and since they had been given the widest circulation by Rose's procedures and public statements, we would not consent to any arrangement of withdrawal by Rose. He would have to surrender in open court and admit that he could not prove his defenses and counterclaims. We on the other hand were ready to prove our charges against him and desired to proceed.

The Judge advised Hays and his client of our position. We were called back into chambers. The Judge urged some resolution that would not require the submission of sordid testimony. His attitude was admirable and I was torn between my duty to co-operate with him in rendering a public service, and my determination to vindicate Eleanor against the unjust accusations that had been hurled at her. I suggested a way out of the dilemma. Let Rose not only withdraw his accusations, but apologize in open court for having made them. Then there could be no misunderstanding about her complete vindication. Otherwise the public might conclude that his withdrawal was not due to his inability to prove his case, but was the result of a mutual compromise. Rose indignantly refused to apologize. I then insisted on proceeding to trial.

All sorts of pleas were made to Eleanor and myself to relent in our demand for an open apology on the record. We refused to yield. When no alternative was open but to proceed with trial, Hays and Rose agreed to make the apology. There was some difficulty over the language, but finally the following sentence was agreed upon: "Mr. Rose expresses his regrets at having made these charges." I also insisted that the withdrawals be "with prejudice." This is a legal phrase which has magical properties. It meant that Rose would not be permitted ever again to make the same charges in any court. It is equivalent to a judgment on the merits which gives finality to the matter. Usually withdrawals of counterclaims can be made "without prejudice," which would have the opposite effect of permitting their reassertion at a later date. I would have none of this. The retreat would have to be unconditional and permanent. This, too, was agreed upon.

When we returned to the courtroom, Hays announced publicly and on the record, Rose's withdrawal of defenses and his claims for divorce against Eleanor, with prejudice. Then he read the apology.

In order to leave not the slightest vestige of doubt of Eleanor's victory and complete vindication, I moved to amend our complaint to include a new charge of cruelty: "The assertion of those . . . charges against Mrs. Rose and others constitutes grounds themselves for separation.

We ask your Honor to say this: That these improper charges themselves . . . constitute mental cruelty."

    JUDGE MCNALLY: "I will grant your motion to amend the pleadings, and I will hold, as a matter of law . . . that the making of charges of infidelity, where there is no proof, constitutes cruel and inhuman treatment."

We limited our evidence to this ground and abandonment. The Judge granted a separation decree in Eleanor's favor and set down for further proceeding the establishment of proper alimony and counsel fees to be awarded her.

At the end of those proceedings when Rose agreed to pay a property settlement, alimony and counsel fees, the Judge again confirmed Eleanor's vindication. He said: "Certain charges were made by the defendant against his wife, the plaintiff. Not a scintilla of proof was suggested or offered in connection therewith, and it is only fair to say there has never been any evidence of misconduct by Mrs. Rose at any time."

When we left the courtroom after Rose's surrender, she received an ovation from a huge crowd that filled the corridors and flowed out endlessly, it seemed. It is an extraordinary psychological fact about public reaction that millions of people will identify themselves sympathetically with one of the contestants in a court or political struggle. It is mystifying why one politician who is charged with moral dereliction or misdeeds will be destroyed forever, while another, as was the case with Mayor Curley of Boston, will be re-elected while he is serving a term in jail. Grover Cleveland was elected President after he acknowledged publicly being the father of an illegitimate child. Other candidates, accused of far lesser moral transgressions, have been defeated and their careers ruined. Jimmy Walker could sin and be cheered. A dozen others in similar position have been disgraced.

I believe that the key which unlocks the public's mood of generosity and sets in motion a rooting interest in the person who is beset with trouble is the ingrained American tradition of fair play. It is as trite as corn and as noble as the religious concept of forgiveness and understanding. We don't like to see people victimized even if they have blundered. Subtle distinctions, which one would think are beyond the mass mind, nevertheless play a part. They are instinctively made by the public. For example, the arrogant accuser is never a hero, even when we approve his achievements. That is why numerous politicians who did far worse than Sherman Adams were let off lightly. It was the fact that he was a martinet, the revelation that he had refused an official who resigned because of a scandal the opportunity to see and explain to President Eisenhower, which set so many people to cheering when he found himself in a similar predicament. He had been too holy in his stricture on others, and public sentiment turned against him.

In litigations that come to public notice, the winning of popular support depends on intricate, psychological factors. The lawyer's art of persuasion must encompass public approval, because, whether we like it or not, it may have real impact within the courtroom. This fact is recognized by the courts that permit a transfer of a case to another jurisdiction if local public opinion is inflamed and prevents a fair jury trial.

There are sharp professional restrictions on counsel against issuing statements to the press. These are sound, first because trial by newspaper is abhorrent to the concept of an objective, impartial trial, and second, because any commitment in the press may constitute an admission to be used in cross-examination or a revelation to the adversary. I have learned much from an opponent's garrulousness, while maintaining a steady policy of hoarding our ammunition for the trial.

There are exceptions to this rule, like all others. Even the Government of the United States, in instituting an antitrust or other proceeding, will issue an extensive statement to the press, not only asserting the allegations in the formal complaint, but giving a highly prejudicial statement of the seriousness of the condition that it seeks to correct or the relief it will seek in the public interest. The defendants may have other views. Must they remain silent while they are branded monopolists, exploiters of the public, or criminals?

Similarly, in the course of litigation, an adversary may issue inflammatory statements to the press. Must the aggrieved party hold his peace while public opinion turns to public contempt or even hatred for him?

There is another area of litigation publicity which is unavoidable and proper. The press has the right to report judicial proceedings. Each time an intermediate motion is argued, reporters sit in the jury box (a practice permited so that they can hear better); they give detailed versions of the arguments as well as the Judge's comments. Here, too, the public is conditioned in favor of one side or another even before a trial has revealed the full contentions of the parties.

My own practice has been to forbid clients to turn to the press to argue their rights. Before I undertook the "Bobo" Rockefeller case, it had been a daily sensation in the newspapers. The first statement made by Mrs. Rockefeller the day after our retainer, was: "I have been instructed by my lawyer to make no statement whatsoever. I intend to follow his advice."

In the Rose case we followed the same procedure of "No comment" at the beginning. But we were dealing with a master publicist in Rose himself. He had earned a reputation through his syndicated column for his pungent, clever, and breezy style. He employed it as we have seen, uninhibitedly, as a weapon against Eleanor. It was easy to maintain silence in the face of most of his barrages because they did him more harm than good. Almost any attack he launched lost some of its momentum before it got off the pad because of the reverse pull of his unchivalrous conduct. A man who is caught with the proverbial blonde is hardly in a position to take the offensive against his wife. Eleanor's loyalty had been proclaimed by Rose, himself, after the first episode. She was the understanding wife. It was Joyce Matthews who did not understand him when she bolted the door and used razor blades. How could Rose expect anything but public revulsion when he "discovered" that his marriage to Eleanor was not binding? This needed no answer. He was violating the gentleman's code, and this can be more deadly than breaking the moral code. It sets in motion that instinct for decent dealing or fair play which is the explanation for what would otherwise be the mystifying inconsistency of public opinion.

Similarly, his announcement in the press that he had changed his will to cut Eleanor out of it raised no fears in our mind as to public reaction. Aside from its retaliatory aspect, such a decision on his part was peculiarly of a private nature and should have been kept so.

One may be forgiven for announcing generosity, but how is public sentiment to be won for an announcement of "disinheritance," no matter how much within his rights he was in doing so?

However, whenever we sensed that Rose might have made inroads into public opinion, such as when he accused her of misbehavior or ridiculed her claim that he was penurious, we broke our silence for retorts aimed at straightening out the record.

I hope the day will come when a code adopted by the courts together with the press will make all comments by the parties or their counsel out of bounds. I once debated the English practice versus the American practice in this respect, at least as it applied to criminal cases. Editors of leading American newspapers opposed my support of the English system. Judge Harold Medina presided as chairman over this discussion held at Columbia University. In England a newspaper publisher and editor may be sent to jail or severely fined for publishing the picture of an accused person. The theory is that this enables witnesses falsely to identify the defendant. Nor will an English newspaper publish any statements by the district attorney or the evidence he is gathering. It will only report the indictment, if one is handed down, or the actual proceedings of the trial. True, this is a limitation upon the coverage of the press, but we must balance the constitutional right of the freedom of the press against the equally important right of the accused to a fair trial. It would be wise, in my opinion, to extend similar protection to litigants in civil actions.

However, until such effective procedure is adopted, I feel it is my duty in any litigation to counteract such prejudicial data as is published against my client. The lawyer must gauge the pulse of the public reaction skillfully and be sufficiently a psychologist to deal with this problem too, for in essence it is just an extension of the jury problem. No matter what the warnings of the Judge, juries learn what the newspapers and others say and may be influenced by them too. As Judge Jerome Frank once wrote in a case where the district attorney had been interviewed by the press: "He could just as well have telephoned every member of the jury."

For that matter, human nature being what it is, and irreverent though it may be to the judiciary, not all judges trying a case without a jury are impervious to the public opinion swirling around them, from the elevator boy to family at home, and from radio and television coverage to newspaper reactions, which may place the burden on them of swimming upstream in rendering an unpopular decision.

Another reason why I consider it part of my function to protect the public record, so to speak, is because clients are particularly sensitive when engaged in a controversy receiving public notice. If they are humiliated, shamed, ridiculed, or made to look contemptible in the public eye, it may avail them little that later they win. Furthermore, their victory may be limited to the relevant issues, but irrelevant coloration may be very painful and never wiped out. Also, such a client is undermined by the abuse and feels he has lost, come what may. He fails to function adequately in a contest requiring his courage and persistence. These are additional reasons why I deem the public opinion surrounding an important controversy a matter of concern in the all-encompassing strategy of persuasion.

By the time Eleanor, her friends, witnesses, and counsel reached uptown after leaving the courthouse, radio reports had heralded her victory. Some newspapers had rushed out with headings so large that they could almost be heard as well as read: ROSE GIVES UP or ELEANOR WINS. When our car stopped for red lights, some individual would recognize her and emit an Indian call, and crowds would assemble instantaneously from nowhere, to cheer and make it difficult for us to move again. I suggested that we proceed to the Algonquin Hotel for lunch at the Round Table, which we would take over on this special occasion. I ate there daily when not in court, and it would be an appropriate place to celebrate. We did so.

Jubilation and screams of congratulations came from all sides. Strangers, friends, and acquaintances crowded over the table to kiss Eleanor, shake her hand, and congratulate her. Feelings were so intense that many women sobbed. It is remarkable how hysteria can be engendered by what was after all a husband-and-wife quarrel. It was obvious that the controversy had been won even more completely in people's minds and hearts than in the courtroom. Wave after wave of emotional good wishes swept over us. They were deeply sincere, as if the triumph belonged to each of the onlookers.

In this atmosphere cocktails were served. Eleanor was no longer in training. She accepted one too. Then toasts were called out from all sides. They acclaimed Eleanor's victory and many of them were critical of Rose. Eleanor spoke up. Everyone expected her to join in the general hilarity. Instead she said, "I wish you wouldn't say those things about Billy. Despite everything he has done, I don't hate him. We had many happy years together. He lost his head over a girl, but that isn't the first time this has happened to a man. I think he did some terrible things, and I think he will be ashamed of himself for doing them. We have won. I feel wonderful. Let's drink to that and let the other things go."

This rebuke toned the guilty down an octave. I was full of admiration for her and said to myself: "There is no substitute for character, and there is no rule about where you find it."

What are the avenues of quiet solution for what should be extremely private disputes?

First, there is reconciliation. This may not be a desirable remedy in some instances. Reconciliation for reconciliation's sake makes no sense. Unless the parties have a reasonable chance to derive happiness from their reconstructed marriage, it is only a trap for continued anguish and ultimate explosion. A lawyer may be proud to have effected a reconciliation, but while the feather in his cap may be an adornment to his professional pride, it is the parties who have to go home and suffer with each other. I no longer advise any reconciliation without some procedure which holds forth promise of eradicating the cause of the breach.

Even the theory that where there are children, the parents should blindly sacrifice themselves to maintain a united home won't stand examination. In the first place there is a moral question of what the relative values of the right to be happy are between adults and children and whether the parents must be sacrificed for their children. Even if this difficult choice had to be made in such terms, and conceding the responsibility of parents for the youngsters they have brought into the world, we know that children learn to live their own lives, and ultimately become "selfishly" independent. This is as it should be, but what a disillusionment for the parent who has sacrificed a lifetime by continuing in a miserable marriage, or by not remarrying, to find that the child's appreciation is limited by the needs of its own independence and that a doting mother or father is actually a handicap to it? Grown people owe consideration to the lesser remaining years ahead of them, and even if the issue were a straight choice between their own and their children's happiness, I am not at all sure that the customary assumption of where their duty lies, does not need careful re-examination. Particularly so, since no one contemplates abandoning the children physically or depriving them of love.

Fortunately the choice is not as difficult as it appears to be. There is a second reason why reconciliation is not inevitable because of children. If there is one thing which child psychologists agree upon uniformly, it is that a child living in an unhappy home is more likely to suffer psychic injury than if the parents were divorced and the child nevertheless had their love. Having consulted experts on this subject, and offered the testimony of leading authorities to this effect, I have learned about the invisible antennae with which children are equipped. They pick up the slightest nuance of tone. A mere glance between the parents, registers deeply in their consciousness. Tensions, no matter how disguised, seem to leave their scent in the air and can be "felt" by the child. It is one of the mysteries of the human mechanism that even a baby in its cradle will be upset by the quarrels between its parents which have taken place out of its hearing and which they carefully hide when they coo over the crib. The scars left upon the child by an unhappy environment may be serious, or they may be overcome by a hardy personality. One never knows. But the risk, even though small, of the child growing up emotionally disturbed, with potential injury ranging from stuttering to homosexuality, and from phobias to insanity and criminality, are certainly considerations against reconciliation for reconciliation's sake. Even if the children's welfare were the sole consideration, they may be better off if their parents are divorced, and they have a new chance at happy environment, than if they are reared in the poisoned atmosphere of contempt between father and mother. A misleading factor is the tendency to hysterics and heartbreaking plea made by children when they are first advised of their parents' decision to part. Many a parent has been unnerved at the last moment by such a tearful and desperate outburst of their children and has returned to a miserable existence. What is overlooked is that most children are as resilient as they are sensitive. Their capacity to recover from emotional trauma is as remarkable as that from physical injury. Nature protects them, provided a blanket of love from both parents is wrapped around them. Who has not observed a child, stunned by a parent's death, recover with almost disgraceful speed from the blow? The strongest water power in the world is a child's tears, but it also dries up fastest. Children divert themselves by new interests with far greater facility than adults. The process of growing is all-absorbing. A divided home is a tragedy, but it may have less lasting effects upon children than the tragedy of a quarrelsome home or, even worse, of a home filled with the meaningful quiet of contempt and neglect.

So even where there are children, there should be no reconciliation without affirmative efforts to correct the relationship that has faltered and collapsed. Of course where there are no children, reconciliation should be clearly conditioned on some corrective measures. What kind?

This depends on the root of the trouble. There can be no generalities which are applicable to the complexity of personalities clashing in intimate relationship. But one is not likely to be far off base if he searches for sexual incompatibility or disinterest.

When I ask a client what she or he considers to be the basic reason for marital crisis, I will get a whole catalogue of explanations from interference by in-laws to miserliness, and from drinking and gambling to temper tantrums. But when I probe long enough, the real reason emerges, and it is almost always the sexual relationship. Indeed, when I am assured that there never has been anything wrong with the physical aspects of the marriage, and I can believe it, I know that it is virtually inevitable that this couple will get together again. The angriest vows that they will not tolerate their suffering another moment, mean nothing. These are the cases in which the lawyers learn one fine morning, in the midst of the proceeding, that their clients have made up and are together again. These are the cases in which the parties remarry after they have obtained a divorce. These are the cases where even the horror of physical beatings (a refined woman appearing in your office with bruised eyes and cut lips, as if she had been through a bout in Madison Square Garden) does not prevent her from returning to her husband. Similarly, where the sexual excitement is overwhelming, I have seen men of immense pride forgive their wives' infidelity time and again, and seek reconciliation. I have seen powerful executives who will not brook any disrespect from the mightiest, stand for insult and incredible public humiliation from their wives in order to hold on to the marriage. When there is physical love, faults are frequently unnoticed or they are deemed cute eccentricities and charming. When there is sexual disappointment, the slightest grievances are magnified and stored up as ammunition for the weekly outburst. One can almost read the chart of sexual adequacy by the trivia that irritate the parties.

So if reconciliation is to be effective, a healthy sexual relationship must be established or rehabilitated. This is not the function of the lawyer —though, for some reason, we are expected to be wise advisers about everything. Sometimes a client will insist on sharing sexual confidences with a lawyer rather than taking specialized advice. Women, particularly, are far less reticent than men in intimate matters. I always approach such inquiry with great delicacy. I explain that I am not prying and want no detail, but a few general answers concerning the sexual relationship with her estranged husband might be helpful. Almost invariably there is mature understanding, and an uninhibited revelation. Men, even the most sophisticated, will rarely respond with similar unembarrassment.

There are two approaches to the sexual problem. One is advice and treatment by a psychoanalyst, the other by a professional marriage counselor. In years past, I have tried the former frequently, and found it almost always unrewarding. In the first place, analysis is too extended a procedure. A marriage that has reached the lawyer's office can rarely settle down for a one- or two-year wait. The problem is urgent. Only where the sexual problem is extreme, involving impotency or homosexual drives, or female frigidity and incompetence, is the psychoanalyst preferable to the family counselor; then the parties may separate and await the medical result if they are so disposed. In most instances, the sexual problem is not as profound. It lies in the maladjustment, psychological approaches, techniques, and misunderstanding of the personalities and habits of the participants. Here a family counselor may be of real service, and the treatment is not lengthy. Sometimes six to fifteen consultative visits will suffice. While the percentage of success is not high, it is gratifying enough to warrant frequent use. It is not unreasonable to delay the divorce for a short time if the parties have any desire to salvage their marriage.

There are, however, definite conditions which must be imposed upon the husband and wife, or they will waste their own time and that of the marriage counselor.

I find it necessary to instruct the husband and wife, because they usually have no understanding of these matters. In the first place, a marriage counselor is not just a wise man who gives fatherly advice; he is a trained scientist in his field. He does not, therefore, approach his mission with a conviction that the parties should be reconciled. If the interviews should reveal that the marriage will continue to be painful and unsuccessful, he does not hesitate to so advise and recommend a divorce. Knowing that much must have bound the parties together, when they married, he seeks to reconstruct a healthy relationship. He does not prejudge, nor is he influenced by the general conviction that reconciliation as such is a good deed. The parties are not being lulled into more years of unhappiness. They are getting an informed judgment of the balance sheet of their marriage. I therefore urge resort to consultation with a marriage counselor, pointing out the added advantages of each separately, and then together, confiding in him without any reservation concerning their sexual incompatibility and otherwise embarrassing intimacies.

Secondly, and most important, no marriage counselor can be of aid unless both parties desire to save the marriage. There must be an acceptance by each of some responsibility for the failure of the marriage.

If only one party wishes to reconcile, the marriage counselor can be of no help. He must have mutual and voluntary desire toward reconciliation. Sometimes one of the parties—let us say the husband—does not want to reconstruct the marriage. In order to avoid criticism, he yields to his wife's entreaty and consents to visit the family counselor. He knows in advance, however, that he is merely going through the motions. He is like the Judge in pioneer days who announced that he would give the defendant a fair trial and then hang him. The husband is ready to announce the failure of the family counselor whenever the visits have concluded. Invariably the counselor will call me at the end of the first or second conference to tell me that the husband is acting in bad faith, that he hasn't the slightest intention of reconciling and that his co-operation is fraudulent. The patients are dismissed on the ground that the procedure is futile. Recognition by the marriage counselor of the patient's simulation is a confirmation of his skills.

I have had a number of remarkable reconciliations under a marriage counselor's guidance where detailed sexual instruction, combined with psychological insight, restored or, perhaps for the first time, created sexual harmony and contented relationship. In some instances the wife was encouraged to make aggressive advances, while in others the very opposite advice turned out to be effective. There are no universal rules. Personalities vary and sexual appetites, like other appetites, are subject to allergies, so to speak. One rule only is fairly constant. Where contempt and disrespect have set in, the sexual relationship rarely prospers. For that reason, almost anyone can read the sexual thermometer by observing the ordinary social and conversational temperature between husband and wife. Some women understand this instinctively. They are feminine-wise. They look adoringly and listen attentively to their husbands. They follow the inscription in age-old wedding rings, "To his virtues be kind. To his faults, a little blind." Even where their high regard is partly simulated, they are usually triumphant in their hold on their husbands. But in this day of independence and emancipation, women frequently forfeit their most powerful weapons, their femininity and their psychological dependence. They vie and compete with their husbands. They deflate his ego. The resulting trauma causes deep psychological reverberations, affecting the sexual relationship in profound ways. Then we expect the psychoanalyst or marriage counselor to unravel the mystery. My inexpert observation is that men are far more sensitive than women in these areas. The toughest businessman will wilt internally from the most casual and unintended assaults by his wife upon his self-importance. Women are a hardier breed. They will even prosper under domination. The reason? I suppose it is a basic rule of nature, and even the man-made or, should I say, woman-made doctrine of emancipation cannot abrogate the natural law.

A most amusing illustration of woman's real power and man's susceptibility to it was a cynical explanation once made to me by a client that she could captivate any man by a simple technique. When he spoke, she opened her eyes in wide wonderment, registering attentive admiration—while her ears were completely closed and she thought of her next day's chores. Invariably the brightest and most discerning men were victimized by her manner. She laughingly illustrated her act upon the next man who sat near her. He was an important executive and I am sure he prided himself on his insight and understanding. Yet he fell like a ton of bricks. He later asked me who the woman was, and remarked that she was quite fascinating. Men are vainer than women, and if their conversational feathers are admired, they preen themselves and strut on happily. Of course, a real love relationship is based on sincerity, but, as a lawyer, having encountered women who are desperately trying to hold their husbands at any cost, I am surprised that they are not more familiar with that feminine lore with which they are supposed to be born. The answer to the bromidic riddle, "I wonder what he sees in her," may well be that she seems to be seeing everything in him.

After every effort at reconciliation has been exhausted unsuccessfully, is a brutal court contest inevitable? Not at all. There are still peaceful ways of disposing of the controversy.

There are three kinds of matrimonial relief: separation, divorce, and annulment.

In a separation proceeding, one of the parties to the marriage demands the right to live apart from the other and not be molested. If resisted, this remedy will only be decreed if the defendant, upon trial, is found guilty of cruelty or abandonment or failure to support. This is the rule in New York and in many other states, but since the laws vary in different jurisdictions, I shall state the New York doctrine as a prototype. Cruelty, incidentally, is not limited to physical violence. It includes mental cruelty. For example, I have obtained separation decrees because a husband has taunted his wife with his infidelity and made invidious comparisons between her charms and skills and those of other women. The Court held this to be mental cruelty warranting a separation decree.

Similarly, I have obtained separation decrees because the husband continuously used vile and obscene language toward his wife or deliberately humiliated her in public, flirting with other women; or repeatedly denied her sexual relations, tormenting her as unworthy of him; or frequently became drunk and ignored her, or abused her parents and friends. All these constitute mental cruelty, and the catalogue can be as long as the ingenuity of man can invent to wear down his wife's nerves and health, without resort to physical violence.

In one case, my client testified that her husband had been particularly solicitous one night about her losing sleep, and had provided her with two sleeping pills. He also worried that his snoring might wake her, and therefore provided wax flints for her ears. Since she rarely used this equipment, his concern about the torment of insomnia raised suspicions in her mind which ordinarily would not be there. She took one sleeping pill, but her anxiety was such that nothing but a lethal dose would have overcome her straining nerves. In the middle of the night, her husband left the bed. She had one eye open all the time and she followed him. He was on the telephone, exchanging breathless love phrases with his blond mistress. He stole back into bed, his wife still pretending to be under the influence of his pills. Thereafter, each time he provided her with pills was notification to her of the strange nocturnal telephone intercourse. If he had sent her a telegram to be present, he could not have been more informative. It was not until she set forth the details in court that he learned how he had alerted a woman's fears at the very time he thought he was lulling her to sleep. The Court held he was guilty of mental cruelty.

In another case, my client described an incident in the hospital a day after she had given birth to her first child. Her husband sent no flowers or gifts. He came into the room in sullen mood. He did not kiss her. Instead, he berated her and demanded that when they returned home, her invitations to her parents and brother must be curtailed. A nurse overheard this tirade and testified to its accuracy. The setting for these words made them mental cruelty.

In another case, the wife, who had previously experienced false labor pains, cried out that she was in labor, and there was physical evidence of a pool around her feet, that she was in danger. The husband scoffed at her hypochondriacal tendency and would not drive her to the hospital. He was guilty of cruelty. Of course, in all these cases these were only vivid symptoms of a long existing disease, but they were the culminating evidence establishing mental cruelty.

The law has recognized, ever since a libel was deemed an assault and battery, that the sensibilities of a person can be subject to real injury. One has only to look at women or men who have been subjected to long sieges of mental cruelty to know that they can wither and show the effects of their torment more than if they had been physically struck. One of the piteous sights in matrimonial controversy is to look at a woman, haggard and overthin from loss of sleep and food, her eyes dimmed and rimmed with red because there are no more tears, quivering and shaken, although not a finger has been laid on her. Yes, mental cruelty is quite a proper addition to the grounds for separation.

A separation decree does not terminate the marriage. Although the parties live apart, their marital vows remain intact. Inheritance laws apply to them as husband and wife. Alimony awards, if the husband has lost the suit, will continue to be paid to the wife. If the husband has won the litigation on the ground that his wife has been cruel to him or abandoned him, no alimony will be awarded except for the support of children if there are any, or for her only if there is danger that she will become a public charge.

A divorce differs from a separation in that the marriage is actually dissolved. Either party may remarry after a specified period. In New York the only ground for divorce is adultery, although a marriage may be dissolved under the Enoch Arden Law if the husband or wife disappears for more than five years and is not known to be living despite efforts by publication to locate the missing spouse. Also, if a husband or wife is imprisoned for life, he or she is deemed civilly dead, and the mere remarriage of the free spouse terminates the prior marriage.

If the husband has been found guilty, an alimony award will be granted in favor of the wife. It will be paid to her until she remarries. Then it ceases, the theory being that her new husband has the responsibility of providing for her. It would be unseemly for the prior husband, by continuing payments, really to help support her new husband. In so far as alimony is concerned, there is no difference between a separation and a divorce. The degree of misconduct is immaterial. Alimony awards are based on the capacity of the husband to pay and maintain his wife in the approximate style to which they were accustomed.

The third remedy is annulment. The marriage is not only ended, it is held never to have come into existence legally. This remedy stems originally from the ecclesiastical courts which granted a *vinculum matrimonii,* and now comes down to us as an annulment of the marriage contract because it was induced by fraud.

The kind of deceit which will justify an annulment depends partly upon whether the marriage has been physically consummated. If the fraud is discovered before the parties cohabit, it will more readily be deemed sufficient ground than if intercourse has taken place. The reason is that if the wife's status has changed, public policy requires that she and any possible child must be protected.

In any event, the kind of fraud which warrants an annulment is the revelation for the first time after marriage that the husband is impotent or that either party is incapable of copulation (the woman, because of physical defect or excessive sensitiveness rendering intercourse impossible); or that either party concealed the existence of a venereal disease, or epilepsy; or that the marriage was entered into during complete intoxication; or where one of the parties concealed incurable insanity; or was under legal age; or was still married to another; or where the parties are within the prohibited degrees of consanguinity (parent and child, brother and sister, and uncle and niece); or was incapable of procreation.

However, courts have refused to consider as adequate grounds for annulment prior lack of chastity (though incest has been deemed proper ground), or misrepresentation of financial status. The courts of different states differ as to whether concealment of a prior pregnancy or even birth of an illegitimate child is sufficient ground for annulment, the dispute hovering around whether this sufficiently affects the new marital status.

Often the testimony in such cases involves sexual deficiencies that warrant the Judge in having the medical testimony heard in chambers where the traditional right of visitors in the courtroom is not observed.

There are two ways of obtaining a separation decree: either by litigation or by a written agreement out of court. So if this be the remedy sought, the parties do not have to go through a trial belaboring each other with accusations of cruelty or abandonment or failure to support. If reason can be maintained, the law permits them to settle their controversy peacefully by signing a contract of separation in a lawyer's office. Such a separation agreement provides for their living apart, alimony, and custody and visitation of the children. It has the same effect as if a judgment of the court had been granted after a trial.

Due to the public policy that marriage contracts are sacred, certain conditions are imposed on their modification. A husband and wife may not enter into a voluntary separation agreement or sue each other for separation if they are still living together. Only if the marriage has deteriorated to the point that the couple is living apart may they proceed against each other or sign a separation agreement. The philosophy behind this rule is that the law will not encourage interference with the marital status. As long as the husband and wife can tolerate each other under the same roof, they may recover from their quarrels and resume their marriage. Every obstacle is thrown in their path to prevent precipitous conduct which breaks up their relationship. Therefore, the complaint in a separation action must allege that the parties have been living in separate abodes, or the action will be dismissed. A separation agreement must contain a similar recital or it is defective. The law assumes that such physical separation establishes the practical fact that the parties no longer can safely live together. The marriage therefore has already been sundered. The law is only confirming what has occurred. It is not providing the legal device for breaking the marriage. In this way public policy considerations have been preserved.

Another condition imposed on separation agreements, which ordinary contracts do not require, is that the wife and children must not be left so penniless that they become public charges. Even if the separation agreement expressly provides that after a certain amount has been paid, the husband is relieved of the obligation to pay alimony—or because the wife has abandoned the husband—she agrees that there shall be no alimony, the clause is ineffectual if circumstances impoverish her and the governmental authorities are faced with the burden of maintaining her. She may then disregard the contract and sue the husband for support. Public policy permits this. This rule makes it necessary for the agreement to protect the wife against herself, and that is a good thing. For example, if she receives a lump sum, it should be so restricted that she cannot squander it at once. The husband will remain liable if she faces destitution. It does not matter that she may have brought the disaster upon herself. The overriding consideration in the eyes of the law is that the state must not be burdened with an obligation that primarily remains the husband's.

These are some of the legal tools available, but wisdom is required to use them wisely. What does a separation really accomplish for the married couple? If a crisis has arisen in the marriage and there is need for time to solve it, a separation provides an intermission for thought and reconstruction. Sometimes the physical violence or mental cruelty has reached a point which makes it impossible for husband and wife to share the same abode. The frictions and tensions mount to explosive pitch. Distance at least provides safety, if not enchantment. A full-scale effort at corrective reconciliation can then be undertaken. This is the first duty. Perhaps the separation will sober the parties to their responsibilities to themselves, their children, and their marriage and make possible a reunion.

Even if this cannot be achieved, a separation affords the parties an opportunity to think through their future more calmly and without the bitterness that derails their mental processes.

But a permanent separation, without more, seems to make no sense at all. It can only breed trouble. If the separation is voluntarily agreed upon without court contest, there may be a "gentleman's agreement" (fortunately it is never called a "lady's agreement") that each will ignore the other's adulterous conduct. This is, of course, contrary to law. Even then there is a risk that one may turn on the other, and in any event neither is free to contract a new marriage and build a new life. Furthermore, if there are children, they grow up knowing not only that their parents are not living together, but that each has other attachments. Children do not need critics as much as they need models, and what a precept both parents hold out for them under an endless separation agreement!

If, on the other hand, the separation is not voluntary, but the result of a suit, in which the wife, let us say, refuses to free her husband by divorce, then the consequences are even more involved and filled with foreboding. Since there is no truce—by virtue of a gentleman's agreement—neither party may commit adultery without the risk of detection. The husband, being frustrated by his wife's refusal to grant him a divorce, feels justified in spying on her to see if she has really resigned herself to a loveless and sexless life for the rest of her years. So while a separation decree does not bar her from going out socially, even in the company of other men, her conduct must be so circumspect that it is not only moral but gives all the appearances of being moral. She may not kiss her escort good night; she may not bring him to her apartment when no one else is there or at inordinate hours; she may not visit his apartment under suspicious circumstances. Not that these acts would be sufficient evidence of adultery in themselves, but they can, depending on their continuousness and degree of indiscretion, at least create an issue for the courts. The law does not require direct proof of adultery because it recognizes that intimacy is not readily to be witnessed. The test is "inclination plus opportunity" under circumstances warranting a reasonable conclusion that adultery was committed. Each case depends on what the jury finds when the irresistibility of the suspicious circumstances comes head on against the persuasiveness of the explanation of innocence. Decisions can be found of every conceivable shade. In one case the proof that the woman and man were seen partly unclad in the bathroom and were together through the night was countered by testimony that he became ill and she tended to him. The jury found her innocent. In another, a clergyman in a secret place was seen embracing a woman, but the jury accepted his version that he was giving his benediction and exhorting her to penance. In another case, under almost identical circumstances, the jury took a more skeptical view of clerical virtue. Of course, we are all familiar with Lord Stowell's opinion that the man did not visit a house of ill fame "to say his paternoster." The rule of probability is usually the decisive factor. It is a common experience for lawyers that juries which do not wish to brand a woman immoral—particularly if she is a mother—will disbelieve the accusations against her, even when they are supported by imposing proof. I have been the beneficiary of such rulings on behalf of my client. Also, I consider it one of the severest tests of a lawyer's persuasive skill to charge a woman with immoral conduct and make it stick.

Those who founded the jury system must have relied on the fact that jurors, being ordinary citizens, would bring to their judicial decisions the compassion and understanding of the layman, rather than the cold impersonal approach of the legally trained mind. We do our best to weed out sympathy and emotion from the judicial system. It is supposed to represent the impartiality of a bloodless, rational approach, but inwardly I think we all rejoice that justice is tempered with some mercy and that it manages to peek from behind its symbolic blindfold, perhaps even to wink impishly at its unbending guardians.

Despite this tolerant approach, husband and wife, living separately under a decree, are forced to live a furtive life, head turned over the shoulder at all times. If they are normal people, the standard of chastity imposed upon them by law is unrealistic. The premarital conflict simply shifts into the area of concentrated spying. The stakes may be high. If either party has refused the other a divorce, particularly in a state like New York where adultery must be proved, he or she is subject to attack if caught in a compromising position. Then alimony previously awarded in the separation action ceases. There are also the "satisfaction" aspects which, because of the burning feelings of frustration and revenge, are sometimes more important than the honor and money involved.

It is always a proper defense to a charge of adultery that the plaintiff, too, is guilty of the same offense. The law then refuses to give either party relief, leaving them just where they were, as if to say a plague on both your adulterous houses.

So the ugly game develops in which each side seeks to obtain incriminatory evidence against the other, if not for purposes of attack, at least to store up defense ammunition for the uncertain future.

Instead of a separation decree ending the relationship between the incompatible couple, it often only provides the stimulus for their watching each other more closely than when they were living together. The preoccupation with the daily habits, the going and coming of the "enemy," steeped as it is in growing hatred, becomes a neurotic task, devoid of self-respect and dignity. The daily detective reports are read with obscene hope. Councils of war are held to make the trailing more efficient. Sometimes the parties take affirmative steps to entrap the victim. If this can be proven, as I did once in a case in which the wealthy parents of the husband placed a charming gigolo on the pleasure cruise of the wife who was traveling to recover after a separation decree, the law will not tolerate the device. Yet, these are the sequelae from the stagnated waters of a permanent separation.

I am surprised by the unworldliness of some parents who are confident that their daughter will commit no indiscretion and therefore that she can hold out indefinitely under a separation decree until the husband makes a proper financial settlement. Young married girls, having experienced the joys of love, are particularly oppressed by loneliness. Being depressed by the failure of their marriage, and human nature being what it is, they are peculiarly susceptible to affection and will take the most grotesque risks when they find it.

I have learned this fact the hard way. In one case, the young wife had been reared by her nationally prominent parents in the best religious tradition. She was a brilliant as well as beautiful girl, having achieved some distinction of her own in science studies. We were in the midst of our legal proceedings against the husband for a separation decree. Due to religious conviction, divorce was not entertained. As always in such matters, I privately warned her to be extremely circumspect in her conduct. If ever I thought the instruction was unnecessary it was in her case, particularly because of her absolute assurance that, irrespective of the pending suit, the thought of immoral conduct would not enter her mind. Nevertheless, I went through the ritual of explaining the stakes involved and the bitterness of her husband and his parents.

One morning at three o'clock my phone rang. It was my client. She was in the most desperate state of all, complete unfeeling calm. She had just been raided by her husband and a squad of detectives. Pictures had been snapped and the technical identification question asked in preparation for the trial. She was in the two-room apartment of a man and alone with him when the detectives, like storm troopers, crashed through the door. She assured me that at least on this occasion, no impropriety had occurred. She and her friend were quite fully dressed. I could only conjecture whether the raid was premature, or too late, or wasted on the wrong night, or whether she was really innocent. When I got her to my office, I learned the facts in confidence and believed that the accusation could be defeated. But my first and far more difficult task was to restore her will to live. She could not face her parents. She thought they could not survive the blow. She was drowning in shame. I broke the news to them in another room while she sat in a stupor of fear in my office. Although the mother fainted, and the father looked worse remaining conscious, they responded with wisdom and deep understanding.

When they came into my office and enveloped their daughter with love and assurance, she took their embraces stiffly and without any emotion. Finally, she burst into hysteria and I knew all would be well. It was eventually, and her parents learned that they had a more wonderful flesh and blood daughter than the marble image they had created for themselves and in her.

In another case, a similar incident developed into a tragedy. This was a litigation fought desperately, as if to the death. The young wife was suing her husband for a separation on grounds of cruelty. The specifications were gruesome, including his lewd mishandling of their infant daughter. She desired a divorce, which he would not give her, and having very wealthy parents, a veritable army was engaged to track him down and expose his adultery. In a preliminary conference in my office, when I had attempted to prevent the controversy from becoming a litigious war, he had given a frighteningly neurotic performance in which, suddenly, he had broken into sobs, and thereafter assured me that any hope of obtaining the required divorce evidence against him was foredoomed because he could, without any difficulty, live a sexless life, and intended to do so.

Nevertheless, he applied more ingenuity in avoiding detection than I have ever encountered. He insisted on exercising his right of visitation by taking the child to a suite in a leading hotel. There he provided a nurse as well, but adjoining this very room was his mistress in a suite rented by his bachelor friend. Thus, he could always blame his friend for the woman next door while his presence was justified by the visit with his baby. I had never before heard of a man hiding behind his own child's skirt.

He was so alert to the possibilities of being trailed that he drove his automobile at the speed of five miles an hour so that anyone following him would be identified by the crawling pace. Even this precaution was not sufficient. He would circle around a block several times, and, as a final test, drive in the wrong direction on a one-way street. He seemed to have dedicated his life neurotically to the litigation, and I would not be surprised that his resulting inattention to his large business enterprises cost him far more than was involved in the controversy. But, of course, it was not money that spurred him on in the battle of attrition.

The circumstances were such that I had good reason to suspect she too was under constant surveillance. I issued the customary warnings to her. Her upbringing and demure behavior was such that I was sincere in assuring her that I had no fears of her misconduct, but rather that she must avoid any situation which an unscrupulous husband might distort. In fact, this was a case in which the scheming, mentally ill husband might attempt to frame her. She must be so circumspect that even a lie could not be foisted on her. She understood, and assured me that she would not go out socially with any man, even in the company of others, and that her life, too, was dedicated to freeing herself and her child from this wicked man.

Later she met a very charming, unmarried man with a responsible position in a professional office. They became friends and were even discussing the possibility of marriage if ever she could free herself from her husband. She had kept this respectable tryst secret from her parents and myself, but not from the detectives hired by her husband who could account for every second of her whereabouts. She forgot her promises about avoiding even the appearance of impropriety. One night after dinner, when her friend was depressed because his father was dying and he had just come from the hospital, he suggested that they go to his apartment where they could talk for a while before taking her home. When she entered his apartment alone, the warning signals went out from the hordes of observers that D day (I suppose standing for detection) had arrived. Within an hour the husband and three detectives, led by the head of the agency, opened the entrance door to the two-story building with a latch key and filed up the very narrow stairway to the room where my client and her friend, fully clothed, were drinking coffee. A downstairs tenant, alarmed by the unaccustomed procession, demanded to know who they were. The noise alerted my client's friend, who thought a robbery was about to take place. On his table lay an iron wrench with which he had placed his new license plates on his car. He seized it, and as the chief detective burst open the door, crashed the wrench over his head, breaking his skull. The heavy man fell backward, sending all those behind him tumbling down the stairs and through the plate-glass window of the lower door. The injured detective feared for his own role and refused an ambulance. Fortunately he survived, but he brought suit for huge damages against the young man who had protected his home from invasion. However, the incident and the resulting suit cooled the young man's ardor because he realized the involvements which accompanied a love affair with a married woman. She, on the other hand, resented the fact that his love was too feeble to withstand the storm that they had encountered. Even after she finally obtained a divorce, their friendship was never renewed.

But once more, the horrified parents and the guilt-struck girl presented as great a problem as the litigation itself. One simply cannot take for granted the dammed-up feelings of people and assume that they will act in accordance with litigation requirements. Such forewarning must be taken into consideration when the original strategy is determined, rather than after the event.

So it follows that a permanent separation is impracticable and unrealistic. It is a status of suspension without a clear ending in sight and therefore becomes bedeviled with mean retributive action.

When either husband or wife want a divorce and the legal grounds to obtain it are not available, what happens? It is not uncommon for such a frustrated person to shop around for relief among different states that provide more lenient divorce laws. Unfortunately there is a wide disparity among the states of the grounds sufficient for a divorce. If a chart were made of these differences in the fifty states, it would look like an unreadable crisscross of divergent reasons, ranging from adultery in all states to incompatability in Alaska and New Mexico; vagrancy in Missouri; crime against nature with man or beast, in North Carolina; mental suffering in California, Colorado, and the Canal Zone; continued absence in Connecticut, Vermont, and New Hampshire; violent and ungovernable temper in Florida; loathsome disease in Kentucky; leprosy in the Hawaiian Islands; wickedness in Rhode Island; intemperance in Arizona, Arkansas, California, Idaho, Wisconsin, South Dakota, Ohio; desertion in forty-five states; impotency in thirty-four states; and varying permutations, winding up with anti-cohabitation beliefs in Kentucky and New Hampshire. Until there is a uniform federal divorce law or the states among themselves pass consistent laws, these differences create opportunity to maneuver, to which desperate people continue to resort.

Let us suppose that a man falls in love with another woman and wishes to shed his wife. She refuses to institute divorce proceedings. Hers is the obstinacy of the rejected, than which there is no greater. Since they live in New York, he can obtain a divorce in court only by proving that she has committed adultery. She has turned all her passion to blocking him from marrying that other woman and has none left for any other purpose, even if she were so disposed, and she is not.

Suppose, then, that the husband goes to one of the favorite "divorce mill" states, Nevada or Alabama. The ground for divorce there is mere mental cruelty and incompatibility. This he can charge and attempt to prove.

He can institute suit in Nevada only if he has established residence in that state. He does so. Only six weeks' residence in a hotel satisfies the technical requirement. He then begins his suit for divorce. The wife is served with the complaint in New York. If she has proper advice, she ignores the document. The reason is that if she replies to it either by personally appearing in Reno to contest the action, or by filing a notice of appearance through an attorney, she confers valid jurisdiction upon the Reno court. Where both parties appear either in person or through a legal representative, the contention that the husband had established a fraudulent residence is waived. A divorce which is then granted in Reno, on the more lenient grounds permissible there, would be deemed valid in every state of the Union. Under our Constitution, each state gives "full faith and credit" to the judicial proceedings of every other state. Even though the grounds for divorce may differ, a divorce decree in another state which had jurisdiction over both parties will therefore be recognized in New York or elsewhere.

However, if the wife does not appear in her husband's action, if she just sits tight and ignores it, the husband will obtain a divorce decree in Reno which will be valid in Nevada but not in New York. Since Nevada did not have jurisdiction over both spouses, New York is not bound to give full faith and credit to its decree. It reserves to itself the right to determine whether the other Court had jurisdiction over both parties. If it did, New York may disagree with the grounds of divorce, but will, as a matter of comity, give recognition to that state's decree. Otherwise, it considers the divorce decree a nullity.

So the husband returns to New York with a piece of paper purporting to sever his marriage which is worthless. A unilateral decree in another state is an empty promise of relief, something like that noted producer's observation that an oral contract is not worth the paper it is written on.

The husband may return and wave the paper before his new "wife" with the same grinning expression of satisfaction with which Chamberlain held aloft the statement signed at Munich, but it is just about as binding. If, indeed, the real wife wishes to underscore her triumph and obtain judicial confirmation of the nullity of the decree, she can do so by instituting an action in the New York Supreme Court for a declaratory judgment. The Court will declare the husband's unilateral divorce in Reno invalid and that she is still his legal wife under the laws of the State of New York. If the husband, relying on the Nevada decree, should have remarried there, the declaratory judgment will also state that such marriage is invalid and that his wife, when he left New York, is still his only legal wife, for all purposes, including inheritance.

This analysis of the legal position makes it appear that the husband has suffered a total defeat (if it is the wife who went off to Reno because she wanted to marry another man, that she had).

But, alas, how different the practical situation is. It is really the husband who has achieved his goal, even by following an invalid procedure. Why? Because he can ignore the wife's Declaratory Judgment and set himself up in an apartment with his new "wife" right in New York. He can then proceed to live as if his divorce and his new marriage were valid. Technically, he is committing adultery, but the legal wife can do nothing about it. If she sues him for divorce, he is delighted to default, and obtain a valid divorce decree in New York. If she sues for separation on the ground that he abandoned her, he also defaults. In either event, alimony will be awarded against him, but he is ready to make such payments. They are not higher because of his defiance of the laws of New York. Furthermore, alimony payments are tax-deductible as an expense and, consequently, are not too painful.

If she goes to the district attorney's office to have him indicted for bigamy, she will be refused because, among other reasons, the crime, if any, was committed in Nevada where the second marriage took place. Of course, the authorities there recognize the divorce and the remarriage in their own state and will therefore not act.

If she asks the New York district attorney whether adultery is not a crime, she will be told that it is, but that for various reasons, a conviction cannot be obtained, and the criminal statute is virtually unenforced. Too many citizens would be under indictment if the law was literally pursued.

Even if the wife finds that there is confusion in the charge accounts of department stores because the new "wife" is using her married name, no relief can be given her. The courts will not grant an injunction against the use of the name either on the letter box or otherwise. The reason for this "hands off" policy is that it is an ancient doctrine of equity that injunctions will not be granted to order people's lives about, or which require continuous supervision over the personal habits and movements of people. It is a highly pragmatic rule. It is based on the philosophy

—which could well guide governments as well as courts—not to extend authority beyond the ability to enforce. An interesting corollary is a precept Napoleon is said to have laid down: "There is no higher immorality than to occupy a place one cannot fill."

Injunction orders are usually negative because then their violation is easy to determine and punish. So a defendant is directed not to interfere with a directors' meeting; not to picket a store that is not involved in a union dispute; not to grant special discounts or give rebates which violate the Robinson-Patman provisions for equal pricing; not to merge with another company and thereby create a monopoly; not to tie in one product with the sale of another so as to violate the antitrust laws, and so on. Even where an affirmative act is intended, the injunction order is usually couched in negative form, for similiar reason. For example, if a star has violated his contract and refused to appear before the cameras, the injunction order will forbid him from working for anyone else. It will not direct him to work for his employer, because it is beyond the sheriff's power, as a practical matter, to lead him to the studio and compel him to emote.

So, the wife finds herself without any practical remedy. She cannot sue her husband for open and notorious adultery because she would defeat her purpose of keeping him tied to her. She cannot stop him from representing to the world that he is married to another woman. She cannot even stop the imposter wife from continuing her disguise as the legal wife.

Not only friends, but even family and children, adjust themselves to the new state of affairs. They visit the betraying husband and his "wife." They go out socially. The wife displays her declaratory judgment. She asks the children to read it and understand the true state of affairs. But rarely does it affect their conduct. The sophisticated standards of the day protect the husband (or the wife if it is she who is in that position). People are not considered outcasts, or morally depraved, because they have sought a solution for their unhappy domestic lives. Sometimes, the sympathy actually shifts to the offending party, whether it be the husband or the wife. "Why does she act like a dog in the manger?" or "Why does he try to hold on to her if she doesn't love him any more?"

The only rights preserved to the wife in a practical sense are her inheritance rights if her husband should die. Then the legal position enshrined in the declaratory judgment comes into full play. But the wait is endless, and her life is frittered away while she keeps a degrading deathwatch.

However, there are offsetting forces. The husband's position remains uncomfortable even during life. Should he have any children from his new marriage, their status is beclouded. The new "wife," too, must live down her sensitivity to the defective status of her "marriage." Few women, no matter what their verbal attitude may be toward the "silly" formalism of marriage, can be happy in an illegitimate relationship. Having an eye for security, they look ahead to the future and see only the legal claims of the real wife when death has removed her antagonist. Curiously, the wife attains her rights symbolizing her closeness only when her estranged husband dies. If it is the wife who has obtained a unilateral decree and remarried, the pressures upon her are even greater. The unrecognized position of her future children casts a pall over her life.

To all of these legal considerations must be added an imponderable force of sheer nastiness. Many a woman, seeing her husband and his mistress cavorting around in fine restaurants and theaters, while she, the real wife, is shut out from life, takes the law into her own hands. She confronts her husband and his "floosie" (which is, of course, her word for the woman) wherever she finds them in public and deliberately creates scenes. Police are called. There are occasional arrests. But she makes sure that they do not live in peace. Her forays will sometimes extend to her husband's office, and the ensuing embarrassment is ocean-deep.

So the contending forces, legal, illegal, emotional and irresponsible, clash with each other until the amicable solution that should have been arranged in the first place is consummated. What is that solution?

Even where the reconciliation effort (including a marriage counselor's advice) has failed, even where a separation agreement, without resort to litigation, cannot be agreed to, a peaceful solution is still possible without a vicious matrimonial contest.

The parties can institute proceedings for divorce according to the local laws of their domicile. In that event the husband should agree to make his wife and children financially secure. The method and techniques for this are little understood.

First, let us look at the moral aspect. Often in these controversies it is the husband who seeks a way out of the marriage. He may protest that there is not another woman in the case, which is untrue, or he may have tired of his wife without any external stimulus. Whether I represent the husband or the wife, my advice is the same. I tell the husband that I have no right to preach morals to him and I don't intend to do so. If he won't reconcile and insists on changing his life in midstream, the least he can do is give his wife and children financial security. He cannot give his wife love, but it is possible for him to give her a nest egg, so to speak, so that, come what may, she will have financial peace of mind. He should make reasonable sacrifices to achieve this. It does not matter too much whether she, by her conduct, has contributed to the marriage debacle. Usually both parties bear some responsibility. For this purpose, I am not concerned with apportioning their guilt. It is the manly and right thing for the husband to accept the burden of financial contribution to his wife's future happiness.

If there are children, he and his wife will be obliged to meet in the future to discuss their education, to attend graduation ceremonies, engagements and marriage. Sometimes they must confer and meet because a child is sick. Their relationship ought to be sufficiently amicable to perform their future duties to their children without embarrassing them or each other.

A just settlement, even beyond the requirements of law, will be appreciated by the children as they grow older. Their respect for their father will increase. Their relationship will be healthier. A vicious contest in the courts, even if the father were to succeed, might cost him the high regard of his own children. The wife, given financial security, will be in a better position to marry and reconstruct her life. If she doesn't remarry, at least she is assured the comforts which will assuage her loneliness. She, too, may in time feel less rancor toward him. Sometimes, if his financial settlement has made it possible for her to marry again, alimony ceases. He is thus unexpectedly rewarded for his generosity.

I conclude by pointing out to him that he is at the fork of the road. He can either turn up a litigation lane, with all its bitterness, years of contest, demeaning publicity and continuous nerve-shattering visits to his lawyer and the courts, or he can choose the lane of peace and good will, deriving inner satisfaction from the fact that he did all he could, even beyond the law's demands, to make the woman who shared his life and bore him children, as secure as mere money could make her.

Having thus prepared the husband for the will to do the decent deed, the next step is to explain the practical means available to achieve it.

Many states like New York do not provide the remedy of property settlement. The court may award only alimony and counsel fees for the wife's representation. It has no power to grant part of the husband's general assets to the wife. Nevertheless, even in these states, public policy encourages the husband, as part of a matrimonial settlement, to give the wife a lump sum of money or other property to provide for her general security. This stems from the old concept that a woman who "has been used" and lost her blush of youth, has a much more difficult road ahead of her than a man. That is why the law in many other respects places a solicitous arm around the woman in matrimonial controversies. She is deemed to be at a decided disadvantage in rehabilitating her life, particularly if she has children. This, despite the recent startling skill of middle-aged women to look attractive, even if they have to run the gamut from therapeutic exercise to therapeutic surgery. Even more effective is their ability to make maturity, poise, and knowledge of life more than compensate for the lost vitality of youth. Some modern women have learned to remain young in spirit, to progress in charm, and hold the line in appearance. Thereby they have made the law's approach to their problems somewhat obsolete, particularly when they put their new assets to use in the business world and often compete successfully with men in earning capacity. However, the law is constructed for the average woman, not the exceptional one, and besides, it has traveled the road of justice for centuries and its pace is notoriously slow. Public policy continues to remain concerned with a woman's welfare in a matrimonial dispute.

This reveals itself in some very practical ways. For example, if the husband, in addition to alimony, gives a property settlement to his wife, the law rewards him with unique tax immunity. The money which the wife receives as property settlement is free from income tax. Unlike alimony payments, which she must report as income and pay tax upon, she keeps one hundred cents of every dollar paid to her as property settlement. The law wishes to encourage her getting a nest egg and makes this contribution to induce such arrangements.

For the same reason, the husband is relieved from paying a gift tax on the amount of property settlement given to his wife. If a happily married husband were to give his wife a large gift, the gift tax would be very sizable. So attractive, therefore, is the elimination of such tax from a property settlement payment that there have been cases where the husband wanted to give his wife a gift of a million dollars, and in order to save the gift tax of about a quarter of a million dollars, he pretended to divorce his wife and gave her the million dollars as a property settlement. Thereafter they remarried. Of course, this is fraud and if detected, the wife receives a lump sum, but the husband receives his lumps in tax and penalty assessment. However, this demonstrates vividly the tax benefits conferred upon a property settlement made in the course of settling a matrimonial dispute. In no other transaction that I am aware of, do such unique tax immunities apply. In no other instance can one of the parties retain every cent given to her free from tax, and the other pay no gift tax on the sum presented.

True, property settlement payments, unlike alimony, are not tax-deductible expenses to the husband. Therefore, as a practical matter, they must come chiefly from his assets. Here again, however, the law steps in to give the husband an encouraging push in the right direction. It permits him to pay the property settlement over a period of ten years. If the time is more than ten years, the payments lose their character as property settlement, and are considered alimony. Then the magical veil is lost. The wife must pay income taxes on the sums received, which, of course, reduces them very substantially. The reason for the ten-year rule is that if some limit were not put upon the time to pay out the property settlement, husbands and wives would always characterize alimony as property settlement. Therefore, the law retains the distinction between alimony and property settlement. One is weekly support for the wife and children. The other is a fund separately paid as security for her future. The husband may pay it all at one time or in installments over a period of ten years, but not one day longer. The time afforded reduces the husband's resistance to making such a sacrifice. He can no longer make the reasonable argument, that to dip into his assets for a large payment would deprive him of his resources for immediate business needs, or leave him too strapped to meet his own new obligations of furnishing a home and maintaining his own security fund. A ten-year period gives him an opportunity to pay in comparatively small installments. Even in modest situations, five thousand dollars a year for ten years, still affords the wife a sum of $50,000, untouched by a dollar's tax. In case of wealthy husbands, property settlements can run into many millions of dollars. Since property settlements may consist of other property than money, husbands have chosen to give stock, real estate, a garage, jewelry, paintings, and often title to the home and furnishings in which they live.

A property settlement may affect the amount of alimony which the wife is ready to accept. If the property settlement is large enough, alimony may be very small. After all, the wife can invest the money she receives and create her own income from it. Even if she is conservative and places her money in tax-exempt securities, she can still receive 3 per cent income therefrom. So the variations are infinite. If the property settlement is impressive and accelerated, the alimony is less; otherwise, it is more. As the property settlement payments are received over a protracted period, the alimony may be reduced according to a scale worked out in advance.

The wife derives a special benefit from property settlement in that, unlike alimony, it does not stop because she has remarried. Therefore, if the woman has a real prospect of an early marriage, she is wise to make sacrifices in the amount of alimony she is to receive and concentrate on property settlement instead. The former will stop when the wedding bells ring, but the property settlement payments will be due even though she is married for the ten years over which they are spread. Sometimes my female client is coy in confiding even in me that she is in love with another man and that a new life awaits her. Ordinarily this fact is of no concern to me. But when I explain the difference in strategy, depending upon whether she will be remarried soon, or there are no such prospects in sight, the confidential fact is quickly smoked out. I then know in what direction to negotiate. Conversely, if I represent a husband and, despite his wife's tearful denials, he suspects that another man's existence has something to do with their own miserable existence, I can learn the truth by either excluding property settlement or reducing it to a minimum. Since she knows that alimony payments will end if she remarries, her attorney offers to keep the alimony very low, if only a property settlement will be given. He might as well send me an advance invitation to the pending marriage.

A property settlement is justified by another consideration. In many states, the wife is vested with a dower right if her husband should die. This means that in New York, for example, she is entitled to receive the income from one-third of his estate if there are children, and if there are none, income from one-half of his estate. In either event she receives a

$2500 cash payment from her portion of the estate. If the husband leaves her more in his will, she can elect to take it, but even if he tries to cut her off without a cent, the law guarantees to her the income from the estate I have just described. The only exceptions are if she has abandoned the husband or he has obtained a divorce or separation decree against her.

The wife's interest in her husband's estate is a right conferred upon her by special statute. Without such a law, it has always been recognized that a man has a right to dispose of his property by will, in any way he sees fit. He can disinherit his wife, or their children, and give all his money to a cat and dog hospital. The test is not whether he acts reasonably. The law will not interfere even with his most unreasonable bequests so long as he is mentally competent and not the victim of duress or undue influence. Mental incompetency has been so defined by the courts as to require proof of his not being in possession of his faculties sufficiently to know generally the nature and extent of his property and the natural objects of his bounty, even though he may choose to ignore them. Mere eccentricity, neurotic behavior, and even emotional instability do not invalidate a man's will. Similarly, undue influence is defined to be such physical or mental pressure as to deprive a man of the exercise of his free will when he signs his last testament. It is really coercion exercised mentally. For example, a daughter refused to give her sick father medicines that would relieve his torturing pain after a leg amputation unless he signed a will leaving his property to her. This was held to be undue influence because the doctor's testimony indicated that his pain was so great that her refusal to relieve it was almost equivalent to holding a gun to his head.

On the other hand, the fact that a man leaves all his money to his mistress because she lavishes herself upon him, is no proof of undue influence. On the contrary, the law considers his gratitude to her an understandable emotion, no matter how much it may disapprove of it in a moral sense. The proof to establish mental disability or undue influence is so exacting that it is only in the very rare case that either of these contentions can be sustained. I have won such cases, but I far prefer to defend them.

Therefore, until the statutes were enacted to protect wives, a husband could cut off his wife in his will with impunity—except for her ancient "dower" rights in his real estate. Now, however, the legislature vests her with a right which even a will can not cut off. This leads me to the property settlement. These vested rights may induce the husband to enter into a financial arrangement with the wife under which, in return for a property settlement, the wife releases all her claims against his estate. In effect, she has sold her rights. The argument can be made that if the husband insists on paying alimony only, he is really buying his wife's interest in his estate without paying a cent for it. This is an additional justification for a property settlement even though the law in many states does not require the husband to give one.

Another technique to accomplish a peaceful settlement is to provide in the agreement that if the wife should remarry, the husband will pay her at that time a sum of money equivalent to five years' alimony—or three years or some other period agreed upon. The theory of course is that when she remarries, the husband's obligation to pay alimony is automatically cut off. Since he would owe her these payments for the rest of her life if she remained single, her marriage confers a great benefit upon him. For this reason, it is not unfair to give her an additional sum of several years' alimony. When I represent the husband, I often agree to this clause because it encourages the wife to remarry.

I have found, particularly in the case of large alimony payments, that the wife is reluctant to yield her permanent income for the sake of a new marriage. She may fall in love with a man of modest means who will be unable to maintain her in her previous style. Although she cherishes the legitimate state of marriage, she offsets this yearning with some hard considerations of the value of permanent alimony. After all, the income she would be giving up is equivalent to a valuable annuity. Being a divorcée, and therefore probably past her earliest romantic notions, security looms large enough to vie with sentiment. So in some cases she lives with the man who would marry her, but doesn't formalize their marriage. Since she is divorced, her prior husband has no claim upon her conduct. Only if there are children of the former marriage who live with her is her mode of life a proper subject for his concern. We shall see later how the law treats this kind of problem. It is a peculiar fact that after a divorce the husband continues to be bound to pay alimony to his former wife if she lives in sin, but is relieved of his obligation to do so if she legitimizes her relationship. Nevertheless, so it is, and the way to overcome this problem is to tempt her with an accelerated payment of several years' alimony if she marries.

A similar problem of income versus inhibition is posed in those rare cases where the husband disinherits the wife if she should remarry after his death. Does he hope to insure her "chastity" thereby, or really to doom her to an immoral love? The law has taken steps to prevent a dead man from stretching out his hand after death to control his property endlessly. He cannot direct its future beyond any reasonable number of lives in being plus twenty-one years. It would be even more appropriate to forbid a man in his grave from directing his wife's right to live a normal life on pain of money forfeiture. Jealousy is one of the least tolerable emotions even during life; exercised from the grave it is simply obscene.

One other legal requirement must be considered before an amicable disposition is made of the unhappy marriage. A divorce may not be arranged even by mutual consent. There is no inherent right to obtain a divorce. It must be granted by the local legislature. Public policy, which is concerned with good morals and the stability of society discourages divorce, although some courts have stated that society is "not interested in perpetuating a status out of which no good can come and from which harm may result." Nevertheless, the Statute of the particular state in which the parties reside must be scrupulously followed. In New York State, the scandalous practice has been engaged in of furnishing spurious proof of adultery, while the defendant defaults. No honorable lawyer will touch such a case. Neither should any decent citizen, no matter how grieved his life. Fraud is never a solution for any problem, and character should not be compromised by expediency. One can spot these collusive defaults from a distance of miles. Like any bad script, the rules of probability have been violated. Detectives take the stand to give the pat testimony required by the decisions. They always describe the corespondent as undressed, trying to cover herself with a sheet, while her nudity could be observed (they never even wear nightgowns in these melodramas); the husband, with only pajama tops, has opened the door because some-one knocked announcing he had a telegram to deliver. So the private eyes gained entrance. Then the classic touch from some of the early cases, "the bed looked rumpled and both pillows dented, as if two people had slept in it."

Some judges, fed up with the obvious collusion or perjury, have protested vigorously and dismissed these cases. However, these rebellions are sporadic. The courtroom set aside for default cases sounds as if it were a recording studio, making the same record day after day.

Instead of a six-week residence in Nevada or a twenty-four-hour residence in Alabama or Mexico, if the husband establishes a real residence in another state by the standards of the State of New York, then his suit for divorce becomes a real threat, even if the wife does not confer jurisdiction upon the "foreign" state. New York will recognize the husband's genuine permanent residence as a proper situs for the divorce action. The wife's default is then at her own peril.

It will not deprive the divorce decree of its validity, any more than if the husband, residing in New York, had begun his divorce action there and the wife had defaulted.

In view of the desirability of avoiding a rancorous court contest, why do husband and wife so often find themselves on stage in a courtroom enacting the most hideous roles?

Often a wife proclaims that she is eager to be rid of her betraying husband and that she would not tolerate him another moment if he came back sniveling with apology. She wants only full and complete financial security. She wishes to punish him in his pocket where it will hurt him most and assuage her pain in the only way it can be.

She doesn't mean a word of it. She is determined not to let him go.

Furthermore, she doesn't know it herself. She is quite sincere when she tells me that if she can obtain a particular sum as alimony for herself, trust funds for the children to provide for their schooling, camp, and rearing, and perhaps a property settlement in a certain range, she will be the happiest woman in the world because she will then be rid of a man who was never worthy of her loyalty and sacrifice. But as the negotiations proceed and we near the goal, she becomes panicky because of the possibility of success. She increases her demands. She is infuriated by some argument that has been made by the opposing lawyer. She finds new grievances which justify a change of attitude. She insists on punitive measures because some trifling incident has offended her sensibilities.

In one case, where millions of dollars had already been offered to my client, she went out one morning to buy some pots and pans in a local store. The proprietor had received the standard notice from the husband's lawyer, as did the department stores, and jewelry establishments, that the husband was no longer responsible for her accounts. He had been forwarding very substantial weekly alimony checks, and this was a legal precaution against larger liability.

She was so angry, that she insisted on raising her demands by one million dollars. Among the lawyers, this became known as the pots and pan incident.

In another case, the wife kept shifting and increasing her demands, and when they were finally met, she demanded the jeweled necklace of her mother-in-law. This, too, was delivered. Having exhausted her resourcefulness for harsh terms, she signed the separation agreement. Nevertheless, she decided later that she was withdrawing from it. She chose to brush shoulders with her husband even if only in a courtroom.

The fact is, of course, that these women do not wish to and cannot give up their husbands. Having been rejected, their pride induces them to say and think that they are determined to end their insufferable marriages. But emotionally, or rather neurotically, they are incapable of letting their husbands go. This unconscious resolution to hold on is lit by fires of jealousy of the interfering woman. While the wife proclaims that her sole interest is in a money settlement, she would really rather starve than make the contribution to her husband's happiness which it is still possible for her to withhold.

Such a frustrated woman dedicates her life to blocking her husband. If she isn't careful she may develop phobias of all kinds. I have observed one symptom that is common to some of them. They hold their heads straight when talking to you, but when anyone speaks up from either side, their eyes shift while they remain rigid. The impression is that of great suspicion, and indeed that is what it invariably is. Such a woman suspects everyone around her. She is constantly aware of plots. She sometimes gets to the point of assuring you that someone is trying to kill her, or steal her papers, or bribe your assistant.

It is a pity, because some of these ladies had no prior history of a persecution complex. Some are women of accomplishment whose charm and stability were never before questioned. The blow of a broken love can do extraordinary damage to its victim. Having learned by experience to recognize the mannerisms of such emotionally shocked women and men, I refuse their retainers, irrespective of the merits of the case, and even though it is within the limited ration of such cases accepted by our office; for I know that the relationship of complete confidence between lawyer and client is not likely to survive in the sick atmosphere of an overtroubled mind.

Another symptom of the neurotic client is that he takes to studying the law applicable to his case. His do-it-yourself attitude is almost as dangerous in law as in medicine. A layman who is obsessed with his disease and studies up on it in order to correct and lecture his doctor, would also perform his own surgery if he could. I like to explain every phase of the law to clients and why our strategy and recommendations are what they are. I respect the intelligence of the client and believe he has a right to know. It develops confidence and trust if he learns that there are no secrets from him. But it is wearing without being rewarding to explain to a client, who, having a smattering of recent self-education in law, pits his ignorance against my knowledge. Such a client derives a vicarious thrill from the fact that he is debating me, even if he "loses."

One day a lady of national prominence flew in from a distant state, by appointment, to place her marital difficulties before me. She seemed quite composed, though tense, and I sat back to hear her story and observe her closely at the same time. To my surprise she touched only lightly on the facts. Instead, she told me that her case was so involved because of the conflict of laws and other factors, that she had for two years made a study of the law applicable to it. She proceeded to outline the legal steps that should be taken to protect her interests. She took out a sheaf of notes from an ample handbag which was really doubling as a brief case and referred to statutes of various states where the litigation might win and the writs that could be obtained. She mispronounced their names, and was hopelessly confused about the law of domicile, residence, and the involved proceedings she outlined. I was so taken aback by the performance, that I stole a glance at my desk clock and decided to test her stamina as well as her learning. Forty-seven minutes later she finished her legal lecture. She sat back and waited for my reaction.

"My dear lady," I said, "we have no vacancy for a lawyer in this office at the present time. If we did, I doubt that I would engage you."

"Of course, I am not a lawyer," she said, "but I have studied my case because I wanted to be helpful."

"Helpful?" I replied. "You have been telling me what the law is for almost an hour. You have given me all sorts of advice, but, my dear lady, I am not in trouble. I don't need any."

I then told her that I would not accept her retainer and gratuitously suggested that she was in sufficient difficulty not to take on the additional task of being her own lawyer as well. She had neither the knowledge nor competence for the task, but even if she had, being emotionally involved, she would be the last person to have an objective view of the problem or its solution. There is an old saying that a lawyer who represents himself has a fool for a client; what is an adequate characterization for a layman who has himself as a lawyer? She needed able counsel, but more important, she needed one who would be strong enough to disregard her pretense of knowledge and guide her firmly. Of course, I knew while I was uttering these words that they were futile. If the lady had had sufficient judgment to accept such criticism, she would not have devoted several years to the neurotic activity of amateur studies in law. André Malraux recently gave this advice to a man who was on his way to a gallery to buy some abstractionist paintings: "Don't buy any. Do it yourself," he told him. The practice of the law is not so haphazard and undisciplined that it will ever yield to a do-it-yourself kit.

The woman who knows that she will not free her husband is much easier to deal with than the one who deceives herself and her counsel by insisting that it is financial security she wants and nothing else. One can attempt to reason with the former by depicting her life dedicated to the harassment of the man she hates, instead of to the rebuilding of a new and happy life for herself. If she rejects this advice, the legal war in court ensues. At least there is an honest acceptance of the fact that it is not within the husband's ability to avoid conflict by voluntarily providing sufficient money for her. Deep passions of revenge have taken over the arena. Such a woman remains in love with her husband and gratifies her feelings vicariously by holding on to him. It is the reverse of the psychological fact that a man will often be led to the pursuit of a woman by her flight from him. (He chases her until she catches him, goes the old saw.) It is true, even if it has become stereotyped in a thousand stories, that a change of attitude by the rejected, will sometimes stimulate a renewed interest. I have in mind one case in particular where a husband refused to continue the marriage. He had no grievance against his wife. Gallantly he spoke in the highest terms of her beauty, charm, and good character, but he was bored with her. The scenes in my office when they were together were heart-rending, not because of a broken marriage, but because she stripped herself of every vestige of pride and pleaded for his love. She offered to adjust herself to any whim he might dictate. She declared her love for him and was willing to accept him on any terms he chose to impose. Her sincerity was baptized in a stream of tears as she humiliated herself without any reservation. He was embarrassed and kindly, but hurt her even more by giving reasons why they could not be happy together. She was entitled to something better than his mere sufferance. She was young and attractive. He urged her to strike out on a new path in life and make some man happy who would be worthy of her. So the sessions went, she protesting her love for him and he suffering on her behalf as well as his own, but adamant.

I represented him, but advised delays, hoping that his heart would be softened by her desperate yearning for him. To no avail. He was pleased to offer her a substantial property settlement and large alimony. He wanted his freedom. After months of negotiation, she pleading for a reconciliation to the very last, a divorce was obtained on proper grounds in the jurisdiction in which they lived.

After what must have been an equivalent to a period of mourning, the wife began to thaw out from her numb self-imprisonment. Occasionally she would accept dates. She was seen by her former husband in theaters and she was smiling. She seemed to be having a pleasant time. Two months later I saw my client and his former wife together in a leading restaurant. Gone was the preoccupied look at the menus, the wall of silence between them, and the empty stare that identifies some married couples. They looked radiant. I greeted them and said I was pleased to see them together. "Oh, we are sorry. We should have told you. We married last week," he said. I noticed that when they left, his manner was not that of a man who was conferring his presence upon the lady, but rather that of an attentive escort. She, on the other hand, carried her head pridefully, as if it had never been lowered in tears.

The wife who will not loosen her grip on her husband is equaled by the husband who will not loosen his grip on his wallet. Each is responsible for the cases that explode in court. The most shocking illustration of a contest that was as unseemly as it was unnecessary follows.

The range of matrimonial proceedings is exceedingly wide. They may involve an infant of sure innocence, or an adult of ghastly guilt. The most incredible case of sexual aberration that I ever encountered concerned a foot fetish. Yes, I asked myself the same question, "What in the world is that?" The wife explained that her husband would make love only to her feet. They, and not she, were the object of his adoration.

She was a beautiful woman with sensitive, even features. The pallor of her skin and whiteness of her teeth contrasted with her black hair, which parted in the center and surrounded her face gracefully. She dressed elegantly, and her bearing was marred only by nervousness. Being intelligent and articulate, she was able to explain the nightmare of her nights with sufficient restraint to limit the embarrassment of recital. It required no insight into character to know that she was telling the truth. Her demeanor and speech were devoid of the hesitancy that sometimes accompanies inventiveness. Whenever she was tested for detail, it was so precise that despite its bizarre content there was no doubt of its accuracy. I later met her husband. Except for a general impression that he was a weak man, no one could have suspected the depths of his sexual needs. His frail build had a dapper quality. He was well spoken and courteous. But, as things turned out, I was compelled to cross-examine him for days on end. Then unfolded a tale out of his own mouth which would have made Krafft-Ebing blush.

He was represented by distinguished lawyers. I was therefore confident at the outset that this, of all cases, would be quietly disposed of and that there would never be the need to prove the horrendous charges. He was extremely wealthy. Her demands were modest, since she wanted to be rid of him. Surely there was no occasion for contest. His counsel soon learned that he was intractable. He denied the charges. He insisted upon trial. His lawyers acknowledged that our financial requests were reasonable and insisted that their client meet them or they would resign from the case. He refused. They withdrew. Other lawyers of high standing took their place. When they learned that their client wanted a public exposure of the controversy rather than a decent settlement, they too withdrew. A third lawyer of splendid reputation undertook the matter. He felt that it was his duty to try the case, since that was the condition of his retainer. However, he sought throughout the proceedings to stop the obscene revelations. So did the Judge. He threw the weight of his authority behind the pleas of all of us that the ordeal was unnecessary. The husband, timid in all other matters, was a rock of determination in this. He wanted to testify. He would have no short cuts.

Curiously enough the wife had predicted that this would happen. I did not pay her any heed, even when she explained that he would derive a special thrill from being pilloried on the stand. As he returned day after day to the witness stand, he was enveloped with excitement. The more I entrapped him and forced admissions out of him, the more he suffered and the more stimulated he became. I have never before or since witnessed such masochism and self-flagellation. It was a disgusting and frustrating experience. If it was our purpose to punish him for his stubbornness, we failed, because the more he was defeated, the more he enjoyed the torment.

When there was no alternative but a trial, I asked the Court to bar the public. Ordinarily it is an absolute right of a citizen to visit any courtroom he chooses. Indeed, the rooms are constructed to accommodate visitors on the back benches. This is no mere courtesy to wandering passers-by. It is an architectural concession to the Anglo-Saxon horror of star chamber proceedings, where justice, or should I say injustice, is meted out behind closed doors and out of the reproving gaze of the ordinary citizen. We jealously guard this right of scrutiny as a preventive of injustice at the source. It would be reversible error for a Judge to shut out the public from his courtroom. But there are exceptions. If the subject matter is so prurient that it would be barred from the newsstand or stage, then the Judge, in the public interest, may conduct the hearings in chambers, or in a closed-off courtroom. Opposing counsel joined with me in the request that the public be barred from the salacious testimony about to be adduced. The Judge agreed, and my guess is that this was the first great disappointment to the husband. However, later, the stenographers' minutes were filed and if he yearned for public airing of his conduct, his wish was ultimately gratified.

While the wife testified, struggling with embarrassment, he sat back in his chair alongside his counsel, thoroughly relaxed, with a bland look of interest on his face as if he were a spectator rather than the ignoble figure of the recital. Only his eyes gleamed. Their excitement had an obscene quality, and I was convinced that when he took the stand he would be too tempted to confess to be able to persist in denials.

My questions drew her into a description of events, as one leads a child into deeper water by gentle persuasion.

Q. Now, I am sure you understand by now that it is with considerable regret that I will have to ask you concerning some matters which ordinarily one would hope to avoid, of a delicate nature, concerning your intimate relations, but I want you to know that the Court understands and everyone else does, and it is a sealed session, so do the best you can and I shall try to be as careful as I can. We don't have to get every detail in, unless counsel insists later on cross. . . . Please tell us first . . . what was the subject matter which caused this difficulty in your relationship?

A. . . . My husband directed his attention and love-making toward my feet, which were the object of his love-making and not myself. . . . It was so bad that I just felt that it wasn't me at all that he was making love to; that I had nothing to do with it; that it was just my feet. I wasn't included in the intimate relationship at all.

Q. What did he do?

A. . . . It was a customary thing . . . for him to approach me by pushing his head under the covers of the bed and going on what he called a treasure hunt, which meant getting my feet and kissing them and caressing them and licking them and sucking the toes and putting them against his face. . . . He asked me to step on his face, which I refused to do. That was revolting—I couldn't step on a human being.

Q. What did he do?

A. And when I refused, he took my feet and pressed them against his face as hard as he could and particularly against his eyes.

His concern about her feet was fanatical. If she stepped out of bed on the carpet "it was very displeasing and distressing . . . to him, and he would go to the bathroom and get a washcloth and soap and wash my foot, and if I put my foot into my shoes, he would wash the inside of my shoe too. . . .

"When I would get out of bed in the morning, my slippers would be underneath the bed and I would feel with my foot for the slipper, and he watched to see that I wasn't really touching the floor. . . . First he washed my foot and then grabbed the shoe . . . and washed the inside. . . . He said I should never, never do that . . . that I knew this was terribly important to him and that I deliberately put my foot on the floor to spite him, and when I assured him that . . . I didn't like to wound him or offend him, and certainly I didn't like the . . . miserable times that followed such episodes . . . he said he believed that I did this to spite him."

Q. Did he tell you . . . why he did not want your foot to touch the floor before it got into the slipper or why he washed the slipper?

A. Yes, he said he didn't want me to touch the floors because they were dirty; people walked around in their shoes on the floor; they came from outside . . . and he wanted to kiss my foot, to put it in his mouth, and he did not want to have those germs in his mouth, that dirt.

Q. Now, was he concerned with any callous forming on your foot?

A. Yes, that was a matter of great concern to him. . . . He would take a razor blade and very carefully remove it . . . not exactly cutting, scraping . . . he would spend a fantastic length of time doing it so carefully that there was nothing but a little bit of white powder that was like Talcum powder left from it. You couldn't see a piece that was cut off, just a little white talcum.

Q. Where would he work on your foot to do this powdering, as you call it?

A. In our bedroom. I would be lying on my bed, with him sitting on the side of the bed, with my foot on his knee, and it was a meticulous and careful thing. . . .

Q. Did he tell you why he wished to do this?

A. Yes, he said he didn't want my feet to be rough and he didn't want me to go to a chiropodist to have it done. He said he preferred to do it "myself." He did not like the idea of a chiropodist handling my foot.

Realizing that the testimony ran so counter to common experience that objective evidence was particularly important to buttress her testimony, I had canvassed every possibility. Once, when she was abroad and they had to walk a great deal in the museums, he had taken her shoes to a cobbler, who had fitted two-inch rubber pads to the sole and heel to soften the impact upon her feet. I wanted them as an exhibit, but a maid, disgusted with their appearance, had obtained her permission to throw them out. Since she had not thought in terms of a trial, she had been unmindful of their evidentiary value, and out went a perfect exhibit into an ashcan. We had better luck in another direction.

Q. Did he ever ask you to . . . have any special cream . . . to soften the bottom of your toes or heels?

A. Yes, he asked me to get a cream.

Q. Did he send you to a doctor?

A. Yes.

Q. To get a special foot cream?

A. Yes.

Q. Did you go to this doctor?

A. I did.

Q. Did he prescribe the cream for the heels of your feet and the bottom of your soles?

A. Yes.

I showed her a jar with a label on it bearing the date, the number of a prescription, and the signature of the doctor. The name of the drugstore that had filled the order was on it. The prescription gave her name, next to which were the words "external use to heels." I offered the jar in evidence. There was not even an objection, and it was marked as an exhibit.

Q. . . . Were there any other practices he engaged in aside from those you described to your feet that were not of an ordinary character?

A. Yes, Mr. Nizer.

Q. You will have to mention it, please, I am sorry.

A. He also awoke me in the morning approaching my ear. . . .

I left several other revelations that were dragged out of her in implicit form only to await his denial. To my astonishment, and perhaps his attorney's too, he later blurted out his confirmation of some of them during his own attorney's questioning and before I even began my cross-examination.

In the meanwhile I turned to another instance of objective evidence. She had bought a reversible bath mat. He gave careful instruction that she should step only on the upper side and not on the one that may have previously touched the floor: "I had taken my shower and was standing on the bath mat drying when he came into the bathroom, and he said, 'Are you sure that you have the right side of the bath mat up?'

"And I said, 'Yes, I am sure,' and he said, 'How can you be sure? There is no way of telling which is the right side.'

"And I said, 'Well, I folded it with the right side and put it on the side of the tub.'

"And he said, 'You can't be sure, but now you can.' And he took the fountain pen out of his pocket and did like this on the bath mat to make an ink mark and said, 'Now you can be sure which is the top side and which is the bottom.'"

Q. When you told one of my associates this, were you asked whether you still had that bath mat?

A. Yes.

Q. Did you go back and look for it?

A. Yes, I did.

Q. Had it been washed in the interim? . . .

A. Of course. . . .

Q. Was there still some sign of the ink despite the washings?

A. Very faint, but there was still some very faint sign of the ink. . . .

Q. I show you this bath mat . . . is this the mat . . . that was reversible and had two sides?

A. Yes. . . .

Q. I ask you whether there is still a slight indication of the ink marking?

A. Yes. . . . It is in the corner.

I offered the mat in evidence, and there was no objection. It was received as an exhibit, and I awaited his denial or explanation on cross-examination.

She explained that he believed the consummation of sexual excitement was weakening. He had so been informed in his youth. This was the subject of much discussion and he was finally persuaded to ask a doctor. Although informed that he was wrong "he said that he still felt it was [weakening] and so he continued that practice."

Q. Before your marriage was there any indication of his, shall I call it, preoccupation . . . to a woman's foot?

A. There was nothing that impressed me as such at the time. It is only looking back that I recall things. . . . If we had been for a walk, for instance, and we came back, he would say, "You are tired. Your feet must hurt walking so long in high-heeled shoes," and take off my shoes and massage my feet, but I took this as a gesture of great tenderness, and it didn't seem to mean anything but that. It never occurred to me that it had any other significance.

After marriage, when she discovered that his interest in her feet was sexual, she remonstrated that his conduct was bewildering to her. He offered an explanation: "He told me . . . that when he was a small boy he and his sister and nurse went on a train trip . . . and that they slept in the same bed, and that he was put . . . at the foot of the bed, and he loved his nurse very much. She was very pretty and he was very attached to her. And he said he began to play with her feet, and she told him he couldn't do that and pushed him away."

Q. Was this his own explanation as to why he had this—

A. Yes. And he said that made him interested in them because she forbade—that it was like taking candy from a baby, that then the candy is desired because it is taken away.

His rationalizations of his abnormalcy were a lesson in the deceptive capacity of the human mind: "And then he said that was his weakness . . . that he liked feet, that people liked different things. Women might be attracted by a man who had mustaches, and I said, 'But that is a very different proposition.'

"And he said, 'Some men like breasts.'

"And I said, 'But breasts are sexual objects, it has something to do with love-making, and feet seem to me to have nothing to do with love-making.'

"And he said, when I protested that I didn't like this thing that he was doing to me . . . that if I loved him I wouldn't object to it.

"And I said, 'But love is a question of sharing something, two people together, and it seems to me if you love me, you wouldn't want to do something that was objectionable to me. I can't understand it.'

"And he said that . . . when I refused him, that was the worst thing that I could do . . . because that was aggravating it and . . . he referred to the same expression he used about the nurse, that it was because she refused him that it became desirable to him, that it was like taking candy away from a baby. If I would just give in to it . . . and if it was satisfied, it would just disappear of itself."

Q. What did you say?

A. I said it didn't sound feasible to me . . . but he pleaded with me . . . and so on occasion I would give in to him. But it didn't get better, it got worse. . . . It was so painful to me . . . I used to numb myself with alcohol to go through with these nights. . . . I then would get up . . . and walk all night long.

The various practices she was subjected to, which he considered erotic, but anyone else would have thought psychotic, wore her down. She lost weight at an alarming pace. Knots formed in her stomach and doctors advised they be X-rayed, but they turned out to be muscles rebelling against inordinate tension. Her stomach acted hysterically. To her physical decline was added disgust, frustration, and despair. She had continuous sobbing spells and thoughts of suicide began to intrude regularly in her mind. Then, in an effort to regain her hold on hope and life, she refused to submit any longer to his oral and pedal practices. Thereafter he waged a bitter campaign of economic retaliation against her.

Now that she was seeking a separation decree, so that she could, in the classic phrase of that remedy, "not be molested by him," he had compelled her to go through the ordeal of this recital. Several times she broke down in tears, after trying desperately to retain composure. The court clerks, stenographer, lawyers on both sides and the Judge showed their sympathy for her. Only the husband sat impassively, as if he were a disinterested, if not bored spectator of a drama that did not concern him. Tragic incidents sometimes evoke humorous anecdotes. During one lunch hour, when I wanted her to be able to swallow some food, and therefore endeavored by good cheer to lift her depression, I told the story of a fraternal lodge meeting at which a sick committee reported on its missions of mercy. The chairman told so harrowing a story of one particular family where cancer, polio, and poverty had struck all at once, that every brother in the room shed tears—all but one. He sat quite stoically through the impassioned recital. At the end of the meeting one of the curious attendees approached him and said, "I notice you weren't moved at all by the committee's report.

Everyone else was. Have you any special knowledge about the case? Don't you think it presents a truly heart-rending picture?"

"Of course it does," he explained, "but I am not a member of this lodge."

Judging by the husband's disinterest, he apparently was not a participant in the suit being tried. He soon learned he was. His lawyer put him on the stand. He was as unstable in his testimony as in his emotions. For example, he was asked whether his wife's testimony was true that he told her he feared sexual consummation because it would weaken him. At first he said he didn't recall such a statement. After lunch recess he was asked the same question and he replied "Yes, I had told her that I believed that that was the case."

On cross-examinations I asked: "Now, what happened during the recess which made your memory so clear that you had such a conversation, when before the recess you said you didn't recall having such a conversation?"

A. I refreshed my recollection.

Q. From what? . . .

A. I thought about it.

Q. You just thought about it?

A. Yes.

Q. In other words, did this happen more than once during this trial, where you would say "No," or "I don't remember," then if you would just think about it, you would remember it; is that the way your mind operates on it?

A. Operates that way very often.

Q. So that at any time that you give me an answer one way or the other, unless I give you a full chance to reflect, it is very possible that after the recess you may think about the opposite answer; is that correct?

A. It's possible.

Q. . . . Did you volunteer to your lawyer and suggest to him "I thought about it, I would like to answer that question again, so please ask it of me again." . . .

A. I believe I did.

Q. . . . How old were you when you had this conversation with your wife and told her, "Yes, that's true, I believe that an orgasm weakens me?"

A. About thirty-six.

Q. Then . . . she said, "Why don't you check it with your doctor?" Did you do so?

A. I did.

Q. Did he tell you this was nonsense?

A. That's right.

On direct examination he had denied his preoccupation with her feet. On cross-examination I asked: "Would you kiss her erogenous parts, as you defined erogenous?"

A. I would prefer to use the word stimulate.

Q. And one of the erogenous parts that you would stimulate was the arch of the foot?

A. One of them. . . .

Q. . . . When you were trying these improvisations of stimulation, did you kiss in order to stimulate?

A. Yes. Kiss, what do you mean?

Q. Any of the erogenous parts?

A. Yes, I would say most of them.

Q. Yes. Now there came a time as a result of your improvisation and kissing erogenous parts when your wife just dreaded, and you felt it, dreaded to have your love-making practiced on her? . . .

A. She certainly rejected me. That is about the best way I can describe it.

Q. She did more than just reject you. She started to drink alcohol right before you started your love techniques, didn't she?

A. She drank, yes.

Q. . . . Right immediately before it, she would start to drink, wouldn't she?

A. I would say yes.

Q. And sometimes her drinking was so heavy that she got sick and you couldn't make love to her?

A. Very often.

Q. Did she ever tell you that the reason for that was that she had to steel herself to these methods of yours?

A. Never.

Q. Did you know that . . . after she had submitted to you . . . she walked . . . through the night?

A. She did that, but I never related it to—

Q. You mean that you were unobservant about that?

A. No, she did that. She worried me very much on a number of occasions.

Q. That she would do after you had practiced your improvisations of titillating erogenous zones?

A. At this moment I can't say that I recall associating the two together, but you may have a point there.

He had explained his concern over his wife's stepping on the garden grass with her bare feet because she might contract a disease. I asked him: "What disease did you say you were afraid of?"

A. I think it is called hookworm.

Q. Do you know of any person in your life who ever got hookworm from a garden? . . .

A. It has been my understanding—

Q. Not understanding. My question is: Do you know of a single person who ever had hookworm?

A. I can't say that I know of any person, no.

Q. . . . Were you ever afraid she would get hookworm on her hands?

A. No.

In our search for witnesses, we thought the masseuse used by the wife might have some knowledge because the husband often lay on the bed, observing the massage casually, but thoroughly alert to that crucial moment when the wife would put her feet in her slippers. If she stepped on the carpet first, he would jump off the bed screaming his protest. The good Swedish masseuse confirmed the fact, describing how startled she had been by the first outburst and how careful she was thereafter. She shrugged her shoulders in an expressive gesture, as if to say, "There are all kinds of lunatics in the world." Just when she was all prepared to testify, she told us sorrowfully that her husband had forbidden her to get mixed up in this court contest. She was beyond entreaty. He would not even see us. We could have subpoenaed her and forced the truth out of her under oath, but we would not do this to the poor woman. She was distressed and under severe castigation by her husband for having "talked too much." We let her be. However, I tried to obtain the admission from the defendant on cross-examination.

Q. You used to watch very closely when that massage was over to see whether she stepped on that rug, didn't you.

A. No.

Q. Didn't you, to put it plainly, bawl out the masseuse because she did not bring the slippers fast enough, and she might step on the rug?

A. No.

Under pressure, his certainty melted.

Q. Are you sure of that?

A. I have no recollection of it.

Q. . . . Do you deny that it could have happened?

A. I think it extremely unlikely. I wouldn't know the connection.

The look in his eyes told me he was wavering. I surprised him by a sudden shift:

Q. The connection was you do admit that you marked . . . a reversible rug with ink to be sure it did not turn over on the other side?

A. That is correct.

We had obtained by this tangential question more than we could have from the direct attack.

He was an astonishing witness in that he would fiercely resist a minor accusation and yet yield easily on a major one. His obsession with sex had exhibitionist tendencies, but he was not too concerned when pressed for admissions. His denials seemed to be merely of a token variety.

I thought there was one element of excitement which he derived from testifying which was normal and which many witnesses experience; that is from jousting with the cross-examiner and scoring against him. However, his method was as immature in this area as in the rest of his personality. His idea of defeating the examiner was to deny a fact simply because the phrasing of the question included an adjective or adverb to which he did not subscribe. So if you asked him whether he was very angry on a certain occasion, he would deny it flatly, but after a long struggle he would admit he was angry, but justify his denial because he was not "very angry" as the question had been put. Such a denial is called a "negative pregnant" in law, meaning that it is filled with the possibility of admission. The phrase is ancient and its metaphoric allusion to pregnancy is a strange departure from the formalism of the common law. A pleader who denies an allegation of a complaint with a negative pregnant is deemed to have admitted it for all practical purposes. What a combination we were treated to—foot fetish and negative pregnants.

It took some time to discover the specious denials the defendant was making. Even his attorney was startled by some of the answers and registered his disgust when a long wrangle ended with an admission, his client smirkingly asserting that he had a right to answer the question the way he did originally because of the precise manner in which it was phrased. Once, when he answered, "I will deny what you say happened," I addressed him directly on the subject: "That is constantly your approach to these questions, and I would appreciate it, in all candor to the Court, if you would not deny a question simply because the precise wording is what you don't agree upon."

He smiled triumphantly, as if we were appealing to him to stop being clever. In his mind's eye he must have thought of himself as having outwitted the world. He continued his tricky denials until the Judge's patience ran out:

COURT: Why don't you tell that to Mr. Nizer? Why do we have to fence with every word?

A. I'm sorry.

This case presents as good an illustration as any I have ever known of the resourcefulness which can be applied to obtaining witnesses to prove a fact. How would one expect to find a disinterested observer of such an intimate practice as foot fetishism? Yet where the truth exists, it can be demonstrated in many ways if only the search is in sufficient depth, both in imagination and effort. We had found a splendid witness in the masseuse, but she slipped out of our hands. We had obtained objective evidence in the jar of cream for the heels and the marked bath rug. But the most exciting tracing of a live witness resulted from an idea that seemed remote in inception, but brought a conclusive witness to the stand. I had studied some of the literature on foot fetishism. It was not plentiful, but I noticed the observation that it can be an expression of a struggle against homosexualism. Such a person, it occurred to me, might take a great interest in his wife's clothes. This turned out to be a correct deduction. She could not buy a dress or a hat without his expression of taste and final approval. I thought therefore that perhaps while buying shoes or during fittings in the home the dressmaker, like the masseuse, might have witnessed some incident involving her feet. She could recall no such occasion. Besides, she said, almost all her dresses were fitted and bought in the leading department stores. Since her husband had invariably accompanied her on these missions, I pressed her as to whether he had ever protested her stepping on the floor in the presence of a dressmaker. She had no such recollection. I almost gave up this remote lead, when she volunteered that there was one particular woman who served her for years in a leading store and she did recall a quarrel with her husband. She would inquire.

She returned breathlessly to state that the clue was correct, but that the woman could not, under company rules, testify against a customer. The general manager of the store was a client of mine. I visited him and asked him to aid us in establishing the truth. He called the witness into his office, and when she told him the remarkable story, he authorized her to tell what she knew if she was subpoenaed. Indeed she was!

One can imagine the shock to defense counsel and the surprise to the Judge when she took the stand. As for the husband, he listened with dispassionate interest.

She was a heavy-set, middle-aged, gray-haired woman. Her friendly sales manner was frozen by the unaccustomed role she was playing. I established preliminarily that she lived with her husband in a fashionable apartment and that she was associated with a famous department store.

Q. What is your occupation?

A. I am in the designers' salon.

Q. How long have you been in charge of this department?

A. I am going into my fourteenth year.

Q. Has the plaintiff been a customer of yours?

A. For some time.

Q. Have you a room of your own where you fit dresses and show them?

A. Yes, I have a very beautiful room.

Q. Tell us briefly how it is fitted.

A. Well, I have very lovely drapes, a very beautiful gray rug.

Q. Is that wall to wall?

A. Yes. Flowers—

Q. That is sufficient for this purpose. Did the defendant ever accompany his wife when she tried on dresses?

A. Yes. Has on several occasions.

Q. Did anything ever occur that was of an unusual nature on one of these occasions?

A. Yes, something very unusual happened. . . . She was trying on dresses, lots of dresses, and her feet began to get a little tired and she wanted to get out of her slippers, and with that her husband said, very angrily, he said, "Oh no, don't step out of your shoes until —wait a minute, you have got something." And he looked at me and said, "Will you please get a towel for my wife." Well, as I didn't have a towel, I told him, why I would be willing, I would go out and get some tissues, tissue paper. The packing desk is not too far from my room. So I went out and I brought in a few pieces of the paper.

Q. What did you do with it?

A. Put it on the floor, and then at that time she naturally stepped out of the slippers onto the tissues.

Q. Then she continued to try on her dress?

A. Naturally.

Q. When she got through was there anything unusual before she got into the slippers? Did she step on the rug?

A. Oh no. Her husband did not want her to step on the rug at all. I am sort of proud of that room because it is a lovely room and it is kept very well because there is someone in there every day to keep it.

Q. Did she have stockings on?

A. Oh yes, she always wore stockings.

Q. Did this happen on more than one occasion?

A. Yes, it did.

Q. Throughout the period of time can you give us approximately, if you remember, how many times that her husband wanted you to get this tissue paper?

A. A couple of times.

Q. Although he came in more than that?

A. Yes, he did. But then I would naturally go and get it and bring it in. After all, they are my customers, and you do that.

NIZER: That is all.

There was no cross-examination.

The Judge decided the case in favor of the wife. He made findings to the effect that the husband had subjected the wife against her will and continued opposition to various unnatural and aberrational erotic practices, that she rejected him with the aid of self-anesthetization by drink, that he then would indulge in temper tantrums and "punish" her with protracted periods of silence and non-communication. He awarded her substantial alimony and counsel fees. Later they were divorced and he paid a larger sum than his prior counsel had pleaded with him to pay and avoid exposure at trial.

Such are the labyrinthian mysteries of human frailty that the husband probably considered it worthwhile to pay an extra sum to have the excitement of sitting on a witness stand and being dissected for all to see the darkness within.

The most shattering moments in life are sometimes purely reflective. The realization suddenly dawns that one has been defeated by life. Some incident, which may not be tragic, sets the mind to work. Then there is conjured up a picture of frustration and emptiness, and the emotions are overwhelmed by the image as if it were the external reality.

No one can reach into the brain of a person a moment before he commits suicide, but I imagine that if we could, we would find in many instances that it was such a distorted conclusion of utter failure and futility which triggered the crime against himself. I use the word distorted because a crisis is only as desperate as an alarmed imagination will make it, and only as temporary as a courageous perspective will compel it to be.

So a man who has held a responsible position in a firm for many years and loses his job, let us say, because his company has gone out of business, and who cannot obtain employment because of his age, may suddenly conclude that he is too old to be useful and that his lifetime of accumulated experience has turned out to be a waste. According to this picture which he paints in his despondent mind, nothing is left but to become a charge upon the city charities or his children. He is suddenly overwhelmed by his plight, which in essence is nothing more than a customary difficulty of getting a job. He may be driven by his exaggerated notion of disgrace to what I would call a nerveless breakdown, or even to an escape from life itself.

The circumstances may vary. Sometimes it is a man of achievement who has gained public recognition and enjoys a prideful status. He runs into a non-productive period. His assets run out and he is forced to consider tapping a friend for a loan. In itself, it is not a critical matter, for as sure as fate, he will work his way out of his financial depression. But at the moment, when he must confess to his surprised friend that he has no money for his rent and needs help, the realization of the state he has sunk to can suddenly unnerve him and make him burst into a flood of unmanly tears.

There may be a blank wall which has nothing to do with money. A wealthy actress may discover that she is no longer in great demand. Instead of recognizing the normal process of her graduation from ingénue status by sheer passage of time and turning her talents to more mature roles or, indeed, away from the stage, she sprouts a picture in her mind of youth having passed her by, of permanent relegation to a has-been existence, of a life empty of admiration and love, without even the echoes of applause. Desperation and a distorted personality may take over. This may become the item of the unaccountable sleeping pill dose. The newspapers ruminate about the mystery. She was rich, beautiful, in good health, and had many friends. There was no disappointment in love. What they do not evaluate is the false image in her mind which closed the door to reality.

I recall how astonished I was by the reaction of a famous vaudeville star who had commanded at least $5000 a week whenever she wished to bestow her favor upon a theater chain. She was offered only $3500 a week, and indignantly rejected the insult. Her agent sorrowfully informed her that another star had been engaged. She was stunned. Then the pictures began to form in her mind of the significance of the incident. Actually it only meant that business was poorer and she was older, but her inflamed mind concluded either that her agent had betrayed her in favor of another client or, worse, that her artistic career had come to an end. There was nothing more to live for. She sank into a mental morass dug by her own misinterpretation of events.

For the same reason even the advent of certain birthdays has a depressing impact. Usually it is the birthday which marks a decade, like thirty, forty, or fifty. After all, the forty-ninth or fifty-first year is not much different from the fiftieth. But there is something about the even number that induces the taking of life inventory. Suddenly all the prior years are telescoped into one conclusion. This results from an acceleration of judgment rather than an objective appraisal. It leads to lugubrious thoughts. "My life is three quarters gone, and where am I?" The rhetorical question may be burdened with thoughts of youth frittered away, health uncertain, beauty or handsomeness fading, and the future only an extension of the decline. The reality may be a healthy balance, for there is growth of personality and development of character, a family established, and the wonder of the approaching vintage years. It all depends on the perspective. There is a chemical power in numbers. Whether it be thirty or sixty, the mind is stimulated to sum up and the emotions to count down.

Similarly, a man or woman who visits a lawyer to present a matrimonial problem is often overwhelmed by the sudden realization of what has happened to love, home, and family. Such a woman may enter my office jauntily and greet me with a gay smile as she sits down to begin the interview. Then the fact that she is in a lawyer's office to discuss the breakdown of her marriage suddenly has its impact. So this is what she has finally come to. Her whole life presses in on her in one moment. Her mind goes back to sweet love, the bridal gown dreamed of since she was ten, the hail of rice happily dodged, the honeymoon when torrents of passion and gentle sweetness vied with each other, the founding of a home with the protracted joys of new acquisitions, the ecstatic agony of childbirth, the unfolding of her child's personality with its humors and charms, the unbearable worry of illnesses, the graduation ceremony when she saw only one child cameoed out from all the others, and then the more prosperous years of better living and travel, the personal excitement shrinking to disinterest, the suspicion of faithlessness sensed from innumerable trivia, and finally the open breach, as if she and her husband were only two partners in a business enterprise who could part, and not two lives interwoven in each other's flesh and thoughts and from which other lives of their bones and blood have miraculously been created, and as if intimacy did not create its own possessiveness so that they and their children belonged to each other and could not be separated. It is all incredible. The final persuasion is the surroundings. She is in a lawyer's office; her home has collapsed. She wants to speak, but her lips quiver, the shoulders heave, and then, despite all efforts at self-control, there is a violent outburst of sobbing. It has all been provoked by the explosive realization of the last step. But, of course, it is an accumulation of nights in which sleep has been displaced by search into memory for explanation, of waking from momentary naps of exhaustion with a pressured feeling around the heart to remind her, before consciousness does, that she is miserable, of days filled with tears that flow unaccountably even when the mind is on daily chores, of living in a fog of despair.

Sometimes these feelings are repressed by sheer determination, so that the exterior appears calm. But the voice is the least subject to discipline. It trembles and fades. It, as well as the eyes, can cry. Usually the first mention of the children causes the emotions to batter down all ramparts of restraint. There is a sudden silence, as if a flood had cut off communication, a struggle of the facial muscles—and then surrender to hysteria.

I consider it a lawyer's task to bring calm and confidence to the distressed client. Almost everyone who comes to a law office is emotionally affected by a problem. It is only a matter of degree and of the client's inner resources to withstand the pressure. Men are as prone as women to become unnerved. They usually hide their concern more effectively, but the toll may therefore be greater. The tension of self-restraint is so great that it presents physical symptoms, such as circulatory interference resulting either in unnatural pallor or fiery-colored skin, twitches of muscles, clenched hands which quiver when they open to light a cigarette, a tapping or swinging foot, as if keeping time to discordant music within, and, of course, the always revealing voice, dammed up with hoarseness, which will not be cleared.

No matter how serious the problem really is, the client usually enlarges it. The distortion is the chief enervating factor. If it can be removed and the difficulty viewed realistically, the anguish will be proportionately diminished. I realize that the task of shrinking a client's anxiety is in the psychological realm, if not indeed in the psychoanalytic, but I do not believe that life lends itself to the separation of the sciences into neatly labeled compartments. It is essential that the client emerge immediately from the depressed atmosphere of fear and defeat which envelopes him, or he will not be able to function in the legal struggle ahead. I consider this my first problem and deal with it directly. For example, to return to the distressed wife—although the effort is similar for the husband, or the businessman attacked in an antitrust suit—I wait until she has finished her recital, and invite her to lean back against the chair on which she sits stiffly. She expects me to give her a legal opinion, and nervous interest momentarily displaces the tearful look in her eyes.

I recall saying to one such client, "This may surprise you, but first I am going to give you some medical advice. There is nothing about this case that cannot be solved legally, but I have observed the strain under which you are laboring. I realize that you have suffered a great emotional shock and are deeply upset. If you permit this tragedy to undermine you so that you become ulcerated or suffer a nervous breakdown, you will only be adding to your troubles; you will make it more difficult to obtain the legal relief to which you are entitled.

"Your husband has done everything he can to hurt you. He cannot do any more. The only one who can hurt you now is yourself. You must get control of yourself. No doctor, no psychiatrist, no lawyer can do it for you. You must help yourself, and the way to do it is to get a proper perspective of this matter. Right now, caught in emotional tides, you think your whole life was crashed down over your head. The world seems to have come to an end. This is the distorted view you have of your problem. Actually, it is not the greatest tragedy that ever befell a woman. I am not making light of your plight. It is a terrible blow, but hundreds of thousands of women have suffered a similar fate and have come out of it, rehabilitating their lives and finding new happiness. At this moment, I know, this seems impossible to you. But you are young and personable, and you will ultimately find someone more worthy of you who will appreciate you. You must get a realistic perspective of this problem and not exaggerate it.

"After all, far worse could have happened. Suppose something terrible had happened to your children, or some crippling disease had struck you or your dear ones. Bad as this situation is, it is not a desperate crisis. You must see it in proper perspective.

"I know this is easier to say than to do, but you can do it, even if you have to go into a room and talk out loud to yourself in front of a mirror. Resolve that you will strengthen your self-discipline, that you are not going to permit your husband's treachery to undermine you, that you will not permit him to triumph through your own disintegration, and that you are going to take hold of yourself and see the thing through in the best way you can for your own sake and for your children's.

"If you will promise to take care of yourself, I assure you everything will come out all right. Whether we undertake to represent you, or some other competent attorney does, you can be protected legally. The real problem is your health and state of mind. If we win while you become ill, it will avail nothing, isn't that so? Will you promise me to make a real effort to gain a true perspective of this situation, and put on inner brakes, so to speak, so that you will regain a little equanimity?"

Words of comfort, skillfully administered, are the oldest therapy known to man. Even primitives, who used chants instead of logic, could instill healing confidence in those possessed by "evil spirits." Today the blessing of intelligence is offset by the curse of hypersensitivity. It is as if the very improvement of the brain is achieved by an inbred process that also heightens the neurotic capacity. Culture and instability, artistry and temperament, brilliance and erraticism—these are civilization's couples. The more our ailments stem from the mind, the more we must resort to the chemistry of words. But the skill of reaching the mind with ideas is not the exclusive province of special practitioners. The reason we exalt common sense is because it derives chiefly from the training school of experience which all of us attend. This makes the observant graduate, who has thereby acquired sharper judgment, a healer in the psychological sense. That is why we turn so often to older people for advice. It is not because they are superior, but rather because they have survived similar storms and have the wisdom of perspective.

I think that is why a lawyer, entirely apart from his technical knowledge, is specially equipped to lead a client to serenity. He telescopes a lifetime of experience in concentrated study of clients in distress. He combines the insight of his observation with the skills of persuasion, which are his special talent, to reach the mind of his anguished client and bring it solace and calm.

I have seen the effect upon different clients hundreds of times. Of course the approach to each differs, depending on the personality involved, and the nature and degree of the distress. On many occasions a client has announced at the end of an interview that he feels so much better already that he cannot quite believe it. This is accompanied by a grateful handshake which, in contrast to the one on arrival, is so dry and vigorous as to constitute a clinical miracle in itself. Not infrequently, too, such a client has called the next day to say that for the first time in weeks he has slept well, and without a sedative. These psychological inroads are not only immensely satisfying, but continue to be mystifying. For one never gets over the tremendous impact of discovering which were the right words for the particular person, and what a radical change an hour's talk can bring about in a person who was crumbling before your eyes. Less important is the pragmatic fact that this is the first step to legal victory. There are shocks ahead on the road of contest, and a protagonist who can stand the bumps is essential if the journey is to be successfully completed. Not infrequently the lawyer must win the battle inside his own client before he can cope with his adversary.

Parents often love their children with the same intensity with which they hate each other. Who gets custody? This question causes extreme emotional incitation. The father vows that he will never part with the children, who love and need him. The mother resorts to the most primitive threat of the animal who will kill for her cubs. As if the acerbation of sundered love were not enough, new elements of unreasonable determination and devotion are added to the controversy.

The law steps in to pronounce some calm edicts about the matter. First and last is the rule that it is the children's welfare and not the parents' desires which govern. Children are not pawns in the struggle between their father and mother. They are not chattel to be disposed of according to which of the parents has triumphed in their own vendetta. They are not to serve either as rewards or punishment. Their own happiness is the criterion to which the parents' rights are subordinated.

Where infants are involved, the mother is invariably the right custodian. Even if she has lost the matrimonial action and been found guilty of adultery, she is still awarded custody. The welfare of the infant being paramount, can anyone doubt that it needs the love and care of its mother? Only in the most extraordinary circumstances, where the mother's depravity would mean the neglect of the infant or subject it to dangerous surroundings, will she be deprived of custody.

Where the children are older, and particularly when they reach their teens, the mother's custody is not taken for granted. The children are permitted to express their wishes. Nevertheless the strong tendency still is to grant custody to the mother. The father's preoccupation with work during the day is itself sufficient to overcome most of his claims. He simply has not the time, as the mother usually has, to rear the children. Therefore, unless she is morally unfit, in the sense that she subjects the children to improper environment or her own bad habits, such as intoxication or looseness with men, the law still favors her as custodian. It goes on the theory that even a bad woman is usually nevertheless a loving mother and that children should not be deprived of that maternal affection which nature implants in the heart of even its unworthy creatures.

Since what is best for the child is the decisive consideration, each case must be examined on its own particular set of facts. Even if the child is old enough to express a preference, its discretion is not too highly regarded. It may have been won over by gifts, or by being catered to against its own interests. Even lack of discipline may be a form of bribe, but no one can argue that the child's welfare is enhanced thereby. Having a better time with one of the parents than with the other may account for the child's choice, but the parent's popularity must be earned by considerations that the Court deems in the real interest of the child. A spoiled child is no tribute to the parent who has campaigned for its affection by surrendering to it.

The Court is even more alert to situations where the child's choice is vehement and an expression of hatred. This often indicates that the child's mind has been poisoned by the other parent. The implanting of ill will and malice in a young heart, which should cherish and respect both parents, is so serious an offense that it virtually precludes the designation of the offending parent as custodian.

I once encountered such an instance in extraordinary form. The parents in the litigation were at each other's throats in an unseemly manner, and the fiercest subject of their conflict was a six-year-old son. The father accused the mother of being unfit to rear him. The mother asserted that the father was given to wild tantrums of temper and had even vented his psychotic anger by administering severe beatings to the child for no reason at all. In the midst of the litigation the father seized the child and refused to return him to the mother. Negotiations and pleas for some arrangement that would not make the sweet-looking boy the terrain of battle, failed. I got out a writ of habeas corpus to compel the return of the child to the mother. The hearing came before Supreme Court Justice Edgar Nathan of New York. He directed that the parents and the child appear before him. As is customary, the child was brought into chambers for a few questions. To the amazement of all of us the little, six-year-old boy, his face distorted with hate, pointed an accusing finger at his mother and yelled: "You're just a whore! That's what you are. I hate you. I hate you. I want to be with Daddy."

The Judge and I examined the child gently. It was soon apparent that he did not know the meaning of the words he uttered and that his lines had been given to him and carefully rehearsed by his father. The poor child's mind had been turned by an insidious campaign of expensive toys which would have filled a small store.

Custody was granted to the mother, who had to drag away the protesting, hysterical child, still screaming imprecations at her which he had memorized and didn't understand. We arranged special treatments for him and he emerged, I hope, not permanently scarred by the incident. Poetic justice fulfilled its rhyme and reason in this case. The father not only lost the separation suit, but, sadly enough, became so embroiled with his financial testimony in his effort to minimize alimony, that he was ultimately indicted and convicted by the Government.

If custody meant exclusive possession of the children, one could understand better the fever that surrounds the word. What parent could resign himself or herself to be cut off forever from the children? However, custody doesn't mean that. The other parent invariably has visitation rights. Custody, therefore, really specifies the roof under which the children will sleep. It does not bar reasonable access to them by the non-custodian parent. This limitation upon custody reduces its concept substantially. Despite awarding custody to one parent, the law does not abandon the fundamental rule that the welfare of the child is the sole criterion in fashioning the applicable edicts. This requires that the child be afforded the presence, companionship, and love of both parents as continuously as possible. To achieve this end the law provides broad visitation rights.

However, even these rights must yield to what is good for the child. Therefore they are circumscribed by innumerable rules that set forth what is reasonable. They vary with the age of the child and the surrounding circumstances. The hours of visitation must not interfere with the feeding and sleeping of the child. Infants, of course, cannot be removed from the mother's home. The visit is localized within the house, and for a limited time.

When the children grow old enough to be taken out, there are careful provisions for their return in proper time, suitable to their age and health. Later, weekend visits may be arranged, provided the father has suitable quarters and environment. The rule for daughters sometimes differs from that for sons.

Then there are the complicated schedules worked out about alternating holidays, and whether the privilege of the Thanksgiving holiday visit is offset by Christmas or Easter. Also, birthday celebrations and vacation periods are split and alternated. Modern camps for children diminish the area of dispute, because custody is often surrendered to a camp counselor, and the camp director tells both parents what their visitation rights are.

Where there is contentiousness between the parents, its bitterness spreads over every aspect of visitation rights. Whether the hours of visitation are to be 6 to 8 or 5 to 7, whether it is Saturday or Sunday, and later which of these days is alternated to each parent, whether notice must be given in advance of each visit, what penalty applies where the visit is skipped, and innumerable other trivia afford the disputants additional ground for combat.

There are more serious conflicts. If each parent remains unmarried, the visit to the custodian's home may be feasible. Even then, if there is ill will between them, the Court will order that the visit take place not in the presence of the other parent, and, if the child is too young, with a nurse or acceptable relative or designated friend. However, if the mother has remarried, she may not wish her former husband to invade her home even to visit his child. The courts respect this sensitivity, particularly of the new husband, and provide for other arrangements, such as bringing the child to some neutral but suitable place for visitation. On the other hand, if the father has remarried and the child is old enough to be taken out of the house, the mother may not wish the child to be enveloped by the new family her husband has acquired. The Court will consider this objection only if the new surroundings are not desirable. Always it is the child's welfare that determines the answer.

If the new marriage of the mother shifts the residence out of the state, the former husband may object to the loss of his right of visitation. He may also raise the point that if custody were shifted to him, the child's schooling and rearing would be enhanced by remaining in its old environment. All this would be weighed by the Court and balanced against the age of the child, the character of its stepfather, and the benefits of its new surroundings. Generally the courts will not countenance the removal of the child from the city in which the parents both resided originally. Once more it is not deemed in the best interests of the child to be deprived of its natural father's love and interest. That, and not the deprived parent's rights, is the chief consideration.

If the husband fails to pay alimony, the wife cannot deny visitation rights to him. His money default is a breach of his contractual obligation, or a court order. He may even in some states be jailed for such non-payment. But his visitation rights won't be forfeited, because that would be punishing the child. All equities yield to this one concern. Therefore, though it may not be considered fair for a husband to fall down on his solemn responsibility to support his former wife and child, one right will not offset another if it is the child who would be affected.

In a matrimonial action, the child is deemed the ward of the Court, which retains jurisdiction to revise both custody and visitation provisions if there is a serious change of circumstances. Sometimes the parent who has custody cannot afford to give the child the benefit of good schooling and rearing, while the other parent, having remarried into wealth, may be able, for the first time, to confer great advantages upon the child. Money is not the decisive criterion, and a respectable argument can be made that hardship may strengthen character and that love in close proximity is more important than luxury. The Court may strike a balance, always with an eye to what is best for the child.

I once obtained an order shifting custody to the husband because his success in business enabled him to offer his sickly child an opportunity for residence in healthy surroundings, opposite a park, with a large room filled with sunlight, and immediate medical attention, all of which the mother could not provide. Since she was remarried, the father could not increase her alimony to make possible these advantages for the child without setting up a new household for her husband, which even he, in good character, declined. The decisive factor was the child's eagerness to live with his father. The mother discovered that the extremely broad visitation rights voluntarily granted her lessened her anguish. Ultimately the child's physical improvement made up for any grief she may have felt when she lost custody. This, however, is the exceptional case. Fundamentally custody and visitation rights are not rearranged by the courts with every shift of circumstance. The child must be given a sense of stability and this, too, militates against changing its abode, or even the routine of visits.

The saying that man proposes, but God disposes is apt in these matters. Lawyers may struggle for weeks with the details of visitation arrangements that are subsequently upset by circumstances neither parent envisioned. At the time of negotiation, the stubbornness of each parent is turned into a holy crusade because love of child is involved. Unreasonableness is glorified as virtue, because the whole subject is vested with martyrdom and sacrifice. Often the parent does not realize that he or she is smarting from the rejection of love by the other and not from the contemplated deprivation for another half hour of the child's presence. But the venom turns into a channel of righteousness over the devotion to the child. In so many instances I have seen the complicated visitation terms ignored later by both parents.

Ironically many a parent has subsequently pleaded with the other "to take the children" for a while so that a vacation trip may be enjoyed without the burden of their presence. Even more ironic, the request has been refused. The original contest for every additional minute has been turned into disagreement as to who should relieve whom, temporarily of course, of the children. The doting mother may have learned that there are other men as well as pebbles on the beach and decided to rebuild her life. She begins to make dates and take trips, and her previous insistence that her closeness to the child was a precious right that she would guard against any encroachment, yields to the practical needs of her new life. It is not that she loves the children less. It is only that the former arbitrary and unreasonable demands, which were motivated by personal frustration rather than by loyalty to the child, become dissolved with time.

Similarly it is not uncommon for a father who has struck a heroic pose of fighting through every court of the land for the privilege of having his son with him on alternate weekends or several weeks in the summer, to surrender those rights repeatedly and even neglect to visit the child in the city on many occasions available to him in the agreement. Once more, it is not that he loves the child less, but rather that his exclusive dedication to it, which was the assumption during the negotiations, has been diluted by the practical needs and temptations of his other interests.

The fact is that in a united home the parents need not strain to confer their love and presence on the children. Even then, absence during the summer in a camp or later in a school is not looked upon exactly as a calamity. But when each parent is living a single life, although there are children about, the fluidity of their existence often conflicts with visitation provisions rigidly fixed in a written agreement. Once again, it is a matter of perspective. At the time that the clauses are fought over, the parents still unconsciously envision themselves living in the same house and resent separation from the children, or else they fail to understand the different conditions that will later prevail. In any event, visitation rights are often honored in their breach rather than in their observance.

Finally there is the all-controlling factor of the children's growth. As their personalities develop, their choices are made with greater discrimination. They can no longer be "bribed" with gifts or with non-resistance to their whims. The stimulation that they receive from one parent is weighed against the other. If they prefer the company of one, it is going to be difficult to read the visitation clause to them which provides impartial, equal division of time. True, their choice is selfish, which is the rule rather than the exception with children, but is this not the very standard that the law provides? Only if the child has been lured by "good times" which are not wholesome, will the court interfere. So it comes about that as the children grow older, the visitation and even custody provisions are automatically revised by their exercise of will and preference.

Among the little tragedies that fill peoples' lives are those caused by the ingratitude of children. How often I have seen a mother dedicate herself to her son, sacrifice herself for him, and rear him to young manhood, only to have him ultimately choose his father, who may have neglected him, but now eagerly reaches out to share the joys of his maturity. Such new-found comradery, in which the son finds his father charming and exciting company and which excludes the mother emotionally, may be a crueler blow to her than even her husband's earlier betrayal. Its pain is increased by the need to hide it. She may not even show her jealousy. She must pretend that she is delighted that he loves his father. It is a sign that she has reared him well and given him character. But when the son chooses to spend Christmas with "Dad" and his new wife, and later gushes about the joyous time he had and, with the insensitivity that comes from unawareness, pays his stepmother compliments for her beauty and wit, the mother feels as if she is standing in front of an abyss of unendurable defeat and pain.

There are areas in human relationships which do not lend themselves to fixed contract provisions. Flexibility is an underestimated virtue. The scientist often assumes some degree of error in order to arrive at a more accurate computation. The builder allows a tolerance for change of temperature. The political or economic scientist is foolhardy if he charts the future in detail. The social scientist, too, must permit some vacuum to be filled by unforeseen emotional reactions. Visitation rights belong to this category of social invention. The more they are specified and augmented with detail, the more they are taxed by unanticipated and changing circumstances. So often, hours and days of harrowing argument are engaged in working out procedures that are inappropriate for events as they later unfold. All the relationships are in flux. The mother and father may remarry. Each may have new children, and the focus of interest may shift or be diluted. The children grow up, and their wishes are different than anticipated. The economic conditions of the parties may change and make a difference.

The sensible solution is to provide general terms and rely on the reasonableness of the parents to adjust their rights in accordance with the actual events that confront them. This requires good will. Where it exists, the more elastic the arrangement, the fairer it turns out to be. Where it doesn't exist, the visitation terms are set forth in rigid inflexibilty. But this is usually the beginning, not the end of the trouble. Either the parents later voluntarily revise their overdetailed blueprint, or they quarrel in the courts once more.

Until we make matrimonial law uniform throughout the land, the conflicts of varying legal standards will create bizarre results. A vivid illustration is the Astor case.

John Jacob Astor was the scion of a famous father. He had dropped the Jacob from his name because, he testified, "it implies great wealth, sixty, seventy, eighty million dollars which I don't have. It was a source of embarrassment to me. . . . Also, triple names always sound impressive and I simply changed it to John Astor."

The Supreme Court of Florida found that his net worth was only "four and three-quarter millions," and that his annual income before taxes "was approximately $250,000 . . . and never varies by more than 5 per cent from year to year." Apparently his "embarrassment" at being considered wealthy did not inhibit him from spending in 1954, as the Court found, $238,000. He "has been accustomed," the Court said, "to live in the luxury that his substantial wealth permits." Among the luxuries he permitted himself was a matrimonial tangle that is practically unique in American law. Its complexity can only be partly gleaned from the fact, which the Court recited, that in one year "he paid attorneys $105,000 . . . for domestic relations litigation."

His difficulties began with love, when he met Dolores Fullman, a magnificent girl of fine breeding and beauty. As he described his own reaction from the witness stand: "I fell in love with her at first sight. . . . I wanted a beautiful, sweet wife, and then I found she was not only beautiful and sweet, but very intelligent, and I fell hook, line, and sinker."

It was not difficult to understand her impact upon him. Although she was tall, shapely, blue-eyed and almost perfectly visaged, she had no self-consciousness about her beauty. Dolly, as she was affectionately known, was gay and at ease and popular with everyone.

It was not as easy to understand his appeal to her. Although only forty-two, he was fifteen years older than she, and a huge, bearish kind of man whose heavy moods matched his bulk. But she testified that when he wooed her "he was sweet and kind, and told me that everyone had always taken advantage of him because he was rich, that they always wanted something out of him. He said he really despised going to all those parties with insincere people—that all he really wanted was a home and family, and normal nice things around him." He came to her home. She was impressed with an Astor humbly courting his intended bride.

During the trial the cross-examiner, Mr. Parker, suggested that there was another allure:

Q. You were not interested in his money?

A. Not particularly, no. I have always had everything I wanted. Mr. Astor can't give me much that I don't have except extravagant jewels and things like that which I could very well do without. No, I am not interested in his money.

The courtship did not prosper for one reason. Astor was still married to his second wife, Gertrude. He had an eight-year-old daughter from this marriage. He was separated from his wife, but he had not obtained his freedom. He decided to secure a Mexican divorce without her consent. With a battery of lawyers and investigators he went to Juarez, Mexico, and obtained a unilateral divorce. Three weeks later he married Dolly in Arlington, Virginia. They sailed off for a honeymoon in Europe. It was, according to later testimony, a trip filled with horror. Her recital of his misconduct was so vivid that the cross-examiner asked:

Q. Why didn't you leave him?

A. For many reasons. I wanted more than anything to have the marriage work. I've had one marriage that didn't work because I was very young. I would have done anything normal, anything at all, to make it work. I didn't want to cause him terrific embarrassment by arriving in New York alone and have all the newspaper reporters come down on me. He said it would be a disgrace, it would ruin his son who was going to college, that I couldn't do that to him, and so forth—and I couldn't.

On the return trip they sat at the Captain's table with Senator Kefauver and his wife, Nancy. Everyone observed that the bonds of matrimony were extremely taut and painful, and each gave Dolly sympathy and friendship. She lasted out the trip and then fled from him, even though: "He told me he had been through an emotional convulsion, that he was better now . . . and he'd make it all up to me. . . ." He refuted her testimony, but one of his own witnesses, the investigator and lawyer, John G. Broady, testified about the history of his deplorable physical condition and its possible neurotic overtones: "I talked to the doctor myself. I was trying to get him in shape to get in the Army or Navy. He wanted to get in the Armed Services. He is a big fellow and looked like he was strong, but he was in his mother's womb when his mother was adrift in a lifeboat in the North Atlantic in icy waters with waters washing around her, and the doctor said that long stay in the lifeboat prior to his birth possibly caused the difficulties. . . . I do know that Mr. Astor, ever since I made his acquaintance in 1936, has had doctors almost continuously."

It would have pleased the most rigid Freudian to trace the possible egocentric and physical characteristics of a man to the Titanic disaster that took his father's life and cast his mother adrift in the icy dark of a heaving sea.

Astor ascribed his weakness, which contrasted with his immensity, to another cause. He testified: "I had typhoid fever when I was thirteen in Italy, and I was taken to Europe and they forgot to give me vaccinations against typhoid—innoculations, rather—and I had a severe case.

"Theoretically I should have died. Thirty per cent of typhoid patients do die, and when I came out of it I was wounded for life, can't stand on my feet for more than forty-five minutes; can't play more than six holes of golf. I gave up golf."

Only six weeks had elapsed between Dolly's marriage and bitter separation. But Gertrude Astor had not sat idly by during this time. She instituted a suit in New York State, where she resided, to declare John's Mexican divorce from her invalid, his subsequent marriage to Dolly a nullity, and that she, Gertrude, remained the true wife of John.

In the meantime Dolly retained me to protect her interests. Conferences with Astor's counsel soon revealed no possible common ground between us. On the contrary they took the position that his Mexican decree was not worth the red wax seal on it, that it was invalid because Gertrude had never appeared in that action, that John Astor was therefore still married to Gertrude, and that Dolly's status during the six weeks of the "honeymoon" and since was not that of a wife. Obviously such a challenge to her marital status had to be met.

It seemed to me that the impending struggle would take place in two jurisdictions, one in the State of Florida where Dolly resided, and the other in New York State where Gertrude was proceeding to protect her position as wife and the huge inheritance potentials that flowed therefrom.

We mapped out our strategy on the basis of these conflicts. I had no doubt that Gertrude would succeed in her action in New York State for a declaratory judgment which would determine that the Mexican divorce was invalid against her and therefore that she was still John Astor's wife. However, I also had no doubt that Dolly would succeed in the State of Florida if she sued there, because John would not be permitted to disclaim the divorce he himself had obtained. If this legal analysis worked out, he would have two legal wives, one in each state. The crucial test would come when Astor's attorneys, as was inevitable, would confront us in a New York Court with the conflict and seek a resolution. I had a plan for that, too.

We began a separation action in Florida, asserting that Dolly was married to John and seeking maintenance for her as his wife. Robert H. Anderson and William C. Steel of the Miami law firm of Anderson, Scott, McCarthy and Preston were our local counsel.

Astor countered by asserting that the Mexican divorce decree that he had obtained against Gertrude was void and therefore that he was still married to her and Dolly was not even his wife. He interposed a counterclaim in which he took the offensive. He asked that the Court annul his marriage to Dolly because of a prior subsisting marriage. Finally, for good measure, even if he lost his other contentions, he asked for an absolute divorce from Dolly on the ground of extreme cruelty. So the issue was joined.

We contended that Astor could not take advantage of the invalidity of the Mexican divorce because he had procured it himself and had induced Dolly to marry him on the strength of it. We invoked the ancient equitable doctrine of estoppel. One may not take advantage of his own wrong deed. He is estopped from so doing.

Florida courts had, on one prior occasion, applied the rule of estoppel in a similar situation. It was not until years later that our office had occasion to establish a similar rule in New York State. In Caswell vs. Caswell I asserted the defense of estoppel against a husband who claimed his prior Mexican divorce illegal. The highest Court of New York upheld this position.

The vital issue in the Astor case depended on the soundness of this rule of law. To overcome this doctrine, Astor presented witnesses who testified that they had warned Dolly that the Mexican divorce was of questionable validity and even that she and John should marry in Virginia rather than Florida because that was a better state from the viewpoint of recognizing Mexican jurisdiction. Dolly presented as a witness an attorney in the office of Astor's Miami counsel who stated that when Dolly's father inquired about the legality of the proceedings, he gave his opinion that they were valid, based on the facts presented to him. In short, Astor attempted to overcome the doctrine of estoppel by demonstrating that Dolly, too, knew of the vulnerability of the Mexican decree.

The trial also involved a full factual review of what happened on the honeymoon trip in the intimacy of their suite. Circuit Judge Vincent C. Giblin presided at the trial and wrote an opinion in which he severely criticized Dolly's motive in marrying Astor. Nevertheless he found that: "She is living separate and apart from him through his fault. I do not believe that she intended or desired such an early termination of the marital relationship. He, however, as he admits, decided, even before the honeymoon had ended, that the marriage was a mistake."

Far more important, the Judge held that Astor "cannot question the validity of the Mexican decree because he not only sought and procured it, but took advantage of it by remarrying. . . . The husband's obligation to support his wife remains. His assumption of the obligation by marrying her was his mistake and not mine, and he should pay the penalty for his aberration."

The Judge also dismissed Astor's counterclaim for a divorce based upon the theory that Dolly had been extremely cruel to him. He directed Astor to pay counsel fees to Dolly's attorneys in the sum of $12,500, but stated that in view of the fact that the marriage lasted only a month and a half and his views as to her motive, she was not entitled to alimony that would give her "luxury to which she has never been accustomed." He awarded only $75 a week. The fortunes of legal contest are not only difficult to predict, but even to assess after they have occurred.

From my viewpoint this was a resounding victory. Keeping an eye on the ultimate goal, we had achieved our first objective. Dolly had been established in Florida as Mrs. John Astor. She was his legal wife. Estoppel had stricken from John's hand the sword that would have severed the marital ties. No matter how small the alimony award, it was a legal acknowledgement of her right to be supported by her husband. It confirmed her marital status. She had not been just a girl traveling with Astor under the mistaken notion that they were married and on a honeymoon. Finally, any gratification he would receive from the fact that only nominal alimony had been awarded her would disappear in the realization that ultimately his huge fortune would be subject to her claim as his wife.

However, it was not easy for Dolly to swallow the indignity of the Judge's opinion about her and its reflection in the pittance granted her as alimony. At first I had some misgivings about appealing the case to increase the award. It might endanger the far more important decision in her favor. But we had to consider the client's sensitivity as well as her rights. Injury to the former might be more painful than to the latter. Sometimes the flattering and sympathetic words of a judge will offset an unfavorable decision. Ego being what it is, a client can derive immense satisfaction from a high appraisal of him by the Court, even though rules of law require his defeat. In the Astor case we had the opposite situation. She won, but the sympathy and understanding we thought she was entitled to, were denied her. We decided to appeal from the inadequate award. If we could increase it even somewhat, the denunciation it implied would be removed.

Since this was our purpose, we moved boldly to announce our challenge in the brief that was filed in the upper Court: "The sole legal question here is whether the award of only $75 per week constitutes an abuse of discretion by the Chancellor. . . . That is the only question that the appellant can legally appeal. She won every other legal issue below. There is, however, embodied in this appeal an incidental, non-legal question which is more important to appellant than the legal question. It is the question of correction of the gravest injustice—unwarranted injury to reputation. That correction can now be made only through the medium of an award consistent with the unappealed finding that these parties live apart through Astor's fault. . . ."

Astor's counsel characterized Dolly as a "gold digger" who had entrapped their client. Disregarding the unpleasant implications to Astor, they contended that no other rational explanation existed for so young and beautiful a girl marrying him. We replied that if Dolly were so motivated, the marriage would not have been as short-lived; crass considerations would have dictated a different course. It was honor and self-respect which accounted for her conduct.

Love is not to be measured by the simple yardstick that an advocate chooses in order to defend a cause. One might as well ask a girl who marries a famous author whether she would have loved him if he had not written his books, or a girl who marries an industrialist whether she would have the same degree of affection for him if he were a clerk. The complex factors of personality, achievement, and standing—yes, and wealth—cannot be separated and isolated for the purpose of a demagogic slogan at a trial.

Would Astor have married the plaintiff if she were ugly? Did he marry her solely to possess her and cast her aside? These would be more relevant considerations if the function of the courts was to evaluate the factors of love and their reasonableness. This is not a province for the Court's determination, I argued. Even psychiatrists may find the question beyond their ken.

It was she, not he, who had been entrapped. It was she who had been deceived by his previous bearlike kindliness. She had fallen in love with him when he was considerate and attentive. His very position of power, renowned name and wealth, made his shy appeal for her affection and her hand in marriage an emotional rather than a calculating experience.

The impact of our argument had to be heavy to overcome a rule of law which stood athwart us. That was that a higher Court will not overrule a decision which is based upon the discretion of the lower Court unless it constitutes a clear abuse of discretion. The right to alimony presents a legal question, but the amount of alimony is a discretionary matter. Astor's attorneys leaned heavily upon this doctrine. Even if the Supreme Court differed with Judge Giblin, it should not overrule him, they argued, because it could not be said he had abused his discretion.

These were the heights we had to scale, and scale them we did. Chief Judge Drew, Judge Roberts and Judge O'Connell concurred in Judge Crosby's opinion written for a unanimous Supreme Court of Florida in which he concluded: "So long as the marriage continues, a husband is under an obligation to support his wife in a manner approximating that which *he* has established. . . .

"Assessment of the amount of an award of alimony to a wife . . . necessarily involves the exercise of judicial discretion. We have repeatedly held that this court 'will not disturb the order of a lower court in the exercise of its judicial discretion unless an abuse of this discretion is clearly shown. . . .' We conclude, however, under the circumstances of this case, and in the light of the Chancellor's finding, that the present status exists through the husband's fault, that the wife's maintenance should be substantially increased in order to conform reasonably with the mode of living that the husband has set for himself."

The Court then reversed that part of the decree which awarded $75 weekly alimony and increased it to $250 a week. It affirmed the decree otherwise and assessed the costs of our appeal upon Astor. Dolly felt vindicated. The Appellate Court had decided that Judge Giblin had abused his discretion in allowing her small alimony.

We had established her marital status and removed the scar she had suffered in the course of combat. I warned her of the inevitable storms ahead. She now exuded confidence in the ultimate outcome. This was a proper psychological frame of mind for her to be in, but I knew that much more would be necessary if we were to hold our position.

Gertrude had by this time obtained a decree in the Supreme Court of New York State declaring John's Mexican divorce invalid, his marriage to Dolly a nullity, and that she was still his wife.

As expected, John now instituted an action in the Supreme Court of New York State against his two "wives," Gertrude and Dolly, seeking a declaratory judgment as to "which of the defendants is the lawful wife of the plaintiff." He contended that he was entitled to know because the doubt affected rights to his property and estate.

We countered by applying for an injunction in Florida to prohibit John from attempting to relitigate a matter already decided in the Florida Supreme Court, namely that Dolly was his wife. However, Circuit Judge Charles A. Carroll refused to enjoin John from proceeding in New York because he was not certain that the previous estoppel ruling in the Florida Court was a decision on the merits, that is, as we lawyers say, *res adjudicata*, meaning that the matter had been finally decided for all purposes. However, he felt that Dolly was being put to new expense to defend herself in New York and authorized an application for counsel fees and suit money on her behalf. This was done and granted, but we had failed in our effort to prevent John from continuing his New York attack.

The chess moves continued with increasing complexity as the lawyers executed novel legal gambits. John had sued both women, asking, "Which one is my wife?" Gertrude now attacked Dolly in a counterclaim, saying "She is not. I am." This move by Gertrude we blocked. We made a motion to dismiss this counterclaim on the ground that Gertrude had not served it on Dolly in New York, and the fact that both had been served by John in New York did not confer jurisdiction upon a counterclaimant. This was a new and fine point, but Supreme Court Justice Aaron Steuer upheld our contention. Gertrude's attack on Dolly was dismissed. So far as Dolly was concerned, we had pruned down the dispute as one between John and herself. This gave us, as we shall see, a great advantage.

The time had come to face up to the crucial issue. John was pressing to have the Court decide which of the two contenders was his true wife. We had long prepared for this hour. Our answer must have taken Astor's breath away. We contended both were.

Our legal syllogism had been carefully worked out. I moved to dismiss his complaint on three grounds.

First, Astor had raised these same contentions about the invalidity of his Mexican divorce and all the rest of that now familiar refrain when Dolly sued him in Florida. Their controversy had been determined. He could not harass her by traveling around in different states to relitigate her status as wife. The law would not permit such legal shopping.

Second, I argued that Astor's action for a declaratory judgment should be dismissed because there was no pending problem requiring decision or, as the law calls it, "no subsisting justiciable controversy." It is well-settled law that if a litigant attempts to anticipate a future problem and asks the Court to determine his rights in advance, the courts may, in their discretion, refuse to act. Astor could not assume that he would die before Dolly and Gertrude, that neither of them would have divorced him prior to death, and therefore on these hypothetical assumptions foresee the problem as to Dolly's right to receive a share of his estate. Courts do not deal with abstract questions predicated upon nebulous contingencies.

Third, both Dolly and John were residents of Florida. New York courts did not look with favor upon actions brought by a non-resident to seek relief concerning the marital status of another non-resident.

Astor's attorney, Barent Ten Eyck, insisted that the Court should tell his client which of the two defendants was his lawful wife. He conceded that New York must give full faith and credit to the Florida decree in favor of Dolly, but contended that due to estoppel, Astor had been prevented from asserting his defense and therefore there had not been a decision on the merits.

As to there being "no justiciable controversy," Astor's attorneys filed a special brief pointing out that there were more than remote contingencies involved. Their efforts to discover immediate problems requiring solution led them to fictitious, if not ludicrous, lengths. Suppose, they said, Astor desired to effect a reconciliation with one of the defendants; he might be committing a crime according to the laws of the state where the other "wife" resided. I replied that Astor seemed to have no disposition to make up with either wife. Furthermore, I could not believe that he would decide to love that wife which the court told him was his. Or suppose, conjured up Astor, he had to decide which wife should sign his income tax return. He would not know. I pointed out that under our statutes, since he was separated from both, he could not file a joint return with either of them. Also, this was not a justiciable issue requiring a trial.

Or suppose, he strained, he wanted to deduct the expense of his alimony payments from his income tax return, which would he claim? Aside from the fact that this, too, was not the kind of issue which required determination, we suggested that since the alimony paid to each wife was under a final separation decree, he would very likely be entitled to deduct both.

Finally he urged that he ought to be relieved of one of his alimony payments. We startled him again by suggesting that each judgment deserved the full faith and credit of the other state and that he must obey both.

The more intricate the legal contentions, the more burdened with technical refinements, the more I seek a moral rationale behind the façade. In this case, it was simply this: Astor had brought about his own dilemma.

He was not to be heard now to complain about it. He should not be permitted to throw his problem into a Court and request it to solve the conundrum resulting from his own machinations. Suppose he got another Mexican divorce from Dolly and married again, and repeated this a fourth and fifth time. Could he just throw the mess into a Judge's hands and say, "Now, you tell me, which one is my real wife?"

The courts do not exist to straighten out the knotted affairs of every eccentric who comes along. They provide a forum for the determination of disputes. But Astor had no more right to cast his bag of matrimonial miscellany into a courthouse and request the Judge to disentangle his affairs than a businessman who had gotten himself involved in numerous enterprises, with conflicting cross-interest, could submit them all to a Court and ask it to extricate him.

Astor has made his two beds, and since he was not going to sleep in either of them, he could not call upon the court to tell him which should have given him rest and happiness, if conditions had been otherwise.

Supreme Court Justice Samuel Gold, who had heard these arguments, dismissed Astor's action. He held that Astor could not "procure relief which would deprive either" Dolly or Gertrude of the alimony awarded each.

However, in the exercise of extreme caution, he permitted Astor to file an amended complaint if he could summon up some new "justiciable issues" requiring the Court's immediate decision.

There was still a gasp left in the dying action. Astor's counsel exploited it to the full. First, they moved for reargument. It was denied.

Then they took advantage of the right to file an amended complaint. We moved to dismiss it on the ground that, in essence, it added nothing new to the original complaint. Again, extensive briefs were filed. Supreme Court Justice Henry Epstein wrote a vigorous opinion dismissing the complaint. He granted our motion for additional counsel fees. There was an appeal. We were upheld.

Now Astor resorted to the very last moves still available to him, before we could announce, in the chess player's triumphant phrase, "Checkmate," the king had no escape. He went back to Florida and instituted a suit against Dolly to annul his marriage to her on the ground that Gertrude's decree in New York bound him to two wives and he was entitled to a reconsideration of the previous decision rendered against him in Florida. After Astor put in his evidence, the Chancellor declared that he saw no reason to re-examine the prior decision. He dismissed the action. Astor appealed. Chief Judge Charles Carroll, writing for a unanimous Court of Appeal, reviewed the long history of three trials, three appeals and innumerable motions, and held that the original Florida judgment was *res adjudicata* as to all matters now raised again. The dismissal was affirmed.

A petition to the Florida Supreme Court was rejected. Astor applied to the United States Supreme Court for certiorari, that is, permission to appeal. It was denied.

Astor had no other place to go. He had added to the prior distinctions of his great family the questionable one of having American courts hold that he was legally married to two women, with alimony obligations to both of them.

We had steered Dolly through all the shoals to the shelter of a valid marital status. But Gertrude herself conferred complete and final victory upon her. She divorced Astor, and Dolly remained his wife with no cloud upon her exclusive title as Mrs. John Astor.

TALENT

Chapter Three

THE CASE OF

THE PLAGIARIZED SONG

"RUM AND COCA-COLA"

"Rum and Coca-Cola" was one of those songs which swept the nation, capturing its imagination and vocal chords. More than 300,000 popular songs are published each year in the United States in search of *that* song whose tricky melody or lyrics make it irresistible. Repetition does the rest. The air waves become saturated with the tune. Flick a radio or television dial at any hour and the chances are high that you are at some stage of its rendition. Orchestras play the song continuously for enthusiastic audiences who yell with delight as the opening bars summon even exhausted dancers to the floor. Singers use the song like old vaudevillians used the flag—to guarantee applause. Motion picture companies weave the song into their newest picture or sometimes weave the picture around the song. Millions of people succumb to the assault on their ears and, while occupied with their tasks, whistle or hum the melody. And the profits for the publisher of the song are huge. Ownership of the song is a precious asset, and challenges to its originality are not uncommon.

The legal charge that a literary or musical work has been stolen from its real creator is called plagiarism. When physical or tangible property is stolen, it changes hands. The owner no longer possesses it. But when a melody is copied, the owner has it, and so has the thief. Furthermore, it can be disguised by some changes and presented as an original work. After all, there are only seven notes in the diatonic scale and twelve notes in the chromatic scale and, despite the miracle of infinite permutations,

234 · My Life in Court

one can always demonstrate a prior similarity to at least a snatch of a new tune. Therefore, to win a plagiarism suit, the plaintiff must establish not merely some similarity with his own prior work, but "substantial copying" therefrom. This subjects the accuser to a fearful task for, if he depends only on partial similarity, the defense can usually demonstrate dozens of still earlier ancestors of the limited combination of notes which is supposed to have been stolen. It takes so little change to create originality that the defendant insists it is the dissimilarities that created the individuality of his song. Indeed, if it were otherwise, it would be impossible to have an original tune, for it is always possible to trace parts of it to prior works. Similarity in part with a previous melody, whether by accident or design, does not disqualify original creation of a work which on the whole is a new combination. It is for this reason, among many others, that plagiarism suits are almost always lost. To win them requires not only a meritorious claim of substantial copying, but extraordinary resourcefulness in batting down ingenious defenses raised by musical experts and historians.

When, therefore, I was approached to bring a plagiarism suit against Leo Feist, Inc., the publisher of "Rum and Coca-Cola," and the song's alleged composers, I was ready to make the customary courteous declination, except for the fact that the man who wanted to sue was Maurice Baron.

He had testified for me as a music expert in several plagiarism suits, and a lawyer, like a soldier, has a special spot in his heart for anyone who has been through a battle with him. Furthermore, Baron was a delightful man and artist. Although he had been a staff composer and associate conductor at Radio City Music Hall in New York City for ten years, had composed more than three hundred compositions, which had been published by leading publishing houses, and had had his opera about François Villon produced in English, he was a Frenchman from his wax-tipped mustache to his Gallic-tipped accent. The French Academy founded by Richelieu and composed of forty of the most distinguished living artists had conferred the title of Officer of the French Academy upon him for his contributions to music. He wore the French Academy Palms, a little violet ribbon, in his lapel. He was a serious artist but he had never lost his charm or whimsical humor. He still thought a woman's extended hand was for kissing, not shaking.

I had high regard for Baron's musical judgment and even higher for his integrity. During preparation and cross-examination in the cases in which he appeared as my musical expert, he never compromised one whit with his musical convictions. This made him an even more formidable witness. Also, he had an imaginative mind and, when I pressed him for visual demonstrations of audible similarity, he responded with considerable inventiveness. So in Harry Von Tilzer's plagiarism action involving those standards, "I Want a Girl—Just Like the Girl That Married Dear Old Dad," "I'll Lend You Everything I've Got Except My Wife," "When

Harvest Days Are Over, Jessie Dear," and "I Love My Wife, but Oh, You Kid!" I had asked Baron to construct steel bars upon which we could hang and shift steel musical notes identified by various colors, so that the "substantial taking" could be demonstrated visually as well as on the piano. He had responded with ingenuity, filling in symbols for rests, keys, tied notes, etc., which would accurately translate the traditional symbols of music into the intelligence of sight.

Also, in the "Starlight" case, now a landmark in musical copyright law, it was necessary in order to win the case to eliminate a requirement of proof which had been insisted upon for a century, namely, that a plaintiff must prove access as well as similarities. In other words, a plaintiff had to prove that the alleged thief of the melody had heard it or seen it—had had access to it. In the "Starlight" case, a witness who was to testify to access became unavailable and, desperate as well as undaunted, I had argued that the similarity of the two tunes was so overwhelming as to preclude coincidence. The plaintiff could, I argued, win even though he did not prove that the defendant had access to his song. Judge Alfred C. Cox of the Federal Court wrote a learned opinion departing from the rules of access, and held that the *internal* evidence of copying was strong enough to establish plagiarism. This case was upheld by the higher courts, despite the music industry's intervention, on the ground that such a new rule would open up the floodgates for fraudulent claims. The testimony of Maurice Baron, my music expert in that case, made the chief impact on the trial court, persuading it that the striking similarity of notes and construction precluded any inference of coincidence and that it established copying.

Maurice Baron was also a publisher of classical and semiclassical music, particularly of French derivation. So, when he asserted that "Rum and Coca-Cola" was lifted from a song in a folio published by him entitled "Calypso Songs of the West Indies," I listened with respectful attention. This was not the claim of some inexpert composer whose imagination was inflamed by greed. This was a charge by a man of complete integrity and expert judgment.

I undertook the suit. It opened up new worlds of exploration. For three years, we followed trails from African Stick Songs to Spanish *pensamientos*, from Mexican and Indian melodies to "King Ja-Ja" of Barbados. In Port au Spain we tracked down the boyhood friends of our composer, Lionel Belasco, who had written the original tune in 1906. We interviewed American soldiers who had been at the airport in Trinidad on the very day when the alleged composer of "Rum and Coca-Cola" arrived on a USO tour.

At the end of three years, the case was tried in a Federal Court. The trial took eleven days. Twenty-eight witnesses took the stand, among them two professors of music as well as other experts, such as Dr. Sigmund Spaeth. Our thorough preparation and resourcefulness was matched by determined opposition, for the property stakes as well as creative pride were high.

I thought it advisable to invent still newer devices for demonstrating similarity of musical construction. At one point Judge Simon Rifkind was moved to comment: "I confess we are going much further into the theory of the structure of music than most of the cases I am familiar with in this field pretend to go. However, I am wondering whether we are beginning an innovation—which may be useful—which is beyond the confines of previous adjudication."

The battle raged back and forth. Cross-examination was fierce. First one side, and then the other, seemed to have scored. As in any hard-fought trial, the courtroom seethed with the drama of surprise and the emotional uncertainties of the witnesses. I believe this particular case presents more than the ordinary piquant and, at times, thrilling developments of a plagiarism contest.

The charge was that "Rum and Coca-Cola" had been copied from "L'Année Passée," a song composed by Lionel Belasco in 1906, when he was a boy in Trinidad. In 1943 Belasco and a singer of folk songs, Massie Patterson, had submitted to Maurice Baron a group of twelve West Indies songs created by Belasco, among which was "L'Année Passée." Baron had freely transcribed them. He had hired a lyric writer to aid Miss Patterson in translating the French patois into English, and then had published the folio as a semi-classical work under the title: "Calypso Songs of the West Indies by Massie Patterson and Lionel Belasco. Free Transcription by Maurice Baron. English Version by Olga Paul."

A year later "Rum and Coca-Cola" was published, with credit for the music and lyrics to a comedian named Morey Amsterdam. The song was first sung by one Jeri Sullavan at the Versailles night club in New York City. It created an immediate sensation. The Andrews Sisters recorded it and two hundred thousand records were sold, all citing Morey Amsterdam as the sole composer. Shortly thereafter, as new sheet music and records of "Rum and Coca-Cola" were made, the credits were changed, and the composers were listed as Morey Amsterdam, Jeri Sullavan and Paul Baron (not Maurice Baron, nor related to him), the head of the music department of Columbia Broadcasting Company.

The music of "Rum and Coca-Cola" was almost identical to that of "L'Année Passée." Before turning to their remarkable similarity, it was necessary to establish the genuineness and originality of Lional Belasco's composition, particularly since he had created it thirty-seven years before it was copyrighted by Maurice Baron.

We brought Lionel Belasco to New York. He was almost seventy years old, but handsome and much younger in appearance. He testified to his early training and career. His mother had been a concert pianist and music teacher. At the age of twelve, Lionel began to compose and had written four hundred ballads, psillos, waltzes, calypsos, and rumbas, becoming the foremost composer produced by the West Indies. From the time he was sixteen, he had conducted his own band. Later he turned professional and toured the West Indies—Barbados, Santa Lucia, Martinique, British Guiana, Dutch Guiana, and Venezuela. He played his own music almost exclusively. The Victor Company recognized his talents and in 1914 sent technicians to Trinidad to record his band, the first recordings ever made on that island. Thereafter he recorded more than three hundred songs for Decca, Columbia, and other companies.

Finally he came to the United States, appeared at Carnegie Hall and Grand Central Palace, on national broadcasting chains, and in several motion pictures made by Paramount Pictures Corporation and Columbia Pictures Corporation.

How had he come to write "L'Année Passée?" He testified as follows:

Q. Did you compose the music and the lyrics of the song "L'Année Passée"?

A. Yes, I did.

Q. What is the meaning of the words?

A. It means yesterday.

Q. That is a rather liberal translation?

A. Last year.

Q. When did you compose it?

A. 1906.

Q. Do you recall any special incident with respect to the composition of the lyrics and the music?

A. I do.

Q. What is it?

A. This song was written around a certain happening in Trinidad. There is a small town, and any little happening around there is quite an incident, quite a happening, I should say. And there was a girl of a family, a very prominent family whose daughter had gone to the Convent, and she ran away from her home with a ne'er-do-well, just a common man in the street, people in entirely different social standings; and she lived with this man for quite a little time, and after he put her out on the street, as we say, a streetwalker. She became a streetwalker. Naturally, in a small community that is sensational, and that was really how the song was written. I wrote it around that happening.

Q. Did you know that family?

A. Yes.

Q. What was the name?

A. Soye. The girl's name was Mathilda.

Q. Did you write the words in English?

A. No, in patois. In those days a lot of those songs were written in patois words. That is, French patois.

Q. Now you are not a singer, but may I ask you to sing the words together with the music as you composed it then in 1906, and then translate the substance of the words for his Honor?

A. [Witness sings in patois.]

Q. Now, just briefly tell his Honor in English the substance of that.

A. Briefly, "Last year I was a little girl, I was a little girl at my mother's home; this year I am a streetwalker."

We did not claim that the words of "Rum and Coca-Cola" were similar. Our claim was limited to the music. But the pathos of the original lyrics had led Maurice Baron to construct a dramatic harmonization adding an unessential discord to a chromatic chord. When the defendant copied the music, he fell into the error of copying some of these chords, totally unsuitable to the gay words of "Rum and Coca-Cola." It was a telltale clue, almost as if we had found a musical finger-print, and I never let up on this point, as we shall see.

Also, the detailed social origin of Belasco's song fixed the date of musical composition persuasively as 1906. Finally it gave authenticity to his story, as facts dug up to the very roots always do.

But I was not content to rest there on the origin of our song. I sought corroboration. Who was present when Lionel Belasco, then twenty-five years old, composed the melody? And to whom did he play it originally? Where are these people? Of course, I was told that almost forty years had passed and, even if he could remember their names, he would not know whether they were dead or, if alive, where they were. I brushed all these protestations aside. If ye seek diligently enough, ye shall find. Nothing is impossible. The following witnesses took the stand: First, Gerald Clark, who led a band called "Caribbean Serenaders." He had lived in Trinidad for twenty-eight years and came to the United States in 1927 where, after graduating from high school, he attended Howard University. He had made more calypso records than any living man for such well-known recording companies as Decca, Brunswick, Victor, Keynote, Gill, and Muni Craft. He had given a calypso concert at Carnegie Hall in 1947. He had played at the Ruban Bleu, Village Vanguard, and other night clubs. He was fifty-five years old.

Q. Did you ever make a study of calypso music?

A. From childhood on I studied calypso music. All of us who played music were interested; we idolized Lionel Belasco as a great composer of Trinidad who had brought the calypso to a higher stage. I played the guitar, and I learned Belasco's tunes and played them on my guitar.

Q. How long did you live in Trinidad?

A. For twenty-eight years.

Q. How long have you known Lionel Belasco?

A. Since about 1904. I was a kid then.

Q. Where did he and you live?

A. He lived in Duke Street and I lived in Woodbrook, not very far away.

Q. Was that in Port-of-Spain?

A. Yes.

Q. Would you say that was a few blocks away?

A. Yes, I would call it a few blocks.

Q. And were you intimate with him in 1906?

A. Yes.

Q. What was the nature of your relationship at that time?

A. As I said, I used to play the guitar, and Mr. Belasco had young fellows who went in there and he taught them to play numbers that he composed, and I used to go around there and he would show me some and I would catch—we all never read music—and I would run home and pick up my guitar and practice on it what I learned from him.

Q. Now when for the first time did you hear a song and the lyrics entitled "L'Année Passée"?

A. Well, I heard it from the time Mr. Belasco composed it—1906 it was.

Q. Did he teach that song to you at that time?

A. Yes. I went there by myself, but I met others there, Cyril Montrose, a fellow by the name of James Minerve, there was Lovey, Donawa. There was quite a few boys.

Q. Now is there any way that you can fix the year as 1906?

A. Well, prior to that there was a tremendous fire. A courthouse—not as large as this—it burned down completely, and perhaps a couple of years before, this Mathilda Soye song was written.

Clark explained that when he mentioned the Mathilda Soye song, he was referring to "L'Année Passée." He, too, had heard the story of Mathilda Soye, and his version coincided with that of Belasco.

There was nothing that Mr. Julian Abeles, counsel for the defendant, could do with this impressive testimony. Indeed, the longer he cross-examined Clark, the larger his testimony loomed. He finally tried the oldest of all gambits.

ABELES: But you looked through the book in Mr. Nizer's office?

A. Yes, I went through a few things in Mr. Nizer's office.

Q. Mr. Nizer went over the case with you, spoke to you about the case?

A. Yes. He wanted to know from me how much I knew about it. There were no further questions on this subject. The witness had avoided the oldest trap of denying he had ever spoken to the attorney about his testimony. For some reason, even truthful witnesses with regard for their oath, hesitate to admit that they have reviewed the case and their testimony with the attorney who puts them on the stand. They think such an

admission may invalidate their testimony and they do not wish to destroy
the case they have come to aid. This reveals the unfortunate and false
impression in many quarters that attorneys concoct the testimony given
by the witness. This is as rare as the bank teller who turns out to be an
embezzler or the doctor who keeps the patient ill to extract money from
him. Such dishonesty is almost certain to bring its own retribution, because invented testimony is always bedeviled by facts that spring up on
all sides to expose it.

On the other hand, a lawyer who will put a witness on the stand
without thorough preparation disserves his client, his profession, and the
truth. He defeats justice, because such a witness will wander about un-
knowledgeably without the benefit of having had his memory refreshed by
documents, the recollection of others corroborated by objective facts, and
the truthful history painfully reconstructed by interviews, deposition, and
written evidence gathered over a period of years, sometimes all over the
world. If I should ask you, without preparation, to tell me what you did
on some particular day only last month, you would either not remember
or your spontaneous reconstruction would be full of holes. But if I had
interviewed your secretary, examined your diary, read the letters you sent
that day, traced the people you were with, pressed your own recollection
for hours at a time and weeded out errors, you could reconstruct the
events of that day with substantial accuracy. It is the only way to approximate the truth.

So, when I prepare a witness and reach the cross-examination drill,
pretending to be a hostile cross-examiner, the following often takes place:
I ask, "Have you ever spoken to anybody about this case before you
testified?" He says, "No." I throw up my hands in amazement. "What
are you doing right now?" I ask. "Well, you don't want me to say that,
do you?" "Of course I do, Mr. Jones. I have told you a hundred times.
Tell the exact truth, about everything. All right, I am a cross-examiner
again. Be on your guard. Have you ever talked to Mr. Nizer about the
testimony you gave in this case?" "Yes." "He went over the case with
you in great detail?" "No, I wouldn't say that."

I step out of character again and demand, "Oh, wouldn't you? Haven't
we poured over every fact for hours and hours? Haven't I asked you to
read certain letters, proved certain dates, recited the testimony of others,
and so on? Tell him so when he asks you. He will ask you how many
times you saw me and how many hours we were together. Let's see,
yesterday we were here until 2 A.M.; don't forget it. On the other hand,
he will try to lead you into an inference that I told you what to say. Tell
him the fact about that, too. What would you say?" "Well, you always
asked me to tell the full truth."

Time and again my witnesses have surprised the cross-examiner and
the jury by the frankest revelation of our preparation, and I have never
known a jury to be prejudiced by it. On the contrary, particularly when

aided by my comments in summation, jurors have appreciated the honesty of the witness, which reflected favorably on his other testimony as well.

In the same category is the cross-examiner's questions, "You are a friend of the plaintiff?" followed by "And you want to see him win this case?" The answers should be similarly candid, though it sometimes takes instruction for witnesses to comply. "I am his friend. I want to see him win this case because I think he is right or I wouldn't be here." Many a lawyer has reeled back from such a reply. It is best for the cross-examiner not to press his luck too far. There is a story—vouched for as not apocryphal—of an overzealous lawyer who insisted that the hostile witness tell him whether he had discussed the case with his attorney during the lunch hour and what was said. After considerable reluctance, the witness, on instruction to answer, replied, "I said to my attorney, 'How can we lose this case with such a shyster on the other side?'"

The second witness we put on the stand to testify to Belasco's creation of "L'Année Passée" in 1906 was Walter Merrick. If an attorney had rubbed his Aladdin's lamp and chosen to create an eyewitness who had achieved such eminence that his word would not be doubted, he would have asked for Merrick. I squeezed every detail out of his story. Let the stenographic transcript of the record tell it:

Q. Are you licensed to practice medicine in the State of New York?

A. Yes, for sixteen years.

Q. Where did you graduate from?

A. Howard University, Washington, D.C. I got my Doctor of Medicine there.

Q. What degree did you graduate with?

A. Bachelor of Science.

Q. What other universities have you attended?

A. I went to England where I did post-graduate work with special references to diagnosis and neuropsychiatry and went to the College of Physicians and Surgeons at London for about another year of post-graduate work.

Q. Also Edinburgh?

A. Yes. I first went to the Royal Infirmary of Edinburgh University.

Q. Have you attended any universities in this country since then?

A. Yes, I returned to the United States of America, got my full citizenship, and did postgraduate work at Post Graduate Hospital attached to Columbia University. There I did postgraduate work with special reference to neuropsychiatry.

Q. Are you associated with any hospital at the present time?

A. Yes, I am. I hold the position of assistant visiting neuropsychiatrist at Harlem Hospital, and also I am head director of the Department of Physical Medicine of Harlem Hospital.

Q. Is that a city post?

A. That is a Civil Service position. I get paid by the City for that one. The other is honorary.

Q. Do you specialize in any field in your practice of medicine?

A. Neuropsychiatry and diagnosis.

Q. Have you written medical articles?

A. Yes, from time to time I have written minor works. But at present I am engaged now at Harlem Hospital on a major work on a theory of mine of cerebral dysrhythmia; epilepsy, really.

Q. Have you also been a teacher, and are you one?

A. I have been a teacher in chemistry at Howard University years ago. And here at Harlem I am lecturer in physical medicine to the nurses and also to the incoming interns. I am just preparing a series of lectures to the residents now.

It was gratifying in more than a litigation sense to find that Lionel Belasco's little childhood friend had become an eminent physician. But the Aladdin lamp had greater surprises than that in store for us.

Dr. Merrick stated that he was born in 1896 in Kingston, St. Vincent, a small island just a few miles from Trinidad. He told how, as a child of four or five years of age, his parents fled with him to Trinidad to escape from a volcanic eruption in St. Vincent, and he remained there for about twenty-four years. He then gave the following account of his interest in music:

Q. Have you ever studied music?

A. I have been studying music since the age of six. I played the quatro, the guitar, the violin, but my real instrument is the piano.

Q. How long have you been playing the piano, sir?

A. Well, since the age of six. I have been playing for about forty-five years.

Q. And you can read music?

A. Yes, fairly well.

Q. Will you tell us where you first learned about West Indian music, and more particularly calypso music?

A. I took quite an interest as a boy in Trinidad, and when I grew up with the young men who were all in love with calypso music. It wasn't calypso music at that time. It was Cambuolay, Kalendar, Paseu; and later on, through the vicissitudes and evolutions, it became calypso music in my time.

Q. When did calypso music originate then?

A. In the early 1900s.

Q. Are you familiar with the field of calypso music, and have you made a study of it?

A. I think I will have to be immodest and say yes. I think I know as much about calypso music as anybody living.

Q. Will you tell us on what you base that?

A. I have studied calypso music from the age of six. The bands rehearsed in a bamboo tent adjoining our property, my mother's and father's land in Belmont. There was not a song composed that I did not go there and hear them sing, and join them, and the fellows would come with me and go around with the band. And I studied. I also went to the Arouba bands. Those were the African bands.

He continued to study calypso music while he was in Trinidad and, much against the wishes of his parents, organized a band which played at all the theaters in the length and breadth of Trinidad—Port of Spain, St. Gernando, San Juan, San Grande—from 1913 until he left Trinidad in 1920.

He went on to explain that he was the first person to elevate calypso music to formal theater presentation and that the Victor and Columbia recording companies had engaged him to record in the United States. While he was at Howard University he wrote songs that were played by other bands. He mentioned "Mango Man," "Creole Carnival Memories," "Rum Joe," and many others. They were played by such well-known bands as those led by Cab Calloway, Duke Ellington, Nat Brusiloff, and Louis Jordan. His outstanding work was a light opera, *Black Empire*, performed in Washington in 1931. It earned him a Rosenwald fellowship to write an opera of West Indian life, but Dean Adams and President Mordecai Johnson of Howard University persuaded him to "stick to my medicine." However, he continued to study calypso music as a hobby.

Q. Have you given lectures on calypso music?

A. Scarcely a week passes where I am not asked to speak somewhere on the origin of calypso music. I have spoken at Columbia University. They have asked me to lecture at their School of Music with special reference to calypso.

Q. Were you ever invited by the Government of the United States to represent this country at a music festival?

A. There was a music festival held on the White House lawn and I was asked to receive the West Indian delegates.

Q. Are you working now on a book dealing with the subject of West Indian music?

A. Yes, with Dr. Alain Locke, professor of Wisconsin University. So we had found a witness to Lionel Belasco's original composition, who was not only an eminent physician but also the world's foremost authority on calypso music, whose opera, *Black Empire*, is considered one of the outstanding works of the colored peoples of the world. Truth is more wonderful than fiction. It is as if one were searching for an eyewitness of an automobile accident and found him to be also a foremost medical authority who could testify both to the occurrence and its medical consequences at one and the same time. Dr. Merrick was so qualified musically that we added him to our battery of experts. I shall refer to those developments later. For the present, I need merely point to his conclusive evidence on "L'Année Passée," which he said he learned from Lionel Belasco in 1906.

Q. Did Belasco teach you "L'Année Passée"?

A. Yes. I was a little fellow, and I copied his style of playing—imitation is the sincerest form of flattery—and even today in the playing of a Spanish waltz or a calypso you can scarcely tell the difference of my playing from Belasco's.

Q. Is there any way that you can fix the date of 1906?

A. I left the Government School and was admitted to the high school in 1908. I was still going to St. Anne's School when it happened, so I fix it about two years before 1908.

Q. Did you know what the words referred to in the first verse?

A. I don't know the name of the young woman, but it was about some young woman, the old story, seduced by the villain in the play, and it was the habit then, and still is the habit, that current events are made the theme of calypsos. Belasco said he wrote, he composed it and I had no reason to doubt him. I did not see him compose it. I believed him. He taught it to me.

The third witness we presented was James Francis Minerve. These Trinidad boys were remarkable. Minerve's record was only slightly less impressive than Merrick's.

He was born in Trinidad in 1882 and was brought up there. When he was about thirty-five, he came to the United States to take up permanent residence. He obtained a B.S. degree from Johnson C. Smith University in North Carolina. He also graduated from the New York School of Physiotherapy and was engaged in active practice for some twenty-seven years. He was chief technician of the physiotherapy department of the Department of Hospitals of the City of New York, a position he had held for twenty-three years, and was the author of *Techniques of Physiotherapy*. At one time he had acted as marriage license clerk for the Panama Canal Judicial Department and interpreter to that department in Hindu and Spanish. He received recognition for these services.

With such a background of responsibility, his recollection of certain boyhood events would not be subject to much skepticism. The Rule of Probability had been brought into play, but now I strove to reconstruct details so that special credence would be given to his remarkable testimony.

I elicited from him that he knew Lionel Belasco in 1906. Even at that early stage, Belasco was known all over the island as a musical composer, indeed the only one in Trinidad. They were neighbors and visited each other almost daily. Several boys gathered together at Belasco's home and he taught them the songs that he had composed. The last song he learned before leaving for Panama in 1906 was "L'Année Passée," and he remembered Belasco telling him the Mathilda Soye story associated with the song.

At the time Dr. Merrick and Minerve were pinning down the date as 1906, we already knew that Leo Feist, Inc., had obtained a deposition of an ancient calypso singer of Trinidad, Philip Garcia, known as Lord Executor, who swore he had heard the melody of "L'Année Passée" in 1893, thirteen years before Belasco claimed to have written it.

When a witness cannot be subpoenaed to court because he is out of its jurisdiction, it is possible in law to obtain his testimony in one of two ways. Either the Court issues an order permitting both counsel to travel to the witness's jurisdiction and examine him there before a local judicial officer, or the Court may make an order permitting both sides to submit interrogatories to the witness by mail, the questions and answers being administered by a local official. This latter method is really unsatisfactory, particularly for the opposing lawyer because he never sees the witness and cannot improvise cross-examination according to the answers. He may only submit written questions based upon the written interrogatories served upon him. It is a great disadvantage for the Court as well as the lawyer not to observe the witness under questioning and thus be able better to judge his credibility. That is why appellate courts will not tamper with the factual findings of the lower Court but only with legal errors. Since an appeal is argued on the basis of the printed record of the testimony and no witnesses appear in person, the upper Court recognizes that it has not the same opportunity as the trial judge or jury to evaluate the evidence.

This salutary rule is well illustrated by the interrogatories of Garcia, the Lord Executor. If his testimony, sent in by mail without my having had an opportunity to cross-examine him face to face, were all there was as against Belasco's word, the case might well have been lost on this point alone. For it is also the law that the plaintiff has the burden of establishing his case by a preponderance of evidence. The scales must tip in his favor. If they tip in favor of the defendant or if they are evenly balanced, the plaintiff has not sustained his burden of proof and must lose.

But we did not leave the matter there. In addition to Belasco, we had presented Gerald Clark, who fixed the date of 1906 by the old-fashioned reckoning (which seems to be the truest method of immigrants) —the fire that burned down the courthouse; Minerve, who fixed the month and year because it was the last song he learned before going off to the Panama Canal in 1906; and Dr. Merrick who confirmed the date by his school record; all of them, including Belasco, set the date of the Soye incident as 1905. Far more important, we were able to prove that Garcia was a derelict and his testimony was irresponsible and might have been bought for a dollar. Clark testified that he had only recently returned from Trinidad where he had met Garcia, the Lord Executor, whom he knew very well because he had once recorded with his band.

Q. Tell us in your own way what his condition was when you saw him.

A. If you will excuse the expression, Lord Executor, as I saw him, he is a bum, and he is incoherent—he is not consistent with a conversation. I can say a little more, he has a repulsive odor. I was glad to get rid of him. I gave him some money and got rid of him, because he begs alms, that is what he does for a living, he begs and I was glad to give him a dollar and get rid of him.

Had Gerald Clark, Dr. Merrick, and James Minerve not been found and presented as witnesses, Garcia's fraudulent testimony might have appeared respectable and offset Belasco's word which, after all, was tainted with self-interest.

This is an illustration for those who ask whether a good lawyer can win a bad case or a bad lawyer lose a good case. The answer is yes. Justice is not an abstract, self-revelatory ideal. It is derived from weighing an infinite number of conflicting facts in the classical scale. If, through lack of perception or even of diligence, vital facts are omitted, the scales will tip truly though unjustly. The truth is necessarily the reconstruction of the past, and the lawyer is the artist entrusted with the task of factual resurrection. Like all artists he must not be expected to achieve perfection. Only in the exact sciences is this possible. But at least he can approximate perfection; if he fails too badly, the face of truth will be distorted. The human mind is a sensitive mechanism, responding not only to the body's nerve cells, but to external stimuli to which it is subjected. It cannot be held responsible for stimuli that never reach it when it renders its judgment of right or wrong.

During the cross-examination drill that I gave Minerve in my office, I tested him with the question, "Do you still remember 'L'Année Passée' after all these years? Could you sing it in the original French patois?" His answers were so delightful that I put the questions to him on direct examination.

Q. Did you learn both the music and the words of "L'Année Passée" at that time in 1906?

A. I did.

Q. Did you sing that song to yourself, to your family throughout the years?

A. Yes, sir. Especially around here in the United States, since I am living here, sometimes at work, I would hum it, and then I would sing it to my wife.

Q. You still remembered it distinctly before you ever met any attorney in this case?

A. I did.

Q. Would you give a demonstration to his Honor? Did you sing it in the French patois?

A. Yes.

Q. All right, the way you learned it. Sing the French patois—you are not a singer, are you?

A. No, I am not a singer.

Q. Nevertheless, how would you hum or sing it to yourself?

A. [Witness sings in French patois.]

Q. You sang the word "jal" instead of "femme."

A. Yes.

Q. What does "jal" mean?

A. "Jal" means a streetwalker.

Q. You don't know how the change came about in this song, do you? You had nothing to do with the translation?

A. I had absolutely nothing to do with it.

Q. Before 1906, when Belasco taught you this song, had you ever heard either the words or any similar melody to this melody?

A. No, sir.

So now I felt we had beaten off the only challenge, that of Garcia, the Lord Executor, to the fact that Belasco had composed "L'Année Passée" in 1906. We had persuasively corroborated Belasco's testimony of his original creation of "L'Année Passée" by presenting boyhood witnesses. We had established our base. Now it was time to move to the attack.

Coincidence is the enemy of the plagiarism claim. Even when there is striking similarity between two tunes, it is theoretically possible that they are independent creations and not copies. Therefore, the task of the plaintiff is to show such amazing similarity as to exclude the possibility of coincidence. As Judge Learned Hand once wrote, if two poets independently wrote "On a Grecian Urn," the first creator in time could not sue the second for plagiarism. But would a court be likely to believe that Keats's masterpiece was also written in identical words by someone else who had never heard of it?

So our task now was to make our old friend, The Rule of Probability, our ally.

Of course, I eagerly awaited the opportunity of cross-examining the defendants, and we shall come to those slashing encounters later. In the meantime we created many devices that would lead the Judge to the conclusion of deliberate copying.

First, Maurice Baron, a recognized expert as well as the plaintiff, gave an audible demonstration on the piano. He played "L'Année Passée" and "Rum and Coca-Cola" one after the other, then alternated two bars from each, and again four bars from each. The test in law is the impression created on a layman, not the expert. Therefore the Judge, though unschooled in music, was able to receive a general impression of similarity.

Then we presented a chart on which, instead of notes on a scale, the names of the notes were listed horizontally—do, re, mi, fa, sol, la, si, do. Each note was differently colored. On the top line were the notes of "L'Année Passée" in proper sequence. Underneath were those of "Rum and Coca-Cola." Not only could one see fa under fa and mi under mi in precisely the same place, but since each note had a different color, the visual identity was striking, even if one were tone deaf.

Then we presented a chart of notes drawn on graph paper like Wall Street charts. The upper line—"L'Année Passée"—moving up or down in accordance with the notes, was black. Underneath was "Rum and Coca-Cola" in a graph line of red. There was a third line in blue representing the first version of "Rum and Coca-Cola" (as distinguished from the published one), which was even closer to "L'Année Passée" by a few notes. Now we were ready to draw some mathematical conclusions:

Q. Are there thirty-six notes in the verse of "L'Année Passée"?

A. Yes.

Q. How many in "Rum and Coca-Cola" are identical and in the same sequence as in "L'Année Passée"?

A. There are thirty identical and in the same sequence.

Q. In Morey Amsterdam's first copyright of "Rum and Coca-Cola" how many notes are identical?

A. Thirty-three out of thirty-six.

Q. Would you say that the similarity in the two lines is so great that in your opinion based on forty years of experience as a musician, such similarity excludes the possibility that they were independently created, or that their similarity is a coincidence?

A. I don't know what the laws of coincidence may be—one in a million that those melodies could be alike. I would not say it is impossible. From a musical point of view, and from a coincidence point of view, there is a law of averages, sometimes it may be, but I will prove by the other elements that it cannot be.

Q. I am limiting you just to melody. We will come to other elements at another time. Is this possibly a coincidence?

A. I would say no.

During the submission of our charts, there were strenuous objections by counsel for the defendants that they were musically misleading and inaccurate.

ABELES: It does not indicate the value of each note.

COURT: In other words, it does not indicate whether it is a sixteenth or eighth or half or full note?

ABELES: Yes, or whether it is held and so on. Two compositions can be made to sound entirely different by putting it in different rhythm and different time values.

COURT: All right. What is the answer?

NIZER: This chart is offered for a limited purpose, a comparison of notes to show them in the same sequence, and that the same notes are used in both.

COURT: In other words, you confess that this does not show time value?

NIZER: That is right.

COURT: Now the next question I want to ask myself is whether the absence of the time values can be so deceptive as to constitute a hindrance rather than a help.

NIZER: Well that is a matter for cross-examination, not admissibility. I think I can eliminate the question because I have other charts—

COURT: Which will show the time?

NIZER: Other charts which together with his singing will demonstrate the time value.

COURT: All right, I will receive it subject to the limitation which I have now heard.

We had anticipated these difficulties, for whenever one abandons historical form for novel illustration, some advantages of centuries of practice are bound to be sacrificed. But we inched our way over numerous similar objections that I will not catalogue, and ultimately all of our charts and illustrations were received in evidence. Having shown thirty out of thirty-six identical melody encounters, we turned to the identity of rhythm and time elements. Maurice Baron testified:

A. The relative value of the notes in both compositions in sequence are approximately alike, with some slight differences which could be traced to the lyric of one or the lyric of the other.

Q. When you say changes in lyrics, do you mean that if there is an extra syllable in the words of one song and not in the other, you put in a little extra note for the syllable?

A. Yes.

As to rhythmic pattern, I attempted to clarify his testimony with a summing-up sentence:

Q. You find in these two songs a rhythmic pattern which in its continuity, consecutiveness, and consistency is unique, as distinguished from the general rhythm of calypsos; is that what you mean?

A. That is correct.

Maurice Baron had written the harmony for "L'Année Passée." He pointed out that it had sixteen chords and that "Rum and Coca-Cola" had fourteen identical chords "in the same places and in the same consecutive order."

But most significant of all, one of the chords written by Maurice Baron was musically harsh, so to speak. It was deliberately made so to give a dramatic effect to the word *fille* (little girl) in "L'Année Passée" and thus emphasized the contrast between an innocent girl and the streetwalker she became the following year. The same dissonant or out chord was found in the identical same spot in "Rum and Coca-Cola," though there was no reason for its existence there. Murder will out. The copier had left his calling card.

Common error is the best evidence of copying in any plagiarism action. If I prepare a directory of doctors in the State of New York, I may copyright it. The law protects my research and labor in gathering the data and listing it alphabetically, even though there is no literary creativeness in it. You may not copy my directory and publish it under your name. If you do, you have infringed my copyright and are liable for damages. Also, I can enjoin you from publishing your directory.

But I have not an exclusive property right in the names I have gathered nor in the idea of listing them alphabetically. So if you do not copy my directory, but go out on your own to do the same research I did, you may publish your directory with impunity.

Suppose, nevertheless, I sue you, claiming that your defense of independent research is a sham and that you sought a short cut by taking advantage of my work and copied it. How can I prove that? There is a simple way. I look for common errors. If on page 82 of my directory I made the mistake of giving Dr. Galbert's address as 90 Clark Street instead of 190 Clark Street, and your directory has precisely the same error, what happens to your claim that you never looked at my directory while preparing yours? Why, the Rule of Probability—though not a legal rule at all—does its deadly work. Since in most directories, despite all checking, there are misspellings and other errors, the copier is in real jeopardy. Indeed, it is not uncommon in certain works which, like directories, are easily reproduced, deliberately to insert errors as watchmen against theft.

In literary and other creative works the problem is more intricate, but the same principle applies. The most dramatic illustration of this type that I ever experienced was in the case of a Pulitzer Prize book, *Sam Houston*. Marquis James, the author, had spent seven years researching the life of Houston of Texas. His scrupulous sense for accurate detail had sent him to the archives of France where Houston had been on an official mission for a while, to many states, and to various Indian territories in Mexico and Texas. His book was a huge success and one of the smaller motion picture companies negotiated for motion picture rights. After $30,000 had been offered and rejected, the deal was called off. The company thereafter produced a film called "The Raven" which was the life of Sam Houston. Richard Dix was the star.

Marquis James was understandably indignant to the point of fury. He asked me to institute a plagiarism suit. I pointed out to him that Sam Houston as an historical character was not his exclusive property, that anyone could write or make a motion picture about him, as indeed dozens of books had been written about him and some pictures produced about him, that the motion picture company would undoubtedly produce a script written by its own staff of writers based on their own research, and that this would constitute a perfect defense. Just as he was at the lowest ebb of frustration because of my advice, I let him in on the magical secret of common error.

"If you have taken any liberty with the facts," I said, "using the license in which an author sometimes indulges, and we find that same imaginative incident in the motion picture as if it were historical fact, you may win. Or you may have some facts in your book which, due to your intensive research, no one else could possibly find. If such a fact is in the motion picture, you may win—always provided, of course, that we meet the test of substantial copying. However, I believe a jury will assume substantial copying (I was, of course, again referring to the Rule of Probability which at that time I had not yet articulated specifically) if we demonstrate common error and therefore some copying."

This advice, as I knew, presented Marquis James with a terrible dilemma. If he were to reveal some fiction in his book, would he not be confessing that his vaunted reputation for meticulous honest research, which had earned him the Pulitzer Prize, was vulnerable? It all depended on the nature of the fiction. I encouraged him to make a list of both categories, fiction and facts not available to any one else, and to discuss them with me. After considerable time he returned.

There was fiction and it was quite innocuous. In one scene Houston develops a terrible fever and the Indians save his life. This is historically true. But Marquis James, having lived in Indian territory in his youth and knowing the practices of various tribes and their languages, filled in the dance of the medicine man, described his dress, and set forth the Indian words of some of the chants. This was purely dramatic license. We looked at the motion picture again in one of the movie houses, and, of course, the producer had not been able to resist this perfect motion picture sequence. There was Richard Dix stretched unconscious on a bed of leaves while the medicine man and the Indians, singing the words of James's chant, danced endlessly into the night around the flames that cast weird shadows on a Hollywood-constructed forest.

Also, James had a list of facts that he had dug out from remote sources which he was certain no one else could find. Some of these came from old seared newspaper clippings in some little towns in Texas; others from interviews with old Indians; others from legislative archives, etc. Unfortunately most of these were not necessary to the motion picture and were not used. However, a few were.

On review of the situation, James and I agreed that his reputation would not be compromised by the revelation of the license he had taken in imaginative reconstruction. We started suit.

The defendant, of course, presented its staff writers who had written the motion picture script "from original sources." They produced an impressive bibliography. I cross-examined gently—almost as boringly as I could—for the object was not to alert the witnesses but to lead them by habit to refer to various source material as the origin of this scene or that. When the trap was fully laid and its bear grasp firm, I demanded that the witness produce the source he had referred to and show me the particular detail.

Suddenly the shelter of generalities was gone. No longer could he blithely cite the title and author of some book on Houston which was in the public domain. Where was the specific fact? He could not find it. Nor could he find any other source, except, of course, James's book, and he had to admit that he had read that book. One script writer denied that he had, though peculiarly enough he had read every other book on Houston ever written. His abnegation was as significant as his colleague's indulgence. The suit was settled without further struggle. James collected, his reputation intact and vindicated.

The doctrine of common error is not readily applicable in a music case. But in "Rum and Coca-Cola" we found its equivalent. That is why we developed the point so carefully. Ordinarily in a simple melody such as a calypso song, the harmony is composed of diatonic chords, that is, simple, harmonious chords. The chromatic or somewhat dissonant chord with added discord is a coloration used for more profound music, particularly opera. Maruice Baron, being a composer of an opera and an outstanding musician, had indulged himself when he wrote the harmony for "L'Année Passée." I asked him:

Q. Now tell his Honor where you constructed a chromatic chord, how unusual it is, and where it is. First do that.

A. In the third bar of both "L'Année Passée" and "Rum and Coca-Cola" you will find a most extraordinary chord for this type of music. It is a diminished seventh chord with added discord. It is under the French word *fille* in "L'Année Passée" and under the English word "feel" in "Rum and Coca-Cola."

Q. How many chords are there ordinarily?

A. Thirteenth is as high as you can go in a chord. You have the seventh, ninth, and thirteenth. On the word *fille* I wrote that chord of thirteenth for an effect. The idea was this: "Last year I was a little girl." That is the whole drama of this thing, that last year she was an innocent girl, and this year she is on the street; and I thought I would produce a certain clash on the word *fille* [going to piano and illustrating].

Q. That diminished seventh chord is deliberately made dissonant, is that right?

A. Yes.

Q. Now the seventh diminished chord is composed of what notes?

A. C sharp, E, G, and B flat.

Q. And that chord in itself, without the melodic note of A at the top to which it is a chord, is dissonant, is it not, even by itself?

A. It is dissonant, but not a thirteenth.

Q. But when it is combined with an A is the clash much greater?

A. Yes, because you have the A and B flat which come so near each other, a half tone, which give a violent—well, clash—

Q. Clash is all right. We understand.

A. Clash. Which is used in a dramatic situation.

Q. To represent foreboding or drama?

A. Yes, the drama of that girl saying, "I was a little girl and now I am a streetwalker."

Q. Very well. Now in "Rum and Coca-Cola" in exactly the same place, on the second beat of the third bar, after simple chords, do you find the same seventh diminished—

A. Yes, exactly the same place.

Q. —chord with the A above?

A. Yes.

Q. And what is the language? Is it tragic language, underneath that?

A. No. It says, "They make you feel so very glad." There is a happy sense.

Q. Here, "They make you feel so very glad," and it is right here that the tragic chord is put in?

A. Yes, and that would not require a thirteenth chord to express it, that joy and gladness.

Once a composer has inserted a chromatic chord among a series of diatonic chords, he cannot easily get back to his simple chords. He must build a musical bridge back, or, as the musicians put it, he must resolve it. There are eight choices for this resolution. Once more Maurice Baron chose an unusual resolution. Remarkably enough, the same resolution was found in "Rum and Coca-Cola."

Q. Did you resolve this seventh diminished chord in the normal way?

A. No, I did not. The normal resolution would have been D minor.

Q. And did you use a false, shall I say—is that a fair word?

A. Yes, that is called a false resolution. I resolved it in a dominant seventh chord of C, second inversion.

Q. Why did you do that?

A. I don't know exactly what made me at that moment choose that chord. It is a question of esthetic choice. The first one I can explain, but the second one probably came naturally to me after the first one.

Q. Now I want you to tell me whether in "Rum and Coca-Cola" the resolution from the seventh diminished chord is identical to yours?

A. Yes, I find that the alleged composer of "Rum and Coca-Cola" again used my irregular resolution in the fourth bar, on the word "glad."

Q. And is that the precise same point?

A. Precisely the same point, the beginning of the fourth measure.

In other words, what was so unusual as to be equivalent to a liberty was found common to both songs. The inference of copying was irresistible. We then offered in evidence a chart that compared all the chords in both songs, the few variations being in color, so that the identity of the color for fourteen of the sixteen chords stood out clearly. We continued to pound away at similarity. Both songs were written in the key of C major.

Q. In your opinion, for popular singing purposes, is C major a natural key for "Rum and Coca-Cola"?

A. No. I find it much too low as a popular number. In my opinion it should have been in D, one tone higher. It is too dark for a gay song, too much around the low notes for "Rum and Coca-Cola." For "L'Année Passée," which is a more dramatic song, I think the color, the key of C, is more appropriate.

"L'Année Passée," not being a conventional calypso, had no chorus. "Rum and Coca-Cola" did, but the chorus of a calypso is a mere interlude. It is the least important part of the song. This was rather easy to establish as it turned out. I drew this admission readily from the defendants' experts. But in our direct case Maurice Baron quickly established that the chorus "is merely an obbligato, that is, a variation on the same theme of the verse. Like in Victor Herbert's 'Napoli,' the singer will hold the high note for a few bars and at the end would go back and revert to the original tune. The proof of this is that you can play 'L'Année Passée' or 'Rum and Coca-Cola' with the left hand, and the chorus of 'Rum and Coca-Cola' and the two melodies will fit absolutely like a glove."

Q. In other words, having the verse, the chorus is merely derived from the same music with a variation?

A. Yes, which is called an obbligato on the same melody, the same number of bars.

Q. Now, if you took the verse of "L'Année Passée," if you took that music, you would get the chorus of "Rum and Coca-Cola" from it?

A. Naturally, or we would not be here today.

To thus minimize the chorus of "Rum and Coca-Cola" I had prepared a special recording in which Maurice Baron played the verse of "L'Année Passée" while simultaneously Massie Patterson sang the chorus of "Rum and Coca-Cola." The record was received in evidence, over objection, and was played on a victrola. The melodies did fit like a glove.

I put the final conclusory question to Maurice Baron:

Q. What in your opinion is the cumulative similarity or dissimilarity between these two songs, basing it not merely upon melody alone, but upon all the elements you have testified to?

A. I find it identical, and the alleged composer of "Rum and Coca-Cola" must have copied my "L'Année Passée" in the published version.

We had steeled ourselves for what we knew would be the first attack on cross-examination. Baron was fully prepared.

The defendants were going to claim that "L'Année Passée" was folk music, stemming from unknown sources, and passed on generation after generation from the lips of the natives. Every country has its fund of folk music, the originators of which are unknown, like "Turkey in the Straw" or "Yankee Doodle Dandy." No one owns such music. It is in the public domain.

While there was no doubt in our minds that Lionel Belasco had created "L'Année Passée" as an original tune, there was an unfortunate foreword in the folio published by Maurice Baron upon which we anticipated the defendants would seize. It was one of those things that shorten the life of a trial lawyer, for it did not mean what it seemed to say, but there it was. It read as follows:

The Editor wishes to make acknowledgment to Miss Massie Patterson and Mr. Lionel Belasco, collectors of these authentic Calypso songs from the lips of the Lesser Antilles natives; also to Miss Olga Paul for her expert version of the Creole lyrics.

These songs, though emanating from various parts of the West Indies, are, nevertheless, familiar to the natives of Trinidad, Barbados, Martinique, Guadeloupe, Santa Lucia, etc.

So here Maurice Baron, in his own words, referred to Lionel Belasco as "a collector of these authentic Calypso songs" and, still worse, added "from the lips of the . . . natives."

When I asked him how he came to write such a foreword, obviously contradictory of the true facts, his explanation combined a commercial reason with a naive and ambiguous use of the English language. It was typically Gallic and, coming from him, persuasive. I strove to have him reproduce his answers on cross-examination exactly as he had given them to me, without attempting to improve them by sophisticated reflection. This is how he withstood the attack on cross-examination:

Q. You told Belasco and Patterson you wanted them to collect songs that were popular with the natives in these islands?

A. No, I never did anything like that.

Q. Didn't you say you only wanted songs popular with the natives of the islands?

A. I wanted them to collect from the collection of songs, the songs most representative of all these West Indies islands, and give me the ones that were on the lips of the natives, not some pseudo songs gotten up about "Rum and Coca-Cola" or whatever it was, but the genuine stuff that Belasco had written there and that the people would know, would be on their lips. That is what I meant by collected or selected.

Q. You did not want any songs that had just been written that were not sung by the natives down there, did you?

A. Oh, of course not.

Q. And you wanted to know the background of all these songs, didn't you?

A. Yes.

Q. Where they came from?

A. Yes.

Q. And based upon that you wrote this foreword, didn't you, in the book?

A. Yes.

Q. "The Editor wishes to make acknowledgment to Lionel Belasco and Massie Patterson, collectors of these authentic Calypso songs from the lips of the Lesser Antilles natives." That is correct, isn't it?

A. Correct.

Q. Belasco and Patterson furnished you with the information which is in this foreword, is that correct?

A. This foreword is a commercial foreword that I made because I did not want the book to look that it was Mr. Belasco's songs only, although I have nothing against Belasco—I think the songs are charming—but I wanted the book to say that these songs represented the folk music of today, which is not old, because it is a new music which has been written by somebody who is still alive for Barbados, Martinique, and all these islands. They are authentic, interesting, and people sing them. They are on the lips of people.

The cross-examiner then turned to the contract between Maurice Baron and Belasco and Patterson in which they again stated that they were the collectors of these songs, but Baron exclaimed: "That is true. Collected in the French sense. I can collect my own things, you know."

When Lionel Belasco was cross-examined about this subject, he denied having anything to do with the writing of the foreword.

Q. You did not give him any of that wording at all?

A. No.

Q. These songs you want to say never emanated from different parts of the West Indies?

A. The wording on that is Mr. Baron's.

Q. But did they emanate from various parts of the West Indies?

A. I wrote those songs.

Q. They were not collected from the lips of the natives of the Lesser Antilles?

A. The natives sang some of them.

Q. No. You did not collect them from the lips of the natives?

A. No, I wrote them myself.

Massie Patterson also had to run the gamut of these questions, but she had a better argumentative sense than the others, and knowing the point, she gave more than she received:

Q. Now, "collected from the lips of the Lesser Antilles natives" does not mean that Mr. Belasco wrote those songs—to you—does it?

A. It does.

Q. It means he wrote them?

A. Yes.

Q. He collected them from the lips of the natives and he wrote those songs?

A. He collected them, about the natives.

Q. "Emanating from various parts of the West Indies"—would that mean to you that Mr. Belasco wrote these songs?

A. Yes.

Q. What does "emanate" mean to you?

A. Come from.

Q. So if he uses the words "emanated from those places," the songs come from those places, is that correct?

A. Came from the places Mr. Belasco wrote about.

Q. If he wrote a song about China, then it came from China, is that right?

A. Well, I am not discussing China.

Q. If you say a song came from Barbados, that means to you it is about Barbados?

A. It is about Barbados and it came—

Q. You never—

NIZER: Wait. Let her finish.

A. If it came from Barbados, and whoever wrote it about Barbados, they can say it emanated from Barbados.

Q. Did you tell Mr Baron that these songs were arrangements of public domain songs?

A. Of course not. How could he call his own compositions public domain?

The defendants' experts continued this attack on "L'Année Passée" as folk music. The trouble with their strategy, however, was that they were playing both sides of the street. On one side, they claimed Belasco was not the composer of the melody because it came from ancient sources and was everyone's inheritance, and on the other side, they claimed that the same melody in "Rum and Coca-Cola" was original and created by Amsterdam and Paul Baron. Their over-all strategy was wrong. They could have conceded copying the melody and still have had a better chance arguing: "Yes, we took it, but it doesn't belong to you It belongs to the world as old folk music, so we had as much right to use it as you did." This would have presented a clear issue Nevertheless I believe the testimony of Belasco, Clark, Merrick, and Minerve would have prevailed and established "L'Année Passée" as an original work that could not be copied with impunity. But at least the defendants would not have made the untenable claim that the identity of the two melodies was a coincidence and that Amsterdam and Paul Baron had never heard the melody of "Rum and Coca-Cola" before they wrote it. Their claim to "originality" helped to destroy their more believable claim that this tune was folk music and therefore in the public domain.

In every litigation it is the lawyer's task not only to fight the issues valiantly, but to choose wisely the battleground on which they will be fought. Such decisions involve an over-all evaluation of the strengths and weaknesses of the impending contest, and often a most courageous decision of the ground on which the battle will be pitched. A blurred strategic sense which chooses a terrain with the enemy on the heights can put to naught the most heroic resistance. I have been the beneficiary of such errors in conception on many occasions over a period of thirty years.

We pursued the proof of similarity with additional experts. Dr. Walter Merrick, the distinguished physician who in his boyhood in 1906 had been taught "L'Année Passée" by Belasco and who was now a foremost authority on calypso music, made the most deadly answer on this subject. I asked him to step to the piano and play the first two bars of "L'Année Passée," continue with the next two bars of "Rum and Coca-Cola" and alternate thus between the two songs until finished. The music sounded as if he had played only one or the other composition without alternating. Then:

Q. What is your opinion about the similarity of the two?

A. They are the same. Not identical, but the same piece of music. There are things that are different, similar, the same or identical. It is the same.

The slight variations that did exist, he explained, were due to an extra syllable here or there in the lyrics. "Rum and Coca-Cola" starts with "If you go to Trinidad." To take care of the words "If you" the music started on an upbeat. Whereas "L'Année Passée" started with "L'An" and did not need a note for "If."

Dr. Merrick gave a clear demonstration of the fatal similarity of the diminished seventh chromatic chord in both songs and the identical resolution of both. By this time it was mere repetition, but has that ever injured the art of persuasion?

Professor Norman D. Lockwood was our final expert. He taught musical composition and theory of music at Columbia University. For eleven years prior to coming to Columbia he was Associate Professor of Music at Oberlin College, and he also taught advanced students studying for their doctor's degree in music at Union Theological Seminary. He was also a noted composer, having won the Prix de Rome of the American Academy in Rome for his composition "Odysseus." He had also received an award from the National Institute of Arts and Letters for creative work in musical composition. He had been honored in many other ways, and was Chairman of the Music Committee of the Festival of American Music.

We pinned a chart on a blackboard so the professor could go to work. On the upper line were the notes of "Rum and Coca-Cola." On the lower line "L'Année Passée." Wherever the notes were identical, he had drawn a red line connecting them. Where different, a blue line. His conclusion: "Frankly, this seems to me almost a joke, an unbelievable similarity between these two tunes. I have worked with composers; I have made countless comparisons in the process of writing music, but never have I seen anything to equal this over a space of eight measures. In all music there are similarities, which we call figures, of a few notes, covering perhaps a measure or two. A great many of the classical works are based on very similar short ideas, but here we have eight bars which are virtually identical."

Q. You said only two notes—

A. My deduction is very simple. Out of thirty-eight possible encounters, thirty-six are identical and only two are essentially different.

Q. In other words, Professor, you don't merely find thirty-six out of thirty-eight notes that are the same, but in the same relationship and sequence?

A. Exactly the same order in which the tones appear.

Having established melodic identity, I turned to rhythm. Where a note of one duration is tied to a note of longer duration, it is called a weak suspension. This device is common to a great deal of music emanating from the Mediterranean regions. However, Professor Lockwood pointed out: "The amazing thing to me is that the weak suspension should occur with almost unfailing regularity in bars 2, bars 4, bars 6, and bars 8 of these two melodies.

"I say this is more than a coincidence because looking over calypso melodies one will find that rhythmic device quite frequently, but nowhere except in these examples is this absolute regularity of every other measure."

Now we turned to the harmony and offered another chart that explained the harmonic pattern of each song, chord by chord. Of course, the diminished seventh chromatic chord came in for a scathing lecture: "Now, if two students should bring to me two harmonizations of the same melody, I would spot immediately as an inconsistency that we find in "Rum and Coca-Cola" a chord belonging to this "L'Année Passée" harmonization, having nothing to do with the chords which belong to "Rum and Coca-Cola."

The resolution of this chord was also in his opinion unusual and its appearance in both songs a flag of the copier. His testimony built to the crescendo of a grand conclusion: "I have compared these two publications in their several aspects, melodic, rhythmic, harmonic, and stylistic and on the basis of the similarities which I have pointed out, I find that the possibility of coincidence in the similarity between the two is out of the question. There is no possibility of coincidence."

Before turning the case over to the defendants to proceed, we struck a sudden and swift blow on access.

Paul Baron, the alleged composer of "Rum and Coca-Cola," was a musical director for the Columbia Broadcasting System. We proved that that company had ordered five copies of the folio containing "L'Année Passée." The order and invoice showing payment are received in evidence. The dates were prior to the claimed composition of "Rum and Coca-Cola." We proved that these five copies were kept in the music library of the

Columbia Broadcasting System. Our witness testified: "They are in shelves, not locked, in alphabetical order, and you may refer to anything you want. If you are a staff conductor, you go there regularly to find whatever music you need for the next program and you look up "c" for calypso and B for Maurice Baron."

So Paul Baron had Belasco's "L'Année Passée" at his fingertips when he sat down inspired to create the same melody. While we had once established in another case that unusual internal similarity could prove copying even without proof of access, the persuasive propulsion of access remains undoubted.

We had a number of additional surprise witnesses, but we kept them in reserve for rebuttal. Now I announced on behalf of the plaintiff, "We rest."

What an inappropriate phrase! The moment the defendants' witnesses begin to take the stand, the plaintiff's lawyer becomes a highly sensitized bundle of nerve ends. He must not only be ready to object on proper legal grounds to testimony or exhibits which should be excluded (even a moment's hesitation is prejudicial because the answer may be blurted out before the court can rule), but he must take speedy notes of the testimony, marking cross-examination ideas next to them which he will correlate with the prepared cross-examination. At the same time his observation of the witness must have X-ray sharpness, giving him instantaneous evaluation of every mannerism, every hesitation, every physical movement of the witness, even to the twitching of a jaw muscle or extra blinking of the eyes. And also he must have stereophonic ears, which interpret every inflection of voice, every emotional revelation of hoarseness, stuttering, inept phrasing, slips of tongue, broken sentences because the witness fears stating the conclusion. (We shall see a perfect illustration of this in the cross-examination of Dr. Sigmund Spaeth.)

All these stimuli of sight and sound, registering on the lawyer's mind, give him after many years of experience a sixth sense, a sort of intuitive judgment of where the witness is vulnerable and how to attack. But the process requires the most intense concentration of which the human mind is capable.

I hope I am generally considered self-disciplined and kindly disposed. There is only one thing that sets me off in uncontrollable anger, and that is the interruption of my concentration when a hostile witness is testifying. Associates who whisper in my ear while I am all ears only for the witness may be violently pushed aside and receive apology later for my involuntary rudeness. They have learned to write a note and leave it near me so that I will not lose even a second of hypnotic attention to the witness's words, pitch of voice, and physical movement, the reactions of the twelve jurors, the attitude of the judge, the reactions of the opposing lawyer, his associates, and even those of the stenographer and court attendants.

So complete is this concentration that at the end of a court day in which I have only listened, I find myself wringing wet despite a calm and even casual manner. And in every trial I will lose from two to ten pounds.

The defendants' first witness was Paul Baron, the man they claimed composed "Rum and Coca-Cola." He had been staff conductor for Columbia Broadcasting System for such musical programs as Chesterfield, Camel, Richard Hudnut, Campbell's Soup, and others. He had composed and published about fifteen songs.

He claimed that a singer, Jeri Sullavan, had given him lyrics written by Morey Amsterdam and asked him to write the music. His lawyer asked:

Q.   Did you compose the music of "Rum and Coca-Cola"?

A.   Yes, I did.

He then claimed that he had two melodies in mind at the time he wrote the music, each of which was very similar to "Rum and Coca-Cola." He had only recently refreshed his mind as to the names of these two melodies. One was a Spanish *pensamiento* and the other a song called "King Ja-Ja." When his attorney offered each of these songs in evidence, I used every legal recourse to exclude them from evidence. Even if this effort turned out to be unsuccessful, I knew the issue would be so highlighted that later cross-examination would be clearer and more effective.

ABELES: I offer the *pensamiento* song in evidence.

NIZER: I object on the ground that this witness claimed that somebody refreshed his recollection about this melody. His recollection might be admissible, but the document which is alleged to have refreshed it does not thereby become admissible. My objection is not merely technical. There is no date on this. Our song was written in 1906. Aside from dissimilarity—I won't go into that at this time—the offer of a document which might be published after 1906 would not be pertinent evidence with respect to the issues before your honor.

COURT: Well, the objection is well taken.

ABELES: I will withdraw the song then.

But Paul Baron proceeded to testify that he recalled the melody of the *pensamiento* and also its title at the time he composed. It finally went into evidence. He then testified that he also had the music of "King Ja-Ja" in mind and that song was offered in evidence:

NIZER: The defendant filed a copyright for "Rum and Coca-Cola" claiming originality and collected large amounts of money for it, and now proceeds on the stand to prove that he was unoriginal.

COURT: I have noticed that already.

But the booklet containing "King Ja-Ja" was also received in evidence. Then his lawyer asked:

Q.   Did you take or copy any part of the music of plaintiff's song "L'Année Passée"?

A.   No, I did not.

Finally he offered the first piano copy of "Rum and Coca-Cola" in evidence. During his examination before trial, I had repeatedly asked for the original manuscript and he said he was unable to find it. I therefore asked for special permission to cross-examine him solely as to admissibility of the document. It is an unusual procedure that permits some cross-question in order to determine whether a proper objection can be made. The court granted my request.

NIZER: You say this was taken from the original score which you wrote?

A. Yes.

Q. Where is the orignial?

A. I don't know.

Q. Didn't you think that in a lawsuit involving the originality of your music that the original document on which you claim you wrote the music was going to be an important paper for your purposes, not ours?

A. Yes. I asked Miss Sullavan about the original score and she had no idea where it was.

Q. You tell us the original score which you claim you wrote of this song has completely disappeared, so far as you know?

A. So far as I know, yes.

Q. Did you write the harmony as it now appears on this copy?

A. Yes, I did.

NIZER: I object to this copy going into evidence. It is not the best evidence. The witness has testified that there was an original, which he wrote in his own hand which was delivered to the Feist Company or to Miss Sullavan. Both are defendants here. I say that in a case involving the authenticity of the original music and its originality of composition, the disappearance, without any explanation of where it is, or calling witnesses to explain that they had it and lost it, is improper. No foundation has been laid for a copy made by some person who does not appear; and particularly in the light of the fact that there were repeated requests over the years for this document in depositions, and at no time was even this copy produced, nor was it claimed that there was such a document. On the contrary, we were told that there is none. Under all these circumstances I object to this.

ABELES: I withdraw it for a moment.

Again the defendant mended his fences and offered the copy in evidence.

NIZER: Same objection. No proper foundation laid; no proper proof for its admissibility.

COURT: What you have said I think goes to its weight, but I think a sufficient explanation for the absence of the original has been made for the purposes of admissibility, whatever effect it may have upon weight. Objection overruled.

So Paul Baron had finally put his copy of the alleged music composed by him into evidence together with the music of a *pensamiento* and "King

Ja-Ja" from which melodies he had derived his own. But now he had to run the gamut of cross-examination. His direct testimony takes up 33 pages of the printed record, the cross-examination 136 pages.

    Q. Now before you wrote the music which you claim you wrote of "Rum and Coca-Cola" you knew that Mr. Amsterdam had been to Trinidad?
    A. Yes.
    Q. And that he heard a song entitled "Rum and Coca-Cola" there; you knew that?
    A. Miss Sullavan told me that.

But he claimed it had been sung in Trinidad to a musicial pattern such as "It Ain't Gonna Rain No Mo'." He insisted that Amsterdam had not given him a demonstration of the tune, whatever it was. I then faced him with his original testimony at the examination before trial:

    Q. My next question was: "And Amsterdam made an attempt to reproduce these tunes?" You replied, "Yes." You later changed that answer to read "Amsterdam gave me his demonstration."
    A. Yes.

There was a long wrestling match over this conflict of testimony, he persisting that Amsterdam had not demonstrated the tune. But finally he weakened and his shoulders were pinned to the mat on this point.

    Q. Did you ask Amsterdam to give a demonstration of the tune the soldiers were singing?
    A. Yes.

What Paul Baron didn't know was that we had some surprise witnesses seated among the spectators in the back of the room. They were soldiers who had sung "Rum and Coca-Cola" in Trinidad at the very time Amsterdam had arrived at the airport. They had not sung it to the pattern of "It Ain't Gonna Rain No Mo'," but to the very music that Paul Baron claimed he was inspired to write on his own!

    Q. You don't consider the tune of "It Ain't Gonna Rain No Mo'" as having any similarity to the music of "Rum and Coca-Cola" do you?
    A. Well, there is a similarity inasmuch as the construction is the same.
    Q. Well, have all waltzes the same kind of construction, Mr. Baron?
    A. As far as tempo is concerned.
    Q. And do all fox trots have the same kind of construction?
    A. If you say the 4/4 tempo is the same, yes.
    Q. What would you say?
    A. All fox trots have the same tempo.
    Q. If "It Ain't Gonna Rain No Mo'" were a copyrighted piece of music, would you feel free to compose "Rum and Coca-Cola" or would you feel you were infringing?

A. No, I wasn't infringing on "It Ain't Gonna Rain No Mo'" melodically.

This last answer knocked down the edifice constructed by the defendant that it was really "It Ain't Gonna Rain No Mo'" which with some changes became the melody of "Rum and Coca-Cola." Paul Baron still persisted that he had composed the melody before he ever heard any demonstration from Morey Amsterdam and therefore could not have copied it. I confronted him with an opposite statement from his examination before trial:

Q. Did you use the tune that Amsterdam sang to you?

A. Since what Amsterdam sang was also the same general sound—but actually I paid very little attention to what he sang.

Q. Did you ask Amsterdam about the tune they were singing in Trinidad?

A. Well, naturally I asked him.

Q. What did he tell you?

A. He tried to give me a very unable demonstration.

Q. Of the tune?

A. Yes, it was a very simple matter from there to put the two together because I vaguely remembered a melodic form that was very common to calypso music.

He still insisted that he wrote the melody before hearing Amsterdam's "unable demonstration" and that the reason he had given the conflicting answer was that my questions "were tricky." I did not permit him even this solace—the frequent cry of a trapped witness. I asked:

Q. My first question was: "What did he tell you?" Do you consider that tricky?

A. I would say the whole general question—

Q. No, I am asking you about this. Is "What did he tell you?" a tricky question?

A. No.

Q. Then "Question: of the tune?" Is that a tricky question?

A. No.

The reason Paul Baron had used the awkward phrase "unable demonstration" was to give the impression that he could not even understand the music that Amsterdam sang to him. I asked him if this wasn't so. He denied it. Then I quoted Amsterdam's answer in his examination before trial: "I can sing anything. If a publisher comes up to me with a song tonight, I will sing it on the program tomorrow."

When Paul Baron originally took the stand, his clean-cut, neat appearance and his sincere, cultured manner had given considerable veracity to his testimony on direct examination. By this time, the cross-examination had already disheveled him. Not only had his shiny black hair become less orderly, but his distressed face, halting speech, and shifting attitudes had cast a serious doubt on his story. This is the kind of cross-examination which "roughs up" a witness, takes him off guard, and raises fears in his own mind as to whether he can hold his ground. But we had barely begun.

It was apparently in the late stages of preparation that the defense had identified the tunes that were in Paul Baron's mind when he sat down to write the music, namely, "It Ain't Gonna Rain No Mo'" and "King Ja-Ja." But afterthoughts are dangerous. They often do not jibe with prior events.

When Paul Baron had testified in an examination before trial, he had not mentioned "It Ain't Gonna Rain No Mo'" or "King Ja-Ja" as his inspiration.

Q. When you made your answers in the examination before trial, you had forgotten about "It Ain't Gonna Rain No Mo'"?

A. No, I didn't say I had forgotten it.

Q. You didn't put it in at the time you made your original answers; you know that?

A. Well, when I saw my mistake I put it in.

Q. What was it that reminded you of the mistake and reminded you of "It Ain't Gonna Rain No Mo'"? Who reminded you?

A. Say I reviewed it in my mind.

Q. It just came to you in your mind?

A. It came to me from remembering certain things that happened.

I pointed out to him that Amsterdam in his deposition had referred to "It Ain't Gonna Rain No Mo'." Was it this which planted the idea in his head? He replied:

A. I don't remember what reminded me of it.

Q. You thought of that quite independently?

A. Yes, sir.

As to "King Ja-Ja" I took a calculated risk. The witness seemed sufficiently shaken to make the gamble worth while. He claimed the melody of "King Ja-Ja" had been a source for his inspiration. The day before, the music of "King Ja-Ja" was on the counsel table and I had noticed that during a recess he had stopped to study it. Could it be that he wasn't even prepared to reproduce that melody without looking at the music? I asked him to step to the piano and play it. Then I asked him to repeat it. He couldn't do it the same way.

Q. Well, that second part isn't the way you played it before, is it?

A. Well you play it ten times, and you get the same thing all the time—a change here or a change there.

Q. Well, I am asking you a simple question. The second part isn't the way you played it a moment ago, is it?

A. I doubt it.

Q. And that is true of the first part you played too, isn't it?

A. That is right.

Now, being convinced that the whole "King Ja-Ja" story was an afterthought, I gave the witness his head, something one should rarely do in cross-examination. The art of cross-examination requires tight reins. No matter how complex the question, it should be so phrased that the witness can answer yes or no. One can't be hurt very much by such a reply. But the witness should rarely be given an opportunity to make a speech. Obviously he will embroider his answer with self-serving declarations. Therefore one can quickly spot a bad cross-examiner if he asks "Why?" or "Will you explain that?" This opens the door, and the witness may buttress whatever weakness has developed in his story. Of course, his opportunity to give his most favorable version has already been granted him on direct examination; there he can expatiate, embroider, color, and justify. The cross-examiner's task is different. He must squeeze admissions or contradictions from hostile lips. He doesn't want the witness to repeat his original story. That is the reason for tight questioning. But every rule has its exceptions. I was so sure Paul Baron was floundering that I gave him that rare opportunity:

Q. Will you describe what it was you saw when you saw a copy of "King Ja-Ja" originally? Was it with a cover? Was it a manuscript? Was it published? Was it sheet music? Were there words in it? I leave it entirely to you, but just describe to the best of your recollection what you saw, will you?

A. I can't.

Now I was encouraged to give him even more latitude.

Q. Do you remember whether it was in printed form or in written note form, manuscript form?

A. I don't remember. It probably was not in printed form because many of these things are put together in a copy of manuscript form.

Q. Again, Mr. Baron, I don't want to know probabilities. I am testing your memory, and if you will tell me where you saw it, or you don't remember, I will accept your answer, but don't tell me about probabilities. I am not interested in what might have happened. Do you remember whether it was on a large or small sheet?

A. I don't remember.

Q. Or the color of the paper?

A. I don't remember.

Q. Or whether it was music paper?

A. I don't remember.

Q. Do you know whether it had words?

A. I don't think so.

Q. Do you recall how many years before you sat down to the piano you think you might have seen "King Ja-Ja"?

A. I don't remember.

Q. Was it a piano copy or otherwise?

A. It was probably just a single line.

Q. Not "probably." Do you remember?
A. No, I don't.
Q. Was it in a book?
A. I don't remember.
Q. Do you remember in what city you saw it?
A. No.

On his examination before trial Paul Baron had referred to a strain of music in his mind, without mentioning "King Ja-Ja." I had asked him to write down that strain on a music sheet. Now I asked him to play that music sheet and he was forced to admit that it bore no similarity to "King Ja-Ja." Again we had demonstrated that "King Ja-Ja" was a concocted afterthought. The final thrust consisted of having him play "King Ja-Ja" and selecting therefrom the "strain of music" which he remembered and which he said inspired music of "Rum and Coca-Cola."

A. I can't find it exactly but you will find here a phrase [playing] in "King Ja-Ja."
Q. Isn't that just a cadence you just played?
A. It is a passing note.
Q. A passing note?
A. Yes.
Q. And you mean that is the strain which you recall? Play those few notes again.
A. Just a moment.
Q. Just do as I say. Mr. Baron, you are a defendant and a witness here, and please stop questioning me. His Honor will rule if any of my questions are wrong, and counsel will object. Please be a witness and not a lawyer. Please play the passing phrase which you said was the same. I think it was three or four notes.
A. [Playing]
Q. How many notes have you played?
A. That is four notes.

While our claim was limited to the taking of the music, not the lyrics, it was significant that the words also, by the same extraordinary coincidence were almost identical with the "Rum and Coca-Cola" lyrics heard by Amsterdam in Trinidad:

Since the Yankees came to Trinidad,
They have the young girls going mad,
The young girls say they treat them nice
And they give them a better price.

They buy rum and Coca-Cola
Go down Point Koomahna
Both mother and daughter
Workin' for the Yankee dollar.

Amsterdam's version was slightly cleaned up by substituting for "And they give them a better price," a less crass sentiment, "Make Trinidad like Paradise."

Now Paul Baron had to run the gamut of questions concerning the changes in credits for the music of "Rum and Coca-Cola." After determined resistance and evasion, the telling admission was wrung from him:

Q. You know what copyright means? You sometimes give credit to a lyric writer or to the music writer.

A. Yes.

Q. In this case you were willing to give Amsterdam credit for the whole thing, the music as well as lyrics, is that right?

A. Yes.

Paul Baron then took the preposterous position that he never knew that the recording made by the Andrews Sisters of "Rum and Coca-Cola" also listed Morey Amsterdam as the sole composer of the music and lyrics.

Q. You never looked at a record?

A. I never looked at the labels properly, no.

Q. You were not interested in whether you got credit on those recordings of the Andrews Sisters?

A. No.

Q. And you say the first time you learned about this fact is right now when I showed you this record?

A. Yes.

Q. At the time these recordings first appeared, this was the biggest recording hit in the country, isn't that so?

A. Yes.

Later Jeri Sullavan was listed as composer with Paul Baron. But she had not contributed anything to the music. So another prejudicial admission was wrung from him:

Q. And so, isn't it a fact that the announcement on the final published copy "Music by Jeri Sullavan and Paul Baron" is an incorrect announcement so far as the facts are concerned; isn't that a fact?

A. The way you put it, yes.

The defendant had gotten into evidence a piano copy of the musical composition allegedly composed by Paul Baron. I had objected because the original sheet had not been produced, and also because Paul Baron had never claimed before that he had a piano copy. The Court, however, ruled that this was a matter for cross-examination. Now Paul Baron had the task of explaining the last moment production of a copy that he could not find for three years, and also what had happened to the original. I sought to throw a shadow of fraud upon the copy produced. Piano copies must, under the Musicians Union's rules, have a union stamp and the signature of the union copyist. This copy had no stamp, and the name of the copyist was printed in pencil in a corner, rather than signed in proper form. The pummeling he received on these subjects together with his statement that he composed the music in "half an hour" made the air in the courtroom thick with skepticism.

The final blow was to read to Paul Baron the following, made on his examination before trial when he did not realize the significance of the question:

Q. In a general way, do you avoid dissonant chords in this harmonization? A. I don't have to avoid them; they just don't occur.

Q. Do I correctly understand, then, that the harmonization was more or less intuitive and suggested directly by the simplicity of the melody itself? A. Yes I might safely say that any composer would have done exactly the same thing."

At that time Paul Baron was not even aware of the discordant seventh chromatic chord and its unique nature. Here I sought no contradiction. I wanted him to confirm this statement. The most alluring question to achieve this objective was:

Q. You stand by that, don't you?

A. Yes, I do.

When I was through with cross-examination, there was no redirect examination. Paul Baron's lawyer made no attempt to rehabilitate him. He just wanted him off the stand as quickly as possible. The Court later wrote in its decision: "Paul Baron's claim to authorship of the composition is a fabrication."

Now Morey Amsterdam took the stand. He was intent upon making wisecracks. In answer to the very first question, "What is your profession?" he replied, "Well, I am a comedian—when they laugh." Performers are usually bad witnesses because their exhibitionistic tendencies are stronger than their desire to persuade. Whenever I represent an actor I go through a terrible struggle to eliminate his ambition to give a starring performance on the stand. Persuasion does not come from affectation or from charm or from wit. It is derived from sincerity. That is why illiterate witnesses or those from humble stations in life, who are awed by the courtroom, may nevertheless be the best witnesses.

In the plagiarism suit involving *The Great Dictator*, Charles Chaplin testified on direct examination for about fourteen hours. He gave one of the greatest acting performances ever seen. But I am sure it was ineffectual with the jury. They were entranced but not convinced. He ran through his imposing list of gestures; he turned on the charm as only a consummate artist can; he simulated dark perplexity and then his face lit up with flashes of sudden recollection; he gazed into the jurors' eyes in long silent exclamation points; and then gave them his famous toothy grin; he made them laugh and sometimes feel very sad; but it was evident he never persuaded them. Being sensitive to audience reaction, he felt the icy winds that blew from the jury toward him, and one could observe his frustration, like that which any actor suffers when his performance leaves his audience cold. The jury was never fooled by his histrionic genius. He settled $100,000.

Amsterdam testified like a comedian far more interested in a quip than in forthrightness. He prospered during his direct examination, which was so brief that it is recorded in only eight pages of the record. But his comic gaiety gave way to ill-disguised embarrassment during a cross-examination that lasted seven times longer.

His background as a performer was impressive enough. He had written comic material for Milton Berle, Fanny Brice, Clark Gable, Frank Morgan, and "innumerable other stars." He had twelve radio shows of his own every week. During the war he had volunteered his services for the USO and traveled to the West Indies. That is how he landed in Trinidad.

While on his way to an Army base to entertain, he passed Point Koomahna where the soldiers used to spend their recreation time. A soldier in his car sang verses to a tune like "It Ain't Gonna Rain No Mo'," and the interlude was "Rum and Coca-Cola kill the Yankee Soldier." He adopted this idea for his entertainment, creating verses that he was delighted to reproduce in song on the witness stand. I expected him to bounce off the chair and bow to imaginary tumultuous applause.

On every isle in Caribbean Sea
Native girl dress peculiarly
She wear grass skirt but that's O.K.
Yankee like to hit the hay.

She wear nothing at all from stomach to face
Just to show heart is in right place
She wear sarong like native should
But sarong is only dish towel that "make good."

I bought a dog in Trinidad
Best damn dog I ever had
He's so smart like real Quiz Kid
Saw a sign say "Wet Paint," so he did.
(He so smart that little pup
Walk on front legs if you hold back ones up.)

In Trinidad out on Green Hill
Lives native man called Papa Bill
He got 65 kids in the Carabeen
He never heard of Ovaltine.
(He got 65 wives but he still feels blue
'Cause he got 65 mothers-in-law too.)

When he returned to the United States he claimed he gave several verses to Jeri Sullavan and told her to get Paul Baron to write a melody. Later, when the song was a success, he asked one of his musicians, "Will you scratch me out a lead sheet," so that he could copyright it. He put his name on it because he thought it was special material "and I figured the melody wasn't important."

He concluded by saying, "There were no calypsos in Trinidad when we were there," and that he had never heard "L'Année Passée." His counsel turned him over for cross-examination with the traditional, "Your witness." This turned out to be prophetic. I struck a quick opening blow:

    Q. Have you ever heard calypso-type singers prior to this litigation?

    A. No, sir.

    Q. I will read to you this question and answer from your deposition before trial, page 32: "Q. Are you acquainted with calypso music? A. I have heard probably about as much of it as anybody else has." Do you recall making that answer?

    A. Yes.

He claimed he had heard the song from one soldier only while driving to a camp. This was to negate the fact that the song was widely known on the island. He repeated this on cross-examination:

    A. I heard a song "Rum and Coca-Cola kill the Yankee Soldier" by one soldier, before I did it, not by others.

    Q. Only by one?

    A. Only by one soldier, a fellow who drove us in the car.

I confronted him with his prior testimony on the examination before trial:

"Q. Did you hear it from others before you publicly sang it at the base? A. Yes I did. Q. From how many persons would you say you heard that song before you publicly rendered it? A. Well, I cannot say the exact amount, but I knew it was well known among the boys or I would not have repeated it."

When I asked him whether he didn't remember having so testified, he replied, "I don't remember what happened yesterday." He had already lost his cockiness. His composure was next to go. He admitted that the first performance which he gave of "Rum and Coca-Cola" was exactly as he had heard it, both words and music; later he wrote his own lyrics which were different. But we produced a booklet published in Trinidad of the earlier lyrics, and they were practically the same as his alleged original version.

    Q. Can you explain how it came about that the first three lines of the first verse of the song as you rendered [heard] it in Trinidad happen to be exactly the same as the first three lines of the verse in the book, the Souvenir Collection?

    A. No, sir, I cannot. I never saw the book until after I returned to this country.

    Q. It is a rather startling coincidence, isn't it?

    A. But it is not the first time it has happened.

He was faced with the same dilemma regarding the chorus.

    Q. And that is also a rather startling coincidence?

    A. Yes, sir.

Amsterdam had once faced another charge that he had stolen a melody called "Oh, My Achin' Back." Strangely enough, his explanation there also involved "It Ain't Gonna Rain No Mo'." I quoted his testimony to him:

"A. Here is the exact story. Astaire and Crosby went over together. Willie Shore was with Astaire. He said, 'Go out and say "Oh, My Achin' Back."' Incidentally they sang it to the melody of 'It Ain't Gonna Rain No Mo'.' I taught him to sing the new melody."

Wasn't it a curious coincidence that once before he had transformed a song from "It Ain't Gonna Rain No Mo'" melody to one charged with plagiarism? Now I went back to "startling coincidences" with respect to the music. The "scratch lead sheet" which he copyrighted was even closer to "L'Année Passée"—by three notes—than the published version of "Rum and Coca-Cola."

Q. Would you consider that a startling coincidence too?

A. A coincidence perhaps but not a startling coincidence.

Then I pointed out that the change from the note A in the scratch sheet to E in the published version was exactly as the soldiers testified they sang it in Trinidad.

Q. Would you consider that a startling coincidence?

A. A coincidence, but not startling.

I confronted him with another clue of the copying:

Q. Suppose I were to tell you that same difference in time value exists on exactly the same note in "L'Année Passée," would you consider that a startling coincidence?

A. A coincidence, but not startling. It is not unusual in music.

Q. There has been testimony here by a musical expert, Professor Lockwood, that out of 38 notes in the music of the verse of "L'Année Passée," 36 notes are the same as in "Rum and Coca-Cola" and in the same sequence; would you say that that was a startling coincidence?

A. Just a coincidence.

Q. Not startling?

A. Not startling.

By this time his position had taxed credulity so badly that his answers could no longer hurt me. So I summed up the situation just to make his denial sound even more hollow.

Q. Let me ask you this: Let us take these three or four coincidences without the word "startling" next to them, and if you put them all together, would you say it was a startling series of coincidences—the fact that they were all combined?

A. No, sir, I would not.

Now I demanded and received a confession of errors.

Q. The statement on the first copyright that you are the sole composer of the music is untrue, isn't it?

A. That is right.

Q. That is a false statement, isn't it?

A. That is right.

When the Andrews Sisters' recording came out, it also listed Morey Amsterdam as the composer.

Q. Well that was not a correct designation, was it?

A. No.

I asked him to sing the words of "Rum and Coca-Cola" to the music of "It Ain't Gonna Rain No Mo'." He floundered. I pressed:

Q. You could not really sing it to the tune of "It Ain't Gonna Rain No Mo'" could you?

A. No. That is why I say it was close to "It Ain't Gonna Rain No Mo'."

Amsterdam had given an interview to *Time* magazine. There he had said that he had "imported" the song to the United States.

A. That is untrue.

Q. And being untrue did you do anything to protest to *Time* magazine for having misquoted you?

A. It wasn't that important to me.

A month later, riding on the tide of fame of the song, he had been interviewed by Earl Conrad of a newspaper called *PM*. The story read:

Q. "Amsterdam said he had picked up the Coke song while he was on a recent theatrical trip in the West Indies. Once he heard some native musicians singing a song with a catchy chorus. He said the West Indians pronounced the words 'motha and dawtah' and 'Wo'king fo' de Yohnkee Dollah.' He bought the rights of the tune, he said, and supplied his own lyrics." That is also a misquote?

A. Yes, sir.

Q. Did you take any steps to correct the impression that had been published that you simply brought back the tune?

A. No.

Q. Nothing at all?

A. No.

We traced the reporter, Earl Conrad, subpoenaed him and put him on the stand in rebuttal. He confirmed the accuracy of every quotation attributed to Morey Amsterdam, including the following sentence in the newspaper story: "The following day we met Amsterdam, who is a stocky, wide-awake chap. There were also three pretty girls, and while Amsterdam was in the bathroom dressing and singing we listened to them discuss the songwriter's possible take on a song hit. Later Amsterdam said he expected to make about $60,000 on the song."

Q. Did he tell you that?

A. Yes, he told that to the whole group that was there.

Conrad's testimony concluded with: "I thought the principal fact of the story was that the song was the sensation of the time, that the man said he had picked it up in the West Indies."

Conrad could not be shaken in cross-examination. Indeed, it came out that he had had interviewed Albert Einstein, Louis Adamic, Father Divine, was the author of several books, and had a fine reputation for integrity.

When Amsterdam stepped off the witness stand, everyone in the courtroom knew, including himself, that he had been discredited. If a comedian is only a comedian when they laugh, a defendant only defends when he is believed. The Court did not. Its written opinion was a complete condemnation of him. It read: "There is no doubt in my mind that Amsterdam brought both the words and the music with him from Trinidad, and it was in substantially that form that the song was published."

Nevertheless, our case could easily be lost on the testimony of the next witness, Dr. Sigmund Spaeth. We had destroyed the defendants' claims of original creation, but the decisive question remained, was our music so original that it would warrant an injunction against "Rum and Coca-Cola" or any other similar melody? Of what avail was it to win all the battles and lose at Stalingrad?

Spaeth was Stalingrad. In dozens of lawsuits involving musical copyrights, plaintiffs had been on the verge of victory only to be repelled by Dr. Spaeth's musical resourcefulness and demonstrations. He was reputed never to have lost a case for a defendant. I knew very well that he would be the Feist Company's last and most important witness and that its real reliance was upon him. I warned my client and legal associates that the real crisis of the case was going to turn on Spaeth's testimony. If it stood, we would fall. If, for the first time, he fell, we would win. I had not overstated the situation one whit. Spaeth's skill presented what appeared to be insurmountable obstacles. He put into evidence twenty-one songs of "common ancestry"; he produced nine songs with the diminished seventh discordant chord on the third bar; he demonstrated with charts that our claim that 36 out of 38 notes were the same was false and that only 12 out of 38 notes were similar; he produced two songs that were far more similar to "L'Année Passée" than "Rum and Coca-Cola"; he demonstrated the weak suspension similarity in a dozen other songs; he disqualified our charts chiefly because they did not properly reflect rhythm and time differences which can make similar notes sound dissimilar; and, above all, he insisted that "L'Année Passée" was copied from folk music which belonged to the world.

The qualifications of an expert are like the pedestal for a statue—the more imposing, the nobler the subject above it appears. Dr. Spaeth built a high pedestal for himself. He had recited his qualifications so often that he could rattle them off in his sleep. His lawyer asked him:

Q. Dr. Spaeth, if you please, what is your vocation?

A. I am a writer, a broadcaster, and lecturer on music, for twenty-seven years.

Q. Have you written any books on music?

A. Yes. Twenty-two so far, and I am finishing the twenty-third right now.

No one was more grateful for Dr. Spaeth's prolific pen than I was. He was to learn that I had become his most studious reader. He described his posts as music critic with leading newspapers like the New York *Times* and the Boston *Transcript*. He had been music critic of *McCall's* magazine, *Esquire, Literary Digest,* and *Life.* He had been on the faculty of Princeton University for two years with Woodrow Wilson. At the time of the trial, he was broadcasting Saturday afternoons from the Metropolitan Opera House. He had been doing so for six years, conducting an opera quiz between acts broadcast "to about 15,000,000 people." For the past twenty-six years he had lectured "in practically all important colleges, including Columbia, New York University, and the University of Hawaii in Honolulu. He was also a composer and lyric writer." Mr. Abeles, defendant's counsel, asked him to name some of his outstanding works.

A. Well, for words there are three in the hit class. "My Little Nest" for which Franz Lehar wrote the music. "Chansonette," music by Friml; that song was later turned into "Donkey Serenade." It was played by Paul Whiteman, at which he introduced the "Rhapsody in Blue" by George Gershwin. That was a great historic occasion and that program included "Donkey Serenade," for which I wrote the lyrics.

His compositions had been published by Schirmer, Fischer, Berlin, Harms, and many others. For nine years he was president of the National Association of American Composers and Conductors. As to his special field: "I have specialized particularly in popular tunes in folk music and in classic, and so on; and I have always been interested in the analysis of tunes, and particularly concentrated on popular music, on which I am at present writing a book."

Q. Have you used records of calypso music for any purpose?

A. Yes, to illustrate calypso as a form of folk music. I have used it in the classroom.

Then Dr. Spaeth got to work on our case. But I shall take the motion picture privilege of a dissolve and bring forward the cross-examination addressed to his qualification. It was designed to give a more realistic appraisal of his stature.

Q. Dr. Spaeth, in the course of your professional activities you have become known as a tune detective, is that right?

A. That title has been applied to me, yes.

Q. And you have performed in theaters as a tune detective giving entertainment and demonstrating that art of being a tune detective?

A. At one time, yes; a good many years ago.

Q. In some vaudeville theaters?

A. Only for guest performances, yes.

Q. And then you also appeared on the radio, on commercial and sustaining programs showing how you do your tune detective work?

A. That is right. I might say I did one week at Radio City Music Hall under Roxy as a tune detective. I have done it for entertainment and for instruction.

Q. Well, also for pay.

A. Well, sometimes yes, sometimes not.

Q. And in addition to Radio City Music Hall, you have appeared in smaller vaudeville theaters, haven't you?

A. Occasionally, yes.

Q. Will you mention some of them please?

A. Well there was one in Casper, Wyoming. I cannot remember the name of the theater.

Q. Who else was on the bill with you?

A. I have not the slightest idea.

Q. Was there an acrobat act on?

A. I don't know, because the way—

Q. All right. You don't know.

A. I don't know. I could give you the bill on Radio City Music Hall.

Q. But I did not ask you that.

A. That is one I remember. Theaters I do not.

Q. And you were booked through a regular professional agent?

A. No, I was not.

Q. You did it yourself?

A. Yes.

Q. How long did your act take?

A. It varied, depending on how much time they wanted for that.

Q. Well, in other words, how much room they had for the act?

A. That is right. If they asked me to do five minutes I could do five minutes, which generally meant one tune like my famous discussion of "Yes! We Have No Bananas." That was a stock stunt. It became almost the song of the year. Every program I would have to bring on "Yes! We Have No Bananas."

Q. Incidentally, "Yes! We Have No Bananas" you traced through three prior classical works?

A. Mostly classical.

Q. And you traced them by taking a bar or two or snatch of melody here or there and traced that back to some old work, is that right?

A. That is right.

Q. And then by taking three snatches of melody from old works you pieced together "Yes! We Have No Bananas"?

A. It became a famous song because I made an entertaining little stunt of taking these snatches of old songs in it; an entertaining stunt. Let us put it that way.

Q. Will you mention some of the commercial sponsors you had on your radio programs?

A. Texas Company, International Silver for a program that was called "Fun in Print."

Q. No, I asked you the programs you had.

A. Another one was Rheingold beer, also on Schaefer beer.

Q. Those were paid engagements in which you performed these musical stunts, is that right?

A. Yes, that is right. I was on salary with the American Piano Company and they paid me a salary as a promotion man, and part of my work was to go with their electric player piano, the Ampico, and on stages of all kinds and other places to do such demonstrations and also to use the records.

Q. So you were booked into various vaudeville theaters in which they did not pay you for the vaudeville, but your compensation came from the piano company?

A. It was on salary.

Q. It was a public relations salary?

A. It was a public relations salary.

This preliminary questioning slid almost imperceptibly into the contradictions between his direct testimony and his books. He was so reluctant to give an affirmative answer that at one point the Court observed: "This expert would make a wonderful virtuous girl, he has such great reluctance to saying 'Yes.'"

Spaeth had torn apart our charts which showed that 36 out of 38 notes were identical in the two songs. He gave a lecture and wound up with a chart he had drawn which showed only 12 out of 38 were the same. His conclusion was: "Thirty-six parallels would constitute practically an identity, whereas twelve represents only a very ordinary similarity."

How had he turned identity into non-identity? By insisting that we had ignored accent and beat and particularly the bar lines. Here is an illustration of his ingenious technique beribboned with erudition: "There are only seven notes altogether in the diatonic scale, but of those seven only six have been used in these two tunes. So if you put those six notes in any position you choose you can always create identity, and the actual identity is the fact that there are six notes, common to the two tunes. No more.

"Therefore, if one note is even slightly out of position so far as a real parallel of the melodies is concerned, *which means a parallel by having parallel bar lines,* parallel beats—melodies run on beats of time, and tones that come on those important beats are parallel."

My task was to destroy this theory that parallel bar lines were the acid test of fair comparison. Could we demonstrate that Spaeth in his own books had ignored the bar lines in concluding that one tune was a literal transcription of the others? Could we get him to admit that you could have a flagrant plagiarism even though the beat was different, and the bar lines didn't match? After a long preliminary struggle this is how we fared:

Q. I ask you to look at it now on page 43 of your book *The Common Sense of Music,* and I ask you whether the middle section of "Yes! We Have No Bananas" is the same as the notes in "I Dreamt I Dwelt in Marble Halls."

A. Well, you see the melody notes. They are really identical. That is an identical melodic line which is syncopated in "Yes! We Have No Bananas" and this is on 6/8 time.

Q. I do not want the melodic line. I am asking a specific question. Are the notes the same in both?

A. "Yes! We Have No Bananas" is started out with two extra notes. Outside of that the notes are identical.

Q. And the rhythm you say was changed?

A. The rhythm is changed, yes.

Q. To what extent was it changed?

A. It is a 4/4 rag time in one song and 6/8 in the other.

Q. Now Mr. Spaeth, if the notes are spread on a different number of bars and the rhythm is different would you call these two songs a literal transcription of one another?

A. A literal transcription of one another is a very different thing from a parallel. I would call it a literal parallel.

This was a good enough admission, but now I was not ready to accept anything less than unconditional surrender.

Q. I didn't ask you that. I asked whether you would say one was a literal transcription from the other despite those differences?

A. No, not necessarily. It could easily be a coincidence.

COURT: That was not the question. The question was a literal transcription.

WITNESS: I still do not know. If you mean in "Bananas" the literal four-bar strains, a literal transcription from the four bars in "I Dreamt I Dwelt in Marble Halls," I would say no.

Q. Reading from your book: "The middle section of 'I Dreamt I Dwelt in Marble Halls' is literally transcribed in the corresponding portion of 'Yes! We Have no Bananas.'" Did you write that?

A. I must have, if it is in print.

Q. And what has caused you to change your mind today that that is not a literal transcription? Can you tell us?

A. Yes, very easily. Because there are two additional notes and still every note of "I Dreamt I Dwelt in Marble Halls" is in there, and that is why, without having referred to my book, I was quite ready to play ball and say it is not literal, because I have two extra notes in "Yes! We Have No Bananas."

Q. I am not here to play ball or to play games. I am here to get the truth. Now I ask you, sir, when you wrote that even though there was a difference of rhythm, and a difference of two notes, that nevertheless, you describe these two as one being a literal transcript from the other. Was that a correct statement when you wrote it?

A. I would say when I wrote it that is what I considered it.

Q. Let us see if we understand the fact. A few notes may have been added in one that did not exist in the other, and the fact that the rhythm has been changed does not, in your opinion, amount to so much that one cannot still be called a literal transcription of the other; is that correct?

A. Well, that is a hard question to answer.

Q. Then answer.

WITNESS: May I play it on the piano?

Q. No, I don't want music. I want an answer. I want music in words.

A. It is difficult to answer in words, because we are talking about a snatch.

Q. You cannot answer that question?

A. The notes in the snatch of "The Bohemian Girl" are all literally repeated in the snatch from "Yes! We Have No Bananas," which, however, has a couple of additional notes, in the strain, which are not in the earlier tune, but there are certain parallel notes quite obvious. It might have been a coincidence, it might have been deliberate—I don't know.

COURT: The question is whether, and I should like to have an answer myself, whether the degree of difference between the snatch of "Bohemian Girl" and the snatch of "We Have No Bananas," namely the change of rhythm and the addition of those two notes, constitute a change of such magnitude as to prevent you from calling one a transcription of the other?

WITNESS: I would agree that it would not prevent me from calling one a transcription of the other.

Different witnesses react differently to cross-examination embarrassment. Spaeth grew more determined under pressure. At one point he complained to the Court: "Mr. Nizer is asking me questions that do not make sense."

No witness could announce his distress more vividly than to accuse his tormentor with being ineffectual. And Spaeth appeared visibly distressed.

Q. Isn't it a fact that you called "Yes! We Have No Bananas" a deliberate, flagrant plagiarism?

A. Never in my life have I referred to it that way.

A few moments later:

Q. . . . Did you ever call this fox trot melody a flagrant plagiarism?

A. That I cannot remember. If I wrote anything like that in this book it is possible. I wrote that when quite a young man, in 1925.

Q. Now that you have become more mature, would you still say that?

A. You see, in a court of law—

Q. Listen to my question. I read on page 37: "This was flagrant plagiarism if you will, but it certainly brought Chopin into the American home." Do you stand by that?

A. Yes, if you will.

Then I struck directly at his basic theory that the bar lines must match in order to make a comparison of notes fair.

Q. Now I ask you to look at the bar lines of these two compositions on page 37 of your book which you have called a flagrant violation and ask you whether they coincide or not?

A. The bar lines do not coincide.

Q. So even though the bar lines are different, you still refer to them as a flagrant plagiarism?

A. I have already explained the word "flagrant" and I used that little phrase "if you will."

Finally he made a complete admission about the validity of our chart.

Q. Now you stated that except for the fact that our chart omitted this second note, there would be very considerable similarity.

A. I would say considerable similarity in any case, yes.

I showed him the compositions that he claimed were ancestors of "L'Année Passée" and more similar to it than "Rum and Coca-Cola," and forced him to admit that there he had ignored differences in beat, accent, rhythm, bar lines, and notes far greater than between the two songs in our case. In each instance at first he proclaimed denial or distinction, but always an illustration from one of his own books, brought him back into line. It was a battle of attrition, made all the more effective by the final collapse on each point. His refusal to cede a point until all alternatives had been rejected and nothing was left to him but an admission, taxed the patience of the Court. It brought such comments as:

COURT: Dr. Spaeth, if you would subside and not run ahead of the question—

COURT: If you say it only once, Dr. Spaeth, we might get it.

WITNESS: It is a very clear musical point here, Mr. Nizer.

COURT: There is no musical point involved here at all except an inability to say yes or no.

In order to create dozens of "ancestors" for "L'Année Passée," Spaeth had emphasized that its melody was composed virtually of three notes:

Q. Now you have referred to the three notes that predominate in
"L'Année Passée." What are those three notes?

A. The G is the most important, and the two adjoining notes,
A and F. You have more of those three than anything else.

I wanted him to admit that one could trace three notes in any composition
to prior ancestors and therefore this was not significant. Here I appealed
to his pride. If I could get him to do his vaudeville routines, I thought it
would prove my point. He readily obliged by pointing out that "Three
Blind Mice" was composed of three notes, Nos. 3, 2, and 1 in the scale,
and he hummed excerpts from a famous lullaby, "Mary Had a Little
Lamb," to demonstrate that they were based on the same three notes;
"Yankee Doodle" used them, but in another order. He claimed that, with
his skill and experience, he could trace three or four notes or a strain in
any given piece of music to some prior work.

But, of course, he could not do it by tracing a number of bars as
distinguished from three notes, and he admitted that "the number of bars
having similar melodic strains" between "L'Année Passée" and "Rum and
Coca-Cola" were eight! So his "ancestors" based on three notes were not
ancestors at all for eight bars. He had disproved his own thesis.

There is a psychological principle which you can demonstrate with a par-
lor game. It rarely fails. You tell someone that you are going to make him
say the word "No" despite his resolve not to do so. No matter what you
say he must not use the word "No," or he loses. You will tell him a brief
story and then ask some questions, which he must answer quickly, but of
course you warn him again, the word "No" must not pass his lips. Then
you begin the story that will be the basis of the questions. "Once in Pei-
ping, there lived an old Chinese who had a wife and seven children. In the
back of the house was a garden—" You stop the recitation and suddenly
say, "You are smiling. You know this. You've done it before." Invariably
the answer is, "No, really I haven't." The first word out of his mouth is the
word "No." Sometimes the comical effect is heightened by the exclamation
"No, no, no," so that the only word he has uttered, within a few seconds
after your warning to him, is "No," repeated several times.

Psychologically a person can only stick to a story he has adopted if he
can concentrate on doing so. But if he can be taken unaware by any device
which breaks his concentration on the particular point, he will betray his
true feelings about the immediate matter broached to him. I have on
many occasions applied this principle in cross-examination. I tried it with
Spaeth.

Of course "Rum and Coca-Cola" was virtually identical to "L'Année
Passée," but Spaeth denied this and raised every possible facile distinction
between the two. If I could catch him off guard by diverting his concentration maybe we could induce him to contradict his own contention.
This is how it was done. I questioned him at length about a Spanish song,

"El Cafecito," which he had put in evidence to show that it was very similar to "L'Année Passée." When his mind was thus riveted on the Spanish song and its similarity to "L'Année Passée" and he was fighting off my suggestions that they were not similar, I suddenly shifted:

    Q. I now ask you is "El Cafecito" also similar to "Rum and Coca-Cola" or not?

    A. There must be some similarity, because "Rum and Coca-Cola"— Well, I won't go on after that.

I stared long and silently at the witness, not moving an inch. Neither did he. Then finally I said in as soft a voice as I could muster: "You would not want to finish that sentence, would you?"

He replied: "Well, I will chiefly say that the chief similarities are with 'L'Année Passée.'"

Much later when I was driving to a conclusion, I revived his broken sentence and asked him if he hadn't really meant that if "El Cafecito" was similar to "L'Année Passée," it must be similar to "Rum and Coca-Cola" because of the striking similarity between the two? He denied it.

Whether Spaeth's confusion was due to the strain of a lengthy cross-examination or to being taken psychologically off guard by the shift of concentration was for the Judge to evaluate.

Spaeth had been eager to get to the piano at various times during cross-examination, as if he would be in his element there and could express himself more clearly. Now I gave him a chance. We had sewed together the sheet music of "Rum and Coca-Cola" and "L'Année Passée" so that they were two opposite pages in a book. Above them we placed a large black cardboard so cut out that you could only see the first two bars of one song and then the next two bars of the other song, and so on alternately. I asked him to play the visible portions. What could be a more dramatic way of illustrating their identity? Spaeth sensed its effectiveness. He faltered in his performance.

    Q. Dr. Spaeth, due to the fact that you have made certain errors in striking notes you had to do it twice?

    A. It is hard to do it. This is the kind of trick I do not do in my entertainments.

    Q. Well, now will you play it continuously, without striking a wrong note?

    A. I will try a little more correctly. It is a little hard. [Plays piano]

It appeared to be reluctance rather than inherent difficulty in performance which hampered him. The combined melody sounded as if either one alone was being played.

Now we stormed the last citadel—folk music. Spaeth claimed that the music of "L'Année Passée" was folk music and therefore not protectable. It belonged to the world. He insisted that the essential ingredient of folk music was that no one knew who the composer was. It came down to us from the past without any identifiable originator.

Since Maurice Baron had described his folio of West Indies songs as folk music, it was our contention that a song written by an identifiable composer like Lionel Belasco could nevertheless achieve the status of folk music.

To disprove Spaeth's definition of folk music I hurled quotations from his many books at him. Had he not written that Stephen Foster's songs, "My Old Kentucky Home, Good Night" and "Old Folks at Home," were folk music, even though their composer was known? He quibbled that he had meant they were "folk type of music" rather than folk music. Had he not written in another book that "There was a real charm also in the folk songs of the Neapolitans actually written by individual composers, often in prize competitions"? Had he not called "Funiculi-Funicula" a folk song even though its composer, Luigi Denza, was known? Had he not in another of his books referred to jazz compositions, such as "St. Louis Blues," as folk music, even though he knew its composer was W. C. Handy?

To escape the weight of these questions, he improvised an explanation that compounded his dilemma.

Q. I did not write it, Dr. Spaeth. You wrote it. Isn't that what you meant?

A. The simple answer is that that book lists the records made for Ampico, and when that book was written, we were doing promotion work for the American Piano Company, and we naturally listed anything that had a folk-like quality of which there was a record. We had records to sell.

Q. You mean to say that this really was not accurate but you stated this in the book in order to sell records, is that right?

A. I think that is a harsh description. In a commercial book in which we are trying to sell records, I would call it permissible.

Q. Even though you don't think it is accurate?

A. It is historically by no means accurate.

Q. Have you ever written in another book (not concerned with selling records of the American Player Piano Company), namely, *Stories Behind the World's Great Music*, page 82: "Outside of Grand Opera, Italian music is best known today by the Neapolitan *folk songs,* most of which are of fairly modern origin and the work of definite individuals"?

A. Yes, I must have. You are reading it.

Q. Did you consider it correct when you wrote it?

A. Yes.

By this time Spaeth's obstinate resistance had spent itself. There is a moment in every struggle when the contestant may suddenly be overwhelmed with a realization of defeat. Until that moment, no one is ever fully beaten. An unimaginative person who cannot glimpse the debacle, may never surrender. It is a rule of life and death too. Many a desperately ill person will astound his doctors by defying all the rules of survival, until an inner sense of surrender will bring about instantaneous collapse. These are not merely psychological matters. There appear to be physiological reasons, such as the secretion of vital fluids, whether adrenalin or still unidentified hormones, which determination stimulates.

Spaeth was ready to quit. When I asked him whether it wasn't striking that the two songs had weak suspension notes in the same sequence, he, for the first time, conceded readily, like a fish that has given its last wiggle and is pulled in docilely:

A. I would say that is striking.
Q. Very striking?
A. A striking similarity. Yes.

I let him go.

The case came to a close after our expert, in rebuttal, analyzed the twenty-one compositions submitted by Spaeth. He showed that there were only three or five or seven note similarities with "L'Année Passée" as compared with thirty-three note similarities between that song and "Rum and Coca-Cola." He challenged the nineteen illustrations submitted by the defendants of the diminished seventh chromatic chord on the ground that they were all in chromatic settings, unlike "Rum and Coca-Cola," which had diatonic chords with only this one exception.

Soldiers from Trinidad testified that prior to Amsterdam's arrival there, "Rum and Coca-Cola" was sung all over the island to the same tune that Paul Baron claimed to have written later in New York.

Extensive legal briefs were submitted by both sides to the Court. Later it rendered an opinion granting judgment to the plaintiff, requiring the defendants "to deliver up for destruction all infringing copies and devices, and all plates, molds, and other matter for making such infringing copies, of plaintiff's said copyrighted song, and all parts of musical instruments on which defendants' infringing song entitled "Rum and Coca-Cola" has been transcribed or recorded, and all plates, molds, matrices and other matter for making such infringing parts of such musical instruments."

The decree in favor of the plaintiff entitled him to recover the costs of the action, reasonable counsel fees, and to have an accounting for all damages resulting from the infringement.

The defendants appealed to the Circuit Court of Appeals, the higher Federal Court composed of three judges presided over by the brilliant Judge Learned Hand. They retained former Secretary of War Robert Patterson to argue their appeal. Patterson had not only been an outstanding Federal Judge before going to Washington, but he was a distinguished and skillful lawyer. He was, indeed, the protégé of Judge Learned Hand, who had sponsored his career. What higher accolade could any lawyer have than that?

On the day of the argument in the Appellate Court, the defendants moved a piano into the courtroom and Dr. Spaeth appeared ready to perform. But the Court ordered the piano removed. The case would be heard on oral argument based upon the printed record of the trial. No witnesses are ever heard on appeals. Only the lawyers present arguments limited to the stenographic minutes of the testimony. The Court stated that no exception would be made.

Judge Patterson argued for reversal with remarkable skill. His young face was marked with deep lines in his cheeks, which added character to his earnestness. I was full of admiration for the simple artfulness with which he built the most telling legal points, developing the facts with just the right emphasis to strengthen his legal contentions.

At the height of his argument, he surprised the Court and me by turning somewhat mysterious. He urged the Court to adopt a rule of law which he disarmingly admitted was unsettled, there being two opposite views of the matter by leading authorities. However, he said, one of these authorities he was sure the Court had high regard for, and he even felt that I would not dispute it. He then read a quotation from an article in the *Columbia Law Review* and concluded: "The author of that article, your Honors, is my distinguished adversary, Mr. Nizer."

Judge Hand threw back his lionesque head, something like Franklin Roosevelt used to do, and roared with laughter. "This ought to be a lesson to the bar in general," he said, teasingly, "not to write treatises in law journals. You never know what side you will be on the next day."

When my turn came to argue, and I had dug out of the rich record all the favorable testimony to overwhelm the defendants factually, I turned to the propositions of law upon which Judge Patterson really based the appeal. In due time I reached the point in the *Columbia Law Review*: "Your honors, I do not profess to have the learning of Judge Patterson, whose opinions as a judge still glitter in the law books, and whose wisdom was recently at the service of our Government in times of peril, when only the foremost talents could meet the crisis. I may say with great sincerity that I have sat drenched in admiration and envy at his skill in marshaling his arguments for a cause which I have previously deemed rather hopeless.

"But there is one subject on which I do claim to be the foremost authority in the world! I will bow to no one, not even Judge Patterson, nor if they could be summoned from the valhalla of judicial heaven, Judge Marshall and all the past great Chief Justices of the United States Supreme Court, in asserting my pre-eminence. That subject, your Honors, is what the author of that article in the *Columbia Law Review* intended to say. I am closer to him and know his innermost thoughts better than anyone else."

I then proceeded to interpret the quoted passage favorably to our contention.

It is not often that such byplay may be indulged in before this court, which not only ranks next to the United States Supreme Court in power, but also has been deemed by many at the bar to be the equal of any court in the land in judicial distinction. But the judges as well as counsel on both sides accepted the exchanges in good humor as a relaxed moment in an austere atmosphere.

Several weeks later the court unanimously affirmed the judgment in favor of the plaintiff.

Judge Patterson's path and mine crossed again in what I may refer to as a tragic epilogue. Some time after our appellate argument, Schine Theatrical Enterprises sent its attorney, Mr. Willard McKay, to ask me to become trial counsel for it in a pending antitrust suit in Buffalo, New York. I could not at that time undertake the conduct of the case and Judge Robert Patterson was thereafter retained. On January 22, 1953, he made his first appearance in the case, before Judge Knight sitting in Buffalo. After the argument he took an American Airlines Convair back to New York. As the plane was nearing its destination it suddenly plunged down over South Elizabeth, New Jersey, falling into several houses on South and Williams Street. The plane burst into flames and exploded, all twenty-three aboard being killed and eight persons in their homes likewise meeting instantaneous death.

I mourned, as did millions of others, the loss of Judge Patterson, who had rendered a unique service to our country as Secretary of War in its most critical hour. I also mourned the loss of an eminent jurist, lawyer, and friend. And mingled with these feelings was the eerie realization that, but for a quirk of fate, I would have been on that plane.

HONOR

Chapter Four

ISSUE OF NAZISM

IN AMERICA

"If you cross the street on a rainy day and an inconsiderate speedy auto spatters mud on you, don't try to wipe it off immediately. You will only spread it all over your clothes. Wait a day or two until the mud dries and it will flick off."

This is the advice I have given to dozens of would-be litigants in libel suits. Though I have tried many such actions, I have more often dissuaded people from bringing such suits. Governors, famous authors, Judges, scientists, and stars have yielded to my entreaty not to sue, even though they had valid libel actions. In most instances the publication that prints the libel has limited circulation, whereas the news of a suit by a prominent person is published broadly throughout the land and even internationally. Thus the libel is spread, for curiosity is more intense about what was said than whether it will be proven false. Furthermore, the issue is kept alive by a vigorous prosecution. There are often examinations before trial, and other proceedings which revive the false statement, jogging the memory of millions who long ago would have forgotten about the matter. Finally, it is rare that a distinguished person, though libeled, suffers actual financial damage. The very pre-eminence of the plaintiff's reputation is a shield against financial hurt. The community continues to hold such persons in high regard. I have pleaded with them to wait only for a little time until the mud caked and the libel flicked off. Then they could achieve a better perspective of the irresponsibility of the source, the imperviousness of their high standing, and the phenomenal forgetfulness of readers.

Of course, there are situations that do not permit such an aloof attitude. Usually these are cases where the libel is destructive of honor, reputation, and the ability to earn a livelihood; or where some large principle is involved, such as the curbing of reckless columnists (the Reynolds–Pegler case or vulgar magazines such as *Confidential*), or the defense of our country as in the Foerster–Ridder case.

Thus far I have spoken only of innocent victims who nevertheless resist the temptation to strike back. There is another class of plaintiffs in libel actions, who sue because a sense of guilt drives them to desperate measures. We know that even half a truth will infuriate, whereas a whole lie may leave one merely contemptuous of the assailant. Undoubtedly such plaintiffs may not be fully conscious of the truth of the libel. They sometimes block out their guilt by self-hypnosis. In such a case, the truer the charge, the more indignant and outraged the denial. There is a tragic irony in such a case. The libeled person brings about his own downfall. He pursues his enemy until he catches him and is then destroyed by him.

The classic case of this phenomenon is Alger Hiss. Had he kept his peace with aloof dignity, the storm might have blown over. But it was Hiss who, like Oscar Wilde, pursued his enemy until he, himself, was caught.

The same psychological demons drove Victor Ridder to his own defeat.

Victor F. Ridder was the publisher of ten newspapers, including the *Journal of Commerce* and the Seattle *Times*. He also published the German language newspaper called the *New Yorker Staats-Zeitung und Herold*.

He was generally regarded as a liberal and social-minded citizen. President Franklin D. Roosevelt had appointed him WPA Administrator in 1935. Mayor Fiorello La Guardia had invited him to address an anti-Nazis rally at Madison Square Garden in 1938 where he appeared with Rabbi Stephen S. Wise, Ambassador William E. Dodd, and others. Governor Herbert Lehman had reappointed him president of the New York State Board of Social Welfare. He was a founder of the Catholic Committee of Big Brothers and of the National Conference of Catholic Charities.

Of such a man Professor Friedrich Foerster had said that he was a Nazi propagandist and Pan-German sympathizer doing Hitler's propaganda work in the United States. Victor Ridder responded by printing a pamphlet denying the charge and saying that Professor Foerster had deliberately and maliciously distorted the truth. It was Professor Foerster who sued for libel! Ridder counterclaimed for $250,000, but withdrew the counterclaim before trial.

This litigation blossomed into one of the most remarkable libel suits in legal history. Distinguished professors appeared as witnesses for both sides. President George N. Shuster of Hunter College testified for Ridder and was obliged to stand a withering cross-examination.

This courtroom drama took place in the bizarre setting of the defendant Ridder, crippled with bone disease, being carried in his wheel chair to the witness stand day after day for cross-examination.

The circumstances were unique. In December 1942, when it seemed that it was only a matter of time before the Nazis would lose the war, a full-page advertisement appeared in the New York *Times* and in the New York *Herald Tribune* entitled "A Christmas Declaration." The layout was a shrewd use of space. More than half the page was taken up with a Dürer drawing of the head of Christ. The printed text was an appeal to the German people to rise against Hitler and reveal their hatred of his tyranny and his abominations. Then the world would understand the true German spirit and innocence. The signatories to this advertisement were Americans of German descent, most of them sincere, patriotic, and innocent about the strategy of Pan-Germanism. However, Professor Foerster spotted among the signers Victor F. Ridder and his two brothers who were co-publishers of the *Staats-Zeitung,* Gustave Wieboldt, G. E. Seyforth, Theobald Dengler, and Carl Witthe, some of whom had praised Hitler as a great leader and had previously asserted that the German people "are voluntarily and completely united behind the Fuehrer."

Professor Foerster saw behind the pious Christmas Declaration a plea for a soft peace, the execution of the Pan-German plan to snatch delayed victory from defeat. His trained eye caught the following sentence among many noble sentiments: "We remind the German people of the mercy and forgiveness that are present in the hearts of people for those who turn against evil."

So he published an "Open Letter" in pamphlet form in sharp criticism of the Christmas Declaration. In it he wrote: "Your declaration contrasts the Nazi system with the ideology of the German people as if they were fundamentally different. The situation is just the reverse. Hitler's system constitutes only the terrible fulfillment of a century of German nationalistic lawlessness."

As far back as 1920, in his book *My Struggle Against Militaristic and Nationalistic Germany,* Foerster had pierced this false distinction between the German people and the Prussians or, as later known, the Nazis. In a remarkable passage, stemming from the conscience of a noble man, he wrote: "I know that new German evil from the core, being myself a Berliner and a Prussian. You will not fool me with all your fibbing of 'those others,' my dear countrymen. I know 'those others' and I know 'us' too. I leave it to those others to recognize and extirpate their own sins. I am a German, fearful for Germany. I am anxious to save Germany from Prussianism.

"The truth is not imprisoned in Allied archives, but in you, the secret archives of your conscience. Only there you can learn precisely what had to happen and what is going to happen again, if you do not recognize the errors down to the last roots and confess in true spirit, with humanity, with truthfulness and with honesty your formidable apostasy from God—and from true Germandom."

Professor Foerster prophesied in writing eleven years before the event that there would be another German holocaust loosed upon the world in about 1938!

The Open Letter published by Professor Foerster had a very limited circulation of only a few thousand. It was not aimed at Ridder particularly. Rather it included him in a small group who had waged "a demagogic pro-Nazi campaign" against Great Britain and the United States. Ridder might well have shrugged off the attack, taking shelter behind his national reputation as a Roosevelt–Lehman–La Guardia appointee and anti-Nazi and liberal. But like the snake that is drawn to the mongoose, he pursued Foerster. He published a special reply in pamphlet form charging that Foerster had published "malicious falsehoods." Then he went to New York County District Attorney Frank Hogan and sought to have Foerster indicted for criminal libel. He failed. He continued to chase Foerster. He approached Dr. Nicholas Murray Butler, President of Columbia University, and Dr. Frank Fackenthal, its Provost, to prevent Foerster from obtaining a post there and maintaining the library of Germanic history. Ridder failed, but he continued his hot pursuit. He approached Mr. Perry Osborn, director of the Museum of Natural History, to cut off funds for the Germanic Library at Columbia University. He failed again. He then sought out Professor Harold Moulton of the Brookings Institution to terminate its sponsorship of Foerster.

Thus he laid a basis for a claim of punitive damages, even if the plaintiff had suffered no actual damage. But more than this, he persecuted Foerster so long that the dear Professor turned and sued *him* for libel. Then the battle was joined. The war was on.

I have referred to my reluctance to undertake libel suits even where the libels were vicious and the plaintiffs famous. How was it then that I was drawn into this case? The libel was exceedingly thin. Even the ugly word "lie" had not been used. Nor was I unmindful of the task that lay ahead. Libel actions are peculiarly lawyer-made suits in the honorable sense of the phrase; that is, they depend so much upon the resourcefulness and thoroughness of preparation. For example, in this case, I had every issue of the *Staats-Zeitung* over a period of fifteen years translated into English. Each news item of signifiance, each editorial, each special feature was translated, indexed and numbered, so that I could call for it at a moment's notice during cross-examination. Even the "Letter Box" feature of the newspaper did not escape analysis and, as we shall see, yielded one item of pure gold. This, in the last analysis, is the "art" of cross-examination—thorough preparation. Neither Ridder nor President Shuster nor Professor Shuler could utter a word that could be contradicted in writing without being instantly confronted with the evidence. I memorized scores of such items and catalogued many by number in my cross-examination notes. The illustrative quotations from the minutes of the trial can best be understood in this light, not as the result of any brilliance, but rather of sheer perspiration. Furthermore, the cumulative effect of several weeks of such cross-examination is to reveal to the jury the witness's lack of candor, his denial or failure to remember even the most innocuous fact until it was dragged out of him by confrontation with a clipping from his own newspaper. And these clippings, like soldiers, marched by the hundreds to the witness stand.

So the task of preparation was enormous; the libel was "provoked" by Professor Foerster's attack on the Christmas Declaration. It was a libel published in defense, not as an initiating offensive; and in effect it merely said Professor Foerster "distorted the truth." Yet I eagerly accepted this case.

The reason can be partly divined from the quotations I have already given from Foerster's works. They reveal the largeness of spirit of the great man he is. I cannot think of any other client whom I was prouder to represent. Unfortunately greatness does not always achieve general fame. Professor Albert Einstein might have been known only to astronomers and physicists but for a quirk of chance which made his a household name, though so few understood why. And he, as he once told me, was bewildered by his fame. This was even before his equation—mass times the speed of light squared equals energy—which ushered in the atomic age.

Recently Ernest Bloch died. Many keen musicians believe he will be the fourth B—Bach, Beethoven, Brahms, and Bloch, yet how many people knew that a genius had passed from the scene.

Friedrich Foerster belongs to this category of truly great men not universally recognized. If you think this is an overestimate, let me tell you about his life. It will serve the additional purpose of revealing to you one of the protagonists of this courtroom drama.

For seventeen years Foerster was Professor of Philosophy and Education at the Universities of Munich, Vienna, and Zurich. His eighteen books and thousands of essays have been translated into fifteen languages, and his eminence was such that twenty books have been written about him and his educational and political work. Most of these and his own works were introduced at the trial and formed a mountain on the counsel table—as if an evidentiary monument had been constructed for the plaintiff.

Behind this façade, this seventy-six-year-old professor sat, imperturbable, kindly, the very image of a scholar. Yet one who had not read about his life would never imagine that this quiet man, looking like an older and more handsome blue-eyed Shakespeare, was a doughty fighter who, time and again, had risked his life for moral principles.

His political training began early. His mother was related to Marshal Helmuth von Moltke, a famous military leader, while his father was a disciple of Alexander von Humboldt, the scientist and humanist. When Friedrich was only thirteen years old he heard violent clashes among the distinguished visitors at his home, for Prussian generals and democrats were both welcome. The two Germanies conducted their quarrels of Pan-Germanism against Democracy in the presence of this impressionable youngster. His mother had said to him, "You have the handsome nose of a Moltke, but, dear child, turn it in the direction of your father."

This he did. In 1914 he charged the Kaiser with "whipping up the aggressive instincts of the German people." He was condemned to three months' fortress imprisonment for his "political offense." He described this on the witness stand as "honorable imprisonment." But the Kaiser found he could not silence him. After completing his sentence, Foerster wrote: "Our unscrupulous power politicians are nothing but doctrinaires of barbarism."

In the midst of World War I, while Foerster was Professor of Education and Philosophy at Munich, he published a book in which he called Bismarckism "the mortal disease of the German people" and the cause of war. He pleaded for Germany to return to her old federative traditions. The philosophy faculty condemned him for placing the responsibility for the war upon Pan-German Philosophy. Only his pre-eminence as a scholar saved him temporarily from the loss of his professorial chair.

In 1917 Emperor Charles of Austria invited Foerster to join him in reorganizing Austria on a true federative basis. Foerster attempted to form a cabinet composed of all Austrian nationalists, thereby eliminating any basis for German hegemony over Austria. The German bloc resisted furiously and sabotaged the effort.

In 1918 Woodrow Wilson asked Professor Foerster to urge the German people to accept his fourteen points and terminate hostilities. Foerster arranged a great public meeting in Munich. The tension was so great that machine guns were placed all about the building to prevent his assassination. In a dramatic plea that transcended nationalism, he urged the acceptance of the fourteen points. The German press denounced him and the program as a "Foerster peace."

At the end of World War I, Foerster resigned his professorship to become Minister Plenipotentiary of the Bavarian Republic at the peace conference in Berne, Switzerland.

When he returned to the University of Munich, he gave special lectures to the faculty and students about the German intellectuals' responsibility for the World War in shamelessly surrendering to the war lords.

He braved the storms of disapproval and toured Germany urging German youth to reject the militaristic Pan-German program.

Foerster, Walther Rathenau, and a number of others were marked for assassination. All but Foerster were killed. A general, remembering his Moltke background, awoke him in the middle of the night, and with nothing but a hastily donned robe, Foerster escaped to Switzerland. He never returned to Germany.

But did he stop his efforts, though warned that he would be killed? He continued to write and act. His books were like rockets, not in their destructive effectiveness, for they failed in that respect, but in the fierce light they cast upon the nature of Pan-Germanism or, its newest name, Nazism. At the trial he testified: "What was Pan-Germanism? Nationalism fell into the German soul like a match into a gasoline tank. Pan-Germanism formed a block all over the world to destroy all the states which had German minorities.

"I admired my military uncles for their unconditional surrender to duty, for their virtues, but it was virtue in the service of the devil, a perverted virtue.

"German militarism is Beethoven in the trenches. That means that music, metaphysics, and the general science techniques, all the German qualities were misdirected in the service of world conquest. I, as a little poor creature, tried to do my work to prevent that, to call up the better tradition. But the wave of madness, a new kind of Islam, without Allah, ran over Germany and brushed away all hopeful beginnings."

In an issue of *Humanity*, a weekly political review offered in evidence at the trial, Foerster wrote on July 8, 1927, that "the masters of Germany will embark upon actual aggression in about 1938." He said that "Germany was like the character in *The Brothers Karamazov* who is bound by fate to commit murder because Germany's preceding crime, World War I, had not been recognized and atoned for as such by the German people."

But he was not content with mere writing. He was also a man of action.

In 1927 the German General Staff planned a coup. They "induced" the German Minister Gustav Stresemann to announce at the League of Nations that Germany had disarmed in accordance with the Versailles Treaty and that therefore the other nations should disarm. Had this deception succeeded, the Nazis would have attacked earlier and perhaps successfully.

Through secret channels Foerster discovered the full details of the enormous rearmament program that was then being effectuated behind the screen of the Weimar Republic. He even learned that the General Staff planned to attack Poland first—as it later did in World War II. He published a complete exposé of these facts, including the precise number of machine guns manufactured as "baby carriages," the number of Stuka dive bomber pilots being trained in so-called innocuous glider schools, and the specific military maneuvers being held in anticipation of the invasion of Denmark, Norway, and France. Foerster hastily published a special treatise of these revelations and arranged with French Minister Aristide Briand to place a copy on the desk of each delegate of the League of Nations on the very morning Stresemann was to speak. When the German Minister arose to assure the world assembly that Germany had disarmed, each delegate had staring him in the face Foerster's document exposing the fraud. Stresemann flew into a rage and cried "Canaille" at Foerster.

In 1932 Foerster was invited to lecture in London before members of Parliament at a meeting of the Royal Society for International Affairs. He sought vainly to destroy Parliament's illusion about Germany. He submitted documentary evidence of Germany's plans for world conquest. He concluded his lecture with these words: "If you don't use your eyes for seeing you will need them for weeping."

In 1936 he appeared before the Protestant Congress in Montpellier, France, and, despite Nazi threats, submitted his documentary evidence of Hitler's scheme of conquest. His warnings went unheeded.

The Carnegie Foundation for Peace sponsored Foerster's trip to the United States in 1940. He was invited several times by our Government to lecture to the President's cabinet, the Department of State, the War Department, and other governmental groups on the German problem and Pan-Germanism.

Indeed, it was on such an occasion that I first met him. As the author of *What to Do with Germany*, I had been asked by Secretary of War Robert Patterson to lecture to a selected group of Government officials gathered at the White House. Professor Foerster shared the platform with me. In the course of research for my book, I had repeatedly come across his name and achievements. It was as if one lone voice was singing in contrapuntal opposition to the Wagnerian thunder of a nation of murderers. Of course, as he wrote, "It goes without saying that there are millions of sturdy Americans of German descent who feel profoundly attached to everything that America stands for." And also that there were hundreds of thousands of Germans in Germany who were horrified by Nazi bestiality, but that was the very core of his argument. These good Germans were helpless and swept over by the tide of planned world conquest. Unfortunately the great majority of German professors, writers, intellectuals, and even the labor unions were immersed in Pan-Germanism and supported the horrors of Hitler–Prussianism.

So, having come to regard Foerster as the fiery conscience of that inarticulate, helpless, better Germany, it was exciting to meet him face to face. Unlike some "great" men who shrink upon intimate contact, Foerster lived up to the noblest image I had of him. Ego, that great motor which drives men to accomplishment, but also injures their perspective so that they imagine themselves suns around which all other events orbit, was almost invisible in his personality. He was so dedicated to the cause of peace and the prevention of attacks upon the world by his own countrymen that he was generous toward anyone who aided this highest goal. As the author of such books as *Christ and Human Life, Applied Christianity, Moral Education,* and *Patriotism, Nationalism and Christianity,* he had achieved religious serenity even in a life of combat. He was without affectation. He was unmindful of his handsome head distinguished by a white beard, a sonorous voice, and strong gleaming teeth that were frequently revealed in a warm smile. He spoke excellent English, although occasionally there was a trace of complex German grammar in it. He was charming, humble, and gay even as he uttered inexorable words. His sincerity and selflessness impressed everyone. And need I, by this time, point out his extraordinary courage, not only about his personal safety, but in facing the derision and contempt which are heaped upon a man who is "traitorous" to his own country when that country serves the devil? I can think of no martyrdom that is more difficult to bear than to tell the awful truth about a people and a country you love.

How could I refuse to help such a man strike a blow for a great though difficult cause?

On direct examination Professor Foerster told his life history. It was intertwined with the awesome history of two world wars. I drew from him a description of the many books he had written in his one-man intellectual war against his countrymen's madness. For example, his book *Authority and Liberty,* written in 1910, was an attempt, he said, "to do justice to the two great necessities of human life, leadership and liberty." His book *Education and Self Education* was an attempt "to lead German fathers and mothers away from the Prussian conception of education and to bring them back to the old humane traditions of the classic era."

COURT: What did you assume to be the Prussian conception?

A. . . . The Prussian method of education was . . . an attempt to subordinate not only the whole life, but the whole education to preparation for war, and to educate young for a narrow-minded kind of patriotism which was doomed to cut them off from any community with the rest of the world and from any respect of foreign traditions.

One of his books had a subtitle, *When I Would Keep Silent It Devoured My Bones.* It was a quotation from Jeremiah. I asked him for its significance. He replied: "It was a painful task to charge one's own nation with the unique responsibility for a tremendous collective crime, but all my studies and observations made during a whole life of fifty years' observations have convinced me of this responsibility, and this book spoke it out for the German people."

Like all true prophets, his words seemed to be timeless. Would that this book were required reading in Germany today. He went on: "The German people cannot reconcile themselves with the rest of the world unless and before it has reconciled itself with truth, and I tried to do justice because I spoke to the German people and appealed to those virtues. I tried to do justice and called by name the great virtues which were incarnated in the Prussian system.

"Without those virtues Prussia would not have been able to conquer the German soul: discipline, sense of responsibility, unconditional surrender to duty.

"But, as I said, all that was in the service of a catastrophic error and a criminal aspiration, and the whole task of re-education of the German people will consist in the effort to liberate the virtues from the vices, from the service of the evil spirit.

"That is the meaning of the book."

Unlike most witnesses, Professor Foerster's demeanor did not change one whit when I turned him over for cross-examination. He was above fencing, quarrelsomeness, or personal hostility. He continued to "lecture" with patience and humility. He had been rebuffed so often in life that he was not surprised by non-receptivity. But neither could he be discouraged by it.

The cross-examiner, Mr. Steckler, endeavored to puncture the Professor's accuracy and scholarliness by taking him through the pamphlet which he had issued and which had attacked the Christmas Declaration advertisement for playing into the hands of the Pan-German plan for a soft peace.

In this pamphlet, Foerster referred to the Steuben Society and the Nazi Bund as of 1933. Since the Bund was organized three years later, Steckler demanded an admission of error.

Q. In 1933 there was no Nazi Bund, was there?

A. Yes, but it was the same people . . . who later took on another name.

Q. You mean to say that all that happened was that the name was changed and nothing else?

A. May I see—may I look through my notes?

Q. Yes, sir.

A. Yes, it was founded in 1933 under the name Bund of Friends of the New Germany, and the leaders were then Spanknoebel and Storm Troop Leader Joseph Schuster, Dr. Griebl and later Fritz Kuhn in 1936; and in the spring of 1936 the Bund changed the name to American German Volkbund. . . .

His pamphlet had stated that the concept of two Germanies is a dangerous myth. The cultural Germany of Goethe and Beethoven had been replaced more than a century ago by the militaristic Prussianized Germany of Von Clausewitz, Von Bismarck, Von Moltke, Von Hindenburg, Ludendorff, Von Seeckt, and Von Brauchitsch. Professor Foerster had cited as "clear proof of this fact" a quotation from the *Berliner Post* in 1912 which read:

"Whom do the hearts of the Germans adore most ardently? Are they Goethe, Schiller, Wagner, Marx? No! They are Barbarossa, Frederick the Great, Blücher, Moltke, Bismarck—the hard men of blood and iron!"

Steckler wanted to know whether this statement was an editorial. Foerster didn't remember. He didn't know what the newspaper's circulation was.

Q. That is clear proof without your knowing who wrote it?

A. Yes, it has no interest who wrote it.

The pamphlet had said to the signers of the Christmas Declaration, "You praise E. M. Arndt, but you do not seem to know that this very Teuton leader devoted his idealistic passion to the aims of an unbounded Pan-Germanism."

Steckler developed the fact that in 1806 Napoleon had occupied the German provinces. Then he asked:

Q. Do you believe that it was wrong for a German to want his country to be freed from France?

A. No.

Q. Do you believe that it is wrong for a German to want Germany united?

A. No.

Q. And still you say that—

A. It depends on what kind of a union.

Q. Well, now, I will let you tell what kind of a union you think that Arndt was talking about.

A. I defined it already yesterday. I said I have nothing to object against a union which takes the different tribes of the German people together which were decentralized after the war of thirty years, but Pan-Germanism begins when they want to annex Switzerland and the Netherlands, and then all countries which contain German minorities. That is Pan-Germanism, which has thrown Germany into conflict with the whole world.

Q. . . . And that is what you believe Ernst Arndt intended?

A. Yes.

Q. And you used these quotations as illustration?

A. Yes, and I can bring more quotations dealing with the Eastern question, where they launched terrible threats against the Czechs.

Q. Against the Czechs?

A. Against the Czechs which ought to be annihilated.

Q. If you have some more, just bring them in.

A. Yes, yes, yes.

After Steckler had made similar sorties against the reliability of Foerster's sources, he shifted to the claim that the quotations in the pamphlet were incomplete and therefore distorted. He read the pamphlet's quotation of a speech by Dr. Walter Thomas that was printed in Ridder's *Staats-Zeitung.* Then he attacked:

Q. . . . Was that a complete quotation?

A. No.

Q. There were a number of sentences and words missing, is that correct?

A. Yes.

Q. There were also parts of sentences missing were they not?

A. Yes.

Q. Just why did you pick out the particular phrases that you put in and leave out others?

A. Because to my mind, what we quoted stands independently for itself alone and the true value is put into full light just by the quotation we gave, and I say that just this whole speech shows the terrible confusion in the mind of the many honorable German Americans, and I shall prove it.

Q. Oh, no, please, you just testified. . . . I move that that be stricken.

COURT: Do not state what you can prove, Professor. . . . If you have other reasons than those stated by you, you may continue your answer.

A. . . . Yes, because we have not to do with mistakes and nice little faults to be covered, we have to do with the conspiracy which has cost the lives of millions of Americans and. . . .

STECKLER: I move to strike it out as not responsive.

COURT: No, your question was, "Why did you do thus and so."

STECKLER: Yes.

COURT: When you ask the witness why, you open up the floodgates of reasoning.

STECKLER: All right, I withdraw that.

A. When I am a member of a family which prepares the burning of the house of a neighbor . . . and I am informed of it, am I obliged to cover the crime of my parents and family? I have to uncover it.

Steckler then read the quotation from Thomas's speech, "We are pleased with, and proud of, a strong united Germany, regardless whether under Bismarck, Ebert, Hindenburg, or Hitler," and continued with the following words which Foerster had omitted, "just as we are proud of a free and strong and progressive America, whether it be under the administration of Roosevelt One, Hoover, or Roosevelt Two." Foerster insisted that the balance of the sentence did not change the meaning. Steckler read the quotation, "We demand the right to cover up real or alleged faults of our origin with the cloak of love and silence," and demanded that Foerster read aloud the succeeding omitted portion, "with which we cover the sins of a brother, a mother or a father, just as we defend America against all written attacks when we are abroad."

Q. And you mean to say and tell the Court and jury that in your opinion, the words that were omitted were meaningless and did not in any way modify the words you quote in the pamphlet?

A. It had no meaning because we had not to deal with mistakes. In the case of mistakes the comparison would be right and allowed, but we had . . . to do with the terrible crime which was prepared, and there was no permission to cover it. We are obliged in the name of a higher law when even our mother and our father, our country, prepares a terrible crime, to uncover it and not to cover it.

The cross-examiner asked Professor Foerster whether he was German, whether his friends were, whether they were educated and had good morals. To all of which the answer was yes.

Q. Now isn't it a fact, Professor, that what you have just said condemns an entire race as a race?

A. I did not say an entire race as a race. I said the leading people . . . the majority of the nation, it is a collective crime and Hitler said it in *Mein Kampf*, "As true as God lives in heaven, World War I was not imposed upon the German people, but desired by the German people," and then he inflamed this same people still more and so this crime has been supported by the majority of the German people, and that does not say that there are not honest Germans who kept apart, but they were a component minority.

Q. Are you quoting Hitler as an authority?

A. . . . Authority for the guilt of the German people.

Foerster admitted that he did not know the origin of the Christmas Declaration, nor who wrote it, nor who paid for its publication as an advertisement.

He was queried about his sources of income. They came from his books. The Carnegie Foundation had paid his passage to the United States and thereafter $1500. The only other payment made to him was a gift from an English friend. "I was in economic need and a Christian representative of English Christianity sent me 200 pounds to help me for the moment." The suggestion was made that he might have been paid by France or other governments. He denied it.

The moment he stepped from the witness stand, we followed with another redoubtable authority, Reinhold Schairer, Professor of Education at New York University and Executive Director of the World Education Service Council, a private organization with twenty directors from various countries, to develop educational exchange among freedom-loving nations. He had been the head of the University Students' Exchange in Berlin, but when Hitler came into power "400 Brown Shirts marched around the Administration Building and took several millions of dollars of accumulated funds." Schairer was dismissed, his pension taken away, and he fled with his Danish wife to Denmark. Finally he received a Rockefeller scholarship and came to the United States.

When he was a young man, his father who was a Lutheran minister gave him some of Professor Foerster's books "with the invitation to go through them most carefully and to learn the real philosophy of education."

In 1917 he met Foerster and later learned of his work against Pan-Germanism. He testified: ". . . Rathenau and Erzberger, as you know, were killed by people who were connected to student organization, and it was very clearly, again and again, outspoken that Foerster would be the next one to be killed."

I attempted to establish Foerster's reputation, which was at stake in the suit.

Q. What was his reputation in academic circles, in universities, among professors, learned men, and scholars, to your knowledge?

A. I think even those who were opposed to him . . . always took him as a man of greatest sincerity and honesty. . . . He was accepted as the very great model and spiritual leader, and everyone knew that he was very strict on all questions of truth and honesty.

Schairer called him "the most outstanding educator of our present time."

NIZER: You may cross-examine.

STECKLER: No questions. [Witness excused]

Dietrich von Hildebrand, Professor of Philosophy at Fordham University, was the next reputation witness. He had known Professor Foerster since 1914. He testified that in the circles he moved, Foerster's reputation was excellent. "I admit," he said, "that those were Catholic circles in the majority and that they would not have invited me if they would have been favoring Pan-Germanism."

Q. . . . What is his reputation generally as a scholar and as a man of integrity and truth?

A. . . . He is considered as an outstanding scholar and as a man of the purest intention, and especially I would stress his devotion to truth.

Q. . . . In other words, under no circumstances at all is a lie permitted or a distortion permitted; there should be truth?

A. Yes.

NIZER: Cross-examination.

STECKLER: No questions. [Witness excused]

Soon after, Professor Hamilton of New York University had stated that "Professor Foerster's integrity is unquestioned. He is a scholar with all that word means," and Steckler had waived examination. The plaintiff rested.

Victor Ridder was wheeled to the witness stand. Despite his unfortunate illness, he exuded vigor. His was the hard-lined face of a man of action who nevertheless, as a publisher, was engaged in words and thought. Professor Foerster's bearded, esthetic face was that of a scholar, who nevertheless was engaged in action. In every way they contrasted with each other. I wonder sometimes whether it is a mere coincidence that the antagonists in great court battles are the antithesis of each other in personality.

Ridder testified to his distinguished background, as a member of the National Executive Board of the Boy Scouts of America; as a member of the New York State Board of Charities, appointed first by Governor Charles S. Whitman and later by Governor Herbert H. Lehman of New York; as founder of the Catholic Committee of Big Brothers; and as administrator of New York City WPA, appointed by President Franklin D. Roosevelt.

He described his trip to Germany in 1933 in the company of Herman Metz, a former Comptroller of New York City, an Army officer in the First World War, and the President of the German American Board of Trade in 1933. Ridder said he went as an individual but "represented the German-American societies here in New York, what we call the German-American Conference."

When he returned from Germany he wrote a series of articles in the *Staats-Zeitung* which had been offered in evidence by Professor Foerster. He proceeded to contradict the translation of some of these articles. The plaintiff's version had him praising Goebbels's "extraordinary wise propaganda." He maintained the word should be "smart" or "clever," not "wise."

He testified that he had resigned from the Steuben Society "in 1940, perhaps" (which he corrected later to be 1942) and that he had never attended any meeting of the Steuben Society which was held together with the Nazi Bund, or any Nazi Bund meeting, or "any meeting at which the Steuben Society or any other society demonstrated for the Hitler regime under the flag of the swastika," or at any meeting at which cablegrams pledging allegiance were sent to Hitler, or at which the aims of National Socialism were openly supported. Thus he denied the assertions in Foerster's pamphlet.

The signers of the Christmas Declaration called themselves Loyal Americans of German Descent. The President was Dr. George N. Shuster, President of Hunter College. Ridder was not a member, but signed the Declaration after talking to Henry Rutz of the Office of War Information. Ridder named Dorothy Thompson as the author of the Christmas Declaration and the American Jewish Congress as the organization that paid for its printing. When Professor Foerster published his reply, Ridder went to District Attorney Frank Hogan of New York County to seek a prosecution for criminal libel against him. Hogan asked him to prepare a statement of his grievance "so that the Legal Department would have something to go on in preparing a case." He did so and printed about sixty or seventy, but distributed about forty copies. It was never printed in his own newspapers.

Then he set forth his anti-Nazi activities. Mayor O'Brien of New York City had talked to him about the public protests which resulted from the announcement that there would be a German Day celebration under the leadership of Heinz Spanknoebel. There was a hearing at City Hall, and Ridder, his brother Bernard, and Samuel Untermeyer, a leader in anti-

Nazi activities, addressed the meeting in protest against Spanknoebel. He concluded his testimony by an impressive recital of his being a speaker at an anti-Nazi rally in Carnegie Hall in New York City in 1938. Mayor Fiorello La Guardia of New York City presided. The other speakers were Henry Wallace, Rabbi Stephen S. Wise, and the Rev. Fulton J. Sheen. The meeting "was a protest against the pogrom against the Jews following the . . . murder of a man named Von Radt, who was an employee in the German Embassy in Paris and whose murder was used by the Nazis as an excuse for a very bitter pogrom, or persecution of the Jews. The meeting was a protest against that, and I spoke there at the request of the Mayor."

Q. And did every speaker discuss the same thing?

A. Pretty largely, yes.

STECKLER: Your witness.

The art of cross-examination is often regarded as a destructive process —the tearing down of the witness. However, it can be constructive in that it builds an edifice out of the admissions wrung from the witness. Sometimes the cross-examiner, in crossing swords with the witness, forces him back and up a step with each attack until the witness stands at the top of a long staircase with no further room for retreat.

The process is involved. The examiner may have to retreat temporarily, renew his offensive from another position, or forego obtaining an admission that he deems vital. Unlike books and motion pictures on courtroom scenes, a brief series of direct questions almost never lead to the crumbling of the witness. This is all too pat and artificial. But the true process is far more exciting, because the contest is genuine. The witness strikes back hard; he volunteers and squeezes into his answers data injurious to the examiner. It is honest give-and-take and, when the witness finally makes a fatal admission, the excitement and impact are all the greater.

Although it might be interesting for the technician to read days and days of cross-examination and follow the labyrinth of questions and exhibits which brought the examiner out of the tunnel of contest into victorious light, this would be too lengthy and taxing a process for the layman. So I shall telescope the process by comment, though realizing considerable loss in the omission of the lengthy wrestling for the truth.

I have referred to constructing an edifice. Historically, it was important to show that Ridder was a German propagandist long before the Nazis came to power. Then his service to the Nazis would fall into a pattern. So I asked him:

Q. And you knew that Hanfstaengl in 1914, 1915, 1916 had spread German propaganda in this country even during the First World War?

A. Yes, I knew that.

Q. You knew that your newspaper had assisted him in that, did you not?

A. Assisted him? We were engaged in a similar activity of working on the German side in the war in 1914 until the United States went into the war.

Q. Didn't you get paid by the German Government?

A. Oh, no, no.

NIZER: I call upon counsel to produce the books we subpoenaed of the check for $20,000 paid to the *Staats-Zeitung.*

There was vigorous objection and Ridder's counsel, Mr. Steckler, announced: "I am unable to produce any records in 1914." Whereupon I showed Ridder a photostat of a check made by a German importer to the *Staats-Zeitung* for $20,000 dated October 12, 1914. Ridder's reply was: "I assume—I cannot assume, I just do not know."

Q. Well, did the *New Yorker Staats-Zeitung* get many checks for $20,000 in one sum in 1914?

A. I do not recall.

Q. It was not for advertising, you know that?

A. I assume it was not.

He suggested that perhaps it was a loan, but he could not recall repayment, and he finally admitted, "I do not recall it as a particular loan."

The notorious Captain Karl Boy-Ed, Naval Attaché at the German Embassy in 1914, who was recalled at the request of the United States, was active with Dr. Hanfstaengl in propaganda work, and Ridder admitted that he had dinner with him "every two or three months, sometimes often, sometimes less often."

Q. Did not Boy-Ed on various occasions make suggestions as to what should be written in the *Staats-Zeitung?*

A. I do not know.

Q. You would not deny that this is so.

A. No, I would not deny it.

Then I shifted to the Nazis. Dr. Robert Treut had been designated by Hitler to unify the Germans abroad. Ridder admitted helping him. At one point he misspoke himself, as many a witness does when pressed with hundreds of rapid-fire questions. He said:

A. The purpose of the Union of Germans Abroad (called U.D.A.) was the unification or the—I won't say the unification, but the contacting of German citizens in foreign countries, roughly.

COURT (Judge Ferdinand Pecora): Well, what do you mean by contacting, for what purpose?

WITNESS: Oh, raising money, getting them interested, regular propaganda contacts, I would say.

Ridder's closeness to Dr. Treut had to be prodded out of him:

Q. Did Dr. Treut visit you in 1933?

A. I do not know.

Q. You do not know?

A. No. He may have.

Q. How long had you known Dr. Treut?

A. Oh, quite a few years.

Q. By "few years" what do you mean?

A. I would say five years, seven years.

Q. Isn't it a fact that you knew him as early as 1922?

A. Maybe.

Q. That would be eleven years, not five.

A. It might be eleven; it might be twelve.

Q. When Dr. Treut came on those occasions, did he visit you?

A. He usually came in to see me when he was in the country, oh yes.

Q. And do you recall that one of the occasions on which he came to visit you was to raise money for German schools in countries no longer part of Germany?

A. You mean in parts of Germany which had been transferred to other countries?

Q. All right; I will take your definition of it.

A. Yes. The answer is yes.

Q. You helped him on that occasion?

A. I helped him.

Q. You became very friendly with him?

A. I would not say—yes, I was quite friendly with him. I liked him.

Having established an old friendship with Treut, I now turned to his real mission under Hitler and Ridder's aid to him.

Q. Didn't Treut come to you personally and ask the assistance of yourself and your newspapers in aiding his function here under the Hitler government?

A. I think—I think he might have, yes, surely.

Q. And even though you recall that he asked you to help him, you do not recall precisely what it was about, is that what you mean to tell us?

A. No, it is too far back.

Q. And he thanked you publicly for the great aid you had given him, you recall that, don't you?

A. I do not recall that.

Q. I read to you from your own newspaper the *Staats-Zeitung* of March 22, 1933, this quotation of Dr. Treut: "However, I should now like to stress also that local Germandom ought to cast aside its timidity about a solid cultural connection with the ancestral stock. The citizen idea can also be overdone." What do you understand the words "ancestral stock" to mean, Mr. Ridder, in that sentence.

A. I would say it meant German ancestry, if it came from Dr. Treut.

Q. Yes; and "the citizen idea can also be overdone," that would mean that being a citizen of the United States should not be taken too seriously; that can be overdone; you still belong to the old country; is that not it?

A. I think that was the implication he had in mind, yes.

Q. Now, did you cut off your relations with Dr. Treut after he made that address?

A. No; I do not know whether I saw him after he made that address or not. Maybe I did.

Q. And you continued to be friendly with him, did you not?

A. Oh, yes.

By a similar series of questions, and after being confronted with his own newspaper report, Ridder admitted that Dr. Treut, on leaving the United States, had praised Ridder highly for helping him make his mission a success. Ridder actually organized the German-American Conference and became president of it. The inference was clear that this conference, in accordance with Hitler's request, through Treut, would not "overdo the citizen idea" but rather remember its "ancestral stock." More than this, Treut designated one Karl Gunther Orgell as Nazi representative of the "Association for Germandom Abroad." Where was Orgell's headquarters?

Q. And when Dr. Treut went back to Hitler, do you know whom he designated to carry on his work here?

A. No, I do not.

Q. Never heard of a man by the name of Orgell?

A. Yes, Karl Gunther Orgell.

Q. Karl Gunther Orgell?

A. Yes, he was my secretary for a while.

Q. Didn't Dr. Treut designate Mr. Orgell as the man to continue the work here?

A. I do not recall.

Q. You do not remember that?

A. No, I do not remember that.

Q. Well, let me read to you—

A. Maybe he did; I do not know.

Q. Let's read from your own newspaper, Exhibit 92: "Mr. Karl Gunther Orgell now again holds the representation of the Association for Germandom Abroad." Does that remind you about it?

A. No.

However, after a tussle, Ridder replied, "I will accept it if it is in my own newspaper to refresh my recollection, but I do not remember it." It later turned out that Orgell had actually shared Ridder's private office.

Q. He had a desk in one part of the room in which you had your office, didn't he?

A. That is right.

Q. He was on the payroll of the *Staats-Zeitung?*

A. Yes.

306 · *My Life in Court*

Q. And was that because he was rendering a service to you as an officer of the *Staats-Zeitung?*

A. No, it was more because somebody had to pay him for doing his work, and we paid him.

Q. You mean that since he was doing work among the societies—

A. In the societies, we paid him.

Q. You volunteered to take care of that?

A. That is right; we took care of it.

It was left to summation to show how clearly this link had been forged. Ridder, as president of the German-American Conference, was the "representative of Germandom." He worked with the Nazi agent who came to strengthen the Fifth Column here. American citizenship was not to be taken too seriously. Once a German, always a German; "ancestral stock" were the words used, but Ridder admitted this meant "German ancestry." Treut returned to Hitler announcing the success of his mission with particular praise for Ridder's assistance. Finally, and most significant, the Nazi Treut designated Ridder to be in charge of "Germandom Abroad." This was done, none too subtly, by designating Orgell as the representative of "The Association for Germandom Abroad" and Orgell became Ridder's secretary, sharing his private office and being paid by him.

But all this was only an atmospheric prologue to the drama that was to unfold.

The moment Hitler came into power, Ridder and his brothers began to visit him. They wore out the planes going back and forth. Victor Ridder saw Hitler and his Nazi associates for a month during April 1933. He returned to visit Hitler again two months later, and repeatedly thereafter in 1935 and 1936. While Victor Ridder was on his way back to the United States from his first trip, his brother and co-publisher Bernard Ridder visited Hitler, and another brother and co-publisher, Joseph, also visited Hitler in interim periods.

Victor Ridder attempted to explain these visits as journalistic enterprise by an American publisher of a German-speaking newspaper. He vigorously denied that he was acting as a representative of the German American Conference (a formal title for the Fifth Column). He was not representing Germandom abroad, he said. But this shield was soon stricken from his hands. The culminating questions were as follows:

Q. Didn't you consider yourself a representative of Germandom?

A. No, no, no.

Q. I read to you from Plaintiff's Exhibit 73, which is the first part of your report of your trip, when you came back from Hitler. I read to you this sentence, "I may consider myself as a representative of Germandom." Do you say that in your own article?

A. I think we used a German word, didn't we? What was the German word?

Q. Now you tell me what the German word is. [Showing exhibit to witness to examine it.] It is right in the first paragraph, Mr. Ridder, may I help you on that?

A. Are you sure you have the right one? Oh, I see, all right.

Q. "*Vertreter das Deutschdom.*"

A. That is right.

Q. You did say you were a representative of Germandom?

A. That is right.

Q. And, a moment ago when you said you did not, that was an inadvertent error?

A. Yes.

The helpful word "inadvertent" was not sarcastic. I was still being gentle with the witness. I have referred to his unfortunate illness—I believe it was tuberculosis of the hip bones—which made it necessary for him to be carried in his wheelchair to the witness stand. His rugged face was lined with anguish and he was obviously in constant pain. The sympathy which, like my own, went out to him from the jurors, was a factor not to be ignored. The problem is less aggravated, but the same, whenever one has to cross-examine an old lady or a pretty young girl. An insensitive cross-examiner may gain his point by reckless attack, but antagonize the jury in the course of doing so. Polite, sympathetic, and deft questioning is required. The cross-examination must not be cross. But there is a point at which even such a witness may be dealt with aggressively, and that is when he has been so discredited that the jury actually enjoys his discomfiture. How does one tell that such a point has been reached? The lawyer must have lateral vision. He must observe the jury's reactions at all times. Most people, when enthralled by a drama being enacted before them, register their emotions very clearly. They grimace, turn away in disgust, snicker at an implausible answer, smile in gratification as the cross-examiner scores, or, conversely, identify themselves with the witness, suffer with him, understand his confusion, and exhibit relief when he has momentarily extricated himself. Sometimes, the mood of a jury will transfer from one to the other, and the lawyer who is so intent on his involved task of questioning as to lose his lateral vision may also lose the jury and the case.

So, I characterized Ridder's error as "inadvertent." There came a time, as we shall see, during later days of cross-examination when I could indulge in an all-out attack upon him.

While in Berlin Ridder visited or, still more significant, was visited by the leaders of the Nazi apparatus. In each instance, he either had a feeble memory or attempted to minimize the event. This was foolish, because he had written a series of articles about his trip and, due to lack of preparation, I assume, he did not remember what he had said. This is as dangerous as a man who has written passionate love letters but pretends barely to recollect his encounter with the lady. After confrontation time and again with his own writings or other exhibits in my hand, Ridder had to yield.

    Q. Wasn't there a special personnel committee appointed by Hitler to receive you?

    A. Oh, no, no, no, you got that mixed up.

    Q. I have?

    A. Yes.

    Q. Did you make this answer to the following question on your examination before trial? "Q. Whom did you see of the party officials?

    A. I saw Goebbels twice. I saw Mr. Schact. I saw Mr. Funk. A man named Frank, Hanfstaengl, I saw a Captain whose name I do not remember whom Hitler referred to as the personnel committee."

    Q. Do you recall making that answer?

    A. Yes.

His pretense that he did not know what position was held by Dr. Dieckhoff, who visited Ridder at his hotel in Berlin, resulted in the following speedy retreat:

    Q. Well, what was Dr. Dieckhoff's position?

    A. I do not recall, but I knew him.

    Q. I read to you from Plaintiff's Exhibit 33, your own article, as published in the *Staats-Zeitung*: "Dr. Dieckhoff, the former Chargé d'Affaires of the German Embassy in Washington." Do you recall him?

    A. Yes.

    Q. Did you know him before that?

    A. Yes.

    Q. He was an old friend of yours?

    A. I had known him for a long time.

    Q. He greeted you as an old friend?

    A. Well, he was an old friend.

    Q. He was at that time pretty important in the Nazi Government, was he not?

    A. I do not know.

    Q. Well, in 1933 wasn't he Minister Director for the Nazis?

    A. I do not know. I know now maybe he was.

Ridder saw "a great deal" of Hanfstaengl, his fellow pro-German propagandist in World War I. He sought to minimize Hanfstaengl's status as a Nazi.

    Q. You would not say he was the head of the foreign press department?

    A. No, I would not—no.

    Q. All right let me read to you from your own article, Exhibit 73:

"Dr. Ernst Hanfstaengl, the head of the foreign press department."
Did you write that?

   A. Yes.

   Q. Well, then, you did know he was the head of the foreign press
department.

   A. In 1933, maybe I did, sure.

   Q. And you knew he was very close to Hitler?

   A. Yes.

After a lengthy wrangle on cross-examination it developed that Ridder had
paid the following glowing tribute to Hitler's close associate: "Many German-Americans will recall that Dr. Hanfstaengl distinguished himself by
his untiring efforts on behalf of the defense of Germany against Allied
propaganda during 1914, 1915, and 1916."

Ridder's witness-stand version of Goebbels ran into the following passages from his articles: "Hardly ever before in history has a people been as
wisely propagandized as Germany in the last year by the National-Socialist
party."

Contrary to his assertion that he was merely reporting an evil genius
of whom he disapproved, his article was a paean of praise to the "world-
renowned" Goebbels, to his "extraordinarily wise—or, as he claimed,
'clever'—propaganda," and to his "unusually quick power of perception."
Ridder hoped that Goebbels would come to the United States where he
would "be very happy to welcome him here in America." This could hardly
be distorted into personal condemnation! Of course, the later proof showed
that the *Staats-Zeitung* reeked with Goebbels's propaganda. Most telling
in the struggle against Ridder's contention that he was merely reporting,
and not approving, was his statement with respect to the 250 newspapers
suspended by the Nazis: "I must admit that among these 250 papers were
also such that I would have suspended myself." This, of course, was an
endorsement of Hitler's policy, rather than the American tradition of a
free press.

The importance of Ridder as the head of "Germandom" in the
United States was recognized by Hitler, who invited him to fly with him
and his entourage to Munich. There was the customary denial and then
confrontation:

   Q. Weren't you invited to fly with the Fuehrer and his entourage?

   A. No.

   Q. Let me read to you from Plaintiff's Exhibit 76: "I heard a good
many interesting things about Hitler's great pilot, Captain Bauer,
about whom so many miracles were told, and thus it was a pleasure
for me to receive a phone call on Saturday morning at eleven, inviting
me to fly with the Fuehrer and his entourage to Munich." Is that
what you wrote?

   A. That included the two planes. It did not include my plane. I
was not to fly with Hitler. I was to fly with this other group.

Q. But it was to fly with Hitler and his entourage in two planes?

A. In the two planes, yes, oh yes.

Q. Didn't you originally understand that it was going to be Captain Bauer, his personal pilot, who was going to take you there?

A. Never.

Q. I see. Now when you arrived at Munich were there a great number of people there who had gathered there and cheered the entire group that arrived?

A. No, the cheers were when Hitler came. I was leaving the airport as his plane came in. I did not wait.

Q. Didn't you write that "the people were there to cheer us" meaning yourself and your group, Hanfstaengl and all?

A. No, why should they cheer me?

Q. Let me read what you wrote in Plaintiff's Exhibit 76: "After a short while the weather cleared up enough for us to land on a field, where in spite of the bad weather, a great number of people had gathered to cheer us."

A. Oh well, I think—

Q. Did you write that?

A. I do not know. I would have to see the original.

Q. All right, I show you the original. Look at approximately the second page of this article of yours, in your own newspaper, and tell me whether the word "us" doesn't appear there. "To cheer us." This is the part [showing] I am referring to, Mr. Ridder. That may help you locate it. "We flew from the Templehoff Airport."

A. Yes.

Q. It says "cheer us".

A. Yes.

Q. That is a correct translation, isn't it?

A. It is a correct translation.

Hitler regarded Ridder as one of his important "Unterfuehrers," in charge of the vital German Fifth Column in the United States, for he included Ridder in the most exclusive of all Nazi functions. Sixty top Nazis and Ridder were invited by Hitler to gather at the Brown House at Munich, the headquarters of the Nazi Party, and hear him outline his policy in a private speech. Ridder's efforts to squirm out of this fatal proof of his true position among the Nazi elite resulted in the following verbal struggle:

Q. Did you consider Hitler's speech a significant speech?

A. Not particularly.

Q. Didn't you, when you returned, write in your report "On that evening of our arrival the Reichschancellor held a long and very significant speech."

A. I did not use the word "significant" in that sense. I used it more in the sense of outlining than in the sense of importance.

Q. What was the German word you used?

A. I do not recall.

Q. I show you the word you used in German, that the Reichs-chancellor made a long and *deutsamen anrede*.

A. That means, point out the path, *deutsamen* meaning "to point".

Q. Doesn't *deutsamen* mean significant?

A. I do not know.

Ridder admitted that those sixty Unterfuehrers, whom he defined as "deputy leaders, the top men in the Nazi party," were "strong-arm men" who were going to resort to violence. He attempted again to take the position that he was a critical observer rather than an admiring participant. This is what became of this contention:

Q. You felt that this group was not going to fight long with words, isn't that so?

A. Well, you had the impression that they were perfectly willing to resort to something besides words.

Q. Well, I ask you directly, didn't you at that time feel that this group would not long fight with words?

A. I do not know whether I want to put it just that way, but the fact is that—

Q. The fact is you did put it that way.

A. If I put it that way it is still very well within what I meant. The impression I got was that they were fighters.

Q. "It is a group which will not long fight with words." Isn't that the description you gave?

A. Yes, I think so, a good description.

Q. You thought they were sort of strong-arm men and gangsters in a way, did you not?

A. Aggressive, I would say, and battlers, I described them.

Q. Um-hum. Well didn't you also write that you were full of admiration for these men?

A. I do not think I used those words, period.

By this time Ridder appeared nervous each time I moved to the counsel table to reach for an exhibit. On this occasion I did not take the steps to the counsel table for contradictory proof. He was immediately embold-ened.

Q. Well, did you feel that you had greater respect for these people than you had before you met them?

A. No, no.

Q. Are you sure of that?

A. I am quite sure of that.

Then the few steps.

Q. Let me read to you from your article: "In this one hour, which I spent in the Brown House, I heard quite a bit which I am glad to admit has brought me a greater respect for this group than I ever had." Did you write that?

A. Yes, I wrote that.

Q. When you said that you had a greater respect for them, did you mean that to be complimentary?

A. I referred to things that I had learned.

Q. Just a moment, Mr. Ridder, please answer my question. Did you mean that you had a greater respect, did you mean that to be complimentary?

A. You will have to take the two sentences together.

Q. Did you mean that you had a greater respect than you ever had?

A. That, oh yes.

Q. When you said that "I am glad to admit"—

A. Yes.

Q. Did you mean by that, that you were pleased with the situation?

A. I meant by that that I was glad to admit—

Q. And among the interesting things that you heard that you were glad to admit gave you a greater respect for this group than ever before was the fact that the Polish Corridor problem was going to lead to war, didn't you?

A. Are you testifying now?

Q. I am asking you the question. Isn't that one of the things you heard, that the Polish Corridor question was going to lead to war?

A. No.

But after five minutes of probing with an evidentiary scalpel:

Q. So, somebody told you, one of these group leaders, whoever the name was, told you that the Polish Corridor problem was going to lead to war?

A. One of them might have, yes.

Q. A moment ago, I think you told us that Hitler told you that, too?

A. He did.

Q. And you considered that confidential?

A. That was confidential.

Q. You were born in this country, Mr. Ridder?

A. I have testified to that effect.

Q. You are, of course, an American citizen?

A. Yes.

Q. And you regarded these statements by Mr. Hitler, and by one of the Unterfuehrers stating that the Polish Corridor problem was going to lead to war, you regarded that as confidential from the United States?

A. I regarded it as confidential. It was their statement.

Q. Hm.

A. Of course, I did.

It turned out that the Nazi leaders, including Hitler himself, told Ridder of their aggressive designs, which he admitted were "confirmed by their whole history up to this day, 1943." Ridder not only treated all this as confidence, but he also deliberately misled the American people by reporting that "Hitler was going to keep Germany safe from war." The *Staats-Zeitung* likewise drummed this theme that Hitler wanted only peace. Lulling an enemy with peaceful assurance while planning attack is a recognized Pan-German technique. As I closed this topic of cross-examination, I left Ridder dangling on his admission that he had written of Hitler: "He was one of the most sincere and honest men I had ever met."

One can never assess what piece of evidence has most impressed a jury. After verdicts, I talk to the jurors to determine which particular factual and psychological onslaughts on their minds resulted in persuasion. Although jurors are extraordinarily right in their conclusion, it is usually based on common sense "instincts" about right and wrong, and not on sophisticated evaluations of complicated testimony. On the other hand, a Judge, trying a case without a jury, may believe that his decision is based on refined weighing of the evidence; but, as Cardozo pointed out in his *Nature of the Judicial Process,* he, too, has an over-all, almost compulsive "feeling" about who is right or wrong and then supports this conclusion with legal technology. Because Judges, sometimes, consciously reject this layman's approach of who is right or wrong and restrict themselves to the precise legal weights, they come out wrong more often than juries.

In any event there was one piece of testimony given by Ridder which shocked me more than others that on their face seemed more condemnatory. If I were a juror, this particular admission would have carried conclusive persuasion with me.

When Ridder was hobnobbing with Hitler and his sixty deputy fuehrers at the Brown House in Munich, he talked to Vorpostenleiter (Advance Post) Leader Wagner of Danzig. Danzig did not belong to Germany and had not yet been seized by it. However, in anticipation of future acquisition, a Nazi Advance-Post Leader existed to prepare the road in accordance with Fifth Column technique.

In his article, "My Trip to Germany," published in the *Staats-Zeitung,* Ridder made this remarkable statement: "I told this gentleman from Danzig that he, though he considered himself the holder of Germany's advance post, was really part of the main army only two hours from the German border, while I, as a member of the German American Conference, consider myself the holder of Germany's advance post 3000 miles away."

Thus Ridder coupled the thought of his heading an advance post for Nazi Germany with the distance separating the post from the "main army." Wagner was only two hours from the protective wing of the German army, while Ridder headed a post 3000 miles from the German army.

Ridder attempted to extricate himself from this self-exposure by semantics. He quibbled with the translation "advance post" and said it might better be read "outpost" in the sense of isolation. He actually worsened his position thereby, for he now contended that he, a prominent American citizen considered himself nevertheless a representative of "Germandom" who, together with all other Germans in the outpost of the United States, were isolated from Nazi Germany and its "main army"! The real meaning, of course, was that Ridder thought Wagner's task was relatively easy because the German army, only two hundred miles away, would soon conquer Danzig and make Wagner the Caesar of that province. But Ridder's task was much more formidable, for how long would it take before the main Germany army could do the same for him?

I do not know what compact Hitler made with Ridder in his "confidential" talks, but there was no difficulty in proving what Ridder did when he returned.

He immediately launched a special Sunday supplement in the *Staats-Zeitung* devoted exclusively to propaganda for the Hitler regime. The weekly supplement was called "The New Germany" and its inaugural issue carried the legend "One Reich, One Will." Ridder, having admitted that he knew from his conversations with Hitler that he was bent on a conquering program which was actually executed in the next ten years, nevertheless dedicated this new Sunday section to "promote understanding for the aspirations and aims of the new regime, and counteract the manifold attacks, denunciations, and suspicions leveled against the Nazi Government."

Ridder admitted under cross-examination that he considered criticisms of "The New Germany" often "unintelligent." Appropriately enough, the first article in this new Sunday section was entitled "The Resurrection of the German People."

Q. And by resurrection, you mean resurrection under Hitler; isn't that what you meant?

A. Yes, oh yes.

At first, Ridder denied that this Sunday section was given free to anyone who asked for it. "Oh, no," he answered. But then the few steps to the counsel table, the contradictory announcement in the *Staats-Zeitung,* the confrontation, and the reversal: "That is correct."

As Professor Foerster had said, the Germans put Beethoven in the trenches; culture was placed at the service of the devil. Here was a typical poem in the Sunday supplement:

Far from the land of the ancestors
We wander thru the world
Under thousands of flags
As it pleased the Lord.
Even though it has disappeared
The land of our ancestors
We are still united
By German blood.

Yet who will stop us
From being German and loyal?
No matter how the world will go,
Even though it may threaten us;
We are loyal and remain
German until death!

Ridder explained that poetry in these issues was designed for entertainment value.

Q. You considered the poem, that "no matter what happens, we are Germans and loyal to the death," you considered that entertainment?

A. Yes, it was put in as—you will find a poem in any Sunday magazine, sure.

Q. Entertainment for children or grown-ups?

A. For grown-ups.

Q. I show you the Sunday section as late as 1936, September, several years later, the first stanza of the poem says:

Let the shining hammers dance upon the red steel,
That the ringing of anvils should resound,
Let the shining hammers fall,
Germany now needs sharp blades.

I ask you, "Germany needs sharp blades"—what does that connote to your mind?

A. I would say that it means that Germany needs strong weapons, or sharp weapons.

COURT: You mean armament?

WITNESS: Rearmament, I would say.

NIZER: In 1936?

A. That is what it would mean to me, if I read it.

Q. Did you consider it entertainment?

A. That was all part of a poem.

Q. For the kiddies?

A. I have already testified that it is for grown persons. They would understand it.

I took Ridder through the various Nazi aggressions, confronting him in

each instance with the approval expressed in the *Staats-Zeitung*. Put together like a mosaic and in retrospect, it had a special impact.

On June 30, 1934, Hitler ruthlessly "purged" Chief of Staff Ernst
Röhm and other leading figures, it being reported that he personally used
his pistol in this series of murders which Ridder admitted shocked the
American press. The *Staats-Zeitung* applauded Hitler's "manliness."
Again, Ridder sought refuge in semantics.

A. I see the word *Mannhaftigkeit*. I think it means rather strength
than manliness.

Q. What does the prefix of that word mean, m-a-n-n?

A. Man.

Q. What does *haftigkeit* mean?

A. I do not know what it means in this connection.

I showed him Funk & Wagnall's Cassell's German dictionary. The only
definition of *Mannhaftigkeit* was manliness.

Q. Are you willing to accept it now?

A. Yes—oh, yes. All right.

When the Nazis seized Danzig, the *Staats-Zeitung* editorial head read:
"The Nazi Victory in Danzig." It not only hailed the union of "this
outlying post of German civilization" with "the Motherland," but it demanded the return of the Polish Corridor to the Hitler Reich: "Accordingly, the solution would have to be 'Danzig together with the Polish
Corridor back to the Reich.'" It developed that the *Staats-Zeitung* was
always attuned to the Goebbels schedule of anticipating the next step in
aggression by raising a propaganda din against a new "intolerable situation."

When Hitler marched into the Rhineland, the *Staats-Zeitung*
editorial was entitled, "Heavily Armed France Threatens." "With fullest
justification Germany has countered these steps with the occupation of
the Rhineland." The editorial excoriated France as being disdainful of
treaties, and the League of Nations as "a tool of France."

When Hitler marched into Austria—after Chancellor Engelbert Dol-
fuss had been brutally put to death in his home—the *Staats-Zeitung*
exulted: "Austria and Its People Return to the German Reich." Editorials
trumpeted, "One People, One Reich," and proclaimed that what had
been denied in 1919 and 1931 through the "stubbornness and short-
sightedness" of the Allies had nevertheless become an actuality through
Hitler's glorious deeds. The *Staats-Zeitung* seemed to be literally bursting
with pride, as its two-page spread of Hitler's picture riding into Vienna
ran into the very margins.

Q. Do you know any editorial that the *Staats-Zeitung* wrote in
which there was a single word of disapproval of the seizure of Austria
by Hitler?

A. I do not know. I have no idea.

Q. You never disapproved of the policy of the *Staats-Zeitung?*

A. No.

Hitler's rape of Czechoslovakia was greeted by the *Staats-Zeitung* with the editorial comment: "After twenty years the dream of Czechoslovakia as one of the great powers is at an end. What was created by short-sightedness, revenge . . . was shattered yesterday under the heavy pressure of pitiless historic logic."

The shocking breach of the Munich Agreement was defended: "The slogan of self-determination, the exaggerated nationalism, are a sweet and intoxicating poison for the small ones, to which all cold reason has to give way."

When Hitler invaded Poland, thus leaving no alternative but total conquest or total defeat, the *Staats-Zeitung* suddenly shifted its emphasis. It condemned the Allies for resisting Hitler because this was the last move on his agenda. Poland was all that was necessary for the "territorial liberation" of Germany; "a secure Reich with no danger of being attacked. . . ." Once Poland was conquered, Hitler would dedicate the Reich to the construction of "state buildings, art temples, workers' dwellings and recreation parks," and the Germans would create a new Periclean era and flood the world with new symphonies and poems. But the Allies "do not want this German art. England did not want the German mentality to turn toward these Athenian peace-goals." England wants to take away "the soul of the German nation."

Within three months after this Pan-German lulling technique, Hitler invaded Belgium, the Netherlands and Luxembourg. Norway and Denmark had been seized "for their protection." In France the Germans had turned the Maginot line, and the Luftwaffe was strafing hordes of civilian refugees without mercy.

At this juncture in world history, the *Staats-Zeitung* Sunday Section of May 19, 1940, argued: "Was it really an ethical partition of the world for eight million Dutch, whose armies could have been annihilated in five days, to own a mighty empire, which they themselves could not defend without the help of the British Navy?

"Time and again we have talked to the winds. The Dutch, saturated and self-sufficient, have simply laughed off the problem of property transference of their colonial possessions to nations which are militarily stronger."

The Letter Box feature of the *Staats-Zeitung* was used to state delicate problems faced by German Americans and to guide them so that they would be loyal to Germandom while keeping out of trouble with Uncle Sam. The jargon of the Letter Box was as personal as advice to the lovelorn.

As early as September 11, 1939, the Letter Box was hinting that German-Americans should not enlist to fight against the Fatherland should the United States become involved in the war. To a "worried reader," the answer was: "Even in 1917, one did not send Germans, if they weren't American citizens, against their homeland, weapons in their hands. Even those Germans who had already become citizens were not sent over to the front, unless they had been incited to such an extent by the systematic war propaganda that they volunteered for it."

So an American citizen of German descent who fought against Germany in World War I was, according to the *Staats-Zeitung*, a dupe of "systematic war propaganda." In a later Letter Box, such an American was called a "queer fellow."

Another answer suggested that German-Americans should not openly make disloyal remarks. "Be clever and wise. Do not hold your necks too near the rotating cross-saw." There was a special exhortation to be cautious in opposing conscription: "Do not act rashly! To be sure, you might renounce your birthright as an American, but there is no chance that by doing so your position would be improved. That would not relieve you from the obligation to report for military service under the new U.S. defense law.

"In case of any heroic declaration you would merely stir up a hornet's nest. You have your ways and means. . . . Always unburden your heart to me whenever you get a notion to do so! But for the present, never bow down! . . . but keep silence!"

The *Staats-Zeitung* even attempted to explain to its readers that its own real intentions were not to be read on the surface. In answer to a complaint—genuine or invented for the purpose—that the newspaper was not aggressive enough in pursuing its Pan-German policy, the answer was: "Do you know what we would risk? Do you know that we have to give consideration to political currents, if we do not want to jeopardize our existence?"

One day after Pearl Harbor the *Staats-Zeitung* editorial addressed "To Our Racial Brothers" advised: "And if they are wise, they will refrain from any discussion of the war, in order to avoid misunderstandings."

Ridder's counsel made the mistake of cross-examining Professor Foerster on this point. Unlike Ridder, the professor never floundered.

Q. And isn't it a fact that that one sentence was only an incidental part of the entire editorial?

A. No, it was not only incidental. It stands alone, and is a special advice, and this advice kills the value of all that has been said. If we cut away the other phrases we cut away a full disguise. If you say to a man "Shut your mouth" then he has something to hide. If they were really loyal, it would not have been necessary to shut their mouth, they could speak on our streets about it. But this shows that they had to hide something, and I can throw the light on the true motives by quoting a phrase from the *Staats-Zeitung*, February 3, 1940, where the *Staats-Zeitung* addressed to the readers the following advice—

STECKLER: If your Honor please, just one minute. . . .
The cross-examination did not pursue the matter further.

Ridder refused to admit that throughout all the years from 1933 to 1940 the *Staats-Zeitung* contained the programs of the German short-wave broadcasts.

Q. Couldn't you look at any issue between 1933 and 1940 and find out whether you have it in there?

A. I cannot leave this place, how can I look it up?

Q. Have you asked any of your associates to do it?

A. No, we intend to tackle that job tonight.

NIZER: Will you obtain that information, Mr. Steckler?

STECKLER: We will try to.

A moment later:

STECKLER: We know it was done in 1933, and if you wanted to check it all the way through, the chances are it was. But I do not think you want to check every year.

NIZER: You can take my research for it, if you wish. I say straight through 1940. They are your papers.

STECKLER: I do not doubt it for a minute.

NIZER: All right.

Ridder, after the customary quibbling, conceded that these broadcasts were conceived in the Nazi Ministry of Propaganda. The link with the Goebbels apparatus was far more direct. After the usual denial, I wrung from Ridder the admission that he received free of charge the dispatches of the Trans-Ocean News Service, which was the official organ of Goebbels's Ministry of Propaganda. Trans-Ocean even paid the cable charges. Later there was a nominal charge of $25 a week, even though Ridder admitted that these dispatches filled at least twenty per cent of his entire news space. Again, after fierce resistance, Ridder was compelled to admit that even these $25-a-week nominal charges were paid directly to the German Embassy.

Furthermore, Goebbels's designee on Trans-Ocean, one William Hoffmeister, also acted as a key editor on the *Staats-Zeitung*.

Q. And how long did Hoffmeister work for you?

A. I do not know. I would have to look it up.

Q. If I refreshed your recollection that he worked for you until late 1943 [long after the United States was at war with the Nazis], would that refresh your memory?

A. No, but it is close enough.

The feature editor of the *Staats-Zeitung* Sunday edition was the notorious Nazi, Heide. He had been denied United States citizenship "on the ground that the applicant was not attached to the principles of the Constitution."

Q. Did you make any inquiry as to—in what way he was not attached to the principles of the Constitution?

A. No, because my brother told me he had gone into the matter, so I accepted his decision.

Q. Now, he is still working for you?

A. Oh, yes.

I have referred to pieces of evidence which carry special conviction to certain minds. Two jurors told me after the verdict that the inability of Ridder to answer the following question injured him in their eyes more than any affirmative admission that he made:

Q. Did you in 1933 use the diplomatic pouch of the German Government to send papers to Germany?

A. I do not know.

Q. Did you in 1933 receive papers from Germany through the diplomatic pouch?

A. I have not the least idea.

Q. You would not deny that you did?

A. I would not affirm or deny it.

These answers are a typical illustration of the unexpected that occurs in cross-examination. This was one question Ridder would have been safe to deny—as he had denied many others where he was proven wrong—for how could I have had contradicting proof on this subject? Also he need not have feared exposure from some item in the *Staats-Zeitung*. It would not be likely to blabber about such an inner-governmental device. But a besieged witness does not have time to reason and weigh. I had simply guessed that Ridder's ties with Hitler were such that communications between them might be carried in the German diplomatic pouch, which is, of course, immune from any inspection. I had planned to insert this question suddenly and fiercely at a proper psychological moment, when the witness was reeling from proven contradictions. In the midst of another subject and while taking those conditioned reflex steps toward the table loaded with exhibits, I wheeled and threw the question at him, only to obtain a non-committal "I would not affirm or deny it."

I have never tried a case in which at some point I did not receive a totally unexpected blow. Whenever things are going well and everyone around me is bubbling with high spirits, during lunch hours or at the end of the day, they hear my warning, "Take it easy. This case isn't over yet. I know that a terrible blow on the back of the head is coming." For some reason it always does. A contradicting document of which we had no knowledge is suddenly produced, or an unexpected powerful witness shows up against us, or one of our own witnesses or a client makes a horrible blunder or—well, or something no one could have foreseen occurs. When it happens, the psychological problem shifts. Then I warn my associates not to permit their distress to be too visible in the courtroom. "Smile," I whisper. And during the next lunch hour, when appetites are feeble, I do my utmost to lift the gloom and remind them of all the favorable testimony that is in the record. "Remember, the atmosphere will clear in another day or two as new evidence comes into the case."

The Ridder trial was no exception to this rule. Despite the mountainous evidence we had produced of his Nazi involvement, Ridder testified about a matter that might well have thrown a serious doubt on our thesis. I will let him tell it as he did on the witness stand under questioning by his own attorney:

Q. Did Spanknoebel ever tell you what his purpose was in coming to the United States?

A. He submitted a letter of authority authorizing him to take over the German language newspapers in the United States and to conduct the activities of the German organizations in the United States.

Q. Who signed that letter?

A. It was signed by two men, Hans Bohle, who was the head of the bureau—

Q. What bureau?

A. The Foreign Bureau of the National Socialist Party, and by Dr. Rey, the head of the German Labor Front.

Q. Where did Spanknoebel show you this letter?

A. In our office.

Q. Were you alone at the time he came in?

A. When he first came in, yes.

Q. Did anybody else come in the room?

A. My brother Bernard joined me afterwards.

Q. And what answer did you give Spanknoebel in connection with his request?

NIZER: Ojection, sir.

COURT: Overruled.

A. My brother said to him, "Spanknoebel—"

COURT: Do not tell us what someone else said.

A. We threw him out of the office.

Ridder then went on to describe a meeting of the German-American Conference where Spanknoebel proposed to hold a trial of Ridder, his brother Bernard, and Dr. Ludwig Obendorf "for what they called our treason to our German blood, and my brother and I went up to defy them."

A. I went to the meeting in company with Inspector Hertzman, whom Mayor O'Brien had sent at my request. When we got there we found Spanknoebel and his group had complete control of the meeting. They had filled the place with about four hundred of their own people, and they thought they could intimidate us.

NIZER: I move to strike that out.

COURT: Strike out the statement as to what they thought.

A. We defied them. My brother made a speech attacking Spanknoebel, telling the people who were there that he was going to lead

322 · My Life in Court

them into trouble. What they were trying to do was contrary to American principles, and we did not propose to have Spanknoebel and his group walk into the organizations, throw the Jews out, take control of them, and make them part of the Nazi Party. We told them that as most of them obviously were not American citizens, they had better find out what went on in America before they tried anything of that kind. . . .

And he further stated to Spanknoebel that within a few days he, Spanknoebel, would be on his way back to Germany. Spanknoebel then replied in his speech, in which he pointed out to the meeting that he was the representative of the German Government here, that he was representing the Party, and that we had no right to interfere with their plans.

Then I got up and made a speech in which I said that these people were speaking a language which people in this country did not understand and that the German-American group in this country would not take on this program. They did not approve of it, that we had lived in harmony and peace with the Jewish element in New York City, and particularly with the German Jews who were all members of our organizations, and we did not propose to have Spannknoebl, or anybody else, to come in and throw them out or throw us out, because we were defending them.

Q. Do you know what happened to Spanknoebel after that?

A. Four days later he was indicted and fled the country.

Q. Did you discuss his activities with any public official?

A. Yes, Mr. George Medalie, the United States District Attorney at that time for the Southern District of New York.

Q. When did you discuss that with him?

A. The day after the meeting.

What was one to do with this testimony? I fell back upon the Rule of Probability. It has never failed me. After lengthy excursions into the probabilities, until the early hours of the morning, I reached the following conclusions and gambled on cross-examination to establish them.

1) *Ridder resented Spanknoebel, but this did not mean that his quarrel with him was an expression of hostility to his superiors. After all, Ridder's newspaper had supported Hitler's conquests throughout the later years, as our voluminous evidence showed.*

2) *If this deduction was right, then Ridder must have taken his grievance, not to the American authorities, but to the Nazi authorities. I would cross-examine him as to whether he had approached high German officials on this matter.*

3) *Ridder must have known that Spanknoebel had been recalled to Germany before he engaged him in open contest. Otherwise, how could he have visited Hitler frequently thereafter and been received in friendly fashion? I would therefore cross-examine in accordance with this probability.*

4) It would not surprise me, therefore, if Ridder had not initiated proceedings with the United States Attorney's office. More likely, Mr. Medalie had called Ridder when the internal struggle for control had been aired publicly at the German American Conference. I would cross-examine deeply on who initiated the United States Attorney's proceedings.

5) As to Ridder's assertion that he was a friend of the Jews, it opened the Staats-Zeitung to proof of its anti-Semitic contents, which otherwise might not be relevant under the issue of his particular libel and the Christmas Declaration.

If all this seems like Sherlock Holmes cerebrations, I may assure you that this is precisely what the Rule of Probability requires, except that here we are dealing with reality, not fiction, and no author is around to fashion the plot neatly. This is how these deductions proved out in the crucible of cross-examination:

Q. Spanknoebel was a rabid Nazi, wasn't he?

A. Very.

Q. And when he came to visit you, you say that he tried to take over your newspaper?

A. That is what I said.

Q. And you told him that his methods with you were wrong and would not win friends for Germany in the United States, did you say that or not?

A. May I say, your Honor, what I did say?

Q. No, did you say that?

COURT: Did you say, in words or substance what Mr. Nizer said?

WITNESS: Possibly in substance, yes.

So, the practical consideration that Spanknoebel's methods "would not win friends for Germany" was an important element in the controversy.

Q. Now, at that time you did not have Mr. Spanknoebel arrested, did you, in July?

A. Arrested?

Q. Yes.

A. How could we have him arrested?

Q. My question is, did you?

A. No, of course we did not.

Q. You did not file a complaint with any public authority against him at that time, did you?

A. Why, no.

Q. And you did not issue any statement to the press about Spanknoebel's demand upon you?

A. Why, no.

Q. But you did get in touch with Berlin, did you not?

A. No, we got in touch with the German Consulate.

Q. Did you have a talk with Dr. Luther [German Ambassador] about it?

A. I had a talk later on in Washington.

Q. Did you tell Dr. Luther anything about the demand which you say Spanknoebel had made upon you to take over the newspaper?

A. Oh yes.

The second deduction had proven correct. Ridder had complained to the Nazi Ambassador to the United States, not to the United States authorities.

Q. Did Dr. Luther communicate with Berlin about it?

A. I do not know.

Q. Didn't he tell you he did?

A. No.

Q. Well, you knew that Spanknoebel's authority to act as a representative of the German Government was revoked, did you not?

A. We found that out the day of the meeting, of the Turn Hall meeting.

We were close to the third objective. Finally Ridder admitted knowing of Spanknoebel's recall at the time he spoke against him:

Q. Well, in any event at the time you and your brother were making speeches against Spanknoebel, you knew his authority had been revoked by the Nazis?

A. Certainly, sure we did.

Q. Now at the time you talked to Dr. Luther, you had not yet talked to the Federal authorities of the United States about it, had you?

A. No.

I now turned to the fourth objective.

Q. At no time did you make a request upon the Federal attorney, or the State attorney to indict Spanknoebel, did you?

A. My brother and I went to see Mr. Medalie.

Q. That was after he had called you, is that not so?

A. Yes, that was after the Turn Hall meeting.

Q. Yes.

A. Oh, sure.

Q. But you did not go to see Mr. Medalie to have Mr. Spanknoebel indicted, is that correct?

A. You mean, well, we do not indict him. We went down there because Mr. Medalie said he thought we should give him the information which we had, and we were glad to do it.

Q. In other words, when this story of this meeting came down then Mr. Medalie called you and your brother down?

A. Yes.

Q. You did not initiate any proceedings against Spanknoebel?

A. No, oh, no.

Q. Now, you had this fight with Spanknoebel?

A. Yes, sir.

Q. Did you visit Germany afterwards?

A. Oh, yes.

Q. What year?

A. I do not remember, 1933, I went. I think I was there—I know I was there in 1936.

Q. Weren't you there in 1934?

A. I think I was, yes.

Q. How many months after this terrible fight with Spanknoebel did you go to Germany?

A. Well, this battle ended in October with his fleeing.

Q. Yes.

A. I suppose I went probably in July or August of the following year.

Q. You were not molested?

A. No.

Q. And you did visit Germany again in 1935?

A. Yes, I was there in 1935.

Q. And in 1936?

A. In 1936, yes.

Q. You were not molested on any of those occasions?

A. No.

To support his testimony that he was anti-Nazi, Ridder also testified that he had "made a public protest in City Hall to Mayor O'Brien" against the Nazi Spanknoebel being the main speaker at a German Day celebration. However, it turned out that he had accepted as a substitute Dr. Griebl, whom he knew "was one of the early Nazis" and a "cohort of Spannknoebl." Again, that deadly trio: the denial, the confrontation, and the admission:

Q. Did you agree to have Dr. Griebl be the main speaker at the German Day instead of Spanknoebel?

A. No.

Q. I show you first the New York *Herold* with a statement by you, and ask you to look at this sentence particularly [indicating] and ask you if that is not a fact? See it there?

A. I do not recall what the word *designieren*—that is right, I did.

Of course, in summation, where the opportunity is afforded, the ramifications of the Spanknoebel matter could be analyzed with clarity. It was after the Spanknoebel "fight" that Ridder praised Hitler's seizure of Danzig, Austria, and Czechoslovakia.

Ridder had opened the door on the subject to anti-Semitism. He claimed he attacked Spanknoebel's anti-Jewish policy. During the trial he forgot this pose. For example, he did not remember it when I asked him:

Q. Could you from 1933, let's say, to 1939, when the war began, point to a single article in that Sunday Section which was anti-Nazi?

A. I have not the slightest idea.

Q. You have not any idea?

A. None.

Q. That is the best you can say as a publisher?

A. That is the best I can say.

The *Staats-Zeitung* reported Bernard Ridder's speech on his return from a personal interview with Hitler: "Mr. Ridder declared to the Fuehrer 'I am 90% Nazi!' 'That is not possible,' exclaimed Hitler and he wanted to know what is represented by the remaining 10%. Mr. Ridder declared to him candidly and openly that he, like many of his American fellow citizens, cannot agree with the German conception in respect of the Jewish question."

The German newspapers reported that Bernard Ridder had said, "I am 100% Nazi." According to the same New York report Ridder said that "Hitler and the men surrounding him are men of great intelligence and personal charm." So Ridder "opposed" anti-Semitism, but thought the anti-Semites were intelligent and charming.

Furthermore, the *Staats-Zeitung* had on occasion fulminated against the Jews. It contained an article excoriating the Jewish people as "the inventors of capitalism." And when a protest parade headed by Major General John F. O'Ryan was held in New York against Nazi persecution of the Jews, the *Staats-Zeitung* reported the marchers as "little men and little women . . . with half-grown and undergrown children," and charged that at least 10,000 of the marchers must have "sworn upon the red flag." Thus, there was the familiar gambit—the Jews were the inventors of capitalism and also Communists sworn to tear it down.

After a severe pounding, Ridder yielded rather than continue the posture that these reports were fair:

Q. I ask you whether you consider the description of those who marched, "little men and little women were rushed past, together with half-grown or ungrown children," a fair newspaper report or whether it was an attempt to create prejudice against those who participated in that march?

A. The answer to the first half of the question is "No," I do not consider it fair reporting.

Q. I read from this same report, "Two things struck the attention of the unbiased observer." You do not consider this reporter unbiased who wrote this up for you?

A. No, he was prejudiced. You can see it right from the editorial.

Q. Can't you?

A. Yes.

Even after the United States was at war with Germany, Ridder's sympathy for the Nazis could not be restrained.

Q. Did the *Staats-Zeitung* raise moneys for the relief of German war prisoners in the United States and Canada?

A. I think we did, certainly.

Q. And that was in 1941?

A. 1941, it might—it might have been 1942, even.

COURT: Did you say in 1942, also?

WITNESS: I do not know whether it was 1941 or 1942.

NIZER: I believe it was, your Honor, in 1942 as well. I was coming to that, sir.

COURT: You mean after America entered the war?

WITNESS: Yes, these were prisoners of war in the United States and in Canada.

I have often heard cynical comments by laymen about lawyers' ethics, how they fashion a witness's testimony and teach him to lie. Aside from the fact that the noble traditions of the legal profession are at least as well observed as those of other professional men I can earnestly report that I have never met a topnotch lawyer whose sense of honor did not meet the highest standards. The reason for this is not compressed within the ethical proprieties of Bar Association rules or the high character required for following the highest calling of all, that of being an advisor. The reason is also to be found in the practical fact that lack of scruples leads to defeat. If an opponent permits his client to lie or if through lack of preparation he is unaware that his client is deliberately lying, he assures his own downfall. A thousand facts spring up to bedevil the lie; I never am so certain of success as when a witness has deliberately fabricated evidence. For, if I am prepared and persistent, such a witness cannot survive. A jury may forgive a witness's error in fact. We all make them. But it will never forgive a deliberate lie.

A good illustration of this principle occurred in this trial. When I asked Ridder whether he knew that his brother Bernard had had a long interview with Hitler, he denied any knowledge of this. I confronted him with a front-page story of the interview in the *Staats-Zeitung* under the byline of Margreve which said: "Berlin, May 20—Hitler's personality, loving passionately peace and order, revealed itself today in a conference, lasting for one hour and three quarters, which Mr. Bernard H. Ridder, president of the Staats-Herold Corporation, had with the Chancellor."

He was all set for this attack. His quick answer was, "That is a fake." Did he really expect this would end the matter? That reply was the platform from which three hours of cross-examination were launched.

Q. Did you publish any statement in the *Staats-Zeitung* saying that this front-page story of an interview with Hitler was a fake?

A. No.

Q. You just permitted the impression to continue with the readers that this long interview and story about Hitler was genuine, even though you knew it was a fake, is that right?

A. No, we decided that it would be waste to rake it up. It was one of those things we were glad to forget as quickly as possible.

Q. You as a publisher believe in the integrity of the news, don't you, Mr. Ridder?

A. Yes.

Q. And you believe if a newspaper makes an error that error should be corrected, don't you?

A. Not always.

Q. Not always?

A. No, we did not correct it.

Q. In other words, according to your standard of ethics as publisher, if a newspaper has a news item which turns out to be a complete fake, you just forget about it and hope everybody else does?

A. Sometimes we do, and sometimes we don't.

Q. Um-hum. This is the standard by which you conduct the publications of your newspapers, is that right?

A. I personally, those are my standards.

Q. I beg your pardon?

A. Those are my standards.

Ridder forgot that his brother Bernard had made speeches about his long interview with Hitler and that, a month after his return to the United States, the *Staats-Zeitung* had reported one of these addresses: "Mr. Ridder conveyed his impressions of his last trip to Germany and drew a characteristic picture of Adolf Hitler, with whom he became acquainted as also with his closest collaborators. . . . Air Minister Goering sent an airplane to Bremen to fetch Mr. Ridder. Everywhere is the new feeling of life met with, so that Mr. Ridder upon his first encounter with Adolf Hitler declared to the Fuehrer: 'I am 90% Nazi.'"

So the *Staats-Zeitung* later confirmed the truth of what Victor Ridder had branded as a Margreve fake story. Thus Ridder was forced into a new series of concoctions, like a man in a morass, struggling furiously and therefore sinking faster. Now he claimed that his brother may have met with Hitler, but hadn't told him.

A. The first time I learned that my brother had an interview was that article you showed me the other day, Mr. Nizer. So I called up my brother and asked him about the interview, and he said, yes, he had had an interview with Hitler.

Q. So you now tell us that the first time you learned that your brother had an interview with Hitler was when I showed you—

A. That is right.

Q. —the *Staats-Zeitung*?

A. Yes.

Q. On Friday afternoon?

A. That is right.

Q. Didn't you ever see that story that he had an interview with Hitler?

A. No, I do not think I was here in June.

Q. Just listen to my question, please.

A. The answer is no.

Q. Suppose you make the answer after I put the question.

A. All right.

Q. Didn't you ever read any place, whether in the *Staats-Zeitung* or any other place, that your brother had had an interview with Hitler and had said, "I am a 90% Nazi"?

A. I do not know.

Now he was in new trouble. The New York *World-Telegram* had printed a series in which Bernard's interview and statement had been published. It turned out that Ridder and his brother Bernard not only read this series, but that Joseph Ridder had personally visited the *World-Telegram* concerning this series. Yet Victor Ridder insisted, for now he was completely surrounded, that even after the *World-Telegram* story he had not asked Bernard whether he had interviewed Hitler.

Finally Ridder contended that he had fired Margreve immediately for writing a fake story. I subpoenaed the *Staats-Zeitung* records. Of course, Margreve was on the payroll for a year thereafter!

Q. Well, you finally found out the story was not faked?

A. Later on, I did, yes.

Such a debacle must not be permitted to grow dim in the jury's mind. Repeatedly thereafter, when I showed Ridder a quotation from his newspaper, I asked, "*This* story was not a fake, was it?" It became a theme whose melody haunted Ridder.

True drama is seldom unrelieved by humor. Perhaps this is the reason why court scenes invariably produce unexpectedly amusing and often hilarious incidents. There were a number of such in the Foerster case. One involved Professor John Shuler.

Professor Foerster, in his attack on the Christmas Declaration as a plea for soft peace for Germany, had traced the Pan-German movement in the United States. He analyzed the functions of the Steuben Society, which had "packed meetings of the America First Committee" and had become "the center of isolationist and un-American agitation." In the course of this argument he pointed out that, "As far back as the 1780s, General von Steuben planned to make a monarchy out of North America with a Hohenzollern Prince at its head." To Foerster, Von Steuben, the hero of the German societies, was a Pan-German and no hero at all. Ridder decided to challenge this version of Von Steuben and to paint him as a great man. Professor Shuler was called to the stand to accomplish this and thus discredit Professor Foerster. Shuler relied on a history "written by Macauley Parker," but he did not have the book with him. I objected and insisted that he produce the book on which he relied. It was soon arranged that he would withdraw from the stand and return the next day with the book. But I had gained an invaluable advantage. I knew what he was going to testify to, and I knew his authority. That night was not one for sleep. I pored over histories on Von Steuben. I found that the good Professor had even been ignorant of the name of his authority. It was not Parker, but Palmer. When Professor Shuler returned and testified to the greatness of Von Steuben, I was not unprepared.

Q. Dr. Shuler, you have been teaching history how long?

A. Oh, forty or forty-five years.

Q. Have you ever written a book?

A. Never did, no.

Q. Did you ever write an article?

A. None that I would like to mention.

Q. What is that?

A. None that I would like to mention. They were not exactly historical articles.

Q. And I think you told us that you went to Johns Hopkins the first time when you were here.

A. Yes.

Q. But you did not graduate from there?

A. No, I was there three years.

Q. And then you said when you went to Columbia to get your Doctor's degree you wrote a thesis for the Doctor's degree, which is the customary way of doing it, is it not?

A. Yes.

Q. And that thesis was on what subject, Doctor?

A. On "The Language of Richard Wagner in His *Der Ring des Nibelungen.*"

Q. And Wagner's *Ring des Nibelungen* is generally considered a symbol of Pan-Germanism, is it not?

A. Something like it.

So his only written work was a thesis in college which was partial to Pan-Germanism. Now I was ready for the main attack.

Q. Now when you were here the first time you mentioned a book and you did not have it with you. Do you recall you gave the name of the book as Parker?

A. As Palmer.

Q. You recall that you called the book Parker?

A. That was a *lapsus linguae*.

Q. A lapse of what?

A. A slip of the tongue—*lapsus linguae*.

Q. Have you read that book carefully?

A. Yes, sir.

Q. You read all of it?

A. Yes, sir.

Q. You say that you looked up the character of Von Steuben and you familiarized yourself with his character. Is his character described in any way in Palmer?

A. Well, yes, oh yes.

Q. And is he considered a very fine man?

A. As a man?

Q. Yes.

A. Jovial, yes.

Q. I mean is he considered a man of integrity?

A. Yes, sir.

Q. By Palmer?

A. Yes, sir.

Q. And a man who was truthful?

A. Yes.

Q. Well now I read to you from page 2 in which the author says, "My first reaction upon discovering that my hero [Steuben] was a systematic, circumstantial, and deliberate liar was one both of disgust and disappointment." You remember that?

A. Yes.

Q. He said, "I was disposed to proceed no further with my book."

A. Correct.

Q. "Here was, indeed, a golden opportunity for a debunker or muckraker, but that sensational role made no appeal to me. My curiosity was aroused, however, and I determined if possible to discover the motive for this remarkable falsification." Do you remember that?

A. Yes, sir.

Q. Will you agree with me that Palmer considered Steuben a liar instead of having integrity? Did he, or did he not?

A. As far as he went, yes, but you did not go far enough.

Q. You mean he becomes an honest man on the next page?

A. No.

Q. . . . I ask you whether Palmer does not think that Von Steuben is a liar? Look at it, sir.

A. Yes, I know the passage, but you did not read all of it.

Q. You read any part else that you say changes that any place in the book.

A. "In due time I was rewarded by discovering that the Baron [Steuben] was not the sole and probably not even the principal father of the fictions."

Q. Let's stop there for a moment. I will let you read on. In other words, Steuben was not the only liar, there were others?

A. Bigger liars than he.

Q. Without worrying about other people, in this case, Doctor, does that change the fact that Palmer thought that Steuben was still a liar?

A. In one respect.

Q. One respect?

A. In one respect, sir.

Q. When he says "systematic liar," does that mean one respect or a lot of respects?

A. I should judge that would mean a lot of respects, but he does not show those other respects, he only shows one.

Now I went after his other authorities:

Q. You recall that you quoted from Kapp?

A. Yes, sir.

Q. Now you know about Palmer's reliability as an author, don't you?

A. Yes, sir.

Q. Now Palmer wrote: "I soon became aware that there were gross misstatements of fact in Kapp's narrative." Remember that?

A. Yes, sir.

Q. Palmer continued, "I discovered that Steuben's pre-American history as Kapp wrote it is largely a myth." Remember that?

A. Yes.

Q. The man you quoted, Kapp, Palmer thinks that he is a liar too, doesn't he?

A. Well, I wouldn't say a liar. I would interpret "myth" there, sir, as being not in accord with historical fact.

Q. . . . In any event a man who writes false history is lying, isn't he?

A. Well, in a sense.

Q. In a pretty large sense?

A. Perhaps so.

Then, after quoting Palmer to show that he, too, reported Von Steuben as having invited Prince Henry of Prussia to set up a monarchy in the United States, I was ready for the final thrust:

Q. Exactly! In other words, Prince Henry was informed by Von Steuben that they could set up a monarchy in America, is that right?

A. [Nodding in the affirmative.]

Q. Please do not shake your head, we have to have the answer. Will you please say—

A. Yes.

Q. . . . Now does that in substance bear out Professor Foerster, that Von Steuben invited Prince Henry to come over here and be the head of the Crown?

A. I challenge Palmer there on that.

Q. Well, didn't you bring in Palmer, Doctor, to cite as an authority on this subject?

A. You mean the whole of Palmer?

Q. Didn't you bring in the whole book with covers on it?

A. I did, yes.

Q. Well, then you said you relied on Palmer, didn't you?

A. To a large extent.

Q. You mean that the very sentence which supports Professor Foerster is the extent to which you do not rely on it.

And so on for an hour. We were all entitled to a light moment.

Shortly after startling admissions came tumbling out of Ridder's mouth, a young man appeared in the back of the courtroom. He sat on a first-row bench near the window, in the humid courtroom, with a pad on his knees, and wrote copiously. A trial lawyer is always alert to any new personality in the courtroom. He may be a witness for his adversary, and any advance intimation may enable the lawyer to prepare for the attack. So assistants are always ferreting out information about any visitor who does not seem to be merely listening to the trial. In this instance the mystery soon solved itself. The note-taking observer introduced himself to me during a recess. He was an FBI agent who had been assigned to the trial when word got out of the developments. He asked for our co-operation in furnishing copies of exhibits and expressed his amazement at some of the revelations.

Ridder's chief witness was Dr. George N. Shuster, President of Hunter College in the City of New York. It was he who was President of an organization known as Loyal Americans of German Descent, which had issued the Christmas Declaration. He testified that Dorothy Thompson had shown him the draft, which he had changed, and the publication of which the American Jewish Congress had financed. He also stated that the Office of War Information of the United States Government had requested its publication.

Then he was turned over to me for cross-examination. He admitted that his information about the American Jewish Congress came from a Miss Schultz and that he never investigated whether the financing came from individuals rather than from that organization.

Q. Did you notice the sentence in the third column, "We remind them [the German people] of the mercy and forgiveness that are present in the hearts of people for those who turn against evil . . ."?

A. Yes, sir.

Q. That was signed by you in December 1942, was it not?

A. Yes, sir.

Q. At that time, Dr. Shuster, it was pretty clear to you that the Nazis were going to lose the war, wasn't it?

A. No, sir.

Q. You mean that after the beginning of January 1943, approximately that time, you still thought that the Axis powers might win the European war?

A. No, sir.

Q. Well then, if you do not mean that, you thought the United Nations would win in December 1942; didn't you feel that way?

A. Yes, sir.

Q. Now, feeling that the United Nations were going to win, in other words, knowing that the tide had turned, you approved a sentence which reminded the German people and the American public that if at this time they would throw off the Nazi, there would be forgiveness for them, is that what you would take by that sentence?

A. Yes, sir.

Q. In other words this was a plea, wasn't it, Dr. Shuster, for forgiveness for the German people?

A. No, sir.

In the opening statement made to the jury, Ridder's attorney had announced that he would present Dr. Shuster as a witness. Thereafter I became an expert on Professor Shuster's copious writings.

Q. Did you ever say in writing or orally that Hitler was an honest, inquiring man?

A. Not that I know, Mr. Nizer.

Q. Did you ever write any place that Hitler is and has been a greatly perplexed, honestly inquiring, and quite unsteady young man?

A. Yes, I did.

Q. Where did you print that?

A. I am sorry. You know my books, apparently, better than I do, Mr. Nizer.

Q. Is the only place you ever said that in your book?

A. I am not sure that I said that, Mr. Nizer.

Q. All right. I read to you from page 40 of *Strong Man Rules* by Shuster. I take it you will acknowledge that is your book?

A. With great pleasure, sir.

Q. With great pleasure?

A. Yes, sir.

Q. All right. I quote, "Hitler is a politician of whom it might be said that if he had not existed it would have been necessary to invent him." Do you remember writing that?

A. No, sir.

Q. I show you page 40 of your book and show you that sentence, and ask you if that refreshes your recollection that you said that?

A. Yes, why don't you read the rest of it?

Q. I am going to. First I ask, did you write that sentence? It is a complete sentence, is it not, Doctor?

A. Yes, sir.

Q. Did you write it?

A. Yes, sir.

Q. . . . Now I continue . . . "Hitler is our friend, the old soldier, designed to go down to history as a cross between Hotspur and Uncle Toby and to be as immortal as either." Do you recall writing that sentence?

A. Yes.

Q. Who was Uncle Toby?

A. Uncle Toby is a knight in *Twelfth Night*.

Q. A knight?

A. A very ridiculous knight.

Q. You considered in 1935, that Hitler was just ridiculous, did you?

A. No.

Q. But when you referred to him as a cross between Hotspur and Uncle Toby, did you mean to say that he was not dangerous?

A. I meant precisely that—Hotspur, if you will recall, Mr. Nizer, was rather dangerous.

Q. I will read this: "Hitler is not a German. Hitler is and has been a greatly perplexed, honestly inquiring, and quite unsteady young man." Do you recall writing that sentence?

A. Yes, sir.

Q. In 1935 you considered Hitler "an honestly inquiring and quite unsteady young man"?

A. Yes.

Q. And by "honestly inquiring" you meant that he was speaking the truth?

A. No.

Q. He was honestly making inquiries?

A. Yes.

Q. You did not consider him malicious at that time?

A. Oh yes.

Q. You had read *Mein Kampf* in 1935?

A. Certainly. If you remember I wrote the notes for *Mein Kampf*.

Q. I read the next sentence, Doctor. "Those are a few of the plain facts, which may turn out to be at least as interesting as some of the fiction currently in vogue." Did you write that?

A. Yes.

Q. By the word "fiction" you meant that the attacks that were being made upon Hitler were, to a great extent, fiction?

A. No.

Q. . . . Didn't you refer by "fiction" to the attacks that were being made upon Hitler?

A. No, sir.

Q. Did you ever write, Dr. Shuster, that the Germans are, and I quote, "a people upon whom the late Mr. Woodrow Wilson played what can only be called a dirty trick"?

A. Yes.

Q. You wrote that in 1935?

A. Yes.

Q. Did you write "What matters is not poor Horst Wessel. Chaps like him have done worse at Harvard and lived it down"?

A. Yes, sir.

Q. . . . Who is Horst Wessel?

A. The author of the Horst Wessel *Lied*.

Q. That was the official battle song or hymn of the Germans, was it?

A. Yes.

Q. And Horst Wessel, you know, was a very disreputable figure, was he not?

A. I would not say that.

Q. Did you know that he conducted a prostitution house?

A. No.

Q. You knew that he was the official hero of the Nazi Party, didn't you?

A. One of the official heroes.

Q. And his song, the Horst Wessel song, was the celebration song of the Nazis?

A. Of the Nazi youth.

Q. You were referring to "poor Horst Wessel" intending to indicate didn't you that Horst Wessel was a character to be sympathized with?

A. No.

Q. When you say "chaps like him have done worse at Harvard and lived it down" you were minimizing Horst Wessel's contribution to evil, were you not?

A. No.

Q. Did you ever write, "Frankly I think that the record tends to show the United States the most militaristic of Western peoples"?

A. Not that I remember.

Q. Let me read from page 56 of your book and then I will show it to you, Doctor. "Frankly I think that the record tends to show the United States the most militaristic of Western peoples. At least there is no other which has fought so many wars from which it could have abstained." I show you that on page 56 and ask you if you wrote that in 1934?

A. Yes, sir.

Q. And when you wrote that . . . do you mean that the United States engaged in wars which it could have kept out of and should not have engaged in?

A. Yes.

Q. Is that what you meant?

A. Precisely.

Q. While calling the United States "the most militaristic of Western peoples," did you also write complaining that the German Army had been limited to 100,000 by the Treaty of Versailles?

A. Yes, sir.

Q. You wanted a larger German Army then?

A. No, sir.

Q. Why did you denounce the Versailles Treaty in limiting the German Army to 100,000 men?

A. Because the limitation of the German Army to 100,000 men meant that at a very bad psychological moment, you released to civilian political life people who were not prepared for any other profession. . . . It would have been wiser to have chosen the other way, provided one did not succeed in establishing complete disarmament in which I profoundly believe.

COURT: What was the other way that you just referred to?

WITNESS: The "other way" was to increase, temporarily, the strength of the German Army from 100,000 men to 200,000 men.

Q. . . . You either had a small German Army or a large one?

A. We estimated you could have a standing army of 250,000 men.

Q. . . . You feel that if the German Army had been permitted another 150,000 men that that would have improved the social conditions of Germany?

A. Not necessarily.

Q. Do you speak German?

A. Yes, sir.

Q. Did you ever write in 1934 that Hitler had integrity?

A. Well, certainly not that I know of.

Q. This is your book, is it not, *Germans* by Shuster?

A. Yes.

Q. Let me read to you a passage from page 262, "Herr Hitler appeared with the answer. . . . But there is no doubting his efficiency. Or his bravery. Or, in spite of inconsistencies, his integrity." Do you recall that?

A. Yes, sir.

Q. Do you still feel that Hitler had integrity?

A. From the point of view—

Q. Do you or do you not? Do you still feel Hitler had integrity?

A. No.

Q. Do you feel that when you gave this judgment it was a wrong one?

A. Your question is not proper.

Q. What is improper about it?

A. You are suggesting a totally different meaning for the word "integrity" than what is in the book. By "integrity" in this book is meant consistency, from the point of view of the German nationalist and not integrity from the moral point of view.

Q. Let me show it to you, the sentence reads—

A. Go ahead, read the whole thing.

Q. Pardon me, Doctor, let's do it slowly and correctly. The sentence reads, "But there is no doubting his efficiency, or his bravery, or in spite of inconsistencies, his integrity." Now is there anything in that which refers to his integrity as being consistent with nationalism, or does it just end with integrity?

A. Precisely, it contains the word "inconsistencies".

Q. Do you think inconsistency and integrity are synonymous?

A. From a logical point of view they are.

Q. But not from a dictionary point of view, are they?

A. If you will be good enough to supply a dictionary I will be glad to answer the question.

Q. I would not supply a dictionary to the president of Hunter College, sir.

A. Thank you, sir.

Q. When you use the word "inconsistency" you mean to say that that has the same meaning as "integrity"?

A. In that context it has.

COURT: Doctor, a reference was made to a book you wrote about the German people being victims of a dirty trick played by Woodrow Wilson. What was the "dirty trick"?

WITNESS: The reference I made was to the failure of Mr. Wilson to establish at Versailles the kind of peace which had initially been advertised to the German people.

NIZER: . . . Did you ever write "Curiously enough, Hitler has come out of the ordeal with a reputation for moderateness and kindliness"?

A. Yes.

Q. What ordeal did he come out of with a reputation for moderateness and kindliness?

A. Mr. Nizer, the ordeal was, I think, if I remember correctly, in the first months of the regime.

Q. And in the first months of the regime weren't the edicts passed in which Hitler dissolved the Parliament and started his pogroms against Jews?

A. Oh, yes.

Q. Um-hum.

A. Everybody in Germany assumed that all the evil things were being done by subordinates and if only Hitler knew about them all would be well. With that unfortunate reputation.

Q. Let's see if you meant that. "Very good people who stagger under heavy blows feel that the great man wanted otherwise and that subordinates frustrated his benevolent designs." The words, "great man" referred to Hitler in that sentence, didn't it?

A. Oh, of course. I point out to you again, Mr. Nizer, as you are well aware, the device of irony is a customary one in literary composition.

Q. Well, let me ask you whether this is irony. Did you ever write in *Like a Mighty Army* by Shuster, page 67, "Even those Americans who are enemies of the Jews—those who sincerely believe that the children of Moses are unscrupulous in business, ill-mannered, and generally distasteful—will scarcely deny that the German government has challenged the ethical feeling of mankind. The facts, or the prejudices (I am not debating the point) fail to come within a mile of justifying a policy which is compounded of savagery and ignorance." Do you recall writing that?

A. Yes, sir.

Q. When you refer to "The facts, or the prejudices (I am not debating the point)," you meant by that whether all those things said about the Jews are true or merely prejudices, you are not going to decide either way?

A. Certainly not, Mr. Nizer.

Q. You intended this to be ironical.

A. No.

Q. You recall writing in your introduction to this book on page 15, "Being a marked individual always, the Jew simply could not venture with impunity into these exposed positions. An American family with these phenomena cannot help deplore the fact that May Day Communist parading in New York and elsewhere is so largely a Semitic manifestation. Surely it must be obvious that when the 'reaction' sets in these United States, anti-Jewish feeling may accompany it." Do you recall writing that?

A. Yes.

Q. And wasn't that an effort by you, ironically or otherwise to associate the Communistic parade with a Semitic or Jewish parade?

A. No, sir.

Q. In May 1933 did you give a lecture before the students of the Bronx Annex of Hunter College?

A. No, sir.

Q. You recall that very definitely, do you?

A. Yes, sir.

Q. Did you ever say "Hitler is indeed no ogre. He has a sensitive heart and will do no harm to anybody"?

A. No, sir.

Q. You know that the *Staats-Zeitung,* Mr. Ridder's newspaper, reported your speech in that way?

A. Precisely, I have already—

Q. Just a moment, let's go slowly. You know that the *Staats-Zeitung* quoted your speech that Hitler is "indeed no ogre." What does ogre mean anyhow, Doctor—monster?

A. I should imagine you were correct in that assumption, Mr. Nizer.

Q. "Hitler is no monster. He has a sensitive heart and will do no harm to anybody." How long after May 12, 1933, when this was published in the *Staats-Zeitung*, did you find out that it had been published there?

A. The date was probably 1944.

Q. You found it out eleven years later?

A. Yes, sir.

Q. It had never been called to your attention before that?

A. Not that I am aware of.

Q. Do you consider the *Staats-Zeitung* an irresponsible newspaper?

A. I consider the *Staats-Zeitung* a newspaper.

Q. Well, may I have an answer to my question?

A. No—

Q. And you refuse to answer the question as to whether you consider the *Staats-Zeitung* a responsible newspaper?

A. I consider the *Staats-Zeitung* a responsible newspaper.

Q. Oh, you do say that even though this report, let me show it to you—

A. I have seen it Mr. Nizer. You do not have to show it to me.

Q. Will you please read the headline?

A. "*Hitler Kein Unmensch.*"

Q. Please translate.

A. "Hitler is no monster says George N. Shuster."

Q. Then there is a whole column of the speech, is that right?

A. Yes, sir.

Q. And you say that you never made that speech?

A. I certainly do say so, yes, sir.

Q. And even though you did not make it and they published the complete speech, you still say that it is a responsible newspaper?

A. I say it is.

Q. Do you?

A. It is as responsible as the New York *Times* which quotes just as badly.

Q. You say you never said Hitler is not a monster?

A. I did not make that speech at all.

Q. You say you never said that in any speech?

A. I might conceivably have said that Hitler was no monster.

Q. Now you not only might have conceivably said it, you wrote it, didn't you, those exact words?

A. Well, as I said before, you are more familiar with my writings than I am.

Q. Is that to my credit or yours, Doctor? I want to point it out to you. Read the whole passage, and I will ask you—"The man is certainly no monster." You wrote that?

A. Yes, sir.

Q. That was not ironic, was it?

A. No.

NIZER: That is all.

Three times Steckler conducted re-direct examination of Dr. Shuster and three times I re-cross-examined. When I asked him whether he considered Arndt's poems Pan-German expressions, he denied that they were. I read a stanza:

So, blow your trumpets,
Come out, Hussars,
You ride, Field Marshal, like the rushing winds toward victory, to the
Rhine,
Across the Rhine, you courageous daredevils, Ride into France.

Q. Does that mean conquest of France?

A. No.

Q. What was he riding into France for, for pleasure?

A. For the Battle of Waterloo, for which we ought to be, all of us, very grateful, Mr. Nizer.

Q. And when in the other poem he talked of Austria, the Tyrol, and Swiss, should we be grateful . . . that the Nazis went into Austria and made an *Anschluss?*

A. . . . Oh, for heaven's sake, no.

Q. Or Munich, or the taking of Czechoslovakia—you would not be grateful for that, would you?

A. Mr. Nizer, you know full well what my attitude is.

COURT: . . . The jury does not.

WITNESS: My answer, of course, is an indignant no.

Steckler asked him whether, after the Christmas Declaration was published, he had not worked in various organizations and societies to separate the guilt of the Nazis from the German people. He replied that he had in some. He named the Catholic Association for International Peace of which he was President: "My attitude toward peace can be defined in one term. . . . I think that all the guilty in the war should and must be punished. But, I am not willing to admit that the only people who are innocent in Germany are members of the Communist Party. I think that Hitler's attack, as I have said on innumerable occasions, was primarily on the Christian churches, both Catholic and Protestant. . . . We had in Germany thousands of clergymen who went to concentration camps. My point is very simply this: These Germans are just as much entitled to walk in hand with us in the reconstruction of a new Europe as are the people who belong to the Communist Party. If that is a 'soft peace,' I am in favor of a 'soft peace.'"

Q. . . . Finish, if you wish.

A. My conception of a good peace for Germany is a peace in which we permit the co-operation with us of the surviving Christian, Jewish, and Trade Union groups.

STECKLER: That is all.

I cross-examined again:

Q. If you had your way, then, you would have the German people today, with the exception of war criminals, taken right back into the family of nations immediately now, just yes or no to that, is that what you plan?

A. No.

Since he had repeatedly contrasted Germans with Communists, as if Professor Foerster didn't profoundly detest the Communists too, I asked him:

Q. Doctor, you have made . . . references to economic theories of one kind or another. And, I ask you whether you ever wrote this, "Again, while I am not enthusiastic about the social conceptions of Dr. Schacht and Herr Göring, it is by no means certain that their experiments are vastly inferior to some of our own." Did you ever write that?

A. May I answer that question, not yes or no, your Honor.

COURT: Well, don't you consider that that can be answered yes or no?

WITNESS: I consider that the yes or no is incriminating. . . . The difficulty with Mr. Nizer quoting from my books is that he selects passages at random and asks me whether I wrote them or did not, with the result if I say I wrote them I stand incriminated before the Court. . . . Yes, I wrote that passage, if that is what you mean.

Q. I read on . . . "The present essay is devoted to the religion which is Hitlerism's one genuinely impressive creation." Did you write that?

A. Of course, I did.

Q. And you consider that Hitler's "one genuinely impressive creation"—

A. Was his religion, is his religion.

Q. You consider Hitler a religious man?

A. May I now have the book?

Q. Answer my question first.

A. Yes, of course I do.

COURT: . . . What did you understand to be his religion when you wrote those words?

WITNESS: Hitlerism is a religion in the sense that Mohammedanism is a religion. . . .

I invited him to point to other passages in his book which might explain his meaning fully. He read at length, citing such sentences as "We must be prepared to see from one to five years more of active propaganda for a view of life which denies, quite as effectively as does Bolshevism, the assumptions upon which Christian civilization is based. . . . If we are candid we shall admit that most of the so-called fundamental challenges to the Church have their origin in the sexual desire. . . . A whole era of anti-Christianity has gone into making this butchery and barbarism. . . . It is impossible for us to sit by idly while the right to live and preach the Testament is denied to millions by the dictatorship of Hitler." "That is one passage," he concluded; "I could go on all afternoon and read some more."

I quoted from a 1933 editorial in *Commonweal*, a magazine with which Dr. Shuster was associated: "In all probability Adolf Hitler is too simple and fearless a man to betray the working population. If he finds that what he believes ought to be done cannot be accomplished, he will resign."

He stated he had never seen it.

Q. Would you approve it?

A. No.

Both sides excused the witness.

The defendants put upon the stand Colonel V. McDermott, the Director of Selective Service in the City of New York. In 1940 he had issued news releases to the newspapers, including the foreign language press. He was asked whether the *Staats-Zeitung* had published them. I objected.

STECKLER: If your Honor please, there was an exhibit in evidence in which—back in May 1940—remarks were made by a columnist to the effect that people if they ate enough and got to weigh 300 pounds they might not be taken in the draft. . . . I feel that I am entitled to show, through Colonel McDermott, that this newspaper . . . co-operated in every way in connection with Selective Service.

The Court overruled the objection and the evidence of such co-operation went in. My cross-examination consisted of three questions:

Q. You do not read German, do you, Colonel.

A. I do not.

Q. And you have never read the *Staats-Zeitung*, have you?

A. I never have.

Q. You do not know what is its editorial policy?

A. I do not.

NIZER: Thank you very much, sir. [Witness excused.]

Throughout the trial, Professor Foerster, seated quietly at the counsel table, was the dominant figure in the courtroom. Although the crowded courtroom reacted to every word in the unfolding drama, he sat, serene and dignified, registering no emotion. It was as if nothing could surprise him, for he knew the facts in advance. Never was there a moment of gloating or triumph on his face. He was above the contest, observing a part of his life's work being vindicated.

The Court allowed counsel several days for summation. There were several hundred exhibits and about three thousand folios of testimony to be collated and transformed into a cohesive and persuasive argument.

One unusual event occurred in the midst of my summation. The courthouse of the Supreme Court is opposite City Hall. It was a hot June day and the windows were open. In the midst of my argument, loud martial music floated into the courtroom, followed by frenzied cheers. General Eisenhower had returned triumphantly from Europe and he was being received at City Hall. I made no reference to the event. Indeed, I was irritated by the interference with my argument. However, when the jury, after only one hour's deliberation, returned with a verdict of $100,000, the full amount requested in the complaint, the following argument was made by Ridder's counsel to set aside the verdict or, at least, reduce it: "Unfortunately, the trial was concluded and the jury entered upon its deliberations on the very day when the City was engaged in welcoming General Eisenhower from his triumph in Germany. After a trial which so deeply explored German militarism and Prussian militarism, it seems to us that that was reflected, the excitement of the day and the excitement of the times were reflected in the verdict of the jury."

He further argued that Professor Foerster "had not conducted himself as a cloistered professor in a college, but had gone out into the open fighting this cause to which he has devoted a great many years of his life and has received epithets and many rebuffs. I shouldn't expect that the names applied to him by the defendant could be hurtful as they might be to one who had not sought out the controversy."

Judge Ferdinand Pecora rendered a long opinion in which he exercised his unique power to reduce the verdict of the jury from $100,000 to $50,000. He referred to Professor Foerster's eminence "which has provided him with an armor against which would fall broken any darts of envy, malice, or ill will. . . . It is an armor of which plaintiff may well be proud. It is an armor that is not easily acquired and where one rightfully wears it, he does so because the rectitude of his life has girt him with it."

The Judge referred to Ridder's efforts to injure Foerster economically by communications with Columbia University and others in the fields of education, but concluded, "Those efforts by the defendant, however malevolently they were motivated, fortunately do not seem to have succeeded in the attainment of their harmful purpose."

More telling was the Judge's finding that "The evidence showed that the libel was circulated among not more than fifty or sixty persons. It was not circulated through the columns of the newspaper . . . but was embodied in a written statement concededly prepared by defendant . . . and circulated only to the extent of the issuance of sixty copies at the most."

The Judge then concluded: "While I do not think that the verdict of the jury in plaintiff's favor was induced by passion or prejudice—for I have already indicated an opinion strongly to the effect that a substantial award to the plaintiff was amply justified by the evidence—still I have found it difficult to avoid the conclusion that the jury in fixing the amount of damages may have been either consciously or unconsciously influenced by a species of patriotic spirit to which the issues peculiar to this action would make a ready appeal.

"I will grant the motion to set aside the verdict of the jury unless the plaintiff consents within ten days to a reduction of the award made by the jury to the sum of $50,000."

Ridder then appealed to the Appellate Division in an effort to set aside the verdict because of alleged legal errors committed at the trial and we sought to sustain the jury's original award. The Judges of the Appellate Division, without rendering a formal opinion, directed a new trial unless the plaintiff stipulated to reduce the award to $15,000. A stipulation to this effect was entered into and the amount of $15,000 was paid.

In so far as Professor Foerster was concerned, he was only academically interested in the struggle over the size of the verdict. He looked upon the entire judicial proceeding as a unique opportunity to wage war on Pan-Germanism in a civilized and intellectual forum. He felt not that he had won or that Ridder had lost, but that truth had been vindicated.

Fourteen years later, on June 2, 1959, Foerster became ninety years old. A small group of distinguished scholars and educators from all parts of the world and a few personal friends tendered him a luncheon. I was asked to preside.

The Professor, having always been troubled with cataracts, was now totally blind. Otherwise, he had scored an unbelievable victory over age. His back was straight and he walked vigorously. His face was pink and unlined, with barely a trace of jowls. His professorial beard was a little whiter, but his lips were red, there being no trace of that bluish hue which is the flag of an old man's declining circulation. His teeth, his very own, were still gleaming and strong. Even when he sat in repose, there was an air of vitality about him. He was not tired. He was serene. He had just finished writing one book and was engaged in another! His life had been a series of defeats, but defeat is education. It is a step to something better.

Professor Dietrich von Hildebrand of Fordham University, who had been a student in Munich under Foerster, told how Foerster's religious teachings had changed his life. Professor Jacques Albert Cuttat, Swiss diplomat and lecturer on Comparative Religion, hailed Foerster as "the conscience of two generations." The actor Eli Wallach read a biographical sketch of Professor Foerster's life.

A glowing tribute from Professor Albert Einstein, delivered at Foerster's eighty-fifth anniversary, was read. It contained the following: "You have always found the courage to speak the truth without hesitation, even if the truth was not too palatable for the groups you intended to reach. You have not shrunk from this sacred duty, even when you knew that you exposed yourself to the enmity of misguided majorities—nay, even if you literally sacrificed yourself to this duty which, alas, is so little appreciated."

Other savants spoke, their philosophical expositions yielding in each instance to emotional appraisal of Foerster as a gallant man. Then Foerster acknowledged the verbal wreaths that had been placed on his brow. He asked for permission to remain seated (not because of feebleness, but because of his teaching habits). He spoke for forty-five minutes with ringing resonance. His voice indicated how young he was, no matter what the calendar read. Foerster's vigor and brightness made us forget his blindness, for even his blue eyes were clear and focused.

He summed up his philosophical beliefs, ranging from pedagogy to sexual ethics (on which he had written leading works), and then turned to his life's mission, the war on Pan-Germanism and the saving of the German people from themselves and their false education. Once more he warned that Germany was unrepentant and had not expiated its sins; that Nazis held key positions in all vital areas of the new Republic; and that we must be alert or we will rebuild Germany and she may join with Russia, her natural ally to destroy Western civilization.

One cannot control the length of one's life, but one can control its depth and width. Foerster had succeeded in these latter dimensions, and nature had bestowed the first upon him.

When he finished, I introduced Professor Alvin S. Johnson, President Emeritus of the New School for Social Research, pointing out that the combined ages of Johnson and the guest of honor totaled more years than the age of the United States. After graceful and heartfelt words about Foerster, Professor Johnson proceeded to astonish the knowledgeable group present by arguing that Germany alone was not to blame, that the United States, England, and France were equally guilty in the blind policies they had followed, that we had blemishes of aggression upon our own historical record, and, of course, so did England and France, and so on through the long list of tiresome false syllogisms, as if the sins of England and France at Munich could be equated with Hitler's sin in creating the crisis (the citizen who is not courageous enough when he faces a vicious murderer is guilty in the same degree as the killer and both should be electrocuted); or, because history is full of past depredations by others, Germany is legally justified in evening up the score in this century by brutal war.

I thought I detected a look of chagrin and hopelessness even on Professor Foerster's face. As I bade him good-bye, I thought to myself, "Professor Foerster, they still don't understand you."

LIFE AND LIMB

Chapter Five

TWO CASES OF NEGLIGENCE

I. DEATH IN BIRTH

Mother and child died in childbirth. Was it the doctor's fault?

One of my legal assistants had left my office to organize his own law firm with two friends. I had given him my blessing and a promise: "If there is anything I can ever do to help you in your career, Bill, don't hesitate to come to see me. You may be sure I will not fail you. Good luck."

This promissory note should not have been made out in blank. When it was presented, I was surprised at the figure that had been filled in. He didn't merely want advice—he wanted me to try a case for him.

He was direct, and his anxiety made him persistent:

"Mr. Nizer, when I left, you offered to help me in my new work. Well, we have a malpractice case against a doctor which is coming to trial, and we are in trouble. The insurance company refuses to pay a cent. We represent the husband of the woman who died in childbirth. The baby died too. We can't even get a doctor to testify for us, though a number of them have told us that they think the obstetrician was negligent. I must ask you for a great favor. I will never ask another. Please try this case for us. We know we can't afford to pay you a retainer, but you can make any fee arrangement you wish out of any verdict. We are willing to waive our fee."

"Of course, I wouldn't think of that, Bill. It has nothing to do with fee. If I do this, I don't want a fee. But you know how few malpractice cases are triable. This one is out of the state. My schedule of trial work would not permit me—"

He interrupted to assure me that the case could be adjourned to suit my calendar requirements.

The more my questions revealed the frailities of the case, the weaker my own position became. "That is why we need you," he said. So I was catapulted by a reckless promise into the most difficult malpractice case I have ever tried.

Doctors are protected by a special rule of law. They are not guarantors of a cure. They do not even warrant a good result. They are not insurers against mishaps or unusual consequences. Furthermore they are not liable for honest mistakes of judgment. The same rule protects dentists and lawyers. The reason that the law builds such a protective barrier for the professional man is that otherwise he would be open game for every patient or client who did not come out well. The peril of being a physician or surgeon would be forbidding. The law recognizes that he must exercise his judgment, about which experts may differ, under challenging circumstances. He is held only to the standard of using his best judgment, even though it may turn out to be wrong. If he applies reasonable skill, no matter how disastrous the outcome, he may not be sued for damages. The law holds that the patient takes an inherent risk when he submits himself to the doctor. There is an implied contract between them in which he is told in effect, "Medicine is not an exact science. I will use my experience and best judgment. You take the risk that I may be wrong. I guarantee nothing."

This rule of law is such a bulwark of defense for doctors that it is almost impossible to win a malpractice case against them. They do not have to prove that they were right. They may, if they wish, admit that in hindsight a different course would have been better. They need only assert that they used their honest judgment in a reasonable manner. That is enough. There are always experts who testify for their fellow doctor that he acted reasonably under the circumstances. Various choices, they say, were open to him. He selected one of them and they testify it was not unreasonable to do so, even if they might have preferred another choice.

This legal shield for the doctor requires the Judge to dismiss the case if the plaintiff has not offered clear proof of negligence. The greatest hazard for one who sues in a malpractice case is that his cause may never "get to the jury." At the end of the plaintiff's case, and before any defense is required, the Judge may, as a matter of law, throw the case out on the ground that no prima-facie case has been made out. This means that not sufficient evidence of negligence has been offered to require the defendant to put in his defense. The plaintiff having failed in the minimum proof required of him, the jury has no issue to determine. The case is dismissed.

How can the plaintiff present sufficient evidence for a prima-facie case? He must produce a doctor who testifies that the defending doctor was guilty of negligence, not merely bad judgment. Such testimony usually guarantees getting the case to the jury. It is difficult enough for the patient to win a jury verdict after the Judge has charged the jury concerning the legal yardstick it must apply; however, the plaintiff at least has a fighting chance. The greater danger is that the Judge will throw out the case because of insufficient evidence without even submitting it to the jury.

So the plaintiff has two preliminary hurdles. First, obtaining a doctor to testify against another doctor; second, having his testimony sufficiently sharp and condemnatory to satisfy the Judge that it meets the minimum requirement of law.

I do not know whether it is a compliment to the medical profession to say that it is almost impossible in most states to induce a doctor to testify against another doctor. That depends on whether you look at the matter from a social viewpoint and the requirements of justice, or from the viewpoint of professional loyalty and comradeship. It is not very difficult to get lawyers or accountants to testify against members of their craft. Perhaps this is because professional ostracism is applied less in those professions than in the medical profession. In some states an attempt has been made to solve this problem. For example, in Maryland the medical societies designate an outstanding medical expert to look into the charge before trial. If he finds merit in the plaintiff's cause, he advises the insurance company to settle. Otherwise, he comes to the defense of the sued physician. Other proposals have been made to have the court appoint an outstanding physician to make a "neutral" report. The defects in these self-disciplinary procedures are many, but this is not the place to analyze them.

It is sufficient to advance the chronicle of this particular suit that in New York, obtaining an expert to testify against an obstetrician is well-nigh impossible. Many doctors to whom we submitted the facts on a hypothetical basis thought the defendant had been grossly negligent. But they would not under any circumstances testify. We were without an expert, and it was suicidal to go to trial without one.

Finally I asked the husband, who was suing on behalf of himself and a first child born to the couple, to comb his relatives, no matter how distant, for a doctor. There was a nephew who had just graduated from medical school and served his internship. He had never delivered a child himself, but he had assisted an obstetrician in two deliveries. He could hardly qualify as an impressive expert against the defendant doctor who had delivered 2600 babies and participated in 15 Caesarean surgeries. But if he could express a medical opinion of gross negligence, we might survive a motion to dismiss at the end of the plaintiff's case.

Then the defendant doctor would have to take the stand. I would have an opportunity to cross-examine him. The only way we could prove negligence was out of the doctor's own mouth. It was a long chance, but it was that kind of a case.

The nephew was finally persuaded that his family relationship ought to take precedence over his concern about professional retribution; the deciding factor was his deep conviction that the defendant doctor was negligent. He was courageous enough to defy tradition on the very threshold of his career.

So we went to trial. In selecting the jury both sides strove to find types sympathetic to their position. The doctor's attorneys looked for men and women who would understand a professional man's vulnerability in the uncertain world of science and the destructive effect of an adverse verdict upon his career. We, on the other hand, desired jurors who would consider the husband deprived of his wife, and the first child, deprived of its mother, above the considerations of injury to the doctor's reputation. Each attorney had six challenges, or rights to reject an unsatisfactory juror. The challenges were exercised to the hilt. So the judicial process operates to eliminate sympathies, whether for one litigant or the other, from the jury box, resulting in jurors more likely to determine the case on the merits rather than on passion or sympathy.

Our first witness was the husband. He testified that the defending doctor had treated his wife during her first pregnancy. Due to her physical formation and condition, he had advised that she was incapable of being delivered of a child by natural birth. The doctor had therefore called in a surgeon who performed a Caesarean operation. It is so called because Julius Caesar was born by surgery rather than natural delivery through the pelvic tract.

Five months later the wife became pregnant again. This time the defending doctor permitted her to labor forty-eight hours until the child was asphyxiated and was stillborn, and the mother died too.

The husband swore that when he saw his wife struggling day and night in labor, he pleaded with the doctor to call in a specialist to perform a Caesarean operation, but the defendant doctor advised against it. So, with the mother in agony, a natural delivery was attempted, until she and the baby expired.

Our young medical expert testified that the child was in a transverse position and that this indicated insufficient measurements of the pelvis. This had required the first Caesarean delivery and was just as necessary for the second delivery. It was his opinion that in such a case the rule is, once a Caesarean, always a Caesarean. There have been cases of as many as five Caesarean deliveries, and this would have been only the second. He testified that the defending doctor's treatment was unskillful, negligent, and unprofessional. In his opinion, the patient had suffered a ruptured uterus and the doctor was guilty of gross negligence.

The doctor's attorney performed his own legal surgery on the witness. It was not difficult to expose his inexperience. How dared this young physician, who had never delivered a child in his life, pit his opinion against a doctor who had been a director of the obstetricians society of his county. He threw at the neophyte witness the fact that the mother had myocarditis and aortic regurgitation, both evidences of advanced heart disease, and compelled him to admit that these might have been the cause of her death, and consequently the child's death too. He drew from him the admission that he had no fact upon which to base his theory of a ruptured uterus. The death certificate recited the cause of death as chronic myocarditis. This condition could have caused a dilatation of the heart during labor.

He belabored the young doctor with hypothetical questions that skill-fully established the serious risks of a Caesarean operation in a patient suffering from a heart condition. It was all a matter of judgment. Did the "expert" witness have any reason to assert that the defending doctor had not used his best judgment? The reply was "No," but he insisted it was negligence not to have called in a Caesarean specialist as in the instance of the first delivery.

We knew that the good young man would not impress the jury. Our hope was only that he would create an issue of fact and compel the defending doctor to take the stand. When we ended the plaintiff's case, the crucial test had to be faced. The doctor's attorney moved to dismiss the complaint, and argued earnestly that the expert testimony had been so discredited as to be worthless in establishing a prima-facie case, which is the legal way of saying the minimum proof necessary to require the defendant to proceed with a defense.

I had submitted an extensive brief demonstrating that the credibility of the testimony was for the jury to pass upon. The weight that should be given to it was also a jury question. As a matter of law, the Judge could not dismiss the case in view of the testimony given by the expert that the defending doctor had been grossly negligent.

The Judge doubted that we had offered sufficient *credible* evidence to constitute a prima-facie case, but he decided to reserve decision until the end of the case. This required the defendant to take the stand. We had achieved our objective by a hair's breadth.

Incidentally, it is the practice of some Judges who doubt the validity of plaintiff's cause, not to dismiss, but to reserve decision, since they are confident a jury will decide for the defendant. If so, the verdict has a more conclusive quality. Appellate Courts will not interfere with a jury's finding of fact, except in extraordinary circumstances where there is not a scintilla of evidence to support the jury verdict. On the other hand, a dismissal at the end of the plaintiff's case raises solely a question of law as to whether the evidence adduced constituted a prima-facie case. The Appellate Courts are liberal in making this test because there is a tendency to permit the plaintiff to have his full day in court and not cut him off without even requiring the defendant to state his answer to the complaint. I believe it was such practical trial and appellate considerations which motivated the Judge in not casting us out at once. However, in reserving decision, he held a sword over our head. Even if the jury brought in a verdict for us, he might still set it aside on the legal ground that there was insufficient evidence on which to base it.

In such a situation the Judge has a psychological investment in a defendant's verdict. He may be unaware of it, but feeling that he has subjected the defendant to an ordeal in the interest of getting a jury verdict, he leans toward the defendant. Throughout my cross-examination, the Judge evidenced this unconscious prejudice against our case. He was impressed with the defendant's professional stature and his expert's high reputation. He wanted no miscarriage of justice—a mordant phrase in this particular case. No doubt he was trying to be judicially impartial, but Judges, like the rest of us, are affected by motivations so deep that they are hidden from their own awareness. I never resented his rulings. I understood his frame of mind, and I felt grateful that he had at least given me an opportunity of cross-examination. It was up to me to cast a doubt in his mind as well as in the jury's collective mind. And then, since doubt wasn't enough, to win them over to the merits of our cause.

The accused doctor took the stand. He had such distinct parallel lines running down his face that they seemed to divide it in sections and gave him a much older appearance than his sixty years justified. Even his plastered-down white hair seemed youthful in contrast to his tracked face. On direct examination his lawyer elaborated on his standing. He was associated with six hospitals, his special skill being obstetrics. He had practiced medicine for twenty years. He had treated plaintiff's family for eighteen years. When the plaintiff's wife became pregnant the first time, he took care of her. The mother had a slight heart murmur, but this was not the reason he advised a Caesarean delivery. It was due to the abnormal position of the child, which, instead of lying head down in readiness to come down the pelvis, was lying crosswise in a transverse position. He testified that there was no malformation or smallness of pelvic opening. Her measurements were normal. He told her she could have more babies, but to wait until her heart was "in much better shape." He denied plaintiff's testimony that the reason he gave for requiring a Caesarean section was that she had a small pelvis.

When she returned pregnant five months after the Caesarean, he found her condition poor. She was tired most of the time, her heart was not as good as previously. Her urine was normal. So was her blood pressure. He then described the events of labor. She entered the hospital on July 13 at 3 P.M. At 5 P.M. she was having false labor pains. There was no contraction of the uterus, but the child was turning. On the morning of July 14, the first real labor pains began. At 4 P.M. she was two fingers dilated. This indicated that progress was normal for the amount of pain. There was no indication for a Caesarean operation.

At midnight he examined the patient. She was asleep. She had very slight pains. She slept well all through the night. There was no indication she was going to deliver the baby.

On the morning of July 15, she was four fingers dilated. Her condition was good. At 11:30 that morning, the membrane had ruptured. The head of the child would come down three hours after the water broke. Her pain was normal. He expected her to give birth at about 2:30. He went back to his office. At 1:30 in the afternoon, he received a call and rushed to the hospital. The baby was ready to be born, but the mother was in collapse. She was clammy, her color poor, her breath short, her pulse poor. The nurse gave her stimulants and oxygen. He delivered the baby. He tried to resuscitate the child with hot and cold water, but it never breathed.

The mother had suffered an acute dilatation of the heart. He explained that the heart had four chambers. If one chamber dilates, it draws blood from the rest of the body. It was this that caused the baby's death.

He treated the mother and child continuously from 1:30 to 3:00 P.M., when the mother died. The death certificate entry of the cause of death was given by him as chronic myocarditis, a heart condition.

He testified that the child had been delivered in a normal, natural way. The cause of its death was what had happened to the mother.

Then in reply to his attorney's further educated questioning, he described the hazards of a Caesarean operation. The surgeon must cut through the skin, muscles, peritoneum, and then the uterus. He stressed the fact that the uterus in its normal condition weighs only 2 ounces and is 2 inches long. But at the time of a Caesarean, it is 13 inches long and 519 times larger than when normal. The surgeon must extract the baby with placenta, bag of water, and umbilical cord. There are the dangers of shock from ether, pneumonia which sometimes follows the ministration of ether, the shock of surgery, hemorrhaging. Also, the surgeon must induce the uterus to stretch down. The percentage of fatality in Caesarean operations is ten per cent. The doctor wished to avoid this risk.

He definitely asserted there was no rupture of the uterus in this case.

He explained that a Caesarean is called for a second time only if the patient has a fibroid which blocks the pelvic canal, or if her measurements are too small to make possible natural birth. Neither of these conditions existed here. He denied the plaintiff's testimony that he had told the doctor to call in a specialist for a Caesarean operation.

He sent a bill for services to the plaintiff, who never paid him. The bill for $141 was a reasonable charge, and included prenatal care.

Then he bore down on the facts which created his legal immunity. He had followed established practices. He had exercised his best judgment. The attorney turned him over to me for cross-examination.

I had observed that in his direct testimony, as contrasted with his pretrial examination, the doctor had cut down the number of hours his patient had labored. I addressed myself to this preliminary matter.

Q. When the patient was admitted to the hospital on the second occasion, she was taken directly to the delivery room, is that not so?

A. Yes, sir.

Q. She was in pain at that time?

A. She complained of pain.

Q. Well, as far as you could see she was in pain, was she not?

A. No, sir.

Q. She was not?

A. Not as far as I could see.

Q. Wasn't she having pains every 15 or 20 minutes?

A. She was complaining of pain, but it was not—it was false labor, a lightening or quickening which may come at any time three or four weeks before delivery of a child.

Q. In other words, you call it false labor pains?

A. Yes, sir.

Q. There is no way of telling a false labor pain from a real pain just by looking at a patient?

A. There is by examination.

Q. Did you examine her the moment she came in?

A. I examined her at five o'clock.

Q. When did she come in?

A. Three o'clock.

Q. And both before and after your examination she was having pains every 15 or 20 minutes, wasn't she?

A. She was complaining of pain, but she wasn't having labor pains.

Q. I did not ask you whether they were labor pains or false labor pains. She was having pains every 15 or 20 minutes, wasn't she?

A. Not to my observation or examination.

Q. Do you recall testifying in an examination before trial in this action, doctor?

A. Yes, sir.

Q. Under oath?

A. Yes, sir.

Q. And do you recall being asked this question in that examination and making this answer: "Q. What was her condition when she entered? A. She was having false labor pains every 15 or 20 minutes. . . ." Do you recall making the answer that she was having those false labor pains every 15 or 20 minutes?

A. Yes, sir.

Q. That was correct, wasn't it?

A. If I said that in the examination before trial, it is correct. . . .

Q. Well, I show you this examination before trial and ask you if that is your signature swearing to it?

A. Yes, sir.

Q. So that from the time she entered until the time she died she had pains; no matter what the description of them is, she had pains, isn't that so?

A. No, to my own examination she had real labor pains from the time her uterus started dilating.

Q. But without this distinction which you draw between false labor pains and real labor pains, she had pains from the time she got into the delivery room every 15 to 20 minutes from the moment she entered until she died, didn't she?

A. No.

COURT: Doesn't the hospital record disclose that she slept well the night before?

NIZER: It does not, your Honor. This witness testified to something he knew nothing about.

Q. I am talking of intermittent pains. I say didn't she have intermittent pains every 15 to 20 minutes, and later every 10 minutes, from the time she entered the hospital until she died?

A. According to her own statement, yes, sir.

Q. You knew her. Did you have any reason to doubt her statement at that time, doctor?

A. No, sir.

So finally he had yielded. In doing so he had revealed to me the kind of witness he was. He would concede nothing until forced to do so. It is good to skirmish with such a witness. The admission he could have made in the first instance had to be dragged out of him with the crowbar of his contradictory testimony in an examination before trial. Now, after another struggle, I combined his reluctant admission with a more vital fact.

Q. She entered the hospital on July 13th at three o'clock?

A. Yes, sir.

Q. So that she was in the delivery room, or, as you call it, the labor room, from July 13th at three o'clock until July 15th at three o'clock, at which time she died?

A. Yes, sir.

Q. In other words, she was in that delivery room a period of 48 hours?

A. Yes, sir.

Q. And when she entered the delivery room she had these pains intermittently at 15 to 20 minutes, is that right?

A. According to her statement.

Q. Which you don't challenge. You have no reason to challenge it, I mean, have you?

A. No, I have no reason to challenge.

The poor woman was in pain for forty-eight hours. What had the doctor done for her? He claimed that on the second day when she began "real" labor, he examined her at "nine o'clock in the morning." I immediately contradicted him from his own prior testimony at his examination before trial:

Q. Now, I read this to you: "Did you make an examination of her at that time? A. Not until four o'clock."

Q. So you did not make an examination at nine in the morning, did you?

A. Not a vaginal examination.

Q. Well, what kind of an examination did you think I was talking of?

A. I don't know, but you can examine a patient externally with a stethoscope, auscultate and palpate.

I could not prove it, but I felt he had slipped out of the contradiction by pretending to have misunderstood my question. I involved him in another conflict with himself almost immediately.

Q. Did she have any real labor pains at midnight on the second day?

A. She did not.

Q. Were you asked the question "Was she having any *real* labor pains at midnight on the second day?" on your examination before trial and did you make this answer: "Just the same as in the afternoon, every 15 or 20 minutes." Do you recall making that answer?

A. That meant false labor pains.

Q. No, it says did she have any real labor pains? That was the question. Do you recall making that answer? Will you look at me, please. . . .

A. Yes. . . .

Q. And those pains were every 15 or 20 minutes, weren't they?

A. Yes, sir.

Q. And those intermittent pains continued right through the third day until she died?

A. Yes, sir.

In obvious distress, he looked toward his counsel like a beset fighter turns to his corner for advice. When I quickly directed him to look at me, he did so. This brought the incident even more sharply to the jury's attention.

When the woman came to him pregnant so soon after the Caesarean operation, he did not advise her against childbirth.

Q. Did you consider it safe for her to have the child at that time?

A. I did, under . . .

Q. Under what?

A. I did.

Q. Were you going to say under the proper care, doctor?

A. No, I wasn't.

Q. Would you say that now, that if she was under the proper care it was safe for her to have a child?

A. It was safe for her to have a child.

Q. If she was under the proper care, doctor?

A. Yes.

Q. She was under your care, wasn't she?

A. Yes, sir.

Earlier in the trial the husband had testified that he spoke to the doctor on the day she died, pleading for a Caesarean operation because she was formed too small to give birth naturally. The doctor denied even talking to the husband that day:

Q. And you never talked to him on July 15?

A. I did not.

I read his prior answer at the examination: "Q. Do you remember having any conversation with the husband on July 15th? A. I had a conversation with him and his sisters."

Q. Do you recall making that answer?

A. No, I don't.

Q. Do you remember reading this examination before you signed it and swore to it?

A. Yes, sir.

Q. Was your memory better then than it is now about this matter?

A. No, sir. . . .

Q. Have you any records to change your mind about that, doctor?

A. No, sir.

Q. And so, without any record of any kind, you now say that your testimony of yesterday that you had no conversation with him is more correct than your testimony at the examination before trial, is that right?

A. Yes, sir.

Q. And your statement in the examination under oath was an error, is that right?

A. That was an error, yes, sir.

I sometimes think of a witness's credibility as a finely knitted quilt. When the edges are snipped, the unraveling ultimately destroys the center. The loosening process was beginning to affect his central story. I felt the time had come for a frontal challenge.

Q. Will you look at your records and tell us what the measurements of the woman were in centimeters?

A. The measurements?

Q. Yes.

A. Her crest was 28 centimeters, her anterior superior spine 25 centimeters, her transverse was 13.5, and her anteroposterior was 11 centimeters.

Q. You have read those from what?

A. From my office card.

Q. And when was that made out?

A. When the patient came and was examined by me.

Q. May I see that, please?

A. [Witness handed card to Mr. Nizer]

Q. When do you say those measurements were written in?

A. When she first came to see me for an examination for the first baby.

Q. Well, you have not got that marked next to that date.

A. Measurements I always put on the side of a maternity card.

Q. Do you observe any change in ink from the writing at the top of that and the writing which begins with the measurements, doctor?

A. No.

Q. You do not think there is any change in the color of the two inks?

A. Well, it is the same ink.

The card was handed to the jury and it was left to them to determine whether one was much darker than the other, thus indicating that the measurements had been written in more recently to counter our theory that she was too small in the pelvic region to give birth naturally. Even so, if he had "doctored" the measurements, he had not done so adequately.

Q. Will you translate those measurements into these terms which are the standard terms for prenatal care, are they not? First, the external conjugate diameter. Which of these is supposed to represent that?

A. My measurements— I don't take— I take the anteroposterior and I take the oblique and I take the transverse and I take the spines and the crest, which are the standard measurements.

Q. Do you claim to have special knowledge in obstetrics?

A. I do.

Q. Well now, aren't there standard measurements for measuring a woman to find out whether she is small or not—and isn't that universally done when a woman comes for prenatal care?

The doctor claimed that he took these standard measurements. In answer to my questions, he said that the external conjugate diameter was 13.5 centimeters and that of the right and left oblique diameter 12.75 centimeters. He denied that, in a normal case, the first measurement should be at least 19 or 20 centimeters and the other one should be at least 17 centimeters. I continued to press him.

Q. I ask you whether the internal conjugate diameter, which you say is 9.5, should not be at least 11.5 centimeters?

A. We allow 2.5 centimeters for that.

Q. But it should be 11.5 shouldn't it?

A. Yes, sir.

Q. And if a woman is not 11.5 centimeters, then she is small, isn't she?

A. No.

Q. Well if you allow 2.5 centimeters, which it should be, how can you say no?

A. Well, we allow that much for the baby coming through, 2 centimeters.

Q. Normally it would be 11.5 centimeters instead of 9, wouldn't it, doctor?

A. Yes.

Q. And this woman had 9.5 you just testified?

A. Plus 2.

Q. Originally you didn't say plus 2, did you doctor?

A. I am sure I did.

Q. You don't mean that. You know you said 9.5 centimeters, didn't you, doctor? Do you want me to read back the record?

A. I would like to.

The Judge anticipated the impending collision and tried to save the the witness, but his excitement deafened him to the subtle warning.

NIZER: May I have permission to read back the record to the witness.

COURT: Then he said subsequently, they allow 2.

NIZER: Yes, but he originally said 9.5 centimeters, and he said he was sure of the measurements. Now, may I have the record back, your Honor, so that I can establish this point to the doctor's satisfaction?

COURT: I don't know whether the doctor is disagreeing with you or not. Subsequently he said there was an allowance of 2.

Q. Originally you said that her measurement—the internal conjugate was 9.5 centimeters, didn't you, doctor?

A. Plus.

Q. Originally you said 9.5 centimeters plus nothing?

A. Yes, with allowance. . . .

Q. Only when I gave you the measurement which I claim was proper, then you said, "We allow 2," isn't that what happened, doctor?

A. I think I said it before that.

NIZER: Now I ask permission to read the record on that. [The prior testimony of the witness in question was read by the stenographer as recorded.]

Q. Well then, doctor, now that you have had it read originally, until I supplied all the measurements I claim were the normal ones, you said it was 9.5 without any qualification, isn't that right, doctor?

A. Yes, sir.

Q. We agree on that now?

A. Yes, sir.

Q. And you added this allowance of 2 after I gave you the measurement of 11.5, isn't that so?

A. Yes.

The duel between a cross-examiner and a witness is rarely conducted from two fixed positions. The contestants are forced to roam in various directions by unexpected thrusts and counterblows. The original scene of the lawyer's attack may be abandoned temporarily, to ward off a tangent escape. Ultimately the struggle is resumed over the ground that is vital to a decision. The lawyer hopes that his less conclusive victories in the course of battle have weakened and exposed the witness for final victory. So the doctor's credibility had suffered severe cuts from the forced admissions that some of the woman's measurements were smaller than normal. His defenses to the main attack that her pelvic size made natural birth impossible, were somewhat disorganized and enfeebled. The preliminary offensive had been sufficiently successful for the critical assault to begin:

Q. Now, as a matter of fact, doctor, it was because you knew that this woman was small that you performed the first Caesarean operation, wasn't it?

A. It was not.

Q. Well now, let us look into that. You say that the reason you performed the first Caesarean operation was that the child was in a transverse position, is that your testimony?

A. Yes, sir.

Q. Where the child is in a transverse position, if the measurements are normal, there is no indication for a Caesarean operation, is there?

A. No sir, not— That can't be answered yes or no.

Q. Can't it?

A. No, sir.

Q. Let me put it again to you. Where the measurements of a woman are normal, but the child happens to be in a transverse position, then an operation is not necessary, is it?

A. Not automatically, no, sir.

Q. As a matter of fact, the transverse position, doctor, is a very unusual situation, isn't it?

A. It is, yes, sir.

Q. Would you say that less than one-half of one per cent of the cases are transverse position?

A. Yes, sir.

Q. So that the very fact that a child is in a transverse position is in itself some indication of an abnormality, isn't it?

A. Yes, sir.

Q. Now isn't one of the leading abnormalities for transverse position the small size of the pelvis?

A. No, sir.

Q. You now testify that the smallness of the woman . . . is not a contributory factor to the transverse position?

A. It may be, but it is not the most prominent.

Q. Well, let us not quarrel about whether it is the most prominent. It is one—

COUNSEL: I object to those comments on his testimony.

COURT: I will sustain the objection. The jury will disregard it.

Q. Is it a contributory factor towards a transverse position of the child that the woman is built small?

A. In some cases.

Q. In the case of a woman who is giving birth to a first child, what do you call it—primipara?

A. Primipara.

Q. That is a medical word meaning the first baby?

A. Yes, sir.

Q. In the case of a woman who is giving birth to her first child, where there is a transverse position . . . doesn't that indicate a pelvic contraction?

A. No, sir.

Q. And doesn't that indicate such a pelvic contraction as indicates necessity of a Caesarean operation?

A. No, sir.

Q. . . . Doctor, would you consider Professor Franklin S. Newell, Professor of Clinical Obstetrics at Harvard University, an authority on the subject of obstetrics?

A. Yes, sir.

Q. You have undoubtedly heard of Newell's famous book, called *Cesarean Section, Gynecological and Obstetrical Monographs?*

A. Yes, sir.

Q. Let me read this sentence from that book to you: "Transverse presentations in primipara . . . are an indication of sufficient pelvic contraction to warrant the assumption that Cesarean section is probably the best method of delivery." Do you disagree with that, doctor?

A. That is a matter of opinion.

Apparently he had remembered the admonition of his counsel, "If in trouble, remember your best shield is that you exercised your honest judgment."

Q. First I ask you whether you disagree with it?

A. Yes.

Q. You disagree with Professor Newell on that?

A. Yes.

Q. But although you disagree with him, you did perform a Caesarean section?

362 · *My Life in Court*

A. After giving the patient time enough to see that she would not deliver herself.

Q. Well, you found it necessary finally, didn't you?

A. I did.

Q. To that extent, Professor Newell seems to be right, doesn't he?

A. He does.

Again the doctor's resistance had turned out to be futile, and he had suffered the indignity of virtually reversing himself. Despite his evasiveness, a syllogism of devastating logic had emerged from his testimony. He had performed a Caesarean on this woman the first time she gave birth. The child had lain in transverse position. This indicated a small pelvic region. If her measurements had been normal, she might still have given birth naturally despite the transverse position. He gave her time to deliver the baby normally. He found she could not, and performed a Caesarean section. Was this not conclusive proof that her bone structure would never permit her to bear a child without a Caesarean? Why had he on the second occasion let her struggle for forty-eight hours to deliver a child that could not possibly pass out of her narrow pelvic structure? To complete the symmetry of the syllogism, I faced him with a negative element of disproof.

Q. What is a version extraction?

A. That is to dilate the cervix and go up and turn the baby around with one hand on the outside or both hands on the inside and to bring the baby down by grabbing hold of a leg and then getting the other leg and bringing the baby out.

Q. . . . Where there is a transverse position, it is possible by manipulation to deliver the child, isn't it?

A. Yes, sir.

Q. Without a Caesarean section?

A. Yes, sir.

Q. Did you try to do that in this case?

A. I did not.

So he did not attempt to extract the baby by hand manipulation, which he would have done had her measurements been normal. Yet he continued to resist the ultimate admission that she was too small, and fell back upon the last refuge—judgment.

Q. Now, if her measurements were normal, you would have made that attempt, wouldn't you?

A. No, sir.

Q. Even if they were normal, you would not have attempted to avoid a Caesarean?

A. Not at that time. It was a question of judgment.

Q. . . . Despite everything you told the jury about how terrible and dangerous a Caesarean operation is?

A. Yes, sir.

There comes a time in cross-examination when the attorney may indulge in the luxury of hurling his challenge in the form of questions, ignoring the witness's denials. When the very air is filled with the improbability of the witness's answers, it matters not that he continues to deny. The questions evoke the jury's approval, and the repeated protestations of the witness only emphasize the untenability of his position. Such a series of questions never convey their full impact in cold print. It is the passion and indignation with which they are asked, while the witness's feeble answers are ignored, as if they were not even heard, which have the effect of an accusatory summation:

Q. Isn't the real reason that no effort was made at a version extraction by manipulation of the hands that the woman was too small?

A. No, sir.

Q. And isn't the real reason you performed the Caesarean the first time that she was too small and you could not get the child out through the natural tract?

A. I delivered her later through the natural tract.

Q. Dead, wasn't it?

A. Due to the mother's condition.

Q. It was dead, wasn't it?

A. Yes, sir.

Q. Blue in the face, wasn't it?

A. No, sir.

Q. Strangulated?

A. No, sir.

Q. Didn't you report on your death certificate that the child died of asphyxiation?

A. The child died of atelectasis.

Q. What is atelectasis?

A. That the lungs do not function. As soon as the baby is born, the baby begins to cry.

Q. It was born dead then, wasn't it?

A. It was.

Q. In other words, you did not deliver it and then it died for failure to function? It was a dead fetus, wasn't it?

A. The lungs failed to function.

I continued to throw questions at him at a steadily increasing rate of speed and in crescendo. His self-discipline and reserve were yielding. He finally made the fatal admission.

Q. Well, when do you consider a transverse position so dangerous that a Caesarean section must be performed and version extraction impossible?

A. If there was a contracted pelvis.

Q. In other words, when there is a contracted pelvis and you have

a transverse position, then you must perform a Caesarean, is that
right? Isn't that what you have just said, doctor?

A. Yes.

Q. And in this woman's case there was a transverse position and
you performed a Caesarean, didn't you?

A. Yes, sir.

This was tantamount to a clear admission that the woman was too small
to give birth naturally. This being so, of course, she could not do so on
the second occasion. Not to perform a Caesarean again was to doom her
to a hopeless struggle, until her uterus burst and she and the baby died.
The resort to "my best judgment" was now hollow and meaningless. He
was careless and reckless, not merely mistaken. I pursued this line of
questioning.

Q. The fact that she was pregnant five months after the Caesarean
section was no handicap in the case?

A. No, sir.

Q. So far as the second pregnancy is concerned, that did not
come too soon from the viewpoint of the uterus?

A. No, sir.

Q. Now on direct examination of your counsel you testified that
this woman had a slight heart murmur, is that correct?

A. Yes, sir.

Q. . . . You would not have described her heart condition as
myocarditis, would you?

A. Yes, sir.

Q. Would you also have described it as an aortic regurgitation?

A Yes, sir.

Q. Now, why on direct examination of your attorney, did you
fail to mention an aortic regurgitation and myocarditis?

A. I wasn't asked the question.

Q. Well, you were asked what her condition was and you described
it as a slight heart murmur, didn't you?

A. Yes, sir.

Q. Well, myocarditis is a very serious heart disease, isn't it?

A. Not necessarily.

Q. . . . You cannot answer directly whether chronic myocarditis
is a very serious heart condition?

COUNSEL: I think that is a very unfair question.

COURT: Yes. He just said it was not.

Q. Is that what you say, doctor, it is not.

A. It is not.

Q. . . . Well, you, as a doctor and a surgeon, would you call a
person who had chronic myocarditis seriously ill?

A. No, sir.

Q. And that heart condition you did not consider serious enough
to prevent a Caesarean section, did you?

A. No, sir.

Q. Did you fail to perform a second Caesarean section on the occasion of her second birth because of her heart condition?

A. No, sir.

Q. The heart condition had nothing to do with it?

A. No, sir.

Q. . . . Was the reason you did not perform a Caesarean section due to her heart condition?

A. No, sir.

There was a purpose for these repetitious questions. I wanted to pin him down so that he could not escape when the trap was sprung. Now it was ready.

Q. Do you recall testifying in a proceeding in the Municipal Court?

COUNSEL: What proceeding?

NIZER: May I ask the witness a question?

A. No, I don't.

Q. Do you recall an action brought by you against the husband [for the medical bill]?

A. Yes, sir.

Q. And you remember testifying under oath, don't you?

A. Yes, sir.

Q. Now do you recall making this answer: "The reason for no second Caesarean was that her heart was in too bad a condition. This was a heart case. She was in too bad a condition to have another Caesarean." Do you recall giving that testimony?

A. No, sir.

Q. Well, if I tell you that I hold in my hands the official minutes of the court stenographer, would you say that you did not say this?

A. I wouldn't say I didn't say it.

Q. . . . Didn't you say the reason for no second Caesarean was that her heart was in too bad a condition? Didn't you say that?

A. If it is in the record, I did.

Q. Well, let me show it to you. It is underlined, doctor [handing record to witness].

A. Yes, sir.

Q. Then you did say that, didn't you?

A. Yes, sir.

Q. . . . So this was an error?

A. Yes, sir.

Q. And your testimony on the examination before trial, that was also an error?

A. Yes, sir.

Q. Was your memory worse or better then than it is today?

A. It was the same.

Q. But you now say the opposite, don't you?

A. Yes, sir.

Cross-examination elicits the truth in innumerable ways—by forcing the witness to abandon his prepared positions and improvise under circumstances of stress, by inducing the witness to elaborate his inventions, by striking down the inventions and leaving the witness exposed, so that the truth is his only available alternative. The resourceful techniques for dislodging a lie are as many as an agile mind can devise. Cross-examination is the only scalpel that can enter the hidden recesses of a man's mind and root out a fraudulent resolve. Psychiatry and drugs may have given us new insights into motivation, but the classic Anglo-Saxon method of cross-examination is still the best means of coping with deception, of dragging the truth out of a reluctant witness, and assuring the triumph of justice over venality. This process is as successful as the lawyer's thorough preparation and skill make it. That is why injustice can occur in the court. There is no scientific yardstick for the truth's evaluation. If the lawyer, as Benjamin Franklin once said, is not glorious because he has not been laborious, or if in his duel with the dragon, his sword is not skillfully wielded, the truth may never come to light. This is what makes almost any trial more fascinating and breathless than the most elaborate creation of the fiction writer. It is genuine contest, suspenseful because the outcome is uncertain, and nothing less than truth and justice hang in the balance. The judge or jury make an affirmative contribution to the exciting drama, by evaluating the witness's performance, not merely in terms of his embarrassment or confusion, or, on the other hand, his successful stubbornness, but by reading behind these emotions, to discover his honesty or perfidy. A confused witness may not be a liar at all, and his human failing may even elicit sympathy. On the other hand, a witness may succeed in holding his ground, but be exposed as a liar. The psychological aspects are intriguing and limitless. The jury's instinct, based on common experience, determines the reaction. It is the lawyer's duty to provide enough grist for the mill. It will be ground fine enough. Of course, the ideal is to compel the witness to confess his lie in a substantial matter, and thus make the task of the jury easy. Even short of that, impressions can be created which lead inexorably to the discovery of the truth.

I believed that the real cause of the woman's death was a ruptured uterus, and not heart failure. I set out on a cross-examination path toward this objective. The doctor, of course, did not know my destination. He parried questions without always knowing the meaning of his own resistance and that sometimes he was running in the wrong direction.

So, for example, he had insisted that the woman's heart condition had nothing to do with his not performing a Caesarean. He had forgotten that this was the very reason he gave for his decision when he testified in the Municipal Court to collect the $28 unpaid balance of the bill. In my opinion, he lied on both occasions. He had used the heart condition as a disguise to cover up the real cause of her death—a ruptured uterus. For, to admit the truth would have revealed her inability to pass the child through the tract naturally and condemned him as grossly negligent for not having performed a Caesarean. I engaged him in medical exploration.

Q. Myocarditis is an inflammation of the muscle of the heart, isn't it, doctor?

A. It is damage to the muscle of the heart, yes, sir, an inflammation.

Q. . . . What is an aortic regurgitation?

A. It is damage to the aortic valves of the heart.

Q. Let us see if we can make it a little clearer. The blood flows through black as it is venous blood, into the right side and through the right ventricle of the heart, is that right?

A. Yes, sir.

Q. And then it is pushed out through a valve, and is oxygenated and becomes red?

A. Pushed from the right auricles out to the lungs.

Q. Into the lungs, where it is oxygenated?

A. Yes, sir.

Q. And then it comes back into the left ventricle and into the left auricle, is that correct?

A. Yes, sir.

Q. And then it is passed through the body?

A. Yes, sir.

Q. And an aortic regurgitation is an injury to that valve of the heart which prevents the blood from being pushed out into the body, isn't that so? Some of it flows back?

A. The valve does not close tight and some flows back.

Q. The result of that is that the heart must use double the pressure to force that blood through the body, isn't that correct?

A. The heart carries enough energy to do that in most cases.

Q. It carries enough energy, but it becomes an enlarged and dilated heart?

A. The muscle wall thickens.

Q. . . . Doesn't that put a strain on the body?

A. No.

Q. Haven't you got severe swelling, edema, in cases of aortic regurgitation?

A. When it is decompensating.

Q. . . . Would you say as a physician and surgeon that a woman who had a chronic myocarditis and an aortic regurgitation could not even carry a child into the ninth month?

A. No, sir. . . . This heart was not decompensating.

He insisted that the compensation of the heart in this woman's case had made it practically normal in function. Little did he know that in "fighting" me on this point, he was heading toward a disastrous conclusion. When he finally saw the end of the road, it was too late.

Q. And was there compensation there one or two hours before the woman died?

A. There was.

Q. So that, so far as the heart was concerned, one or two hours before she died it was still all right, wasn't it?

A. It was.

Q. But then suddenly she died, didn't she?

A. Yes, sir.

Q. So suddenly that you were in an office a short distance away and by the time you came over she was almost through, wasn't she?

A. She was in a state of collapse, yes.

Q. So that happened very suddenly, didn't it?

A. Yes, sir.

Q. Now, doctor, isn't the sudden collapse after being apparently well, typically the sign of a ruptured uterus?

A. . . . Not the collapse such as this woman had.

Q. You distinguish between the collapses?

A. Yes, sir.

Q. But answer my question anyhow. Isn't it a typical case of a ruptured uterus when a woman is well right up to a short while before she dies and then suddenly she collapses and dies?

A. Not necessarily.

Q. Necessarily or not necessarily . . . most of the time that is a characteristic occurrence in a ruptured uterus?

A. Yes.

Q. And this woman's blood pressure was normal, wasn't it, two hours before she died?

A. Yes, sir.

Q. And her pulse was normal two hours before she died, wasn't it?

A. To the best of my knowledge, it was.

Q. Well, according to your own records it was, wasn't it?

A. Yes, sir.

Q. And you yourself reported when you saw her at 11:30 in the morning—she died at 3—her condition was all right, didn't you?

A. It was.

I changed the subject to pierce his credibility and keep him off balance so that the truth could spill out of any other hidden pockets of deception.

Q. What is a pelvimeter, doctor?

A. That is an apparatus for taking the measurements of the pelvis.

Q. Just the pelvis, or can you measure the size of the infant's head with it? You can do that, can't you?

A. Not before the baby is born.

Q. Can't you? Isn't it approved practice where there is any doubt as to the proper position of the infant or its size to actually find its head?

A. Yes, sir.

Q. And to measure it by a pelvimeter?

A. That can't be done.

Q. That is your opinion, is it?

A. Yes, sir.

Q. This is De Lee's book on *Principles and Practice of Obstetrics,* one of the standard works in the profession?

A. It is used by a great many men in the profession.

Q. Professor De Lee I think you will acknowledge as an outstanding authority on obstetrics, is he not?

A. I do.

Q. I find here the statement: "Direct measurement of the fetal head has been practiced, and Perry has invented a cephalometer for the purpose. Such an instrument is entirely unnecessary, the ordinary pelvimeter giving equally good results." Do you disagree with that statement?

A. . . . It may be done in certain cases, not all cases.

Q. You didn't put that qualification on it before, did you?

DEFENSE COUNSEL: I object to that.

COURT: I will sustain the objection.

NIZER: I respectfully except.

The purpose of stating an exception to the Judge's ruling is to preserve the point for appeal. Unless the lawyer makes such a declaration, he may not argue subsequently that a reversible error was committed by the Judge. If he is silent, he is deemed to have acquiesced and thereby waived the point. In some courts, this rule has been changed. The lawyer need not "advise" the Court that he disagrees, by saying "I except." His rights are reserved in any event.

I now approached the most telling point in demonstrating that the doctor had disguised the true cause of the woman's death, a ruptured uterus, because it would be medical confirmation of his negligence. A study of the rules of the Health Department revealed a startling fact. The doctor was taken completely off guard by it.

Q. The general phrase, myocarditis or chronic myocarditis, is a very general one, isn't it?

A. It is, yes, sir.

Q. It is quite ambiguous in medical phraseology?

A. Yes, sir.

Q. The Health Department, as a matter of fact, does not permit any more the phrase "chronic myocarditis" to be put upon a death certificate as the cause of death, does it?

A. It does.

Q. It does?

A. Yes, sir.

Q. Don't you know, doctor, that there is printed on the back form of death certificates of the Health Department the instruction that you may not use the word "myocarditis" as the cause of death, because it is too general; it means anything? You can put anything under that, don't you know that?

A. As the primary cause of death; as the secondary cause of death, you may.

Q. But you cannot use it as the primary cause of death; you have got to give the real reason and not just say "myocarditis"?

A. Yes, sir.

Q. . . . You know that is the fact?

A. Yes.

Q. Yet you put it down as the primary cause in the case of this woman?

A. Yes, sir.

Q. And not as the secondary cause?

A. No, sir.

Q. Do you know, doctor, from your experience as a physician making out death certificates, what is the reason for that rule that you cannot put down myocarditis as the primary cause of death?

A. I don't know the reason for it.

Q. Well, if I told you that the reason was that you could hide any cause of death under a general phrase "myocarditis," would you say that was the reason for prohibiting it?

DEFENSE COUNSEL: I object to that question.

COURT: Yes, I will sustain the objection.

Although I was prevented by this ruling from spelling out his attempt to cover up the primary cause of death, I believed the jury had done what the human eye does, extends a partial line so as to make a complete image. I had noticed that the doctor's record had no notation of a cardiogram. Since he gave myocarditis as the cause of death on the death certificate, this seemed to me a fair subject for inquiry.

Q. After finding that this woman had chronic myocarditis and aortic regurgitation, did you at any time take a cardiogram?

DEFENSE COUNSEL: I object to it as not within the issues.

COURT: Yes, I will sustain the objection.

NIZER: I respectfully except.

Q. Doctor, wouldn't the condition, as revealed by a cardiogram, be an important factor in determining the necessity of a Caesarean operation?

DEFENSE COUNSEL: The same objection.

COURT: I will allow that.

DEFENSE COUNSEL: I except.

A. No, because a cardiogram has been discredited. We don't do cardiograms as much as we did because cardiograms have been shown to give no information outside that would help in a case of this type.

Q. When was the cardiogram discredited, doctor?

A. Cardiograms are discredited by a great many men at the present time.

Q. When?

A. The last eight or nine or ten years.

COURT: In confinement cases?

WITNESS: In all cases of heart a great many men disagree and believe that the cardiogram is of no benefit whatsoever.

Q. Well, it is an aid in determining the condition of a heart trouble, isn't it?

A. It is not any aid. It is just to carry out and assist your diagnosis.

Q. Yes, it is an assistance. Do you draw the distinction between assistance and aid, doctor?

A. You make a diagnosis of heart trouble, and then you have a cardiogram which just carries out and perhaps lets you know a little more about the heart.

I put the crucial questions.

Q. Well, a lady who has been pregnant and who has had a Caesarean operation performed, and you say she has myocarditis and an aortic regurgitation, isn't it important to find out whether her heart condition has become worse thereafter? Is it or is it not important, doctor?

A. It is important.

Q. And isn't the cardiogram one of the methods by which you can determine whether her heart condition has become worse or better?

A. Not always.

Q. I did not ask you always. Isn't it one of the methods, doctor?

A. One of the assistants, yes.

Q. Now you did not take one, did you?

A. No, I did not.

I read to him his testimony in the Municipal Court in which he had said: "The reason for no second Caesarean was that her heart was in too bad a condition. This was a heart case. It was in too bad a condition for another Caesarean."

Q. I think you told us that that was an error when you testified?

A. Well, I had the heart case in mind at all times.

Within a moment he had shifted again.

Q. Then, do you now say on reflection that the heart condition had something to do with your decision not to perform the second Caesarean?

A. No, it didn't.

Q. But she did have this heart trouble?

A. But that is not an indication for a Caesarean.

Q. Oh, it is not?

A. It is not.

Q. A chronic myocarditis is not an indication for a Caesarean, is that your testimony?

A. It is not.

Q. All right, let me read this to you from Professor Newell, whom you say is an authority: ". . . persons who are believed to be suffering from myocarditis, whether acute or chronic, are better risks for Caesarean section than for labor, since a prolonged difficult labor not infrequently results in acute cardiac dilatation, which is always serious and may prove fatal." Do you agree with that doctor?

A. Well, that isn't this case.

Q. Do you agree with this statement I have just read to you? Once more opposing counsel and a sympathetic Judge tried to cut me off. But I persisted—and by now with some anger.

COUNSEL: I object to it.

COURT: Mr. Nizer, you do not want him to subscribe to something that does not fit the facts in the case, that is, in his opinion?

NIZER: As to whether it fits the case is certainly a matter for the Court and jury, but I am asking this witness after he has testified that a heart condition has nothing to do with a determination of a Caesarean, and he has testified that there was a heart condition in this case on the second occasion—I face him with the statement of an authority that such a heart condition indicates a Caesarean rather than labor, because in labor they die from dilatation of the heart, which he himself had testified is the reason for this death. I think I am entitled to an answer on cross-examination.

A. There are just as many authorities that are against that as are for it.

Q. I asked whether you agreed with Professor Newell?

A. No, I don't agree with him in this case.

Q. You did testify, didn't you, that in this case the death was caused by an acute dilatation?

There were a storm of objections and Court rulings. I braved the inclement judicial weather and moved forward on the witness who now openly showed his distress. His lawyer's shrill objections only revealed the hysteria that was gripping the witness stand.

Q. Did you say that the blood was taken away from the infant because of an acute dilatation of the heart, doctor?

A. I did—sudden collapse of the patient.

Q. An acute dilatation, is that it?

A. Yes, sir.

Q. And where there is myocarditis, isn't there the danger of an acute dilatation if you permit labor?

A Not necessarily.

Q. I did not ask you whether necessarily. I asked you where there is a chronic myocarditis, as in this case, and you permit labor, isn't there the danger of acute dilatation of the heart?

A. Yes.

The doctor insisted that the mother collapsed before the delivery of the dead child. The more I challenged him on this fact, the more certain he became.

Q. Now, are you sure that the collapse of the mother preceded the birth of the strangulated baby, came before it?

A. The collapse, yes, it did come before the birth of the baby.

Q. You are positive of that, are you?

A. Yes, sir.

Q. I read your testimony under oath in the other proceeding: "Immediately *after* the delivery, the patient had a collapse." Did you so testify?

A. I did so testify, I guess, but I didn't have the records.

Q. You mean this was an error, too?

A. The patient was in a state of collapse when I called. That is why the nurse called me at 1:30.

Q. Was it an error?

A. It must have been. . . .

There was one other point I wished to establish to indicate his negligence. He had left the woman's bedside despite her grueling struggle in labor, and returned only in answer to an emergency call. This was not an accusation involving some medical theory. Here he could not plead his exercise of judgment concerning a scientific matter. It involved dedication to his task. How could he have left the patient, wringing wet with perspiration in her heaving efforts, over a forty-five-hour period, to evacuate a child imprisoned in her contracted pelvis? I do not believe it was cruel disregard on his part. Rather it was his ignorance concerning the tragedy that was taking place. Yet was it not such recklessness as was equivalent to negligence? Surely his prior experience in performing a Caesarean section on this woman should have given him some intimation that, after forty hours, a crisis was impending.

I once tried a malpractice case against a surgeon who was called in to examine a child born with webbed fingers on her right hand. Believing that by a freak of nature skin had joined the fingers, and that it could be snipped away, he did so unhesitatingly. Thereby he cut off the fine veins which ran through the connecting skin, and the infant's fingers sloughed off from lack of blood supply. The condition of webbed fingers, called syndactyly, is a rare one. I found a monograph on the subject in a remote German treatise. Even when I cross-examined the surgeon, he still did not understand the enormity of his conduct. He felt he was a victim of a fate that could have befallen any other surgeon. This was little consolation for the pretty little girl who grew up without fingers on her right hand. Nor could I summon up any "understanding" for the doctor's plight. It seemed to me that devotion to his professional duty required him to search the annals of medical history before he jumped to any conclusion.

Yet the doctor in this case left the woman whom he saw in prolonged agony, because he thought she would give birth several hours later. Forgetting his wrong medical opinion, where was his humane obligation to be immediately available in her desperate struggle? I knew the jury would understand this, even if it understood nothing else. So I concluded with this cross-examination:

Q. At 11:30, when you left the hospital, did you think that the child was going to be born at noon?

A. I thought the child would be born in maybe two or three hours.

Q. And so you left?

A. Certainly.

Q. . . . And you did not come back until you got a telephone call that the patient was in collapse?

A. I left orders to call me as soon as it was necessary.

Q. And you did not come back until you got a telephone call that the patient was in collapse?

A. Until it was necessary to come over, that is when I came. After obtaining an admission that "in the case of a ruptured uterus, the child is inside and floating around," and that when it is gotten out "its head would be blue," I announced: "That is all."

My adversary then called for the defense a distinguished medical expert, who traversed the legal lane marked "reasonable exercise of judgment." He was cautious not to endorse the defendant's conduct fully, but rather to point out the difficult choices which he faced and to characterize his decision as a reasonable one. He was far less restrained— indeed wholehearted—in appraising the defendant's outstanding reputation in his profession.

The defendant had stressed the fact that the dead child had finally come out of the pelvic tract. He therefore contended that the pelvic region was not too small for natural delivery. By my first question on cross-examination, this inference was destroyed.

Q. . . . It is possible, if the child is low enough, to take it out even after a ruptured uterus by forceps without an operation?

A. Oh, yes.

Obviously, a dead child, which can be handled with brutal strength without fear of injury, can be dragged out of an orifice which a tender, living child could not pass through. I had only one other objective. It was achieved in exactly three questions on cross-examination, the last of which was:

> Q. I take it that you have been accustomed from your experience in depending upon larger measurements for a normal pelvis [than the defendant testified he found in this woman]?
>
> A. Yes, that is correct.
>
> NIZER: That is all.

Both sides rested. Once more the defendant's counsel moved to dismiss the complaint on the ground that we had failed to establish a case. But now there was no longer any doubt. We had proved enough out of the mouth of the doctor himself, and his expert, to raise serious questions of fact about his negligence. We were entitled to have the jury determine these questions. The Judge so ruled.

We summed up to the jury. The doctor's lawyer wove an adroit plea around the uncertainties, the mysteries, and the perils of the medical science. He hammered home repeatedly the high reputation of his client, and the honest exercise of his judgment. He dissected again the testimony of the novice we had put on the stand to give a contradictory medical opinion. He contrasted the inexperience of our young doctor, a nephew of the deceased woman, obviously doing the family a good turn, with the eminence of the defendant and his expert doctor witness.

He pleaded with the jury not to destroy the reputation of the defendant, earned over a period of twenty years, during which he had successfully delivered 2600 babies into the world. Women in childbirth may collapse, like any man or woman can suffer a heart attack without notice, or a patient unaccountably expire during a simple surgery. Doctors were not omnipotent. They could only use their skills and judgment honestly. They could not be blamed for every mishap in medicine. Throughout the centuries women had died in childbirth, and no way had yet been found to guarantee that such accidents as happened to this woman would not occur. We cannot in retrospect blame the doctor for what he is not responsible for.

The Judge, he told them, would charge the jury on the law and they should apply those legal rules which safeguard doctors from unjust claims. There will always be some disastrous results, and the professional standing of the defendant should not be destroyed because of the unavoidable occurrence of a dilatation of the heart. The deceased woman and her husband knew that her heart was impaired. The suing husband might as well be held responsible for risking her pregnancy so soon after the first child. Nobody was to blame. She might have come through fine. She didn't. That is a tragedy, but not the responsibility of the doctor. The burden of proof was upon the plaintiff to establish his charge of gross negligence by a clear preponderance of the evidence. This he had failed to do.

The defendant's lawyer pleaded for vindication of the doctor's lifetime activities. He demanded a verdict for the defendant.

"You may now address the jury, Mr. Nizer," said the Judge.

The plaintiff has a decided advantage in summing up last. He can analyze the argument just heard by the jury and point out the facts it omitted and the omissions in proof it assumed existed. He can squeeze the artifice and bombast out of it. An adversary's argument may constitute lustrous drapes for the jury to gaze upon, but the answer may lift those coverings and reveal the gaping holes underneath. The shimmering surface that had hypnotized the jury's eye and stirred its emotions then gives way to a renewed contact with reality. The jury's mind is made receptive again to logic and truth.

When I am required to sum up first, I endeavor to prepare the jury so that it will not yield to the blandishments of my adversary. I remind the jury that he will have the last word and that I will not be permitted to reply. I tell them that I must depend on their recollections to correct any misstatement of fact which my opponent, who follows me, may make. I must rely on their discriminating judgment to reject any false arguments. Then, as I proceed to build my own case, I anticipate the contentions of my adversary. I announce his slogans and attempt to destroy them, asking the jurors to become my watchmen when they hear such sophistry, and reject it as an insult to their intelligence.

This technique of stealing an opponent's thunder can be devastatingly effective. When the facts are sound and only demagoguery is to be feared, it is an exhilarating experience if I have guessed my opponent's arguments and even his style of presentation, to hear him echo what I have already warned the jurors against. He stutters as he realizes that the words that come out of his mouth have a familiar and hollow ring. The jurors pride themselves on spotting the simulated argument. It is disheartening for an opponent to hear his best contentions fall dead immediately upon their utterance, while the jurors smile disdainfully at his demagogic effort. It is a test of the greatest skill to spike an adversary's guns by proper anticipation and make truth survive his most eloquent harangue.

When one sums up last, the challenge is not as ominous. I endeavored to clear the atmosphere by accepting the burden which was ours. We did not claim that the doctor was a guarantor of the safe delivery of the child. We knew he was liable only if he was so careless in his professional work as to constitute gross negligence.

On the other hand a doctor is not impervious to responsibility if his conduct has been inexcusably reckless and ignorant. We were not dealing here with a mere error of judgment concerning a close medical question.

We were confronted by a case of reckless disregard of the ordinary standards of medical prudence. As a result a woman had died. Her child was dead. A husband had been bereft of his wife and a first child denied his mother. The doctor's good reputation could not give him a license to disregard his professional duties so brazenly as to cause the death of his patient. He was not to be held to a standard of perfection, but neither could his good reputation give him immunity for inexcusable negligence resulting in the loss of life.

Against this background I analyzed the proof, quoting repeatedly from the stenographic minutes which the doctor's attorney had ignored. He had built his argument on sheer emotionalism. I would build mine on the facts, which had their own octane content. As I constructed the edifice of negligence, brick by brick, I paused to flatten down particular plinths with emphasis.

The woman's first pregnancy had been marked by the fact that the child lay crosswise, in transverse position, instead of up and down. The doctor attempted to avoid a Caesarean section, but "after giving the patient time enough to see that she would not deliver herself," he was obliged to take the child from her body by surgery. I reread his admissions that in some respects she had small measurements. I quoted the opinion of his expert doctor that her pelvic space was smaller than he considered normal. I also quoted Professor Newell's book, that a transverse position of the baby in itself indicated a contracted pelvis and was, indeed, the result of insufficient space. I read the defendant's admission to this effect, an admission he made only when he had no more room to evade. It all spelled out a clear case of the woman's bone structure, too narrow to deliver a child naturally through the pelvic tract.

The woman returned pregnant with a second child. Significantly, it was again in transverse position. Every reasonable indication was that the same physical structure that prevented natural delivery of the first child, would prevent it in the case of the second. Yet he proceeded to permit the woman to labor. Even then, when he had given "the patient time enough to see that she would not deliver herself," to use his description of her first labor experience, he did not perform a Caesarean as he did the first time. Stubbornly he let her press in vain against bones that would not permit the child to pass through—twenty hours—thirty hours—forty hours—forty-five hours—forty-eight hours—until her uterus burst. Was this not gross and inexcusable negligence? Why it was *criminal* negligence!

The doctor's insistence that she could have delivered naturally was disproven by admissions of the truth dragged from him on cross-examination. For example, if her pelvic region was normal in size, he could have taken the child from her by a version extraction, that is, by turning the child around with his hands and permitting it to come out of the tract naturally. The only time such procedure is impossible is when the measurements are too small. In this case he did not even attempt a version extraction. Was this not an admission by conduct that she was too small and had to have a Caesarean?

I analyzed the doctor's deliberate lies. He denied that the husband had pleaded with him on that last fatal day to perform a Caesarean. He claimed he had not spoken to him, until I faced him with his contradictory testimony.

The doctor testified time and again that the woman's heart condition had nothing to do with his decision not to perform a Caesarean, until I confronted him with his flat statement under oath in another proceeding that "the reason for no second Caesarean was that her heart was in too bad a condition."

He denied that she died from raptured uterus. Then why had he violated the rules of the Health Department by stating on the death certificate that the cause of her death was myocarditis? Such a vague and general description is forbidden because it can be used to disguise the true cause of death. Yet, knowing this regulation, he resorted to this deception, rather than state the specific cause. Was it not because he wished to avoid writing "ruptured uterus," which would reveal his negligence in not performing a Caesarean? If he had not had a guilty conscience, he would not have disguised the death entry, violating the rule printed on the death certificate.

Even if we assumed that his casualness in the face of all the danger signs was due to ignorance, how can we explain his not even being with the woman when her uterus was ruptured, the child was asphyxiated, and the mother collapsed before dying? How could he have calmly left the woman, agonizing in her forty-fifth hour, with the promise to return when called? Was not such blasé unconcern totally inconsistent with the duty of a physician? Not only did he not see the evident need for Caesarean surgery, but he blithely left the scene so that no one was there when the emergency struck. This was incredible negligence.

Only when I had analyzed every one of his shifts, evasions, and contradictions, and read his answers in each instance from the stenographic minutes, did I turn to the heart-rending results from his misconduct. By this time the jurors had been caught up with resentment and anger against the doctor. Now these turned into sympathy for the victims, the dead mother and child, and the live husband and orphan. The emotional impact that had been mounting, finally revealed itself in tears as several of the jurors wept openly as I concluded.

The Judge charged the jury on the law. I steeled myself for an uncomfortable hour, because I knew he would bear down on the rules which protected doctors in malpractice cases. The jury listened earnestly, and then retired to reach its verdict. Eleven hours later they returned to announce that they were hopelessly deadlocked. The Judge declared a mistrial. He then summoned the jurors into his chambers to inquire of them what had happened. All counsel attended.

Amazement was added to my disappointment when I learned that from the first moment the jurors were unanimous in a verdict for the plaintiff. I was even more astonished when I learned that they were not split because of the amount of the verdict. What then had divided them? Some jurors feared that evidence of the doctor's negligence was so overwhelming that if they decided against him, he would thereafter be criminally indicted and convicted! They did not want him to be thus disgraced and go to jail. They thought this would be too severe a penalty for an outstanding physician. Of course it would be, but where in the world did they get the idea that the civil verdict for damages would lead to criminal proceedings? They reminded me that in summation I, too, had said he was guilty of *criminal* negligence. Indeed I had. In the course of struggling to satisfy the jury that the extreme test of gross negligence had been met, I had characterized his conduct as so reckless and unprofessional as to be criminal negligence. Of course I had not intended this statement to be literal. It was merely a forensic device to pound home the fact that we had met the burden the law placed upon us in a malpractice case. The phrase "criminal negligence" was a reference to the degree of proof, not to pursuit of the doctor in a criminal court. Nevertheless, my first rush of anger and disgust at the jury's lack of comprehension and ignorance gave way to a realization that it had demonstrated sensitivity and wisdom. And, as always, if it had erred, it was the lawyer's fault. It was I who had planted or encouraged the fear in its mind by my use of the phrase "criminal negligence." I had failed to explain in summation that all that was involved was money damages, that no criminal proceedings could possibly follow because criminal intent would have to be proved, and, of course, there was none. True enough, it seemed bizarre in retrospect to have worried about calming the jury on the subject of criminal responsibility when we were desperate to prevent our complaint from being dismissed because we might not be able to meet the severe standards of civil liability. Yet it was a lesson I never forgot. Since then, more than ever, I measure the nuance of every word I utter in the presence of a jury. I take nothing for granted. Trials are the wonderland of the unexpected. I never dreamed that we would have a hung jury because we had overproved our case.

The Judge set the case down for retrial. But this was not necessary. The insurance company settled the case. So the jury's wish that the doctor's reputation be not destroyed has been achieved. The jury's "stupidity" and my contribution to it, which originally frustrated us, had turned out well after all. Justice works in wondrous ways its miracles to perform.

II. THE WORTH OF A MAN

When John Donelon departed for work on November 22, 1950, kissing his wife and his four-year-old son Brucie heartily, he did not know that his name would be on the front page of all the newspapers that evening.

At the end of that day's work he rushed from his office for the 6:13 train to Merrick, showed his $17 monthly Long Island Railroad commutation ticket, and took his seat in the customary last car which stopped nearest to the parking space where his wife would await him. Three minutes later the front engine of a twelve-car load of passengers, traveling behind him, and headed in the same direction, crashed into the rear car of his train. Since its fifty-five-year-old motorman, William Pokorny, died instantly, the cause of the collision remained mysterious. The engine sheared through the car in front like a telescope which folds one section into another. Amidst the shattering glass and crushed steel were heard the horrifying abbreviated shrieks of seventy-five people who were ground and mutilated to death. Among them was John Joseph Donelon. It was the grimmest disaster in the history of the Long Island Railroad.

I represented the widow in the suit against the Long Island Railroad Company. It came to trial in the New York State Supreme Court, Nassau County, before Mr. Justice Francis G. Hooley and a jury.

The law recognizes that it is impossible to pay damages for a human life. No award can adequately repay a widow for a loving husband, or an orphan for his missing father. The law abhors damages based upon mere speculation. It does not countenance a limitless recovery without any guides for measurement except rampant sympathy. Pragmatic rules have therefore been formulated, limiting the recovery in a death action solely to the pecuniary loss of income suffered by the widow and child. It is as if the law said: "We are helpless to provide a genuine substitute for the loss of life. We can only use money to repay the loss of money, not love, devotion, or comradeship. We will compel a guilty defendant to pay the wife what we can reasonably estimate she would have received from the deceased had he lived." This rule of law can work out harshly. An old man, with short span of life as predicted by the mortality tables, may, if killed, make available to his widow or family very small financial balm for his death. So, too, a retired man, or a woman who earned nothing (the cost of substituting for her house services would be the chief measure of damages), are poor risks for substantial awards. The difficulties of proving damages for the death of a child are even greater under this limited rule of pecuniary damages.

This is why a person severely injured may often recover far larger damages than his estate could if he were killed. Juries may award damages for pain and suffering to the living, but only loss of income to the family of the dead.

So the question was, what would Donelon have contributed financially to his wife had he lived his normal span of years? How long would she have lived to receive this income? What were the conditions of his health, his expectations for increased earning ability, and his devotion to his family which would insure their getting a substantial portion of what he earned? What was his capacity for growth, and what were his ambitions, persistence, and industriousness to achieve that growth in terms of earning power?

The Long Island Railroad Company conceded its negligence. There is a doctrine in law expressed in the ancient Latin phrase *res ipsa loquitur,* the thing speaks for itself. When one enters a train there is the undertaking on the part of the Railroad Company to provide safe passage. The fact that the disaster occurred, without further proof, was *res ipsa loquitur.* We were therefore relieved of the burden of proving the railroad's negligence. But the proof of damage, in the sense of deprivation of financial income, posed an extremely difficult problem. John Donelon was thirty years old. He had earned only $35 a week in his previous job, received increases up to $80 a week over a five-year period, and was earning $100 a week at the Weintraub Agency, an advertising firm, for only five weeks when he was killed. How much of this $100 could be attributed to his wife and son in measuring the monies of which they were deprived by his death? And how could we demonstrate his true earning capacity in the years ahead of him, had his life not been snuffed out?

We applied ourselves to these tasks so intently that the Court announced time and again it was on novel ground and repeatedly warned me that the unprecedented nature of the evidence might cause reversible error. Although the Court ruled out much evidence because there was no warrant for it in prior experience, he was persuaded on many occasions to strike out in new directions. The result was a dramatic reconstruction of a man's personality, capacity, and potential which created a unique standard of proof. In this effort, the clashes with a tough adversary accustomed to orthodox evidence, provided contrapuntal conflict to the main contest.

Our first witness was the widow. She was thirty years old, and the tragedy had enhanced her beauty by touching it with maturity. Like most people who have suffered deeply, the telltale marks were not furrows or lines, but were in the eyes. Her gaze revealed awareness of the cruelty of life. All experience seems to be an abrasive that wipes innocence and naïveté off our faces, adding a knowing if not sad cast to our eyes. But her demeanor was not solemnized by recollection. Her recital was accompanied by a gay spirit as she recalled life with her husband. This recapture of the mood when he still lived (abreaction) gave poignance to her testimony which no flood of tears could have created. I felt the jury was moved more deeply by her brave smile than it would have been by any hysterics:

Q. When did you first meet Jack Donelon?

A. I met Jack about a year before I married; at a friend's wedding; his brother was the best man and I was the maid of honor.

He was twenty-two years old. He was six feet one inch in height, weighed 170 pounds. Her description of him was:

A. Dark hair, ruddy complexion, good teeth, quick step. . . .

Q. What were his personality traits?

A. He had an outgoing personality, was cheerful, well liked. . . . He was keen, full of fun, very good sense of humor, energetic.

Q. You have told us about your devotion to one another . . . what do you base your statement on? . . .

A. He was always affectionate and devoted to myself and to the child. When he would come home late at night, he'd always remember to bring something; a *House Beautiful* magazine, because he knew I was interested in decorating our home, or some coffee ice cream, because we both liked that. These are the small things. And he always brought presents for Brucie, of course, on pay day. He had, for instance, tool kits and garden implements just like Daddy had, and a set of golf clubs.

Q. Now will you tell us what his relationship was with Brucie . . . tell us what they did together.

A. Well, they were devoted. . . . Bruce was Jack's shadow. If Jack was there it didn't matter where I was. . . . In the wintertime they would take Bruce's wagon and go for firewood, we had a little fireplace. . . . They mowed the lawn together, they went for walks, and Jack used to take him down to see the boats. We lived quite near to water. They used to do all things together. He read to him a great deal too.

Q. Did Jack sing?

A. Yes. He had no special talent for it, but in the morning he and Bruce used to—they were the type, both of them, who woke immediately and would sing and dance and they were very gay of disposition. I am not quite like that. I like to have my cup of coffee first, but Jack would be shaving and he and Bruce would sing and have fun together. . . . Bruce would wait for him at night, watch for him, and run out to meet him.

In this way, by a description of trivia, we gave the jury an insight into the joys of their relationships. One cannot depict the happiness of a family by generalities about devotion and affection. The profound feelings of warmth and intimacy can only be comprehended by setting forth in vivid detail the interplay of the drab as well as the inspirational incidents of daily living.

What is true of joy is true also of pain. It cannot be reconstructed by such stereotyped questions as are usually asked in a courtroom. "During those two weeks in the hospital did you suffer any pain?" The answer is "Oh, yes, great pain." But does this really give an understanding of the suffering?

In such cases I subpoena the hospital records and go through every nurse's entry. "3 A.M. Patient groaning. Gave codeine." I refer to the gruesome details of the bedpan and the need for redoing the sheets; the patient's own cries which awoke him; an injection being prescribed by the doctor; the vomiting spells followed by profuse sweating and weakness, the nausea and headaches, the shooting pains "like needles," the gas pains and inserted tubes, and all the rest of the discomforts and agonies which collectively are referred to as pain. Nature protects us against the recall of pain. We may describe a happy event and at least partly be flooded again with joy in retrospect. Fortunately the recollection of pain does not revive the feeling of anguish. The lawyer who seeks to recover damages for that pain must struggle to overcome this handicap. Partly with the aid of the jury's own experience, it can be induced to fuller understanding and evaluation of the suffering for which mere damages are to be awarded.

Appellate Courts have, on a number of occasions, reduced verdicts in negligence cases I have tried on the ground that they were excessive. The law suspects that a large verdict may be the result of passion or sympathy. I have always felt that while an award may be disproportionate in comparison with those for similar injuries, in other cases, they were not too high in any other sense. They reflected a jury's feelings, based on sensitive understanding of the ordeal through which the injured person had passed and, in case of permanent injuries, will continue to suffer every second of every day for long, long years to come. When nature's psychological blocks against such full comprehension have been overcome, the injured victim should not be deprived of adequate damages by invidious comparison with less fortunate victims. So no detail was too small for the picture of their lives I sought to reconstruct. Like photographs telegraphed by dots across the sea, the more dots, the clearer the definition.

Q. . . . Did you do your own cooking, Mrs. Donelon?

A. Yes, I did.

Q. Did Jack ever help you?

A. Yes, he was interested in cooking. When we had guests especially, he thought that no one could mix a salad dressing the way he could; mine didn't seem to compare.

Q. . . . Did Jack subscribe to any magazines?

A. Yes, he read mostly magazines that I find rather dull—*Newsweek* and *U. S. News & World Report*, I think they call it, and *Time*. He read them from cover to cover.

Q. . . . What newspapers did he read regularly?

A. He read the *Times*, the *World-Telegram* at night, the *Tribune*.

Q. Every day?

A. Every day.

Q. What interests did Jack have in his home?

A. He had many interests in his home. He was very enthused about having a home of his own—it was a lifelong desire, you might say, that he had realized.

DOYLE: I move to strike this all out.

COURT: If the jury believes it, it tends to show that he had an active interest in his home rather than in outside activities. I think we will take it, Mr. Doyle. Exception to you.

A. He would do the usual things that one does around a new house. He reversed the utility room so that it would be easier for me to get in to do the wash . . . and he was quite a fanatic on the subject of varnishing the house. Our house was cedar shingle and was varnished instead of painted, you know, and he varnished, I would say, about three times in a year and a half. He liked to keep it looking just right, and he was always busy around the house.

Q. Did you have a lawn in front of the house?

A. Yes. Well, he mowed the lawn and Bruce would help, of course, at least thought he would help. He would hold part of the handle and they would go around together.

Q. Did Jack do any planting? Was he a gardener too?

A. Well, that was his newest hobby and his happiest one, I believe. We weren't in the position where we could pay a landscape gardener as much as we would have liked to—

DOYLE: I move to strike this out.

COURT: Strike that out about what financial position they were in.

Q. Tell us just what he did.

A. He planted rose bushes and azalea bushes around the house . . . and I remember that one thing in particular we were enthused about, he got a small, inexpensive packet of morning glory seeds, and of course neither of us were experienced in this sort of thing, and they turned out to be very beautiful—they covered the front of the house, and many passers-by stopped and commented. That pleased him.

To demonstrate John's desire for improvement, we established that he had attended lectures at the Advertising Club in New York City and completed a course at the Dale Carnegie Institute for public speaking. We offered his "diploma" in evidence. It may not have proved that he had acquired eloquence, but it was eloquent proof of his ambition to better himself. Doyle objected continuously that such evidence was not sufficiently direct on the subject of pecuniary damage. After further excursions into the personality, traits, and habits of the deceased, the Court said frankly: "In any event, Mr. Doyle, we may be on some new ground here in this action as to the evidence that should go in. Take your exception.

To augment his salary at the advertising agency, John worked a few nights a week at Lee-Vur Furniture Company selling on a commission basis.

Q. Did he also bring about his own contacts, his own friends to come over and buy?

A. . . . He didn't like to make any profit on his friends. He would tell them about the furniture place, but he didn't take the commission on them.

What we lost in negating commissions, we gained in giving an insight into his character.

Before submitting Mrs. Donelon to cross-examination, I showed her a sheaf of documents and asked her where she found them. She said they were in a box of miscellaneous papers left by her husband. I did not offer them in evidence because I could not qualify them as yet. I merely asked that they be marked for identification. I intended to connect these papers with other testimony that would make them admissible. The mystery of their contents was to explode at the end of the case. The Judge thought they contained the most remarkable evidence of potential earning capacity ever offered in a death action.

Mr. Walter Doyle took over on cross-examination. He was a burly, dark, heavy-set man, as agile on his feet as with his tongue. His aggressive manner and sarcastic voice were offset by an openness of face and Irish charm which kept breaking through despite his glowering approach to the witness.

There are as many types of trial lawyers as there are varying personalities of men. At one end of the spectrum is the soft-spoken lawyer who approaches even a hostile witness in a kindly manner, who is respectful to his adversary and deferential to the judge. Even when he inserts the knife in cross-examination, he does so bloodlessly. Yet his calm and almost fatherly demeanor can, by its very reasonableness, be persuasive with a jury. At the other end of the spectrum is the lawyer who is bold, loud, and hostile, who permits his sarcasm to spill over his adversary, and who crosses swords even with the presiding Judge. But he can set the atmosphere around him aflame, and these flames can jump over into the jury box and set fire to the convictions of the jurors.

Doyle belonged to this latter school. Railroad attorneys usually do. Their forte is keeping damages down by aggressively challenging the exaggerations of the plaintiff. Whether they are cross-examining a doctor who has testified to permanent injuries, which they believe will cease to be permanent when the verdict has been rendered, or piercing the exaggerated claims of loss of income, they are expert in registering cynical disbelief. The occupational hazard of such lawyers, or should I call it occupational equipment, is to develop a sneering manner and a ridiculing voice. They earn their bread by the sweat of their browbeating. Even their movements in the courtroom are crisp and mock the slowness of formalism, as if to say, "Let's cut out all this pompous attempt to enlarge everything and bring this down quickly to size." A typical illustration is for such a cross-examiner to say to a doctor, who has testified to endema, contusions, abrasions, and hematoma, "that means, doctor, that she had a few scratches, a little swelling, and a blue mark, doesn't it?" After many years of representing railroads in negligence cases, such lawyers sometimes acquire the secondary characteristics of their professional work and are unable to shed their aggressive cynicism. It becomes part of their personality. It would not surprise me if, after a day in court devoted to minimizing testimony, such a lawyer, upon coming home, replies to his wife's greeting "Good evening, dear," by a sharp rejoinder that it is not yet evening, and that it may turn out to be a pretty miserable one when it does arrive. I know a politician who is so accustomed to striking a mysterious, confidential pose that when he meets you, he beckons for your ear, and then from one corner of his mouth (it is the only way he can talk) asks in a hushed whisper, "How are you?"

Doyle quickly drew from the witness the fact that her husband had worked in a shipyard during the war. After the war he was out of work.

Q. Mrs. Donelon, during the summer of 1950 it is a fact that your husband was unemployed?

A. Partially unemployed.

Q. The only thing he had for six months . . . was this commission business, selling furniture, is that right?

A. That's right.

Q. He worked there only some nights and weekends, is that right?

A. Yes.

Q. What job did he have as his regular employment during that period?

A. He didn't. He was between jobs and that furniture job helped us along. He was looking for just the right opening.

Q. Among his papers when he died did you find any copies of any letters that he wrote looking for work in the advertising business during this six months? . . .

A. His seeking— May I just express myself here?

Q. No, I am asking about copies of letters. That is the question.

A. No, I don't recall any. Mostly he went around looking, you know, to the proper agencies.

Q. Are there any here—any copies of applications for work that he made during that period?

A. I don't know whether I have any. . . .

Q. They are not here?

A. No.

Q. Do you know that he earned gross, during the year 1950, $3,825.84?

A. Yes, but it wasn't a full year.

Q. And for a full year, 1949, that he earned $4,219.07, do you know that?

A. I wouldn't remember the figures exactly, but if you have them in front of you—

Q. Of that, of course, he paid for his own clothes, he bought a pair of shoes or a necktie occasionally, did he not, like the rest of us?

A. He did.

Q. And he had his share of whatever the cost of running the house was, the food and laundry and all the rest?

A. As far as the food . . . when you cook it doesn't matter whether it is for two or three, since we are getting down to this fine point.

Q. Working day and night and painting the house three times in the year, didn't you cook a little bit for him?

A. Well, of course I did.

Q. . . . Mr. Donelon had only been with Weintraub about five weeks before his death, isn't that right?

A. Yes.

So the cross-examination continued to minimize all aspects of her husband's potentialities and his earnings. Before he came to work with the Weintraub agency, he had held a job with National Export Agency for five years. Mr. Kruming was its president. But had he written any letter of recommendation for her husband when he left? Had she any copies of any letters he "may have written to people in the advertising business," looking for a job?

A. He went for interviews, sir.

Q. No, no, madam, have you any such papers?

A. No.

Q. Did you find any in whatever files or places it was that these various exhibits you bring here were found?

A. No.

DOYLE: I think that is all.

To reveal to the jury how thin the cloud of skepticism was which Doyle had emitted, I asked Mrs. Donelon only one question on re-direct examination.

Q. You were asked whether there were any recommendations by an executive of the National Export Advertising Agency where your husband worked. Who is the president of that organization?

A. Paul Kruming.

NIZER: That is all. [The witness was excused.]

NIZER: Mr. Paul Kruming will you please take the stand.

The witness testified that Donelon checked advertising in foreign countries for such companies as The American Safety Razor Corporation, the Borden Company, Westinghouse Electric International Company, Quaker Oats Company, H. J. Heinz Company, the Warner-Lambert Pharmaceutical Company, and others. Later he placed advertising in foreign publications. His salary rose from $35 as a learner to $80 in a five-year period.

    Q. In your opinion did he have a good future in the advertising business?

    A. I believe that with the training that he had he did have a good future.

He left the firm because the possibility of becoming an account executive was limited and he desired to better himself.

    Q. Were you ready to recommend him at all times highly?

    DOYLE: Object to that.

    COURT: If we say the jury has a right to look into his expectations, I think this is competent. Objection overruled. Exception to Mr. Doyle.

    A. I would have recommended him.

Doyle was at him at once with a series of questions aimed at his credibility.

    Q. Have you any record of any idea that Mr. Donelon ever submitted?

    A. I have not.

    Q. . . . Have you any record of any recommendation that you wrote for him at any time after he left you?

    A. No.

    Q. Have you the final notation that was made at the time that he did leave you?

    A. We never make one.

    Q. You never make one? . . . You have put in your whole life in the advertising field, is that right?

    A. That's right.

    Q. And people come and go, do they not?

    A. Yes.

    Q. . . . Do you say to this Court and jury that you never make a notation of the reason for a person leaving your employ?

    A. Yes.

    Q. That is your statement?

    A. Yes.

He pummeled Kruming on his failure to place Donelon in another job when he knew he was leaving. The intended inference was that he could not recommend him.

    Q. Did you make any overtures on his behalf with any of your competitors or other agencies?

    A. No, I did not.

    Q. . . . And this you say was a progressive employee that you just did not happen to have a place for, is that right?

    A. Right.

    Q. For that type of man who would work for you for five years, did you make a single phone call or write a single letter to try to get him placed?

A. I don't believe so.

Q. Is there any doubt about it? The fact is you did not, isn't that right?

A. The fact is that I might have and can't remember, because I would have been willing to.

Q. . . . And after he left your employ, can you give me the name of one single person in any agency that you talked to about it?

A. I cannot.

I was not concerned with this attempt to becloud Donelon's record as a satisfactory employee, because we had a series of witnesses who would inundate the defendant on this issue. And we had special proof concerning that mysterious sheaf of papers which we appropriately were saving for the end.

Our next witness was Bernard Kahn, who was in charge of the production of television commercials for the William H. Weintraub agency. The Judge lightened the atmosphere with the observation, "We might talk to him about those long commercials," and the witness responded, "I try to keep them short, your Honor." Then we settled down for some poignant as well as informative testimony. Despite objection we established that Kahn had served in the Air Force in China, Burma, and India and had been hospitalized. His awards for valor were kept out of the record.

Since he had been responsible for recommending Donelon to his firm, he was permitted to state his standards for selecting employees: "I hire people who are young. I hire people with ideas. I place a premium on fresh thinking; as we all know, advertising is nothing more than ideas, and we are always looking for people who can grow with my department."

Kahn was only twenty-nine years old. We did not succeed in establishing his salary and that of other young executives in order to indicate Donelon's potentiality at this firm. The Court was constantly called upon to make rulings of admission or exclusion which involved a fine balance between relevance and prejudicial impact. For example, Kahn's heroism in battle might prejudice the jury in his favor and yet contribute little to his credibility—therefore excluded. His earning power had relevance, but his background as a college graduate and experienced advertising man might make such evidence an inapplicable analogy and prejudicial—therefore excluded. So, rules of evidence are in essence determined by common sense, but this does not necessarily simplify them. The weights for or against admissibility are often so close that the perspective from which the scales are viewed determines which way they appear to tip.

Kahn was a neighbor of Donelon's, and their back-fence acquaintance-ship led to family friendship which suburban life stimulates, I suppose, to overcome isolation. Even before Jack came into the Weintraub office, he and Kahn would meet at Pennsylvania station regularly to ride home. They played "a little game" on the train: "We'd pick up a magazine in Penn Station, the latest copy of *Life* or the *Saturday Evening Post*, and on the way home we would thumb through the magazine and examine the ads and try to decide why this ad was a good one, why this was a bad one, and if it was good what made it good, and if it was bad what would improve it. We did that several nights a week."

Q. On the night of the accident, how was it that you were not with him?

A. Well, I had to get some work out . . . and we were going to take the 6:13 together that night and I asked him to wait for me to get the 6:25, but he was anxious to get home, so he went ahead and I stayed.

So Donelon had refused to wait twelve minutes and had rushed for the death train. Had he waited for his friend, we would not be in court, and he would have merely had an anecdote about his narrow escape. Who has not experienced this feeling of eerie fate when, let us say, a mountainous truck whizzes by from nowhere brushing your clothes? The incident may be mentioned casually over a cocktail. One more inch and a life would have fallen like a blazing star from the sky, disrupting all the satellite lives orbiting around it. Even lesser accidents, involving a broken arm or leg make one yearn to relive the fateful moment again so as to avoid the tragedy by a second try. But life is inexorable. It seldom gives us two chances. As a skeptic once said, "Nature's way of giving you warning is death."

A short time after Donelon came into the Weintraub organization, Kahn's superior, Mr. Norman, sent him a memorandum about the new employee. I offered it in evidence.

DOYLE: I object to it. Unsigned, incompetent, irrelevant, immaterial, and not binding on this defendant.

NIZER: Mr. Doyle asked for a memorandum before from Mr. Kruming.

DOYLE: Let us sum up now.

NIZER: Please do not speak that way, sir. I am addressing the Court in answer to a question. There is no reason for discourtesy to me. After establishing that the memorandum was sent in the regular course of business, Judge Hooley said: "There is only one thing that bothers me. Is Mr. Norman going to be here?"

NIZER: He will, sir, and I will connect it with him too. . . .

COURT: All right, subject to connection and his appearance here so that he may be cross-examined in regard to the communication, we will take it. Mr. Doyle's objection is overruled and he has an exception.

I then read Mr. Norman's memorandum to the jury: "This is just to let you know that your boy, Jack Donelon, is doing a real fine job. Thanks for bringing him in. He is just the remedy we needed for this export headache and, unless I miss my guess, he is going to be a pretty important guy around here before too long."

What had Donelon done to earn this accolade? Kahn described his contributions "beyond his normal functions." The agency handled B. T. Babbitt Incorporated, which produces Bab-O, the kitchen cleanser. Kahn testified: "Jack submitted an idea for a little character called 'Sink Smog.' He made a villain out of him which Bab-O would chase away, and that idea was adopted for printed advertising and for television." We offered in evidence the advertisements with that impish character, Sink Smog, designed to be an incongruous compromise between villainy and cuteness. Naturally he took flight as soon as Bab-O, looking almost glitteringly sexy, appeared on the scene.

Another problem facing the advertising experts was the creation of a newspaper advertisement for the Henry J., one of the Kaiser-Frazer automobiles. Donelon suggested the headline that was accepted. The witness testified: "It read 'The Henry J. Solves America's New Car Payment Problems.' This was a low-priced car and the problem was to drive home forcibly to people that here was a car that every family could afford, and everybody submitted headline ideas, and this was chosen. It was Jack's."

The most ingenious of Donelon's imaginative creations, though not yet accepted, was for Airwick, a household deodorizer. "This is an idea for a premium. The customer is invited to send in a label and 25 cents and he gets this wall bracket which Jack designed, and on here are Jack's own notes about how the thing should be constructed and what it should look like. This was to be cut out in the shape of a daizy on top, and this was a wall bracket for the kitchen. The Airwick bottle would slip inside. . . . It was to be constructed so that no competitive product would fit in." We offered in evidence the specifications in Donelon's handwriting, and they were received.

The cross-examiner turned his arsenal of skepticism upon the witness, from lifted eyebrows and sarcastic voice to disdainful gestures and amused sneer. Mrs. Donelon had been given a secretarial job at his office after her husband was killed. The implication was that, due to sympathy, the witness was exaggerating in a further effort to aid the widow. Then the Kaiser headline was challenged.

Q. So that within two weeks after he joined the agency you say that he conceived this idea?

A. The headline, yes, I do. That is what I said.

Q. And there is no record of his connection with it anywhere that we can bring here to this court and jury, is there?

A. There is a record in my recollection and the recollection of another vice-president of the organization.

Q. Is there anything in writing that we can bring to this jury?

A. Those sorts of records do not exist.

Q. Now, you say that while you and he were riding on the train you had a game that you played dealing with the pros and cons of ads in newspapers?

A. That is correct.

Q. Never talked baseball, did you?

A. Yes, we talked baseball.

Q. Ever get into a little pinochle game instead of concentrating on advertising?

A. Never.

Q. Never. Four or five nights a week you would play this game?

A. I said about three nights a week.

Doyle turned to face the audience in the rear of the room as he put the next question. The witness was in no mood to take the dramatics without protest.

WITNESS: Are you addressing me or the—

DOYLE: Yes, all these questions are put to you, Mr. Witness.

I would have preferred Kahn not to turn clever and rebuke the attorney, but like a baseball manager, I had to back up my player:

NIZER: Will you face him, he cannot hear you.

DOYLE: I beg your pardon?

NIZER: You turn your back on him.

WITNESS: Will you restate that?

Q. Don't you know that during this period when you were riding the train with him, the claim is made that he worked nights and weekends as a furniture salesman?

A. He used to stay downtown on Thursday nights, he used to go in on Saturdays, and maybe one other night every other week.

After a brief skirmish as to why the memorandum from Mr. Norman was not initialed by him or stamped "Received," Doyle made a final effort to suggest the witness's bias.

Q. Were you instrumental in obtaining for Mrs. Donelon her employment with the Weintraub agency?

A. No. The company is that sort of company, they thought that—

DOYLE: . . . I am through.

NIZER: That is all. I thank you very much, sir. [The witness was excused.]

In rapid succession two other executives from the Weintraub agency took the stand. Norman B. Norman, a vice-president, also taught advertising at the Columbia University Graduate School of Business. He had hired Donelon, and his description of him combined academic with pragmatic standards. "My impressions of Mr. Donelon were that he suited the kind of character and personality that we were interested in hiring in our agency, which principally are intelligence, alertness, and preferably youthful—

DOYLE: Move to strike all of this out as not responsive to the question. . . .

NIZER: I think it is.

DOYLE: We are getting treatises in every one of these answers. . . .

COURT: . . . I think generally we are getting the standards which the witness fixes as the qualifications which he looked for in hiring employees, and we do know that he hired this man. No, I will let it stand.

WITNESS: In addition . . . he had to show a promise of growth in the agency. At that time we knew we were expanding rapidly and were far more interested in obtaining people who had a bright future. . . . I felt he could visit with clients and carry the responsibility of working with them because of his compatibility and agreeable manner and straightforwardness. . . .

Doyle did the best shrinking job he could.

Q. Do you know that Donelon's only education was three years in high school?

A. I understand that is correct.

Q. Did you ever read the book, *The Hucksters?*

NIZER: I object to this, your Honor, as quite irrelevant.

COURT: Sustained. What has it to do with this case?

DOYLE: All right.

Q. Now have you a single memorandum of any work that this man did on either the Revlon account or Maiden Form account?

A. We don't conduct our business that way.

So it went—until our next witness, Warren B. Dubin, another executive of the agency took the stand. Through him we continued to reconstruct verbally the flesh and blood of the man who was no more.

DUBIN: We want a man, as Mr. Donelon was, who is neat, who is fairly good-looking so that there isn't any repulsiveness. There wasn't in his case. He was a fine, handsome fellow. We want a man who is diplomatic, who is polite—at the same time who is firm, as Jack Donelon was. . . .

Q. What is your opinion of Mr. Donelon as an advertising man?

A. . . . I think he had an excellent future . . . he was bound to get ahead.

NIZER: Your witness.

Doyle scored by showing that the man who had replaced Donelon was still earning $100 a week, although two years had passed. I countered by showing that the replacement did not perform the same services as Donelon and that Mr. Norman had to carry many of the burdens previously entrusted to Donelon.

To reconstruct a man's personality one must turn in every direction to find the stimuli that affected him, and his reciprocal impact upon the sources that fed him. My search led me to a remarkable witness. He was

Pastor Joseph A. Belgum, rector of the Norwegian Lutheran Deaconess Home and Hospital. He had received a Master of Science degree in psychiatric social work from Columbia University. He was editor of the *Lutheran Inner Missons Tidings*, a publication of the Lutheran Church.

Q. How did you come to meet Mr. Donelon?

A. I had preached in St. Stephen's Lutheran Church on . . . shelter-care program and . . . family service, and I put a call out for volunteers to assist in the effort. . . . Mr. and Mrs. Donelon responded after the service.

Q. What kind of work did they do?

A. . . . Mrs. Donelon served as a baby sitter, relieving the house mothers, taking care of the children, while Mr. Donelon assisted me in the publicity and promotional work. . . . He made an organizational chart of our agency and how it fitted into the total picture of 29 Lutheran agencies serving 422 Lutheran churches in the metropolitan area.

Q. Did they arouse much interest, these charts?

A. Very much. They were both mimeographed and distributed to all the member agencies and parishes, as well as being blown up into a large display that covered half of a wall.

I produced a copy and, over Doyle's objection, the Judge permitted it to be received in evidence as indicating Donelon's versatility. I then introduced a folder prepared by Donelon which was used in the solicitation of funds evidencing further assistance he had given to the pastor.

Having thus built a factual pedestal, I ventured to place an opinion statue on it. I elicited from Pastor Belgum that he found Donelon both imaginative and skilled, with a special facility for taking a complicated array of things and simplifying them. He described Donelon's personality as a very attractive one and was impressed by his ability to get along well with people.

In cross-examination Doyle attempted to establish that Donelon was only one of many laymen who are engaged in some sort of activity on behalf of their church. This effort was blocked by my objection to the question on the ground that the issue was not how many other good men there are but whether the decedent was a good man, an objection which was sustained by the Court.

The witness stepped from the stand. Immediately I called another clergyman to take his seat. As they passed each other, they exchanged greetings. It is not often that a mission of truth is graced with so much mercy. The new witness was John R. Taylor, Pastor of the Lutheran Church in Merrick, Long Island. He had a scrubbed, ruddy face which shone with good spirits. The aura of God's work seems to reflect itself on the cheeks of His ministers as often as in their eyes.

Pastor Taylor testified to Donelon's efforts on behalf of the Men's Club formed by the 930 members of the Pastor's congregation. He then spoke of the sincere, religious atmosphere in the Donelon home which he had visited and the close family relationship existing between Donelon and his wife. In his opinion Donelon was a devoted husband and father who carried out in a practical way the tenets of the Christian faith.

The cross-examiner was wise not to attack Pastors Belgum and Taylor. Testimony cannot be evaluated merely by logical content. Sometimes it moves on the wings of emotion to enter the jury's heart as well as mind. Then it becomes so profoundly embedded as to be impervious to attack. More than this, the juror adopts a possessive attitude toward his conviction, and resents any challenge to it as an attempt to disrupt the truth. A lawyer must learn to recognize such a situation or he is lost. The test is subtle, but not to the sensitive mind. If his cross-examination does not sound as if it is directed toward the individual on the stand, but to a noble institution he represents, or to a virtuous ideology of which he is a symbol, then beware. Even if the witness were destroyed in such combat, it is the lawyer who loses, because the jury's sympathy for the victim, with whom it has emotionally identified itself, causes it to resent his tormentor. Call this prejudice if you will, but it is the mechanism that triggers "unaccountable" jury verdicts. It is the lawyer's task to understand and avoid the pitfalls of the intellectual triumph accompanied by an adverse verdict. His client expects him to be a pragmatist, not a martyr.

Sometimes I shudder to read of the heroics of a lawyer who defies a local community, heaps fire on its citizens' heads for their disgraceful prejudice, and makes a speech in court which he hopes will be incorporated in the anthologies of noble pleas—while his poor clients rot in jail, or still worse, are hung. If he would risk his own life for his principles, I would bow my head in admiration and contribute to his monument. But he is not in Congress or in the lecture hall. He is in a courtroom where his skills must be dedicated to the holy task of saving his client. What worse way is there to do so than to inflame the jurors and the Court? Defiance and a jutting jaw are not the customary techniques of persuasion.

Aside from negative caution, there are affirmative devices for cleansing the jurors' minds from an irrelevant emotional stimulant. The most effective is to neutralize the prejudice by turning it to one's favor. Trying cases in many states of our country, I have encountered local pride and prejudice. In important cases there are always prominent local law firms with whom I am associated for the trial. They act as a shield to some extent, but the prejudicial question remains, "Why is it necessary to import a New York lawyer?"

I never fail to take cognizance of this understandable prejudice. I do not pretend it does not exist. I address the jury on this subject, pointing out that due to my familiarity with the facts, it was thought I might be of assistance to the distinguished local counsel who represented our client; that the jurors had sworn to do impartial justice between the parties, and I had full faith in the sanctity of their oaths; that if this were a contest between the lawyers, I would concede and not be there. But it was the client's rights which were to be decided, and therefore I stood confident before them because I knew nothing would interfere with their sense of justice and good citizenship in determining that issue and nothing else. Sometimes, if our adversary has made snide reference to "this lawyer from New York," the answer may be bolder. What kind of case has he which requires him to resort to such tactics to influence the jury? Has he not underestimated the intelligence of the jurors? For myself I know something about the noble traditions of their state. I quote from one of its Revolutionary or Civil War heroes. If flags are to be waved, it is good to unfurl them for great traditions worthy of America. It is a fascinating experience to turn the switch and direct the prejudicial torrent against the man who initiated it.

Doyle was therefore wise not to enter into combat with the clergymen witnesses. In summation to the jury the opportunity was available to him to praise these wonderful men who naturally came to help their parishioner, but how much, he could argue, did they really contribute to the question of pecuniary damage? Naturally we all sympathized with the widow and orphan in such a tragedy, but the jurors must follow the law, and the Judge would charge them that verdicts cannot be based on sympathy. There are financial yardsticks, and they had taken a juror's oath to be guided by them and them alone. This would be his proper approach to turn aside gently the compassion of the pastors, and appeal to the jurors' religious obligation to their oaths to do justice according to the rules of law. Religion would be the harnessed force for the defense instead of against it. I knew this was the meaning of the silence of the experienced railroad attorney.

But he was not able to practice the same restraint in the face of the next attack. We had come to the surprise element in the case, the identification of the mysterious documents found among Donelon's papers.

In the course of preparing the case, we had scoured every scrap of paper which came into view. We were also on a continuous hunt for people who could contribute some light to the personality that had vanished into darkness in one crashing instant. When we examined the box of papers Donelon left, we found all sorts of miscellanea, from advertisements he had put aside for study, to his war decoration. Most of the papers sent us on false leads. Still we traced them assiduously. After all we had a terrible problem on our hands. The decedent had earned only $100 a week, and that for a mere five weeks. Before that he had earned $80 a week after five years' experience with a firm that had started him with $35 a week. The jury would be required to take into consideration deductions for his own needs, even from these meager earnings. How much could be left for Mrs. Donelon in view of his low salary?

Furthermore, even though it is the law in most states that the jury may not consider the widow's possible remarriage and consequent new income, it is difficult to weed out such a possibility from a jury's mind when it is exercising its discretion on pecuniary damages. Mrs. Donelon was pretty, personable, and intelligent. It would not be difficult for the jury to believe that she would reconstruct her life with a new marriage in the not too distant future.

Sometimes, due to crowded Court calendars, these death cases come to trial three or four years after the accident. I have had the unpleasant experience—from a damage viewpoint—of coming to court with a client who had already remarried. On other occasions the widow had been "keeping company," and the cross-examiner had not failed to draw the inference that love was only marking time until the verdict had been rendered.

Whatever the reason may have been, the railroad company would not offer more than $25,000 in settlement of the case. Our task was to concentrate on Donelon's potentialities, rather than on his earning capacity at the time of his death.

One can therefore imagine my interest in a series of documents found in his cardboard box which apparently contained percentile ratings for retail selling, practical judgment, native intelligence, and other characteristics and capacities. The handwriting on the documents was not that of Donelon. His wife was certain of that. Indeed his name nowhere appeared on the documents. Where had he picked up these papers? Why had he kept them? She could not give the slightest clue. We put them aside as worthless, but my mind kept coming back to them. What an entrancing possibility they presented. Suppose we could prove Donelon's capacity by scientific test—as if he had had some God-given intimation of his impending disaster and had left the only legacy he could for his wife and child!

I dug more deeply into her memory with endless questions. Had he ever taken a course in psychology? Had he ever submitted himself to an aptitude test? Had he studied this subject and used these documents as a guide? Had he any books on this general topic? Could she recognize whose handwriting was on these papers?

The answers were uniformly frustrating. She knew of nothing of this nature and was sure, in view of their closeness, that if it had happened she would know. I was almost unreasonably angry with her for not being able to supply a key to the magic box we might be holding in our hands.

Time and again I put the documents aside as valueless. But they remained in focus in my mind no matter what else in the case was in the forefront. Once I attempted to find any other handwritten letters or notes in her possession which might, by comparison, identify the writing on the mysterious papers. To no avail. Neither did her inquiry among Jack's friends and acquaintances, no matter how remote, provide a glimmer of light.

One day, like an indomitable suitor who derives satisfaction from repeating the question to the lady, though he knows the answer in advance,

I asked her again whether she had had a brainstorm about these documents. She shook her head patiently as if to say, "How many times will you ask me?" I ruminated out loud about what a coup it would be if these papers really referred to Donelon, and how we could never forgive ourselves if she had had a lapse of memory which deprived us of the most remarkable evidence we could possibly have in the case and which we desperately needed. "Can you, perhaps, think of any friend or acquaintance of his who ever studied psychology? Maybe he could give us a lead." There was the customary hopeless blank look, but within a moment it turned worried. I watched her intently, motioning to my law partner, Sidney Davis, to be immovable. I did not want her memory marred by the slightest distraction. Gradually her frozen face became animated with a faint recollection. "We once had a neighbor," she said with the slowness of one drawing a slender string out of a box, "who was quite a scholar. It might be he studied psychology. I don't know." We pounced upon the tiny clue with avidity. We visited him at his home in Brooklyn where the Donelons once resided. This sent us to New York University. Having given lectures there, I was in a position to stimulate an extraordinary search and cooperation.

The rules of evidence are forbidding obstacles in such an enterprise. Time and again our sleuthing was blocked by a missing link that we knew would bar the proof. Certainly Doyle could be expected to give us no quarter in such a matter. We brought our legal resources to bear on the problem. Later, we submitted memoranda of law to the Judge, to supply such authority as we could in support of our unique effort. Now we were ready to do the best we could. We called Myron E. Berrick to the stand.

Q. Mr. Berrick, what is your profession?

A. I am a clinical psychologist.

Q. What institution are you associated with?

A. The Franklin Delano Roosevelt Memorial Hospital at Montrose, New York. It is a Government veterans' hospital.

He had received his Master's degree and was now attending the four-year course for the Doctor of Philosophy degree in psychology at New York University. Approximately ten students were admitted to these studies. He was one of them. The course involved an integrated program in which he received his internship and practical experience working in hospitals and mental clinics while studying at the university for his doctorate.

Q. Have your studies included testing techniques?

A. Yes. All through the program we are instructed and given experience in psychological tests of all types. . . .

Q. There are subjective and objective tests to determine a man's intelligence?

A. That's right, intelligence, capacity for learning, for growth. . . .

There are two types of tests, those that are self-administered, in which the subject selects the answer, either correct or incorrect, that is on a printed booklet, and they are termed objective tests, in that the subject makes his own decision and there is no selective factor, no interaction between him and the examiner. The subjective tests are those of the inquiry type, where you ask the subject questions, he responds, and then you score his responses as to whether or not they are correct or incorrect.

Q. Are these tests of capacity and intelligence administered only in classrooms and hospitals under testing conditions?

A. Oh, no, not at all. These tests have found wide use in industry, in the Army, Navy, Marines. A young lad in high school looking around for his future would, on the basis of these tests, know what fields he would tend to do the best in. . . . The medical schools, dental schools, engineering schools have different tests which are selected.

Q. Are they also used in industry?

A. Yes, they are widely used for selection of personnel and executives. . . . They found wide use during the last war in selection of female help where women were intrained for industry, but through the basis of tests it was found that many women had abilities that they had never understood and were able to use effectively in various jobs in factories.

Q. Could you mention some of the companies in the business world that use these?

DOYLE: If your Honor pleases, I think we have had enough of this gentleman's background.

COURT: Yes.

DOYLE: So that we understand he is not a medical doctor, and I object to any proof along these lines in this case as incompetent, irrelevant, and immaterial.

The legal skirmish ended with my squeezing out permission to limit the answer to a few firms. Berrick mentioned International Business Machines, Ford Motor Company, and Bell Telephone. Now we moved to the critical area.

Q. When did you first meet Mr. Jack Donelon?

A. In 1946. We were neighbors.

Q. In March 1949 did you give certain aptitude intelligence tests to Mr. Jack Donelon?

A. I did.

DOYLE: Object to it as incompetent . . . not the proper proof, and on the further ground that the qualifications are not sufficient and proper for the submission of proof of this type.

COURT: At the time you gave the test, you were a student?

WITNESS: That's right, sir.

COURT: I would not want a medical student to come on, in fact he would not be permitted to come on.

NIZER: He is laying the foundation, your Honor. I have . . . Professor Glenn, who is the head of the department here. I have got to connect the document which was marked for identification. I promised your Honor to do so, and this is the connection of it.

COURT: All right. We will just take the test without his giving his opinion.

NIZER: I do not intend to have him give his opinion . . . that is why I have Professor Glenn here. I just want to identify the document.

DOYLE: I submit that you would not permit an unlicensed intern to come in here and testify even that he gave a test.

NIZER: . . . Judge, there is already testimony that these tests are objective. They require no discretion on the part of the giver. They are printed forms which are answered and scored.

COURT: Objection overruled.

We had survived the first serious attack which we feared might block off the entire evidence. We recognized Berrick's disqualification to testify about the tests as if he were an expert. We had sought refuge in the legal exception that no interpretation or judgment on the part of the tester was required. That was why we limited ourselves to the objective tests. There were some legal precedents which indicated that mere ministerial functions could be described even by a student. To prevent reversible error, I bore down on this distinction.

Q. Mr. Berrick, I am going to ask this question over again to make it very clear. You told us that these tests which you gave to Mr. Donelon were objective?

A. That's right, sir. The subject takes a pin and punches a hole next to the response that he thinks is correct. That pin hole is recorded on a chart that is printed on the last page. When the test is finished, you open the page, and your correct responses are recorded by the subject himself.

Q. So that there is no discretion involved on the part of the tester in giving these tests that you gave?

A. None whatsoever.

Q. . . . What was the occasion for your giving Mr. Donelon these tests?

There was a vigorous outcry of objection.

COURT: . . . If we get into a situation where this witness is using discretion and making conclusions, his testimony will not be admitted.

DOYLE: Exception, please.

NIZER: I shall comply fully with your Honor's direction.

A. As part of my training I was given a course in the use of a standard battery of objective tests. . . . I was instructed to administer these tests to a subject, to prepare a graph showing his scores in percentiles, to submit the completed tests and my chart to the instructor, who then checked it and returned the forms to Professor Glenn.

Q. He is the head of that department?

A. Yes.

Q. Is he the gentleman in the courtroom [indicating]?

A. That's right.

Q. You were permitted to pick any subject to administer these tests?

A. That's right. Mr. Donelon was a neighbor. I told him about it and he willingly volunteered to be the subject, so I used him as the subject.

Q. Then, on the basis of the scores, which is pure computation mathematically—is that correct?—

A. That's right.

Q. —you prepared this document which I show you, and which has previously been marked as plaintiff's Exhibit 7 for identification.

A. That's right.

Q. Is that your handwriting on that?

A. Yes, this is my handwriting.

Q. And everything on that piece of paper was prepared by you from these scores, right?

A. That's right, sir.

Q. Just recording the scores in percentiles?

A. Yes.

I offered the papers in evidence. Doyle objected so strenuously that the Court asked, "Do you want any preliminary cross-examination about it?" Doyle accepted the unusual privilege.

Q. Mr. Berrick, is there anything on this paper which the deceased placed there, any pin holes? . . .

A. No, sir, not on that sheet.

Q. This is an opinion sheet from somebody, is it not?

A. It is a record of the scores the subject obtained.

Q. It is an opinion sheet, it is somebody's opinion of the results of the test?

A. It is not an opinion. It is the result. It is a graphic presentation called the profile chart.

Q. . . . Who computed the scores on that paper? You?

A. The scores are in the test booklet itself, sir.

Q. . . . Who made the computation, who made the interpretation whether it be 2 times 2 or 3 times x?

A. The arithmetic was mine.

If there was any discretion or judgment involved, the document would be excluded. Then Professor Glenn could not give his opinion about the profile chart. We were still hanging in the balance. The Court took over the questioning. He looked at copies of the tests that had been given to

Donelon. One of them was called the Army General Classification Test. It was an intelligence test and was answered by punching holes into the paper. Another was answered by drawing a circle around one of the alternative words. We finally emerged from the darkness of doubt.

COURT: So that you arrive at these percentages without passing in any way upon the mentality or qualifications of the young man, but merely seeing what the pin holes are he makes, and which you count—how they work out in percentage?

WITNESS: That is right, sir.

COURT: Mr. Doyle, I am going to take it.

DOYLE: I respectfully except to your Honor's ruling.

COURT: . . . This may be offered in evidence subject to connection by a qualified psychologist. Is that right?

NIZER: Yes, your Honor. [Received in evidence as Plaintiff's Exhibit 7.]

NIZER: Why is it called the Army General Classification Test?

A. This was a test prepared for the use of the Armed Forces to screen men, to place them in positions where their major abilities could best function.

Q. How many men were given these tests, approximately?

A. In the last war over 12,000,000 men.

Q. And who used to administer these tests to the Army?

A. The clerks in the Army.

Q. Just any sergeant?

A. Anyone, that's right.

COURT: Did the Army make its dispositions of its men according to these tests?

WITNESS: Yes, sir. For example, in the selection of officer candidates there was a minimum score of 117 that had to be attained, and also in the selection of radar men, aircraft mechanics.

COURT: The reason I ask is that my son spent a year in France and he put on one of these things that he could speak French, so they sent him to England for the duration of the war.

DOYLE: Or telegraphers became bakers.

COURT: Yes.

This comment of the Court, eagerly joined in by Doyle, threw a more skeptical light on the tests than was achieved in cross-examination. There may have been good reason why, despite his knowledge of French, the Judge's son was specially equipped for an important function in England. Of course, his son was not there to be cross-examined, and if he were, I would have attempted to pass off the comment as light banter and added my hypocritical laughter to the jest. I turned the witness over to Mr. Doyle for final cross-examination.

Q. Who else was present besides you and Donelon when the test was given?

A. No one, sir. Under testing conditions—

Q. That is the answer, "No one," right?

A. That's right.

Q. . . . And these percentages which appear on here are your percentages, is that right?

A. No. These are the percentages that appear—

Q. Let us put it this way.

NIZER: Please let him answer. I think he should not be interrupted.

COURT: Unless he withdraws the question.

DOYLE: I withdraw it.

NIZER: You withdraw the question?

DOYLE: Yes, Mr. Nizer, I withdrew the question.

He promptly announced that he had concluded with the witness. I put one question on re-direct examination.

Q. You were asked whether there was anybody else present but you and Mr. Donelon when you gave the tests. Do the instructions on the printed forms . . . have anything to say about who shall be present?

A. Yes, sir. They are quite specific. The testing room is to be quiet, the test to be administered to one person in the Army. There were usually cubby-holes in which each testee went. . . .

Over all legal obstacles, we had succeeded in getting into evidence the papers found in Donelon's box, although they did not bear his name or his handwriting. I felt like a swimmer who enters the ocean on a steep beach and is driven back and knocked over by the fiercely breaking waves, until he finally gets past them and finds the water manageable. The going would now be easier with Professor William D. Glenn on the stand to interpret documents marked in evidence. He had the professional manner of precise speech combined with the tolerance of the rational approach. First we developed his impressive background as an authority. He had a Doctor's degree in psychology from the University of North Carolina. He was a Fellow of the American Psychological Association and many others. He was Professor of Psychology at New York University and Director of the Testing and Advisement Center of the University, which furnished psychological services to industrial organizations as well as the public. This Center had serviced department stores such as Bloomingdale's and Gimbels, banks such as Chase National and the National City, the New York Life Insurance Company, and the National Library Association, among many others. It had aided the American Management Association in selecting executives for United States Steel and Corning Glass.

Q. What does the testing service do?

A. We examine the problems in connection with personnel selection, make recommendations of the test or procedures to be used, and train their staff members to carry on the work.

Now we directed our attention to Berrick and Donelon. As part of the course, Berrick was required "to give to some outside person" certain tests and submit them to Professor Glenn's department. The summary of these tests is called the Profile Graph. I showed him Exhibit 7, the Profile Graph of Donelon and asked "Will you please take each of these percentiles and interpret them for us briefly, telling us what they tell about Jack Donelon?"

After the last desperate objection had been overruled and exception noted, Doyle sat down frustrated and angered by the impending introduction of the most unusual scientific demonstration of a dead man's potentiality that was probably ever offered in a court room. One could see him sharpening his teeth for cross-examination as the testimony unfolded. The jury leaned forward, a sure sign of its fascination, as Professor Glenn gave his first answer.

A. To start at the beginning here, under the topic "Intelligence" in the Army General Classification Test, Mr. Donelon has a percentile of 99. He is in the top one per cent of the population with which he is compared for men of his age. . . . Test of practical judgment, Mr. Donelon made 70 percentile. That means he is in the top 30 per cent. Anything above 50 per cent or below 50 per cent would be above or below average.

Q. That is, in practical judgment he was 20 percentile above average?

A. And in general intelligence he was 49 percentile above average.

Q. What would the top one percentile in intelligence mean—is that an extraordinary score?

A. That is a very unusual score.

Q. Very high?

A. It is very, very high.

Q. Is the practical judgment where he ranks 70 very high?

A. That is high. Practical judgment is subject to modification, it is something you can learn. General intelligence is something you cannot learn.

Q. That measures your native intelligence?

A. That's right.

Q. Has nothing to do with education, would it?

A. No, the test is designed to be free of cultural and educational factors. . . .

Q. Go ahead, sir, please, with the Profile Graph.

A. In the Detroit retail selling inventory, the result was 96 percentile. That puts him in the top four per cent.

Q. What does the test purport to do?

A. That is a test of the ability to do retail selling. . . .

Q. Is that used by large department stores and others to indicate that kind of personality and ability?

A. It was designed for that specific purpose.

Q. Has it been found, in your experience, Professor, to be correlated to the successful people in these fields?

A. It has.

Q. Thank you, sir. Go right ahead.

A. Personality, which is suitable for retail selling, Donelon was in the 98 percentile, that is the top two per cent.

Q. Is that very high, Professor?

A. You couldn't get much higher. Now his intelligence of the type required for retail selling was 87 percentile. His ability to do checking accurately is 98 percentile. His ability to do arithmetic accurately is in the 94 percentile. All of those factors are important in retail selling. That was found by experience. A survey of working speed and accuracy uses checking, code translation, finger dexterity, and counting. All of those are fine movements that are subject to speed. Take them one by one, the total score when you add them all up was 98 percentile, which is very high. . . . Now in finger dexterity he was 10 percent below average.

Q. He was weak there?

A. Weak there. May I point out that ten percentile below the average is within the range of average. We would consider from 40 to 60 as the range . . . so he is not really defective.

Q. Yes?

A. Counting rapidly, he was 65 percentile, that is above average. Now interest is the next area.

Q. What do we mean by interest?

A. Well, an individual's ability or achievement in any field depends to a great extent upon how interested he is in that field. The reason a great many people do not do well has been found to be that they are not motivated in a particular area, just disinterested. In this connection I ought to point out too that disinterest is as much a positive factor as interest. In order to be interested in one thing, you must be more or less disinterested in something else, its opposite, so to speak, and that shows up here. His interest in personal and social affairs was in the 99 percentile. That is extremely high. His interest in mechanical affairs was only in the 15 percentile. You will note that ties up with his lack of finger dexterity. He doesn't do those things as well as he does other things. His interest in business procedures was 85 percentile, quite high. In the arts, music, painting, and so forth, it was 85 percentile. His interest in the sciences was in the tenth percentile, very low. That ties up also with finger dexterity and mechanical interests.

Q. In other words, he had a disinterest?

A. A disinterest. There was a disinterest in manipulative procedures, manipulative acts that would also tie up with finger dexterity, mechanical interests. There is agreement all the way through there. His interest in computational material was only in the 20 percentile. That would tie up in the same area. . . . The level of his interest, the maturity, the seriousness with which he is interested in the personal–social, the business, the arts, the verbal material, was 99 percentile. That means he was a grown man in his attitude toward these areas.

Q. In other words, that is the kind of man who would progress more rapidly, is that such an indication, Professor?

A. Very serious achievement. He was in earnest. In personality, which is obviously important in any achievement, the test called Mental Health Analysis, the degree to which he possessed mental health, was in the 90 percentile. He is in the top 10 per cent of stable, normal individuals, and had freedom from these factors: behavioral immaturity, which means he no longer acted as a child; emotional instability, which means that you would expect him to be mature, have control of himself, and do the grown-up thing in situations of stress and strain; feelings of inadequacy, just 40 percentile. Such feelings, of course, are the basis of achievement very frequently.

As he continued to testify, a painting of Donelon emerged, not of his external appearance, but of his inner qualities. Perhaps it was more like an X ray, because Professor Glenn's interpretive reading was necessary to give meaning to the lights and shadows of Donelon's personality: "freedom from nervous mannerisms, 70 percentile," "ability to form close personal relationships, 97 percentile," "ability to deal with other individuals, and to be tactful, courteous, 99 percentile," "ability to take part in social groups, 95 percentile," "satisfactory work and recreation, 60 percentile," "outlook and goals, 99 percentile."

Q. What would that mean?

A. I can quote from the manual.

Once more there was strident objection, but the document was in evidence and the Court gave him permission to read from it.

A. Outlook and goals is described as the mentally healthy individual who has a satisfying philosophy of life that guides his behavior in harmony with socially acceptable ethical and moral principles. He also understands his environment and the cause-and-effect relationship which shape his destiny as a member of a social group.

Q. In that category, you say he was what?

A. In the top one per cent of the group of which he was a part.

Q. How many individuals have you, as the Director of the Testing Bureau of New York University, given these tests to?

A. In the last six years we have had over 40,000 people. We have a staff of 65 people, of course.

I attempted to show that these tests have been proven to be accurate in their predictions. Naturally I was flooded with objections by Doyle. The

Court upheld him on the ground that the witness could not have personally checked these results and would therefore be testifying to hearsay. I was eager to get this testimony before the jury. It was a vital link in the persuasive chain.

COURT: Are we not going pretty far? How many has he kept track of and compared their development with his prediction?

NIZER: I do not mean merely the 40,000, your Honor. I am offering proof by one of the leading authorities about the experience of these tests.

I approached the subject from another direction and, to the accompanying music of objection and colloquy, established that there are scientific organizations that prepare these tests, such as the Psychological Corporation, Science Research Associates of Chicago, and California College Test Bureau. They are composed of prominent psychologists and statisticians. It costs "approximately $30,000 at a minimum to develop one of these tests."

Q. Has there been any attempt to correlate the tests and percentiles which they result in with actual experience of what happens to these men?

A. . . . We make periodic studies. We select from our files a certain number of cases so that they will represent the total group. As much as two years after the tests have been used, we follow up those and get responses from as much as 87 per cent of the ones we write to, to find out the relationship between the prediction of the tests and the actual outcome. We do that about one study a year in order to check our own performance.

Q. What have you found from such studies supervised by you?

A. . . . We found that the tests do predict success in particular fields, as indicated by the results. We also use those results to correct and change and improve our procedures.

COURT: Do you find any that you predicted great things for some who did not turn out so well?

WITNESS: Yes, sir.

COURT: Go ahead.

NIZER: How would you sum up the potential of Mr. Donelon as revealed in the exhibit you have before you—Plaintiff's Exhibit 7?

DOYLE: I object to that, if the Court pleases, as not within the issues, incompetent, irrelevant, and immaterial, and no proper foundation laid.

COURT: On the question of expectations, which the Court conceives to be a proper subject for the jury here, the objection is overruled.

DOYLE: I respectfully except.

At last our efforts were about to come to final fruition. Those sheets of paper in a cardboat box, with unidentified handwriting, which had led us to a neighbor on Ocean Avenue, Brooklyn, and then to his teachers in New York University and their storaged files, to endless interviews in an effort legally to connect the evidence with Donelon, the late hours of library research, and the theory of objective testing which eliminated the opinion of a non-graduated student—these mysterious scraps of paper were now to result in a scientific judgment of what Donelon might have become, had he lived. Professor Glenn gave his summary: "In the area of intelligence he is an extraordinarily capable individual, capable of considerable growth, tremendous growth in the area of practical judgment and aptitudes, all of those areas are high, extremely high. His interests were integrated at a mature level and related to his abilities. He is an extremely well-adjusted individual from whom you would expect good judgment, a balanced life, and were he sent to us by an organization—

DOYLE: Now I object to this.

COURT: Yes, sustained.

NIZER: Finish your opinion as to his potential without reference to what you might have recommended.

A. My evaluation of his capacity for growth, for success, based on these findings, is that it was extraordinarily high.

NIZER: Your witness.

The cross-examiner mounted two attacks against the Professor: first, a demonstration of the tenuous oral tie which qualified the profile graph as that of Donelon; second, ridicule of the tests themselves. He succeeded quickly in attaining his first objective.

Q. Is there a duplicate or a record of Plaintiff's Exhibit 7, which has been referred to as the profile sheet, at New York University?

A. Not to my knowledge, sir.

Q. Have you in your own personal files any record of this test?

A. No, sir.

Q. Is there anything on these test papers that bears the name Donelon. . . .

COURT: It is conceded there is not.

NIZER: I concede that, your Honor.

Q. What happened to the particular papers that were in front of Donelon when he marked them?

A. . . . The scores were taken from them, placed on a profile, and then the sheets on which the marks were would be destroyed.

Q. In other words, we have nothing here . . . that has been in any way marked by Donelon, is that right?

A. We have the profile which sums up the marks made by Mr. Donelon.

Q. Professor, after hearing the testimony, you know that there is nothing on this profile sheet by Donelon. This was written by a student of yours after being in your classes about six months, isn't that right?

A. Yes, sir.

Q. . . . Is there any record of the profile at New York University?

A. No, sir.

Q. So that what you are working from here, in addition to your general knowledge, of course, Professor, is a sheet brought here by a next-door neighbor of this plaintiff; right?

A. That's right, sir.

Q. As far as your records in your department in New York University are concerned, you can find no record of an examination of John Donelon, can you?

A. No, sir, we cannot find it.

There was no doubt that the profile graph rested on the validity of oral testimony, first Mrs. Donelon's, that she had found the papers in her husband's box, and then Mr. Berrick's, that he had given Donelon the tests and submitted the profile graph to his teacher as part of his "outside" practice as required by the course. I had no doubt that the jury would accept the authenticity of Berrick's profile graph as explained by him. Doyle's emphasis of the lack of a written record in Donelon's handwriting or of the original test sheets with his pin marks in them was legitimate cross-examination. He had pointed a warning finger at the difficulties we had encountered in qualifying our proof under proper legal standards. But he raised some suspicions which were unjustified and which, on re-direct examination, I eliminated. So later I asked Professor Glenn:

Q. First, will you tell me the practice of the university with respect to the actual tests which are given by the students to a subject; what is done with the tests themselves?

A. When they are given to individuals, they are kept two years and destroyed.

Q. There was no exception made in that practice in the case of Donelon or Berrick?

A. No exception.

I showed that we had searched high and low for the original test papers and that I had served a subpoena for them. How desperately we had wanted them! We were not sure for a long time that we could get the profile chart into evidence without them. But the University had destroyed these tests, as it had those submitted by other students. In any event there was no significance to the fact that these papers were "missing."

On Doyle's second mission in cross-examination, that of casting doubt upon the science of testing, a battle of acerbity ensued. His ridicule was met by the Professor's resentment. The witness considered psychological tests as scientifically established as, let us say, the Darwin Theory, and Doyles' contempt for them as retrogressive as Bryan's challenge to evolution. The demeanor of Professor Glenn changed sharply as he was poked with ridicule. His professional equanimity gave way to angry retort. The man in front of him was attempting to make his life's work seem ludicrous. He was angered by the cross-examiner's sarcasm. Doyle's voice registered its most metallic disbelief as he began.

Q. Now this test, marked 21-C, is a test of practical judgment, is it?

A. That's right, sir.

Q. Let me read you this series: "What should you do if your clothing caught fire? (a) Call for help; (b) Pour water on it; (c) Roll up in a rug; (d) Get a fire extinguisher." You say that is a typical question to determine the capabilities of a business man of twenty-eight years of age, do you?

A. May I ask sir, if that is question No. 1 in the booklet?

Q. The number is 4.

A. The items increase in difficulty—

Q. Now doctor, please.

A. I can't answer that question without seeing more than you will allow me to, sir.

Q. Will it help you, that is all I want to know?

A. Yes, it will help me.

Q. Now you say these become more difficult as you go to the back of the book?

A. That is true.

Q. All right. There are forty-eight in all, am I right?

A. That's right.

Q. Let me read you 45, Doctor, and tell me whether or not this in your opinion is a question which is helpful in determining the practical judgment of a twenty-eight-year-old businessman: "If you were caught in an elevator would you (a) Break the door; (b) Climb through the top; (c) Wait to be rescued; (d) Call for help."

A. Yes, sir, that would be helpful.

Q. That would be helpful?

A. Yes, sir.

Q. Now let me read you 47, the next, and the most difficult one; "What should you do when you are criticized by your superior? (a) Explain the situation; (b) Pay close attention to what he says; (c) Try to shift the responsibility; (d) Try to remedy the failing." That also would be helpful to you in determining, without ever having seen the man, the capabilities of a twenty-eight-year-old businessman?

As he answered, Professor Glenn bowed slightly to offset the incredulity in Doyle's voice:

A. Quite helpful, sir.

Q. Did you do any work with the Army during the war?

A. Yes, sir, in this war, the Navy, sir.

Q. All right, and I take it that they had about the same comparative tests?

A. Same procedures, that's right.

Q. How many cases do you know of men who in life were trained as mechanics, carpenters, or machinists, or what not, who were converted to cooks as a result of these psychology tests in the Service?

A. I wouldn't know of a single one, sir.

Q. You never heard of one?

A. Never heard of one, not a single one.

Q. Do these Army tests get more difficult as you go through the back of the book too, Professor?

A. I would have to define difficulty, but they do.

Q. Let me read you Question 16 here. Would you say that this would be helpful in determining the capabilities of a twenty-eight-year-old businessman? "A man bought five and a half pounds of meat at 10 cents a pound. How much did the meat cost?" Would that help you?

A. Yes, sir.

COURT: It must have been a long time ago.

DOYLE: And only in an Army non-profit report.

Q. This is Question 54 out of ninety; Professor: "Tom has 15 packages of cigarettes and Bill has 8 packages of cigarettes. Tom has how many more packages of cigarettes than Bill?" Does that help you in determining the capabilities of a twenty-eight-year-old businessman, Professor.

A. Yes, sir, every question there would help me.

Doyle was addressing the witness by his title more and more frequently, but with growing condescension until the word "Professor" seemed to have an invidious meaning. The answers grew more defiant in tone. Suddenly the lawyer changed course sharply, attempting thereby to surprise the witness, and, of course, embarrass him too.

Q. Incidentally have you a fee for coming here today?

A. I expect to be paid for my time, sir.

Q. How much?

A. That has not been set, I believe; typical consulting fee.

Q. What is it based on, what do you expect to be paid on?

A. You would like to know what I usually get for, say, a day's work?

Q. I do not care what you usually get. What is the consideration on which your fee in this case is to be— Withdrawn. Yes, tell me what your monthly salary is with NYU, please.

NIZER: I object to monthly salary, your Honor. He is talking about fees.

COURT: There are two different types of service. He should get some more, Mr. Doyle, for being subject to cross-examination here by yourself. Suppose we ask him what he expects to get here, what he will charge if he is asked to send a bill.

NIZER: You may answer that.

I did not object because an expert's fee is relevant in considering his disinterestedness. I have in some cases drawn out of an opposing witness the fact that his fee varied, depending on the success of the lawsuit. Obviously the jury may consider his stake as affecting his objectivity.

WITNESS: I would expect to receive not less than $100.

Q. Doctor, back to the Army chart here, this is No. 81 out of ninety. "A sentry has eight hours' sentry duty each night. He goes on duty at 9 P.M. What time does he get off?" Would that help you in determining the capabilities of a twenty-eight-year-old businessman?

A. Yes, sir. Those tests were given to 12,000,000 people.

Q. I say, will they help you as a professor in a university?

A. Yes, sir.

Q. To determine whether a twenty-eight-year-old man—

A. Definitely.

Q. —can tell whether a man goes on duty at nine o'clock knows what hour he will get off after working eight hours?

A. Yes sir. That would be helpful.

Q. On this Retail Selling Inventory, that is to tell whether or not you can sell retail, Professor?

A. That's right.

Q. Does this question help you in determining whether a man can sell a fur coat or not: "Do you often just like to get away and be alone?" Does that help you?

A. . . . Yes, but not necessarily a fur coat.

Q. Will this help you also in the retail field: "Do you prefer a movie to a dance?"

A. Yes, sir, that would help you.

Q. How about this one: "Do you often find yourself daydreaming?" Would that one help you?

A. Yes, that would help me. Every one in every booklet there would help me, sir.

Q. . . . Professor, in conclusion . . . have you anything which will connect you or New York University with this panel sheet whatsoever?

A. Nothing with the name Donelon on it, sir.

DOYLE: That is all.

On re-direct examination, I attempted to expose the unfair technique of the cross-examiner. Some of the tests had hundreds of questions. A football question happened to be a sample question on the cover, to illustrate what the subject was required to do. Yet by isolating it, Doyle had attempted to ridicule the entire test. Professor Glenn frankly conceded the experimental nature of this new science. "Sometimes we do not know why these tests work. For instance in selecting saleswomen for Christmas work in a department store, we found that the woman who had $3000 insurance made better sales clerks than those who didn't. We haven't the slightest idea why. It is just a fact that they did."

There is an anecdote about Edison and his random experimentation, unlike the techniques of modern inventors who approach their problems more scientifically. When he was trying to find the best substance to serve as an electric-bulb filament, he made thousands of tests. A friend commented upon his continuous failures. Edison replied that he did not view the matter in such lugubrious fashion. He had been successful in discovering hundreds of substances which were not suitable. In a similar way, psychological research has been greatly pragmatic; the endless sifting of questions, combined with sequence and time factors, until the highest predictive results are obtained. The reason for success might lag behind the achievement.

When I asked Professor Glenn why the questions about clothes catching on fire would help in determining the subject's judgment, he answered simply. "Because it is one of forty-eight that have been shown to be predictive."

Q. Mr. Doyle asked you whether you would hire an executive . . . on the strength of a series of tests, and you said it was done. Will you tell us your experience? . . .

A. The tests show quite clearly whether the individual will be a successful man for a job for which he is being selected.

Q. You said you want to define what you meant when you said the questions in the test became more difficult. I would like you now to have that opportunity.

A. . . . Each question is picked to measure a particular characteristic, and they are presented in a certain order. That is what I meant when I said the test has to be constructed, it has to be built. And what is known as the validity, that is, whether this item will actually measure what it is supposed to measure, is very carefully determined on the basis of experience before the tests are ever used. Whether it will get the same result, is also carefully tested by these experienced techniques.

I felt the atmosphere was clearing, and so I also changed course. My purpose, however, was not to surprise the witness, but to put him at ease. Also at this point a touch of humor, if possible at Doyle's expense, would further restore the balance in our favor.

Q. Incidentally, at one point, you were called a psychiatrist by Mr. Doyle.

DOYLE: That is my error; if I said it, I am sorry.

Q. You would mark Mr. Doyle "H" for humility in admitting that error, would you not, Professor?

DOYLE: That I say is irrelevant.

NIZER: All right.

Q. What is the distinction between a psychiatrist and a psychologist, sir.

A. A psychiatrist is a medical man with an M.D. degree who treats people with mental disorders and emotional disturbances. A psychologist deals with normal people. He does not do treatment, but he studies behavior. We do a great deal of . . . testing for psychiatrists, but we do not do psychiatric work.

COURT: Psychologists do not use couches, I take it.

WITNESS: That's right, sir.

I returned to Doyle's efforts to ridicule the tests, attempting to expose the demagogic technique. I showed that in cross-examining Professor Glenn on the retail selling series, he had selected two or three out of 400 questions which had been carefully constructed in significant sequence, and depended on the factor of instantaneous answers.

Q. Have these tests, which were given to the Army and Navy, proven their usefulness from a viewpoint of scientific testing?

A. Naval aviators who made better scores . . . made more successful aviators. All the people in the Armed Forces were classified in terms of the level of occupation which they could handle successfully.

Q. Now, of course, you do not claim that every selection ever made was perfect; you do not make any such claim, do you, Professor?

A. No, indeed.

Q. What are you claiming for these tests of native intelligence?

A. That we can increase the accuracy of prediction by a very, very marked percentage.

NIZER: That is all, sir.

But it was not all. Doyle exercised his right of re-cross-examination. Apparently he felt that his inroads upon the witness had been canceled out. Once more he extracted individual questions from an arranged sequential battery, hoping thereby to cast a reflection on their scientific value.

Q. Does it help you in determining the capabilities of a twenty-eight-year-old businessman . . . that 48 divided by 3 is 16. Does that help you?

A. It helps me.

Q. . . . Does it also help you . . . that 2 times 17 minus 4 gives the answer 30?

A. It does.

DOYLE: That is all.

Now the door had been opened to further re-direct examination. I was determined to clarify the Professor's thesis. I gave the witness new rein. He explained: "That is a test of the individual's ability to do simple calculations very rapidly. There are thirty-nine of them. He has to do those in a certain time, the time factor being important. It is very important that he shift from multiplication to addition to subtraction to division."

I struck at the heart of the matter.

Q. Is a scientific application of these principles which you have described based upon a comprehensive treatment of the subject, or can it be isolated with individual pinpointed questions?

A. Every aspect of the test is a part in determining its value. The fact that page No. 2 precedes page No. 3 gives page No. 3 a value that it would not have if you reversed the order. They are constructed very carefully on the basis of experience. If you disturb that order or pattern they have no significance until you re-experience them.

NIZER: Thank you, sir, that is all. [The witness was excused.]

The acid test of the impact of the testimony on the defendant came within an hour. During a recess, we were approached in the corridor for settlement.

The technique of settling cases with insurance companies presents its own psychological problems worthy of special studies by the Professor Glenns. Those in charge of evaluating cases for the insurance companies have discovered by experience that many lawyers for the injured come to trial unprepared. This increases the advantage of the defendant, who has had on-the-spot investigators gathering evidence while the plaintiff was lying helpless in a hospital. Also the insurance company is represented by experienced trial counsel who specialize in this type of case. Finally, clogged trial calendars cause delays—often for three or four years. Exploiting these factors, the insurance company adjuster plays a shrewd game. I discovered in my early days as a lawyer that, no matter what settlement figure I put upon the case, the answer invariably was, "Why that is out of the question." When I inquired what counter offer would be made, I was told: "We are so far apart, there is no use our making any offer. If you will come down to earth and submit a reasonable figure, we will consider it." Spurred on by the client's anxiety for immediate cash in hand, I would suggest a lower settlement sum. Once more, irrespective of how reasonable it was, the insurance adjuster threw up his hands in dismay, and refused to make a counteroffer, because he didn't want to "insult" me by stating his evaluation, which was so radically different from mine. However, again, my eagerness for settlement was whetted by the suggestion that I make a more modest proposal.

I soon learned that this method of unilateral bid was a rather common practice among the insurance companies. Ultimately they succeeded in having a sacrificial offer on their records, from which point, when the case finally reached trial, they could proceed to negotiate, demanding further reduction in the interest of compromise. Even then, if they sensed that the plaintiff's lawyer was inadequately prepared, they would remain adamant at least until the plaintiff's case had been presented. If it did not go smoothly, the ground was even riper for a cheap settlement. After this pattern of settlement negotiation had become clear to me, I refused to engage in it. I warned my clients, before accepting their retainer, that the insurance company would exploit the period of time available and that settlement would be impossible until trial. Furthermore, I advised that the best result could be obtained by trial rather than by settlement.

It should be noted that in certain cases of extreme hardship, a motion for preference will be entertained by the Court and an immediate trial granted. However, the facts warranting such remedy must be unique, such as the impoverished condition of the plaintiff who, because of injury, cannot work. Otherwise, moving ahead over hundreds of other claimants would be an injustice to them.

As my clients continued to recover substantial verdicts, the insurance companies learned that their statistical data on the relative unpreparedness of certain lawyers, did not bind me. I refused to be prejudiced because of "average experience." Those cases which I tried were fully prepared, and we frequently recovered several times the highest amount offered by the insurance company even during trial when the strength of our case was more evident. Thus it came about that I reversed the procedure to which I had been subjected. If the insurance company wanted to engage in settlement talks, it would have to make the offer, not I. If I considered it inadequate, I would submit my request. If I heard that familiar song, "We are so far apart that there is no use our giving you a figure. Why don't you submit something more reasonable?", I politely declined, and announced that we would await a jury's determination. I never bid against myself, after those first few years.

So, behind the scenes, even during the very process of trial, the tug and pull of settlement talks goes on. Such negotiations must be confidential. It is prejudicial error if a litigant testifies to any settlement proposals. The law recognizes that men may wish to buy their peace even though they do not consider themselves liable. Public policy approves the adjustment of disputes and therefore protects both parties from any revelation to the jury of such negotiations. Otherwise the jury might draw the inference that one party deemed himself negligent, or that the other considered his case worth far less than he was demanding in court. Neither inference would be justified. The parties may be willing to make sacrifices to avoid litigation, but this should not prejudice their rights to a fair trial. Furthermore, as a practical matter, settlement discussions would be rare, if the penalty for holding an unsuccessful one was that the jury would learn of the concessions which both parties were ready to make. The stance of uncompromising righteousness during trial need not be compromised by the necessary sacrifices for amicable adjustment.

It is even deemed a prejudicial error, requiring a reversal of any judgment, if the jury has learned from any witness or lawyer that the defendant carries insurance. The law recognizes the tendency of a jury to be less concerned with an insurance company's money than with that of an individual defendant. To avoid generosity stemming from such prejudice, the trial is conducted as if the dispute was private, and limited to the plaintiff and the defendant, without reference to the insurer's indemnity.

The only concession made to the plaintiff is that in selecting a jury, he may ask whether any of the jurors holds stock in any insurance company issuing public liability policies. By special statute in most states, this question is permitted. Otherwise, a juror who has a financial interest in such a company and guesses that the defendant is insured, may be prejudiced in his favor. The result of the law's solicitude for both contestants is that no question may be asked which leads to the revelation that insurance exists, such as "an insurance investigator visited me" or "I was examined by the insurance company doctor." The prospective juror may nevertheless sense from the permitted question about his possible stock interest in any insurance company, that the defendant is covered by insurance.

Balancing the scales of justice, as they flutter between the rights of the conflicting parties, is no easy matter. Sometimes, as in this instance, the weights are so feathery that one detects the lady of justice inadvertently biting her tongue as she strives with meticulous care to bring the scales to rest.

I shall not discuss the many additional refinements that come about from this disclosure rule, such as what happens if the cross-examiner, by a reckless question, draws out the fact that there was an insurance company investigator on the scene. Why should the plaintiff suffer a mistrial for a question posed by his opponent? He does not. This is an exception to the rule that revelation is fatal.

A similar dilemma results from the clash of public policy with liability proof. Ordinarily one would think that in a negligence case the plaintiff would be permitted to offer evidence of repair of a defective machine or property after an accident. Logically such proof constitutes an admission of a prior defective condition. Yet, such evidence of subsequent repair is excluded in many states. Why? Because it is in the public interest that defendants be encouraged to make safe any possibly dangerous condition. If we punish them for doing so, by admitting evidence of their repairs against them, would they not be reluctant to make any change until the trial was over? Then, frayed carpets on stairways would not be replaced, gates would not be constructed around dangerous machines, and perhaps other people might be injured. Therefore the case must be tried on the original facts, irrespective of later repairs. The law permits defendants to insist that the original condition was safe, even though they may have taken "extra precautions" after the accident to change them.

So the law strives to maintain a balance between the rights of the individual and the public interest.

For similar reasons, our settlement talks during recesses and after court sessions were kept out of gaze and knowledge of the jury. We would battle in court and confer secretly after adjournment. Following my settlement principles, I threw the burden upon the defendant. What increases was it willing to propose? Step by step the offers went up, sometimes in painful stages—$30,000—$40,000—$42,500—$50,000. I kept Mrs. Donelon informed, but advised her firmly to reject these proposals. I was confident that our case had improved greatly and that the risk of submitting to a jury verdict should be accepted.

When the offer reached $75,000, I grew more cautious. Mrs. Donelon continued to state that she would do only as I recommended, and I felt the weight of responsibility more keenly. It was not my money with which I was gambling, it was hers. I discussed the possibilities earnestly with her, applying the most conservative standards. Nevertheless, we decided to hold out for more. The Judge had been advised by both counsel of these developments, and he, too, had misgivings about the risks she might be taking with the jury, the delay of appeals and possible reversal, requiring a new trial. Still we rejected the offer.

Then occurred a new development that put the case in a different perspective. How does one prove the life expectancy of a person who has been killed? It is customary to refer to the American Experience Table which is annexed to the Civil Practice Act of the state. All we had to do was offer in evidence these predictions of life expectancy for Donelon and his wife, both of whom, being thirty years old, would, according to this table, have thirty-five and one-third more years to live. The law facilitates this proof by statutory provision. In a similar way, the provisions of the charter of a city, or state statutes, need not be formally proved in the state to which they apply. The Court will take cognizance of their authoritativeness, and they may be read into evidence. However, the statutes of another state, or of a foreign government, must be proved, like any other fact, by an expert from that state or government.

I was determined not to accept the mortality tables annexed to the Civil Practice Act. I felt that they were old, and therefore obsolete. The span of life had increased through the years, and I wanted to prove the latest figures, which would add to the life expectancy of both John and Muriel Donelon. If the jury could assume in its calculations that John would have lived several years longer than the American Experience Table predicted, the damages would be greater, and I was fighting for every dollar that might be due my client. I therefore attempted to modernize the mortality table, and for this purpose I required an outstanding authority.

I engaged one of the foremost consulting actuaries and put him on the stand before I called Berrick or Glenn. His name was Richard Fondiller.

His qualifications were outstanding. He had been an actuary for thirty years and had been consulted by various life insurance companies like Equitable Life of New York and Pittsburgh Life Insurance Company. He had been assistant actuary of the New York State Workmen's Compensation Commission. He had been consulted by various states like New York, Ohio, Colorado, Idaho, and Nevada. He had also been engaged by the United States War Department to investigate, as an actuary, the mortality and life expectancy in various plans of the United States Atomic Commission, and generally the mortality and expectation of life throughout the United States. Significantly he had testified as an expert on actuary tables and life expectancy for the Erie Railroad and for the Pennsylvania Railroad. He had calculated tables that were in effect in fourteen states, including New York. Having established his expert knowledge, I put the simplest questions to him to accommodate the jury's digestibility of technical facts.

Q. Now, Mr. Fondiller, what is life expectancy?

A. Life expectancy is the average number of years which the persons of a group will live thereafter. For example, if you took a group of one million lives at age twenty, the expectation of life is the number of years on the average which each of those million lives will live after age twenty. In other words, it might be a period of forty-five years thereafter, on the average, and that is the expectation of life.

Q. What is the function of an actuary?

A. The function of an actuary in insurance is to make various studies of mortality tables, rates of death, probability of death, expectation of life, all of which leads up to the calculation of premium rates for insurance and for pension rates.

Q. Now, in your opinion, what is the most authoritative and modern table dealing with the subject of life expectancy?

A. The United States Life Tables.

Q. What are those?

A. They were calculated from the census which was taken in the year 1940, and I should say at this point that the results of the 1950 census have not been published. Therefore, we have to rely upon these 1940 census life tables, which comprise the entire population of the United States, approximately 140,000,000 persons. These officials tables are published by the United States Department of Commerce in 1946 and give authoritative figures based upon this very large experience.

Q. So that in your opinion this has the broadest base and is the most modern of the various tables which are used in measuring life expectancy?

A. Yes, sir.

Q. Now turning to that table, will you please tell us what the life expectancy would be of a male thirty years old according to that table issued on figures of the United States Government?

At this critical moment, when we were seconds away from our objective, his answer was blocked. The Judge vigorously upheld the objection.

COURT: I have never used anything except the American Experience Tables of Mortality. That is the one that was created by an Act of the Legislature, and as I understand it they have yearly revisions when necessary. I do not know why we should leave the tables printed in the law books. . . .

NIZER: The point, your Honor, is to have the most modern and largest base, and the tables that are printed there, which your Honor refers to, are old. That is the trouble with them. You know that life expectancy increases through the years, Judge.

COURT: Yes, surely, but here it says that . . . space is provided for annual amendments, which I take to mean that they do change these as life expectancy grows.

NIZER: I do not think that is so, Judge, that is the trouble.

COURT: The American Experience Tables of Mortality came about by Act of the legislature. I have never in my years of practice and seventeen years here on the bench used any tables other than the tables that I find at the end of the Civil Practice Manual. . . . I sustain the objection.

I fought on despite the ruling, but I did so deferentially because I knew I was trying to break a precedent, and the Judge's resistance was understandable.

NIZER: Now, your Honor, I would like to be heard on that a little more carefully, because the jury has a right to consider . . . the truth of life expectancy, based upon experience of the most modern tables. The trouble with the tables [in the book] is that they date back to 1868. Life expectancy has increased in the past fifty years enormously. I am going to have a base for that . . . and have the expert qualify why this newer table is the most authoritative. . . .

The Judge refused to change his mind. "I would rather take it out of the book than have you find an actuary somewhere that may disagree with the book. Every death case that has ever been before me has been satisfied to use these tables. . . . Mr. Nizer, you may have reversible error here if I grant your request. You will not have if I follow the tables set forth in the books. But when I go out and follow the testimony of some actuary, I have no doubt an enterprising lawyer could find another actuary who would have a better table somewhere more favorable to him."

NIZER: That would be subject to cross-examination and the credence of the jury. I do not think there are any better than the United States Census, but I will not pursue it, Judge.

COURT: I am going to follow the American Experience Tables of

Mortality in the book, and I am going to exclude any evidence of expectancy of life unless it appears in the table.

NIZER: Judge, I certainly bow to your ruling, but—

COURT: I may be wrong, but I am going to follow what I regard as a safe course. I am not going to pioneer this.

I took my exception and excused Mr. Fondiller from the stand. But pioneers cannot afford to accept defeat. The following nights, Davis and I labored doggedly into the gray mornings on memoranda of law which might change the Judge's mind. The Judge was a scholar, and his curiosity overcame any pride of opinion he may have had. While the next witness, Berrick, was on the stand, we could see the Judge's law clerk busily bringing law books to him which contained authorities in support of our reasoning concerning mortality tables. The Judge was reading these volumes, while listening with one ear to the examination of Berrick, so that he could make evidentiary rulings.

Then, one day, in the midst of Berrick's examination, the Judge made a surprising announcement. "Let me get rid of some of these books before you proceed further. I sent for the Laws of 1868, and the Tables of Mortality based on American Experience . . . and strangely enough, they give the same expectation for a person of the age of this decedent and his wife as they do in the table annexed to the Civil Practice Act. For that reason I am disposed now to take proof . . . as to who made this table, from the witness who was last on the stand. All of us recognize that the expectancy of life has increased here in America, thanks to the doctors, since 1868, and I thought in ruling as I did previously that the early revisions meant something, but the fact that it is substantially the same as is set forth in 1868 at the time the tables were set up indicates that there has not been any change herein."

The Judge had reversed himself. The door was open for proof that the life expectancy of Donelon was longer than the official American Experience Tables predicted. After Professor Glenn left the stand, we brought our actuarial expert, Mr. Fondiller, back to the seat from which he had been dismissed without being permitted to give the crucial answer.

Q. Mr. Fondiller, you have told us about the United States Life Tables based on the 1940 census issued by the United States Government. Do you recall your testimony on that?

A. Yes.

Q. Under that table what is the life expectancy of a male at the age of thirty?

A. Thirty-eight and eighty hundredths years or almost thirty-nine years.

Q. What would be the number of years of life expectancy of a female of the same age of thirty, as read from those tables?

A. Forty-two and twenty-one hundredths, or approximately forty-two years.

DOYLE: That I move to strike out as not within the issue.
COURT: Her expectancy of life?
DOYLE: Yes.
COURT: It is within the issues.
DOYLE: I respectfully except.

When I tried to bring the tables further up to date from 1940 to 1948, by citing the statistics from the later Federal reports the Judge sustained objection. Nevertheless we had increased Donelon's life expectancy from thirty-five to thirty-nine years and hers from thirty-five to forty-two years. This meant that the jury had four more years to consider in evaluating his potential income, and her pecuniary loss.

But the gain was much greater than that. We had broken through an ancient precedent and proved that the American Experience Tables were obsolete. The effect upon the Long Island Railroad Company was a shattering one. Seventy-five persons had died in the same wreck that had taken Donelon's life. Hundreds of cases were pending against the Railroad Company. If the enlarged longevity calculations were computed for all of them, the cumulative effect of additional damages would be tremendous. We had shown the way, but how would other plaintiffs learn about it? If there were a large jury verdict and a consequent inevitable appeal, the novel point would be passed upon, and enter the law books. Then the new rule that a plaintiff could bring the mortality tables up to date would become officially recorded as a judicial opinion and knowledge of it would spread. If on the other hand the case was settled before a jury rendered a verdict, the chance of the Judge's ruling receiving wide currency was very slight.

Indeed, life and casualty insurance companies generally might well be concerned by exposure of the out-of-date mortality tables. Were not hundreds of millions of dollars of premiums being collected on the basis of actuarial tables of longevity that lagged behind the times? Some day, perhaps in just as incidental a manner, the inaccuracy of these tables and the premiums based upon them may meet the proper challenge.

I had not counted on this pressure upon the insurance company in our case, but it was an unexpected by-product of our resourcefulness. First, the defendant had been stunned by the scientific proof of Donelon's capacity for growth. As if he had prepared for his death, he had taken a battery of tests to establish his potentiality and we had gotten it into evidence.

Now the defendant had an additional stimulation for immediate settlement. The tempo of adjustment talks quickened. Much of the psychological byplay was dropped. We were no longer given the ultimatum that the final offer had been made and that it would be withdrawn unless immediately accepted. We did not have to call the bluff as often, nor engage in similar counter tactics. I sensed a genuine eagerness, almost anxiety, to settle the case. The offers rose to $80,000, then in larger leaps to $90,000. This we were assured with angry sincerity was the last offer. I felt we had reached the end of the settlement rope, and the choice of acceptance or risk of jury verdict was acute.

Mrs. Donelon continued to express blind faith in my judgment. She would accept or refuse, as I advised, without any regret or recrimination. This only increased my concern in deciding for her. I explained that I was confident of a higher verdict from the jury, but there was no assurance of this. I was deeply troubled in advising her to reject the offer, only because I knew how precious every dollar was to her and Bruce. A settlement meant immediate and certain cash—no appeals and no delays.

I hoped she would be influenced by my analysis to indicate a preference, but she wished to be guided, whatever the consequence. This was touching, but also painful. I had to say that if the responsibility was solely mine, I would advise going to the jury. She had no delayed reaction of regret. Instead, she enthusiastically closed the discussion with the statement that she had followed me up to this moment; she was glad to continue to do so. She even tried to comfort me, "Don't worry, Mr. Nizer, if anything goes wrong, I know you have done your best and I shall be satisfied." I winced at the mere thought that my guess about the jury might turn out to be wrong. Yet it was my duty to get her every cent I could. It was a responsibility I could not shirk. I reported to our adversary that we rejected his offer of $90,000. He turned somewhat surly and said he would meet us in court for summation.

That night, with more intensity and anxiety than I have labored in cases involving millions of dollars, I prepared my summation to the jury. I knew what these dollars we had refused would mean for the rest of Muriel and Bruce Donelon's lives. I was determined to sharpen my skills to their finest edge to sway the jury to a large verdict. It was another one of those nights when I never touched my bed. In the morning I washed and shaved and went to court, prepared to make the most persuasive argument of which I was capable.

When I was about to enter the courtroom, Doyle approached me. He was in his most affable and charming mood. "What *do* you want in settlement?" he asked with admirable directness, compelled no doubt by the fact that there was no more time for jockeying.

"Does this mean, Doyle, that you are ready to increase the $90,000 offer, or is it your keen curiosity at play?"

"If you'll be reaonable, I'll see if I can get the company to better it."

"Fair enough," I said. "Let's meet with the Judge. He said he would help us if we got close."

We sought a conference with the Judge in his chambers and reported the situation. He sensed Doyle's readiness to make sacrifices to settle the case, and also my deep concern about the responsibility I was bearing in holding out. He entered on his mission of compromise with great skill. He warned Doyle that a very large jury verdict might be in the offing and warned me that I had a duty not to pull the string too tight where so substantial an offer was available. He induced me to lower my demand from $150,000 to $125,000, and pushed the defendant up to $95,000. I held out firmly. My summation was ringing in my head. I was not eager to deliver "the oration." Rather, I felt that the hazard of rejecting the offer of $95,000 was not too great because even if a jury were to disappoint us, it would not bring in a verdict much lower. The facts and emotional appeal assured us of that. Furthermore, I sensed that Doyle "had" to settle the case. I could not be sure he had been instructed to do so, but a large jury verdict would jeopardize settlements in all the other pending death actions. Certainly they would not have evidence of a profile graph, or the testimony of an actuarial expert increasing life expectancy over the standard tables. If word got out that a jury had brought in a large verdict in a case of a man who earned only $100 a week, what would it cost the insurance company to dispose of its other cases?

These imponderable factors encouraged me to be stubborn, even when Doyle exasperatedly and with a gesture of final exhaustion said that he would recommend to his superiors a settlement of $100,000. I stood fast and insisted on proceeding to summation. The Judge met separately with each counsel, and then advised me that Doyle was ready to recommend to his superiors a settlement of $112,500, but that this was his final proposal. He urged me to bring Mrs. Donelon before him. He would advise her to accept, thus sharing my responsibility and reducing my zeal to get every last dollar for her.

After hearing the Judge's fatherly advice, Mrs. Donelon looked to me, her head poised to bow yes or turn to no, as I would indicate. Although I was confident that a jury would give her more—else why had the Railroad made this offer—the bird-in-the-hand theory applied especially to a widow and child. Also, the saturation point of justifiable risk had been reached. The Judge had frankly stated to Mrs. Donelon that he had made unusual rulings in which precedent had been broken and that no one could be sure how the upper courts would view them. Even if the jury verdict was higher, how much would it be worth to have money in hand, without the delay of appeal and risk of reversal? I approved, and her head nodded in reflex action.

The Judge then paid gracious obeisance to our representation, stating that it was the best prepared and tried case that had ever come before him. He could elicit no dissent from her, though I knew how large a part fate had played when five years before, Berrick had asked Donelon to be his psychological guinea pig.

We filed into the courtroom. The jury stood respectfully until the Judge was seated. "Members of the jury, the Court is pleased to say to you that the parties have amicably settled their differences. The Court encourages these settlements. No high pressure is used on either side.

Parties make their own bargain. You must not feel that your time is wasted because you did not have a chance to pass upon it. . . . You have done your share in bringing it about. The case goes out of the Court forever; there are no appeals, no retrials. Thank you, very much."

Later, Mrs. Donelon burst into tears as the realization crowded in upon her that the termination of the lawsuit somehow gave finality to the tragedy she had suffered. It was as if Jack still lived in some mysterious way while the contest was alive; with its close, the stark reality of his neverness made its full impact. Often an event will open the mind to full comprehension of a fact that psychologically had been blocked out because it was too painful to accept.

When Mrs. Donelon had stoically adjusted herself to her loss and new-found loneliness, she made a most unusual request of me. She wanted Brucie to know the kind of man his father was, and above all what kind of man and father he would have been, had he lived. The record of the trial was not a legal document to her; it was a full-sized portrait in greatest detail of Jack's personality, character, goodness, and bright future, and of his relationship with her and her son. Could I obtain the minutes of the trial, so that Brucie could read them and understand and cherish his father?

I, of course, fulfilled her wish. It was the most beautiful compliment a lawyer ever received.

PROXY BATTLE

Chapter Six

THE STRUGGLE

OVER LOEW'S

I have a friend who has son trouble. His boy is a gifted engineer, twenty-five years old, but will not work at any trade or profession which you would find listed in a directory. He has set his heart on finding a treasure. No mere dreamer, he. He is ambitious, industrious, persistent, and thorough. He has collected every book and any published data on sunken ships off the shores of distant lands. He has traced golden treasures on pirates' boats and precious jewel boxes on modern liners which lie under water.

He has also investigated the stories of treasures buried in land and has laid his hands on innumerable maps and instruction sheets left by abdicating kings, resigned ministers, absconding generals, and an assortment of robbers and misers.

His engineering skills have enabled him to devise plans to reach and extract these fortunes from the hulls or hills in which they lie buried.

When my friend, who was bewildered by his son's eccentric preoccupation, sought solace, I told him there were hundreds like his son, but they sought corporate treasures. They too had developed techniques for seizing great fortunes. Usually they sought out businesses that had become sick and, with relatively few shares of stock, attacked management and dislodged it. Often the coup was speedy and bloodless. Sometimes, if the management resisted vigorously, an appeal would be made to the thousands of stockholders spread throughout the nation to vote out the prior management and elect them as the new operators of the enterprise. This technique is called a proxy fight, because the shareholder does not attend the election to vote personally; he sends his vote to one of the contending forces who cast it by proxy.

Thus, by concentrating as little as ten or twenty per cent of the stock in their hands, small determined groups have been able to seize great industrial complexes. With the majority of the shares diffused and the shareholders leaderless they have obtained working control of the enterprises.

Although the Government has set up an agency—the Securities & Exchange Commission—to regulate proxy contests, and although there are always the courts as a last resort, the great stakes involved stimulate ruthless warfare not unlike the do-or-die daring of pirates of old. The techniques are more subtle. One kills by publicity, by bankers' pressures, by financial squeezes and economic strangleholds. One uses all the artifices of the democratic process to persuade the voting stockholder that his interests lie with the insurgents. But when the management of the enterprise has been captured, the insurgents enjoy not only the power and emoluments of officers and directors with the attendant opportunities for capital gains on the stock market and stock options for themselves, but also the influence and standing which come with heading a famous company.

Yes, my friend's son, if only he knew, might have turned his heart's desire into business channels. Nor need he have sacrificed the lure of great reward. The pirate's gold boxes are a pittance compared to the capture of a national business enterprise.

This chapter is devoted to the true story of such a quest and its outcome. The struggle was commensurate with the large stakes. It evoked all the noble and ignoble qualities of men when they are engaged in desperate battle, all in a drama more exciting than fiction could possibly contrive.

Loew's Incorporated was a quarter-of-a-billion-dollar industrial empire. It produced motion pictures under the trade name of Metro-Goldwyn-Mayer. A lion called Leo has roared thousands of times in the opening title scene to herald symbolically a production of majestic quality. The company also owned more than a hundred theaters in the United States and Canada, music publishing companies, a recording company, a radio station, interests in television stations, and a motion picture studio in England. It had an army of almost 14,000 employees: 8500 in the United States, and 4900 foreign personnel situated in forty-seven countries.

The gross receipts derived by Loew's Incorporated from its worldwide activities averaged $178,000,000 each year for the past ten years.

But a shrewd operator would also observe other assets. Many a man who is heavily insured is worth more dead than alive. This may also be true of a corporation. Loew's Incorporated had valuable real estate holdings. It owned 185 acres of land in Culver City, California—some of it found to be oil-producing. On this land were twenty-eight buildings containing production stages, laboratories for producing films, a building for the manufacture of cartoons, property rooms, scene docks, permanent street sets and backings, dressing room buildings, various office buildings for the housing of writers, directors, and administrative officers, machine shops and woodworking shops. It also had the real estate owned by the theater company operating one hundred theaters in choice sites.

The same shrewd operator's keen eye would also observe the recording studio for re-recording pictures in foreign languages. This is really a magic factory where any language in the world is skillfully adjusted in dialogue to accord with the vowel and consonant movements of an American star's lips, so that Marilyn Monroe or Gregory Peck appear to be speaking Japanese, Chinese, French, or Portuguese.

Another asset that would not escape covetous eyes would be the new values of old films leased to television stations. Loew's has licensed seven hundred of its motion pictures produced prior to 1948 for an unexpected windfall exceeding fifty million dollars.

For almost forty years Loew's Incorporated had been the pre-eminent motion picture company. Its management had been so successful that its 26,000 stockholders contentedly endorsed whatever it desired. However, Loew's, the greatest motion picture organization of them all, fell into trouble. To understand how this came about, I must explain that the Loew's dynasty had both a king and a president. The two fell out, and a struggle for power eventuated, in which both were destroyed. The field was left open for pretenders. The history of this proxy contest is the attempt of the king and his allies to regain his throne. Anachronistically it resulted in one of the bitterest fought contests in the history of American industry.

The king was Louis B. Mayer. His long sharp nose and balding head gave him an eager but predatory look not unlike an eagle. He not only presided with an all-powerful scepter over the Metro-Goldwyn-Mayer studio, but, since Metro was the prime company, he was virtually the king of all Hollywood.

The President was Nicholas M. Schenck. He was short, soft-spoken, and deceptively harmless in manner. Mayer's flamboyance and volubility were offset by Schenck's retiring disposition. But, aside from Schenck's integrity in his personal and business life, their differences were more surface than deep. Actually they were both keen and courageous in battle.

In this industrial constitutional monarchy, Schenck directed the vast Loew enterprise from his office in New York. Theater operations, domestic and foreign distribution, publicity, radio station and music companies all came under his brilliant leadership. He also, of course, had technical authority over the studio in Hollywood, but he was wise enough to modify it and not to irritate Louis B. Mayer, the ruler of that domain. So long as the Metro studio maintained its acknowledged pre-eminence, the company prospered and this divided authority between the executive and the manufacturing department continued in a sort of uneasy truce.

But as the years went by, Mayer, whose vanity exceeded that of his most narcissistic star, found the adulation that his position commanded insufficient. He tired of merely being the king of Hollywood. He sought new interests, and found the race track a new realm to conquer. He began by buying and breeding horses as a hobby. One day he called for his accountant and asked how he was faring in his adventure in horse flesh. He was told that he was in the red over $300,000.

"I decided that this was no longer a hobby," he told me once. "I decided to make it a business." He did, and ultimately sold his stable for millions of dollars of profit. But this effort required concentration and a new dedication. In addition to his personal preoccupations, at least until he married, this new enterprise absorbed his flagging energies. He was approaching seventy. As he thrilled to the excitement of the race track, he became more bored with the studio. He ignored it in favor of his new love. Whenever anyone wanted to speak to the king, to approve the many pronunciamentos that had to be issued in his name, he could not be found in his office. It became a famous phrase in Hollywood to say that Mayer could be located on Stage 14—that meant he was at the Santa Anita race track.

With the growth of television in 1947, the halcyon days of Hollywood ended. Now motion pictures had to be of high entertainment quality, or they met a dismal reception at the box office. It was a time for creative showmanship and energetic application, but Louis B. Mayer was satiated with honors, stuffed with money, and disinterested in the studio. In 1947, 1948, and 1949, while he was in sole charge of the studio, the great Metro-Goldwyn-Mayer lost millions of dollars in production.

President Schenck asserted his prerogatives. He had suffered long and not so silently with Mayer's insubordination and arrogant independence. Now he challenged the king of Hollywood and, in a fierce struggle, deposed him.

The hurt to Mayer's pride was indescribable. Here was one of the founders of the company, who had received throughout the years fifteen million dollars in the form of salary, share of profits, guaranteed annuity benefits, and who had in addition participated in the form of partnership income in more than twelve million dollars paid to the firm of L. B. Mayer & Co. and its predecessors; who had been publicized on the front pages of the nation's newspapers annually as the highest earning executive in the world; who, in the sacred caste system of Hollywood's hierarchy, stood at the very apex; and who had been forced to hand in his resignation. What a humiliation for a man of his unique stature, and what a bitter cup for one of his temperament. This man who could cry copiously when wooing a star onto the roster; who could faint at a moment's notice, leaving a resistant star or competitor horrified and guilty as he lay unconscious on the carpet; who could go into incredible foaming rages, or whimper through the night like a little child whose heart was breaking; this undisputed master of the princes and princesses of the screen, had been maneuvered into a position where he was left with no alternative but to resign.

He dedicated his life to revenge. He pledged his immense fortune to a program of retribution. With each inhalation and exhalation he made, he renewed his vow to destroy his enemy and return in triumph to the company that bore his name. A demoniacal, all-consuming hatred drove him toward this last objective of his life. Without understanding this, the events that followed would be incomprehensible.

A great revolution has occurred in the production of motion pictures. Until recent years each studio had a roster of famous stars, directors, writers, and producers. At one time Metro-Goldwyn-Mayer had more such outstanding personalities under contract than all the other studios combined. From Garbo and Clark Gable to Myrna Loy and Spencer Tracy, from Jean Harlow and William Powell to Norma Shearer and John Gilbert, "the Company with more stars than there are in heaven" was Metro.

In those days the unique talents of such producers as Irving Thalberg, Hunt Stromberg, and David O. Selznick were nourished by the exclusive availability on the Metro lot of the foremost writers, directors, scenic designers, and composers. A producer could push a button and bring Joan Crawford, Hedy Lamarr, John Barrymore, or Walter Pidgeon into his office for their new roles; push another button and assign Greer Garson, Marie Dressler, Rosalind Russell, Robert Montgomery, and Wallace Beery to other roles; push another button and assign Sidney Franklin or Jack Conway to direct the picture.

It was a great honor for an artist to be invited to join the Metro family. By long-term contracts and options, Metro assured itself of an unexcelled pool of talents.

As the years went by, salaries for these artists soared, but no salary has ever risen higher than the tax that was designed to accompany it. Artists became disgruntled. With few exceptions, stars' earning lives are limited to a small number of years. If no harvest can be reaped in that short span, what happens to their security? This argument has been presented time and again on behalf of actors, writers, and even prize fighters, to Congress in support of proposals for tax exceptions. But the answer has invariably been negative, based on the old argument of bad precedent. There are many businessmen, too, who make one large profit and then have years of drought. Where shall we stop with exceptions?

So stars sought their own remedy. Independent producers of motion pictures soon provided the answer. They offered the star not only a salary, but an interest in the picture. The profits to the actor were deemed capital gains and subject to only twenty-five per cent tax. Furthermore, they spread the income over several years instead of concentrating it in one taxable fiscal year. Agents for artists further developed this technique for compensation. Soon the star was not even content with a percentage of profits. He demanded a percentage of gross receipts, so that if the picture lost money he would nevertheless receive a capital gain. Other resourceful ideas were developed. Artists organized their own production corporations and took long-term salary payments from their own companies, as well as capital-gain profits from the venture.

The result was an exodus of stars and creative artists from the studios in which they had been employed for years. Any small entrepreneur who acquired an important script and who was willing to give up fifty per cent or more of his profit to the star and cast, could wean them away from their old employer and arrange bank financing on the strength of his package.

A vivid example of the irresistible lure for capital gains was Darryl F. Zanuck's resignation as the head of the Twentieth Century-Fox Film Studio, where he commanded a fabulous salary, to become an independent producer and license his films for distribution to the very studio he had managed. He was better off financially being a colonel in the king's army, than king. This was, of course, just as true for other producers, directors, and, above all, actors. Free-lancing became the desired estate, where once it was a sign of failure. Participation deals became the order of the day.

As the pool of artists flowed away from all studios, the most precious streams came from Metro.

Nicholas Schenck found it difficult to adjust himself to the audacity of actors and directors demanding "a piece of the picture." They were employees. By what right did they claim to become owners of the property? Did they finance the production? Did they take the risk if there was a loss? Did they concern themselves with the huge overhead of the studio? He and his associates had developed the Metro trademark. He had pride in its greatness. In most instances he could trace the star's development to Metro's solicitous care and training and to the unique story properties, cast, and other talents lavished upon the vehicle in which the actor appeared. He could demonstrate that artistic schooling, followed by publicity and exploitation build-up, had frequently taken a gangling and ignorant girl and made her the most desired and admired woman in the world. Who had taught that girl how to walk? Who had straightened out her teeth and capped them into a smile of perfection? Who had taught her how to pronounce words and improve her voice? Who had clothed her glamorously with the specially prepared creations of the greatest *couturiers*, imported and employed on the Metro lot?

How many directors had developed ulcers trying to teach this impassive girl how to depict the great emotions?

He could recall the unknown, awkward young men who had been promoted by millions of dollars of studio effort so that their names were better known to the populations of the world than that of the President of the United States. Metro had given fame and fortune to these boys and girls and made them stars, and now they threatened to leave the studio unless they were given a percentage participation in their next picture. What ingratitude! Was Metro to become a mere financing organization in which for all its risks, it would receive only a part of the profits? This would be betrayal of the stockholders.

The argument seemed sound enough, but when a theory collides with a fact, the result is a tragedy. The fact was that a new day had dawned. Television had made huge picture investments more hazardous than ever before, and the best insurance for these risky ventures was great star power. So as the risk increased, the need for the star, the outstanding director, the great script writer, increased too. The price went up, and the price was percentage participation—not mere salary. Stars could not be obtained any other way.

Small companies and independent producers "raided" the stars with attractive partnership deals. The Metro trade-mark was no longer a guarantee of the highest quality, unattainable by a competitor. On the contrary, unknown companies like Allied Artists and newly created corporations weaned away the foremost stars from Metro and other studios. The heavens had become pretty cloudy for Metro. One could hardly see a star twinkle. To add to its difficulties, Dore Schary, who had succeeded Louis B. Mayer at the studio, was not producing a sufficient number of successful box office attractions. He was intent on making pictures of great significance and high purpose and some wag accused him of selling out Metro for a pot of message.

Jimmy Stewart made a picture for Universal Film Corporation on a large participation basis. Word flashed through the industry that his interest would exceed one million dollars. And it would not even be taxable as ordinary salary. Actors' eyes shone without the aid of make-up. Their agents set new sights for them. The scramble for percentages was accelerated. Even independent producers began to complain at the inordinate demands. Every secondary artist, director and author wanted a share in the picture, and after all there was only one hundred per cent to divide.

The combined effort of television competition, which shrank the motion picture audience, the loss of its great roster of stars and artists, the poor product which emanated from the once peerless studio, and the hard-artery policy of looking backward to its historical greatness, rather than forward to the challenge of the untried, resulted in the precipitous decline of Metro. From its accustomed position of primacy in Hollywood's aristocracy, it sank to the lowest plebeian depths. In ten years from 1946 to 1956 the earnings dropped from $3.66 a share to ninety-one cents a share.

Stockholders restlessly probed for reasons for the debacle. Suits were instituted attacking the mountainous drawings and interests of Louis B. Mayer, although he was long gone from the studio, and charging nepotism and mismanagement. Nicholas Schenck was forced to retire from the presidency, although he remained Chairman of the Board. Louis B. Mayer had had his first great triumph over his enemy—Schenck had fallen. Soon the path would lie open for his re-entry into Hollywood, marching at the head of his legions. Napoleon had not returned to Paris with greater pomp than Mayer planned after his recapture of Loew's, Incorporated.

Schenck's resignation from the presidency left a big void, but there was a natural successor. He was Arthur M. Loew, the son of the founder of the business, Marcus Loew. He was tall and athletically thin. His debonair appearance—aided by a hairline mustache—was offset by a soft voice and manner which revealed inner shyness.

He was head of foreign distribution of Metro pictures throughout approximately fifty countries. His department had been highly profitable. He was, by knowledge, experience, and the prestige of his name, the most authoritative person for the post.

But Arthur Loew did not want the job. He was wealthy and, more important, power was no lure either. He felt no need to conquer any worlds. While his philosophy included usefulness as well as play—chiefly tennis and yachting—and therefore a willingness to travel and supervise sales, it did not include the sacrifice required for rebuilding the once peerless corporation. What was required of him was not sweat, blood, and tears. Air conditioning, peace, and manliness eliminated these sacrifices in mere corporate strife. But slave hours, ulcers, and nervous breakdown were the potential price and Arthur Loew neither had, nor would he offer the stomach for it.

The directors of the company—still friendly to Schenck—looked around for another President. They thought of Lew Wasserman, an executive of a leading talent agency, Music Corporation of America. Agents, because of their control of stars, had become the most powerful figures in Hollywood. This was one of the ironic by-products of the revolution in picture-making. An agent had once been a mere salesman trying to place his actor under contract to a studio. He had cooled his heels in outer offices, and it was a distinction for him to obtain a conference even with studio executives of secondary rank. Now, in the new era of participation or package deals, it was he who was in command. Presidents of companies visited his office and sought his good will. Perhaps, then, an outstanding agency executive like Wasserman would best fit the requirements of the presidency.

Abe Schneider, Treasurer of Columbia Pictures Corporation (he has since become its President), and generally recognized as one of the younger executives of great potential, was also considered for the high post.

These and various others either were not available or were objected to by one faction or another.

The man Nicholas Schenck wanted to succeed him was Charles Moskowitz, Treasurer of Loew's. But he was under charges in various legal proceedings because his brothers and relatives were interested in corporations doing business with the company. Candy concessions in the Loew Theatres, sales of carpet and other functions in operation involved Moskowitzes, Schencks, or their strain. Although later careful investigation revealed not an iota of impropriety in these dealings, and indeed showed that the corporation had often profited in price from these relationships, the very charge of nepotism, combined with the company's decline, was fatal.

Schenck and the Board of Directors pleaded with Arthur Loew to take the helm if only for one year until a man with adequate qualifications could be found. He yielded to their entreaties, but with reluctance. Morale at the studio, now headed by Dore Schary, was low. Cash in the till was low, and bank loans had to be arranged. The momentum of preeminence which once had pushed the company to new ascents, was gone. Like a plane that either goes forward or falls, the company was not even standing still—it was plummeting.

Before the year was up Arthur Loew insisted that the Board of Directors find another President. He wanted to go back to his foreign department. After the continuous crises in the top post, he sought to get away from it all in the Foreign Legion, so to speak.

After various replacements were unsuccessfully canvassed, the eyes of the board turned to one of their own ranks. He was Joseph R. Vogel, general manager of Loew's Theatres outside New York City. He had begun with the company at the age of 14 as a part-time usher. Could one find a lower estate than that? Even Alger's heroes looked like boys with silver spoons in their mouths by comparison. His compensation had been the privilege of seeing the motion picture without charge. Little did he know then that some day he would be paid thousands of dollars a week to watch movies and evaluate them.

At the age of seventeen he became a treasurer and an assistant manager. Those were the days when motion pictures were used as chasers, to empty the theater between vaudeville shows. Since then the industry has come a full cycle from drive-outs to drive-ins.

At the age of eighteen and a half, Vogel became manager of Loew's Theatres, New York City. He had established a reputation even then for showmanship. The Singer Midgets, a famous vaudeville act, traditionally would not work more than two shows a day. But Vogel discovered their weakness for cigarette coupons, with which house furnishings could be obtained free, and played upon it until they accepted heaps of coupons for an extra performance. Marcus Loew and Nicholas Schenck marveled at the unprecedented high receipts at their Victoria Theatre and visited this young manager to discover the secret of success, just as they would have been sure to investigate the reason for failure. Vogel found it difficult to explain that the midgets preferred Sweet Corporal green coupons over Uncle Sam's greenbacks. No manager had ever succeeded with the latter, but he had with the former.

His rise kept pace with his energies and resourcefulness and was therefore steep and speedy. At the age of twenty-six he was promoted to the home office to be assistant to Col. E. A. Schiller, the head of the Theatre department. Soon he was placed in charge of the Poli-New England Theatres, then the Loew's Pittsburgh and New Orleans Theatres, and later the Loew's State and Capitol Theatres, flagships of the circuit, situated on Broadway in New York City. Ultimately, as his talents made inevitable, he became General Manager of Loew's Theatres at a salary of three thousand dollars a week.

Under his direction, over a period of ten years, Loew's Theatres, considered by many experts to be the greatest theater organization in the world, earned a profit of seventy-five million dollars.

In the business world, success is necessarily achieved at the expense of competitors. Therefore respect and admiration are earned more frequently than affection. Whenever I hear disparaging comments about a highly successful man, I wonder if the bitterness may not have been engendered by being bested in fair combat.

Vogel was the exception to the rule; he enjoyed universal popularity. This was due not only to his forthrightness and fair dealing, but to an engaging personality. In appearance he bore a striking resemblance to the entertainer, Phil Baker, from light blue eyes to a warm smile. His voice was soft, and suitable to his modest demeanor. His geniality and affability, together with his more solid qualities, translated themselves into charm. Throughout the struggle that followed, the concession made by his fiercest enemies—so often that it became cloying—was, "Of course he is a nice man. Everyone likes Joe. So do we."

Men who graduate from that apocryphal university known as the School of Experience, usually continue to take postgraduate courses. Unlike some degree-holding college graduates, their education does not stop upon receipt of their diploma. As Dr. Nicholas Murray Butler, former President of Columbia University, once put it, "Most men die at twenty-five and are buried at sixty-five."

Vogel continued his self-education over a period of forty years. The diffident, unschooled boy became a well-spoken, gracious man. In the words of Emerson, "An original gentleman—who if manners had not existed, would have invented them." His work obliged him to observe the vagaries of public taste in motion pictures. The surprises, no less than the expected verdicts taught him as it did other pioneers in the industry, much about entertainment. It gave him a sixth sense, an intuitive judgment about a box office attraction, which is the closest one can come to scientific evaluation in an unpredictable field. So even though he had no production experience, he knew better than most what the studio should produce.

He was the natural choice to fill out the four months of Arthur Loew's term and then attempt the reconstruction task on a permanent basis. He, too, was reluctant to undertake the job of heartache and headache, but his life was intertwined with the company. He could not refuse the call from the Board of Directors, composed of his superiors and associates over a period of forty years. Somewhere, too, in the mixed emotions of fear, duty, and loyalty there was an understandable pride in ascending to the presidency of a world-wide organization, in which he had started—if it is possible to put it that way—one step below its lowest rung.

Louis B. Mayer regarded the rise and fall of Presidents with satisfaction. First Schenck, then Arthur Loew, and all within a year. They were toppling even before they were pushed. He must have thought of them as transient French ministers, until he, the strong man, was ready to take over. He had no concern about Joe Vogel, "a nice guy," who would be swept out of the way easily. As for Schenck, he was still holding on to the title of Chairman of the Board, but it was plain to the whole industry that he had lost power. Mayer would complete his execution with special relish.

Mayer's plans were therefore directed to a proxy fight at the next annual stockholders meeting only four months away, in which he would attack Schenck's regime and be restored to power himself. Since the opposition lay virtually prostrate in confusion and disorganization, his strategy board, comprised of brilliant lawyers, corporate accountants, and experts on proxy contests, must have felt that the fight might be won without a contest. The management—no one was too sure who that really was, except for Vogel who had just come on the scene—might be unable to make a reasonable appeal to the stockholders. It was vulnerable to many charges. The greatest motion picture company in the world was in decline. How could the Board of Directors, which had presided over this debacle, defend its record? How could Schenck? How could Vogel, who, though not responsible for the past, would be identified with it?

However, Mayer too was vulnerable. He was now 72 years old, and his final years at the studio had been a failure. His strategists decided to keep him behind the scene until the triumph was assured. This gave rise to an artful plan to use the largest single stockholder of the company, one Joseph Tomlinson, as the spearhead of the drive. A contest, if any was necessary, was to be fought in his name.

Tomlinson was a Canadian. He was President of Consolidated Truck Lines, Ltd., and of a road-building company. He had never had any association with the entertainment world. However, the lure of Hollywood must have been considerable, for he invested three and one-half million dollars in Loew's stock and acquired 180,000 shares. Out of nowhere had appeared the largest single stockholder of the company.

Tomlinson was a huge man about fifty years of age, with a long nose, matted-down hair, and a thick reddish brown mustache. His speech was sharp and unadorned with any nicety. He combined plain gruff talk with amiable good sportsmanship. When he slapped you on the back you could not determine whether you had been attacked or greeted. He could have been transplanted from Canada to Texas and taken root instantly.

Mayer sent an emissary to him. He was Stanley Meyer, a young man, about thirty-five years of age. Meyer had managed theaters for his father, and later with the aid of his uncle, Matty Fox, had achieved some distinction as the producer of the motion picture *Dragnet*. But Mayer must have known him best as the son-in-law of Nate J. Blumberg, at one time President of Universal Pictures Corporation. Whatever the reason for young Meyer becoming Mayer's protégé, he entrusted to him the mission of making an alliance with Tomlinson, who was to spearhead the attack against the company. So there appeared among dramatis personae another strange character. Meyer acted at all times as if he wore chaps. When he talked, he looked down shyly and dug his toe into the imaginary soil like Gary Cooper. His broad face and nose had a handsome Indian cast, except for the blue eyes, which were so light that they were disconcerting. He adopted a modest, almost obeisant manner toward the important men with whom he now came in contact, but he was so conscious of his power that one almost imagined he was carrying a banner with the words "Louis B. Mayer's spokesman."

Tomlinson was flattered and honored to learn that Louis B. Mayer wanted him to become his associate in taking control of the company. His large stockholding had pushed the door slightly ajar so that he could peer into Hollywood's magic palace. Now, suddenly the king had invited him to become his chief minister and share the throne room. In his fondest dreams he could not have imagined such good fortune. He, a Canadian roadbuilder, was to become a great figure in the land of the most beautiful women in the world. He was to preside over the most glamorous enterprise in all industry. Although he could not aspire to the presidency of the company because he knew nothing about the motion picture business, he could be the Chairman of the Board, or perhaps, chief executive at the studio, since Louis B. Mayer would be behind him as advisor. He joined eagerly with Mayer. From that moment, the offensive —in Tomlinson's name—took on disciplined purpose and meaningful direction. Mayer and Tomlinson had stock, money, and experts in all fields, from law to public relations.

The Bylaws of the corporation provided for cumulative voting. This meant that every share of stock could be multiplied for voting purposes by the number of directors who were to be elected. If a stockholder wished, he could cast these cumulated votes for one candidate or divide them among as many as he wished. So, for example, if there were thirteen directors to be elected, Tomlinson's 180,000 shares could be multiplied by thirteen, which would give him 2,340,000 votes to cast in one block. By proper mathematical calculation he could concentrate his votes to assure the election of one or perhaps two directors. If joined in by other large stockholders, the representation could be extended.

The annual stockholders meeting was to take place in February. On December 14, a written ultimation was delivered to President Vogel. It demanded his surrender.

This letter, sent in Tomlinson's name, is a vivid illustration of the type of warfare waged in ousting management.

While the letter was addressed to Vogel, it was written for the consumption of stockholders and the general public. It was therefore a blend of high moral purpose, demagoguery, and solicitude for the poor mulcted stockholder.

It began by announcing a proxy fight:

"Dear Mr. Vogel:

I have come to the conclusion that it is necessary for me to communicate with my fellow stockholders in our mutual interest. Specifically I intend to seek the election of a Board of Directors, truly representative of the stockholders' interest and capable of directing the affairs of the company free from the inherited blight of mismanagement, waste and nepotism, which the present board, whose composition is dominated by employees, perpetuates, and which you, under the present board, are incapable of escaping."

Tomlinson then announced that he "was in control of 250,000 shares of your company, which is approximately 5% of your outstanding capitalization." The translation into cumulative voting was left to the reader.

There followed a demagogic argument that cast a revealing light on the other postures in the letter. It read: "Let me also say that I believe that the hope of not only the United States but the world lies in winning the great struggle through which it is passing in dealing with 'isms' and adverse forces around the world.

"The winning force to do that is the managerial corps of American business, in fact the managerial corps of all business. Nobody can or will do it as much as they. If this group should lose the confidence and support of the American people, all is lost for all of us. Therefore stockholders in American corporations, particularly, are the strongest bulwark to protect and defend what we hold dear. It is this which motivates me in what I have to say."

So spoke the Canadian Tomlinson. If Vogel and his Board didn't get out, they were aiding "isms" and endangering world peace!

This was followed by an illustration of the kind of inflammatory charges that would be made against the management if it didn't haul up a white flag and slink silently away.

"The company has been operated in a way that seems to serve the special interests of the managers, their relatives, their friends, their lackeys. . . ."

The evil relationship is insidious and far-reaching throughout the company and persists. . . . Only a new and sound directorate, uncontaminated by misguided loyalties and habit patterns can hope to cope effectively with the problem of cleaning house."

If the directors had any mind to resist, they were informed that criminal charges might be hurled at them. The letter continued: "Frankly, I feel that the Loew Management is so bad that it threatens all American business in the same way that the infidelity and mismanagement of Sam Insull and Howard Hobson brought about a legislative reaction against all business, and put tremendous handicaps on initiative, opportunities and ambitions of many an American management."

This was real hatchet-swinging. Howard Dietz, a director and head of Advertising and Publicity of the Metro-Goldwyn-Mayer Pictures Corporation (and a gifted lyric and script writer who, together with Arthur Schwartz, had written many of America's popular songs), as well as several other directors, desired to sue for libel. In the meantime they faced charges that would be publicly made, if they did not get out.

"The Loew Company, for years," continued the letter, "until Louis B. Mayer left it, was considered the 'Tiffany' of business." One need not have been perplexed about who, behind the scenes, was responsible for that thought. Once more the attack continued. "Generally speaking, the Loew's management's attitude has been one of 'we are managing this company and we are going to manage it to suit ourselves and our own interests.' The so-called changes which have recently taken place within the last 12 months have not changed anything basically. Some people have shifted around, but have done nothing, because of the factors I mentioned, can do nothing really constructive except to change the background on a scene without changing the act or the play. The same prompters are in the wings and are still maneuvering for their own and unhidden purposes."

There followed a clever effort to align the banking firms with the insurgents. "The influences and power of this cabal have been so strong as to compel banking houses, such as Lehman Brothers and Lazard Freres, who represent hundreds of thousands of shares, to withdraw their partners from the Board of Directors because they could not agree with the policies of management. So long as the Schenck, Moskowitz and Dietz influence remain, you are unable to accomplish the changes expected of you."

The letter concluded by announcing that Tomlinson had retained Benjamin A. Javits (brother of U. S. Senator Jacob Javits of New York) as "my counsel to help me in this fight, if there should be the necessity for one."

In true ultimatum fashion, Vogel was given 48 hours to capitulate: "If by that time [Monday, December 17 by 5 P.M.] you find it inconvenient or if you decline to work for a constructive plan or program with which all can be satisfied, which I believe it is possible to do, then I shall have to proceed to the next step without further delay."

A series of meetings began with counsel and advisers. It was soon discovered that Tomlinson wanted nothing less than complete control of the corporation. All executives of the company were to resign from the Board of Directors, and a new Board was to be organized which would be satisfactory to the Tomlinson group.

Louis B. Mayer was to return as chief factotum and "adviser" to the studio. Tomlinson was to become Chairman of the Board. Stanley Meyer was to be the executive head of the studio in Hollywood or President!

These demands were too severe and were rejected. A livable compromise was sought. Crisis conferences were held every night into the early hours of the morning. Each telephone ring brought a new alarming rumor. Public relations experts acted like intelligence services to the embattled forces, bringing back "inside" information of a concession that might be made, or a biographical tracing of new directors being proposed by the opposition.

The bankers' position was crucial. In proxy contest they would not only control hundreds of thousands of votes, but the prestige of their support could be decisive. Each side sent powerful intermediaries to sound them out. The banks were in an anomalous position. On one hand they opposed the old management of Schenck and Arthur Loew and felt that Vogel was too identified with the old regime. On the other hand they were not enamored with the unknowledgeable Tomlinson, accompanied by the prospect of Louis B. Mayer's return. Nevertheless rumors of pacts between the bankers and the Tomlinson group exploded regularly in the secret meetings that were taking place in hotel suites, law offices, private dining rooms, and other rendezvous. The Tomlinson faction boldly claimed that Lazard Freres and Lehman Brothers had thrown their support to it and that management was doomed if it chose to engage in a proxy fight.

Then occurred one of those strange accidents that so often affect the fate of a battle. While Vogel and his counsel and advisers were meeting late one evening with Tomlinson and Javits, Vogel's secretary announced that Mr. Andre Meyer of Lazard Freres was calling Mr. Tomlinson. The call appeared to confirm the alliance that had been trumpeted by Tomlinson and his counsel for several days. In the atmosphere of tension and attrition, that telephone ring, following a series of disheartening reports of defections, sounded as if the bells of victory were pealing for the opposition. It turned out later that Andre Meyer was simply returning Tomlinson's call and that no significance was to be attached to his action, but the psychological effect of the incident may well have played a part in the subsequent decision.

To Vogel this threat of open warfare at the next stockholders meeting could not have come at a more unfortunate time. It involved nothing less than the complete disruption of his many plans for the rehabilitation and revitalization of the company over whose destiny he had so recently assumed control. Although the numerous charges circulating against the existing directors were irresponsible and baseless, he recognized that the accusations against them would reflect on the company as well as the individuals. Indeed one of the tasks on which he was then engaged was the reconstitution of the Board to make it an effective aid to management.

Vogel had good cause to be suspicious of Tomlinson's motives, and he deeply resented the method of his approach. But he was desperately anxious to avoid a bitter, costly proxy fight at the very moment when all his energies were required for solution of the overwhelming problems facing management. He also recognized that Tomlinson's position as the largest single stockbroker of the corporation, and the size of his financial investment, entitled him to some consideration, however inept he might have been in asserting his position.

He therefore put aside a natural reluctance to negotiate with Tomlinson. What made his decision a particularly valiant one was the fact that he was ready to sacrifice his own pride and self-respect to protect the corporation. Continued discussions finally resulted in a compromise solution under which a new Board of thirteen directors would be constituted composed of objective, high-minded men who would be partial to neither faction. Six of such directors would be suggested by the Tomlinson group, and six by the Vogel group, each approved by the other. A thirteenth neutral director would also be agreed upon in advance.

It was a difficult choice Vogel had to make—either resist at all costs, bringing on an immediate contest, or compromise in the hope that time would buy harmony. If things had worked out well, it was statesmanlike to bide for time to heal the wounds. If they did not, then the compromise was ineffectual appeasement. Often the wisdom of decision rests not on the factors at the moment it is made, but on subsequent events. If successful, we say the executive had vision. If not, he was a visionary.

Still, I know of no higher fortitude than stubbornness in the face of overwhelming odds. The reason victory is sometimes snatched from "impossible" situations, is that crises distort the facts and make them look more lugubrious than they are. The mysterious logic of a strong will can be superior to mathematical computation. The reason, I suspect, is that facts are man-made images of events and can be as distorted as the eye that forms them. Imponderable factors of emotion, health, temporary exhaustion, and surroundings can change the face of truth.

There is an aphorism about a farmer who before sunrise on a cold and misty morning, saw a huge beast on a distant hill. He seized his rifle and walked cautiously toward the ogre to head off an attack on his family. When he got nearer, he was relieved to find that the beast was only a small bear. He approached more confidently and when he was within a few hundred yards the distorting haze had lifted sufficiently so that he could recognize the figure as only that of a man. Lowering his rifle, he walked toward the stranger and discovered he was his brother.

In the course of controversy, anxiety begets sleeplessness, and exhaustion feeds fear and panic. Situations are seen through a haze of hopelessness, and even brotherly faces may appear to be monsters.

The six directors named by Tomlinson were Tomlinson himself, Stanley Meyer, Ray Lawson, a Canadian neighbor and friend of Tomlinson's, and three intimate friends of Louis B. Mayer: Louis Johnson, once his attorney, and former Secretary of Defense, K. T. Keller, former President of the Chrysler Corporation, and Fred F. Florence, Chairman of the Executive Committee of the Republic National Bank of Dallas.

The six directors proposed by the Vogel group were Vogel, George A. Brownell, a partner in the John W. Davis law firm, William A. Parker, chairman of the Board of Incorporated Investors, Inc., John L. Sullivan, once Secretary of the Navy, George L. Killion, President of the American President Lines, Ltd., and Frank Pace, Jr., Executive Vice-President of General Dynamics Corporation and a former Secretary of the Army.

The thirteenth director was Ogden Reid, President and Editor of the New York *Herald Tribune* at that time, and thereafter the United States Ambassador to Israel.

As to the reputation and distinction of these men there could be no doubt. But this overlooked a basic proposition in human nature. One who owes his appointment to an old friend will unwittingly be sympathetic to his grievances and receptive to his suggestions, particularly when that friend, Louis B. Mayer, was a famous figure in the industry of which the director had no knowledge whatsoever.

Also there were opportunities for special pleading. Mayer would have the ear of a Keller, a Johnson, and a Florence and fill it with his enormously persuasive and emotionally charged tirades.

Experience has demonstrated that arbitrators designated by respective contestants, despite their acknowledged integrity, almost always see the justice of their appointer's position. The subtleties of gratitude and loyalty have an unfortunate way of affecting the mind, often without the awareness of the principled man behind the mind. We believe with heart and soul what we want to believe. Fundamentally, this is the essence of persuasion. If one can be made to wish emotionally that a certain result should obtain, he will find any argument appealing which achieves that goal. This is what Judge Benjamin Cardozo referred to as the judicial process—the "instinctive" reaching of a conclusion and thereafter the reasoned process to justify it. I find not only jurors highly susceptible to this approach, but even the most sophisticated Judges. If the moral atmosphere can be created which cries out for remedy, a long-standing precedent may be broken by conservative Judges to right the wrong. That is why I never let my guard down, no matter how firm the legal principle is that I espouse, if the equitable aspect of the case gives me concern, and conversely why I will venture forth boldly on a legally questionable proposition if the facts stir the conscience for relief. We shall see later in this case as good an illustration of this precept as could possibly be imagined.

The great weakness was that in all this galaxy of directors, only Vogel was in the motion picture business. None of the executives who headed the various departments of the vast-flung company had a seat on the Board. It was one thing to remove the former officials, many of whom had thirty and forty years' experience in the industry; it was another to designate as successors, men who had no real experience in an entertainment enterprise.

The annual meeting of the stockholders took place February 28, 1957. Vogel for the first time presided as President. He had been in office only four months. He presented the "harmonious" slate of thirteen directors, and each was declared elected by 4,567,000 votes.

The democratic process in a business enterprise is subject to the same foolishness and wisdom as that in government. The little stockholder has his moment in the limelight. Sometimes he can be embarrassingly searching in the questions he puts to his president. Sometimes he is an exhibitionist who wastes the time of the meeting with demagogic speeches. Two incidents are recorded in the minutes of the meeting which were typical. One provided a telling touch of humor. A stockholder by the name of Heiss questioned the President about his production plans. He was pleased with Vogel's sincere reply. But before he sat down he wished to record a prophecy: "Well, congratulations. I wish you good luck. If you haven't got ulcers now, you will get them later."

Another stockholder by the name of David Bell, who held proxies for 14,000 votes, elicited a statement from Tomlinson which became invaluable in later legal proceedings. Bell began with an expression of good will: "I think management should be complimented on the fact that there was no proxy fight. I also think the opposition who placed some members on the Board are also to be complimented on that score. I wonder if Tomlinson, who had made some public statements in the course of getting these various men on the Board would get up and say something which would help the other stockholders." [Applause]

MR. TOMLINSON: I would be very happy to say a few words. My effort in the first place was to see that the stockholders of this company got a fair break. When it became apparent, in my opinion, that a satisfactory reconciliation could be made and save the company the vast expense and waste which would take place if a proxy fight was carried out, *I was very happy to sit with Mr. Vogel.*

That afternoon Tomlinson called a private caucus of directors and proposed that Vogel be removed as President and Stanley Meyer be designated in his place. How much the defeat of that proposal was due to the reluctance of the new directors to act precipitously without any real facts upon which to base their judgment or to the fact that, under the Bylaws, the President could not be removed except for cause, will probably never be known.

Two days later I entered the picture. Vogel visited me to retain me as special counsel for the corporation.

He had been stunned by Tomlinson's conduct. The compromise he had made in connection with the reorganization of the Board of Directors was in reliance upon the solemn promise that this would bring co-operation and peace. He was eager to get on with the business of the company. There was so much to do. He wanted to put politicking and internal strife behind him and do a job.

He had been least concerned with the introduction of friends of Louis B. Mayer to the Board of Directors. They were fine men and would respond to his good faith, he thought. I was touched by the wholesome sincerity of the man. All his life, he had practiced the idealistic yet practical philosophy of being fair and forthright, and had stimulated reciprocal responses even from sharpshooters. I thought of Lincoln's reply when someone asked him whether he didn't intend, now that he was in power, to destroy his enemies: "Certainly. I will make them my friends."

Vogel had been supremely confident that he could win over Tomlinson, Meyer, and all the rest. He was sure the bankers would respond to his earnestness and achievements. He had done it all his life, and he would do it again. The trouble was that he had never encountered this type of situation before. He was a businessman and clung tenaciously to the theory that honest performance and results would win his critics over to his banner.

I took quick inventory of the situation and found it serious. Even assuming that Vogel's designees held fast, despite the pressure that might be put on them, the opposition had six votes or a majority depending on Reid. The balance of power was so precarious that if one of the "friendly" directors should be unable to attend a meeting, the majority instantly shifted to Tomlinson. Also, the opposition was no longer on the outside. They were within the citadel and, as directors, could engage in harassing tactics which would make it impossible for Vogel to function.

I had a long-standing resolution not to step into the middle of a controversy or litigation which I had not handled from the start. I did not mind undertaking uphill battles no matter how steep if I could deploy the forces from the inception.

I was distressed to find the precarious posture of the case. I had known Vogel for many years. His reputation for integrity was peerless. He had offered himself as President in the darkest hour of his company and now he was fighting a desperate political battle. I could not refuse his earnest plea that I come to his side. Indeed, I voluntarily abandoned my requirement for an advance retainer fee because I did not want to supply Vogel's enemies with additional grievances. I also left the reasonableness of the fee to the discretion of the Board of Directors, depending on the extent of the services and the result obtained. This was not only calculated to disarm the Tomlinson group, but had a humorous aspect too. If I could stave off their plan, the result would be better and the fee more deserved. It reminded me of an occasion when a Nazi group of Christian Fronters (which is what they desecratingly called themselves) was indicted by the Federal Government for subversion. They sought me out to defend them. They had a litigation kitty of $100,000, and offered it to me. I don't know what pixie humor beset me, but I said: "I will accept your retainer on the following condition: You will deposit $100,000 in a bank; if I lose the case, the fee will instantly be turned over to me; if I win, I will receive nothing!

It took a little while for these estimable gentlemen to interpret the proposal correctly. For, despite Bar Association resolutions which make it proper for a lawyer to defend the most heinous murderer or sneaky Communist, I will not represent a man whom I detest. He is entitled to able counsel, and there are many such, but I cannot split my personality or fragment my convictions.

Not all was red in the balance sheet of Vogel's chances. There was first his popularity throughout the motion picture industry. If the struggle could be turned in such a way as to permit this force to be brought into play, an enormous reservoir of good will was available. It could be harnessed like water power.

There was a dedicated corps of executives and employees who had a fervent feeling for the company akin to patriotism for one's country when it is in jeopardy. Chief among these was Benjamin Melniker, general counsel and Vice-President, and later Robert O'Brien, the newly designated Treasurer to succeed Moskowitz.

There was a special public relations expert on the scene, David Karr, and his staff, who provided the skill so necessary to the conflict that was in the offing. Karr, who is now President of Whitney-Fairbanks Company, had written a book on proxy contests, and his professional competence and hardness were badly needed. For in addition to operating as a businessman trying to earn profits for his stockholders, Vogel now had to be a general, beleaguered by guerilla troops who had fought their way into the capital city and threatened to extinguish his peaceful and constructive endeavors.

A short cut to seizing a company is to make life so difficult for its executives that they resign. Tomlinson opened up such a drive against Vogel and his associates. First, he demanded that the corporation provide him, as a director, free of charge, an office on its premises. Vogel assigned to him a large room on the twelfth floor of the Loew offices at 1540 Broadway, New York City.

Tomlinson moved in with three attorneys, and representatives of an outstanding accounting firm. He literally took off his coat and went to work on the management.

Under his authority as a director, Tomlinson demanded immediate delivery to his office of every conceivable corporate report and data covering long periods, sometimes extending to as much as twenty years. These demands included the expense and entertainment accounts of all officers and executives; interoffice correspondence of all kinds, production costs on motion pictures that had lost money; the write-off cost of stories that had never ripened into motion pictures; all contracts with producers, stars, or executives, and records of exercise of options; production and distribution schedules and costs; records of advertising expenditures; television contracts, music-recording contracts, and operation records, and wagonloads of vouchers and documents of every conceivable description.

The departments were suddenly flooded with these written demands. To comply immediately would mean the virtual cessation of corporate business. Many of the documents were in warehouses. Others were needed for daily use. Others were highly confidential, and the head of the department sought approval from his superiors before relinquishing them.

Could legal action be taken to stop these inordinate and unreasonable demands? It could. But for strategic reasons, I advised full and unrestricted compliance. We were in such a bad posture that we could only gain by our opponent's mistakes. The truth was that Tomlinson was not acting, as he would claim, to ferret out wrongdoing, but to harass and interfere with corporate business and tire out management. If we could lead him on, his bad faith might become evident. I noticed, for example, that the headquarters on the twelfth floor was calling for all legal folders of suits that had been brought against the company. A file was called for by name of a baseless litigation by a stockholder twenty years ago, which the company had won. What possible constructive function could such an inquiry serve? Was not the real purpose to read the accusations, even though they had been discredited?

Vogel was in full accord with the strategy of giving Tomlinson everything he requested. "If he can find anything wrong," he said, "I want to know about it too. I'm not responsible for what the prior regime did, and

I don't want to give the impression that I am shielding it. I want everybody to know that I am trying to do the right thing."

The more we complied, the more Tomlinson requested. He could not draw a refusal out of us.

Then the campaign was intensified. If the voluminous papers called for were not delivered immediately, telephone calls were made to the head of the department demanding action. These phone messages were not only unreasonable, but often deliberately rude.

On one occasion, William Parker, a director, happened to be in the general counsel's office, when an arrogant demand was trumpeted across the phone so loudly that he could hear the insult at the other end of the room. He insisted on accompanying Melniker to Tomlinson's office and confronting him with the unwarranted nature of his conduct toward top executives of the company. Parker later submitted an affidavit of this incident in the court proceedings.

Men who had served the company thirty years and more, and had pride in its distinction, were assaulted disrespectfully by an outsider who suddenly had come upon the scene. They were belabored with insult and humiliated by contemptuous treatment. The temptation was irresistible, either to adopt the low road and go "up there and punch him in the nose; who does he think he is talking to," or preserve dignity and resign with the philosophical solace that life wasn't worth such indignities.

I strove to give a different perspective to the situation. The roles of man and mouse were reversed in this case; the man would take the punishment in order to defeat the enemy. Vogel promised them a happier day. They hung on.

Now, however, the third phase of the offensive began. It was even more insidious than the previous ones. Its target was Vogel, himself. It consisted of a letter campaign, addressed to him with copies simultaneously sent to all directors.

From the mass of documents delivered to him, Tomlinson spelled out grievances of all kinds which were the subject matter of these letters. Each letter was designed to sound an alarm which would strike terror not only in the hearts of management, but of all directors who might bear responsibility for the serious derelictions that were set forth.

When this offensive was ready, it was launched—like Montgomery's batteries at El Alamein—on a concentrated time schedule. There was no sporadic fire. For several days, a letter shot was fired regularly each twenty-four hours. Toward the end of the campaign, two letters went out each day.

On the face of them these letters had a sincere businesslike ring. Seemingly they were conservatively stated and solidly based on fact. They gave every appearance of being written in good faith to stave off some disastrous conduct upon which Vogel seemed intent. Their chief purpose was to create a state of alarm over the incompetence, if not, indeed, the bad motives, of the management, and to give fair warning before the corporate assets were dissipated by stupidity and malfeasance. They also put enormous pressure on the directors. Why should they be involved in affairs so fraught with scandal?

I could tell how clever these letters were by my own reaction when I read each day's missile. The impact was enormous. "This is a most serious charge," I thought, "and apparently supported by fact. If it stands up, we must be frank in reply, thanking Tomlinson for bringing the matter to our attention, and promising immediate action." But when we called for explanation from our executives and accountants, we found that we had a perfect answer. Then, it was all we could do to restrain our anger. We merely set forth the facts that disposed of the charge, but once more, our strategy was to hold our real fire. Our six-to-six division of the Board was so precarious that it was still advisable to hoard our ammunition.

Yet, so artfully contrived were these daily letters that each succeeding one gave me a new shock. "This time, they probably have something," I would think, but to my relief, upon inquiry for the facts, the answer was complete and devastating. Nevertheless, the pressure on management and the directors was painful. Suppose you were a director and you received the following letter by registered mail, return receipt requested:

Dear Mr. Vogel:

I understand that you plan to transfer the pre-1949 film library to a Liberian Corporation. . . .

The purpose of this letter is to request that all steps looking toward putting the program into effect promptly be halted. . . .

In my view, the new directors should pass specifically on the question of whether the corporation should incur the risk of placing $60,000,000 worth of assets in a foreign corporation. They should certainly review the decision to enter into this transaction without prior clearance from Internal Revenue, in view of the fact that the consequences could be severe, amounting to an immediate liability of as much as $15,000,000 if the ultimate ruling is adverse. . . .

I am so strongly of the view that no further action should be taken on this matter until the new board has been fully informed of the proposal and the problems which it raises, that I hereby request that you inform me by letter by the end of the current week, what your plans are in this regard.

I am taking the liberty of sending a copy of this letter to the other members of the Board.

Very truly yours,
Joseph Tomlinson

As a director, if you received such a letter, you would have a right to be deeply concerned. The charge was that the corporation might sustain a fifteen-million dollar tax loss by its reckless conduct. A promise had been made that you, as a new director, would have an opportunity to review this matter, particularly since it involved the transfer of sixty million dollars of assets to a foreign corporation (Liberia, of all places). Quite right that Tomlinson should demand of Vogel that he stop trying to rush this transaction through in violation of his promise to submit it to you and the directors.

But what were the facts? We prepared them in the form of a report by general counsel to Vogel, which he sent to Tomlinson and all directors. It contained the following information: For a long time, Alvord and Alvord, outstanding Tax Counsel for the company, had studied the matter of corporate reorganization and the transfer of the pre-1949 library of motion pictures to a Liberian company. Alvord's report had been sent to each director.

At one of the directors' meetings, Tomlinson had demanded to know why the Alvord plan was not moving along faster. It had to be explained to him that a favorable tax ruling from the authorities in California was being awaited, before the motion pictures could be taken out of the state.

Later, another expert tax firm, Olvaney, Eisner and Donnelly, was consulted about the Alvord plan, and approved it. The company was thus assured that the sale of sixty million dollars worth of motion pictures would legally and properly involve a capital gains tax of fifteen million dollars, instead of an income tax of thirty million dollars. There were tax precedents for such a plan, approved by the Government, and Vogel was moving forward to save fifteen million dollars for the corporation.

Only a week before Tomlinson wrote his accusing letter, he and one of his attorneys, Ernest Cuneo, had talked to Melniker about this matter and had been told: "At the last meeting, your position was why wasn't this transaction closed yesterday, and now you want to hold it up." He was assured, nevertheless, that the Liberian transaction would not be consummated until the Board of Directors passed on it at the next meeting.

Vogel sent a covering letter with the report in which he attempted to simplify the facts and give true coloration to Tomlinson's conduct.

It was intended to submit the Liberian matter to the Board at its next meeting before any further action was taken.

You, Mr. Stanley Meyer and your attorney, Mr. Cuneo, were specifically so informed.

Furthermore, your position at the last Board meeting was that we ought to accelerate this transaction.

It is therefore difficult for me to understand the present alarm you have sounded, with copies of your letter to all directors.

Nor can I understand your reference to an immediate tax liability of

$15,000,000, *when you are actually referring to a tax saving which you fear may not be achieved.*

Above all, was it wise for you to set forth in writing a doubt as to the tax situation, which might later be distorted by tax authorities so as to prejudice the corporate interests?

This last sentence was the nub of the matter.

One more illustration of the letter campaign will suffice. Tomlinson charged that the company had purchased a twenty-five per cent interest in a television station for $750,000 and that now he "was astounded to discover" that the television station "is practically bankrupt." So the directors were given the impression that through negligence or chicanery, the company had poured out three quarters of a million dollars to buy some stock in an insolvent company.

Vogel again sent a detailed report of the transaction in reply. It appeared that Minneapolis had four television stations. It was the thirteenth largest market in the United States. Three of the stations would not pay an adequate price for the Loew pictures. The fourth, now called KMGM, because of the importance of the transaction to it, met the price of $1,725,000. However, as part of the payment, the KMGM stockholders wanted Loew's to become affiliated with it by buying twenty-five per cent of the stock for $750,000. Since the price available from the competitors was far less, Loew's felt the deal was acceptable. It took unique precautions, however, in view of the financial weakness of the station, to provide that its payments for the stock were dependent on prior receipt of cash for the films.

On the other hand, with the Metro films, the station might prosper, as others had, and Loew's twenty-five per cent interest would then be very valuable.

Vogel wrote a covering letter to reduce the complicated facts to simple understanding:

1). *We have gotten a better price by about $650,000 from station KMGM than could have been possible from any other station in the area.*

2). *We have acquired a 25% interest in what could be a very valuable property worth several million dollars.*

3). *We have thus far paid out to the KMGM stockholders the sum of $37,500 for our stock interest, and at the same time we have received $82,500 as payment for our pictures.*

4). *The purchase agreement provides that we are to pay for the stock over a period of years. However, if we do not receive our regular license fee from KMGM in any month, we are relieved of our obligations to make our stock payments, and in addition, the full license fee for all our pictures becomes due and payable, unless such default is cured within 21 days.*

5). *The exceptionally large license fee of $1,650,000 plus $75,000 for print costs, sets an excellent precedent for future deals.*

Sincerely,

Jos. R. Vogel

Copies to all directors.

Some time later Vogel met Tomlinson, who ruefully conceded that this deal was a splendid one for the company. But in the meantime, word had been broadcast that Vogel was squandering money buying stock in a collapsing corporation. The directors had to plough through the complexities of the transaction to come out in the light.

Even if Tomlinson were confused or in doubt, why had he not talked to Vogel privately and learned the facts? Good faith surely would have required consultation on these matters before making serious charges and alarming the other directors, especially as Vogel had made it so clear that he was anxious to discover, and correct, anything prejudicial to the interests of the company. But instead, the letters kept streaming out by registered mail with copies to all directors. Shoot first and find out later.

During this letter campaign, Vogel was in Hollywood. He had gone to the studio to cope with the production problem. He had let out Dore Schary, and now proceeded to apply his own standards of showmanship, which he believed could combine artistic integrity with box office appeal. On this very first trip to the Coast, he ordered *Ben-Hur* to be put into production. He knew that the way he wanted it done would cost between twelve and fifteen million dollars, but he considered this less of a gamble than any of the one and two million pictures. He recalled that when Metro first produced *Ben-Hur* in 1934, it was one of twenty-four pictures released that year. Metro was then at the apex of its achievements. Yet, *Ben-Hur* grossed more money than all the other pictures combined. Vogel, while operating the Theatre Company, had repeatedly urged a modern *Ben-Hur*. His pleas were unheeded. Now that he was in charge, he insisted on this venture despite the amazed looks on the faces of his associates at the studio and New York. The company was short of cash and going downhill with huge losses at the studio. How could it risk a fifteen-million dollar investment in one picture?

I had found Vogel conservative and given to understatement in all matters, except one. It was *Ben-Hur*. When I discussed the matter with him, he was uncharacteristically didactic: "I tell you, Lou, *Ben-Hur* will be the greatest picture and the greatest money-maker in the history of entertainment. There is no risk in this venture. It will break every box office record ever made."

Such confidence and enthusiasm carried him through stormy directors' meetings where the cost of *Ben-Hur* provided an inviting target for criticism.

Vogel canceled out a number of Schary productions, even though this involved accepting losses because of the preparation expense previously incurred. He was trying to stave off the making of pictures that did not gross their production cost, not to speak of distribution and advertising expense. At the same time, he cut studio overhead by about two million dollars. All this had to be done with one hand, while with the other, he strove to shore up the sinking morale at the studio.

These were harrowing tasks. They involved the strain of breaking old customs and relationships. Important artists who had been with the company many years, but had been unsuccessful recently, had to be taken off the contract lists. Promotions had to be discriminatingly made, and stimulus given to executives in new posts. Vogel was working day and night at these exacting tasks, made more difficult because of emotional factors in terminating old associations.

While all this was going on, we would telephone him from New York to advise him of the daily letter received from Tomlinson. We all agreed on the necessity for answering each charge within twenty-four hours. There were two reasons for this. First, the allegations must not be permitted to seep in. The letters were so designed that a long lapse to gather the replying data might harden the convictions of the recipients. The second reason was psychological. Every shot must bring an immediate answering barrage. Repeatedly, executive heads of departments worked into the early morning hours to sift reports or communicate with others in Hollywood or in Europe in order that Melniker and I could prepare the answering letter through the rest of the night. But it had to go out within twenty-four hours from the receipt of the charge. If the exact-timed regularity of the attack was to wear us down, our promptness of reply revealed stamina that might discourage the attacker. Also, who knows the inner weakness of the adversary? Perhaps he would find the backfire wearing on *his* nerves? As we went on, this latter possibility became more real. The replies were in each instance completely devastating. How would Tomlinson look to his co-directors after an unwarranted campaign of obstructionism?

Due to our time schedule of reply, we had to call Vogel at all hours, read the accusation, which must have made his heart sink, and then present the facts and covering letter which would be sent. These long telephone sessions became filled with mutual expressions of sympathy. I felt deeply the injustice of haranguing him with these varied complex subject matters (the accuser could pick his spot for attack over the extensive territory of Loew's operations) when he was exhausting himself in the forbidding tasks at the studio. He, on the other hand, was thinking of us. It was three hours earlier at the Coast, and the time there was one in the morning. We bemoaned our fate mutually at the sniping to which we were being subjected while trying to serve the stockholders, but felt better in the camaraderie of suffering. So, the letters came and the answers were made with the regularity of the orbit of the moon.

The remarkable fact that emerged was that Tomlinson could not find a charge that would stick. The expense accounts did not even supply material for a letter. Indeed, we learned that the company owed money to Charles Moskowitz, who had been the favorite target in suits charging nepotism and exploitation of the corporation. Ironically enough, the telephone charges unpaid to him were for calls made from Miami (while he was on vacation) to Tomlinson, to supply data requested of him. The only entertainment expenses that might have been deemed heavy were paid to Louis B. Mayer. Of course, Tomlinson promptly forgot them.

The affairs of the company for a period of at least twenty years had been subjected to X-ray scrutiny by accountant and lawyers, and not a speck of scandal had been found. If it were there, undoubtedly it would have been bugled not only in letter, but in affidavits subsequently filed in court. There just wasn't anything.

I represent industries and companies of all varieties, and I think their executives would thank their lucky stars if a thorough combing of their books and records over many years revealed no more than the Tomlinson investigation. Whatever might be said for the business judgment of the prior regime, it had a right to be proud of its impeccable conduct.

Suddenly, Tomlinson and his staff picked up their belongings and left the twelfth floor, never to return. The campaign of letters dried up the same day. He had run out of material, and the bombs he had launched had turned out to be duds. The psychological pressure had also reversed itself. He was being exposed daily as a mere harasser and obstructionist. Furthermore, the strategy of daily attack required Tomlinson's constant attendance at his investigation headquarters. Tomlinson had a boat waiting in sunny waters; he yearned to be on it. With the disingenuousness which gave him a certain charm, he told me one day that he would be damned if he would spend the spring holed up in 1540 Broadway.

We had survived the blitz. It was the enemy who was worn out in the battle of attrition. Tomlinson left behind him a trail of bad faith. For, if he had really believed that the corporate affairs needed exposure and correction, would he have quit on a Tuesday morning? He had merely waged a campaign of intimidation. It had failed and had left him looking silly and in need of a vacation.

But before we had time to congratulate ourselves, the next drive began.

It was an attempt to obtain control of the Executive Committee of the company. This committee had the power under the Bylaws to conduct the business of the corporation in between directors' meetings. It was the very nerve center of the organization. If the Tomlinson group could obtain a majority on it, the President would be completely stymied and a proxy fight for control of the Board might be unnecessary.

Tomlinson now openly demanded that he be made Chairman of the Executive Committee and that Stanley Meyer and Louis Johnson be designated on it, thus giving him a control of three out of the five members. The Board of Directors had the power to designate this committee, and Tomlinson's demand, therefore, constituted an early test of whether the Board would support management or the insurgents.

The political maneuvering was intense. Distinguished intermediaries were used by both sides to hold the lines tight, or make encroachment on the directors of the other side. Ogden Reid, the thirteenth director, was under particular pressure. If the Board divided six and six, his vote would be decisive. The phones didn't stop ringing as reports of the wavering or firmness of this director or that came through. Conferences were being held constantly, often late at night in hotel rooms, at which directors on opposing sides met with Reid or in other groupings in an effort to swing the tide. The bankers were importuned to throw their weight to one faction or the other. One would have thought a national election was being held. Attention was riveted on votes rather than on corporate business.

The directors' meeting that would decide the composition of the Executive Committee was to take place on March 28, 1957, at 2 P.M. At 4 A.M. of that day, we seemed assured of victory by one vote. Knowledge of the letter campaign and the accompanying personal insults to executives had had its effect. Our public relations experts were meeting threat with threat, and there were stories circulating that I was preparing a conspiracy suit against Tomlinson and whoever aided him in his attempt. At 12 noon, Louis Johnson called me and asked whether Fred Florence and he could have an immediate meeting with Vogel and myself before the meeting began. We met in Vogel's office. We could have peace, we were told. "The sixty-four dollar question," said Johnson quite bluntly, "is: Can Louis B. Mayer come back into the company?"

Florence echoed the thought, indicating the prestige which would accrue to the company from Mayer's great name. Vogel told them about Mayer's record, and rejected the proposal. Acknowledging defeat, Tomlinson withdrew his slate. The directors then designated Vogel, George Killion, Ogden Reid, and Frank Pace. Despite the treatment he had received from Tomlinson, Vogel proposed that he be made the fifth member of the Executive Committee because of his substantial stock interest. Tomlinson declined. Either control, or continued warfare, and warfare it was.

Shortly after this failure to capture the Executive Committee, Vogel began to receive telephone calls and personal reports advising him that word was being spread in all quarters that he was incompetent and unequal to the task of running a huge company like Loew's. These undermining stories were richly garnished with false tales of his ineptitude. Stories appeared in the Press of the dissatisfaction with management in high quarters. The bankers were reported on good authority to feel that Vogel had to be replaced. One of the techniques was to link Vogel with the prior administration, quote from various unproven complaints against it, and create the confusion that these were charges against him.

If the United States wants to discover the fastest jet propulsion, let it learn how to harness rumors. They have wings and fly with incredible speed in all directions. Like radio waves which travel around the world seven times in one second, rumors, particularly if they are evil and skillfully launched (which means they must be told in strict confidence), permeate the very air. A haze of malevolence enveloped management and made it difficult for it to breathe.

We actually yearned for the good old days when we were subjected to the letter campaign. You can come to grips with a specific charge in writing. But how does one combat vilification from anonymous sources? Directors, friends, executives of different companies, and others whose concern was hypocritical, kept advising us of the malicious whispers that were circulating. Often they brought the accompanying news that peace could be bought if Vogel would step out as President and become Chairman of the Board or head of the foreign department, under a contract that would give him financial security, while Louis B. Mayer would return as adviser to the studio, and Tomlinson or Stanley Meyer would become President or executive head of the studio under Mayer's guidance. This was the blueprint for the seizure of the Loew empire. No matter who we talked to, this "solution" was communicated to us. It began to sound like a record. We had only to bid someone good day, when the record was played to us.

Worst of all was the actual obstruction of corporate business. The new era of motion picture production in which valuable "packages" were put together with star, author, and director participating in the profits, intensified the keen competition among the companies for these deals. The lifeblood of production was to acquire an outstanding book, play, or story and attract popular artists into the venture. Such plans were carefully guarded secrets. If word got around that a certain deal was in contemplation, competitors redoubled their efforts to acquire the star whom they desired for another venture, or perhaps for the same one. Also, stars were subject to "advice" and influence from high quarters as to whether a planned production might or might not turn out successfully. In short, secrecy was essential to the successful culmination of deals.

When Vogel submitted his plans for large enterprises to the Executive Committee and to the Board of Directors, he discovered that the deals vanished under his fingers. On many occasions, he was advised in confidence by the executives of other companies or by the stars themselves that word had leaked out about the transaction and that Mayer and others had dissuaded the artist from making it, or that a competitor having been tipped off to the terms, had jumped in and bettered them. I shared Vogel's maddening frustration, but for an additional reason. We could not betray the sources of our information without putting our friends in jeopardy. We knew the facts, but could not prove them.

Meetings of the Board of Directors became the testing ground for the opposing forces, rather than business sessions. One who entered the Board room might have thought he was attending a cabinet meeting at the White House. There sat a former Secretary of Defense, Louis Johnson, a former Secretary of War, Frank Pace, Jr., and a former Secretary of the Navy, John L. Sullivan. In addition, there were distinguished business-men: Keller, former President of the Chrysler Corporation; Killion, President of a large shipping line; Parker, President of a large investment trust; Reid, the publisher of the New York *Herald Tribune*; and Florence, an important banker.

But the sessions of the Board were marked and marred by factional strife. Some members of the Board would hold their own caucuses in the midst of a directors' meeting. A recess would be called for, and a clique would gather in a corner of the room or outside the door to discuss strategy, and then return. Sometimes, the formality of recess was not engaged in. Several directors would simply walk off for a private conference. The so-called Vogel directors (although he had not even met most of them before he designated them) would endeavor to placate the Tom-linson faction. Killion, particularly, was adroit in smoothing over the crises that were constantly arising. The result was that there were little eddies and pools of conferring directors in all parts of the room and in the hall-way while Vogel waited for the meeting to reconvene. The interruptions were sometimes more continuous and cohesive than the meeting.

When Vogel was berated and particularly harassed, I would speak up. On one occasion, Tomlinson proposed that the company hire a new firm of accountants. He suggested the very firm that he had retained when he operated from the twelfth floor during the letter campaign. Vogel was agreeable to the selection of any outstanding accounting firm, his attitude being as always, "We have nothing to hide." But quite rightly he opposed the hiring of a firm that had assisted Tomlinson, however unwittingly, in a drive against the management. Johnson, Keller, Lawson, and Stanley Meyer immediately backed Tomlinson's proposal and roundly chastised Vogel for insinuating that an accounting firm of national reputation was not suitable for the company. I spoke up vigorously against such sophistry. The objection was not to the standing and ability of the firm, but to its association with one of the factions in the corporate strife which made it ineligible to represent the company. Keller was so irritated with my argu-ment that he made a motion to expel me from the room. There was an up-roar, then some private meetings which filled the corridor. The motion was withdrawn. Keller was partially right. A director has the privilege of having his attorney present to advise him except when the Board votes to hold a closed executive session. But the law is that only a director may address the meeting. His attorney may do so only with the consent of the Board.

In any event, there was a compromise achieved by artful intervention. Keller and Johnson could suggest any other accounting firm of distinction, and Vogel would approve. Arthur Andersen & Co. was chosen.

One night, I had a dream. Dr. Vogel was standing over a weak patient, trying to give him a blood transfusion, but his enemies kept knocking the needle out of his hand. At the next directors' meeting, I saw the dream enacted. Vogel had brought a deal with the well-known Hecht-Hill-Lancaster organization to the point of consummation. This was a company formed by the star, Burt Lancaster, and other talents, which had produced a number of hit pictures and achieved an outstanding reputation. This company was most eagerly sought by the studios. To Metro, the Hecht-Hill-Lancaster Company had special value. Not only was it an outstanding production unit of proven potential, but it made available Burt Lancaster to play the part of *Ben-Hur* in Vogel's pet project. Vogel and his knowledgeable associates had worked out an arrangement that they knew would be very advantageous to the company and boost its production prestige. Vogel had negotiated in secrecy. Now the complicated terms were agreed upon, and all that was needed was quick approval by the Board of Directors.

When he explained the proposed contract to the Board, Tomlinson and Stanley Meyer protested vociferously and were supported by Johnson and Keller. The deal involved millions of dollars, and it was easy enough to strike postures of alarm, particularly by the uninformed. It was as if Louis B. Mayer—who was tripping up deals in California, as we had been constantly informed—had stretched his arm into the Board room in New York and blocked Vogel from conducting the business of the company. The argument deteriorated into acrimonious exchanges, and Vogel feared that if the proposal was rejected, or even tabled, that the Hecht-Hill-Lancaster people would be humiliated and prejudiced. He was eager to preserve their good will. So he withdrew the proposed contract from the Board, hoping thereby to quell the storm, prevent the internal strife from leaking out, and close the deal some other day. But Tomlinson had no intention of sitting on his triumph in silence. Word went out that Loew's had turned down the Lancaster deal. Vogel was humiliated and frustrated. Not only had he lost a highly desirable contract, but other producing units and stars shied away from Loew's. Its president was in trouble and could not put through the deals he made.

Vogel had just come back from the Coast where he had shored up sinking morales, risked the demolition of several incipient Schary productions, and lined up a production program, which would attract producers and stars and give momentum once more to the studio. Now, those painfully achieved advances were threatened by this uninformed and unreasonable opposition.

The most poignant newspaper stories I know are those that describe farmers toiling for a year over a crop, nursing and tending it as if it were a precious child, and then standing by helplessly as a cold spell kills it before their very eyes. Vogel must have felt like that.

I had been working out a legal strategy during the fierce skirmishes, only a few of which I have recounted. They were really holding operations. It was obvious that the evenly divided Board, at best, provided us no solid base for attack or defense. Much greater ingenuity and resourcefulness was called for. One step that I was considering was a suit against the obstructing directors for conspiring to injure the company. We were handcuffed by our own desire not to advise the world of the internal feud that was rending the company. Though the trade knew there was some trouble, a suit would blazon the rift to the stockholders and public.

This hovering threat of a conspiracy suit may well have been responsible for a completely unexpected development that delighted as much as it amazed us. One morning I received a transcontinental telephone call from Stanley Meyer. He began by telling me that his father-in-law, Nate Blumberg, former President of Universal Pictures Company, had told him, when I became counsel for Loew's, to confide in me. "Dad," as he called Blumberg, had said flattering things about my integrity and alleged prowess and advised him never to be on the other side of me, and if he ever was in any kind of trouble, to place himself in "Uncle Lou's hands." He continued to call me "Uncle Lou," a family relationship I had never earned, but which, under the circumstances, I was not eager to disown. He proceeded then to tell me how, as a protégé of Mayer, he had joined with Tomlinson in an attempt to drive Vogel and management out of the company so that they could obtain control. He praised Vogel as a fine man and able executive who had been unjustly treated, and expressed his regret at having had any part in such tactics. I heard what I knew was true, but my ears were disbelieving because the words were coming from one of the participants himself. When he was finished and had answered my questions, I said, "Stanley, I appreciate your candor in telling me all this. I hope you don't intend this to be confidential."

"Not at all, Uncle Lou," he replied, "I am telling the truth and I don't care who knows it."

I asked him whether he would be willing to repeat his statement directly to Joe Vogel. He said he would be delighted to do so. I arranged a time late in the afternoon for such a telephone conference. When I told Vogel of the development, he was torn between confidence in me and incredulousness. I asked him, Melniker, and Carleton Skinner (an executive assistant to George Killion) to be at my desk at the appointed hour. If Meyer had had a change of heart and refused to take the call, I would not have blamed my client for believing that the strain of contest had affected me.

But, true to his word, Meyer was waiting for the call at the Van Nuys number he had given me.

I have an executive phone that can act as a loud-speaker so that everyone in the room can hear what the party on the other side is saying and anyone can speak and likewise be heard at the other end of the line. It is a helpful device for conferences. All can participate in the discussion, and it is unnecessary to repeat to one's associates what has been said. I have never used the loud-speaker without first notifying the other side. I consider it improper and a betrayal to do otherwise. For the same reason, I will not have a recording device attached to a telephone or in any other form. I shun such mechanisms like a plague. To those who contend that if the truth is spoken, no harm is done even by a secret recording, the answer is that this is a hypocritical and unsound argument. If one side only knows that a recording is being made, the other may not take the pains to correct a misstatement, or may even for the purpose of persuasion, humor the speaker by treating the subject lightly, in order to get to the more crucial issues. So, one side is stating his position meticulously, the other casually, or not at all. The resulting opportunity for distortion is unlimited. The truth can only be disserved by such an uneven presentation.

Furthermore, not being on guard, the speaker may make derogatory statements about his own client or friends in the course of serving their cause. It is not uncommon for a lawyer to comment on the temper, stubbornness, or even unreasonableness of his client, which requires that a concession be made to him. But when he does so, it is on the implied promise of confidence, so that candor can prevail. To record such embarrassing conversation is not only to violate the confidence, but to set a trap. Truth is neither the issue nor a proper excuse for such dishonorable conduct. To put it plainly, secret recordings give unfair advantage, even though both participants are honest in statement. I find it distressing that their use appears to be increasing. Fortunately, I believe I can detect that a recording is being made by the artificiality of the conversation. When my caller begins to talk like a bad playwright constructing his first act, full of unnatural recitals of past events, when he engages in a detailed review of what had just been said and seeks my confirmation of his accuracy, or when his speech is devoid of all the customary informal short cuts and is precise and dressed up with the self-consciousness of one who is about to have his photograph taken for posterity, my sensitive ear tells me all is not well. Few people are great actors, and it takes more talent than is generally recognized to make a recording unilaterally without self-exposure.

I began my conversation with Stanley Meyer by telling him who was at my desk and that I had my loudspeaker on so that what he said would be heard by all of us. Did he mind? Not at all. I asked him to report what he had told me that morning. He did so unhesitatingly, with embellishments and flourishes which constituted a fascinating confirmation of what we had previously suspected from rumor, or pieced together through imagination, or simply guessed.

Louis B. Mayer had made an alliance with Tomlinson because he was the largest individual stockholder and would give proper representation to the attack. They planned to seize control of the company, but Mayer was to remain behind the scene until victory was assured. Stanley Meyer was a protégé of Mayer's and acted as his secret intermediary. After the compromise that gave them six directors on the Board, they thought the company would just fall into their hands. Stanley Meyer would become President, and Mayer, after a triumphant return, would be an adviser at the studio. Tomlinson would either be Chairman of the Board, or technical head at the studio. The fact that they attained parity on the Board by mere threat of a proxy fight, convinced them that final victory was hours away. That is why immediately after the stockholders' meeting that elected the compromise slate, they called a caucus to remove Vogel and designate Meyer as President. There was some resistance to the unseemly haste of the coup. A little time would put a better face on the expulsion of Vogel. Then one of the lawyers apparently learned that under the Bylaws, the President could not be removed during his term of office except for cause, although all other officers could be thrown out arbitrarily. However, experienced hands knew that if the proper pressure was applied, Vogel would have to quit. Dozens of other Presidents had been unable to stand the gaff of highly developed techniques to make life miserable and unbearable for an official who had no clear control of the Board of Directors. The pressure had then been applied. It was at this point, Meyer said, that he rebelled. He advised Tomlinson against the nasty campaign that had been waged, nor did he approve of the wholesale demands for voluminous records, accompanied by insult and epithet to drive the executives to distraction and resignation. He condemned the letter campaign as dishonest and stupid. He said he had so told Tomlinson, but the latter was convinced that one more push would put him in control of the quarter billion dollar prize. Now, he was pleased to say, Tomlinson had more respect for his judgment.

He regretted particularly that Vogel had been abused. He considered him one of the finest men he had ever met and a wonderful executive. There was no doubt that he should remain at the helm. He disavowed any further aspiration to the presidency, modestly referring to his youth, and making light of his qualifications. He did, however, believe he could be valuable as the head of the new television department or, if Louis Mayer did come back to the studio, as an assistant to him. This was the only intimation of a reward he hoped to reap for offering his friendship to us.

He addressed Vogel directly, saying, "Everyone in the industry knows, Joe, that you're not only a wonderful fellow but that your record as the head of Loew's Theatre organization and your experience in the industry make you the best possible president that any motion picture company could have."

It was an interesting endorsement, considering its source.

He told us that he was "fed up" with Tomlinson's tactics. Vogel was serving the stockholders' interests, and "Dad" had told him to approach Vogel and me and take our guidance. He was, therefore, eager to demonstrate his friendship. That is why he was talking so freely and would be pleased to testify, if necessary, to the truth.

When he concluded, I again thanked him, and Vogel expressed his appreciation. Meyer replied that he was only doing what was right because he wanted to make amends for his own participation in the affair. He offered to repeat what he had said to anyone we wished.

As matters developed, I did not institute a conspiracy suit against the Tomlinson group. Requirements of timing and unexpected developments dictated other strategy. Stanley Meyer must have felt that he had unnecessarily revealed all to buy our good will. Later, when it appeared to him—and with good reason—that Louis Mayer was about to triumph after all, he reverted to his original role. Then it was that we threw his statement in his teeth. Vogel, Melniker, Skinner, and I submitted affidavits in court of what he had told us. Not a word was said in reply denying the statement he had made to us. What a curious episode. One of the enemy crosses our lines because he acknowledges our cause is just. Then, when ultimate victory appears to be on the other side, he retreats to join his comrades. However, he could not take with him the evidence of intrigue which he had so volubly supplied.

At this point an unforeseeable and extraordinary incident occurred which placed us in new jeopardy.

Frank Pace, Jr., recommended to Vogel that the management consultant firm of Robert Heller & Associates be engaged by Loew's to recommend more efficient procedures and review and report on personnel. That company had performed such a task for the War Department when Pace was Secretary of War. Keller was enthusiastic for the proposal because Robert Heller & Associates had reorganized the Chrysler company procedures.

The moment I heard of the suggestion, I was concerned. I saw the possibility, no matter how remote, that the lines of ultimate battle between Tomlinson and Vogel might be altered by outside intervention. If the Heller report were favorable, we would have gained little. We were willing, without it, to stand on Vogel's record of achievements, made despite the backsniping and interference to which he had been subjected. If, on the other hand, the report should criticize Vogel, we would be faced with a neutral judgment for the first time. That would be an impossible obstacle to overcome in the uphill climb we faced.

We stood to lose. We could not gain. Melniker, whose sound judgment was always a source of strength, had precisely the same opinion as I did. It fortified me in believing that I was not merely being swept by a hunch. I pointed out to Vogel my concern over the hiring of Robert Heller & Associates. He thought we should pursue the suggestion since Pace favored it. Would I not please interview Mr. C. R. MacBride, the executive who would be in charge of the Heller investigation?

I met MacBride at my office. He was tall, light, and handsome. He was as impressive in speech and manner as he was imposing in appearance. He explained the nature of his services, the number of men who would be assigned to the task, whom they would interview, and how their report would be sifted and synthesized. I cut through the techniques and candidly stated my concern. This would not be the ordinary task. The corporation was being torn asunder by divisiveness. The directors were men of high standing and considerable influence. One vote could shift the balance of power. There was a campaign against Vogel. I had no qualms about his ability, but I was deeply worried lest in such an inflamed situation, any recommendation might give comfort to our opposition unjustly.

MacBride told me that he had the highest regard for Vogel. Frank Pace and others had spoken in glowing terms of his dedication to the corporate interest, his integrity, and his experience. If necessary he intended to talk to Vogel's opponents and win them over to harmony. He cited illustrations of similar service in other situations. I thanked him for the long interview and immediately went across the street to see Vogel. I told him I was as concerned as ever about hiring the Heller Company. I questioned what MacBride's attitude would be if, as well might happen in our precarious situation, our opponents obtained a majority and constituted management. Would he then consider that his principles required him to support the opposition? It did not appear that the merits of the controversy would carry the day, but rather that management control would determine the recommendation.

Whatever misgivings Melniker and I had, yielded to the reality of the situation. Since Pace and Reid both favored hiring Heller, of what avail would Vogel's resistance be, even if he were ready to make it? He would be outvoted by a clear majority of directors, whose good faith in this matter could not be challenged. Indeed, his opposition might create overtones of fear on his part. So Heller was engaged.

On July 12, 1958, a momentous day in the history of Loew's, the meeting of the Board of Directors was held in Hollywood instead of New York. This had been planned for a long time. It was Vogel's idea that the directors ought to visit the studio and see first hand the magical aspects of the business about which they knew so little; the immense carpenter shop with its technicians who could not only build anything, but make anything look like something else; the miniature department, the enemy of perspective, which could construct a block-long set in reduced scale with such detailed veracity that the rest of the world seemed suddenly to be thyroidally enlarged; the red screen, a mere sheet in front of which actors emoted, but which made it possible to show that very scene in front of the Tower of Pisa, or the Taj Mahal, or the subway entrance at Times Square, as the director wished; the sound studio where plastic surgeons of the larynx gave depth to thin voices and timbre to flat ones, and grafted other voices on to the lips of the beauteous stars not blessed in throat; and where dexterous scissors snipped tape to insert a new note or correct a pronunciation; the lighting department with its infinite variety of new bulbs which gave drama even to a shadow, and constellatory brilliance without the heat which might mar the layers of cream on the star's face; the wardrobe department with its thousands of costumes from caveman's leopard skin with appropriate stone mace, to elaborate velvet and silk regalias of the French Court with wigs of every design, color, and size; with costumes for a thousand Indians differing according to tribe, or for thousands of Confederate soldiers of different ranks, or for Napoleon's bedraggled troops in Moscow, or for the new spaceman's outfit correct to every scientific detail; the prop department which could furnish any room from a kitchen to a dazzling ballroom of any period and of every country; could supply railroad cars of 1890, the original Ford T, or the interior of a new atomic submarine; the sets, where one suddenly came upon Wall Street, and walked down the cavernous blocks reproduced with such fidelity that each towering building was recognizable, but turned out to be cardboard fronts ingeniously stippled and treated to look like marble, stone, granite, aluminum, or copper, even when disbelievingly inspected and touched; and by turning the corner, suddenly emerging on a huge Southern estate with its immense rolling lawns (all artificially laid in plastic material), its colonial house looking regal and yet dilapidated as befits the script; and by walking a few feet to the left coming upon a lake where gigantic wind machines were whipping up the waves, and pouring tons of rain on a foundering ship while dynamos created lightning flashes in a sunny Hollywood day.

Vogel wanted the directors to meet with the magicians who made all this possible, and then to have lunch with the executives, producers, and directors on the lot. Finally, he wanted them to meet the famous stars and watch them perform on the stages of the great plant.

Although doctors tell us that there are only four blood types in the human race, I am sure some day they will discover a fifth, composed of showman's blood. It makes a race apart. Vogel belonged to it, and he believed that if the businessmen on his Board were immersed in the glamour of the enterprise, their blood would change too; their eyes would light up with wonder—and wonder is innocence. Fascination was an ingredient of love, and he hoped these men would learn to share his love for the business.

So the good-will tour to the Coast was carefully planned. After a brief directors' meeting, they would be taken on a grand tour of the studio in special cars and under the most expert guidance. They would lunch in the great commissary with executives on one side of them and actresses bedecked in costume on the other, thus transporting them into different periods of history with only one common ingredient, the breathless beauty of the stars.

Vogel planned to present the Hecht-Hill-Lancaster deal once more to the Board meeting, and obtain its approval. He was still dreaming about *Ben-Hur*. Perhaps in this euphoric atmosphere, he could push it through. It was a rare piece of shrewd handling—but anything for the company he loved.

With this picture in mind Vogel, knowing that I wished to visit my mother in Bethlehem, New Hampshire, did not find it necessary for me to attend the Board of Directors' meeting in Hollywood.

One of the handicaps of having directors who are not in management is that few of them reside near the company's headquarters. To attend a meeting in New York, Killion had to come from San Francisco, Parker from Boston, Keller from Detroit, Tomlinson and Lawson from Canada, Meyer from Van Nuys, California, and Florence from Texas. Only Brownell and Reid were in New York City. It was therefore difficult to convene a meeting that all could attend. Regular Board meetings were supposed to be held on the third Wednesday of each month. Rarely could this be managed. Vogel, always acting in good faith, had freely rearranged meeting dates to accommodate Tomlinson and his group. He realized that the hairline balance on the Board made it necessary for Tomlinson to have his supporters present, and he assisted in making this possible. It was the only fair thing to do. Neither he nor I would countenance taking advantage of the absence of one of the directors to put through an amendment to the Bylaws or in any other way strengthen the position against Tomlinson. On the other hand, Vogel could not afford to take any chances and felt it essential to have "his" directors at the meeting, in order to protect himself.

Well, on July 12, neither Sullivan nor Pace could come to California. The Tomlinson group had a clear majority. Also, they knew I was not going to be there. Finally, Hollywood was the home of Louis B. Mayer. He would be there.

The night preceding the meeting, there were feverish activities in the home of Louis B. Mayer. Tomlinson, Meyer, Keller, Lawson, attorneys, and public relations experts, swarmed in and out. The air was charged with excitement. Rumors like those radio waves were traveling around the world seven times in one second. Vogel was getting warnings by phone and from panicky visitors who rushed to him breathlessly; the Board was going to remove him as President the next day!

I was seated on the porch of our Bethlehem home, flanked on one side by a beautiful apple orchard and on the other by a forest of pine trees. Nothing could be more idyllic. Suddenly the phone breached the peace. My office advised me of the report.

Bethlehem, New Hampshire, is part of the White Mountains. Except for the Burma Hump, it is the most inaccessible place in the world—at least, it seemed so that night. The nearest airport is in Berlin, New Hampshire, and only two motor planes of the Colonial Air Lines take you on limited routes. I could not hire a private plane to the Coast; none would pick me up anywhere in those mountain ranges. I could not even get back to New York quickly. It is a tedious overnight train ride and trains do not run regularly. An automobile dash to New York would take too long for a plane connection to reach California in time for the emergency. If Louis B. Mayer had arranged my isolation, he couldn't have done it better.

I telephoned my partners in New York, and one of them was on a plane to the Coast within sixty-five minutes. I decided to stay put and operate by telephone. It was better than being en route, and completely cut off from events. Also, we were all being swept by the frantic pace of events. Hysteria is the enemy of solution. I would make a virtue of my imprisonment in the hills. It was a good place to be calm and think. I went into the apple orchard, and, like a true philosopher, sat on a hickory bench under the laden boughs and reflected.

Out of my reverie a train of thoughts emerged. Vogel could not be removed except for cause. There was none. Therefore, we could challenge his ouster as illegal. But, wait a minute. Suppose they invented a cause that would reduce the issue to one of judgment, and courts don't interfere with the exercise of a director's judgment, unless his bad faith is established. That would be too difficult to prove. There must be something more solid to cling to. Did not "cause" mean that notification had to be given of charges so that Vogel could defend himself? Of course. The subject of Vogel's removal was not on the agenda. However none was necessary. A Board meeting can take up any business that comes before it. Too bad. Hold it—this isn't a general meeting. It is a special meeting. It had to be if it was held on any other day but the third Wednesday of the month. Notice of a special meeting must set forth the special matters that will be considered. You can't take up anything at a *special* meeting that isn't on the written agenda. No proposal to remove Vogel was on the notice of this special meeting. Excitement was surging through me. I knew that feeling of painful exhilaration when a good idea is about to be born. Hold on. Can't the directors waive a defect in the notice? They have a majority. They'll waive it. The excitement ebbed out of me. It was a false labor pang. No, a majority of directors can waive a defective notice of general meeting, but I think—at a special meeting, all directors must be present before a subject not listed on the notice of meeting may be considered. Sullivan and Pace were absent, therefore the defective notice could not be waived. It was unfair to take up a subject that might have assured the presence of the absent directors. Right. The rationale is there. If this is the law, Vogel not only can refuse to entertain the motion to remove him, he can warn the directors that their illegal conduct will subject them to personal liability. If they are warned in advance and persist in deposing the President, any stockholder can sue them for damages to the corporation. I dashed to the telephone and called my office in New York. It was ten o'clock at night, but I knew a squad would be there. It always was. Unlike Jimmy Walker who used to answer complaints that he didn't attend to City business by saying, "Nonsense, you can see lights in my office for hours after I have gone to sleep," I was accustomed to setting the pace for the "night shift."

I got three attorneys on the conference phone and held forth. I do not believe in assigning a bare legal problem without full explanation of the setting in which it lies. The bane of a large law office is that lawyers sit in their legal cubby holes and are told to research a specific proposition of law, or prepare a bill of particulars, or perform other legal specialties, all in a vacuum. They rarely see the client. They lack the stimulation of the human factor. They do not know all the surrounding facts—and who can tell when an irrelevant fact is transformed by the alchemy of resourcefulness into golden relevance? I arrange for my assistants to sit in at conferences with the client, if possible, from the first moment. I see to it that they have every coloration in the case from the appearance of our witnesses to the personality of opposing counsel. A lawyer engaged in the art of persuasion can no more afford to restrict the materials that he will use than an artist can afford to exclude colors from his palette. So in this spirit, I did not simply assign research of the legal question, "May a Board of Directors at a special meeting, at which several directors are missing, consider a matter not listed on the notice of the meeting?" Rather, I presented the whole course of events about to be consummated in a few hours. I explained the need for a resourceful stopgap to prevent the deposal of the president. After that, we had a battle plan in full readiness. The surprise coup in California had to be thwarted first, or all was lost. I steeled myself for the reactions that I knew were coming, but which I have always encouraged. "If you don't attack me, our adversary will," I said. "Don't be tactful. Punch any holes you can in the idea."

"Well, Mr. Nizer, assuming we find this is so, isn't this a pretty thin technicality?" said one of them.

They must have been surprised by my asperity, but they knew it was not personal. "Technicality?" I remonstrated. "This is no technicality, it is a rule of law based on principle. If you call a special meeting, there must be a reason for it. Otherwise, why not wait a month, or more likely, a few weeks, for the regular meeting? The reason that compels the convening of a special Board meeting should, therefore, be set forth in precise terms. This gives the directors an opportunity to consider the matter in advance, or even consult counsel or experts. If it is urgent enough to summon a special meeting, it is only right that the directors should be informed of the emergency. That is why a notice of a special meeting must set forth the agenda with particularity, whereas a general meeting need not.

"Now, look at the morals of the situation. I call a special meeting to approve, let's say, the Hecht-Hill-Lancaster contract. Two directors don't come. They are willing to leave this matter to the rest of the Board. They see nothing vital in the situation. Then another motion is sprung— one of supreme importance, nothing less than the ousting of the entire management. If the absent directors had known, nothing would have stopped them from attending. Assume their votes would have been for management. Can they be lured by silence into non-attendance? Is not the rule of law we are discussing, a basic protection of corporate morality? Is it not a highly conceived aid of fair play and justice? It is the Tomlinson faction that is hypertechnical. They are taking advantage of the accidental absence of two directors to achieve a purpose not envisioned by the stockholders. We are asserting a protective rule of law to prevent their aggrandizement."

So I went on. I believe I get more out of developing the facts and arguments for my associates than they do. It is a process of self-persuasion which gives substance as well as form to a naked idea. Sometimes, if the logical syllogism breaks down during my recital, I will interrupt myself with a criticism, and my associates are thereby made aware of the testing process of my recital. I am not merely informing them, I am challenging myself. "Check me on the law," I concluded, "I'll take care of the morals."

The phone rang every few minutes with the latest from California. The rumors were tripping over each other in haste and piling up. Mayer is going to appear personally at the meeting and take over. . . . Noah Dietrich is now lined up as the new President. . . . It may be Sam Briskin. . . . Tex McCrary is in Hollywood. He is slated to replace Karr. . . . All top executives are going to be out. . . . Melniker is out. . . . The Nizer firm will be discharged immediately. The ominous recurrent theme rumbling underneath the funeral music was always the same; you can still have peace if Louis B. Mayer becomes adviser to the studio and Vogel steps down from the presidency, while Tomlinson and Meyer move up into key posts. We knew the melody and we knew the simple lyric—"You can have peace if you surrender." Only now I imagined I could hear the new stanza:

> You have no choice in this mess,
> We'll throw you out if you don't say yes.

When California got off the wire, New York was able to squeeze in. The legal report was perfect. No motion to remove Vogel could legitimately be made, majority or no majority. As President, he had the right to declare such a motion out of order on the ground that it had not been scheduled for consideration in the notice of the special meeting. Furthermore, this defect in the notice could not be waived or corrected at the meeting, unless *all* directors were present. Even if óne director were absent, the defect was fatal. The motion would have to wait until all could be notified. If the directors acted illegally and deposed the President, the resulting paralysis of the corporation could cause huge damages, perhaps millions of dollars. A director who violated the law deliberately would lose the immunity customarily conferred on him when he acts in good faith. He would act at his peril in voting Vogel out improperly. He could be personally liable for damages. The legal authorities were clear. The decisions of the Courts in analogous cases were read to me over the phone. There was no doubt we had a valid position.

A statement was prepared for Vogel to read declaring any motion to remove him illegal. I foresaw the possibility that Melniker might be excluded from the meeting. Vogel would be on his own. I feared only one possibility in this desperate holding action—that he would yield to some compromise, perhaps proposed by one of the friendly directors. My heart went out to him for the ordeal he was to face the next day. Having fully explained the rule of law our opponents had overlooked, I gave him a narrow track to ride on and implored, commanded, and begged him not to get off that track, no matter what happened: "We can't foresee all contingencies. But whatever they are, stick to your guns. Do not recognize any motion to remove you, or even to table such a motion. The moment you deviate from this position, Joe, you waive the defective notice. Then, if they renew the motion, you are trapped. So don't recognize any business that is not scheduled on the notice of the special meeting. Don't hesitate to remind the directors that they act at their own risk if they proceed against your ruling. Tell them counsel have so informed you and you are giving them fair notice. If someone takes over the meeting by force, simply repeat your statement that you declare his action out of order and hold on to your gavel."

Though only a few hours were left of the night, the next day came agonizingly slowly. When it came, we learned that we had underestimated the enemy. Despite all our preparation, we were struck a surprise blow of such devastating force that it blew Vogel, the entire management, and me a mile high in the air.

There is an old saying, invented no doubt by assassins who did not want their careers foreshortened, that when you shoot at the king, be sure you kill him. This rule is true in corporate struggles for control. When the move to depose management is finally taken it is usually fatal if it falters.

After a late night session, Tomlinson, Meyer, and their associates, were still meeting continuously the next day. None of them showed up for the tour of the studio. Their absence could be disguised for a while during the world tour taken within the 197 acres of studio sets, but when the special luncheon, attended by executives and artists took place, six of the eleven seats at the table were vacant. The empty seats looked like Grand Canyons. Aside from the discourtesy, they were eloquent announcements of the internecine warfare that was raging. The producers and stars had also heard rumors of the imminent putsch, and while they considered it good manners to pretend ignorance of the family quarrel, which the head of the house was eager to hide, they now shared Vogel's embarrassment. The strife was too evident. Show people are always depressed when the audience is thin, but the slight is not personal. In this instance, it was. A pall fell over the day's program. Vogel had been confident that the shimmering beauty and wonder of the studio would soften the hardest heart. He was a businessman himself, but there were other values than accountants' columns, and in show business profits are derived from dreams more than from drives. Perhaps the directors would be touched with the magic of the enterprise to a new understanding that imagination and emotion are not the enemies of financial success. Now he had come face to face with the realization that his opponents lived in another world. He could not even communicate with them.

The studio personnel, from top executive and star to ordinary employees, held a secret caucus of their own. They decided to drop the pretense of their ignorance. If it was war, they wanted to enlist. They designated a committee of the most influential producers and artists to visit Vogel immediately. A touching scene followed. They told Vogel they knew of the plot to have Louis B. Mayer returned to the studio. The despot who formerly ruled was disliked by almost all personnel. Morale would be shattered. There would be wholesale resignations. Vogel knew, as they told him, that those who addressed him were not only independent in wealth and fame, but would be eagerly sought by other studios at increased income. But they had been with Metro all their artistic years. Like Vogel, they loved the company and wanted to save it from Mayer's spite, Tomlinson's acquisitive instincts, and Meyer's ambition. Since Vogel had taken over, the studio, which had lain prostrate, had sat up and lost its anemic look. The transfusions of new production plans by a man with forty years' knowledge of this particular patient's vitality, had created a new morale. Now they saw the whole structure threatened. They wanted Vogel's permission to attend the directors' meeting that was about to take place and plead with the Board not to destroy the company; to permit the reconstruction to continue, so that Metro once more would be the greatest motion picture organization in the world; to tell the directors what Vogel meant to the company. He was one of them, and there could be harmony and progress. They would implore the Board unashamedly not to destroy the great company they loved. Emotion swept the meeting. One of the producers began to cry; Vogel barely controlled himself from shedding tears, too. But he rejected the proposal, while expressing his gratitude. The directors might misunderstand such a visit and believe it was organized or stimulated by him. Perhaps, too, he had concluded that the Tomlinson group was impervious to sentiment, and appeals to relent would be interpreted as weakness.

The directors assembled for the Board meeting. Louis Johnson, bald-headed and sallow-faced, was to be the leader of the Tomlinson group. As a lawyer and consummate political figure, toughened in battle, he had the courage, calm, and bluntness for the task. Keller was rough and powerful; he could run over the opposition with anger and assertiveness. Tomlinson hid his nervousness with airiness. The moment had come to finish the campaign he had waged. Meyer was happy to be with the titans. He would not speak, but great rewards were in store for him. His own associates didn't know that when he thought a counteroffensive was about to be waged, he had called the opposition and begged off. Lawson was dignified but uncomfortable, serving his neighbor, Tomlinson, who had placed him on the Board. Florence was beholden to his friend, Louis B. Mayer, but always was troubled with the whole affair.

On the other side of the table sat Killion, shrewd and charming, unhappy over the attack that was coming. He had been lured with proffers of the Presidency during a time when the survival of the old regime was in the balance. But character had made his choice easy. He had preferred to go down with the ship captained by Vogel rather than traffic with his opponents. Now he was exhilarated by the opportunity to match wits with Johnson, whom he cordially disliked. William Parker, the Boston-bred gentleman, with a fine head, from his distinguished gray hair to his handsome, sensitive features, was slowly soft-spoken, but inwardly he burned with indignation at the crude tactics of the adversaries. Integrity and loyalty made him a tower of strength to Vogel. Brownell, a distinguished lawyer, whose firm had represented Loew's for many years, was sympathetic to Vogel, but worried about being involved in a bitter proxy contest. Ogden Reid, only thirty-three years old, darkly handsome, with a fine voice, was still an enigmatic figure. He appeared to be doing his best as the "deciding vote" to consult with both sides and bring peace.

At the head of the table sat Vogel, facing the worst hour of his life. He was particularly pent-up because he had been subjected to the most ominous rumors, the emotional plea of his studio comrades and the burden of carrying out legal instructions.

As we had foreseen, the first move was to declare an executive session and ask Melniker to leave the room. Vogel proposed the Hecht-Hill-Lancaster deal again, pleading for its importance and value to the Company. He explained that a star like Burt Lancaster would enhance the *Ben-Hur* production immeasurably, and that conservative as he was in prediction, that picture might gross thirty million dollars! If the contract was not going to be approved by the Board, he would like to withdraw it and not have it put to a vote. He owed this to the Hill company.

Tomlinson and Johnson with some show of heat advised that they would oppose the deal. Meyer and Keller joined in. It was evident the majority at that meeting would kill the deal. Vogel withdrew the proposal. The defeat was swift and sharp.

At various meetings since Heller & Associates had been engaged, MacBride made an interim report of progress. He had supported Vogel in his reforms and aided him in personal problems. He reflected Vogel's earnestness in building the company. So the next order of business was another interim report. Vogel called MacBride into the room. He made his recommendations orally. He suggested a replacement for Howard Dietz, head of the Advertising and Publicity Department, and also for Charles Reagan, head of the Sales Department. He reported that the Treasurer, Charles Moskowitz, had already been asked to retire and that, in view of the outstanding qualifications of Robert O'Brien, he approved Vogel's recommendation of O'Brien to replace him.

Reid asked MacBride whom he would recommend to head the Sales Department, and he replied Richard Harper, who was then assisting in the Television Department. Reid urged that David Karr's services as Public Relations Counsel be terminated and asked MacBride whether he had a replacement in mind. He replied that he recommended that Tex McCrary of McCrary and Finkelstein, be engaged in his place. Mac-Bride further recommended that Orton Hicks be made head of the new Planning and Research Division, and George Murphy, assistant to the President. Then, without any warning, came the great explosion. Mac-Bride recommended that Vogel be replaced as President!

This was like a prearranged signal for an all-out attack. Tomlinson insulted Vogel by accusing him of having done nothing since he came into office to get rid of the laggards and incompetents. Lawson wanted to know from Vogel where he had spent his time, on the Coast or in New York. Johnson asked whether Tex McCrary had a press release ready concerning this meeting. It turned out that McCrary was waiting in the outer room with a fully prepared statement in his pocket.

Killion was the first to recover in this mad rush of events. He asked who McCrary was and by what authority he was going to issue a release. He praised Karr and said that the Board had not yet approved MacBride's recommendations, and furthermore he thought the Heller report should be in writing so that it could be studied.

Johnson demanded that the Board act immediately on MacBride's oral report, particularly in approving the recommendation to replace the President. The shock of MacBride's report, the cumulative surprise of recommendations ousting all other executives and designating specific replacements—including McCrary with a press release ready to announce his demise—overwhelmed Vogel. He could barely catch his breath.

Killion and Parker, equally stunned, recovered sufficiently to ask for a recess, which was granted. It must have appeared to the opposition that

Vogel and his few supporters saw the handwriting on the wall. The Mac-Bride recommendation had provided the perfect "cause" for removal, and a clear majority was ready to enforce it. "Give them a chance to surrender," they must have thought. If they want a face-saving gesture now, we'll still supply it. Let Vogel accept the terms he knows so well. Let him "move up" to the Chairmanship of the Board. Louis B. Mayer will return as adviser to the studio; Tomlinson and Meyer will divide the offices between them. Vogel can profit. He will receive financial security, and he need not suffer the indignity of being thrown out of office. The official statement will skillfully present the matter as a harmony plan—just like the last one—for the benefit of the corporation.

While the Tomlinson group was awaiting an invitation for a conference, Vogel met with Killion, Parker, and Melniker. Killion advised getting time by any resourceful device possible. Even if only forty-eight hours could be gained, Vogel would have a chance to meet with me and regroup our forces. He suggested entering into negotations which would delay the vote. Parker, too, felt that if Vogel could escape that meeting still President, there would be some opportunity to maneuver.

But they had a new President on their hands already, although they didn't know it. His name was Vogel, but he was not the same man. MacBride, Tomlinson, and his cohorts had finally stirred Vogel to abandon the precept by which he had guided his entire life—if you are fair and decent, you will be treated fairly. He need no longer submerge his instinct to fight because of the corporate interest. The two had merged. The corporation's welfare now demanded that he assert his prerogatives. There was a prepared legal position upon which to fall back. "They can't throw me out," he announced. "If they do, we'll sue them for every cent they have and protect the corporate interest at all costs. I don't want any conference with them. I am going to fight."

In his earlier days Vogel had been somewhat of a boxer. As a theater manager in tough neighborhoods he had flattened more than one roughneck with a single punch. Now he smacked a fist against his palm with such force that it made a resounding noise. It was a gesture we were to see often thereafter. I always imagined it was a physical release from his frustration as the struggle became more desperate. In his mind's eye, Tomlinson's jaw must have been where his palm was, and Tomlinson toppled over each time.

Vogel insisted on reconvening the meeting without further ado. The Tomlinson group was taken aback. They were even more surprised when Vogel with no trace of his hesitant, kindly manner, as if he apologized for presiding over so august a body, but with a firm angry voice, read the statement I had prepared: "The notice of the meeting pursuant to which this meeting is held indicated very clearly that this is a special meeting of this Board.

"It is perfectly clear, I have been so advised by counsel, that this being such a meeting, no extraordinary action can be undertaken by this Board except for routine and ordinary business, particularly in view of the fact that we do not have a full Board present.

"All those matters which were specifically listed in the agenda for this meeting may properly come before this Board at this meeting.

"I must, therefore, rule that any matter not on the agenda is out of order on the ground that it is not authorized by the Charter or Bylaws and such procedure would be contrary to settled law.

"In my capacity as President of this corporation and as presiding officer of this meeting, I must strongly inform you that I have been informed by all counsel representing this corporation, on the basis of their careful research and considered opinions, that if this Board should persist in considering an action upon such a matter outside the agenda, that it would be taking an action illegal in every respect. You cannot attempt in this illegal manner at this special meeting, and in the absence of a full Board being present, to take any such action.

"I am President of this corporation and I have been vested with authority to protect the stockholders of this company. I expect fully to discharge the responsibilities of my office and my obligation to the stockholders and I shall expect you gentlemen, as directors, to conduct yourself with proper regard for ordinary procedure and the requirements of the law."

Vogel had defied them. Now it was their turn to be stunned—apparently we had learned of the attack and prepared a defense to block it. It was a technicality—sure enough, but the stakes were too high to make a mistake. Vogel's ouster must be legal. Furthermore, Reid and Florence particularly would have no part of the immediate removal. It was the Tomlinson group who now called for a recess.

They found a justification for yielding. They now had the Heller report recommending Vogel's replacement. A majority on the Board seemed assured even if all directors were present. Would Pace, for example, reject the recommendation of the consultant firm he had brought into the company? Even Reid and Brownell could not very well ignore a report from the most reputable source. Why take risks because of two weeks' delay? Then the next regular meeting would take place and the technicality that was thwarting them now would have been bypassed. It was they who sought a way out. They welcomed Brownell's face-saving suggestion to have the Board appoint a committee to study the Heller recommendations and report back at the next regular meeting. But Vogel was implacable. When Brownell moved for the appointment of such a committee and Johnson seconded it, he ruled it out of order.

There was another recess. It began to look like the good old days when miniature directors' meetings were being held all over the place. Now Brownell pleaded with Vogel that his motion was reasonable and not injurious to him. Killion saw its advantage. It gave time—precious time. But Vogel adamantly refused to yield an inch. The plan had worked. The opposition, with a clear majority in hand, was afraid to consummate the putsch. They had lost the element of surprise.

After the whirling conferences had made everybody dizzy, Brownell reported that it was the unanimous desire of the directors to keep Vogel with the company, but to strengthen the executive department. Therefore he would press his motion to appoint a committee to study and report on the Heller recommendations. Johnson seconded the motion. Whatever this ambiguous statement meant (and it was later the subject of violent contradictions in court, Tomlinson claiming that all directors had agreed that Vogel should be replaced), Vogel was riding that single track. He declared that the subject matter was not on the agenda for the special meeting and therefore was out of order. He was gaining strength as the opposition floundered. The process of attack had reversed itself. It was an early object lesson in the advantage of leadership.

Johnson was so upset by the turn of events that he lost his head, a rare act for him. There he was with a clear majority and the best conceivable "cause" for removing management, but he was stymied by a preposterous technicality about a notice of a special meeting, and even Meyer and Tomlinson were amenable to delay. Now that they were willing to yield and study the report until the next meeting, Vogel would not even recognize that motion. Who had the majority here anyhow? Who was boss? How could Vogel, instead of collapsing, lay down the law to them? It was enough to drive a man mad. Johnson announced that if Vogel didn't recognize the motion, he would, and take a vote. On what theory this could be done, even Johnson could never explain. Nor could his many distinguished counsel. We had goaded them into a preposterous position —and all because they were eager to achieve a delay of the very matter they had come to execute.

Vogel now had a recording too. He played it again: "I declare your motion out of order and will hold you responsible for any illegal action you take. . . ."

Johnson usurped the function of Chairman and took a vote. He declared that there was no opposition and that the motion to study the Heller report was unanimously passed. No one had talked up. Killion and Parker smilingly realized that Vogel was having his cake and eating it too. They were delighted to have the Heller report sidetracked until the next meeting and so they didn't vote against the motion. On the other hand, they knew the meaning of Vogel's rejection of the procedure. When Vogel played his record again, Johnson, still acting as Chairman, unauthorizedly, asked for the composition of the committee. Keller proposed Reid, Pace, Tomlinson, and Johnson. Johnson called for a vote and announced that there was no opposition, the President not voting, and that the committee had been designated. Vogel, putting the needle back on the record, ruled the motion and entire action out of order.

He declared that he had not recognized the committee and that it had been illegally designated. Tomlinson, Johnson, Keller, and Meyer must have been thoroughly sick of the tune by this time. When the meeting adjourned, Vogel walked out of the room, still President.

We had no time to congratulate one another on the miraculous escape. The next meeting was a short way off and we could be sure there would be no technical defects to save us again. But we were ready with our plan and Vogel ordered it put into effect. The Bylaws gave the President the "power to call special meetings of the stockholders for any purpose." We were not going to await the next directors' meeting. If Tomlinson and Johnson thought we were like the heroes of a Greek drama who, knowing their fate, moved resolutely toward it, they had mistaken our instinct for survival. We were determined to shift the scene of the next act. It would not be in the confines of a Board room, but in the open spaces where resided 26,000 stockholders. We would appeal to them.

This required a public announcement of the quarrel. Vogel no longer had any inhibitions about making it. Indeed, where formerly he always held in reserve the possibility of *rapprochement* and therefore insisted on restraint, now he was boiling with anger and was the most aggressive in our group. The form of the announcement was important. Like an opening statement by counsel in court, it could create favorable momentum. How we needed it. The Heller report weighed heavily on our thoughts. We would have to overcome it and turn the contest back to one between Tomlinson and management. This required boldness as well as dignity. Most advisers thought the statement should be limited to the Tomlinson group and not mention Louis B. Mayer. He was still a powerful figure. Why take him on? Why force him into the battle? Give him a chance to retreat if he should choose not to be involved in a prolonged contest. Also, the bankers might be displeased by a rabid press release. So it went. One can summon up cogent arguments for most positions.

Vogel urged the most vigorous offensive possible. Name Mayer; make him the chief actor of the piece as he is, and Tomlinson and the others his puppets. It is the truth and will carry conviction. There is a psychological principle that your stature is measured by that of your opponent. If we picked the lesser figures we would shrink in size. More important, we would lose the stance of confidence which an audacious challenge to Louis B. Mayer would create. No one had dared tackle him before in the public arena. Vogel would have to establish his own new image as a leader in the public mind if we were to attract the stockholders to our banner. For similar psychological reasons we adopted another daring strategy. Let us ask the stockholders to remove Tomlinson and Meyer from the Board because of their conduct.

Until three thirty in the morning Vogel, Melniker, Karr, Dietz, and I prepared the statement that Vogel would issue announcing the attack. It stunned the financial world and delighted the motion picture world. To Vogel's surprise, it made him the industry's hero. No one had thought that he could stand up to the forces that were moving to crush him. The odds against him were overwhelming and, besides, he was "too good" a man to put up a struggle. With trepidation but resignation, the industry, and Hollywood in particular, expected Vogel to be swept aside as the titans Nicholas M. Schenck and Arthur Loew had been swept aside by the irresistible coalition of financial forces. Though many felt anguish over the thought, they accepted the inevitablity of the great Loew's being taken over by interests foreign to the business—all except Mayer, who would have his revenge and his final triumph, which almost all begrudged him. In this moment of despair over the demise of the industry's greatest company, there came an announcement. To everyone's astonishment it was not a dressed-up declaration that Vogel had made another "compromise" that would ease him out of the company and surrender it. It sounded like a thousand trumpet calls to battle. Vogel defied the unconquerable enemy. He put the finger on Mayer as the secret conspirator and challenged him to come out in the open and fight. He told the public the whole story. He had a plan of battle. He was determined; he was unafraid. Loew's might be saved after all. This was the chief reason for the emotional reaction in the industry, and among a good part of the public.

None of us evaluated sufficiently the impact of Vogel's announcement. We believed it was the proper, bold strategy, necessitated by our distressful position, but we had not anticipated the adulatory reaction that heartened us and pointed the way to untapped reservoirs of available support. What was in Vogel's announcement that had struck so deep a chord?

It began with a simple declaration of objective, putting the leading actors immediately into focus: "On behalf of Loew's Inc. I am calling the stockholders into a special meeting September 12th to remove Joseph Tomlinson of Canada and his associate Stanley Meyer from the Board of Directors. Tomlinson and Meyer with the constant guidance of Louis B. Mayer have been actively attempting to seize control of this great public company and against the interests of the stockholders. The stockholders and the entire motion picture industry are well aware of Mayer's record when he was in supreme command at the studio. During his term of 27 years he received over twenty million dollars in compensation. In the last three years of Mayer's sole authority as the studio's head, in 1947, 1948, and 1949 the pictures released lost about nine million dollars. This is the man who at the age 72 is attempting to recapture his position through the Tomlinson-Meyer machinations."

After outlining the serious repercussions upon the corporation, the proposed solution was set forth: "At the special meeting which is being called, the stockholders will also be asked to enlarge the Board from 13 to 19 seats, and to fill the new and vacant posts so that an effective working majority of independent directors can be given to management. A full slate of candidates of the highest standing in their respective fields will be presented."

This was our plan to get out of the strait jacket where one absent director turned management into a minority, or where an adverse view of one of the friendly directors or of the "neutral" director frustrated the President's program. How could any management continue to function always perched on the edge of a cliff, fearful that it might be pushed over at any time?

The statement set forth the proposals for peace repeatedly offered by Mayer, Tomlinson, and Meyer and branded them as an ultimatum to surrender. Then there was set forth for the first time to public gaze a full revelation of the tactics employed against Vogel. The public was told what had really been going on behind the outer façade of normal operations. Vogel described how he had "launched a thorough-going program to bring the company back to its former eminence. Housecleaning was the order of the day and I took action on many matters. . . . I speeded our television licensing and created an organization at the studio to produce directly for TV. I established a policy of making all purchases through competitive bidding. Our staff worked round the clock seven days a week to accomplish the important things that had to be done. I shall report in detail on the progress of our management despite harassment, and I shall be frank and say much more could have been done if I had not been obstructed."

The statement closed with an introspective observation and an appeal not to Mayer or Tomlinson, but to the Loew's family of employees. "For a long time I remained silent. This was due to my desire not to expose our internal quarrels to public gaze lest this injure our company. Such forbearance was mistaken for weakness. As often is the case, it accelerated new attacks in the hope that one more blow might wear down the management, cause resignation of Board members, and that our company might fall into the hands of the attackers. When it became clear that more injury would be done to our company by paralysis than from exposure, I determined to submit the facts to our stockholders.

"In the meantime I appeal to all artists, executives, and employees to perform their duties enthusiastically. Ours is a great company. I shall take all necessary steps to protect the stockholders' interests. You and management represent the only knowledgeable pool of manpower in this situation.

"When the stockholders have spoken, we will be able together, and with added executive and artistic power, to go forward unhampered by internal strife."

But our opponents had no intention of permitting the stockholders to speak. Certainly not until the year was up and they were in complete control. They weren't going to sit by blithely and watch us construct an escape hatch called a special stockholders' meeting. They had a plan of their own.

Those who cheered Vogel did not know about the Heller report. It was still a private skeleton in our closet. As long as we could lance with Mayer and associates, we had a moral position. But how could we contest with Heller and Associates? The accusations of the Tomlinson group were obviously colored by partisanship, but the Heller firm had a national reputation for integrity and impartiality. What would a stockholder think of an adverse recommendation from this impressive source?

We had hoped against hope that the oral report made by MacBride at the July 12 meeting might not be his final word. But on July 25 MacBride sent his written report to all the directors. Its first recommendation was: "Mr. Joseph Vogel should be relieved of his responsibility as President and Chief Executive officer of the corporation. The recommended replacement is Mr. Samuel Briskin."

It further recommended that Mr. Louis B. Mayer be elected Chairman of the Board, and Stanley Meyer, assistant to the President, but "assigned full time to work with Mr. Mayer at the studio."

As to counsel: "Mr. Benjamin Melniker should be relieved of his duties of Vice-President as soon as a qualified replacement can be found. The firm of Phillips, Nizer, Benjamin and Krim should be discharged as counsel for the corporation as soon as a qualified replacement can be found."

MacBride also recommended that the general sales manager, Charles Reagan, should be replaced by Richard Harper; Price, Waterhouse & Co. should replace Arthur Anderson & Co. as the firm's accountants; and Howard Dietz should be replaced as Vice-President in charge of Advertising and Publicity.

As to Public Relations Counsel, the arrangement with David Karr should be terminated and the firm of Tex McCrary, Inc., retained.

It was the sober opinion among our inner group that the Heller report seriously endangered our position in the proxy battle. Its eminent source would attract the stockbrokers who controlled tens of thousands of proxies of their clients. Worst of all, in any court contest our moral position on which I leaned so heavily was completely negated. A Judge might look with jaundiced eye on the contentions of outsiders trying to fight their way into a company, but it was bound to be impressed with a report issued by a consulting firm that had reorganized the War Department for the United States, the United States Steel Corporation, and other great enterprises, and had been brought into Loew's by the very management it found it necessary to condemn.

Inertia breeds despair. I find that action, even if not too well conceived, at least stimulates hope. We were not going to sit on our haunches and let the Heller report run riot over us. On July 26, when one of the directors read MacBride's recommendations to me, I called a conference to review the new threat which hung like a sword over our heads. We asked MacBride to meet with us. Perhaps we could learn enough about the developments to guide us in overcoming them. Fortunately, he was in the city and we had an immediate interview. I threw a hundred questions at him. He recommended that Briskin replace Vogel as President. Had he ever met Briskin? He admitted he had not, nor had anybody in Heller Associates. He considered Briskin a temporary stopgap appointment.

This answer was filled with such promise that I decided to come back to it much later, when I had built an enclosure around it.

When I pointed out Vogel's achievements as chief of the Theatre department, which had earned $75,000,000 over a ten-year period, and his recent accomplishments despite internal corporate handicaps, he readily conceded Vogel's qualifications. He even volunteered that Samuel Goldwyn, and many others to whom he had talked, thought Vogel was a wonderful man and a very able businessman.

Then why did he recommend his removal? Because Vogel was unable to unite the Board of Directors. The corporation had to have a Board which worked together with the President if it was to function properly. I argued that this might be the fault of some of the directors rather than the President. I used a homely analogy. "Suppose a marauder enters my house and wishes to attack my wife and me. Who is to be thrown out, the marauder or those whom he threatens?" MacBride rejected the analogy. The corporation must have peace, he argued, and unless the management had a working majority it could not function.

Throughout this questioning, his earlier answer that Briskin was intended to be a stopgap President only, was in the forefront of my mind. This appeared to be a key that might unlock a door behind which lay great promise. I wanted to be sure I did not fumble at the lock in the darkness of uncertainty. I was waiting for psychological light to make the effort. It seemed to me the moment had arrived.

Words, like other living things, give off an aroma. There was a scent in the air, but I could not quite identify it. It was not belligerence I smelled. Could the perfume be a desire to do justice to Vogel's position? It was too much to hope for, but we had gained enough by indignation. I changed course sharply.

Since his objective was to have a President who would be supported by a majority of the Board, why not await the verdict of the stockholders? After all, they *are* the corporation and in a few weeks they would determine the controversy. If they elected a Board which would support Vogel, would not MacBride recommend his retention as President? He assured me he would. "Then why do we need a stopgap President?" I asked. "Let's await the special stockholders' meeting and election."

He agreed this made sense. I asked him whether he would mind if I dictated this understanding for him to sign. He said he would want to submit it to his attorney first.

We summoned a secretary. The audience in the adjoining room, which had been keeping an anxious vigil, was mystified by the call. They spent the next hour in excited speculation. I wished I could give them word, but I dared not break the spell in our room for even an instant. I dictated MacBride's position endorsing Vogel and retaining him as President, should the stockholders give him a majority on the Board. MacBride agreed that I had given a completely accurate account of our conversation. He suggested, however, that instead of signing the statement, Melniker should write asking him for an elaboration of his written report of July 25, 1957, and he would then reply in the terms I had dictated. He pointed out that his report had concluded with "We will, of course, be glad to discuss our recommendations either orally or in writing on any or all of these recommendations should it be deemed advisable."

After Melniker's letter requesting elaboration of MacBride's position was dictated, we invited him to dictate his reply. He did so, and it was in precise accord with the statement of our conversation. I was still concerned about approval by his lawyers. Despite his reluctance, I insisted that we were entitled to know whether the letter he dictated would actually be sent or not. He finally reached his attorneys in Cleveland who suggested certain minor revisions, to which I agreed. After a second telephone conversation in which MacBride assured his attorney that everything in the letter was correct, he hung up and said, "It is all right. The letter will be sent." He was flying back to Cleveland that afternoon. Before he went, he initialed the final version agreed upon as correct. That same evening he signed a letter in Cleveland on his firm's stationery, and it was immediately delivered.

An observer must have been stationed outside Melniker's office, because immediately after MacBride left, our eager friends burst into our room from the other side. "What happened?" was the meaning of the din that resulted from the overripe suspense. Although overcome with excitement and emotion, Melniker could be heard to say: "Heller has withdrawn its report. They are endorsing Vogel for the presidency."

Once more the multiple inquiries clashed into a cacophony, but it spelled out incredulity: "Heller has what?"

"It's a fact," I said. "MacBride has initialed a letter of retraction. It will go out to all directors tonight." Melniker read the letter which all directors received the next morning.

July 26, 1957

Board of Directors
Loew's Inc.
1540 Broadway
New York, New York

Gentlemen:

In a letter received today from Mr. Benjamin Melniker, Vice President and General Counsel of your Company, we were asked about our recommendations to the effect that certain officers of the Company be relieved of their duties.

The major reason, others being inconsequential, for our recommendation that Mr. Vogel be relieved as President was based upon the fact that he was unable to unite a divided Board and thus do away with the disorganization resulting from the bickering of the Board of Directors.

If Mr. Vogel receives an effective working majority of Directors as a result of stockholder action at the Special Stockholders' meeting which has been called for that purpose among others, we would recommend that Mr. Vogel remain as President, and be given full opportunity to carry out his program.

It is our view that . . .

A voice yelled, "For God's sake, get Joe on the phone." The order was given to call Vogel on the coast, while there were cries of "Let him read on." Melniker continued:

It is our view that Mr. Vogel is a very competent executive, and were it not for the conflict in the Board we would have recommended unqualifiedly his retention as President and Chief Executive Officer.

These opinions . . .

A cheer went up from listeners in so many keys and pitches that the shrillness summoned stenographers, clerks, and other employees to the room, which was overflowing. Again there were loud demands—more impatient than angry—to be quiet.

These opinions [continued Melniker] are the independent judgment of Robert Heller and Associates and myself which have been formulated entirely apart from your inquiry.

The recommendation contained in our letter of July 25th, 1957, that Mr. Melniker and the firm of Phillips, Nizer, Benjamin & Krim be replaced as legal counsel was based solely upon our conviction that if Mr. Vogel was to be replaced under the circumstances, it would not be in the best interests of the Company to retain those so closely and intimately associated with Mr. Vogel.

Also, if Mr. Vogel remains as President with majority support of the Board, the other recommendations in our letter of July 25th, 1957, *would no longer apply, and any future recommendations should be based on performance in the light of such changed conditions.*

Very truly yours,

C. R. MacBride

Now everybody really gave vent to pent-up emotions. The intensity of feeling revealed what everyone knew deep inside, that the Heller report had doomed us. Now that it had been reversed, the deadliness of the handicap could be acknowledged and the corresponding magnitude of relief fully realized. The most powerful adrenalin is a feeble stimulant compared to the psychological lift derived when defeat, ugly and irresistible, is by some quirk of fate transformed into beautiful victory. This was why the revelers could not contain themselves. The previous depression made the swing to exhilaration more extreme. Rejoicing stopped only when it was announced that Vogel was on the telephone. I reported the news to him and assured him, "No, I'm not kidding," "Yes, it is in writing," "No fooling, Joe, all the directors will receive it in the morning." The Heller report was no longer the verdict from on high that Mayer and Tomlinson were right and that he, Vogel, had no business being President; Mac-Bride's report at the July 12 meeting, which seemed as final as it was fatal, had been undone. Not least among the satisfactions was the effect the MacBride letter would have on our adversaries. Karr put it in words when he said that if he had to steal into one of their homes, he would do it just to watch the expression on their faces when they read the letter. On July 25, MacBride writes that Vogel should be let out; on July 26, that he should stay. It was their turn to be flabbergasted, and imagination ran riot depicting how amazement and distress would contest with each other for possession of their faces.

Indeed, Tomlinson immediately expressed his indignation to Robert Heller & Associates, but he was coldly told to "write for elaboration" and he would receive an answer. He did so. The next day all the directors received the following:

July 26th, 1957

Gentlemen:

In answer to our letter to the Board of July 25th, 1957, we have today received a letter from Mr. Joseph Tomlinson, a director of your company, requesting that we indicate the reasons which led to the recommendation made in that letter, that Mr. Joseph Vogel should be relieved of his responsibilities as President and Chief Executive Officer of the Company.

In working on an assignment for any client, Robert Heller and Associates always recognize that primary responsibility is to the stockholders of that company.

Well before the Board meeting held on July 12th, 1957, it had become clear to us that the President of your company did not have sufficient consistent support of the Board to enable him properly to discharge his duties as Chief Executive Officer. Thus, many operating decisions normally left to the judgment of the President had to be submitted to the Board with the result that his recommendations were frequently disregarded. This situation, already acute when we started work on May 6, 1957, deteriorated rapidly to the point where the President and his subordinates were virtually powerless to take prompt and effective management action which they considered advisable.

Repeated efforts had been made by several Directors and ourselves to organize a working majority of the Board in support of the President so that he could exercise normal management prerogatives. All such efforts have failed.

Obviously, the situation existing as of July 12th, 1957, was not in the best interests of the stockholders.

In an effort to resolve this unfortunate impasse a new management slate was presented orally to the Board of Directors at its meeting in Los Angeles on July 12, 1957, which recommendations were reduced to writing in our letter of July 25, 1957. We believed that agreement might be reached on that slate by a working majority of the Board of Directors. Subsequent developments have indicated the unlikelihood of such an agreement.

If such is the case, then clearly the only result attained by allowing those recommendations to stand would be further dissension and disruption of effective management—to the continuing detriment of the stockholders.

Therefore, under the circumstances we withdrew the recommendations contained in our letter of July 25th, 1957.

As the situation has developed we believe the best interests of the company can be served only by ascertaining the wishes of the stockholders. A call has already been issued by the President for a stockholders' meeting on September 12, 1957. At that time, responsibility for control of the Company's operations can be clarified.

Very truly yours,
C. R. MacBride

So now we had two letters withdrawing the recommendations against Vogel, Melniker, Dietz, Reagan, and the others. In addition, we had the opinion from this eminent source that the stockholders, and not the directors, should decide the fate of the company. The odds against pulling out of the Heller disaster had been prohibitive. It had happened; it was a good omen. I did not know how as yet, but the chances were that Vogel would weather the storm. But inwardly, I felt like a surgeon who has made a deft incision, clamped the arteries, and is in the midst of delicate procedure when the attending students in the amphitheater burst into applause for the patient's survival. He was still on the table and his pulse was not too strong. It was not wise, however, to dampen the high spirits which pervaded our camp. It was good for the morale of the company, from the studio to the lowest office echelon.

Then from an unexpected quarter we were struck the worst blow of all. Two of our "friendly" directors resigned. We were left in a hopeless, shrunken minority. Our opponents could call a directors' meeting to assert their clear majority. They had only to go to a judicial bank, so to speak, to collect their victory.

To go back a bit, when the move to oust Vogel at the California meeting failed, Johnson, acting as if the deed had been done, usurped the President's prerogative and accepted a motion appointing a committee "to study" the Heller report and report back at the next meeting. A committee consisting of Pace, Reid, Tomlinson, and Johnson was designated. Pace had originally recommended Heller; Reid had already shown regard for MacBride's recommendations. And so the Tomlinson group confidently expected an approval of the recommendation to fire Vogel.

This committee met. MacBride was present. He had not yet reversed himself. Pace and Reid knew that an attempt to throw Vogel out meant a proxy fight. They had observed his change of mood. He was going to fight on the beaches of the judiciary, the fields of public opinion, and in the homes of 26,000 stockholders. He would never surrender. They knew that as directors, they would be involved in the contest, and stand in the cross fire of recrimination. They could not afford to be in such a fight; Pace, because he was just then ascending to the presidency of the General Dynamics Corporation, which could look back on its distinguished past and look forward into space itself for its future; and Reid, because as a publisher he was highly sensitive to public opinion. In any event, since both Pace and Reid were determined not to be involved in a proxy contest, their only alternative was to resign, unless they could bring about a compromise between the two warring factions.

Tomlinson and Johnson were not disposed to grant an inch. They had Heller's recommendation that Vogel should be discharged. This supplied the one missing ingredient, proper "cause" to remove him, as the Bylaws required. They also felt they had a majority to enforce the report. Victory was theirs, and they weren't going to be talked out of it. They were veterans of the arena—toughened by experience, learned from defeat, and uncompromising in victory. Vogel had escaped by a technicality in California, but his doom was sealed, and no intermediary was going to make them relent by "appeals to reasonableness." While they treated Pace and Reid as inevitable adherents to the winning side, their ultimatum, to be carried to Vogel, was "complete surrender." He must quit. Mayer, Tomlinson, Meyer, and Briskin or Dietrich would take over. Unable to make any headway, Pace and Reid decided to withdraw from the zone of hostilities before the war broke out. They issued a joint statement of resignation. This changed the original alignment, so that Vogel had five directors, Tomlinson six, and there was no "neutral" director.

Worse was to come. George Brownell, one of the oldest serving directors on the Board, and whom Vogel considered knitted to him by sentiment as well as merits, also sent a letter of resignation. Vogel, spurred on by our dismay, pleaded with Pace to withdraw his resignation for just two months, until after the special stockholders' meeting. Vogel had sat with Pace on the Board of the Theatre Company, and when he transferred to the Presidency of Loew's, had asked him to serve on the Loew Board. He admired Pace and considered him his friend and well-wisher. Yet now, when he pleaded desperately that Pace's resignation shifted the balance in the Board irretrievably, Pace would not even delay his resignation. If the new Vogel were inclined to look back longingly to his prior standard that friendship begets friendship, he received another blow to steel him to the cruelty of life.

So now the alignment of directors was Tomlinson 6—Vogel 4. Vacancies to be filled—3. On such kindergarten mathematics did the control of hundreds of millions of dollars of property rest.

Crises, like cancers, are of different types. Some are benign and can be excised. Some are malignant but at least do not spread. Others metastasize. Our crisis was of this character; it crept everywhere.

Under the Bylaws, directors were empowered to fill vacancies on the Board. They could do so by mere majority. So the Tomlinson group would now fill the three vacancies with their nominees, and the alignment would become: Tomlinson 9, Vogel 4. The crisis of imbalance had multiplied itself to a better than 2-to-1 majority. We looked in another direction and there were its evil cells again.

Being in control, the Tomlinson group had other powers. Even if they couldn't discharge Vogel, because Heller's reversal had left them without "cause," they could simply bypass him and discharge all the other executives without "cause" as the Bylaws permitted. Melniker, Dietz, the studio executives, and I, as counsel, would be fired instantly. How could Vogel hold out with all of his shields removed, surrounded by hostile executives who would ignore him and by a Board that would gloat at his discomfiture? Besides, how long would it take under these circumstances to find a "cause," whether insubordination or disobedience to the Board? There was a limit to endurance in the face of irritations and provocations.

We looked at the corporate body and realized that the ugly crisis had spread to another unexpected quarter. Having a majority, Tomlinson could, by resolution of the Board, cancel the President's call for a special stockholders' meeting.

Another look, more horror. Suppose even the special stockholders' meeting did take place, on the theory that the President's right to call it could not be reversed by the Board, we were no longer management. In a proxy contest the "ins" have an enormous financial advantage over the "outs." It costs a minimum of $150,000 and often from $250,000 to $500,000, to wage a proxy fight. There are numerous mailings to the stockholders, the hiring of proxy solicitors, lawyers, public relations experts, special SEC counsel, and other expenses. It is industrial war, and like war in general, terribly costly. The corporation pays these expenses to protect management in a proxy fight. The insurgents must furnish their own war chest. If they win and become management, the corporation may reimburse them for, presumably, the stockholders have decided that their election was in the corporate interest. If they lose, they rarely are repaid. The risk of the battle is that they may pay out-of-pocket up to a half million dollars, in some instances a million and more. Digging for oil is expensive. So are proxy battles.

So Tomlinson and his group, having become management, would be entitled to have the corporation pay their proxy expenses for a lavish campaign. The Vogel group would become the insurgents and have to raise its own funds. Where was the money coming from? Tomlinson and Mayer had money. There was no one on our side who could put up any substantial sum. So it went. The crisis was metastasizing itself.

The fact remained that, until the vacancies on the Board were filled, Tomlinson had a majority of only two. If we could win away one of his directors, the Board would be deadlocked five-to-five. Tomlinson would not have the majority with which to fill the vacancies.

My eyes fell on Fred Florence. The possibility of weaning him away in view of his relationship with Louis B. Mayer was so remote that, in ordinary circumstances, I would dismiss it as an arrant thought in the course of sifting ideas. But we were *in extremis*. Besides, what had been the odds that MacBride would withdraw his recommendation? I set myself the task. Vogel and I had met Florence for breakfast a short time before, when he tried to persuade us that the prestige of Louis B. Mayer was an asset we ought to have on our books. Florence was tall, thin, and it was difficult to tell whether it was his seventy-odd years or his courtly manner which bent him slightly. He was the head of a highly reputable bank in Dallas, and he combined the dignity of his position with a Southern gentleman's diction and grace. His inclination was to favor Vogel, whose code and courtesy he liked. But he prized loyalty as a great virtue, and that he owed to Louis B. Mayer, not to say gratitude for business reasons. Yet, what did we have to lose but our pains?

It was a Sunday morning. I propped myself up in bed and got on the telephone. I prefer to work from a reclining position. Even in my office, my large, soft chair tilts, and a hidden footrest under the desk permits me to incline sufficiently, without offending any client's notion of dignity. If couches were permitted in courtrooms I would be a real terror. I have since found justification for my lazy posture in medical articles which suggest that it takes the strain off the heart and increases stamina as well as thinking powers. For me it is sufficient that it is an aid to equanimity. It is awkward to go into a tantrum from a flat position, isn't it?

I had arranged through important friends for Florence at least to accept my call. He assured me he would have been pleased to anyhow, a gesture he must have regretted in the next several hours, because I called him back five times. My only chance was not to win his mind by outside impact, but to stir his own sense of moral right sufficiently to overcome his devotion to Mayer. He owed his first loyalty to his conscience. If that demanded that he vote with Vogel, how could he fail to respond to the voice within him?

He was not feeling well, so I was obliged to temper my approach and interrupt myself at appropriate times to be sure I was not overtaxing him. I summoned all the persuasive powers I had to my presentation. I revealed to him Stanley Meyer's confession to Vogel, Melniker, and myself. I re-enacted the campaign that had been waged against Vogel and asked Florence rhetorically whether anyone had the right to be an ally of such combatants, even in silence. His duty was to speak up, for did not his Southern tradition require him to be a gentleman in victory and a man in defeat? I recalled to him the way in which Tomlinson's adherents sprang on Vogel in California, taking advantage of the absence of two of Vogel's directors. I told him we noted and appreciated his obvious distaste for that abortive coup and even assumed he had helped to defeat it by postponement. I summoned up his standards of honor and told him that Louis B. Mayer would respect him more if he voted against the cabal, than if he yielded to it. Was it not his absolute integrity which Mayer cherished?

I demonstrated that the deadlock he would create by voting with us would not defeat Mayer. It would merely give the stockholders an opportunity to decide the contest. Thus he would be serving the cause of corporate democracy. Mayer would some day be grateful to him, because forcing his way to power would give him neither peace nor real satisfaction. Being brought back to power by the stockholders would be a genuine and lasting triumph. So I continued to appeal to his profound sense of propriety while trying to still the inner call of loyalty to his friend.

Time and again I felt I was making inroads. Being a banker, it was his habit to count a thousand before making up his mind. He said he would think it over, or speak to his lawyer and call me back, or would I call him in half an hour. I suspected that he was calling Mayer to get approval for the independent exercise of his judgment. Or perhaps his code required that if he were going to vote against Mayer, he at least advise him. This was all conjecture. I know only that after each recess, I had to regain lost ground all over again. It became increasingly difficult to recreate the emotional atmosphere in which the flames of persuasion could reach his inner citadel of conscience. I exhausted myself with every conceivable plea, from the virtue and honor of Socrates to the principles of the Confederacy. The long exchanges between us, alternately subtle and blunt, set off a struggle within him. He complained of feeling tired and ill from the talks. At one point he called his doctor and told me he would call back. When he did, it was his physician who was on the phone. He said that I had disturbed his patient in some extraordinary way; that he had a fever and that he wasn't well enough to take such aggravation; that Mr. Florence wanted to convey this message to me, "I cannot do as you ask, but I appreciate very much what you have told me. I will not vote against Mr. Vogel. Therefore I am sending a letter of resignation immediately." The doctor added that whatever the reason was, his patient had been shaken too much by this matter. It was endangering his health. He was endorsing his decision to resign at once. Furthermore he would not permit Mr. Florence to talk to me. So there was no use calling again. I conveyed my sincere good wishes to his patient. I hung up defeated. There were no more miracles. Tomlinson's majority had been cut from 6-to-4 to 5-to-4, but that one vote was as good as 220 million if you counted it in dollars.

When I reported the development to Vogel, he remarked that at least one of their directors had quit too. But he ruminated, if only Pace or Brownell had remained for a few weeks it would now be 5 to 5. He smashed his fist into his open palm, and I could guess whose face was in it this time.

"What are we going to do now?" came from all sides. The situation was too tragic to tell the story that this question evoked in me: A railroad man applied for the job of stationmaster and was given a severe examination to determine his fitness for the post. "Suppose," said the examiner, "two trains were coming at each other on the same track and you saw them in the distance. What would you do?"

"I would rush on to the tracks with red flags and wave them to stop."

"Suppose you had no red flags?"

"I would tear the shirt off my back and signal them with it."

"Suppose it was night and they couldn't see your shirt?"

"Oh, then I would wave my lantern, of course."

"Suppose you were out of oil?"

"I would gather some wood immediately and build a fire signal on the track."

"Suppose it was raining hard?"

"Then I would call my wife."

"Your wife? What for?"

"I would say, 'Come right over, honey, you're going to see the damndest wreck anyone ever saw.'"

We were not yet at the point of hopelessness, where exasperatedly we would call viewers for the ensuing wreck. I yearned for an apple tree under which to think—indeed, I needed a whole orchard.

Time was short. Tomlinson and Johnson were moving quickly to exploit the decisive advantage that had been thrust at them by the unexpected resignation of "Vogel's directors." Their lawyers mapped out the mopping up. They were not going to wait even a month for the next directors' meeting. The Bylaws permitted two directors to call a special meeting of the Board on short notice. They did so. The agenda on the notice of meeting sent by telegram and mail, was a blueprint for seizing control of the company. First, the Board was to act on the Heller report. We could still permit ourselves a dying chuckle. The reversal letters of MacBride had come in after the meeting had been called. Instead of adopting the report and firing Vogel immediately, they would now have to reject the report. No matter how dark the hour, these retraction letters by MacBride still had the possibility of being the turning point in the case. Second, the Board would fill the vacancies created by the resignation of directors. Third, it would consider whether there should be a special stockholders' meeting as requested by Vogel.

It was plain to see. The insurgents would elect new directors and swell their majority, so that death, illness, or accident to one of them would not deprive them of control. They would then cancel the President's call for a special stockholders' meeting, fire the present administration, excepting possibly Vogel, who might be retained in some role other than president, and install themselves as management in final triumph.

The storm was upon us. But there are brainstorms too. I had one and tested it out on my associates in one of those sessions where I try to persuade myself while informing them. Simplicity is usually the identification mark of a good idea, and at least to that extent this one had possibilities. It had only three steps in its logical development. First step: There were originally thirteen directors, therefore a quorum was seven; unless a quorum was present, the directors had no power to act, and they could only adjourn the meeting for another date. Second step: If the Vogel directors didn't show up at the meeting, there would be only the five Tomlinson directors, two short of quorum. Third step: Any action the Board took except to adjourn would be illegal. Q.E.D., as the algebraic and calculus professors used to exclaim when their mathematical flights came to ground safe and sound. But unfortunately, it was not *quod erat demonstrandum*. There was one terrible flaw. The Bylaws provided: "A vacancy in the Board of Directors may be filled by the directors in office, *though less than a quorum*."

So the five Tomlinson directors, though less than a quorum, could fill the vacancies, and then having both a quorum and a majority, go on to take over management.

The Legal dialogue often approaches the symmetry of a solution and then reveals its own flaw. This is the excitement of practicing law, far more than the culminating forensics in the courtroom. It is the struggle of the mind to cope with overawing physical forces, to pierce and shatter the hugest boulders with an idea, to overcome superior numbers and strength with nothing but thought.

I lifted the spirits of my associates with a vague promise. "I think I have a way out of that phrase 'though less than a quorum,' but I will not argue it now. It needs much more legal research." I assigned the task in specific terms, and later dug into that search myself in our library, from the windows of which I saw the morning light up the Hudson River on more than one occasion.

In the meantime, the first step in the syllogism had to be legally verified. Could the Vogel directors deliberately boycott the meeting and thereby prevent it from having a quorum? What were the sanctions for such conduct, if any? Of course we could simulate the claim that because of the short notice, none of our directors could come. Indeed this would have required little artifice. Vogel was at the studio signing up Audrey Hepburn to star in *Green Mansions*. Killion was in San Francisco negotiating an important ship contract for the American President Lines. Parker and Sullivan were both busily engaged. However, I rejected such a device. If we could have saved management by their being present, we knew, and so would any court, that they would be there. I was still depending on a strong moral position ultimately to heal all our legal insufficiencies, and I would not sully it with hypocritical pretense. I wanted to take the position that we deliberately stayed away from the meeting, and rightly so. We did not intend to confer power on five directors seeking to defeat the right of 26,000 stockholders to vote, or permit them to seize control of a corporation because as a result of their conduct two directors had resigned. This was a posture I could maintain with righteousness, rather than avert the judge's gaze while I whimpered that by sheer coincidence our four directors just couldn't make it.

Research developed that there was no obligation upon a director to attend every meeting. Only if he continuously neglected his duties could he be removed. There was no other sanction. If a whole group failed to attend, it might be accused of conspiring to obstruct corporate business, as undoubtedly the Tomlinson forces would charge, but this did not overly disturb me. I would fall back on the basic rightness of our cause. Who is calling whom an obstructionist? We had, through agonizing patience, built a vivid record of our opponents' interference with management and corporate affairs. Now it would stand us in good stead. Let them dare call us obstructionists. We would establish in truth that we were staying away from the board meeting to protect the corporate property and give its owners the right to determine its destiny at a special stockholders' meeting.

So while the law with respect to a director's absenting himself was not perfect, it was satisfactory. I gave definite instructions that our four directors should not attend the special board meeting called by Tomlinson and Johnson. I appeased their fears that deliberate abstention might subject them to personal liability, and wrote each a legal opinion to that effect. One thing was certain. That meeting would have no quorum of seven when its five members first convened.

We were going to call it a rump meeting, and charge that all its actions were unauthorized. As to the right to fill vacancies "though less than quorum," I was working feverishly with a staff of attorneys to confirm a theory I had.

The Tomlinson faction had planned ahead with meticulous care. They had experienced the frustration of being blocked by a technical objection in California. They would permit no more slips between the cup and the lip, for the nectar in the cup was too delicious and the lip too dry and eager, after all these months of pursuit. Now that victory was in sight, the costs of the final battle were inconsequential. So they augmented their ranks of counsel without stint.

Since Loew's was a Delaware corporation, they engaged one of the foremost law firms in Wilmington, Delaware—Logan, Marvel, Boggs & Thiesen, obtaining the personal representation of Arthur G. Logan, its senior, who had once been the law partner of the presiding Chancellor (as the Judge is called in an equity court), and Aubrey B. Lank, as well as other associates. They also retained Louis Johnson's Washington law firm and his able associates. They further retained Milton Pollack of New York, an attorney experienced in corporate struggles. Their legal program was prepared to the last detail.

So confident were they that victory was assured that Louis B. Mayer who, up to this time, was saying, "Who, me?" to all charges that he was behind the Tomlinson drive, decided that this was the moment to come out into the open. The manner in which the curtain was drawn apart for him to step into the limelight was not only the lawyers' work; the best screenwriter of Hollywood must have had a hand in it.

The day of the special directors' meeting arrived. We feared that after the meeting the newly elected officials might try to take physical possession of the Loew offices in New York. Vogel was on the Coast. His office was empty. Suppose that Tomlinson or Briskin sat down at his desk and began to function, or suppose Louis Johnson, accompanied by a guard, walked into Melniker's office, showed him the Board's certificate of designation as counsel, and ordered him to get out.

We engaged twenty-five private detectives from a large agency and gave them careful instructions. We wanted no incidents. There was to be no violence. Each would be stationed at a strategic floor entrance and at certain outer offices. With them would be a Loew representative to identify the visitor. If he signaled that it was one of the opposition, his path was to be blocked courteously but firmly. No claim of authority or threat was to be countenanced. He was to be told that only a sheriff or marshal with a court order would be recognized. He was then to be led to an elevator, one of which was reserved solely for this purpose.

We also gave careful instruction to the Secretary of the corporation, who would attend the meeting. He would be our ears and eyes and report what transpired. Then a small group of us sat in Vogel's office awaiting developments and ready for any emergency.

Suddenly one of the attorneys stationed with a guard dashed into our office. His face was drained of any color. "Louis B. Mayer is in the building. He just arrived with a flock of reporters and cameramen," he exclaimed breathlessly.

"Are you sure? Do you know him well enough? Vogel mentioned only last night that Mayer was in Hollywood."

"I'm positive. I heard him talking to the reporters while he posed. He said he was going upstairs to take back his company. He's on his way to the Board room now!"

Two others ran headlong into the room. "Have you heard the news? Mayer flew in. He's here. He's going to attend the Board meeting!" Another reported that Mayer told the press, "I have come back because I am lonely for Leo the Lion."

Yes, it was true. The newspapers later carried pictures of Mayer getting into a plane in California for his flight to New York to recover the child he had reared. It showed him waving good-bye to his well-wishers, like Lincoln when he departed for the Capitol. It showed him arriving at the airport in New York, greeted by an army of newspapermen who had been alerted to the drama about to be unfolded. Later it showed him entering the Loew Building, with various quotations from him: "I am home again," "I am here to restore Loew's to the top again," "I have decided to take back the company I built." But the favorite of all was a picture of him looking rather soulful, and the quotation was, "I am lonely for Leo the Lion." With this loneliness gnawing at his heart, he proceeded upstairs to the Board room.

As he passed each floor, as he got out of the elevator surrounded by a squad of lawyers and reporters, as he walked toward the meeting, flashlights lit and blinded his way. To him they must have seemed Roman candles, and the pursuing crowd, the entourage of the emperor. Each step of his journey was reported to us. There was awe and fright in the voices that gave us the news. I was surprised by the magic that clings to prestige. The all-powerful man, the man whose name was in the famous title, Metro-Goldwyn-Mayer, the king of Hollywood, was in our midst. He cast an aura of authority, which was like victory itself. Like other kings who had stilled frenzied mobs by their very appearance, Mayer's physical presence gave the illusion that opposition was futile. All the mystery of power resided in him.

I was deeply impressed too, but for another reason. I knew that
Mayer would never go this far in putting himself at the head of the
Tomlinson movement unless he was assured by his personal lawyers and
friends in Hollywood and by the batteries of attorneys in New York and
Delaware that the plan was certain of success. He could not afford to take
any chance. Even in California, where he was around the corner, and
victory seemed imminent, he had played it safe. How right he had been.
Something had intervened and he would have looked foolish had he
made a premature move. Now that he had flown three thousand miles
with all the accompanying fanfare, there was no doubt in his mind or in
the minds of his lawyers and experts, that the triumph was complete.
This is what gave me a pang. I knew how desperate our plight was and
that we were hanging by a thread, but I had evolved a battle plan,
nevertheless. Could it be that there were other flaws in it than I knew?
Mayer's presence gave me reason to doubt myself. That is what disturbed
me most.

The Board room was filled to overflowing. There were more lawyers
in the room than directors. Every word and motion had been rehearsed
under legal supervision. The minutes of the meeting had been typed in
advance. Instead of recording the events, an attorney had the script before
him and simply saw to it that the proceedings were in exact accordance
with the minutes.

First, Louis Johnson was designated chairman. Greenfield, the Secretary of the company, announced, as we had instructed him to do, that
there was no quorum of seven present and therefore the meeting was not
validly constituted. He advised that only a motion to adjourn was in
order. Johnson overruled him and designated one of his attorneys, Ailes,
to act as Secretary.

Johnson called on Greenfield to produce the written resignations of
Pace, Reid, Brownell, and Florence. He refused. Johnson declared that
such resignations had been sent, and that under a specific section of the
Bylaws, they were effective without formal acceptance.

He then asked all counsel present whether under Delaware law the
Board had the power to fill the four vacancies. He was formally advised
that under Section 223 of the Delaware Law a majority of the remaining
directors was authorized to fill the vacancies. Since there were nine directors left, the five present constituted a majority.

Motion was then made to fill two vacancies. Louis B. Mayer and
Samuel Briskin (whose arrival had gone unnoticed amidst the trumpets
and banners for Mayer) were elected directors. They were then ushered
into the room. Photographers recorded the historic moment of Louis B.
Mayer taking his seat at the governing body of the Loew's company,
and then were dismissed. After Mayer and Briskin had qualified and
signed waivers of notice of meeting (no detail was overlooked), it was
declared that there were now seven directors present.

Then it was that the chairman asked Mr. Logan, who headed the legal squadron, whether in his opinion there was a legally constituted quorum. He was informed that indeed there was.

They proceeded to the agenda. A discussion was had "concerning the conduct of the office of President, Mr. Joseph R. Vogel." The script had originally called for the adoption of the Heller report and the dismissal of Vogel. But in the meantime they had received MacBride's letters withdrawing the recommendation that he be relieved as President and urging Vogel's retention if he obtained an effective working majority of directors as a result of stockholder action at the forthcoming special stockholders' meeting. It was a very embarrassing moment. They fled from the subject in an ungainly manner. The minutes record the following disposition in one sentence. "The chairman stated that in view of the absence of Mr. Vogel there was no purpose in discussing the Heller report at this time."

A likely story. The sense of gallantry which they pretended caused them to withhold action against Vogel when he was not present, did not prevent them from immediately proceeding to emasculate all his authority, notwithstanding his absence.

Having bypassed the removal of Vogel, they had smoother sailing. They took over control of the Executive Committee—which once they had attempted to do and had been rebuffed. Now it was easy picking. They designated Stanley Meyer and Joseph Tomlinson to fill the places of Pace and Reid. To make sure that in the absence of either of these new appointees, Vogel would not transact any business, they passed a resolution suspending the Executive Committee and withdrawing all its powers. Only the Board could transact business in the meanwhile, and, of course, the Board now consisted of seven Tomlinson votes and four Vogel votes.

To be sure that Vogel would be helpless to act, a resolution was passed which forbade him from making any contract involving more than $25,000 or for a term of more than one year without the consent of the Board of Directors in advance. They knew, of course, that in the motion picture business this was equivalent to telling him to stay home. The introduction of this resolution was particularly offensive. It read, "In view of the condition of the company . . ." The implication was that the company was in financial distress. They were to hear plenty about this reckless language. They were building our moral position every moment, if only we would have the opportunity to utilize it.

Then came the main thrust. They called off the special stockholders' meeting. The reason, as stated in the minutes, was ingenuous. "It was the consensus of the meeting that there should be no impairments of the efforts which the Board is making to secure effective administration of its policies by the officers and employees of the company, and that a special meeting of the stockholders would involve sufficient disruption of these efforts to make such a meeting inadvisable and contrary to the best interest of the company and its shareholders."

This statement would fool nobody. It meant that they weren't going to permit the stockholders to decide the controversy. Having seized power, they didn't want an election. Every step which legal ingenuity could devise to accomplish this result was taken. They passed a resolution advising the SEC in Washington that Vogel had filed proxy material for a special stockholders' meeting without authority, that it is "repudiated and ordered withdrawn."

They formally retained Logan as counsel for the company in Delaware, and Pollack in New York. Then, just to be sure, they passed a resolution forbidding "the expenditure of any funds of the company for the preparation of proxy material or solicitation of proxies with respect to the Special Meeting" (which they had already called off). With this parting shot they left the old management for dead, and departed. They did not attempt any seizure of offices. Not yet. Instead, they held a press conference announcing the demise of the old regime, and presumably that Mayer's loneliness had been assuaged.

The first thing to do was to have the old management let out such a vigorous yelp that no one could doubt it was still alive. We hastily prepared a statement for Vogel which would serve this purpose. It read: "The Tomlinson-Mayer faction held a rump meeting of five directors out of the thirteen elected by the stockholders. The meeting, of course, was illegal. A quorum of seven is required by the Bylaws. Only five attended. The major piece of business of this meeting was to try to stop the stockholders' meeting which I have called for September 12. I am sure our stockholders will be interested in learning that this is what Mayer, Meyer, and Tomlinson consider most important. That stockholders' meeting will take place despite these efforts to block it. . . . [Louis B. Mayer's] program has simply shifted from obstruction to usurpation. We at Loew's and our counsel, Louis Nizer, are absolutely confident of the outcome. We will hold everyone who participated in this plot legally accountable. We are thankful for the wave of support from all quarters of the industry and the public at large. . . ."

This statement at least heartened our own camp. We had survived the psychological blitz of Louis Mayer's appearance and the "take-over" meeting. But the skillfully conceived plan of the opposition called for one more move. They sued us! We were hauled into the Chancery Court of Delaware on a petition by Tomlinson seeking a declaration that Mayer and Briskin were legally elected directors and that we were therefore interlopers and usurpers.

There was a special reason why Tomlinson rushed into the Delaware Court. The very same legal question, namely, whether directors, though less than a quorum, could fill vacancies, had been decided by the Chancellor of that Court. The decision had been that they could. It fitted the Mayer-Briskin election like a glove. So their strategy was to get the same ruling and, then, with court authority behind them, proceed to throw us out physically.

Word percolated through various sources that we had been outwitted and trapped. Mayer, Tomlinson, and some of their lawyers were telling influential friends in Wall Street, in industry, and in the press that a precedent existed in Delaware which we didn't know about, which disposed of the legal question in their favor, and that they had so maneuvered the situation that they now came precisely under the rule of that case. "This time Nizer is going to get the beating of his life. He has overlooked this authority, and he will look foolish in court. There is no way out. The matter is open and shut."

The name of the case was kept secret. These confidential revelations of our dilemma came to us from many quarters. While a few may have been conveyed in malice, some emanated from high sources that were as friendly as they were concerned. The rumor had not been planted for the purpose of its undermining effect. I was convinced that the exultation in our opponents' ranks was genuine.

The case that guaranteed them victory was the Chelsea Exchange Corporation case. Secret indeed! I had lived with that case for weeks. I had sent for the original record of its proceedings, and had obtained the briefs of opposing counsel. I had spent many nights poring over every word in the opinion. I had sat in research with as many as seven lawyers until the early hours of the morning, seeking some way to extricate ourselves from its conclusive decision.

Mayer's lawyers had not ensnared us into the Chelsea-case trap by rushing in with a suit in the Delaware Court. Loew's was a Delaware corporation, and the issue had to be fought out there. Research had demonstrated conclusively that we could not shift the jurisdiction to another state. We had to meet Chelsea head on. We had known that since the resignations of Pace and Brownell left us in a minority. That is why I had gotten to know every lane and turn of the Chelsea case and grappled with its every nuance.

On one occasion, when Tomlinson was gloating about his victory and not only counting but savouring his chickens before they were hatched, someone expressed blind confidence in me. He replied, "All he has to do is convince the Court that four is larger than seven." The poor man didn't know it, but four *is* larger than seven, if justice requires that it should be. There are infinite numerals and words in her scales which she may add or subtract to prevent wrongdoing.

We filed a cross petition to declare that Mayer and Briskin had been illegally elected directors, that all other action taken at the rump meeting was invalid, and that the Mayer-Tomlinson group should be enjoined from interfering with the special stockholders' meeting scheduled for September

12. The battle was joined. Now all concentration shifted to the new arena, the Court.

The legal rules were all against us; the Chelsea case which permitted directors, although less than a quorum, to fill vacancies; the rule that the majority on the board of directors has the power to appoint management; and the age-old mathematical rule that five is larger than four and that seven certainly is.

Yet matters were not hopeless. If the "conscience of the Chancellor" (what a significant English phrase!) could be stirred by the basic injustice of it all, who knows how many angels might be made to stand on the point of a needle. Of course, it was my task to build plausible bridges for the passage from the traditional legal terrain to novel ground. I had used all my surveyor instruments on the Chelsea case and had prepared a blueprint. It was drawn with such technical exactitude as would have delighted a sixteenth-century metaphysician. But I was not going to be drawn into an argument on the Chelsea rule as if this were the real or whole contest. This was what our legal opponents desired and expected. Indeed, they saw no other issue. This was a pure legal question, if ever there was one. They had fashioned their legal papers to make it so. They moved for summary judgment, which meant that the case was to be determined as a matter of law. The general background facts were not material. Whatever the history of events, the basic facts necessary to the determination of the legal question were conceded. There came a time when, due to resignations, the directors filled the vacancies; did they have the power to do so although less than a quorum? That was the sole legal question. And, of course, there was the Chelsea decision that we were not supposed to know about, which held that they did. That's how neat it was to the Tomlinson lawyers who had prepared their strategy and legal briefs.

For my part, I was well aware of the rule that on a summary judgment application the Court will consider only those facts germane to the legal question and not general equitable recitals. Nevertheless, I proceeded to dictate to a battery of stenographers, through a forty-eight-hour continuous period, affidavits for Vogel, Killion, Melniker and myself, which set forth the entire history of events. This detailed recital was too bulky in typewritten form. We printed it overnight. It was 114 pages in length. It became the bible of our case in the many courts we were destined to preach.

So confident were our opponents that these affidavits were irrelevant that they did not reply to them. Apart from the difficulty they would have experienced in formulating an effective answer, they also feared that a factual reply might make pertinent the long preceding struggle and confound the simple legal question. They told the Court that these affidavits should not be accepted, being merely an attempt to color the case and prejudice the Chancellor. The sole issue, they insisted, was whether the remaining directors had the legal right to elect Mayer and Briskin.

I may say that our associates expressed the prayer that my dictation of "the bible" would not be a complete waste. They spoke as good lawyers are accustomed to speak. "How can we get all this history in? What has it really got to do with the legal question? Whether the five directors who filled the vacancies are villains or not has nothing to do with the case. We can't dispute that they were directors at the time they voted for Mayer and Briskin. The only ground we have to stand on is that they weren't a quorum. Develop your argument against Chelsea, and the other legal arguments. Don't go far afield. An able judge is likely to resent your attempt to drag in the Brooklyn Bridge. It will react against you. Besides, what good will it do even if he listened to you and agreed with your interpretation of the facts? If the Chelsea case is law, he must apply it."

This was not the first time nor, I am certain, will it be the last that I have been warned against legal unorthodoxy. I knew the force of the argument, but it did not move me. "You cannot win this case on the hocus-pocus of Chelsea. A Court will not deviate from its prior decision, unless—" I paused and bore down on every succeeding word "—unless the Court is so stirred by the derelictions of our opponents that it feels compelled by its conscience to thwart the consummation of their scheme. Then our argument against Chelsea, which is technically adequate, may appeal to him. Only then can we hope that he will decide that four of us are, in effect, a majority of nine and that we are still management, and therefore that we can use corporate funds in the proxy fight."

"Do you think any Judge would ever do all that?" said one of my partners. "I really must admire you, Lou. You are the world's greatest optimist."

"I am promising nothing. A Judge [I mentioned his name] met me yesterday and said he thought the odds against us were 1000 to 1. He didn't think we had a case. So I know what we are up against. But there is no other way of winning this case than by drawing the factual history into the dispute and insisting that the legal question involving the Chelsea rule is not the sole determinative factor. Let me put it simply. Our cause is just. That's our strength. I am going to tell the whole story or be thrown out of court in the attempt."

To ease the way for the Court's consideration of the entire matter, we took advantage of an opportunity for a judicial ruling in the New York Supreme Court. We knew that the Delaware Court was not bound by a decision in another state, and I did not intend to irritate the Delaware Chancellor by any such claim, but if we could obtain a favorable decision in another jurisdiction, it would have a moral impact.

Many stockholders were clamoring to come to the aid of the Vogel regime. They designated as counsel former Judge Ernest Hammer and Harold Lehrman to seek an injunction against interference with the special stockholders' meeting on September 12. They asked me for statistical data upon which to base their petition. I was pleased to supply them with it. There were 7966 stockholders residing in the State of New York. They owned more than three million shares, or about sixty-three per cent of the Loew stock. Surely, the Court had jurisdiction to protect these New York residents in their request to have the stockholders' meeting held without interference.

The motion for an injunction against interference with the stockholders' meeting came before Judge Herbert Spector of the New York Supreme Court. I appeared on behalf of Loew's to support the motion. Pollack argued against the motion, but refused to appear for Tomlinson and Johnson and thus confer jurisdiction over them. Seated on the side, listening intently, was a stocky, dark-haired man, with a flattened nose. He was distinguished-looking in a striking sense, as outstanding lawyers usually are. I asked who he was, and was told that it was Mr. Arthur G. Logan. He was witnessing a preliminary test and undoubtedly sizing me up as an adversary.

I did not intend to hoard any ammunition, especially since the issues were not the same as in Delaware. I set forth the conduct of the rump group in full color. It was to that extent a rehearsal for the decisive day approaching in Delaware. It was important to obtain the injunction for use later, if there should be an attempt at physical dispossession. That, too, would be interference with the meeting. Despite the powerful contention that only Delaware had jurisdiction over the internal strife of one of its corporations, the moral suasion of our story carried the day. I was more convinced than ever that in such a presentation lay our hope. Loew executives who heard the argument came back encouraged and confident. It is one thing to know in your heart that you are right; it is another to hear the facts paraded in such a way that everyone around you is swept by the martial music. The Court was marching too. A short time later Judge Spector issued a sweeping injunction against any interference with the special stockholders' meeting. He acknowledged that the question of the quorum and the validity of the Mayer-Briskin election had to be determined by the Delaware Chancellor.

The press and public were impressed by the outcome of our first legal skirmish. Our proxy solicitation picked up steam, like a candidate's headquarters when the first primary victory is reported.

Our opponents took the defeat hard. They had no doubt of the outcome in Delaware, but they feared that the New York injunction might create a conflict in the enforcement of their Delaware decree and delay their taking possession of the company. They therefore rushed reinforcements and heavy armament to the broken-through sector. Resourcefully they moved on behalf of Tomlinson's relatives, Charlotte and William Tomlinson, and other friendly stockholders, representing $250,000 of Loew stock, to intervene in the action. This enabled Pollack to make new moves without submitting Tomlinson himself to the jurisdiction. Learned briefs were filed to demonstrate that internal corporate conflicts must be determined in the state where it is organized and that New York had no jurisdiction.

Simultaneously they appealed to the Appellate Division from Judge Spector's injunction order. There they applied for a stay on the ground that the ultimate issue was soon to be argued and decided in Delaware. Special applications were heard by Chief Judge Bernard Botein and Judge Francis Bergen sitting on behalf of the Appellate Court since it was in recess during the summer. At the same time the Tomlinson forces moved before another Judge of the New York State Supreme Court for permission to have other stockholders intervene and oppose the injunctive relief.

In view of the emergency, orders to show cause were obtained giving short notice of these many applications. Sometimes we would be required to submit arguments on the very shortest of notice. We were kept busy dashing around from one Court to another, to meet every conceivable technical thrust that resourceful counsel could devise. Our offices kept grinding out briefs through the night to supply the Courts with authorities. On one day I made three arguments in three different courts within four hours. Additional pressure was put on us. Johnson and Tomlinson served notice that at the next meeting of the Board the agenda would include the discharging of various executives and employees and also filling the two other vacancies on the Board. We turned this thrust against them. Since we were appearing before the Courts to oppose the modification of the injunction order, we applied for its enlargement to protect us from new aggressiveness.

When the last ingenious move had been exhausted and rulings had been made by eight Judges of the New York Courts—Judges Peck, Rabin, Valente, McNally, Botein, Bergen, Epstein, and Spector—the injunction in our favor stood. It was actually enlarged by a provision forbidding "the removal or suspension of officers of the Corporation or filling vacancies of directors, prior to the hearing and determination of the motion."

The New York Court, however, carefully reserved the right, which we conceded, of the Delaware Chancellor to decide the main legal questions. There are Delaware cases which hold that the decision of a Court of competent jurisdiction of another state is "entitled to great weight" and "special consideration." That is all we claimed for our New York victory. It enabled us to clothe the figure of justice we would present to the Court with a bit of judicial ermine.

The attorneys had clashed in preliminary battle. Their forensics were like the opening drum roll that beckons in the symphony. We headed for the Court of Chancery of the State of Delaware in Wilmington, New Castle County, for the decisive struggle.

Just as there are family and school traditions, there are also judicial traditions. The Court of Chancery of Delaware is heir to one. It has not come about by accident. Many of the great corporations of our country have availed themselves of the advantages of the Delaware Corporation Law. Once organized there, legal controversies must be determined in its courts. It has therefore been of the utmost importance that the reputation of the Chancellor for legal scholarship, understanding of business structure and practice, and, above all, high character and transcendent integrity should give confidence to incorporators. Otherwise, attorneys throughout the nation would be reluctant to leave the haven of their own jurisdictions which are familiar to them and incorporate in Delaware. The Delaware bar, the Governor, the universities, and the leading citizens of the state have made certain that the Vice-Chancellor who, after apprenticeship in that high post, will ultimately ascend to the Chancellor's seat, is a man who combines the highest attainments. So, the tradition.

Chancellor Collins J. Seitz is remarkably young to have attained a judicial post of such eminence. He is about fifty years of age and his neatly side-parted, straight, shining black hair and clean-cut, pale, even features made him look even younger, if not at times boyish. His chief characteristic is serenity, but even it cannot disguise his enthusiasm for the task as he listens to the argument with eager patience. Even if one had not read his lucid and learned opinions in other cases, one would be deeply impressed with the Judge before him.

I have never seen greater concentration in repose. His eyes never left Logan's or mine for one instant during the four hours of argument. The courtroom was stuffed with legal talent. Eighteen lawyers sat at our respective counsel tables. Tomlinson and Meyer had flown in to be present. Other executives filled the forechamber. In the rear were the press, more than twenty representatives, and visitors who had come from California, New York, and other states to hear the arguments. In this tense setting, with assistant counsel scribbling notes for the arguers, whispering to each other, and turning to their files for documents and law books, and with the audience restive too, there were diverting noises and movements. They caused the strict, blue-coated court attendants to signal admonitions for silence. But the courtroom may as well have been empty so far as the Chancellor was concerned. His eyes were riveted—riveted fast—on the lawyer standing alone before him at the lectern underneath the Judge's bench. They were understanding rather than piercing eyes, set in an otherwise impassive face.

Only on a few occasions did he interrupt to put a brief question. It was so incisive that it constituted as much of a challenge as if a lengthy criticism had been uttered. It gave notice to the discerning mind that the Chancellor was not only following the argument intently, but was racing ahead to warn of the defects in the road being traveled. The Chancellor gazed so steadily upon the lawyer that if, as yogis are supposed to do, he could prevent the blink of the eyelids, one felt he would do so not to lose even a subliminal instant. He seemed to listen with his eyes, to appraise and sift with them—above all, to anticipate with them. I felt, after a while, that it would not have been necessary to fill in the entire argument. Once its direction was indicated, he knew the rest, but, unlike other keen minds, did not suffer through the recital. He patiently evaluated its form.

Dramatists use the device of dropping the curtain to denote the passage of time. The audience knows that life goes on for months or years behind that momentary darkness. The novelist uses asterisks for the same purpose. When one is before a wise and attentive Judge, he ought to be able to begin a point, and by some legal signal, indicate that the Judge's sense of anticipation makes unnecessary a full statement and that he will therefore proceed to the next point. Some Judges exercise this privilege on behalf of the lawyer. Unfortunately, however, the very Judges who are thus impatient, may also be arbitrary and cut off recital of fact or even of law of which they have no knowledge. I recall an Appellate Judge once saying to a young lawyer who was expounding the law, "Surely, you will give the Court credit for being familiar with so elementary a proposition."

"Oh, no," replied the neophyte. "That is the mistake I made in the Court below."

Logan addressed the Court first, in support of his request to declare Louis Mayer and Briskin legally elected directors. He spoke in a deliberately matter-of-fact style, as if to say, "Let's cut out all the folderol and get right to the heart of things." This suited his main thesis that a simple question of law was involved, and the Chelsea case was the answer.

At the end of his argument, Logan reserved part of his time for reply. He had heard me argue in the New York Supreme Court, and he deemed it advisable to have the last word. When Logan sat down, the atmosphere he had striven to create existed. This was a power struggle. The strong had won it. They had done so legally. The law was clear. Now the losers came whimpering into court pleading that the law should be ignored. They would want a minority to exercise the rights of a majority. Even our sympathizers in the courtroom acknowledged that the legal position made our cause hopeless.

From the moment I arose to place my papers on the lectern, and began in the traditional way, "May it please your Honor (when we really mean, "May it persuade your Honor"), I felt the appraising and, at first, bemused eyes of the Chancellor upon me. I pitched my tone respectfully low and kept it devoid of any oratorical flourish. This was to be an engagement of the minds, and whatever emotion would arise would stem from the facts, the sincerity of the arguer and the reaction of the Judge, and from no other device.

The petitioners were eager to have this legal question considered in a factual vacuum. Why? Within twenty days the 26,000 stockholders of

504 · *My Life in Court*

the company would have the opportunity to determine the destiny of their company.

Mr. Logan talked blandly of vacancies on the Board. They were not ordinary vacancies caused by illness or preoccupation. They were the result of direct pressures by Tomlinson and part of a scheme to obstruct corporate business. I read from Killion's affidavit: "I am a busy man. As president of a company which operates forty steamships in the worldwide trade, I find that most of my working hours are required by my business. Yet, almost daily I would be called by Mr. Tomlinson or other directors to whom I had talked concerning matters which usually had less to do with the business of Loew's Inc. than with the compaign against Mr. Vogel. The pressures brought to bear upon me were extraordinary. Important business associates of mine were called to induce me to change my mind. It was made clear that I was to be put in a position of great embarrassment if I stood by the principle I had enunciated. I learned that other directors were being subjected to similar pressure. Surely I can understand why some of the directors resigned."

It was not difficult to read the true meaning behind the words that Killion's important associates had been approached to put pressure on him. This was a form of duress. The directors who, unlike him, resigned rather than be subjected to such threats, were pushed off the Board by the Tomlinson group. Could they exploit their own wrongdoings by filling such vacancies and then lift themselves by their own bootstraps and claim that the newly elected directors gave them a quorum?

Despite my resolution for restrained argument, I felt the indignation within me speed my words into torrents and lift my voice to emotional pitch. I also found my arms lifting from their grip on the lectern occasionally, to give emphasis to a thought as if it were on a banner and were held aloft for clearer view. Such involuntary gestures, compelled by genuine feeling, are the only ones permitted to a speaker. No matter how awkward they may be, they are right. It is only the studied gesture that is wrong, and it matters not how photogenically it is made. I aspire only to stand still when I speak and let the words strike such sparks as they can. But when I listen to a radio recording of any of my speeches and hear my fingers angrily pounding the table as if a drumbeat accompanied the climactic words, or when I see a photograph of the event and my arm is in mid-air, I am surprised but not displeased. The inner compulsion of a gesture is its justification. So I realized suddenly that my resolve to make a measured argument had been broken, but the fires within should not be doused. The courtroom had that attentive stillness that bodes well. When I would pause, the unusual quiet created a contrast like a clock that stops and its soundlessness makes a waking sound.

It was against this background that I was now ready to discuss Chelsea. I did so almost cavalierly as I took off to demonstrate that it was not even applicable to our case. My voice resumed its calm and my manner became more fitting for the required technical analysis. Lucidity, not emotion, was the prime objective.

In the Chelsea case there was only one Bylaw concerning the filling of vacancies. It provided that the directors could act although less than a quorum were present.

The Loew Bylaws had two articles for filling vacancies on the Board. The petitioners only cited one; it was Article V and permitted less than a quorum to act. But there was also Article II which required a quorum for all actions of the Board of Directors and listed the filling of vacancies on the Board as one of its powers.

So one article required a quorum of seven. The other said less than a quorum would suffice. It is an ancient rule of construction that where two articles appear to be in conflict, they should be so interpreted as to give meaning to each. It is not to be assumed that the drafters of the Bylaws simply didn't know what they were doing and created conflicting Bylaws.

Chancellor Seitz had recognized this rule in an opinion which I quoted: ". . . Where there is a choice between a construction comporting with 'fairness and reasonableness' as compared with a construction which will lead to unreasonable results, the former construction will be adopted."

How can meaning be given to these two Bylaws, one of which required a quorum and the other not? By recognizing that where the total number of directors had been reduced to less than seven, so that it is impossible ever to convene a quorum, there the directors, although less than a quorum, may fill vacancies. In other words, an exception is provided in the unusual event that an airplane accident, death, or resignation reduces the thirteen members on the Board of Directors to less than seven. Then they may fill vacancies, although less than a quorum. But in the present Loew situation, there are nine directors in office. Five could not act. Article II of the Bylaws required seven. The exception didn't apply.

This interpretation would reconcile the two Bylaws and give sense to each. One was for the ordinary situation where there was a vacancy and more than a quorum of directors existed. Then they must be present or they can't act. The other was for the unusual situation where the Board had shrunken in numbers to less than a quorum. No quorum could ever be gathered. Then the remaining directors, though less than a quorum, could act.

So I continued to construct a legal bridge for an escape from the Chelsea case. If the Judge felt compelled by the equities to abandon or distinguish the Chelsea decision, we had presented a plausible and technically sound argument to do so. It was his desire to undertake the journey which was important. The bridge was there if he wished to cross it.

When I had finished my argument, I felt, more than heard, the breaking of the silence with murmurs that, in a courtroom, are the respectful substitute for applause. It was not for me. In truth, it was for the fact that the heart's desire found legal support. When our inner scales tell us what justice dictates, but we are informed that such a result is impossible, and then it appears possible, the triumph of right inside us find its echo on our lips.

When Logan made his reply argument, I thought I detected a change in his deliberately prosaic delivery. He still insisted that there was only a narrow legal question and that I had artificially enlarged it.

The argument over, the audience stood respectfully while the Chancellor, with vigor not associated with his calling or his immovable demeanor, bounded down the steps to his antechamber. Then nervous hands reached into accustomed pockets and lit cigarettes all over the room. There was the release of general hubbub. Mr. Pollack approached me and said that Tomlinson wanted to shake my hand and congratulate me, but he feared I would not receive him. Would I? Certainly. He came from the other side of the room, and in that hearty, direct manner of his, shook my hand and uttered the most generous compliments in so loud a voice that the reporters took copious notes for their human interest stories of good sportsmanship. We left for New York in hopeful spirits.

On August 26 we heard it from the ticker. The tape in laconic fashion, appropriate to its preoccupation with numerals, reported: DELAWARE COURT DECIDES LOEW'S CONTEST SWEEPING VICTORY FOR VOGEL. CHANCELLOR SEITZ HOLDS LOUIS B. MAYER AND SAMUEL BRISKIN ILLEGALLY ELECTED DIRECTORS. ALL PROCEEDINGS OF TOMLINSON RUMP MEETING DECLARED INVALID. . . .

While the tape was running, already destined to be the confetti of celebration, David Anderson of our Wilmington counsel (Berl, Potter and Anderson) was on the phone, his conservative voice hiding his excitement as best it could, relaying the news. Within an hour he would have the opinion. We arranged to have it read to us on the telephone while a squad of stenographers duplicated it.

It was a twenty-two-page opinion, closely reasoned, scholarly and as translucent in logical development and clarity as the most exquisite crystal. This is not a victor's pink-glassed tribute; losing counsel thought so too.

Logan took an immediate appeal to the Supreme Court of the State of Delaware. Then he applied for a stay pending the hearing of the appeal. In a significant decision, the Court refused a stay, but accelerated the appeal date.

The Tomlinson group, as explosively energetic as a satellite thrust, then instituted another action in the name of Ralph B. Campbell, a stockholder, seeking to enjoin the holding of the stockholders' meeting, forbidding the Vogel group from using company moneys in the proxy contest, requiring the Vogel directors to attend a directors' meeting so that a quorum would be present, and attacking all proxies received by the

Vogel group on the ground that they were obtained by misrepresentation in the solicitation letters that were being sent out.

It soon developed that Campbell was an ex-partner of Tomlinson and that this was another device to argue before Chancellor Seitz for entirely different relief while an appeal was pending from his prior decision.

Our opponents poured proceedings upon us. Tomlinson moved to intervene in the Campbell action to have the Court authorize payment by the corporation to him for his proxy expenses. Since he was on the majority of the Board, he represented management, he argued, and Vogel was the outsider.

We had just won what appeared to be final triumph in the Courts. Of course, we knew that the risk of an appeal still existed, but the very air around the Loew building and at the studio in Hollywood was filled with victory. I imagined, from watching some of them, that all 14,000 employees were walking with heads high in what was suspiciously close to a strut. The newspapers heralded the decision in glowing terms. But there was something about this case that resembled a ride on a roller coaster in its succeeding dips and ascents.

Here we were on high, but suddenly facing an ominous descent. A new suit threatened the cancellation of our proxies and the stockholders' meeting itself. It put in jeopardy our right to finance the proxy contest with corporate funds. We might still be in the position of having won a Pyrrhic victory. Our opponents had been stung by defeat to new efforts. They were tireless and resourceful. A fanatic is one who, having lost sight of his objective, redoubles his effort. Our opponents had redoubled their efforts, but had not lost sight of their objective.

While we were endeavoring to match energy with our adversaries, working around the clock on legal briefs addressed to the complex questions they had raised, and while I was preparing myself for another lengthy presentation before Chancellor Seitz, we received the first push down the sharp descent of the legal roller coaster.

Mr. Anderson, our Wilmington counsel, was on the phone to advise me that Chancellor Seitz had just issued a temporary injunction in the new Campbell suit forbidding the use of corporate moneys on behalf of Vogel's proxy contest, and also prohibiting the use of corporate employees in soliciting or otherwise aiding Vogel in gathering proxies.

The Chancellor had given Anderson a half hour to come to his chambers before he issued the injunction. There had been no real argument because the Judge had the right to issue such a temporary stay ex parte, that is, on one side's application alone. This order would stand until he had decided the case after argument.

We were like an army that is suddenly advised that all supplies have been cut off. Also, this order had a psychological effect. It was a bad omen of the Chancellor's views of our ability to sustain our position.

Once more, we had to overcome the pall that fell over our forces. Karr, who was as effective in private planning as in public relations, suggested that the problem be put before the industry committees which had been organizing spontaneously and offering to help in any way they could. Here was a chance to harness the good will Vogel enjoyed, and put it to practicable use. Also, it was a shrewd move from a morale viewpoint. To give hundreds of Vogel's friends and rooters an opportunity to join in the contest realistically was to lift the spirit of the besieged. We felt as if we had allies in all the hills, and, indeed, we had. Prominent theater operators, like Harry Brandt, organized stockholder protective committees. Checks began to flow in from $10,000 denominations to $1000. One committee retained prominent Wilmington counsel, Clair J. Killoran. Above all, this plan made it possible for the motion picture industry to register its conviction that Vogel's fight was its fight. The industry responded with a burst of enthusiasm to solve the financial crisis. Vogel vowed that every cent would be returned to the generous contributors.

Once more we headed for the Wilmington Chancery Court to ward off a destructive attack. Once more we were under the gaze of the Chancellor for hours as we argued the complex questions raised by imaginative, tireless adversaries.

There were three matters only that concerned us deeply. First, that the stockholders' meeting on September 12 should not be disturbed. Second, that our precious proxies be not canceled. Third, that Vogel's group be deemed management and entitled to the use of corporate moneys to sustain its position in the proxy battle.

The Chancellor by his questions and comments from the bench indicated that Tomlinson and Meyer may have had insufficient opportunity to defend themselves against the charges of removal. He pointed to the minority status of the Vogel group and its control of the books and records of the company and the advantages this afforded in a proxy contest. Having himself spiked Tomlinson's majority by striking down Mayer and Briskin as directors, the fulcrum of his sensitive equitable balance now tended to lift the defeated side.

This time we returned to New York with misgivings concerning the outcome. Our uneasiness turned to alarm when Anderson, our counsel in Delaware, beat the ticker tape announcement to advise us that the Chancellor had postponed the stockholders' meeting from September 12 to October 15. The issues were so novel, the briefs so voluminous, that he needed more time to make a decision.

Vogel had been driving relentlessly to obtain favorable proxies for the September 12 meeting. The letdown of a postponement was severe. We knew that time gave the Tomlinson army of counsel and advisers more opportunity to maneuver. Worst of all, Chancellor Seitz knew that time was of the essence. We had stressed, over and over again, the daily injury suffered by the corporation from the uncertainty of litigation. Was not therefore his postponement an indication that he might grant the injunction against holding the special stockholders' meeting? There is only torment in conjecture of this kind. I find that one's predisposition, whether toward optimism or pessimism, determines the prognostication. We read meanings into the postponement of which the Chancellor probably never dreamed. Yet, with so much at stake, one could not prevent anxiety expending itself in interpretation no matter how enervating the exercise. Each day there was eager inquiry of the Chancellor's secretary whether the decision that would determine our destiny was ready. For weeks we hung on a thin thread of suspense.

Then on September 18 we were advised that the Chancellor had completed his written opinion. It would be filed the next morning. If one could, that night, have measured the feelings of the clients, their attorneys and advisers, on both sides of the controversy, he would have plumbed the hopes and fears which beset man when his fate is in the balance.

The next day we huddled around my loudspeaker telephone while Anderson read Chancellor Seitz's thirty-seven-page opinion from the court clerk's office. It was a careful and detailed review of the involved legal arguments, but what interested us most were the conclusions which sounded like the coda of the most beautiful symphony we had ever heard:

"No preliminary injunction will issue to enjoin the holding of the meeting, now fixed for October 15, 1957.

"The corporation will be preliminarily enjoined from recognizing or counting any proxies held by the individual defendants unless the corporation supplies the Tomlinson board members the stockholders' list as herein provided.

"No preliminary injunction will issue to restrain the corporation from paying reasonable sums incurred by the Vogel group in soliciting proxies.

"A preliminary injunction will issue restraining the corporation from permitting the use of its personnel and facilities for the solicitation of proxies by the Vogel group.

"No injunction will issue to compel the individual defendants to attend directors' meetings."

The Court had restored to us the three things Napoleon said were necessary to win a war: money, money, money. As if we were a majority, we could use corporate funds in the proxy contest with Mayer and Tomlinson. Every cent contributed by our friends, when the original injunction deprived us of the sinews of war, was returned to them. It is one of the rare occasions when those who made financial contributions to a cause, discover that they have made no sacrifice. They had kissed their checks good-bye, never expecting a homecoming. Their return inspired even greater efforts on behalf of Vogel.

Five days later, while the echoes of celebration were still bouncing off the walls, a United States Marshal visited the Loew's offices and served a twenty-one-page complaint in a new suit by Tomlinson to cancel all of Vogel's proxies on the ground that they had been obtained by misleading solicitation letters, and asking the Court to impound all votes. This litigation was not instituted in the Delaware Chancery Court, but in the United States District Court on the theory that the SEC, a Federal agency, had refused to bring such action.

The Mayer-Tomlinson council of war had shifted the battle to the Federal Court. It threatened our votes. It dragged Vogel into court instantly for hostile questioning. All this legal music squeezed our wind like a closing accordion. The day after Vogel's examination, we were due to argue Tomlinson's appeal in the Supreme Court of Delaware. The day thereafter, we were now commanded to argue before Federal Judge Kirkpatrick in Washington to ward off the attack on the proxies.

A lawyer makes inner appraisals of his adversaries, even in the turmoil of contest. I was full of admiration for their resilience and sheer tirelessness, not to speak of their imaginativeness. It seemed impossible to gain final legal victory. Like Antaeus, who was smashed to the ground by Hercules, only to derive strength from contact with the earth (because he was the son of Gaea—the earth) and arose again and again refreshed, the Tomlinson faction appeared to attack with new vigor each time it was thrown by an adverse legal decision. Would it be necessary to hold this modern Antaeus high in the mid-air, as Hercules had done, until victory was achieved?

Tomlinson's attorneys examined Vogel and Reid for a full day. We sat late because we had to travel to Washington that night.

Logan encountered the new Vogel who returned blow for blow. Although Vogel had been prepared in another through-the-night session, he did not have to struggle with his memory to recall the complex facts. They were in his bloodstream. All the months of suffering from humiliating insults, from frustrating obstructionism; all the months that seemed like a lifetime of nightmare because they had taken him from a world of good will and affection and cast him into a world of ruthlessness, made him a perfect witness. He poured out the facts justifying his charges in such a steady stream that at one point, Logan, taken aback by the attack, shouted, "Be quiet," a rather strange admonition from one who had moved heaven and earth to get Vogel to a witness chair to make him speak. It is not surprising that Logan barely referred to the examination in his later argument before Judge Kirkpatrick. For Vogel attributed the resignations of Pace and other directors to harassment from Tomlinson's tactics, which required fortitude and sacrifice on their part beyond the reasonable call which one had a right to make upon a director's service.

Next day, we drove from Wilmington to Dover where the Supreme Court of the State of Delaware is situated. The Court House was built in 1787, and still stands quaint and beautiful. Except for an additional wing to the building, to house the clerical and other facilities necessary to the thriving enlargement of judicial business over the past century and a half, the edifice has been preserved in its original state. The court-room in which the appeals are heard has a magnificent, ornate oak rostrum set unusually high for the three Judges, counsel table and chairs whose hard wood is scooped from use into gentle curves, and a narrow spectator's bench in the rear, seating only six. The room, with its original floor planks, is small, except for a high Colonial ceiling from which hangs a gaslight candelabra, now converted to electricity. The low windows open on ancient big-limbed trees and an expanse of lawn called Dover Green, where the Revolutionary Militia was organized and trained.

We still live by the realities of our senses, and to see and touch, yes, and almost smell the mustiness of the past, was to be transported centuries back. I had a passing vision of the hundreds of lawyers through the generations who had stood at that advocate's table and fought their hearts out for their clients. While immersed in my thoughts, I heard three evenly spaced knocks on a door, and in my mind's eye saw three ancient judges labor slowly up to the austere bench. There they stood, as immovable as ghosts, while the court clerk, in a breaking voice, an-nounced, "Hear ye, hear ye, hear ye, the Supreme Court of the State of Delaware is now in session. Come forth and ye shall be heard. God bless these United States, God bless the State of Delaware and all its inhabi-tants. God bless this honorable Court."

The Judges sank into their soft chairs. The Presiding Judge cleared his throat, and announced: "We will hear the appeal to Tomlin-son versus Loew's." I came out of my reverie. The Judges were not those who had originally sat in the Court when it was built. They were alert and vigorous. This was not to be an argument about riparian rights to a dried stream bed. It was the final stage in the determination of the fate of one of our country's greatest and most modern industries.

Logan stepped to the podium. Representing the appellant, he argued first. He soon demonstrated the versatility of style that leading advocates possess. I would have expected him, as in his prior arguments, to address the Court in subdued tones. The very surroundings compelled a hushed approach. But there rankled in him the series of defeats that he had suffered. This time he exploded in a torrent of words. It was the most effective argument I heard him make.

His client had a majority of five, but Vogel's minority of four was permitted to determine policy and control the company. How could this be? Since when is four a majority of nine? . . .

At a directors' meeting to fill vacancies, Vogel's four directors absent themselves and then charge that the meeting didn't have a quorum.

The five who attend are penalized because four would not perform their duty. Did this make sense? . . .

When the five fill in vacancies by electing Mayer and Briskin under a Statute and Bylaw which says that they may do so "although less than a quorum," Chancellor Seitz says they acted illegally because they were less than a quorum. How can he fly in the face of express language? . . .

The Chelsea case says he can't, but the Chancellor disregards it. What right does he have to change the established law? . . .

Finally, the minority of four is called management (while the majority of five is shunted aside) and the minority is permitted to use corporate funds in the proxy contest. Is not this outrageous? . . . Aren't these decisions topsy-turvy? . . .

Logan's frustration made him breathless and emotional. His indignation seemed like an outcry of pain in the sedate atmosphere. He demanded a reversal of Chancellor Seitz's decision.

In my presentation, I brought the pitch down to a low C and the pace to andante. Before I had even gotten into the first movement, Chief Judge Clarence A. Southerland reached for the main theme with one of those cutting-away-the underbrush questions that keen judges use so effectively during oral argument: "But they *do* have a majority haven't they, counsel?"

I paused and replied slowly: "Your Honor and I are directors and are attending a meeting. We are part of the majority in a divided Board. There is a recess, and we go to the open window to get some air. The window sill is low and as we bend over to look out, the leader of the minority faction approaches us from the rear and gives us a shove. Before he can hear the thud below, he turns and says to the remaining directors, 'Let's resume the meeting, gentlemen. We now have a majority.' Has he, your Honor?"

I thought I detected a faint smile on the Judge's face. I proceeded to develop the full argument of the tactics and pressures which resulted in the shifting of the majority. During the recital of events and citations of law, I would pause along the road to refresh myself and the Court with words from Chancellor Seitz's opinions. To Logan's challenge that there was no legal warrant for the orders against him, I was able to cite at least one distinguished authority, Chancellor Seitz. There is a legal anecdote of the Judge who was defied by a lawyer during argument and told that the highest Court of the state had only the day before decided the same proposition and that therefore the Judge had no power to contravene this very latest authority. The Judge immediately announced his decision against the belligerent lawyer, and said, "Have you anything later than that?" We did have the very latest authority.

At the conclusion of the argument, I indicated that the special stockholders' meeting was to take place in one week. While it was embarrassing and audacious for counsel to suggest to the Court that it hasten its consideration of the appeal, it was critical that there be no cloud over the meeting in which 26,000 stock owners would vote. I respectfully urged a prompt decision within the week.

The argument over, each group of attorneys filled several automobiles and took off for Washington, D.C., where the injunction application in the Federal Court would be heard the next day. We were riding the circuit, like a troupe of performers, only this was not play-acting. It was the final stage of a desperate war of attrition in which the very last round of ammunition was being fired point-blank. We hoped it was the last. Five different applications to stay the stockholders' meeting had been denied by the courts. Twenty-six hours of oral argument had been consumed on two motions, one appeal, hearings before the SEC and examinations before trial. Eighteen legal briefs, hundreds of pages in length, had been filed. I had personally viewed innumerable sunrises, after all-night industry and vigil. Tension and anxiety had added nerve-strain to the problem of endurance. We were all close to exhaustion.

The Federal Judge who was to hear the injunction application was William H. Kirkpatrick, Chief Judge of the Eastern District of Pennsylvania, who, because of the emergency in time, had convened the session in Washington. I had tried an antitrust suit before him in Philadelphia, which had twice gone to the United States Supreme Court, before we could hold our victory. He was therefore familiar with my weaknesses, and I with his strengths. Judge Kirkpatrick is, technically, of retirement age, six feet tall and straight, with a stand-up crop of short gray hair, silver-rimmed eyeglasses, and an old-fashioned casual, scholarly demeanor, symbolized by a green eyeshade which he wears over his forehead like a bookkeeper. He likes to hold informal conferences in his chambers, where he keeps a huge cardboard over his knees and fills in the prepared squares with judicial observations and tentative findings as if they were chess moves. He has a brilliant, blind law secretary with an incredible index of cases in his mind. Woe to those who run afoul their combined nine senses.

The arguments were heard in the courtroom of the Federal Court House, where the finest grained marble speeds the sounds to magnificent, high, wood-paneled ceilings, which bounce them back in muffled density, requiring a microphone system on the bench and at the lectern to be properly heard. So, grandeur can be the enemy of acoustics, something for modern opera houses and music auditoriums to remember.

For hours, we battled back and forth across the familiar terrain. Logan and his associate, Ailes, tried to make it appear that there were new issues raised by "misrepresentation" in our solicitation letters. We demonstrated these accusations had already been passed upon and held to be baseless. The stockholders' meeting was only six days away. I pleaded for a speedy decision.

On a Saturday morning only four days after we argued in Dover, the three Appellate judges, Southerland, Wolcott, and Bramhall, handed down a unanimous opinion affirming Chancellor Seitz.

That same Saturday, Judge Kirkpatrick telephoned both sides to announce his decision denying Tomlinson's motions. So, three days before the stockholders' meeting, two courts, responding to our plea for immediate decision, refused to recognize the Tomlinson majority or the election of Mayer and Briskin. There were no further legal obstacles to the stockholders' meeting. Saturday, October 12, ought to be commemorated by Loew's as V day—for Vogel.

Word began to sieve through to us that Louis B. Mayer had become seriously ill. Since it developed that he had leukemia, no one can say that there was any relationship between the crushing defeats he suffered and his fatal disease. But I have observed through the years with deep concern, the emotional impact of litigation on clients' or adversaries' health. It would not surprise me if it should be discovered some day that the torment of uncertainty over great stakes, whether honor, money, or satisfaction, have a direct effect on the glandular system and lay the victim open to illnesses of all kinds.

These thoughts ran through my mind when I heard the sad news about Mayer's death within months after these court decisions. Where his desire for revenge had been so neurotically intense, where his exuberance at victory, which he thought was certain, was touched with ecstasy, where the subsequent legal decisions struck him down as a director, throwing him out a second time from his company, and where these violent swings from complete triumph to despair had humiliated him and etched bitterness in his heart as if with acid, who can say what mysterious endocrinal effects his body suffered? It might have pleased his dramatic sense to think that he had martyred himself in a struggle to recapture his company. We can only hope it wasn't so.

Vogel submitted to the Board a resolution of profound regret that a founder of the company, who in his early years, had conferred so many of his talents upon it, had passed from the scene. It was sent to the widow with the sincere sadness of all of us. At Loew's, the bitterness of contest had given way to the reflection of the futility of the struggle for power, and the finality of death.

The only way in which we could obtain a real majority on the Board in the midst of the year, was to enlarge it. If we simply filled the vacancies, we could only re-establish the six-to-six balance. That is why we proposed an amendment to increase the number of directors from thirteen to nineteen. This required that we propose a slate of candidates which would appeal to the stockholders. We looked about for outstanding men and designated Charles H. Silver, President of the Board of Education of the City of New York, and previously an important business executive; Bennett Cerf, versatile as publishing executive and entertainer with pen and tongue; Ellsworth C. Alvord, a foremost tax specialist; J. Howard McGrath, former Attorney General of the United States; Francis W. Hatch, Vice-President of Batten, Barton, Durstine & Osborn, Inc., an advertising agency; Charles Braunstein, head of a diamond concern; and appropriately enough some executives of the company, Melniker and O'Brien.

I asked my friend and client Arde Bulova, head of the Bulova Watch Company, whether he would make himself available. Unfortunately he was not feeling well and he sensed that his illness might not be temporary, which indeed it wasn't, for later, after a heroic effort in which he submitted himself to experimentation for a new cancer cure, he succumbed. But he authorized me to invite General Omar Bradley, who was then Chairman of the Board of Bulova Research and Development Labs, Inc.

I arranged a meeting between the General and Vogel. Of course the General was informed of the precise situation, so that he knew he would be opposed in a proxy contest. Needless to say he did not shy away from a scrap. He liked Vogel and his cause, and he lent his name to the slate of new candidates. The General had proved that he was an able administrator when he reorganized the Veterans Administration. He proved to be equally keen in business when he succeeded Bulova, and he has since demonstrated a firm grasp of business problems at Loew's. To his reputation as the generals' general has been added the accolade of the businessmen's businessman.

Now all we needed was votes. While the legal battles were raging, Vogel and his cabinet organized a national campaign to obtain stockholders' approval. Committees formed within the industry to solicit owners of even one share of stock. Throughout forty years Vogel had inspired good will wherever he went. Now, at the critical moment, this affection and sympathy for him, like little drops of water, flowed from all directions forming tiny streams. They trickled into great rivers and finally cascaded in powerful torrents of proxies.

October 15, the day the Courts had been asked so often to interfere with, came unmolested. It was the day that the stockholders of Loew's were convened in special session by their President to act in an emergency in which the company found itself. There was no time to wait until the annual meeting in February. An attempt had been made to remove the President and obtain control of the "government." The President, left in a minority, had appealed to the people, the stockholders. Now they had an opportunity to rise in their wrath and put supporting troops, in the form of additional directors, alongside him so that he could take the reins of government again and function.

To provide adequate space, Loew's State Theatre at Broadway and

Forty-fifth Street in New York City was closed for business, and served as a meeting room. On the orchestra floor, immediately in front of the stage, a long table was set up with chairs for the President and his advisers and a stenotypist who would take down all proceedings. A microphone system was installed so that the President could be heard in the cavernous orchestra and balcony which seated thousands. On the side, was a special table for two officers of the Bankers Trust Company, who were to act as inspectors of election and who had filed their statutory oaths to conduct the election properly. Their counsel and experts sat alongside them. They would be required to rule on the validity of the proxies cast—for example, whether a proxy was invalid because the stockholder was not on the list at the time the books were closed for voting eligibility. Under law, a stockholder may send in his proxy as many times as he wishes. The theory is that as he receives letters and data from the contesting sides, he may change his mind. He is free to do so. It is his last proxy only which counts. The inspectors of election determine all questions that may arise from conflicting proxies. Also, the authority of a brokerage house to vote the stock of its customers must be established. The SEC regulations to assure the integrity of corporate elections are detailed and effective. Democracy in government might do well to learn from the safeguards for democracy in business.

On the stage, behind the worn, maroon velvet curtains, was a staff of computers and neutral experts supplied by the Bankers Trust Company, who under bond and oath made the compilations of the millions of votes that were to be cast. The bustle behind the scene was as furious as in any election headquarters on the decisive day.

Ushers with hand microphones were stationed in the aisles. They supplied the instruments to stockholders recognized by the chair. There are professional stockholders' organizations which send representatives to corporate meetings. They come equipped with their own electrical megaphones so that even if not recognized by the President, they could demand to be heard over the tumult. Several of these "professionals" turned up and added to the din and demagoguery. One of them, a woman, appeared cloaked in a large Florida beach towel, announcing through her blaring megaphone that since some of the directors had just returned from their yachts on the Caribbean, she would at least symbolize the poor stockholders' return from Miami. On the whole, however, the stockholders are serious and responsible, and look with disgust upon the antics of the too common man in the democratic process.

It is customary at noon to serve free box luncheons to the attendees. Also, there are times when a recess of several hours may have to be taken for counting and making complicated decisions. Then one of the company's outstanding motion pictures is shown on the screen to fill in the time.

In the front row of the orchestra sat General Bradley, Bennett Cerf, and the other candidates for election as new directors so that they could be introduced in person to the meeting. With them sat the loyal Vogel minority, Killion, Parker, and Sullivan. The first twenty rows of the orchestra, across the two aisles, were completely filled almost one hour before the meeting was to begin. We did not ascribe any significance to this. We were soon to learn how wrong we were.

Our opponents had demonstrated time and again that they would never give up, but their persistence and ingenuity exceeded even our developed sense of anticipation. What they had not achieved through the courts, they were determined to accomplish by another tactic. We were confronted with legal obstruction and mob hysteria.

The spotlight from the balcony lit up the front table. It was the signal to begin the meeting. Vogel stepped to the microphone and began reading his formal opening statement, announcing that a stockholders' list had been duly filed and that Mr. Carse and Mr. Ulm of the Bankers Trust Company would act as inspectors of election. Apparently upon signal, the attack began.

VOICE: Mr. Chairman, I raise the question of the absence of a quorum.

CHAIRMAN VOGEL: Please let me finish and you can bring that objection up when I finish.

He tried to go on. Hands and voices rose in all directions in the first twenty rows, one right after the other in timed succession. The stenographic minutes could catch only part of the bedlam:

VOICE: Mr. Chairman—

A STOCKHOLDER: Don't interrupt. He has the floor.

VOICE: If there is no quorum, there is no meeting.

Vogel advised him there was a quorum at the adjourned September 12 meeting and it was not necessary to ascertain in advance that there was one at this meeting "and I so rule."

VOICE: Mr. Chairman—

CHAIRMAN VOGEL: You are out of order, sir.

VOICE: No, sir, it is a point of order. I am not out of order.

CHAIRMAN VOGEL: I have ruled.

VOICE: You have ruled and you may be wrong.

A STOCKHOLDER: I don't see why you don't give that man a chance to speak.

CHAIRMAN VOGEL: I will give him a chance.

A STOCKHOLDER: You want everybody to be as brief as possible, and you took a good share of it.

MR. GILBERT: A point of order.

CHAIRMAN VOGEL: I will listen to you at a later time. You are out of order.

A STOCKHOLDER: A point of order is always in order.

CHAIRMAN VOGEL: I have ruled on this, please sit down. I will listen to you later.

VOICE: We appeal your ruling to the floor.

MR. KILLION: Mr. Chairman, I move the adoption—

VOICE: We appeal the ruling to the floor. We appeal the ruling to the floor.

Despite the commotion, Killion read the resolution to be voted on, an amendment to increase the directors from thirteen to nineteen. Parker seconded it. Neither could be heard in the deafening shouts that came from all directions. Men stood and shook their fists while they condemned the President's ruling. The attempts of the majority of stockholders to quiet the hecklers only aided them, because the cries of condemnation joined indistinguishably with the protests, to increase the din. It soon became evident that the obstructionists were no mere rabble. They identified themselves as lawyers.

CHAIRMAN: Are you an attorney, sir?

VOICE: I am.

He presented legal arguments in support of his protest. There were revocations filed with the inspectors of election.

VOICE: If these revocations are valid they may defeat the presence of a quorum, so that there is a real question here.

He read a section of Bylaws and argued that the meeting was proceeding illegally. Another lawyer obtained the floor.

VOICE: I am an attorney, I want to know one thing—is there a quorum present at this meeting? . . .

CHAIRMAN VOGEL: You have stated your point, you have said it twice. . . . Can we give somebody else a chance?

VOICE: May I, Mr. Vogel, appeal your ruling to the floor and ask that we take a vote as to whether it is the order of business to determine whether there is a quorum.

CHAIRMAN VOGEL: I ruled on that.

The yells continued from all parts of the auditorium until it was impossible to be heard or proceed. If the quorum vote of more than 2,500,000 shares was taken first, hours would be wasted and the meeting tied into a knot and adjourned. If it wasn't, the scheme apparently was to create sufficient confusion to make continuation of the meeting impossible.

I was called upon to answer the legal question. I had pulled out of my file the injunction order of the Supreme Court of the State of New York which forbade anyone to interfere with the holding of the meeting. I had enough experience in public speaking to know that the audience could not be stilled by yelling above the noise. Rather I stood still for a while and addressed them quietly, so that they would have to become quiet if they wished to hear. Curiosity is a tranquilizer. I advised the meeting that the certified quorum at the September meeting was sufficient for this one, and besides a quorum would be certified later. In any event a stockholder could preserve his remedy if there were a defect. The audience had become hushed. Then I struck at the obstructionists: "It is one thing for a stockholder to insist upon asserting his rights. Right or wrong he has the right to speak. It is another thing to obstruct a meeting by having men placed throughout the meeting in such a way as to cause confusion and prevent the meeting from taking place. [Applause]

"And let me make it clear that this matter was tested in the Courts. . . . I have here certified copies of the orders of the Supreme Court of the State of New York and anyone who prevents the determination of this meeting by stockholders will be in contempt of court, and we will serve a copy of that order upon anyone who interferes, not because he opposed me—that is your privilege, and you will be given full opportunity, but if there is a calculated scheme throughout this room, as there was ten minutes ago of men jumping up and trying to prevent you from having your say, I call your attention to this court order, and you who may be guilty of this will be served with it before the day is over." [Applause]

I read from the court order and then concluded: "This has been a bitter contest through many courts and the oppositon has had its fair opportunity to present all of its arguments and has the same opportunity again today if they wish it. That is their privilege; but the President has appealed to you to conduct this meeting in an orderly manner, and when he has ruled on a point of order it is no use having five people stand up and scream. That will not progress the meeting.

"You have your rights reserved to you and I appeal to you to comply with the President's spirit, which is that you may state your opposition and then sit down and let somebody else speak, and let's come to a vote and decide this through the stockholders." [Applause]

The obstructionists feared to run afoul of the Supreme Court order. The campaign of disrupting the meeting ceased.

There was full debate in orderly fashion during which Tomlinson spoke bitterly, and the bankers' representative opposed the enlargement of the Board. Then there was an adjournment to tabulate the votes. The amendment to enlarge the board to nineteen directors was carried by 3,445,083 to 519,435!

The Vogel slate for new directors was then nominated. Lehman and Lazard Freres nominated Samuel Briskin and expressed their lack of faith in the Vogel management. The debate was vigorous and full of recrimination. At 7:30 P.M. an adjournment was taken until 8:30 to tabulate the votes on the new directors. The entire slate was elected, each director receiving over 3,500,000 votes. Due to cumulative voting in which Tomlinson and the banks gave their support to Briskin, he was elected too.

Vogel proudly announced the new composition of the enlarged Board: "I can't say how much I thank you all for your confidence, and I want you to know that I am going to do everything in my power to merit that confidence. All my associates will break their necks to do a job for you, I promise you." [Applause]

That night we stayed up late at Dinty Moore's restaurant just to calm down slowly with the realization that Vogel's minority had turned into a two-to-one majority.

Board meetings took on a different character. Tomlinson, Meyer, Johnson, Keller, and Lawson still registered their opposition, but at the appropriated time Vogel called for a vote and his program was adopted. He was able to concentrate completely on business.

Within four months, however, the annual election of February was upon us. Now, there was an opportunity to eliminate more of the dissidents. Johnson and Keller were eliminated from the new slate of directors and were replaced by Ira Guilden and his associate Philip Roth. Lawson and Stanley Meyer similarly were replaced by Louis Green and Jerome Newman. Green's arrival on the scene was due to the fact that he had a deal to buy out Tomlinson's stock. Also, he was associated with Andre Meyer of Lazard Freres in some transactions and had his good will. He therefore brought to Vogel a unique proposal; Tomlinson, who because of cumulative voting could not be removed from the Board, would be eliminated by the acquisition of his stock. At the same time the good will of the bankers might belatedly be acquired.

Green was a self-made man who had not left out the working parts. At our first conference he revealed a facet of his personality by saying, "Listen, fellas, I am a man like this. With me 2 plus 2 is 4. It is not $3\frac{7}{8}$. It isn't $4\frac{1}{2}$, it is 4." I marked this down as a quaint expression which some men are given to—I know a man who comments on his lack of awe for an opponent by saying, "After all he puts on his pants one leg at a time like the rest of us."

But Green was so enamored with his "2 plus 2 is 4" equation that he repeated it every half hour. I almost advised him one day that according to an advanced mathematician in California, 2 plus 2 is really not 4. I thought, however, it would be too cruel to destroy a man's philosophy with such a revelation. Although Green was an old classmate acquaintance of Vogel's, and gave every assurance of his sentimental rather than business desire to be in Loew's, he insisted on Newman's coming into the venture. Newman, his associate, prided himself on reading balance sheets with a more discerning eye than Toscanini could read a score. Soon he was calling for reports and data and making investigations. Then he began to write critical letters. He discovered a $7.50 license fee for a motion picture and chastised the management for so inadequate a price, without knowing that this was just a service charge for supplying a picture to a Naval Hospital. Shades of Tomlinson!

Newman approached the President of another company to discuss joint operation of studios. Green swore by Newman. Board meetings became contentious again. Tomlinson and Green naturally gravitated toward each other. We were relegated once more to factionalism, even thought the opposing faction was a minority.

As the new election approached, Green, Newman, and Tomlinson made demands for more representation on the Board or they threatened a proxy fight.

We met in numerous conferences, where the same old game was played of selecting "independent" directors, who would not be "subservient" to Vogel. Surely we had learned our lesson; we would not surrender our hard-earned majority under any circumstances. Green then publicly announced that he was going to wage a proxy fight and filed the necessary papers therefor with the SEC and engaged prominent counsel for the contest. The newspapers once more featured the battle in Loew's.

We countered with the most audacious move of all. We proposed to the stockholders that they eliminate cumulative voting. We were warned on all sides that such a proposal would give respectability and enormous support to Green. Many law professors and financial experts deemed cumulative voting a desirable protection for the little stockholder. It gave him representation on boards which he might otherwise not obtain. Like proportional representation in politics, it increases the power of the minority. No doubt cumulative voting can be desirable. But it can be abused, as it was in the case of Loew's, to force upon the Board men whom the stockholders deemed inimical to their interests. We decided to tell the facts to the stockholders and trust to their good judgment and their confidence in Vogel's good faith. He was not trying to perpetuate management. He was attempting to do away once and for all with obstructionists, so that his regime could be tested by its achievements.

The stockholders responded magnificently. They eliminated cumulative voting. They reduced the Board to fifteen, electing Vogel's nominees, Nate Cummings and John Snyder. Tomlinson, Meyer, Briskin, Green, and Newman all fell by the wayside. Johnson, Keller, and Lawson had already disappeared from the scene. Vogel was given a Board of Directors which was unanimous in its good will and confidence in him. Of course, he was not the kind of man who wanted to eliminate earnest criticism. He wanted no rubber stamps, and the caliber of the directors was assurance against blind acquiescence. But all backbiting and politics stopped. A cohesive group of businessmen sit around the table with their President and debate, modify or approve his program solely on the basis of their business judgment.

What has been the result? Losses of $2,306,000—after interest and taxes—suffered in 1957, have been turned into a profit for the first three quarters of 1961 of $9,442,000—after interest and income taxes. This means a swing of over $11,000,000. Cash and securities (exclusive of foreign currencies) in 1957 of about $8,000,000 has been improved by June 1961 to $29,000,000, while indebtedness has been reduced by many millions.

Vogel's victory has been the stockholders' victory. After 141 consecutive quarterly dividends, Loew's was unable to make dividend payments for two years after June 1957. Beginning with September 1959, quarterly dividend payments have been resumed. In the year 1960 the company showed the highest profit in twelve years. The first three quarters of 1961 have almost equaled this mark and the full year is expected to show the highest earnings in fifteen years, including those years in which the earnings of Loew's Theatres were included.

Vogel not only reduced fixed expenses by about $8,000,000 a year, but at the same time, improved the grosses on the pictures. Showmanship has been combined with taste to create artistic as well as box office successes such as *Cat On a Hot Tin Roof* and *Gigi*, which won the Academy Award as the best picture of 1958. And *Ben-Hur*, the $15,000,000 Vogel "folly," won eleven Academy Awards in 1960. His prophesy of a $30,000,000 gross will easily be doubled. Many experts predict that this one picture may, in time, gross $75,000,000, and even more. It is almost certain to be financially the most successful piece of entertainment in the history of motion pictures. This was done by the man that Mayer and Tomlinson said was not capable of running the company.

When I meet Tomlinson again I intend to tell him a story. It is about the Canadian who owned a champion bulldog. Its inbred blood had, however, turned it into a ferocious killer. The greatest care had to be exercised or it would tear apart any dog it saw. It had a long list of victims to its record, and its owner's ill-disguised pride. One night the Canadian entered a bar with his bull, and seeing a large yellow dog lying near a table, he seized his own animal just in time and yelled, "Who is the owner of that dog? Take him away. This dog will kill him." The owner, who happened to be a lawyer, gazed down at the friendly, languishing animal at his feet and said, "He's mine. That's all right."

"All right!" screamed the Canadian. "Listen, mister, I am giving you fair warning. This bull is a champion. He's killed seven dogs. I won't be able to hold him much longer. Take that mutt away if you want him alive."

"Oh," said the lawyer casually, as he looked down at his sleepy dog, "he can take care of himself."

Infuriated by the defiance, the Canadian yelled, "O.K., you asked for it," and released the straining, growling bull who, with fangs bared, in one fierce leap was upon the friendly animal. Just as he was about to seize his throat, the yellow dog lifted his paw and smote the bull so hard across his snarling, saliva-flowing snout that he flew backward and crashed against the bar senseless.

The Canadian was as stunned as his champion brute. "Say," he finally stammered, "what kind of a dog is that?"

The lawyer replied, "I don't know. I picked him up in Africa. At that time he had a lot of hair around his neck."

Vogel has recaptured his ideals. He has shed the mails and armor he learned to wear so painfully. Now that he is in unchallenged power, he desires once more to go forth armed only with good will and a smile. The magic has been restored. Friends become intimates; acquaintances become friends; enemies, if any, have short lives once they have met him and enter into a long life of amity. His is the philosophy that sucess cannot really be enjoyed unless it is accompanied by good wishes and good will. I believe so too. Let us hope that nothing will happen again to disillusion either of us.

The principle by which I have guided my legal work is that law is truth in action. It is man's highest achievement, because it is the only weapon he has fashioned whose force rests solely on the sanctity of reason. The more it is codified, the more it is in danger of petrifying. Its primary function, to do justice, becomes circumscribed by rules and precedents, which all too often interfere with its attainment. In order to give stability to law, our legislatures enact statutes to forewarn us, and our courts issue judicial opinions to guide us, but these become immense catalogues that can obstruct the view of simple justice. Their very complexity requires interpretive processes that provide new areas for conflict and error. The journey through the forest, which was to give us shade and shelter, becomes a hazardous undertaking in itself, and so diverts us that we may forget our original destination. Sometimes the circling affects our directional sense. Then we emerge where we least expect, but proclaim it is our true destination. So justice may be disserved by the very servants furnished to protect her. A man-made compass is subject to error from interfering magnetic forces and other causes, and a good navigator would still do well to check his position by the verity of the stars.

So, as a lawyer, I have aspired to master the involved mechanics of professional excellence, but I have striven not to permit them to master me. They are only the techniques for achieving an end, setting truth in action so as to achieve justice. To become so enamored with the paraphernalia of law as to lose sight of its noble objective is the great legal disease. I believe the true legal philosopher tends to simplicity. He uses his technical knowledge to clear away the obstructions to the fresh look. He employs his sophistication to recapture his naïve sense of values. He knows that the authority of a prior case has only the persuasive force of an analogy and that facts, like faces, are never the same.

Lawyers and Judges constantly talk of bare legal questions. I doubt that there are any. Behind them are human beings in strife with one another. Life, property, dominion over children, all that is precious may be involved; and the interacting forces have beaten against each other. Their history is recorded in facts. The legal solution should be affected by every detail of that background. Isolated from it, justice may be done in the abstract, but injustice may be done to the litigants. To win his case, the lawyer must align the two.

I like to think that the scales which the blindfolded figure of Justice holds in her hands are the symbol of scales within each of us. We weigh right and wrong, not by erudite legal processes, but by simple moral precepts. Their source is varied, partly untraceable, and cloaked with the mystery of conscience. They derive from early religious training, from ethical standards absorbed in the home and in society, from cultural values learned from books and teachers, and from what we call common sense because it is based on the wisdom of common experience.

Whatever their source, these moral standards for measuring right and wrong are the target of the persuader. If they are activated favorably, whether in a neighbor or in a million neighbors (who then become depersonalized under the title of public opinion), or in a jury, or in a Judge, they are irresistible. Precedents, no matter how hoary, and rules of law, no matter how firmly established, will yield before them. The same mental processes which fathered the rules and which are now found to be obstructing the desired result will, with equal facility, be used to modify them or, if this be too dangerous, to preserve them, discovering distinctions, however, which make them inapplicable to the particular case in hand. There is no limit to the resourcefulness and agility of the human mind when it is tipped by these inner scales.

The legal contests I have described are illustrations of these principles, which, in the laboratory of my professional work, have always proven themselves.

When a case is concluded I make a conscious effort to empty my mind of it, as if to make room for absorption of new facts. The process is never complete. The past "litigation" merely recedes into the background of memory, while new problems receive priority of concentration.

So I symbolically closed the book on the Loew's contest and signaled my secretary to usher in two visitors from Chicago who had flown into New York by appointment. The cause of their anxiety was an anti-trust suit which threatened their enterprise.

I leaned back and wondered what new legal adventure awaited me.